PHP Cookbook™

Other resources from O'Reilly

Related titles
Building Scalable Web Sites
Essential PHP Security
Learning PHP
Learning PHP and MySQL
PHP Hacks™

PHP in a Nutshell
Programming PHP
Upgrading to PHP
Web Database Applications
   with PHP and MySQL

oreilly.com
oreilly.com is more than a complete catalog of O'Reilly books. You'll also find links to news, events, articles, weblogs, sample chapters, and code examples.

oreillynet.com is the essential portal for developers interested in open and emerging technologies, including new platforms, programming languages, and operating systems.

Conferences
O'Reilly brings diverse innovators together to nurture the ideas that spark revolutionary industries. We specialize in documenting the latest tools and systems, translating the innovator's knowledge into useful skills for those in the trenches. Visit *conferences.oreilly.com* for our upcoming events.

Safari Bookshelf (*safari.oreilly.com*) is the premier online reference library for programmers and IT professionals. Conduct searches across more than 1,000 books. Subscribers can zero in on answers to time-critical questions in a matter of seconds. Read the books on your Bookshelf from cover to cover or simply flip to the page you need. Try it today for free.

SECOND EDITION

PHP Cookbook™

David Sklar and Adam Trachtenberg

O'REILLY®

Beijing · Cambridge · Farnham · Köln · Paris · Sebastopol · Taipei · Tokyo

PHP Cookbook™, Second Edition

by David Sklar and Adam Trachtenberg

Published by O'Reilly Media, Inc., 1005 Gravenstein Highway North, Sebastopol, CA 95472.

O'Reilly books may be purchased for educational, business, or sales promotional use. Online editions are also available for most titles (*safari.oreilly.com*). For more information, contact our corporate/institutional sales department: (800) 998-9938 or *corporate@oreilly.com*.

Editor: Tatiana Apandi

Production Editor: Adam Witwer

Copyeditor: Adam Witwer

Proofreader: Sada Preisch

Indexer: Joe Wizda

Cover Designer: Karen Montgomery

Interior Designer: David Futato

Illustrators: Robert Romano and Jessamyn Read

Printing History:

November 2002:   First Edition.

August 2006:   Second Edition.

 This book uses RepKover™, a durable and flexible lay-flat binding.

ISBN-10: 0-596-10101-5

ISBN-13: 978-0-596-10101-5

[M]

Table of Contents

Preface

PHP is the engine behind millions of dynamic web applications. Its broad feature set, approachable syntax, and support for different operating systems and web servers have made it an ideal language for both rapid web development and the methodical construction of complex systems.

One of the major reasons for PHP's success as a web scripting language is its origins as a tool to process HTML forms and create web pages. This makes PHP very web-friendly. Additionally, it is eagerly promiscuous when it comes to external applications and libraries. PHP can speak to a multitude of databases, and it knows numerous Internet protocols. PHP also makes it simple to parse form data and make HTTP requests. This web-specific focus carries over to the recipes and examples in the *PHP Cookbook*.

This book is a collection of solutions to common tasks in PHP. We've tried to include material that will appeal to everyone from newbies to wizards. If we've succeeded, you'll learn something (or perhaps many things) from *PHP Cookbook*. There are tips in here for everyday PHP programmers as well as for people coming to PHP with experience in another language.

PHP, in source code and binary forms, is available for download for free from *http://www.php.net/*. The PHP web site also contains installation instructions, comprehensive documentation, and pointers to online resources, user groups, mailing lists, and other PHP resources.

Who This Book Is For

This book is for programmers who need to solve problems with PHP. If you don't know any PHP, make this your second PHP book. The first should be *Learning PHP 5*, also from O'Reilly.

If you're already familiar with PHP, this book helps you overcome a specific problem and get on with your life (or at least your programming activities.) The *PHP Cookbook* can also show you how to accomplish a particular task in PHP, such as sending email or writing a SOAP server, that you may already know how to do in another language. Programmers converting applications from other languages to PHP will find this book a trusty companion.

What Is in This Book

We don't expect that you'll sit down and read this book from cover to cover (although we'll be happy if you do!). PHP programmers are constantly faced with a wide variety of challenges on a wide range of subjects. Turn to the *PHP Cookbook* when you encounter a problem you need to solve. Each recipe is a self-contained explanation that gives you a head start toward finishing your task. When a recipe refers to topics outside its scope, it contains pointers to related recipes and other online and offline resources.

If you choose to read an entire chapter at once, that's okay. The recipes generally flow from easy to hard, with example programs that "put it all together" at the end of many chapters. The chapter introduction provides an overview of the material covered in the chapter, including relevant background material, and points out a few highlighted recipes of special interest.

The book begins with four chapters about basic data types. Chapter 1 covers details like processing substrings, manipulating case, taking strings apart into smaller pieces, and parsing comma-separated data. Chapter 2 explains operations with floating-point numbers, random numbers, converting between bases, and number formatting. Chapter 3 shows you how to manipulate dates and times, format them, handle time zones and daylight saving time, and find time to microsecond precision. Chapter 4 covers array operations like iterating, merging, reversing, sorting, and extracting particular elements.

Next are three chapters that discuss program building blocks. Chpater 5 covers notable features of PHP's variable handling, such as default values, static variables, and producing string representations of complex data types. The recipes in Chpater 6 deal with using functions in PHP: processing arguments, passing and returning variables by reference, creating functions at runtime, and scoping variables. Chapter 7 covers PHP's object-oriented capabilities, with recipes on OOP basics as well as PHP 5's new features, such as magic methods, destructors, access control, and reflection.

After the data types and building blocks come six chapters devoted to topics that are central to web programming. Chapter 8 covers cookies, headers, authentication, working with query strings, and other fundamentals of web applications. Chapter 9 covers processing and validating form input, displaying multipage forms, showing forms with error messages, and guarding against problems such as cross-site scripting and multiple submission of the same form. Chapter 10 explains the differences between DBM and SQL databases and, using PHP 5's PDO database access abstraction layer, shows how to connect to a database, assign unique ID values, retrieve rows, change data, escape quotes, and log debugging information. Chapter 11 covers PHP's built-in sessions module, which lets you maintain information about a user as he moves from page to page on your web site. This chapter also highlights some of the security issues associated with sessions. Chapter 12 discusses all things XML: PHP 5's SimpleXML extension and revamped DOM functions, using XPath and XSLT, and reading and writing both RSS and Atom feeds. Chapter 13 explores topics useful to PHP applications that integrate with external web sites and client-side JavaScript such as retrieving remote URLs, cleaning up HTML, and responding to an Ajax request.

The next three chapters are all about network interaction. Chapter 14 details the ins and outs of consuming a web service—using an external REST, SOAP, or XML-RPC service from within your code. Chapter 15 handles the other side of the web services equation—serving up REST, SOAP, or XML-RPC requests to others. Both chapters discuss WSDL, authentication, headers, and error handling. Chapter 16 discusses other network services such as sending email messages, using LDAP, and doing DNS lookups.

The next section of the book is a series of chapters on features and extensions of PHP that help you build applications that are robust, secure, user-friendly, and efficient. Chpater 17 shows you how to create graphics, with recipes on drawing text, lines, polygons, and curves. Chapter 18 focuses on security topics such as avoiding session fixation and cross-site scripting, working with passwords, and encrypting data. Chapter 19 helps you make your applications globally friendly and includes recipes localizing text, dates and times, currency values, and images, as well as working with text in different character encodings, including UTF-8. Chapter 20 goes into detail on error handling, debugging techniques, and writing tests for your code. Chapter 21 explains how to compare the performance of two functions and provides tips on getting your programs to run at maximum speed. Chapter 22 covers regular expressions, including capturing text inside of HTML tags, calling a PHP function from inside a regular expression, and using greedy and nongreedy matching.

Chapters 23 and 24 cover the filesystem. Chapter 23 focuses on files: opening and closing them, using temporary files, locking file, sending compressed files, and processing the contents of files. Chapter 24 deals with directories and file metadata, with recipes on changing file permissions and ownership, moving or deleting a file, and processing all files in a directory.

Last, there are two chapters on topics that extend the reach of what PHP can do. Chapter 25 covers using PHP outside of web programming. Its recipes cover command-line topics such as parsing program arguments and reading passwords. Chapter 26 covers PEAR (the PHP Extension and Application Repository) and PECL (the PHP Extension Community Library). PEAR is a collection of PHP code that provides functions and extensions to PHP. PECL is a similar collection, but of extensions to PHP written in C. We use PEAR and PECL modules throughout the book and Chapter 26 shows you how to install and upgrade them.

Other Resources

Web Sites

There is a tremendous amount of PHP reference material online. With everything from the annotated PHP manual to sites with periodic articles and tutorials, a fast Internet connection rivals a large bookshelf in PHP documentary usefulness. Here are some key sites:

The Annotated PHP Manual: http://www.php.net/manual
> Available in 17 languages, this site includes both official documentation of functions and language features as well as user-contributed comments.

PHP mailing lists: http://www.php.net/mailing-lists.php
> There are many PHP mailing lists covering installation, programming, extending PHP, and various other topics. A read-only web interface to the mailing lists is at *http://news.php.net/*.

PHP Presentation archive: http://talks.php.net
> A collection of presentations on PHP given at various conferences.

PEAR: http://pear.php.net
> PEAR calls itself "a framework and distribution system for reuseable PHP components." You'll find lots of useful PHP classes and sample code there. Read more about PEAR in Chapter 26.

PECL: http://pecl.php.net
> PECL calls itself "a repository for PHP Extensions, providing a directory of all known extensions and hosting facilities for downloading and development of PHP extensions." Read more about PECL in Chapter 26.

PHP.net: A Tourist's Guide: http://www.php.net/sites.php
> This is a guide to the various web sites under the *php.net* umbrella.

PHP Knowledge Base: http://php.faqts.com
> Many questions and answers from the PHP community, as well as links to other resources.

PHP DevCenter: http://www.onlamp.com/php
> A collection of PHP articles and tutorials with a good mix of introductory and advanced topics.

Planet PHP: http://www.planet-php.net
> An aggregation of blog posts by PHP developers and about PHP.

Zend Developer Zone: http://devzone.zend.com
> A regularly updated collection of articles, tutorials, and code samples.

SitePoint Blogs on PHP: http://www.sitepoint.com/blogs/category/php
> A good collection of information about and exploration of PHP.

Books

This section lists books that are helpful references and tutorials for building applications with PHP. Most are specific to web-related programming; look for books on MySQL, HTML, XML, and HTTP.

At the end of the section, we've included a few books that are useful for every programmer regardless of language of choice. These works can make you a better programmer by teaching you how to think about programming as part of a larger pattern of problem solving:

- *Learning PHP 5* by David Sklar (O'Reilly)
- *Upgrading to PHP 5* by Adam Trachtenberg (O'Reilly)
- *Programming PHP* by Rasmus Lerdorf, Kevin Tatroe, and Peter MacIntyre (O'Reilly)
- *Essential PHP Tools* by David Sklar (Apress)
- *Advanced PHP Programming* by George Schlossnagle (Sams)
- *Extending and Embedding PHP* by Sara Golemon (Sams)
- *HTML and XHTML: The Definitive Guide* by Chuck Musciano and Bill Kennedy (O'Reilly)
- *Dynamic HTML: The Definitive Guide* by Danny Goodman (O'Reilly)
- *Mastering Regular Expressions* by Jeffrey E. F. Friedl (O'Reilly)
- *XML in a Nutshell* by Elliotte Rusty Harold and W. Scott Means (O'Reilly)
- *MySQL Reference Manual*, by Michael "Monty" Widenius, David Axmark, and MySQL AB (O'Reilly); also available at *http://www.mysql.com/documentation/*
- *MySQL*, by Paul DuBois (New Riders)
- *Web Security, Privacy, and Commerce* by Simson Garfinkel and Gene Spafford (O'Reilly)
- *HTTP Pocket Reference*, by Clinton Wong (O'Reilly)
- *The Practice of Programming*, by Brian W. Kernighan and Rob Pike (Addison-Wesley)
- *Programming Pearls* by Jon Louis Bentley (Addison-Wesley)
- *The Mythical Man-Month*, by Frederick P. Brooks (Addison-Wesley)

Conventions Used in This Book

Programming Conventions

The examples in this book were written to run under PHP version 5.1.4. Sample code should work on both Unix and Windows, except where noted in the text. We've generally noted in the text when we depend on a feature added to PHP after version 4.3.0 or 5.0.0.

We also call out when a feature will be available in an yet-to-be-unreleased version of PHP, including PHP 6. In those cases, please double check our code, as things can change during the development cycle.

Typesetting Conventions

The following typographic conventions are used in this book:

Italic
> Used for file and directory names, email addresses, and URLs, as well as for new terms where they are defined.

`Constant width`
> Used for code listings and for keywords, variables, functions, command options, parameters, class names, and HTML tags where they appear in the text.

`Constant width bold`
> Used to mark lines of output in code listings and command lines to be typed by the user.

`Constant width italic`
> Used as a general placeholder to indicate items that should be replaced by actual values in your own programs.

Comments and Questions

Please address comments and questions concerning this book to the publisher:

> O'Reilly Media, Inc.
> 1005 Gravenstein Highway North
> Sebastopol, CA 95472
> (800) 998-9938 (in the United States or Canada)
> (707) 829-0515 (international/local)
> (707) 829-0104 (fax)

We have a web page for this book, where we list errata, examples, or any additional information. You can access this page at:

> *http://www.oreilly.com/catalog/phpckbk2*

To comment or ask technical questions about this book, send email to:

> *bookquestions@oreilly.com*

For more information about books, conferences, Resource Centers, and the O'Reilly Network, see the O'Reilly web site at:

> *http://www.oreilly.com*

Acknowledgments

Most importantly, a huge thanks to everyone who has contributed their time, creativity, and skills to making PHP what it is today. This amazing volunteer effort has created not only hundreds of thousands of lines of source code, but also comprehensive documentation, a QA infrastructure, lots of add-on applications and libraries, and a thriving user community worldwide. It's a thrill and an honor to add the *PHP Cookbook* to the world of PHP.

Thanks also to our reviewers: Wez Furlong, James Nash, and Mark Oglia.

Thanks to Chris Shiflett and Clay Loveless for their important contributions. Without Chris, Chapter 18 would be much slimmer. Without Clay, there'd be no Chapters 11, 20, 21, or 26. A special thanks to our tireless editor Tatiana Apandi. Her masterful synthesis of the iron fist and the velvet glove provided the necessary glue to orchestrate the successful completion of this edition. Without Tatiana, this book would have ended up as a 27-page pamphlet completed sometime in 2012.

David Sklar

Thanks once again to Adam. We've been working together (in one way or another) for 11 years and PHPing together for 10. There is no one with whom I'd rather have written this book (except, to be completely honest, maybe Ben Franklin, if he could somehow be brought back to life).

Thanks to the folks at Ning for providing (among other things) an opportunity to do fun things with PHP.

To my parents and my sister—thank you for your steady support and love, as well as for being unwitting test subjects when I need to try out explanations of technical things that I hope are intelligible to non-geeks.

For patience, inspiration, and a toad, thanks to Susannah, who continually amazes me.

Adam Trachtenberg

I can't believe I've been using PHP for 10 years. I still remember the first time I used the language formerly known as PHP/FI. Writing web applications in PHP was so much easier than what I had used before that I immediately dumped everything else. The defining moment for me was when writing text to the error log didn't require a complicated sequence of steps involving file handles, but sending a string of text to function straightforwardly named `error_log( )`. Genius.

A big shout out to David. I would not—and could not—have written this without him. I, and *PHP Cookbook*, owe you a big debt of gratitude.

It's tough to complete with Ben Franklin. However, please know that I, too, support the turkey as the official animal of PHP.

Thanks to everyone at eBay for providing me with such a great opportunity to work with so many amazing people that make up the entire eBay community.

Thanks to my parents, family, and friends for their support and encouragement.

Thanks to Elizabeth Hondl. I love you so very much. Stay tuned for my next book, the *Maritime Disaster Cookbook*.

Clay Loveless

I would like to thank Adam Trachtenberg, David Sklar, Tatiana Apandi and the rest of the crew at O'Reilly for making this book possible, and for including me in the process. Special thanks to my wife, Kendra, and my son, Wade, for allowing the time for me to be included.

Chris Shiflett

Thanks to Adam and David for writing such a great book and for giving me the opportunity to contribute.

CHAPTER 1

Strings

1.0 Introduction

Strings in PHP are sequences of bytes, such as "We hold these truths to be self-evident" or "Once upon a time" or even "111211211." When you read data from a file or output it to a web browser, your data are represented as strings.

PHP strings are binary-safe (i.e., they can contain null bytes) and can grow and shrink on demand. Their size is limited only by the amount of memory that is available to PHP.

 Usually, PHP strings are ASCII strings. You must do extra work to handle non-ASCII data like UTF-8 or other multibyte character encodings, see Chapter 19.

Similar in form and behavior to Perl and the Unix shell, strings can be initialized in three ways: with single quotes, with double quotes, and with the "here document" (heredoc) format. With single-quoted strings, the only special characters you need to escape inside a string are backslash and the single quote itself. Example 1-1 shows four single-quoted strings.

Example 1-1. Single-quoted strings

```
print 'I have gone to the store.';
print 'I\'ve gone to the store.';
print 'Would you pay $1.75 for 8 ounces of tap water?';
print 'In double-quoted strings, newline is represented by \n';
```

Example 1-1 prints:

```
I have gone to the store.
I've gone to the store.
Would you pay $1.75 for 8 ounces of tap water?
In double-quoted strings, newline is represented by \n
```

Because PHP doesn't check for variable interpolation or almost any escape sequences in single-quoted strings, defining strings this way is straightforward and fast.

Double-quoted strings don't recognize escaped single quotes, but they do recognize interpolated variables and the escape sequences shown in Table 1-1.

Table 1-1. Double-quoted string escape sequences

Escape sequence	Character
\n	Newline (ASCII 10)
\r	Carriage return (ASCII 13)
\t	Tab (ASCII 9)
\\	Backslash
\$	Dollar sign
\"	Double quotes
\0 through \777	Octal value
\x0 through \xFF	Hex value

Example 1-2 shows some double-quoted strings.

Example 1-2. Double-quoted strings

```
print "I've gone to the store.";
print "The sauce cost \$10.25.";
$cost = '$10.25';
print "The sauce cost $cost.";
print "The sauce cost \$\061\060.\x32\x35.";
```

Example 1-2 prints:

```
I've gone to the store.
The sauce cost $10.25.
The sauce cost $10.25.
The sauce cost $10.25.
```

The last line of Example 1-2 prints the price of sauce correctly because the character 1 is ASCII code 49 decimal and 061 octal. Character 0 is ASCII 48 decimal and 060 octal; 2 is ASCII 50 decimal and 32 hex; and 5 is ASCII 53 decimal and 35 hex.

Heredoc-specified strings recognize all the interpolations and escapes of double-quoted strings, but they don't require double quotes to be escaped. Heredocs start with <<< and a token. That token (with no leading or trailing whitespace), followed by semicolon a to end the statement (if necessary), ends the heredoc. Example 1-3 shows how to define a heredoc.

Example 1-3. Defining a here document

```
print <<< END
It's funny when signs say things like:
    Original "Root" Beer
    "Free" Gift
    Shoes cleaned while "you" wait
```

```
or have other misquoted words.
END;
```

Example 1-3 prints:

```
It's funny when signs say things like:
    Original "Root" Beer
    "Free" Gift
    Shoes cleaned while "you" wait
or have other misquoted words.
```

Newlines, spacing, and quotes are all preserved in a heredoc. By convention, the end-of-string identifier is usually all caps, and it is case sensitive. Example 1-4 shows two more valid heredocs.

Example 1-4. More here documents

```
print <<< PARSLEY
It's easy to grow fresh:
Parsley
Chives
on your windowsill
PARSLEY;

print <<< DOGS
If you like pets, yell out:
DOGS AND CATS ARE GREAT!
DOGS;
```

Heredocs are especially useful for printing out HTML with interpolated variables, since you don't have to escape the double quotes that appear in the HTML elements. Example 1-5 uses a heredoc to print HTML.

Example 1-5. Printing HTML with a here document

```
if ($remaining_cards > 0) {
    $url = '/deal.php';
    $text = 'Deal More Cards';
} else {
    $url = '/new-game.php';
    $text = 'Start a New Game';
}
print <<< HTML
There are <b>$remaining_cards</b> left.
<p>
<a href="$url">$text</a>
HTML;
```

In Example 1-5, the semicolon needs to go after the end-of-string delimiter to tell PHP the statement is ended. In some cases, however, you shouldn't use the semicolon. One of these cases is shown in Example 1-6, which uses a heredoc with the string concatenation operator.

Example 1-6. Concatenation with a here document

```
$html = <<< END
<div class="$divClass">
<ul class="$ulClass">
<li>
END
. $listItem . '</li></div>';

print $html;
```

Assuming some reasonable values for the `$divClass`, `$ulClass`, and `$listItem` variables, Example 1-6 prints:

```
<div class="class1">
<ul class="class2">
<li> The List Item </li></div>
```

In Example 1-6, the expression needs to continue on the next line, so you don't use a semicolon. Note also that in order for PHP to recognize the end-of-string delimiter, the `.` string concatenation operator needs to go on a separate line from the end-of-string delimiter.

Individual bytes in strings can be referenced with square brackets. The first byte in the string is at index 0. Example 1-7 grabs one byte from a string.

Example 1-7. Getting an individual byte in a string

```
$neighbor = 'Hilda';
print $neighbor[3];
```

Example 1-7 prints:

```
d
```

You can also use curly braces to access individual byte in a string. That is, `$neighbor{3}` is the same as `$neighbor[3]`. The curly brace syntax is a newer addition to PHP. It provides a visual distinction between string indexing and array indexing.

1.1 Accessing Substrings

Problem

You want to know if a string contains a particular substring. For example, you want to find out if an email address contains a @.

Solution

Use `strpos( )`, as in Example 1-8.

Example 1-8. Finding a substring with strpos( )

```
<?php
```

```
if (strpos($_POST['email'], '@') === false) {
    print 'There was no @ in the e-mail address!';
 }

?>
```

Discussion

The return value from `strpos()` is the first position in the string (the "haystack") at which the substring (the "needle") was found. If the needle wasn't found at all in the haystack, `strpos()` returns `false`. If the needle is at the beginning of the haystack, `strpos()` returns 0, since position 0 represents the beginning of the string. To differentiate between return values of 0 and `false`, you must use the identity operator (===) or the not–identity operator (!==) instead of regular equals (==) or not-equals (!=). Example 1-8 compares the return value from `strpos()` to `false` using ===. This test only succeeds if strpos returns `false`, not if it returns 0 or any other number.

See Also

Documentation on `strpos()` at *http://www.php.net/strpos*.

1.2 Extracting Substrings

Problem

You want to extract part of a string, starting at a particular place in the string. For example, you want the first eight characters of a username entered into a form.

Solution

Use `substr()` to select your substring, as in Example 1-9.

Example 1-9. Extracting a substring with substr()
```
<?php
$substring = substr($string,$start,$length);
$username = substr($_GET['username'],0,8);
?>
```

Discussion

If `$start` and `$length` are positive, `substr()` returns `$length` characters in the string, starting at `$start`. The first character in the string is at position 0. Example 1-10 has positive `$start` and `$length`.

Example 1-10. Using substr() with positive $start and $length
```
print substr('watch out for that tree',6,5);
```

Example 1-10 prints:

```
out f
```

If you leave out `$length`, `substr( )` returns the string from `$start` to the end of the original string, as shown in Example 1-11.

Example 1-11. Using substr( ) with positive start and no length
```
print substr('watch out for that tree',17);
```

Example 1-11 prints:
```
t tree
```

If `$start` is bigger than the length of the string, `substr( )` returns `false`..

If `$start` plus `$length` goes past the end of the string, `substr( )` returns all of the string from `$start` forward, as shown in Example 1-12.

Example 1-12. Using substr( ) with length past the end of the string
```
print substr('watch out for that tree',20,5);
```

Example 1-12 prints:
```
ree
```

If `$start` is negative, `substr( )` counts back from the end of the string to determine where your substring starts, as shown in Example 1-13.

Example 1-13. Using substr( ) with negative start
```
print substr('watch out for that tree',-6);
print substr('watch out for that tree',-17,5);
```

Example 1-13 prints:
```
t tree
out f
```

With a negative `$start` value that goes past the beginning of the string (for example, if `$start` is −27 with a 20-character string), `substr( )` behaves as if `$start` is 0.

If `$length` is negative, `substr( )` counts back from the end of the string to determine where your substring ends, as shown in Example 1-14.

Example 1-14. Using substr( ) with negative length
```
print substr('watch out for that tree',15,-2);
print substr('watch out for that tree',-4,-1);
```

Example 1-14 prints:
```
hat tr
tre
```

See Also

Documentation on `substr( )` at *http://www.php.net/substr*.

1.3 Replacing Substrings

Problem

You want to replace a substring with a different string. For example, you want to obscure all but the last four digits of a credit card number before printing it.

Solution

Use `substr_replace()`, as in Example 1-15.

Example 1-15. Replacing a substring with substr_replace( )

```
// Everything from position $start to the end of $old_string
// becomes $new_substring
$new_string = substr_replace($old_string,$new_substring,$start);

// $length characters, starting at position $start, become $new_substring
$new_string = substr_replace($old_string,$new_substring,$start,$length);
```

Discussion

Without the `$length` argument, `substr_replace( )` replaces everything from `$start` to the end of the string. If `$length` is specified, only that many characters are replaced:

```
print substr_replace('My pet is a blue dog.','fish.',12);
print substr_replace('My pet is a blue dog.','green',12,4);
$credit_card = '4111 1111 1111 1111';
print substr_replace($credit_card,'xxxx ',0,strlen($credit_card)-4);

My pet is a fish.
My pet is a green dog.
xxxx 1111
```

If `$start` is negative, the new substring is placed at `$start` characters counting from the end of `$old_string`, not from the beginning:

```
print substr_replace('My pet is a blue dog.','fish.',-9);
print substr_replace('My pet is a blue dog.','green',-9,4);

My pet is a fish.
My pet is a green dog.
```

If `$start` and `$length` are 0, the new substring is inserted at the start of `$old_string`:

```
print substr_replace('My pet is a blue dog.','Title: ',0,0);

Title: My pet is a blue dog.
```

The function `substr_replace( )` is useful when you've got text that's too big to display all at once, and you want to display some of the text with a link to the rest. Example 1-16 displays the first 25 characters of a message with an ellipsis after it as a link to a page that displays more text.

Example 1-16. Displaying long text with an ellipsis
```
$r = mysql_query("SELECT id,message FROM messages WHERE id = $id") or die();
$ob = mysql_fetch_object($r);
printf('<a href="more-text.php?id=%d">%s</a>',
       $ob->id, substr_replace($ob->message,' ...',25));
```

The *more-text.php* page referenced in Example 1-16 can use the message ID passed in the query string to retrieve the full message and display it.

See Also

Documentation on `substr_replace( )` at *http://www.php.net/substr-replace*.

1.4 Processing a String One Byte at a Time

Problem

You need to process each byte in a string individually.

Solution

Loop through each byte in the string with `for`. Example 1-17 counts the vowels in a string.

Example 1-17. Processing each byte in a string
```
<?php
$string = "This weekend, I'm going shopping for a pet chicken.";
$vowels = 0;
for ($i = 0, $j = strlen($string); $i < $j; $i++) {
    if (strstr('aeiouAEIOU',$string[$i])) {
        $vowels++;
    }
}
?>
```

Discussion

Processing a string a character at a time is an easy way to calculate the "Look and Say" sequence, as shown in Example 1-18.

Example 1-18. The "Look and Say" sequence
```
<?php
function lookandsay($s) {
    // initialize the return value to the empty string
    $r = '';
    // $m holds the character we're counting, initialize to the first
```

```
    // character in the string
    $m = $s[0];
    // $n is the number of $m's we've seen, initialize to 1
    $n = 1;
    for ($i = 1, $j = strlen($s); $i < $j; $i++) {
        // if this character is the same as the last one
        if ($s[$i] == $m) {
            // increment the count of this character
            $n++;
        } else {
            // otherwise, add the count and character to the return value
            $r .= $n.$m;
            // set the character we're looking for to the current one
            $m = $s[$i];
            // and reset the count to 1
            $n = 1;
        }
    }
    // return the built up string as well as the last count and character
    return $r.$n.$m;
}

for ($i = 0, $s = 1; $i < 10; $i++) {
    $s = lookandsay($s);
    print "$s <br/>\n";
}
```

Example 1-18 prints:

```
1
11
21
1211
111221
312211
13112221
1113213211
31131211131221
13211311123113112211
```

It's called the "Look and Say" sequence because each element is what you get by looking at the previous element and saying what's in it. For example, looking at the first element, 1, you say "one one." So the second element is "11." That's two ones, so the third element is "21." Similarly, that's one two and one one, so the fourth element is "1211," and so on.

See Also

Documentation on for at *http://www.php.net/for*; more about the "Look and Say" sequence at *http://mathworld.wolfram.com/LookandSaySequence.html*.

1.5 Reversing a String by Word or Byte

Problem

You want to reverse the words or the bytes in a string.

Solution

Use `strrev( )` to reverse by byte, as in Example 1-19.

Example 1-19. Reversing a string by byte

```php
<?php
print strrev('This is not a palindrome.');
?>
```

Example 1-19 prints:

```
.emordnilap a ton si sihT
```

To reverse by words, explode the string by word boundary, reverse the words, and then rejoin, as in Example 1-20.

Example 1-20. Reversing a string by word

```php
<?php
$s = "Once upon a time there was a turtle.";
// break the string up into words
$words = explode(' ',$s);
// reverse the array of words
$words = array_reverse($words);
// rebuild the string
$s = implode(' ',$words);
print $s;
?>
```

Example 1-20 prints:

```
turtle. a was there time a upon Once
```

Discussion

Reversing a string by words can also be done all in one line with the code in Example 1-21.

Example 1-21. Concisely reversing a string by word

```php
<?php
$reversed_s = implode(' ',array_reverse(explode(' ',$s)));
?>
```

See Also

Recipe 23.7 discusses the implications of using something other than a space character as your word boundary; documentation on strrev( ) at *http://www.php.net/strrev* and array_reverse( ) at *http://www.php.net/array-reverse*.

1.6 Expanding and Compressing Tabs

Problem

You want to change spaces to tabs (or tabs to spaces) in a string while keeping text aligned with tab stops. For example, you want to display formatted text to users in a standardized way.

Solution

Use str_replace( ) to switch spaces to tabs or tabs to spaces, as shown in Example 1-22.

Example 1-22. Switching tabs and spaces

```php
<?php
$r = mysql_query("SELECT message FROM messages WHERE id = 1") or die();
$ob = mysql_fetch_object($r);
$tabbed = str_replace(' ',"\t",$ob->message);
$spaced = str_replace("\t",' ',$ob->message);

print "With Tabs: <pre>$tabbed</pre>";
print "With Spaces: <pre>$spaced</pre>";
?>
```

Using str_replace( ) for conversion, however, doesn't respect tab stops. If you want tab stops every eight characters, a line beginning with a five-letter word and a tab should have that tab replaced with three spaces, not one. Use the pc_tab_expand( ) function shown in Example 1-23 into turn tabs to spaces in a way that respects tab stops.

Example 1-23. pc_tab_expand( )

```php
<?php
function pc_tab_expand($text) {
    while (strstr($text,"\t")) {
        $text = preg_replace_callback('/^([^\t\n]*)(\t+)/m','pc_tab_expand_helper', $text);
    }
    return $text;
}

function pc_tab_expand_helper($matches) {
    $tab_stop = 8;

    return $matches[1] .
    str_repeat(' ',strlen($matches[2]) *
```

```
                    $tab_stop - (strlen($matches[1]) % $tab_stop));
    }


    $spaced = pc_tab_expand($ob->message);
    ?>
```

You can use the **pc_tab_unexpand( )** function shown in Example 1-24 to turn spaces
back to tabs.

Example 1-24. pc_tab_unexpand( )
```
    <?php
    function pc_tab_unexpand($text) {
        $tab_stop = 8;
        $lines = explode("\n",$text);
        foreach ($lines as $i => $line) {
            // Expand any tabs to spaces
            $line = pc_tab_expand($line);
            $chunks = str_split($line, $tab_stop);
            $chunkCount = count($chunks);
            // Scan all but the last chunk
            for ($j = 0; $j < $chunkCount - 1; $j++) {
                $chunks[$j] = preg_replace('/ {2,}$/',"\t",$chunks[$j]);
            }
            // If the last chunk is a tab-stop's worth of spaces
            // convert it to a tab; Otherwise, leave it alone
            if ($chunks[$chunkCount-1] == str_repeat(' ', $tab_stop)) {
                $chunks[$chunkCount-1] = "\t";
            }
            // Recombine the chunks
            $lines[$i] = implode('',$chunks);
        }
        // Recombine the lines
        return implode("\n",$lines);
    }

    $tabbed = pc_tab_unexpand($ob->message);
    ?>
```

Both functions take a string as an argument and return the string appropriately modified.

Discussion

Each function assumes tab stops are every eight spaces, but that can be modified by
changing the setting of the $tab_stop variable.

The regular expression in **pc_tab_expand( )** matches both a group of tabs and all the
text in a line before that group of tabs. It needs to match the text before the tabs because
the length of that text affects how many spaces the tabs should be replaced with so that
subsequent text is aligned with the next tab stop. The function doesn't just replace each
tab with eight spaces; it adjusts text after tabs to line up with tab stops.

Similarly, `pc_tab_unexpand( )` doesn't just look for eight consecutive spaces and then replace them with one tab character. It divides up each line into eight-character chunks and then substitutes ending whitespace in those chunks (at least two spaces) with tabs. This not only preserves text alignment with tab stops; it also saves space in the string.

See Also

Documentation on `str_replace( )` at *http://www.php.net/str-replace*, on `preg_replace_callback( )` at *http://www.php.net/preg_replace_callback*, and on `str_split( )` at *http://www.php.net/str_split*. Recipe 22.10 has more information on `preg_replace_callback( )`.

1.7 Controlling Case

Problem

You need to capitalize, lowercase, or otherwise modify the case of letters in a string. For example, you want to capitalize the initial letters of names but lowercase the rest.

Solution

Use `ucfirst( )` or `ucwords( )` to capitalize the first letter of one or more words, as shown in Example 1-25.

Example 1-25. Capitalizing letters
```php
<?php
print ucfirst("how do you do today?");
print ucwords("the prince of wales");
?>
```

Example 1-25 prints:
```
How do you do today?
The Prince Of Wales
```

Use `strtolower( )` or `strtoupper( )` to modify the case of entire strings, as in Example 1-26.

Example 1-26. Changing case of strings
```php
print strtoupper("i'm not yelling!");
// Tags must be lowercase to be XHTML compliant
print strtolower('<A HREF="one.php">one</A>');
```

Example 1-26 prints:
```
I'M NOT YELLING!
<a href="one.php">one</a>
```

Discussion

Use ucfirst( ) to capitalize the first character in a string:

```
<?php
print ucfirst('monkey face');
print ucfirst('1 monkey face');
?>
```

This prints:

```
Monkey face
1 monkey face
```

Note that the second phrase is not "1 Monkey face."

Use ucwords( ) to capitalize the first character of each word in a string:

```
<?php
print ucwords('1 monkey face');
print ucwords("don't play zone defense against the philadelphia 76-ers");
?>
```

This prints:

```
1 Monkey Face
Don't Play Zone Defense Against The Philadelphia 76-ers
```

As expected, ucwords( ) doesn't capitalize the "t" in "don't." But it also doesn't capitalize the "e" in "76-ers." For ucwords( ), a word is any sequence of nonwhitespace characters that follows one or more whitespace characters. Since both ' and - aren't whitespace characters, ucwords( ) doesn't consider the "t" in "don't" or the "e" in "76-ers" to be word-starting characters.

Both ucfirst( ) and ucwords( ) don't change the case of non-first letters:

```
<?php
print ucfirst('macWorld says I should get an iBook');
print ucwords('eTunaFish.com might buy itunaFish.Com!');
?>
```

This prints:

```
MacWorld says I should get an iBook
ETunaFish.com Might Buy ItunaFish.Com!
```

The functions strtolower( ) and strtoupper( ) work on entire strings, not just individual characters. All alphabetic characters are changed to lowercase by strtolower( ) and strtoupper( ) changes all alphabetic characters to uppercase:

```
<?php
print strtolower("I programmed the WOPR and the TRS-80.");
print strtoupper('"since feeling is first" is a poem by e. e. cummings.');
?>
```

This prints:

```
i programmed the wopr and the trs-80.
"SINCE FEELING IS FIRST" IS A POEM BY E. E. CUMMINGS.
```

When determining upper- and lowercase, these functions respect your locale settings.

See Also

For more information about locale settings, see Chapter 19; documentation on `ucfirst()` at *http://www.php.net/ucfirst*, `ucwords()` at *http://www.php.net/ucwords*, `strtolower()` at *http://www.php.net/strtolower*, and `strtoupper()` at *http://www.php.net/strtoupper*.

1.8 Interpolating Functions and Expressions Within Strings

Problem

You want to include the results of executing a function or expression within a string.

Solution

Use the string concatenation operator (.), as shown in Example 1-27, when the value you want to include can't be inside the string.

Example 1-27. String concatenation

```php
<?php
print 'You have '.($_REQUEST['boys'] + $_REQUEST['girls']).' children.';
print "The word '$word' is ".strlen($word).' characters long.';
print 'You owe '.$amounts['payment'].' immediately';
print "My circle's diameter is ".$circle->getDiameter().' inches.';
?>
```

Discussion

You can put variables, object properties, and array elements (if the subscript is unquoted) directly in double-quoted strings:

```php
<?php
print "I have $children children.";
print "You owe $amounts[payment] immediately.";
print "My circle's diameter is $circle->diameter inches.";
?>
```

Interpolation with double-quoted strings places some limitations on the syntax of what can be interpolated. In the previous example, `$amounts['payment']` had to be written as `$amounts[payment]` so it would be interpolated properly. Use curly braces around more complicated expressions to interpolate them into a string. For example:

```php
<?php
print "I have less than {$children} children.";
print "You owe {$amounts['payment']} immediately.";
print "My circle's diameter is {$circle->getDiameter()} inches.";
?>
```

Direct interpolation or using string concatenation also works with heredocs. Interpolating with string concatenation in heredocs can look a little strange because the closing heredoc delimiter and the string concatenation operator have to be on separate lines:

```php
<?php
print <<< END
Right now, the time is
END
. strftime('%c') . <<< END
 but tomorrow it will be
END
. strftime('%c',time() + 86400);
?>
```

Also, if you're interpolating with heredocs, make sure to include appropriate spacing for the whole string to appear properly. In the previous example, `Right now the time` has to include a trailing space, and `but tomorrow it will be` has to include leading and trailing spaces.

See Also

For the syntax to interpolate variable variables (such as `${"amount_$i"}`), see Recipe 5.4; documentation on the string concatenation operator at *http://www.php.net/language.operators.string*.

1.9 Trimming Blanks from a String

Problem

You want to remove whitespace from the beginning or end of a string. For example, you want to clean up user input before validating it.

Solution

Use `ltrim( )`, `rtrim( )`, or `trim( )`. `ltrim( )` removes whitespace from the beginning of a string, `rtrim( )` from the end of a string, and `trim( )` from both the beginning and end of a string:

```php
<?php
$zipcode = trim($_REQUEST['zipcode']);
$no_linefeed = rtrim($_REQUEST['text']);
$name = ltrim($_REQUEST['name']);
?>
```

Discussion

For these functions, whitespace is defined as the following characters: newline, carriage return, space, horizontal and vertical tab, and null.

Trimming whitespace off of strings saves storage space and can make for more precise display of formatted data or text within <pre> tags, for example. If you are doing comparisons with user input, you should trim the data first, so that someone who mistakenly enters "98052" as their zip code isn't forced to fix an error that really isn't one. Trimming before exact text comparisons also ensures that, for example, "salami\n" equals "salami." It's also a good idea to normalize string data by trimming it before storing it in a database.

The trim( ) functions can also remove user-specified characters from strings. Pass the characters you want to remove as a second argument. You can indicate a range of characters with two dots between the first and last characters in the range:

```php
<?php
// Remove numerals and space from the beginning of the line
print ltrim('10 PRINT A$',' 0..9');
// Remove semicolon from the end of the line
print rtrim('SELECT * FROM turtles;',';');
?>
```

This prints:

```
PRINT A$
SELECT * FROM turtles
```

PHP also provides chop( ) as an alias for rtrim( ). However, you're best off using rtrim( ) instead because PHP's chop( ) behaves differently than Perl's chop( ) (which is deprecated in favor of chomp( ), anyway), and using it can confuse others when they read your code.

See Also

Documentation on trim( ) at *http://www.php.net/trim*, ltrim( ) at *http://www.php.net/ltrim*, and rtrim( ) at *http://www.php.net/rtrim*.

1.10 Generating Comma-Separated Data

Problem

You want to format data as comma-separated values (CSV) so that it can be imported by a spreadsheet or database.

Solution

Use the fputcsv( ) function to generate a CSV-formatted line from an array of data. Example 1-28 writes the data in $sales into a file.

Example 1-28. Generating comma-separated data

```php
<?php

$sales = array( array('Northeast','2005-01-01','2005-02-01',12.54),
                array('Northwest','2005-01-01','2005-02-01',546.33),
                array('Southeast','2005-01-01','2005-02-01',93.26),
```

```
                  array('Southwest','2005-01-01','2005-02-01',945.21),
                  array('All Regions','--','--',1597.34) );

    $fh = fopen('sales.csv','w') or die("Can't open sales.csv");
    foreach ($sales as $sales_line) {
        if (fputcsv($fh, $sales_line) === false) {
            die("Can't write CSV line");
        }
    }
    fclose($fh) or die("Can't close sales.csv");

    ?>
```

Discussion

To print the CSV-formatted data instead of writing it to a file, use the special output
stream php://output, as shown in Example 1-29.

Example 1-29. Printing comma-separated data

```
    <?php

    $sales = array( array('Northeast','2005-01-01','2005-02-01',12.54),
                    array('Northwest','2005-01-01','2005-02-01',546.33),
                    array('Southeast','2005-01-01','2005-02-01',93.26),
                    array('Southwest','2005-01-01','2005-02-01',945.21),
                    array('All Regions','--','--',1597.34) );

    $fh = fopen('php://output','w');
    foreach ($sales as $sales_line) {
        if (fputcsv($fh, $sales_line) === false) {
            die("Can't write CSV line");
        }
    }
    fclose($fh);
    ?>
```

To put the CSV-formatted data into a string instead of printing it or writing it to a file,
combine the technique in Example 1-29 with output buffering, as shown in Example 1-30.

Example 1-30. Putting comma-separated data into a string

```
    <?php

    $sales = array( array('Northeast','2005-01-01','2005-02-01',12.54),
                    array('Northwest','2005-01-01','2005-02-01',546.33),
                    array('Southeast','2005-01-01','2005-02-01',93.26),
                    array('Southwest','2005-01-01','2005-02-01',945.21),
                    array('All Regions','--','--',1597.34) );

    ob_start();
    $fh = fopen('php://output','w') or die("Can't open php://output");
    foreach ($sales as $sales_line) {
        if (fputcsv($fh, $sales_line) === false) {
```

```php
        die("Can't write CSV line");
    }
}
fclose($fh) or die("Can't close php://output");
$output = ob_get_contents();
ob_end_clean();
?>
```

See Also

Documentation on fputcsv( ) at *http://www.php.net/fputcsv*; Recipe 8.12 more information about output buffering.

1.11 Parsing Comma-Separated Data

Problem

You have data in comma-separated values (CSV) format—for example, a file exported from Excel or a database—and you want to extract the records and fields into a format you can manipulate in PHP.

Solution

If the CSV data is in a file (or available via a URL), open the file with fopen( ) and read in the data with fgetcsv( ). Example 1-31 prints out CSV data in an HTML table.

Example 1-31. Reading CSV data from a file

```php
<?php
$fp = fopen('sample2.csv','r') or die("can't open file");
print "<table>\n";
while($csv_line = fgetcsv($fp)) {
    print '<tr>';
    for ($i = 0, $j = count($csv_line); $i < $j; $i++) {
        print '<td>'.htmlentities($csv_line[$i]).'</td>';
    }
    print "</tr>\n";
}
print '</table>\n';
fclose($fp) or die("can't close file");
?>
```

Discussion

In PHP 4, you must provide a second argument to fgetcsv( ) that is a value larger than the maximum length of a line in your CSV file. (Don't forget to count the end-of-line whitespace.) In PHP 5 the line length is optional. Without it, fgetcsv( ) reads in an entire line of data. (Or, in PHP 5.0.4 and later, you can pass a line length of 0 to do the same thing.) If your average line length is more than 8,192 bytes, your program may run faster if you specify an explicit line length instead of letting PHP figure it out.

You can pass fgetcsv( ) an optional third argument, a delimiter to use instead of a comma (,). However, using a different delimiter somewhat defeats the purpose of CSV as an easy way to exchange tabular data.

Don't be tempted to bypass fgetcsv( ) and just read a line in and explode( ) on the commas. CSV is more complicated than that, able to deal with field values that have, for example, literal commas in them that should not be treated as field delimiters. Using fgetcsv( ) protects you and your code from subtle errors.

See Also

Documentation on fgetcsv( ) at *http://www.php.net/fgetcsv*.

1.12 Generating Fixed-Width Field Data Records

Problem

You need to format data records such that each field takes up a set amount of characters.

Solution

Use pack( ) with a format string that specifies a sequence of space-padded strings. Example 1-32 transforms an array of data into fixed-width records.

Example 1-32. Generating fixed-width field data records

```php
<?php

$books = array( array('Elmer Gantry', 'Sinclair Lewis', 1927),
                array('The Scarlatti Inheritance','Robert Ludlum',1971),
                array('The Parsifal Mosaic','William Styron',1979) );

foreach ($books as $book) {
    print pack('A25A15A4', $book[0], $book[1], $book[2]) . "\n";
}

?>
```

Discussion

The format string A25A14A4 tells pack( ) to transform its subsequent arguments into a 25-character space-padded string, a 14-character space-padded string, and a 4-character space-padded string. For space-padded fields in fixed-width records, pack( ) provides a concise solution.

To pad fields with something other than a space, however, use substr( ) to ensure that the field values aren't too long and str_pad( ) to ensure that the field values aren't too short. Example 1-33 transforms an array of records into fixed-width records with .-padded fields.

Example 1-33. Generating fixed-width field data records without pack()

```php
<?php

$books = array( array('Elmer Gantry', 'Sinclair Lewis', 1927),
                array('The Scarlatti Inheritance','Robert Ludlum',1971),
                array('The Parsifal Mosaic','William Styron',1979) );

foreach ($books as $book) {
    $title  = str_pad(substr($book[0], 0, 25), 25, '.');
    $author = str_pad(substr($book[1], 0, 15), 15, '.');
    $year   = str_pad(substr($book[2], 0, 4), 4, '.');
    print "$title$author$year\n";
}

?>
```

See Also

Documentation on pack( ) at *http://www.php.net/pack* and on str_pad( ) at *http://www.php.net/str_pad*. Recipe 1.16 discusses pack( ) format strings in more detail.

1.13 Parsing Fixed-Width Field Data Records

Problem

You need to break apart fixed-width records in strings.

Solution

Use substr( ) as shown in Example 1-34.

Example 1-34. Parsing fixed-width records with substr()

```php
<?php
$fp = fopen('fixed-width-records.txt','r') or die ("can't open file");
while ($s = fgets($fp,1024)) {
    $fields[1] = substr($s,0,10);  // first field:  first 10 characters of the line
    $fields[2] = substr($s,10,5);  // second field: next 5 characters of the line
    $fields[3] = substr($s,15,12); // third field:  next 12 characters of the line
    // a function to do something with the fields
    process_fields($fields);
}
fclose($fp) or die("can't close file");
?>
```

Or unpack( ), as shown in Example 1-35.

Example 1-35. Parsing fixed-width records with unpack()

```php
<?php
$fp = fopen('fixed-width-records.txt','r') or die ("can't open file");
while ($s = fgets($fp,1024)) {
    // an associative array with keys "title", "author", and "publication_year"
```

```php
    $fields = unpack('A25title/A14author/A4publication_year',$s);
    // a function to do something with the fields
    process_fields($fields);
}
fclose($fp) or die("can't close file");
?>
```

Discussion

Data in which each field is allotted a fixed number of characters per line may look like
this list of books, titles, and publication dates:

```php
<?php
$booklist=<<<END
Elmer Gantry             Sinclair Lewis1927
The Scarlatti InheritanceRobert Ludlum 1971
The Parsifal Mosaic      Robert Ludlum 1982
Sophie's Choice          William Styron1979
END;
?>
```

In each line, the title occupies the first 25 characters, the author's name the next 14
characters, and the publication year the next 4 characters. Knowing those field widths,
you can easily use `substr( )` to parse the fields into an array:

```php
<?php
$books = explode("\n",$booklist);

for($i = 0, $j = count($books); $i < $j; $i++) {
  $book_array[$i]['title'] = substr($books[$i],0,25);
  $book_array[$i]['author'] = substr($books[$i],25,14);
  $book_array[$i]['publication_year'] = substr($books[$i],39,4);
}
?>
```

Exploding `$booklist` into an array of lines makes the looping code the same whether
it's operating over a string or a series of lines read in from a file.

The loop can be made more flexible by specifying the field names and widths in a
separate array that can be passed to a parsing function, as shown in the
`pc_fixed_width_substr( )` function in Example 1-36.

Example 1-36. pc_fixed_width_substr( )

```php
<?php
function pc_fixed_width_substr($fields,$data) {
  $r = array();
  for ($i = 0, $j = count($data); $i < $j; $i++) {
    $line_pos = 0;
    foreach($fields as $field_name => $field_length) {
      $r[$i][$field_name] = rtrim(substr($data[$i],$line_pos,$field_length));
      $line_pos += $field_length;
    }
  }
  return $r;
```

```
    }

    $book_fields = array('title' => 25,
                         'author' => 14,
                         'publication_year' => 4);

    $book_array = pc_fixed_width_substr($book_fields,$books);
    ?>
```

The variable $line_pos keeps track of the start of each field and is advanced by the
previous field's width as the code moves through each line. Use rtrim( ) to remove
trailing whitespace from each field.

You can use unpack( ) as a substitute for substr( ) to extract fields. Instead of specifying
the field names and widths as an associative array, create a format string for
unpack( ). A fixed-width field extractor using unpack( ) looks like the
pc_fixed_width_unpack( ) function shown in Example 1-37.

Example 1-37. pc_fixed_width_unpack( )

```
    <?php

    function pc_fixed_width_unpack($format_string,$data) {
      $r = array();
      for ($i = 0, $j = count($data); $i < $j; $i++) {
        $r[$i] = unpack($format_string,$data[$i]);
      }
      return $r;
    }

    $book_array = pc_fixed_width_unpack('A25title/A14author/A4publication_year',
                                        $books);

    ?>
```

Because the A format to unpack( ) means "space-padded string," there's no need to
rtrim( ) off the trailing spaces.

Once the fields have been parsed into $book_array by either function, the data can be
printed as an HTML table, for example:

```
    <?php
    $book_array = pc_fixed_width_unpack('A25title/A14author/A4publication_year',
                                        $books);
    print "<table>\n";
    // print a header row
    print '<tr><td>';
    print join('</td><td>',array_keys($book_array[0]));
    print "</td></tr>\n";
    // print each data row
    foreach ($book_array as $row) {
        print '<tr><td>';
        print join('</td><td>',array_values($row));
        print "</td></tr>\n";
```

```
        }
        print '</table>\n';
        ?>
```

Joining data on `</td><td>` produces a table row that is missing its first `<td>` and last `</td>`. We produce a complete table row by printing out `<tr><td>` before the joined data and `</td></tr>` after the joined data.

Both `substr( )` and `unpack( )` have equivalent capabilities when the fixed-width fields are strings, but `unpack( )` is the better solution when the elements of the fields aren't just strings.

If all of your fields are the same size, `str_split( )` is a handy shortcut for chopping up incoming data. Available in PHP 5, it returns an array made up of sections of a string. Example 1-38 uses `str_split( )` to break apart a string into 32-byte pieces.

Example 1-38. Chopping up a string with str_split( )

```
<?php
$fields = str_split($line_of_data,32);
// $fields[0] is bytes 0 - 31
// $fields[1] is bytes 32 - 63
// and so on
```

See Also

For more information about `unpack( )`, see Recipe 1.16 and *http://www.php.net/unpack*; documentation on `str_split( )` at *http://www.php.net/str_split*; Recipe 4.8 discusses `join( )`.

1.14 Taking Strings Apart

Problem

You need to break a string into pieces. For example, you want to access each line that a user enters in a `<textarea>` form field.

Solution

Use `explode( )` if what separates the pieces is a constant string:

```
<?php
$words = explode(' ','My sentence is not very complicated');
?>
```

Use `split( )` or `preg_split( )` if you need a POSIX or Perl-compatible regular expression to describe the separator:

```
<?php
$words = split(' +','This sentence  has   some extra whitespace   in it.');
$words = preg_split('/\d\. /','my day: 1. get up 2. get dressed 3. eat toast');
$lines = preg_split('/[\n\r]+/',$_REQUEST['textarea']);
?>
```

Use `spliti( )` or the `/i` flag to `preg_split( )` for case-insensitive separator matching:

```php
<?php
$words = spliti(' x ','31 inches x 22 inches X 9 inches');
$words = preg_split('/ x /i','31 inches x 22 inches X 9 inches');
?>
```

Discussion

The simplest solution of the bunch is `explode( )`. Pass it your separator string, the string to be separated, and an optional limit on how many elements should be returned:

```php
<?php
$dwarves = 'dopey,sleepy,happy,grumpy,sneezy,bashful,doc';
$dwarf_array = explode(',',$dwarves);
?>
```

This makes `$dwarf_array` a seven-element array, so `print_r($dwarf_array)` prints:

```
Array
(
    [0] => dopey
    [1] => sleepy
    [2] => happy
    [3] => grumpy
    [4] => sneezy
    [5] => bashful
    [6] => doc
)
```

If the specified limit is less than the number of possible chunks, the last chunk contains the remainder:

```php
<?php
$dwarf_array = explode(',',$dwarves,5);
print_r($dwarf_array);
?>
```

This prints:

```
Array
(
    [0] => dopey
    [1] => sleepy
    [2] => happy
    [3] => grumpy
    [4] => sneezy,bashful,doc
)
```

The separator is treated literally by `explode( )`. If you specify a comma and a space as a separator, it breaks the string only on a comma followed by a space, not on a comma or a space.

With `split( )`, you have more flexibility. Instead of a string literal as a separator, it uses a POSIX regular expression:

```
<?php
$more_dwarves = 'cheeky,fatso, wonder boy, chunky,growly, groggy, winky';
$more_dwarf_array = split(', ?',$more_dwarves);
?>
```

This regular expression splits on a comma followed by an optional space, which treats all the new dwarves properly. A dwarf with a space in his name isn't broken up, but everyone is broken apart whether they are separated by "," or ", ". print_r($more_dwarf_array) prints:

```
Array
(
    [0] => cheeky
    [1] => fatso
    [2] => wonder boy
    [3] => chunky
    [4] => growly
    [5] => groggy
    [6] => winky
)
```

Similar to split( ) is preg_split( ), which uses a Perl-compatible regular expression engine instead of a POSIX regular expression engine. With preg_split( ), you can take advantage of various Perl-ish regular expression extensions, as well as tricks such as including the separator text in the returned array of strings:

```
<?php
$math = "3 + 2 / 7 - 9";
$stack = preg_split('/ *([+\-\/*]) */',$math,-1,PREG_SPLIT_DELIM_CAPTURE);
print_r($stack);
?>
```

This prints:

```
Array
(
    [0] => 3
    [1] => +
    [2] => 2
    [3] => /
    [4] => 7
    [5] => -
    [6] => 9
)
```

The separator regular expression looks for the four mathematical operators (+, -, /, *), surrounded by optional leading or trailing spaces. The PREG_SPLIT_DELIM_CAPTURE flag tells preg_split( ) to include the matches as part of the separator regular expression in parentheses in the returned array of strings. Only the mathematical operator character class is in parentheses, so the returned array doesn't have any spaces in it.

See Also

Regular expressions are discussed in more detail in Chapter 22; documentation on `explode( )` at *http://www.php.net/explode*, `split( )` at *http://www.php.net/split*, and `preg_split( )` at *http://www.php.net/preg-split*.

1.15 Wrapping Text at a Certain Line Length

Problem

You need to wrap lines in a string. For example, you want to display text in `<pre>`/ `</pre>` tags but have it stay within a regularly sized browser window.

Solution

Use `wordwrap( )`:

```php
<?php
$s = "Four score and seven years ago our fathers brought forth
on this continent a new nation, conceived in liberty and
dedicated to the proposition that all men are created equal.";

print "<pre>\n".wordwrap($s)."\n</pre>";
?>
```

This prints:

```
<pre>
Four score and seven years ago our fathers brought forth on this continent
a new nation, conceived in liberty and dedicated to the proposition that
all men are created equal.
</pre>
```

Discussion

By default, `wordwrap( )` wraps text at 75 characters per line. An optional second argument specifies different line length:

```php
<?php
print wordwrap($s,50);
?>
```

This prints:

```
Four score and seven years ago our fathers brought
forth on this continent a new nation, conceived in
liberty and dedicated to the proposition that all
men are created equal.
```

Other characters besides \n can be used for line breaks. For double spacing, use "\n\n":

```php
<?php
print wordwrap($s,50,"\n\n");
?>
```

This prints:

```
Four score and seven years ago our fathers brought

forth on this continent a new nation, conceived in

liberty and dedicated to the proposition that all

men are created equal.
```

There is an optional fourth argument to wordwrap( ) that controls the treatment of words that are longer than the specified line length. If this argument is 1, these words are wrapped. Otherwise, they span past the specified line length:

```php
<?php
print wordwrap('jabberwocky',5);
print wordwrap('jabberwocky',5,"\n",1);
?>
```

This prints:

```
jabberwocky

jabbe
rwock
y
```

See Also

Documentation on wordwrap( ) at *http://www.php.net/wordwrap*.

1.16 Storing Binary Data in Strings

Problem

You want to parse a string that contains values encoded as a binary structure or encode values into a string. For example, you want to store numbers in their binary representation instead of as sequences of ASCII characters.

Solution

Use pack( ) to store binary data in a string:

```php
<?php
$packed = pack('S4',1974,106,28225,32725);
?>
```

Use unpack( ) to extract binary data from a string:

```php
<?php
$nums = unpack('S4',$packed);
?>
```

Discussion

The first argument to pack( ) is a format string that describes how to encode the data that's passed in the rest of the arguments. The format string S4 tells pack( ) to produce four unsigned short 16-bit numbers in machine byte order from its input data. Given 1974, 106, 28225, and 32725 as input on a little-endian machine, this returns eight bytes: 182, 7, 106, 0, 65, 110, 213, and 127. Each two-byte pair corresponds to one of the input numbers: 7 * 256 + 182 is 1974; 0 * 256 + 106 is 106; 110 * 256 + 65 = 28225; 127 * 256 + 213 = 32725.

The first argument to unpack( ) is also a format string, and the second argument is the data to decode. Passing a format string of S4, the eight-byte sequence that pack( ) produced returns a four-element array of the original numbers. print_r($nums) prints:

```
Array
(
    [1] => 1974
    [2] => 106
    [3] => 28225
    [4] => 32725
)
```

In unpack( ), format characters and their count can be followed by a string to be used as an array key. For example:

```php
<?php
$nums = unpack('S4num',$packed);
print_r($nums);
?>
```

This prints:

```
Array
(
    [num1] => 1974
    [num2] => 106
    [num3] => 28225
    [num4] => 32725
)
```

Multiple format characters must be separated with / in unpack( ):

```php
<?php
$nums = unpack('S1a/S1b/S1c/S1d',$packed);
print_r($nums);
?>
```

This prints:

```
Array
(
    [a] => 1974
```

```
            [b] => 106
            [c] => 28225
            [d] => 32725
        )
```

The format characters that can be used with pack( ) and unpack( ) are listed in Table 1-2.

Table 1-2. Format characters for pack( ) and unpack( )

Format character	Data type
a	NUL-padded string
A	Space-padded string
h	Hex string, low nibble first
H	Hex string, high nibble first
c	signed char
C	unsigned char
s	signed short (16 bit, machine byte order)
S	unsigned short (16 bit, machine byte order)
n	unsigned short (16 bit, big endian byte order)
v	unsigned short (16 bit, little endian byte order)
i	signed int (machine-dependent size and byte order)
I	unsigned int (machine-dependent size and byte order)
l	signed long (32 bit, machine byte order)
L	unsigned long (32 bit, machine byte order)
N	unsigned long (32 bit, big endian byte order)
V	unsigned long (32 bit, little endian byte order)
f	float (machine-dependent size and representation)
d	double (machine-dependent size and representation)
x	NUL byte
X	Back up one byte
@	NUL-fill to absolute position

For a, A, h, and H, a number after the format character indicates how long the string is. For example, A25 means a 25-character space-padded string. For other format characters, a following number means how many of that type appear consecutively in a string. Use * to take the rest of the available data.

You can convert between data types with unpack( ). This example fills the array $ascii with the ASCII values of each character in $s:

```
<?php
$s = 'platypus';
```

```
$ascii = unpack('c*',$s);
print_r($ascii);
?>
```

This prints:

```
Array
(
    [1] => 112
    [2] => 108
    [3] => 97
    [4] => 116
    [5] => 121
    [6] => 112
    [7] => 117
    [8] => 115
)
```

See Also

Documentation on pack( ) at *http://www.php.net/pack* and unpack( ) at *http://www.php.net/unpack*.

1.17 Program: Downloadable CSV File

Combining the header( ) function to change the content type of what your PHP program outputs with the fputcsv( ) function for data formatting lets you send CSV files to browsers that will be automatically handed off to a spreadsheet program (or whatever application is configured on a particular client system to handle CSV files). Example 1-39 formats the results of an SQL SELECT query as CSV data and provides the correct headers so that it is properly handled by the browser.

Example 1-39. Downloadable CSV file

```php
<?php

require_once 'DB.php';
// Connect to the database
$db = DB::connect('mysql://david:hax0r@localhost/phpcookbook');

// Retrieve data from the database
$sales_data = $db->getAll('SELECT region, start, end, amount FROM sales');
// Open filehandle for fputcsv()
$output = fopen('php://output','w') or die("Can't open php://output");
$total = 0;

// Tell browser to expect a CSV file
header('Content-Type: application/csv');
header('Content-Disposition: attachment; filename="sales.csv"');

// Print header row
fputcsv($output,array('Region','Start Date','End Date','Amount'));
// Print each data row and increment $total
foreach ($sales_data as $sales_line) {
```

```
        fputcsv($output, $sales_line);
        $total += $sales_line[3];
    }
    // Print total row and close file handle
    fputcsv($output,array('All Regions','--','--',$total));
    fclose($output) or die("Can't close php://output");

?>
```

Example 1-39 sends two headers to ensure that the browser handles the CSV output properly. The first header, Content-Type, tells the browser that the output is not HTML, but CSV. The second header, Content-Disposition, tells the browser not to display the output but to attempt to load an external program to handle it. The filename attribute of this header supplies a default filename for the browser to use for the downloaded file.

If you want to provide different views of the same data, you can combine the formatting code in one page and use a query string variable to determine which kind of data formatting to do. In Example 1-40, the format query string variable controls whether the results of an SQL SELECT query are returned as an HTML table or CSV.

Example 1-40. Dynamic CSV or HTML

```
    <?php

    $db = new PDO('sqlite:/usr/local/data/sales.db');

    $query = $db->query('SELECT region, start, end, amount FROM sales', PDO::FETCH_NUM);
    $sales_data = $db->fetchAll();
    $total = 0;
    $column_headers = array('Region','Start Date','End Date','Amount');
    // Decide what format to use
    $format = $_GET['format'] == 'csv' ? 'csv' : 'html';

    // Print format-appropriate beginning
    if ($format == 'csv') {
        $output = fopen('php://output','w') or die("Can't open php://output");
        header('Content-Type: application/csv');
        header('Content-Disposition: attachment; filename="sales.csv"');
        fputcsv($output,$column_headers);
    } else {
        echo '<table><tr><th>';
        echo implode('</th><th>', $column_headers);
        echo '</th></tr>';
    }

    foreach ($sales_data as $sales_line) {
        // Print format-appropriate line
        if ($format == 'csv') {
            fputcsv($output, $sales_line);
        } else {
            echo '<tr><td>' . implode('</td><td>', $sales_line) . '</td></tr>';
        }
        $total += $sales_line[3];
```

```
    }
    $total_line = array('All Regions','--','--',$total);

    // Print format-appropriate footer
    if ($format == 'csv') {
        fputcsv($output,$total_line);
        fclose($output) or die("Can't close php://output");
     } else {
        echo '<tr><td>' . implode('</td><td>', $total_line) . '</td></tr>';
        echo '</table>';
     }
    ?>
```

Accessing the program in Example 1-40 with format=csv in the query string causes it to return CSV-formatted output. Any other format value in the query string causes it to return HTML output. The logic that sets $format to CSV or HTML could easily be extended to other output formats like XML. If you have many places where you want to offer for download the same data in multiple formats, package the code in Example 1-40 into a function that accepts an array of data and a format specifier and then displays the right results.

CHAPTER 2

Numbers

2.0 Introduction

In everyday life, numbers are easy to identify. They're 3:00 P.M., as in the current time, or $1.29, as in the cost of a pint of milk. Maybe they're like π, the ratio of the circumference to the diameter of a circle. They can be pretty large, like Avogadro's number, which is about 6×10^{23}. In PHP, numbers can be all these things.

However, PHP doesn't treat all these numbers as "numbers." Instead, it breaks them down into two groups: integers and floating-point numbers. Integers are whole numbers, such as −4, 0, 5, and 1,975. Floating-point numbers are decimal numbers, such as −1.23, 0.0, 3.14159, and 9.9999999999.

Conveniently, most of the time PHP doesn't make you worry about the differences between the two because it automatically converts integers to floating-point numbers and floating-point numbers to integers. This conveniently allows you to ignore the underlying details. It also means 3/2 is 1.5, not 1, as it would be in some programming languages. PHP also automatically converts from strings to numbers and back. For instance, 1+"1" is 2.

However, sometimes this blissful ignorance can cause trouble. First, numbers can't be infinitely large or small; there's a minimum size of 2.2e−308 and a maximum size of about 1.8e308.* If you need larger (or smaller) numbers, you must use the BCMath or GMP libraries, which are discussed in Recipe 2.14.

Next, floating-point numbers aren't guaranteed to be exactly correct but only correct plus or minus a small amount. This amount is small enough for most occasions, but you can end up with problems in certain instances. For instance, humans automatically convert 6 followed by an endless string of 9s after the decimal point to 7, but PHP thinks it's 6 with a bunch of 9s. Therefore, if you ask PHP for the integer value of that number, it returns 6, not 7. For similar reasons, if the digit located in the 200th decimal place is significant to you, don't use floating-point numbers—instead, use the BCMath and

---

* These numbers are actually platform-specific, but the values are common because they are from the 64-bit IEEE standard 754.

GMP libraries. But for most occasions, PHP behaves very nicely when playing with numbers and lets you treat them just as you do in real life.

2.1 Checking Whether a Variable Contains a Valid Number

Problem

You want to ensure that a variable contains a number, even if it's typed as a string. Alternatively, you want to check if a variable is not only a number, but is also specifically typed as a one.

Solution

Use `is_numeric()` to discover whether a variable contains a number:

```php
<?php
if (is_numeric(5))          { /* true  */ }
if (is_numeric('5'))        { /* true  */ }
if (is_numeric("05"))       { /* true  */ }
if (is_numeric('five'))     { /* false */ }

if (is_numeric(0xDECAFBAD)) { /* true  */ }
if (is_numeric("10e200"))   { /* true  */ }
?>
```

Discussion

Numbers come in all shapes and sizes. You cannot assume that something is a number simply because it only contains the characters 0 through 9. What about decimal points, or negative signs? You can't simply add them into the mix because the negative must come at the front, and you can only have one decimal point. And then there's hexadecimal numbers and scientific notation.

Instead of rolling your own function, use `is_numeric()` to check whether a variable holds something that's either an actual number (as in it's typed as an integer or floating point), or it's a string containing characters that can be translated into a number.

There's an actual difference here. Technically, the integer 5 and the string 5 aren't the same in PHP. However, most of the time you won't actually be concerned about the distinction, which is why the behavior of `is_numeric()` is useful.

Helpfully, `is_numeric()` properly parses decimal numbers, such as 5.1; however, numbers with thousands separators, such as 5,100, cause `is_numeric()` to return false.

To strip the thousands separators from your number before calling `is_numeric()`, use `str_replace()`:

```php
<?php
is_numeric(str_replace($number, ',', ''));
?>
```

To check if your number is a specific type, there are a variety of related functions with self-explanatory names: is_float( ) (or is_double( ) or is_real( ); they're all the same) and is_int( ) (or is_integer( ) or is_long( )).

To validate input data, use the techniques from Recipe 9.3 instead of is_numeric( ). That recipe describes how to check for positive or negative integers, decimal numbers, and a handful of other formats.

See Also

Recipe 9.3 for validating numeric user input; documentation on is_numeric( ) at *http://www.php.net/is-numeric* and str_replace( ) at *http://www.php.net/str-replace*.

2.2 Comparing Floating-Point Numbers

Problem

You want to check whether two floating-point numbers are equal.

Solution

Use a small delta value, and check if the numbers have a difference smaller than that delta:

```php
<?php
$delta = 0.00001;

$a = 1.00000001;
$b = 1.00000000;

if (abs($a - $b) < $delta) { /* $a and $b are equal */ }
?>
```

Discussion

Floating-point numbers are represented in binary form with only a finite number of bits for the mantissa and the exponent. You get overflows when you exceed those bits. As a result, sometimes PHP (just like some other languages) doesn't believe that two equal numbers are actually equal because they may differ toward the very end.

To avoid this problem, instead of checking if $a == $b, make sure the first number is within a very small amount ($delta) of the second one. The size of your delta should be the smallest amount of difference you care about between two numbers. Then use abs( ) to get the absolute value of the difference.

See Also

Recipe 2.3 for information on rounding floating-point numbers; documentation on floating-point numbers in PHP at *http://www.php.net/language.types.float*.

2.3 Rounding Floating-Point Numbers

Problem

You want to round a floating-point number, either to an integer value or to a set number of decimal places.

Solution

To round a number to the closest integer, use `round( )` :

```
$number = round(2.4);    // $number = 2
```

To round up, use `ceil( )`:

```
$number = ceil(2.4);     // $number = 3
```

To round down, use `floor( )`:

```
$number = floor(2.4);    // $number = 2
```

Discussion

If a number falls exactly between two integers, PHP rounds away from 0:

```
$number = round(2.5);    //  3

$number = round(-2.5);   // -3
```

You may remember from Recipe 2.2 that floating-point numbers don't always work out to exact values because of how the computer stores them. This can create confusion. A value you expect to have a decimal part of "0.5" might instead be ".499999...9" (with a whole bunch of 9s) or ".500000...1" (with many 0s and a trailing 1).

PHP automatically incorporates a little "fuzz factor" into its rounding calculations, so you don't need to worry about this.

To keep a set number of digits after the decimal point, `round( )` accepts an optional precision argument. For example, perhaps you are calculating the total price for the items in a user's shopping cart:

```
<?php
$cart = 54.23;
$tax = $cart * .05;
$total = $cart + $tax;        // $total = 56.9415

$final = round($total, 2);    // $final = 56.94
?>
```

To round a number down, use the `floor( )` function:

```
$number = floor( 2.1);  //  2

$number = floor( 2.9);  //  2

$number = floor(-2.1);  // -3

$number = floor(-2.9);  // -3
```

While to round up, use the `ceil( )` function:

```
$number = ceil( 2.1);  //  3

$number = ceil( 2.9);  //  3

$number = ceil(-2.1);  // -2

$number = ceil(-2.9);  // -2
```

These two functions are named because when you're rounding down, you're rounding "toward the floor," and when you're rounding up, you're rounding "toward the ceiling."

See Also

Recipe 2.2 for information on comparing floating-point numbers; documentation on `ceil( )` at *http://www.php.net/ceil*, on `floor( )` at *http://www.php.net/floor*, and on `round( )` at *http://www.php.net/round*.

2.4 Operating on a Series of Integers

Problem

You want to apply a piece of code to a range of integers.

Solution

Use a `for` loop:

```php
<?php
for ($i = $start; $i <= $end; $i++) {
    plot_point($i);
}
?>
```

You can increment using values other than 1. For example:

```php
<?php
for ($i = $start; $i <= $end; $i += $increment) {
    plot_point($i);
}
?>
```

If you want to preserve the numbers for use beyond iteration, use the range( ) method:

```php
<?php
$range = range($start, $end);
?>
```

Discussion

Loops like this are common. For instance, you could be plotting a function and need to calculate the results for multiple points on the graph. Or you could be a student counting down the number of seconds until the end of school.

The for loop method uses a single integer and you have great control over the loop, because you can increment and decrement $i freely. Also, you can modify $i from inside the loop.

In the last example in the Solution, range( ) returns an array with values from $start to $end. The advantage of using range( ) is its brevity, but this technique has a few disadvantages. For one, a large array can take up unnecessary memory. Also, you're forced to increment the series one number at a time, so you can't loop through a series of even integers, for example.

It's valid for $start to be larger than $end. In this case, the numbers returned by range( ) are in descending order. Also, you can use it to retrieve character sequences:

```php
<?php
print_r(range('l', 'p'));
?>

Array
(
    [0] => l
    [1] => m
    [2] => n
    [3] => o
    [4] => p
)
```

See Also

Recipe 4.3 for details on initializing an array to a range of integers; documentation on range( ) at *http://www.php.net/range*.

2.5 Generating Random Numbers Within a Range

Problem

You want to generate a random number within a range of numbers.

Solution

Use mt_rand( ):

```
// random number between $upper and $lower, inclusive
$random_number = mt_rand($lower, $upper);
```

Discussion

Generating random numbers is useful when you want to display a random image on a page, randomize the starting position of a game, select a random record from a database, or generate a unique session identifier.

To generate a random number between two endpoints, pass mt_rand( ) two arguments:

```
$random_number = mt_rand(1, 100);
```

Calling mt_rand( ) without any arguments returns a number between 0 and the maximum random number, which is returned by mt_getrandmax( ).

Generating truly random numbers is hard for computers to do. Computers excel at following instructions methodically; they're not so good at spontaneity. If you want to instruct a computer to return random numbers, you need to give it a specific set of repeatable commands; the fact that they're repeatable undermines the desired randomness.

PHP has two different random number generators, a classic function called rand( ) and a better function called mt_rand( ). MT stands for Mersenne Twister, which is named for the French monk and mathematician Marin Mersenne and the type of prime numbers he's associated with. The algorithm is based on these prime numbers. Since mt_rand( ) is less predictable and faster than rand( ), we prefer it to rand( ).

If you're running a version of PHP earlier than 4.2, before using mt_rand( ) (or rand( )) for the first time in a script, you need to seed the generator by calling mt_srand( ) (or srand( )). The *seed* is a number the random function uses as the basis for generating the random numbers it returns; it's used to solve the repeatable versus random dilemma mentioned earlier. Use the value returned by microtime( ), a high-precision time function, to get a seed that changes very quickly and is unlikely to repeat —qualities desirable in a good seed. After the initial seed, you don't need to reseed the randomizer. PHP 4.2 and later automatically handle seeding for you, but if you manually provide a seed before calling mt_rand( ) for the first time, PHP doesn't alter it by substituting a new seed of its own.

If you want to select a random record from a database, an easy way is to find the total number of fields inside the table, select a random number in that range, and then request that row from the database, as in Example 2-1.

Example 2-1. Selecting a random row from a database

```php
<?php
$sth = $dbh->query('SELECT COUNT(*) AS count FROM quotes');
if ($row = $sth->fetchRow()) {
    $count = $row[0];
} else {
    die ($row->getMessage());
```

```
    }

    $random = mt_rand(0, $count - 1);

    $sth = $dbh->query("SELECT quote FROM quotes LIMIT $random,1");
    while ($row = $sth->fetchRow()) {
        print $row[0] . "\n";
    }
    ?>
```

This snippet finds the total number of rows in the table, computes a random number inside that range, and then uses LIMIT $random,1 to SELECT one line from the table starting at position $random.

Alternatively, if you're using MySQL 3.23 or above, you can do this:

```
    $sth = $dbh->query('SELECT quote FROM quotes ORDER BY RAND() LIMIT 1');
    while ($row = $sth->fetchRow()) {
        print $row[0] . "\n";
    }
```

In this case, MySQL randomizes the lines, and then the first row is returned.

See Also

Recipe 2.6 for how to generate biased random numbers; documentation on mt_rand( ) at *http://www.php.net/mt-rand* and rand( ) at *http://www.php.net/rand*; the MySQL Manual on **rand( )** is found at *http://www.mysql.com/doc/M/a/ Mathematical_functions.html*.

2.6 Generating Biased Random Numbers

Problem

You want to generate random numbers, but you want these numbers to be somewhat biased, so that numbers in certain ranges appear more frequently than others. For example, you want to spread out a series of banner ad impressions in proportion to the number of impressions remaining for each ad campaign.

Solution

Use the pc_rand_weighted( ) function shown in Example 2-2.

Example 2-2. pc_rand_weighted( )

```
    <?php
    // returns the weighted randomly selected key
    function pc_rand_weighted($numbers) {
        $total = 0;
        foreach ($numbers as $number => $weight) {
            $total += $weight;
            $distribution[$number] = $total;
```

```
    }
    $rand = mt_rand(0, $total - 1);
    foreach ($distribution as $number => $weights) {
        if ($rand < $weights) { return $number; }
    }
  }
?>
```

Discussion

Imagine if instead of an array in which the values are the number of remaining impressions, you have an array of ads in which each ad occurs exactly as many times as its remaining number of impressions. You can simply pick an unweighted random place within the array, and that'd be the ad that shows.

This technique can consume a lot of memory if you have millions of impressions remaining. Instead, you can calculate how large that array would be (by totaling the remaining impressions), pick a random number within the size of the make-believe array, and then go through the array figuring out which ad corresponds to the number you picked. For instance:

```
$ads = array('ford' => 12234, // advertiser, remaining impressions
             'att'  => 33424,
             'ibm'  => 16823);

$ad = pc_rand_weighted($ads);
```

See Also

Recipe 2.5 for how to generate random numbers within a range.

2.7 Taking Logarithms

Problem

You want to take the logarithm of a number.

Solution

For logs using base *e* (natural log), use **log( )**:

```
$log = log(10);          // 2.30258092994
```

For logs using base 10, use **log10( )**:

```
$log10 = log10(10);      // 1
```

For logs using other bases, pass the base as the second argument to **log( )**:

```
$log2  = log(10, 2); // 3.3219280948874
```

Discussion

Both `log( )` and `log10( )` are defined only for numbers that are greater than zero. If you pass in a number equal to or less than zero, they return `NAN`, which stands for "not a number."

See Also

Documentation on `log( )` at *http://www.php.net/log* and `log10( )` at *http://www.php.net/log10*.

2.8 Calculating Exponents

Problem

You want to raise a number to a power.

Solution

To raise *e* to a power, use `exp( )`:

```
$exp = exp(2);       // 7.3890560989307
```

To raise it to any power, use `pow( )`:

```
$exp = pow( 2, M_E);  // 6.5808859910179

$pow = pow( 2, 10);   // 1024
$pow = pow( 2, -2);   // 0.25
$pow = pow( 2, 2.5);  // 5.6568542494924

$pow = pow(-2, 10);   // 1024
$pow = pow( 2, -2);   // 0.25
$pow = pow(-2, -2.5); // NAN (Error: Not a Number)
```

Discussion

The built-in constant `M_E` is an approximation of the value of *e*. It equals 2.7182818284590452354. So `exp($n)` and `pow(M_E, $n)` are identical.

It's easy to create very large numbers using `exp( )` and `pow( )`; if you outgrow PHP's maximum size (almost 1.8e308), see Recipe 2.14 for how to use the arbitrary precision functions. With `exp( )` and `pow( )`, PHP returns `INF` (infinity) if the result is too large and `NAN` (not a number) on an error.

See Also

Documentation on `pow( )` at *http://www.php.net/pow*, `exp( )` at *http://www.php.net/exp*, and information on predefined mathematical constants at *http://www.php.net/math*.

2.9 Formatting Numbers

Problem

You have a number and you want to print it with thousands and decimals separators. For example, you want to display the number of people who have viewed a page, or the percentage of people who have voted for an option in a poll.

Solution

Use the `number_format()` function to format as an integer:

```
$number = 1234.56;
print number_format($number);    // 1,235 because number is rounded up
```

Specify a number of decimal places to format as a decimal:

```
print number_format($number, 2); // 1,234.56
```

Discussion

The `number_format()` function formats a number by inserting the correct decimal and thousands separators for your locale. If you want to manually specify these values, pass them as the third and fourth parameters:

```
$number = 1234.56;
print number_format($number, 2, '@', '#'); // 1#234@56
```

The third argument is used as the decimal point and the last separates thousands. If you use these options, you must specify both arguments.

By default, `number_format()` rounds the number to the nearest integer. If you want to preserve the entire number, but you don't know ahead of time how many digits follow the decimal point in your number, use this:

```
$number = 1234.56; // your number
list($int, $dec) = explode('.', $number);
print number_format($number, strlen($dec));
```

The `localeconv()` function provides locale-specific data, including number format information. For example:

```
setlocale(LC_ALL, 'zh_CN');

print_r(localeconv());

Array
(
    [decimal_point] => .
    [thousands_sep] => ,
    [int_curr_symbol] => CNY
    [currency_symbol] => ¥
```

```
[mon_decimal_point] => .
[mon_thousands_sep] => ,
[positive_sign] =>
[negative_sign] => -
[int_frac_digits] => 0
[frac_digits] => 0
[p_cs_precedes] => 1
[p_sep_by_space] => 0
[n_cs_precedes] => 1
[n_sep_by_space] => 0
[p_sign_posn] => 1
[n_sign_posn] => 4
[grouping] => Array
    (
        [0] => 3
        [1] => 3
    )

[mon_grouping] => Array
    (
        [0] => 3
        [1] => 3
    )

)
```

Use the decimal_point, thousands_sep, and other settings to see how to format a number for that locale.

See Also

Chapter 19 for information on internationalization and localization; documentation on localeconv( ) at *http://www.php.net/localeconv* and number_format( ) at *http://www.php.net/number-format*.

2.10 Formatting Monetary Values

Problem

You have a number and you want to print it with thousands and decimals separators. For instance, you want to display prices for items in a shopping cart.

Solution

Use the money_format( ) function with the %n formatting option for a national currency format:

```
$number = 1234.56;
setlocale(LC_MONETARY, 'en_US');
print money_format('%n', $number);     // $1,234.56
```

For an international format, pass %i:

```
print money_format('%i', $number); // USD 1,234.56
```

Discussion

The money_format( ) function formats a number by inserting the correct currency symbol, decimal, and thousands separators for your locale. It takes a formatting string and
a number to format.

For easy formatting, use the %n and %i specifiers, for in-country and international
standard currency displays, respectively.

To get the correct country format, change the locale, as shown in Example 2-3.

Example 2-3. Displaying currency using standard formats
```
<?php
$number = 1234.56;
setlocale(LC_MONETARY, 'en_US');
print money_format('%n', $number);    // $1,234.56
print money_format('%i', $number);    // USD 1,234.56

setlocale(LC_MONETARY, 'fr_FR');
print money_format('%n', $number);    // 1 234,56 Eu
print money_format('%i', $number);    // 1 234,56 EUR

setlocale(LC_MONETARY, 'it_IT');
print money_format('%n', $number);    // Eu 1.235
print money_format('%i', $number);    // EUR  1.235
?>
```

If your locale is not set, the function returns the same string you provide. For more on
setting locales, see Chapter 19.

You can also use printf-like formatting options, including (to wrap negative numbers
inside of parentheses, and ! to suppress the currency symbol, as shown in Example 2-4.

Example 2-4. Displaying currency using custom formats
```
<?php
$number = -1234.56;
setlocale(LC_MONETARY, 'en_US');
print money_format('%n', $number);    // -$1,234.56

print money_format('%(n', $number);   // ($1,234.56)

print money_format('%!n', $number);   // -1,234.56
?>
```

A complete list of options, including left and right precision, fill characters, and disa-
bling grouping is available at *http://www.php.net/money-format*.

This function uses the underlying Unix strfmon( ) system function , so it is unavailable
on Windows machines.

For more on currency formatting, including a substitute algorithm for Windows, see Recipe 19.6.

See Also

Recipe 19.6; documentation on `money_format( )` at *http://www.php.net/money-format.*

2.11 Printing Correct Plurals

Problem

You want to correctly pluralize words based on the value of a variable. For instance, you are returning text that depends on the number of matches found by a search.

Solution

Use a conditional expression:

```
$number = 4;
print "Your search returned $number " . ($number == 1 ? 'hit' : 'hits') . '.';

Your search returned 4 hits.
```

Discussion

The line is slightly shorter when written as:

```
print "Your search returned $number hit" . ($number == 1 ? '' : 's') . '.';
```

However, for odd pluralizations, such as "person" versus "people," we find it clearer to break out the entire word rather than just the letter.

Another option is to use one function for all pluralization, as shown in the `pc_may_pluralize( )` function in Example 2-5.

Example 2-5. pc_may_pluralize( )

```php
<?php
function pc_may_pluralize($singular_word, $amount_of) {

    // array of special plurals
    $plurals = array(
        'fish' => 'fish',
        'person' => 'people',
    );

    // only one
    if (1 == $amount_of) {
        return $singular_word;
    }

    // more than one, special plural
    if (isset($plurals[$singular_word])) {
```

```
        return $plurals[$singular_word];
    }

    // more than one, standard plural: add 's' to end of word
    return $singular_word . 's';
}
?>
```

Here are some examples:

```
$number_of_fish = 1;
print "I ate $number_of_fish " . pc_may_pluralize('fish', $number_of_fish) . '.';

$number_of_people = 4;
print 'Soylent Green is ' . pc_may_pluralize('person', $number_of_people) . '!';

I ate 1 fish.
Soylent Green is people!
```

If you plan to have multiple plurals inside your code, using a function such as
pc_may_pluralize( ) increases readability. To use the function, pass
pc_may_pluralize( ) the singular form of the word as the first argument and the amount
as the second. Inside the function, there's a large array, $plurals, that holds all the
special cases. If the $amount is 1, you return the original word. If it's greater, you return
the special pluralized word, if it exists. As a default, just add an "s" to the end of the
word.

2.12 Calculating Trigonometric Functions

Problem

You want to use trigonometric functions, such as sine, cosine, and tangent.

Solution

PHP supports many trigonometric functions natively: sin( ) , cos( ), and tan( ):

```
$cos = cos(2.1232);
```

You can also use their inverses: asin( ), acos( ), and atan( ):

```
$atan = atan(1.2);
```

Discussion

These functions assume all angles are in radians, not degrees. (See Recipe 2.13 if this
is a problem.)

The function atan2( ) takes two variables $x and $y, and computes atan($x/$y). However, it always returns the correct sign because it uses both parameters when finding
the quadrant of the result.

For secant, cosecant, and cotangent, you should manually calculate the reciprocal values of sin( ), cos( ), and tan( ):

```
$n = .707;

$secant     = 1 / sin($n);
$cosecant   = 1 / cos($n);
$cotangent  = 1 / tan($n);
```

You can also use hyperbolic functions: sinh( ), cosh( ), and tanh( ), plus, of course, asin( ), acosh( ), and atanh( ). The inverse functions, however, aren't supported on Windows.

See Also

Recipe 2.13 for how to perform trig operations in degrees, not radians; documentation on sin( ) at *http://www.php.net/sin*, cos( ) at *http://www.php.net/cos*, tan( ) at *http://www.php.net/tan*, asin( ) at *http://www.php.net/asin*, acos( ) at *http://www.php.net/acos*, atan( ) at *http://www.php.net/atan*, and atan2( ) at *http://www.php.net/atan2*.

2.13 Doing Trigonometry in Degrees, Not Radians

Problem

You have numbers in degrees but want to use the trigonometric functions.

Solution

Use deg2rad( ) and rad2deg( ) on your input and output:

```
$cosine = cos(deg2rad($degree));
```

Discussion

By definition, 360 degrees is equal to 2π radians, so it's easy to manually convert between the two formats. However, these functions use PHP's internal value of π, so you're assured a high-precision answer. To access this number for other calculations, use the constant M_PI, which is 3.14159265358979323846.

There is no built-in support for radians. This is considered a feature, not a bug.

See Also

Recipe 2.12 for trig basics; documentation on deg2rad( ) at *http://www.php.net/deg2rad* and rad2deg( ) at *http://www.php.net/rad2deg*.

2.14 Handling Very Large or Very Small Numbers

Problem

You need to use numbers that are too large (or small) for PHP's built-in floating-point numbers.

Solution

Use either the BCMath or GMP libraries.

Using BCMath:

```
$sum = bcadd('1234567812345678', '8765432187654321');

// $sum is now the string '9999999999999999'
print $sum;
```

Using GMP:

```
$sum = gmp_add('1234567812345678', '8765432187654321');

// $sum is now a GMP resource, not a string; use gmp_strval() to convert
print gmp_strval($sum);
```

Discussion

The BCMath library is easy to use. You pass in your numbers as strings, and the function returns the sum (or difference, product, etc.) as a string. However, the range of actions you can apply to numbers using BCMath is limited to basic arithmetic.

Another option is the GMP library. While most members of the GMP family of functions accept integers and strings as arguments, they prefer to pass numbers around as resources, which are essentially pointers to the numbers. So unlike BCMath functions, which return strings, GMP functions return only resources. You then pass the resource to any GMP function, and it acts as your number.

The only downside is when you want to view or use the resource with a non-GMP function, you need to explicitly convert it using `gmp_strval( )` or `gmp_intval( )`.

GMP functions are liberal in what they accept. For instance, see Example 2-6.

Example 2-6. Adding numbers using GMP

```php
<?php
$four = gmp_add(2, 2);          // You can pass integers
$eight = gmp_add('4', '4');     // Or strings
$twelve = gmp_add($four, $eight); // Or GMP resources
print gmp_strval($twelve);      // Prints 12
?>
```

However, you can do many more things with GMP numbers than addition, such as raising a number to a power, computing large factorials very quickly, finding a greatest common divisor (GCD), and other fancy mathematical stuff, as shown in Example 2-7.

Example 2-7. Computing fancy mathematical stuff using GMP

```php
<?php
// Raising a number to a power
$pow = gmp_pow(2, 10);              // 1024

// Computing large factorials very quickly
$factorial = gmp_fact(20);         // 2432902008176640000

// Finding a GCD
$gcd = gmp_gcd (123, 456);         // 3

// Other fancy mathematical stuff
$legdendre = gmp_legendre(1, 7);   // 1
?>
```

The BCMath and GMP libraries aren't necessarily enabled with all PHP configurations. BCMath is bundled with PHP, so it's likely to be available. However, GMP isn't bundled with PHP, so you'll need to download, install it, and instruct PHP to use it during the configuration process. Check the values of `function_defined('bcadd')` and `function_defined('gmp_init')` to see if you can use BCMath and GMP. If you're using Windows, you need to be running PHP 5.1 or higher to use GMP.

Another options for high-precision mathematics is PECL's `big_int` library, shown in Example 2-8.

Example 2-8. Adding numbers using big_int

```php
<?php
$two  = bi_from_str('2');
$four = bi_add($two, $two);
print bi_to_str($four)             // Prints 4

// Computing large factorials very quickly
$factorial = bi_fact(20);          // 2432902008176640000
?>
```

It's faster than BCMath, and almost as powerful as GMP. However, while the GMP is licensed under the LGPL, big_int is under a BSD-style license.

See Also

Documentation on BCMath at *http://www.php.net/bc*, big_int at *http://pecl.php.net/big_int*, and GMP at *http://www.php.net/gmp*.

2.15 Converting Between Bases

Problem

You need to convert a number from one base to another.

Solution

Use the base_convert( ) function:

```
$hex = 'a1';                              // hexadecimal number (base 16)

// convert from base 16 to base 10
$decimal = base_convert($hex, 16, 10); // $decimal is now 161
```

Discussion

The base_convert( ) function changes a string in one base to the correct string in another. It works for all bases from 2 to 36 inclusive, using the letters a through z as additional symbols for bases above 10. The first argument is the number to be converted, followed by the base it is in and the base you want it to become.

There are also a few specialized functions for conversions to and from base 10 and the most commonly used other bases of 2, 8, and 16. They're bindec( ) and decbin( ), octdec( ) and decoct( ), and hexdec( ) and dechex( ):

```
// convert to base 10
print bindec(11011); // 27
print octdec(33);    // 27
print hexdec('1b');  // 27

// convert from base 10
print decbin(27);    // 11011
print decoct(27);    // 33
print dechex(27);    // 1b
```

Another alternative is to use printf( ), which allows you to convert decimal numbers to binary, octal, and hexadecimal numbers with a wide range of formatting, such as leading zeros and a choice between upper- and lowercase letters for hexadecimal numbers.

For instance, say you want to print out HTML color values:

```
printf('#%02X%02X%02X', 0, 102, 204); // #0066CC
```

See Also

Documentation on base_convert( ) at *http://www.php.net/base-convert* and sprintf( ) formatting options at *http://www.php.net/sprintf*.

2.16 Calculating Using Numbers in Bases Other Than Decimal

Problem

You want to perform mathematical operations with numbers formatted not in decimal, but in octal or hexadecimal. For example, you want to calculate web-safe colors in hexadecimal.

Solution

Prefix the number with a leading symbol, so PHP knows it isn't in base 10. The following values are all equal:

```
0144  // base 8
 100  // base 10
0x64  // base 16
```

Here's how to count from decimal 1 to 15 using hexadecimal notation:

```
for ($i = 0x1; $i < 0x10; $i++) { print "$i\n"; }
```

Discussion

Even if you use hexadecimally formatted numbers in a for loop, by default all numbers are printed in decimal. In other words, the code in the Solution doesn't print out "..., 8, 9, a, b, ..." To print in hexadecimal, use one of the methods listed in Recipe 2.15. Here's an example:

```
for ($i = 0x1; $i < 0x10; $i++) { print dechex($i) . "\n"; }
```

For most calculations, it's easier to use decimal. Sometimes, however, it's more logical to switch to another base—for example, when using the 216 web-safe colors. Every web color code is of the form *RRGGBB*, where *RR* is the red color, *GG* is the green color, and *BB* is the blue color. Each color is actually a two-digit hexadecimal number between 0 and FF.

What makes web-safe colors special is that *RR*, *GG*, and *BB* each must be one of the following six numbers: 00, 33, 66, 99, CC, or FF (in decimal: 0, 51, 102, 153, 204, or 255). So 003366 is web safe, but 112233 is not. Web-safe colors render without dithering on a 256-color display.

When creating a list of these numbers, use hexadecimal notation in this triple-loop to reinforce the list's hexadecimal basis, as shown in Example 2-9.

Example 2-9. Printing out all the web-safe color codes

```php
<?php
for ($rr = 0; $rr <= 0xFF; $rr += 0x33)
    for ($gg = 0; $gg <= 0xFF; $gg += 0x33)
        for ($bb = 0; $bb <= 0xFF; $bb += 0x33)
            printf("%02X%02X%02X\n", $rr, $gg, $bb);
?>
```

Here the loops compute all possible web-safe colors. However, instead of stepping through them in decimal, you use hexadecimal notation, because it reinforces the hexadecimal link between the numbers. Print them out using `printf( )` to format them as uppercase hexadecimal numbers at least two digits long. One-digit numbers are printed with a leading zero.

See Also

Recipe 2.15 for details on converting between bases; Chapter 3, "Web Design Principles for Print Designers," in *Web Design in a Nutshell* by Jennifer Niederst Robbins (O'Reilly).

2.17 Finding the Distance Between Two Places

Problem

You want to find the distance between two coordinates on planet Earth.

Solution

Use `pc_sphere_distance`, as shown in Example 2-10.

Example 2-10. Finding the distance between two points

```php
<?php
function pc_sphere_distance($lat1, $lon1, $lat2, $lon2, $radius = 6378.135) {
    $rad = doubleval(M_PI/180.0);

    $lat1 = doubleval($lat1) * $rad;
    $lon1 = doubleval($lon1) * $rad;
    $lat2 = doubleval($lat2) * $rad;
    $lon2 = doubleval($lon2) * $rad;

    $theta = $lon2 - $lon1;
    $dist = acos(sin($lat1) * sin($lat2) + cos($lat1) * cos($lat2) * cos($theta));
    if ($dist < 0) { $dist += M_PI; }

    return $dist = $dist * $radius; // Default is Earth equatorial radius in kilometers
}

// NY, NY (10040)
$lat1 = 40.858704;
$lon1 = -73.928532;

// SF, CA (94144)
$lat2 = 37.758434;
$lon2 = -122.435126;

$dist = pc_sphere_distance($lat1, $lon1, $lat2, $lon2);
printf("%.2f\n", $dist * 0.621); // Format and convert to miles
?>
```

Discussion

Since the Earth is not flat, you cannot get an accurate distance between two locations using a standard Pythagorean distance formula. You must use a Great Circle algorithm instead, such as the one in `pc_sphere_distance( )`.

Pass in the latitude and longitude of your two points as the first four arguments. First come the latitude and longitude of the origin, and then come the latitude and longitude of the destination. The value returned is the distance between them in kilometers:

```
// NY, NY (10040)
$lat1 = 40.858704;
$lon1 = -73.928532;

// SF, CA (94144)
$lat2 = 37.758434;
$lon2 = -122.435126;

$dist = pc_sphere_distance($lat1, $lon1, $lat2, $lon2);
printf("%.2f\n", $dist * 0.621); // Format and convert to miles
```

This code finds the distance between New York City and San Francisco, converts the distance to miles, formats it to have two decimal places, and then prints out the result.

Because the Earth is not a perfect sphere, these calculations are somewhat approximate and could have an error up to 0.5%.

`pc_sphere_distance( )` accepts an alternative sphere radius as an optional fifth argument. This lets you, for example, discover the distance between points on Mars:

```
$martian_radius = 3397;
$dist = pc_sphere_distance($lat1, $lon1, $lat2, $lon2, $martian_radius);
printf("%.2f\n", $dist * 0.621); // Format and convert to miles
```

See Also

Recipe 2.12 for trig basics; the Wikipedia entry on *Earth Radius* at *http://en.wikipedia.org/wiki/Earth_radius*; and the article "Trip Mapping with PHP" at *http://www.onlamp.com/pub/a/php/2002/11/07/php_map.html*.

CHAPTER 3

Dates and Times

3.0 Introduction

Displaying and manipulating dates and times seems simple at first but gets more difficult depending on how diverse and complicated your users are. Do your users span more than one time zone? Probably so, unless you are building an intranet or a site with a very specific geographical audience. Is your audience frightened away by timestamps that look like "2002-07-20 14:56:34 EDT" or do they need to be calmed with familiar representations like "Saturday July 20, 2000 (2:56 P.M.)"? Calculating the number of hours between today at 10 A.M. and today at 7 P.M. is pretty easy. How about between today at 3 A.M. and noon on the first day of next month? Finding the difference between dates is discussed in Recipes 3.5 and 3.6.

These calculations and manipulations are made even more hectic by daylight saving (or summer) time (DST). Because of DST, there are times that don't exist (in most of the United States, 2 A.M. to 3 A.M. on a day in the spring) and times that exist twice (in most of the United States, 1 A.M. to 2 A.M. on a day in the fall). Some of your users may live in places that observe DST, some may not. Recipes 3.11 and 3.12 provide ways to work with time zones and DST.

Programmatic time handling is made much easier by two conventions. First, treat time internally as Coordinated Universal Time (abbreviated UTC and also known as GMT, Greenwich Mean Time), the patriarch of the time-zone family with no DST or summer time observance. This is the time zone at 0 degrees longitude, and all other time zones are expressed as offsets (either positive or negative) from it. Second, treat time not as an array of different values for month, day, year, minute, second, etc., but as seconds elapsed since the Unix epoch: midnight on January 1, 1970 (UTC, of course). This makes calculating intervals much easier, and PHP has plenty of functions to help you move easily between epoch timestamps and human-readable time representations.

The function `mktime( )` produces epoch timestamps from a given set of time parts, while `date( )`, given an epoch timestamp, returns a formatted time string. Example 3-1 uses these functions to find on what day of the week New Year's Day 1986 occurred.

Example 3-1. Using mktime( ) and date( )

```php
<?php
$stamp = mktime(0,0,0,1,1,1986);
print date('l',$stamp);
?>
```

Example 3-1 prints:

```
Wednesday
```

In Example 3-1, `mktime( )` returns the epoch timestamp at midnight on January 1, 1986. The l format character to `date( )` tells it to return the full name of the day of the week that corresponds to the given epoch timestamp. Recipe 3.4 details the many format characters available to `date( )`.

In this book, the phrase *epoch timestamp* refers to a count of seconds since the Unix epoch. *Time parts* (or *date parts* or *time and date parts*) means an array or group of time and date components such as day, month, year, hour, minute, and second. *Formatted time string* (or *formatted date string*, etc.) means a string that contains some particular grouping of time and date parts—for example, "2002-03-12," "Wednesday, 11:23 A.M.," or "February 25."

If you used epoch timestamps as your internal time representation, you avoided any Y2K issues, because the difference between 946702799 (1999-12-31 23:59:59 UTC) and 946702800 (2000-01-01 00:00:00 UTC) is treated just like the difference between any other two timestamps. You may, however, run into a Y2038 problem. January 19, 2038 at 3:14:07 A.M. (UTC) is 2147483647 seconds after midnight January 1, 1970. What's special about 2147483647? It's $2^{31} - 1$, which is the largest integer expressible when 32 bits represent a signed integer. (The 32nd bit is used for the sign.)

The solution? At some point before January 19, 2038, make sure you trade up to hardware that uses, say, a 64-bit quantity for time storage. This buys you about another 292 billion years. (Just 39 bits would be enough to last you until about 10680, well after the impact of the Y10K bug has leveled the Earth's cold fusion factories and faster-than-light travel stations.) The year 2038 might seem far off right now, but so did 2000 to COBOL programmers in the 1950s and 1960s. Don't repeat their mistake!

3.1 Finding the Current Date and Time

Problem

You want to know what the time or date is.

Solution

Use `strftime( )` or `date( )` for a formatted time string, as in Example 3-2.

Example 3-2. Finding the current date and time

```php
<?php
print strftime('%c');
```

```
print "\n";
print date('r');
?>
```

Example 3-2 prints:

```
Wed May 10 18:29:59 2006
Wed, 10 May 2006 18:29:59 -0400
```

Use getdate( ) or localtime( ) if you want time parts. Example 3-3 shows how these functions work.

Example 3-3. Finding time parts

```
<?php
$now_1 = getdate();
$now_2 = localtime();
print "{$now_1['hours']}:{$now_1['minutes']}:{$now_1['seconds']}\n";
print "$now_2[2]:$now_2[1]:$now_2[0]";
```

Example 3-3 prints:

```
18:23:45
18:23:45
```

Discussion

The functions strftime( ) and date( ) can produce a variety of formatted time and date strings. They are discussed in more detail in Recipe 3.4. Both localtime( ) and getdate( ), on the other hand, return arrays whose elements are the different pieces of the specified date and time.

The associative array getdate( ) returns the key/value pairs listed in Table 3-1.

Table 3-1. Return array from getdate( )

Key	Value
seconds	Seconds
minutes	Minutes
hours	Hours
mday	Day of the month
wday	Day of the week, numeric (Sunday is 0, Saturday is 6)
mon	Month, numeric
year	Year, numeric (4 digits)
yday	Day of the year, numeric (e.g., 299)
weekday	Day of the week, textual, full (e.g., "Friday")
month	Month, textual, full (e.g., "January")
0	Seconds since epoch (what time( ) returns)

Example 3-4 shows how to use getdate( ) to print out the month, day, and year.

Example 3-4. Finding the month, day, and year

```
<?php
$a = getdate();
printf('%s %d, %d',$a['month'],$a['mday'],$a['year']);
?>
```

Example 3-4 prints:

```
May 5, 2007
```

Pass getdate( ) an epoch timestamp as an argument to make the returned array the appropriate values for local time at that timestamp. The month, day, and year at epoch timestamp 163727100 is shown in Example 3-5.

Example 3-5. getdate() with a specific timestamp

```
<?php
$a = getdate(163727100);
printf('%s %d, %d',$a['month'],$a['mday'],$a['year']);
?>
```

Example 3-5 prints:

```
March 10, 1975
```

The function localtime( ) returns an array of time and date parts. It also takes an epoch timestamp as an optional first argument, as well as a boolean as an optional second argument. If that second argument is true, localtime( ) returns an associative array instead of a numerically indexed array. The keys of that array are the same as the members of the tm_struct structure that the C function localtime( ) returns, as shown in Table 3-2.

Table 3-2. Return array from localtime()

Numeric position	Key	Value
0	tm_sec	Second
1	tm_min	Minutes
2	tm_hour	Hour
3	tm_mday	Day of the month
4	tm_mon	Month of the year (January is 0)
5	tm_year	Years since 1900
6	tm_wday	Day of the week (Sunday is 0)
7	tm_yday	Day of the year
8	tm_isdst	Is daylight savings time in effect?

Example 3-6 shows how to use localtime( ) to print out today's date in month/day/year format.

Example 3-6. Using localtime( )

```php
<?php
$a = localtime();
$a[4] += 1;
$a[5] += 1900;
print "$a[4]/$a[3]/$a[5]";
```

Example 3-6 prints:

6/23/2006

The month is incremented by 1 before printing since `localtime( )` starts counting months with 0 for January, but we want to display `1` if the current month is January. Similarly, the year is incremented by 1900 because `localtime( )` starts counting years with 0 for 1900.

See Also

Documentation on `strftime( )` at *http://www.php.net/strftime*, `date( )` at *http://www.php.net/date*, `getdate( )` at *http://www.php.net/getdate*, and `localtime( )` at *http://www.php.net/localtime*.

3.2 Converting Time and Date Parts to an Epoch Timestamp

Problem

You want to know what epoch timestamp corresponds to a set of time and date parts.

Solution

Use `mktime( )` if your time and date parts are in the local time zone, as shown in Example 3-7.

Example 3-7. Getting a specific epoch timestamp

```php
<?php
// 7:45:03 PM on March 10, 1975, local time
$then = mktime(19,45,3,3,10,1975);
?>
```

Use `gmmktime( )`, as in Example 3-8, if your time and date parts are in GMT.

Example 3-8. Getting a specific GMT-based epoch timestamp

```php
<?php
// 7:45:03 PM on March 10, 1975, in GMT
$then = gmmktime(19,45,3,3,10,1975);
?>
```

Discussion

The functions `mktime( )` and `gmmktime( )` each take a date and time's parts (hour, minute, second, month, day, year) and return the appropriate Unix epoch timestamp. The components are treated as local time by mktime( ), while gmmktime( ) treats them as a date and time in UTC. These functions return sensible results only for times within the epoch. Most systems store epoch timestamps in a 32-bit signed integer, so "within the epoch" means between 8:45:51 P.M. December 13, 1901 UTC and 3:14:07 A.M. January 19, 2038 UTC.

In Example 3-9, $stamp_future is set to the epoch timestamp for 3:25 P.M. on June 4, 2012. The epoch timestamp can be fed back to strftime( ) to produce a formatted time string.

Example 3-9. Working with epoch timestamps

```php
<?php
$stamp_future = mktime(15,25,0,6,4,2012);

print $stamp_future;
print strftime('%c',$stamp_future);
?>
```

Example 3-9 prints:

```
1338837900
Mon Jun 4 15:25:00 2012
```

Because the calls to mktime( ) in Example 3-9 were made on a computer set to EDT (which is four hours behind GMT), using gmmktime( ) instead produces epoch timestamps that are 14,400 seconds (four hours) smaller, as shown in Example 3-10.

Example 3-10. Epoch timestamps and gmmktime( )

```php
<?php
$stamp_future = gmmktime(15,25,0,6,4,2012);

print $stamp_future;
print strftime('%c',$stamp_future);
```

Example 3-10 prints:

```
1338823500
Mon Jun 4 11:25:00 2012
```

Feeding a gmmktime( )-generated epoch timestamp back to strftime( ) produces formatted time strings that are also four hours earlier.

In versions of PHP before 5.1.0, mktime( ) and gmmktime( ) could accept an optional boolean seventh argument indicating a DST flag (1 if DST is being observed, 0 if not). In PHP 5.1.0 and up, whether daylight savings time is being observed is controlled by the currently active default time zone, set with date_default_timezone_set( ).

See Also

Recipe 3.3 for how to convert an epoch timestamp back to time and date parts; documentation on mktime( ) at *http://www.php.net/mktime* and gmmktime( ) at *http://*

www.php.net/gmmktime, and on `date_default_timezone_set()` at *http://www.php.net/date_default_timezone_set*.

3.3 Converting an Epoch Timestamp to Time and Date Parts

Problem

You want the set of time and date parts that corresponds to a particular epoch timestamp.

Solution

Pass an epoch timestamp to `getdate()`: `$time_parts = getdate(163727100);`.

Discussion

The time parts returned by `getdate()` are detailed in Table 3-1. These time parts are in local time. If you want time parts in another time zone corresponding to a particular epoch timestamp, see Recipe 3.11.

See Also

Recipe 3.2 for how to convert time and date parts back to epoch timestamps; Recipe 3.11 for how to deal with time zones; documentation on `getdate()` at *http://www.php.net/getdate*.

3.4 Printing a Date or Time in a Specified Format

Problem

You need to print out a date or time formatted in a particular way.

Solution

Use `date()` or `strftime()`, as shown in Example 3-11.

Example 3-11. Using date() and strftime()

```php
<?php
print strftime('%c');
print date('m/d/Y');
?>
```

Example 3-11 prints something like:

```
Mon Dec  3 11:31:08 2007
12/03/2007
```

Discussion

Both `date()` and `strftime()` are flexible functions that can produce a formatted time string with a variety of components. The formatting characters for these functions are listed in Table 3-3. The Windows column indicates whether the formatting character is supported by `strftime()` on Windows systems.

Table 3-3. strftime() and date() format characters

Type	strftime()	date()	Description	Range	Windows
Hour	%H	H	Hour, numeric, 24-hour clock	00–23	Yes
Hour	%I	h	Hour, numeric, 12-hour clock	01–12	Yes
Hour	%k		Hour, numeric, 24-hour clock, leading zero as space	0–23	No
Hour	%l	/	Hour, numeric, 12-hour clock, leading zero as space	1–12	No
Hour	%p	A	A.M. or P.M. designation for current locale		Yes
Hour	%P	a	A.M. or P.M. designation for current locale		No
Hour		G	Hour, numeric, 24-hour clock, leading zero trimmed	0–23	No
Hour		g	Hour, numeric, 12-hour clock, leading zero trimmed	0–1	No
Minute	%M	i	Minute, numeric	00–59	Yes
Second	%S	s	Second, numeric	00–61[a]	Yes
Day	%d	d	Day of the month, numeric	01–31	Yes
Day	%e		Day of the month, numeric, leading zero as space	1–31	No
Day	%j	z	Day of the year, numeric	001–366 for `strftime()`; 0–365 for `date()`	Yes
Day	%u	N	Day of the week, numeric (Monday is 1)	1–7	No
Day	%w	w	Day of the week, numeric (Sunday is 0)	0–6	Yes
Day		j	Day of the month, numeric, leading zero trimmed	1–31	No

Type	strftime( )	date( )	Description	Range	Windows
Day		S	English ordinal suffix for day of the month, textual	"st," "th," "nd," "rd"	No
Week	%a	D	Abbreviated weekday name, text for current locale		Yes
Week	%A	l	Full weekday name, text for current locale		Yes
Week	%U		Week number in the year, numeric, first Sunday is the first day of the first week	00–53	Yes
Week	%V	W	ISO 8601:1988 week number in the year, numeric, week 1 is the first week that has at least 4 days in the current year, Monday is the first day of the week	01–53	No
Week	%W		Week number in the year, numeric, first Monday is the first day of the first week	00–53	Yes
Month	%B	F	Full month name, text for current locale		Yes
Month	%b	M	Abbreviated month name, text for current locale		Yes
Month	%h		Same as %b		No
Month	%m	m	Month, numeric	01–12	Yes
Month		n	Month, numeric, leading zero trimmed	1–12	No
Month		t	Month length in days, numeric	28, 29, 30, 31	No
Year	%C		Century, numeric	00–99	No
Year	%g		Like %G, but without the century	00–99	No
Year	%G	o	ISO 8601 year with century; numeric; the four-digit year corresponding to the ISO week number; same as %y except if the ISO week number belongs to the previous or next year, that year is used instead		No

Type	strftime( )	date( )	Description	Range	Windows
Year	%y	y	Year without century, numeric	00–99	Yes
Year	%Y	Y	Year, numeric, including century		Yes
Year		L	Leap year flag (yes is 1)	0, 1	No
Time zone	%z	O	Hour offset from GMT, ±HHMM (e.g., −0400, +0230)	−1200–+1200	Yes, but acts like %Z
Time zone		P	Time zone offset including colon (e.g. −04:00, +02:30)	−12:00 –+12:00	
Time zone	%Z	T	Time zone, name, or ab-breviation; textual		Yes
Time zone		e	Timezone identifier, e.g., America/New_York		
Time zone		I	Daylight savings time flag (yes is 1)	0, 1	No
Time zone		Z	Seconds offset from GMT; west of GMT is negative, east of GMT is positive	−43200–43200	No
Compound	%c		Standard date and time format for current locale		Yes
Compound		c	ISO 8601–formatted date and time		Yes
Compound	%D		Same as %m/%d/%y		No
Compound	%F		Same as %Y-%m-%d		No
Compound	%r		Time in A.M. or P.M. nota-tion for current locale		No
Compound	%R		Time in 24-hour notation for current locale		No
Compound	%T		Time in 24-hour notation (same as %H:%M:%S)		No
Compound	%x		Standard date format for current locale (without time)		Yes
Compound	%X		Standard time format for current locale (without date)		Yes
Compound		r	RFC 822–formatted date (e.g., "Thu, 22 Aug 2002 16:01:07 +0200")		No

Type	strftime( )	date( )	Description	Range	Windows
Other	%s	U	Seconds since the epoch		No
Other		B	Swatch Internet time		No
Formatting	%%		Literal % character		Yes
Formatting	%n		Newline character		No
Formatting	%t		Tab character		No

[a] The range for seconds extends to 61 to account for leap seconds.

The c formatting character was added to date( ) in PHP 5.0.0. The N, o, and e characters were added to date( ) in PHP 5.1.0. The P character was added in PHP 5.1.3.

The first argument to each function is a format string, and the second argument is an epoch timestamp. If you leave out the second argument, both functions default to the current date and time. While date( ) and strftime( ) operate over local time, they each have UTC-centric counterparts (gmdate( ) and gmstrftime( )).

In PHP 5.1.1 and later, there are some handy constants that represent the format string to be passed to date( ) for common date formats. These constants are listed in Table 3-4.

Table 3-4. Constants for use with date( )

Constant	Value	Example	Usage
DATE_ATOM	Y-m-d\TH:i:sO	2010-12-03 T06:23:39-0500	Section 3.3 of the Atom Syndication format (*http://www.atomenabled.org/developers/syndication/atom-format-spec.php#date.constructs*)
DATE_COOKIE	D, d M Y H:i:s T	Fri, 03 Dec 2010 06:23:39 EST	HTTP Cookies (as defined at *http://wp.netscape.com/newsref/std/cookie_spec.html*)
DATE_ISO8601	Y-m-d\TH:i:sO	2010-12-03 T06:23:39-0500	ISO 8601 (as discussed at *http://www.w3.org/TR/NOTE-datetime*)
DATE_RFC822	D, d M Y H:i:s T	Fri, 03 Dec 2010 06:23:39 EST	Email messages (as defined in *http://www.faqs.org/rfcs/rfc822.html*)
DATE_RFC850	l, d-M-y H:i:s T	Friday, 03-Dec-10 06:23:39 EST	Usenet messages (as defined in *http://www.faqs.org/rfcs/rfc850.html*)
DATE_RFC1036	l, d-M-y H:i:s T	Friday, 03-Dec-10 06:23:39 EST	Usenet messages (as defined in *http://www.faqs.org/rfcs/rfc1036.html*)
DATE_RFC1123	D, d M Y H:i:s T	Fri, 03 Dec 2010 06:23:39 EST	As defined in *http://www.faqs.org/rfcs/rfc1123.html*
DATE_RFC2822	D, d M Y H:i:s O	Fri, 03 Dec 2010 06:23:39 -0500	E-mail messages (as defined in *http://www.faqs.org/rfcs/rfc2822.html*)

Constant	Value	Example	Usage
DATE_RSS	D, d M Y H:i:s T	Fri, 03 Dec 2010 06:23:39 EST	RSS feeds (as defined in *http://blogs.law.harvard.edu/tech/rss*)
DATE_W3C	Y-m-d\TH:i:sO	2010-12-03 T06:23:39-0500	Same as DATE_ISO8601

The formatting characters for `date( )` are PHP-specific, but `strftime( )` uses the C-library `strftime( )` function. This may make `strftime( )` more understandable to someone coming to PHP from another language, but it also makes its behavior slightly different on various platforms. Windows doesn't support as many `strftime( )` formatting commands as most Unix-based systems. Also, `strftime( )` expects each of its formatting characters to be preceded by a % (think `printf( )`), so it's easier to produce strings with lots of interpolated time and date values in them.

For example, at 12:49 P.M. on July 15, 2002, the code to print out:

```
It's after 12 pm on July 15, 2002
```

with `strftime( )` looks like:

```
print strftime("It's after %I %P on %B %d, %Y");
```

With `date( )` it looks like:

```
print "It's after ".date('h a').' on '.date('F d, Y');
```

Non-date-related characters in a format string are fine for `strftime( )`, because it looks for the % character to decide where to interpolate the appropriate time information. However, `date( )` doesn't have such a delimiter, so about the only extras you can tuck into the formatting string are spaces and punctuation. If you pass `strftime( )`'s formatting string to `date( )`:

```
print date("It's after %I %P on %B%d, %Y");
```

you'd almost certainly not want what you'd get:

```
131'44 pmf31eMon, 15 Jul 2002 12:49:44 -0400 %1 %P o7 %742%15, %2002
```

To generate time parts with `date( )` that are easy to interpolate, group all time and date parts from `date( )` into one string, separating the different components with a delimiter that `date( )` won't translate into anything and that isn't itself part of one of your substrings. Then, using `explode( )` with that delimiter character, put each piece of the return value from `date( )` in an array, which is easily interpolated in your output string. Example 3-12 does this, using a | character as a delimiter.

Example 3-12. Using explode() with date()

```php
<?php
$ar = explode('|',date("h a|F d, Y"));
print "It's after $ar[0] on $ar[1]";
?>
```

See Also

Documentation on date( ) at *http://www.php.net/date* and strftime( ) at *http://www.php.net/strftime*; on Unix-based systems, *man strftime* for your system-specific strftime( ) options; on Windows, see *http://msdn.microsoft.com/library/default.asp?url=/library/en-us/vclib/html/_crt_strftime.2c_.wcsftime.asp* for strftime( ) details.

3.5 Finding the Difference of Two Dates

Problem

You want to find the elapsed time between two dates. For example, you want to tell a user how long it's been since she last logged onto your site.

Solution

Convert both dates to epoch timestamps and subtract one from the other. Example 3-13 separates the difference into weeks, days, hours, minutes, and seconds.

Example 3-13. Calculating the difference between two dates

```php
<?php
// 7:32:56 pm on May 10, 1965
$epoch_1 = mktime(19,32,56,5,10,1965);
// 4:29:11 am on November 20, 1962
$epoch_2 = mktime(4,29,11,11,20,1962);

$diff_seconds  = $epoch_1 - $epoch_2;
$diff_weeks    = floor($diff_seconds/604800);
$diff_seconds -= $diff_weeks   * 604800;
$diff_days     = floor($diff_seconds/86400);
$diff_seconds -= $diff_days    * 86400;
$diff_hours    = floor($diff_seconds/3600);
$diff_seconds -= $diff_hours   * 3600;
$diff_minutes  = floor($diff_seconds/60);
$diff_seconds -= $diff_minutes * 60;

print "The two dates have $diff_weeks weeks, $diff_days days, ";
print "$diff_hours hours, $diff_minutes minutes, and $diff_seconds ";
print "seconds elapsed between them.";
?>
```

Example 3-13 prints:

```
The two dates have 128 weeks, 6 days, 14 hours, 3 minutes,
and 45 seconds elapsed between them.
```

Note that the difference isn't divided into larger chunks than weeks (i.e., months or years) because those chunks have variable length and wouldn't give an accurate count of the time difference calculated.

Discussion

There are a few strange things going on here that you should be aware of. First of all, 1962 and 1965 precede the beginning of the epoch. Fortunately, mktime( ) fails gracefully here and produces negative epoch timestamps for each. This is okay because the absolute time value of either of these questionable timestamps isn't necessary, just the difference between the two. As long as epoch timestamps for the dates fall within the range of a signed integer, their difference is calculated correctly.

Next, a wall clock (or calendar) reflects a slightly different amount of time change between these two dates, because they are on different sides of a DST switch. The result subtracting epoch timestamps gives is the correct amount of *elapsed* time, but the perceived human time change is an hour off. For example, on the Sunday morning in April when DST is activated, what's the difference between 1:30 A.M. and 4:30 A.M.? It seems like three hours, but the epoch timestamps for these two times are only 7,200 seconds apart—two hours. When a local clock springs forward an hour (or falls back an hour in October), the steady march of epoch timestamps takes no notice. Truly, only two hours have passed, although our clock manipulations make it seem like three.

If you want to measure actual elapsed time (and you usually do), this method is fine. If you're more concerned with the difference in what a clock says at two points in time, use Julian days to compute the interval, as discussed in Recipe 3.6.

To tell a user the elapsed time since her last login, you need to find the difference between the login time and her last login time, as shown in Example 3-14.

Example 3-14. Finding elapsed time since last login

```php
<?php
$db = new PDO('mysql:host=db.example.com', $user, $password);
$epoch_1 = time();
$st = $db->prepare("SELECT UNIX_TIMESTAMP(last_login) AS login " .
                   "FROM user WHERE id = ?");
$st->execute(array($id));
$row = $st->fetch();
$epoch_2 = $row['login'];

$diff_seconds  = $epoch_1 - $epoch_2;
$diff_weeks    = floor($diff_seconds/604800);
$diff_seconds -= $diff_weeks   * 604800;
$diff_days     = floor($diff_seconds/86400);
$diff_seconds -= $diff_days    * 86400;
$diff_hours    = floor($diff_seconds/3600);
$diff_seconds -= $diff_hours   * 3600;
$diff_minutes  = floor($diff_seconds/60);
$diff_seconds -= $diff_minutes * 60;

print "You last logged in $diff_weeks weeks, $diff_days days, ";
print "$diff_hours hours, $diff_minutes minutes, and $diff_seconds ago.";
```

See Also

Recipe 3.6 to find the difference between two dates with Julian days; Recipe 3.10 for adding to and subtracting from a date; documentation on MySQL's `UNIX_TIMESTAMP( )` function can be found at *http://www.mysql.com/doc/D/a/ Date_and_time_functions.html*.

3.6 Finding the Difference of Two Dates with Julian Days

Problem

You want to find the difference of two dates measured by what a clock would say, not the actual elapsed time.

Solution

Use `gregoriantojd( )` to get the Julian day for a set of date parts and then subtract one Julian day from the other to find the date difference. Then, convert the time parts to seconds and subtract one from the other to find the time difference. If the time difference is less than 0, decrease the date difference by one and adjust the time difference to apply to the previous day. Example 3-15 shows how to do this.

Example 3-15. Finding date differences with Julian days

```php
<?php
$diff_date = gregoriantojd($date_1_mo, $date_1_dy, $date_1_yr) -
             gregoriantojd($date_2_mo, $date_2_dy, $date_2_yr);
$diff_time = $date_1_hr * 3600 + $date_1_mn * 60 + $date_1_sc -
             $date_2_hr * 3600 - $date_2_mn * 60 - $date_2_sc;
if ($diff_time < 0) {
    $diff_date--;
    $diff_time = 86400 - $diff_time;
}
?>
```

Discussion

Finding differences with Julian days lets you operate outside the range of epoch seconds and also accounts for DST differences.

Example 3-16 does the calculation with date parts from arrays.

Example 3-16. Calculating difference with arrays of date parts

```php
<?php
// 7:32:56 pm on May 10, 1965
list($date_1_yr, $date_1_mo, $date_1_dy, $date_1_hr, $date_1_mn, $date_1_sc)=
    array(1965, 5, 10, 19, 32, 56);
// 4:29:11 am on November 20, 1962
list($date_2_yr, $date_2_mo, $date_2_dy, $date_2_hr, $date_2_mn, $date_2_sc)=
    array(1962, 11, 20, 4, 29, 11);
```

```
$diff_date = gregoriantojd($date_1_mo, $date_1_dy, $date_1_yr) -
             gregoriantojd($date_2_mo, $date_2_dy, $date_2_yr);
$diff_time = $date_1_hr * 3600 + $date_1_mn * 60 + $date_1_sc -
             $date_2_hr * 3600 - $date_2_mn * 60 - $date_2_sc;
if ($diff_time < 0) {
    $diff_date--;
    $diff_time = 86400 - $diff_time;
}
$diff_weeks = floor($diff_date/7); $diff_date -= $diff_weeks * 7;
$diff_hours = floor($diff_time/3600); $diff_time -= $diff_hours * 3600;
$diff_minutes = floor($diff_time/60); $diff_time -= $diff_minutes * 60;

print "The two dates have $diff_weeks weeks, $diff_date days, ";
print "$diff_hours hours, $diff_minutes minutes, and $diff_time ";
print "seconds between them.";
?>
```

Example 3-16 prints:

```
The two dates have 128 weeks, 6 days, 15 hours, 3 minutes,
and 45 seconds between them.
```

This method produces a time difference based on clock time, which is why the result shows an hour more of difference than in Recipe 3.5. May 10 is during DST, and November 20 is during standard time.

The function `gregoriantojd( )` is part of PHP's calendar extension, and so is available only if that extension is loaded.

See Also

Recipe 3.5 to find the difference between two dates in elapsed time; Recipe 3.10 for adding and subtracting from a date; documentation on `gregoriantojd( )` at *http://www.php.net/gregoriantojd*; an overview of the Julian day system is at *http://tycho.usno.navy.mil/mjd.html*.

3.7 Finding the Day in a Week, Month, or Year

Problem

You want to know the day or week of the year, the day of the week, or the day of the month. For example, you want to print a special message every Monday, or on the first of every month.

Solution

Use the appropriate arguments to `date( )` or `strftime( )`, as shown in Example 3-17.

Example 3-17. Finding days of the week, month, and year

```
<?php
print strftime("Today is day %d of the month and %j of the year.");
```

```
print 'Today is day '.date('d').' of the month and '.date('z').' of the year.';
?>
```

Discussion

The two functions date( ) and strftime( ) don't behave identically. Days of the year start with 0 for date( ), but with 1 for strftime( ). Table 3-4 contains all the day and week number format characters date( ) and strftime( ) understand.

Table 3-4. Day and week number format characters

Type	strftime( )	date( )	Description	Range	Windows
Day	%d	d	Day of the month, numeric	01–31	Yes
Day	%e		Day of the month, numeric, leading zero as space	1–31	No
Day	%j	z	Day of the year, numeric	001–366 for strftime( ); 0–365 for date( )	Yes
Day	%u	N	Day of the week, numeric (Monday is 1)	1–7	No
Day	%w	w	Day of the week, numeric (Sunday is 0)	0–6	Yes
Day		j	Day of the month, numeric, leading zero trimmed	1–31	No
Day		S	English ordinal suffix for day of the month, textual	"st," "th," "nd," "rd"	No
Week	%a	D	Abbreviated weekday name, text for current locale		Yes
Week	%A	l	Full weekday name, text for current locale		Yes
Week	%U		Week number in the year, numeric, first Sunday is the first day of the first week	00–53	Yes
Week	%V	W	ISO 8601:1988 week number in the year, numeric, week 1 is the first week that has at least 4 days in the current year, Monday is the first day of the week	01–53	No
Week	%W		Week number in the year, numeric, first Monday is the first day of the first week	00–53	Yes

To print out something only on Mondays, use the w formatting character with date( ) or the %w string with strftime( ), as in Example 3-18.

Example 3-18. Checking for the day of the week
```
<?php
if (1 == date('w')) {
    print "Welcome to the beginning of your work week.";
}

if (1 == strftime('%w')) {
```

```
    print "Only 4 more days until the weekend!";
}
```

There are different ways to calculate week numbers and days in a week, so take care to choose the appropriate one. The ISO standard (ISO 8601), says that weeks begin on Mondays and that the days in the week are numbered 1 (Monday) through 7 (Sunday). Week 1 in a year is the first week in a year with a Thursday in that year. This means the first week in a year is the first week with a majority of its days in that year. These week numbers range from 01 to 53.

Other week number standards range from 00 to 53, with days in a year's week 53 potentially overlapping with days in the following year's week 00.

As long as you're consistent within your programs, you shouldn't run into any trouble, but be careful when interfacing with other PHP programs or your database. For example, MySQL's DAYOFWEEK( ) function treats Sunday as the first day of the week, but numbers the days 1 to 7, which is the ODBC standard. Its WEEKDAY( ) function, however, treats Monday as the first day of the week and numbers the days from 0 to 6. Its WEEK( ) function lets you choose whether weeks should start on Sunday or Monday, but it's incompatible with the ISO standard.

See Also

Documentation on date( ) at *http://www.php.net/date* and strftime( ) at *http://www.php.net/strftime*; MySQL's DAYOFWEEK( ), WEEKDAY( ), and WEEK( ) functions are documented at *http://www.mysql.com/doc/D/a/Date_and_time_functions.html*.

3.8 Validating a Date

Problem

You want to check if a date is valid. For example, you want to make sure a user hasn't provided a birthdate such as February 30, 1962.

Solution

Use checkdate( ):

```
$valid = checkdate($month,$day,$year);
```

Discussion

The function checkdate( ) returns true if $month is between 1 and 12, $year is between 1 and 32767, and $day is between 1 and the correct maximum number of days for $month and $year. Leap years are correctly handled by checkdate( ), and dates are rendered using the Gregorian calendar.

Because checkdate( ) has such a broad range of valid years, you should do additional validation on user input if, for example, you're expecting a valid birthdate. The longest confirmed human lifespan is 122 years old. To check that a birthdate indicates that a user is between 18 and 122 years old, use the `pc_checkbirthdate( )` function shown in Example 3-19.

Example 3-19. pc_checkbirthdate( )

```php
<?php
function pc_checkbirthdate($month,$day,$year) {
    $min_age = 18;
    $max_age = 122;

    if (! checkdate($month,$day,$year)) {
        return false;
    }

    list($this_year,$this_month,$this_day) = explode(',',date('Y,m,d'));

    $min_year = $this_year - $max_age;
    $max_year = $this_year - $min_age;

    print "$min_year,$max_year,$month,$day,$year\n";

    if (($year > $min_year) && ($year < $max_year)) {
        return true;
    } elseif (($year == $max_year) &&
                (($month < $this_month) ||
                (($month == $this_month) && ($day <= $this_day)))) {
        return true;
    } elseif (($year == $min_year) &&
                (($month > $this_month) ||
                (($month == $this_month && ($day > $this_day))))) {
        return true;
    } else {
        return false;
    }
}

// check December 3, 1974
if (pc_checkbirthdate(12,3,1974)) {
    print "You may use this web site.";
} else {
    print "You are too young to proceed.";
    exit();
}
?>
```

The function first uses `checkdate( )` to make sure that $month, $day, and $year represent a valid date. Various comparisons then make sure that the supplied date is in the range set by $min_age and $max_age.

If $year is noninclusively between $min_year and $max_year, the date is definitely within the range, and the function returns `true`. If not, some additional checks are required. If $year equals $max_year (e.g., in 2002, $year is 1984), $month must be before the current month. If $month equals the current month, $day must be before or equal to the current day. If `$year` equals `$min_year` (e.g., in 2002, `$year` is 1880), `$month` must be after the current month. If `$month` equals the current month, `$day` must be after the current day. If none of these conditions are met, the supplied date is outside the appropriate range, and the function returns `false`.

The function returns `true` if the supplied date is exactly `$min_age` years before the current date, but `false` if the supplied date is exactly `$max_age` years after the current date. That is, it would let you through on your 18th birthday, but not on your 123rd.

See Also

Documentation on `checkdate( )` at *http://www.php.net/checkdate*; information about Jeanne Calment, the person with the longest confirmed lifespan, is at *http://en.wikipedia.org/wiki/Jeanne_Calment*.

3.9 Parsing Dates and Times from Strings

Problem

You need to get a date or time in a string into a format you can use in calculations. For example, you want to convert date expressions such as "last Thursday" into an epoch timestamp.

Solution

The simplest way to parse a date or time string of arbitrary format is with `strtotime( )`, which turns a variety of human-readable date and time strings into epoch timestamps, as shown in Example 3-20.

Example 3-20. Parsing strings with strtotime( )

```php
<?php
$a = strtotime('march 10'); // defaults to the current year
$b = strtotime('last thursday');
$c = strtotime('now + 3 months');
```

Discussion

The grammar `strtotime( )` uses is both complicated and comprehensive. It uses the GNU Date Input Formats specification, which is available at the following address: *http://www.gnu.org/software/coreutils/manual/html_chapter/coreutils_27.html*.

The function `strtotime( )` understands words about the current time:

```php
<?php
$a = strtotime('now');
print strftime('%c',$a);
$a = strtotime('today');
print strftime('%c',$a);
?>
```

```
Mon Aug 12 20:35:10 2002
Mon Aug 12 20:35:10 2002
```

It understands different ways to identify a time and date:

```php
<?php
$a = strtotime('5/12/1994');
print strftime('%c',$a);
$a = strtotime('12 may 1994');
print strftime('%c',$a);
?>
```

```
Thu May 12 00:00:00 1994
Thu May 12 00:00:00 1994
```

It understands relative times and dates:

```php
<?php
$a = strtotime('last thursday');    // On August 12, 2002
print strftime('%c',$a);
$a = strtotime('2001-07-12 2pm + 1 month');
print strftime('%c',$a);
?>
```

```
Thu Aug  8 00:00:00 2002
Mon Aug 12 14:00:00 2002
```

It understands time zones. When the following is run from a computer in EDT, it prints out the same time:

```php
<?php
$a = strtotime('2002-07-12 2pm edt + 1 month');
print strftime('%c',$a);
?>
```

```
Mon Aug 12 14:00:00 2002
```

However, when the following is run from a computer in EDT, it prints out the time in EDT when it is 2 P.M. in MDT (two hours before EDT):

```php
<?php
$a = strtotime('2002-07-12 2pm mdt + 1 month');
print strftime('%c',$a);
?>
```

```
Mon Aug 12 16:00:00 2002
```

If the date and time you want to parse out of a string are in a format you know in advance, instead of calling strtotime( ), you can build a regular expression that grabs the different date and time parts you need. Example 3-21 shows how to parse "YYYY-MM-DD HH:MM:SS" dates, such as a MySQL DATETIME field.

Example 3-21. Parsing a date with a regular expression

```php
<?php
$date = '1974-12-03 05:12:56';
```

```
preg_match('/(\d{4})-(\d{2})-(\d{2}) (\d{2}):(\d{2}):(\d{2})/',$date,$date_parts);
?>
```

This puts the year, month, day, hour, minute, and second into $date_parts[1] through $date_parts[6]. (preg_match( ) puts the entire matched expression into $date_parts[0].)

You can use regular expressions to pull the date and time out of a larger string that might also contain other information (from user input, or a file you're reading), but if you're sure about the position of the date in the string you're parsing, you can use substr( ) to make it even faster, as shown in Example 3-22.

Example 3-22. Parsing a date with substr( )
```
$date_parts[0] = substr($date,0,4);
$date_parts[1] = substr($date,5,2);
$date_parts[2] = substr($date,8,2);
$date_parts[3] = substr($date,11,2);
$date_parts[4] = substr($date,14,2);
$date_parts[5] = substr($date,17,2);
?>
```

You can also use preg_split( ), as in Example 3-23.

Example 3-23. Parsing a date with preg_split( )
```
<?php $ar = preg_split('/[- :]/',$date);
var_dump($ar);
?>
```

Example 3-23 prints:
```
array(6) {
  [0]=>
  string(4) "1974"
  [1]=>
  string(2) "12"
  [2]=>
  string(2) "03"
  [3]=>
  string(2) "05"
  [4]=>
  string(2) "12"
  [5]=>
  string(2) "56"
}
```

Be careful: PHP converts between numbers and strings without any prompting, but numbers beginning with a 0 are considered to be in octal (base 8). So 03 and 05 are 3 and 5, but 08 and 09 are *not* 8 and 9.

In PHP 5.1 and later, preg_match( ) is faster than strtotime( ) in parsing a date format such as "YYYY-MM-DD HH:MM:SS." In earlier versions of PHP, strtotime( ) is slightly faster. If you need the individual parts of the date string, `preg_match( )` is more convenient, but `strtotime( )` is obviously much more flexible.

See Also

Documentation on `strtotime( )` at *http://www.php.net/strtotime*. The rules describing what `strtotime( )` can parse are at *http://www.gnu.org/software/coreutils/manual/html_chapter/coreutils_27.html*.

3.10 Adding to or Subtracting from a Date

Problem

You need to add or subtract an interval from a date.

Solution

Depending on how your date and interval are represented, use `strtotime( )` or some simple arithmetic.

If you have your date and interval in appropriate formats, the easiest thing to do is use `strtotime( )`, as in Example 3-24.

Example 3-24. Calculating a date interval with strtotime( )

```
<?php
$birthday = 'March 10, 1975';
$whoopee_made = strtotime("$birthday - 9 months ago");
?>
```

If your date is an epoch timestamp and you can express your interval in seconds, subtract the interval from the timestamp, as in Example 3-25.

Example 3-25. Calculating a date interval with epoch timestamps

```
<?php
$birthday = 163727100;
$gestation = 36 * 7 * 86400; // 36 weeks
$whoopee_made = $birthday - $gestation;
?>
```

Discussion

Using `strtotime( )` is good for intervals that are of varying lengths, such as months. If you can't use `strtotime( )`, convert your date to an epoch timestamp and add or subtract the appropriate interval in seconds. This is mostly useful for intervals of a fixed time, such as days or weeks. Example 3-26 adds seven days' worth of seconds to a timestamp.

Example 3-26. Another date interval with epoch timestamps

```
<?php
$now = time();
```

```php
$next_week = $now + 7 * 86400;
?>
```

Using this method, however, you can run into problems if the endpoints of your interval are on different sides of a DST switch. In this case, one of your fixed-length days isn't 86,400 seconds long; it's either 82,800 or 90,000 seconds long, depending on the season.

See Also

Recipe 3.5 for finding the difference between two dates in elapsed time; Recipe 3.6 for finding the difference between two dates in Julian days; documentation on strtotime( ) at *http://www.php.net/strtotime*.

3.11 Calculating Time with Time Zones

Problem

You need to calculate times in different time zones. For example, you want to give users information adjusted to their local time, not the local time of your server.

Solution

For simple calculations, you can explicitly add or subtract the offsets between two time zones, as in Example 3-27.

Example 3-27. Simple time zone calculation

```php
<?php
// If local time is EST
$time_parts = localtime();
// California (PST) is three hours earlier
$california_time_parts = localtime(time() - 3 * 3600);
?>
```

In PHP 5.1.0 and later, use date_default_timezone_set( ) to adjust the time zone that PHP uses. Example 3-28 prints the current time twice—once as appropriate for New York and once for Paris.

Example 3-28. Changing time zone with date_default_timezone_set( )

```php
<?php
$now = time();
date_default_timezone_set('America/New_York');
print date('c', $now);
date_default_timezone_set('Europe/Paris');
print date('c', $now);
?>
```

On Unix-based systems with earlier versions of PHP, if you don't know the offsets between time zones, just set the TZ environment variable to your target time zone, as in Example 3-29.

Example 3-29. Changing time zone with an environment variable

```php
<?php
putenv('TZ=PST8PDT');
$california_time_parts = localtime();
?>
```

Discussion

Before we sink too deeply into the ins and outs of time zones, we want to pass along the disclaimer that the U.S. Naval Observatory offers at *http://tycho.usno.navy.mil/tzones.html*. Namely, official worldwide time zone information is somewhat fragile "because nations are sovereign powers that can and do change their timekeeping systems as they see fit." So, remembering that we are at the mercy of the vagaries of international relations, here are some ways to cope with Earth's many time zones.

The time and date functions were overhauled in PHP 5.1.0, and one of the best parts of that overhaul was greatly improved time zone handling. The added date_default_timezone_get( ) and date_default_timezone_set( ) functions make it a breeze to twiddle time zones to get appropriately formatted output. There is also a new configuration directive, date.timezone, that sets the default time zone to use if you don't call date_default_timezone_set( ).

With these functions available, all you have to do before generating a formatted time or date string with date( ) or strftime( ) is make sure that the currently set default time zone (either from date.timezone or date_default_timezone_set( )) is the one you want to use. If you're building an app that is used by people in multiple time zones, a handy technique is to make the default time zone GMT and then explicitly set the appropriate time zone (based, perhaps, on user preference) before creating a date or time string. This makes it clear in your code that you're generating a time zone–specific value.

The time zones that PHP understands are listed in Appendix H of the PHP Manual (*http://www.php.net/timezones*). The names of these time zones—such as America/New_York, Europe/Paris, and Africa/Dar_es_Salaam—mirror the structure of the popular zoneinfo database.

If you're using an earlier version of PHP, you have to do the time zone math yourself. For a relatively simple treatment of offsets between time zones, use an array in your program that has the various time zone offsets from UTC. Once you determine what time zone your user is in, just add that offset to the appropriate UTC time and the functions that print out UTC time (e.g., gmdate( ), gmstrftime( )) can print out the correct adjusted time. Example 3-30 adjusts the time from UTC to PST.

Example 3-30. Adjusting time from UTC to another time zone

```php
<?php
// Find the current time
```

```
$now = time();

// California is 8 hours behind UTC
$now += $pc_timezones['PST'];

// Use gmdate() or gmstrftime() to print California-appropriate time
print gmstrftime('%c',$now);
?>
```

Example 3-30 uses the $pc_timezones array defined in Example 3-31, which contains offsets from UTC.

Example 3-31. Offsets from UTC

```
// From Perl's Time::Timezone
$pc_timezones = array(
  'GMT'  =>  0,            // Greenwich Mean
  'UTC'  =>  0,            // Universal (Coordinated)
  'WET'  =>  0,            // Western European
  'WAT'  =>  -1*3600,      // West Africa
  'AT'   =>  -2*3600,      // Azores
  'NFT'  =>  -3*3600-1800, // Newfoundland
  'AST'  =>  -4*3600,      // Atlantic Standard
  'EST'  =>  -5*3600,      // Eastern Standard
  'CST'  =>  -6*3600,      // Central Standard
  'MST'  =>  -7*3600,      // Mountain Standard
  'PST'  =>  -8*3600,      // Pacific Standard
  'YST'  =>  -9*3600,      // Yukon Standard
  'HST'  =>  -10*3600,     // Hawaii Standard
  'CAT'  =>  -10*3600,     // Central Alaska
  'AHST' =>  -10*3600,     // Alaska-Hawaii Standard
  'NT'   =>  -11*3600,     // Nome
  'IDLW' =>  -12*3600,     // International Date Line West
  'CET'  =>  +1*3600,      // Central European
  'MET'  =>  +1*3600,      // Middle European
  'MEWT' =>  +1*3600,      // Middle European Winter
  'SWT'  =>  +1*3600,      // Swedish Winter
  'FWT'  =>  +1*3600,      // French Winter
  'EET'  =>  +2*3600,      // Eastern Europe, USSR Zone 1
  'BT'   =>  +3*3600,      // Baghdad, USSR Zone 2
  'IT'   =>  +3*3600+1800, // Iran
  'ZP4'  =>  +4*3600,      // USSR Zone 3
  'ZP5'  =>  +5*3600,      // USSR Zone 4
  'IST'  =>  +5*3600+1800, // Indian Standard
  'ZP6'  =>  +6*3600,      // USSR Zone 5
  'SST'  =>  +7*3600,      // South Sumatra, USSR Zone 6
  'WAST' =>  +7*3600,      // West Australian Standard
  'JT'   =>  +7*3600+1800, // Java
  'CCT'  =>  +8*3600,      // China Coast, USSR Zone 7
  'JST'  =>  +9*3600,      // Japan Standard, USSR Zone 8
  'CAST' =>  +9*3600+1800, // Central Australian Standard
  'EAST' =>  +10*3600,     // Eastern Australian Standard
  'GST'  =>  +10*3600,     // Guam Standard, USSR Zone 9
  'NZT'  =>  +12*3600,     // New Zealand
  'NZST' =>  +12*3600,     // New Zealand Standard
```

```
    'IDLE' => +12*3600          // International Date Line East
);
```

On Unix systems, you can use the *zoneinfo* library to do the conversions. This makes your code more compact and also transparently handles DST, as discussed in Recipe 3.12.

To take advantage of *zoneinfo* in PHP, do all your internal date math with epoch timestamps. Generate them from time parts with the `pc_mktime()` function shown in Example 3-32.

Example 3-32. pc_mktime()

```php
<?php
function pc_mktime($tz,$hr,$min,$sec,$mon,$day,$yr) {
    putenv("TZ=$tz");
    $a = mktime($hr,$min,$sec,$mon,$day,$yr);
    putenv('TZ=EST5EDT');   // change EST5EDT to your server's time zone!
    return $a;
}
?>
```

Calling `putenv()` before `mktime()` fools the system functions `mktime()` uses into thinking they're in a different time zone. After the call to `mktime()`, the correct time zone has to be restored. On the East Coast of the United States, that's `EST5EDT`. Change this to the appropriate value for your computer's location (see Table 3-5). Manipulating environment variables, however, can cause problems in multithreaded environments. If you're using PHP with a multithreaded web server, it is an extremely good idea to upgrade to at least PHP 5.1.0, so you can use `date_default_timezone_set()`.

Time parts are turned into epoch timestamps by `pc_mktime()`. Its counterpart, which turns epoch timestamps into formatted time strings and time parts, is `pc_strftime()`, shown in Example 3-33.

Example 3-33. pc_strftime()

```php
<?php
function pc_strftime($tz,$format,$timestamp) {
    putenv("TZ=$tz");
    $a = strftime($format,$timestamp);
    putenv('TZ=EST5EDT');   // change EST5EDT to your server's time zone!
    return $a;
}
?>
```

Example 3-33 uses the same system function–fooling `pc_mktime()` does to get the right results from `strftime()`.

The great thing about these functions is that you don't have to worry about the offsets from UTC of different time zones, whether DST is in effect, or any other irregularities of time zone differences. You just set the appropriate zone and let your system libraries do the rest.

Note that the value of the $tz variable in both these functions should not be a time zone name but a *zoneinfo* zone. *zoneinfo* zones are more specific than time zones because they correspond to particular places. Table 3-5 contains mappings for appropriate *zoneinfo* zones for some UTC offsets. The last column indicates whether the zone observes DST.

Table 3-5. zoneinfo zones

UTC offset (hours)	UTC offset (seconds)	zoneinfo zone	DST?
−12	−43,200	Etc/GMT+12	No
−11	−39,600	Pacific/Midway	No
−10	−36,000	US/Aleutian	Yes
−10	−36,000	Pacific/Honolulu	No
−9	−32,400	America/Anchorage	Yes
−9	−32,400	Etc/GMT+9	No
−8	−28,800	PST8PDT	Yes
−8	−28,800	America/Dawson_Creek	No
−7	−25,200	MST7MDT	Yes
−7	−25,200	MST	No
−6	−21,600	CST6CDT	Yes
−6	−21,600	Canada/Saskatchewan	No
−5	−18,000	EST5EDT	Yes
−5	−18,000	EST	No
−4	−14,400	America/Halifax	Yes
−4	−14,400	America/Puerto_Rico	No
−3.5	−12,600	America/St_Johns	Yes
−3	−10,800	America/Buenos_Aires	No
0	0	Europe/London	Yes
0	0	GMT	No
1	3,600	CET	Yes
1	3,600	GMT−1	No
2	7,200	EET	No
2	7,200	GMT−2	No
3	10,800	Asia/Baghdad	Yes
3	10,800	GMT−3	No
3.5	12,600	Asia/Tehran	Yes
4	14,400	Asia/Dubai	No
4	14,400	Asia/Baku	Yes

UTC offset (hours)	UTC offset (seconds)	zoneinfo zone	DST?
4.5	16,200	Asia/Kabul	No
5	18,000	Asia/Tashkent	No
5.5	19,800	Asia/Calcutta	No
5.75	20,700	Asia/Katmandu	No
6	21,600	Asia/Novosibirsk	Yes
6	21,600	Etc/GMT-6	No
6.5	23,400	Asia/Rangoon	No
7	25,200	Asia/Jakarta	No
8	28,800	Hongkong	No
9	32,400	Japan	No
9.5	34,200	Australia/Darwin	No
10	36,000	Australia/Sydney	Yes
10	36,000	Pacific/Guam	No
12	43,200	Etc/GMT-13	No
12	43,200	Pacific/Auckland	Yes

Countries around the world don't begin and end DST observance on the same days or at the same times. To calculate time appropriately for an international DST–observing location, pick a *zoneinfo* zone that matches your desired location as specifically as possible.

See Also

Recipe 3.12 for dealing with DST; documentation on `date_default_timezone_set( )` at *http://www.php.net/date_default_timezone_set*, on `date_default_timezone_get( )` at *http://www.php.net/date_default_timezone_get*, on `putenv( )` at *http://www.php.net/putenv*, on `localtime( )` at *http://www.php.net/localtime*, on `gmdate( )` at *http://www.php.net/gmdate*, and on `gmstrftime( )` at *http://www.php.net/gmstrftime*; the time zones that PHP knows about are listed at *http://www.php.net/timezones*; *zoneinfo* zone names and longitude and latitude coordinates for hundreds of places around the world are available at *ftp://elsie.nci.nih.gov/pub/*—look for the most recent file whose name begins with *tzdata*; many links to historical and technical information about time zones, as well as information on the `zoneinfo` database, can be found at the following address: *http://www.twinsun.com/tz/tz-link.htm*.

3.12 Accounting for Daylight Savings Time

Problem

You need to make sure your time calculations properly consider DST.

Solution

If you're using PHP 5.1.0 or later, set the appropriate time zone with date_default_timezone_set( ). These time zones are DST-aware. Example 3-34 uses date_default_timezone_set( ) to print out an appropriately DST-formatted time string.

Example 3-34. Handling DST with date_default_timezone_set( )

```
<?php
// Denver, Colorado observes DST
date_default_timezone_set('America/Denver');
// July 4, 2008 is in the summer
$summer = mktime(12,0,0,7,4,2008);
print date('c', $summer) . "\n";
// Phoenix, Arizona does not observe DST
date_default_timezone_set('America/Phoenix');
print date('c', $summer) . "\n";
?>
```

Example 3-34 prints:

```
2008-07-04T12:00:00-06:00
2008-07-04T11:00:00-07:00
```

With an earlier version of PHP, you must use another method. The *zoneinfo* library calculates the effects of DST properly. If you are using a Unix-based system, take advantage of *zoneinfo* with putenv( ), as shown in Example 3-35.

Example 3-35. Handling DST with zoneinfo

```
<?php
// Denver, Colorado observes DST
putenv('TZ=America/Denver');
// July 4, 2008 is in the summer
$summer = mktime(12,0,0,7,4,2008);
print date('c', $summer) . "\n";
// Phoenix, Arizona does not observe DST
putenv('TZ=America/Phoenix');
print date('c', $summer) . "\n";
?>
```

If you can't use *zoneinfo*, you can modify hardcoded time zone offsets based on whether the local time zone is currently observing DST. Use localtime( ) to determine the current DST observance status, as shown in Example 3-36.

Example 3-36. Handling DST with explicit offsets

```
<?php
// Find the current UTC time
$now = time();

// California is 8 hours behind UTC
$now -= 8 * 3600;

// Is it DST?
```

```
$ar = localtime($now,true);
if ($ar['tm_isdst']) { $now += 3600; }

// Use gmdate() or gmstrftime() to print California-appropriate time
print gmstrftime('%c',$now);
?>
```

Discussion

Altering an epoch timestamp by the amount of a time zone's offset from UTC and then using gmdate( ) or gmstrftime( ) to print out time zone–appropriate functions is flexible —it works from any time zone—but the DST calculations are slightly inaccurate. For the brief intervals when the server's DST status is different from that of the target time zone, the results are incorrect. For example, at 3:30 A.M. EDT on the first Sunday in April (after the switch to DST), it's still before the switch (11:30 P.M.) in the Pacific time zone. A server in Eastern time using this method calculates California time to be seven hours behind UTC, whereas it's actually eight hours. At 6:00 A.M. EDT (3:00 A.M. PDT), both Pacific and Eastern time are observing DST, and the calculation is correct again (putting California at seven hours behind UTC).

See Also

Recipe 3.11 for dealing with time zones; documentation on date_default_timezone_set( ) at *http://www.php.net/date_default_timezone_set*, on putenv( ) at *http://www.php.net/putenv*, localtime( ) at *http://www.php.net/localtime*, gmdate( ) at *http://www.php.net/gmdate*, and gmstrftime( ) at *http://www.php.net/gmstrftime*; a detailed presentation on DST is at *http://webexhibits.org/daylightsaving/*.

3.13 Generating a High-Precision Time

Problem

You need to measure time with finer than one-second resolution—for example, to generate a unique ID or benchmark a function call.

Solution

Use microtime(true) to get the current time in seconds and microseconds. Example 3-37 uses microtime(true) to time how long it takes to do 1,000 regular expression matches.

Example 3-37. Timing with microtime( )
```
<?php
$start = microtime(true);
for ($i = 0; $i < 1000; $i++) {
    preg_match('/age=\d+/',$_SERVER['QUERY_STRING']);
}
```

```
$end = microtime(true);
$elapsed = $end - $start;
```

Discussion

Support for the optional argument `microtime( )` was added in PHP 5.0.0. Without that argument, with an argument that doesn't evaluate to `true`, or in an earlier version of PHP, `microtime( )` returns a string that contains the microseconds part of elapsed time since the epoch, a space, and seconds since the epoch. For example, a return value of `0.41644100 1026683258` means that 1026683258.41644100 seconds have elapsed since the epoch.

Time including microseconds is useful for generating unique IDs. When combined with the current process ID, it guarantees a unique ID, as long as a process doesn't generate more than one ID per microsecond. Example 3-38 uses `microtime( )` (with its string return format) to generate just such an ID.

Example 3-38. Generating an ID with microtime()
```php
<?php
[list($microseconds,$seconds) = explode(' ',microtime());
$id = $seconds.$microseconds.getmypid();
?>
```

Note that the method in Example 3-38 is not as foolproof on multithreaded systems, where there is a non-zero (but very tiny) chance that two threads of the same process could call `microtime( )` during the same microsecond.

See Also

Documentation on `microtime( )` at *http://www.php.net/microtime*. The `uniqid( )` function is good for generating unique IDs.

3.14 Generating Time Ranges

Problem

You need to know all the days in a week or a month. For example, you want to print out a list of appointments for a week.

Solution

Identify your start date using `time( )` and `strftime( )`. If your interval has a fixed length, you can loop through that many days. If not, you need to test each subsequent day for membership in your desired range.

For example, a week has seven days, so you can use a fixed loop to generate all the days in the current week, as in Example 3-39.

Example 3-39. Generating the days in a week

```php
<?php
// generate a time range for this week
$now = time();

// If it's before 3 AM, increment $now, so we don't get caught by DST
// when moving back to the beginning of the week
if (3 < strftime('%H', $now)) { $now += 7200; }

// What day of the week is today?
$today = strftime('%w', $now);

// How many days ago was the start of the week?
$start_day = $now - (86400 * $today);

// Print out each day of the week
for ($i = 0; $i < 7; $i++) {
  print strftime('%c',$start_day + 86400 * $i);
}
?>
```

Discussion

A particular month or year could have a variable number of days, so you need to compute the end of the time range based on the specifics of that month or year. To loop through every day in a month, find the epoch timestamps for the first day of the month and the first day of the next month. In Example 3-40, the loop variable **$day** is incremented a day at a time (86,400 seconds) until it's no longer less than the epoch timestamp at the beginning of the next month.

Example 3-40. Generating the days in a month

```php
<?php
// Generate a time range for this month
$now = time();

// If it's before 3 AM, increment $now, so we don't get caught by DST
// when moving back to the beginning of the month
if (3 < strftime('%H', $now)) { $now += 7200; }

// What month is this?
$this_month = strftime('%m',$now);

// Epoch timestamp for midnight on the first day of this month
$day = mktime(0,0,0,$this_month,1);
// Epoch timestamp for midnight on the first day of next month
$month_end = mktime(0,0,0,$this_month+1,1);

while ($day < $month_end) {
  print strftime('%c',$day);
  $day += 86400;
}
?>
```

See Also

Documentation on `time( )` at *http://www.php.net/time* and `strftime( )` at *http://www.php.net/strftime*.

3.15 Using Non-Gregorian Calendars

Problem

You want to use a non-Gregorian calendar, such as a Julian, Jewish, or French Republican calendar.

Solution

PHP's calendar extension provides conversion functions for working with the Julian calendar, as well as the French Republican and Jewish calendars. To use these functions, the calendar extension must be loaded.

These functions use the Julian day count (which is different than the Julian calendar) as their intermediate format to move information between them. `cal_to_jd( )` converts a month, day, and year to a Julian day count value; `cal_from_jd( )` converts a Julian day count value to a month, day, and year in a particular calendar. Example 3-41 converts between Julian days and the familiar Gregorian calendar.

Example 3-41. Converting between Julian days and the Gregorian calendar

```php
<?php
// March 8, 1876
$jd = gregoriantojd(3,9,1876);
// $jd = 2406323

$gregorian = cal_from_jd($jd, CAL_GREGORIAN);
/* $gregorian is an array:
array(9) {
  ["date"]=>
  string(8) "3/9/1876"
  ["month"]=>
  int(3)
  ["day"]=>
  int(9)
  ["year"]=>
  int(1876)
  ["dow"]=>
  int(4)
  ["abbrevdayname"]=>
  string(3) "Thu"
  ["dayname"]=>
  string(8) "Thursday"
  ["abbrevmonth"]=>
  string(3) "Mar"
  ["monthname"]=>
  string(5) "March"
```

```
  }
*/
?>
```

The valid range for the Gregorian calendar is 4714 BCE to 9999 CE.

Discussion

To convert between Julian days and the Julian calendar, use the `CAL_JULIAN` constant, as shown in Example 3-42.

Example 3-42. Using the Julian calendar

```php
<?php
// February 29, 1900 (not a Gregorian leap year)
$jd = cal_to_jd(CAL_JULIAN, 2, 29, 1900);
// $jd = 2415092

$julian = cal_from_jd($jd, CAL_JULIAN);
/* $julian is an array:
array(9) {
  ["date"]=>
  string(9) "2/29/1900"
  ["month"]=>
  int(2)
  ["day"]=>
  int(29)
  ["year"]=>
  int(1900)
  ["dow"]=>
  int(2)
  ["abbrevdayname"]=>
  string(3) "Tue"
  ["dayname"]=>
  string(7) "Tuesday"
  ["abbrevmonth"]=>
  string(3) "Feb"
  ["monthname"]=>
  string(8) "February"
}
*/

$gregorian = cal_from_jd($jd, CAL_GREGORIAN);
/* $gregorian is an array:
array(9) {
  ["date"]=>
  string(9) "3/13/1900"
  ["month"]=>
  int(3)
  ["day"]=>
  int(13)
  ["year"]=>
  int(1900)
  ["dow"]=>
  int(2)
```

```
    ["abbrevdayname"]=>
    string(3) "Tue"
    ["dayname"]=>
    string(7) "Tuesday"
    ["abbrevmonth"]=>
    string(3) "Mar"
    ["monthname"]=>
    string(5) "March"
  }
  */
  ?>
```

The valid range for the Julian calendar is 4713 BCE to 9999 CE, but since it was created in 46 BCE, you run the risk of annoying Julian calendar purists if you use it for dates before that.

To convert between Julian days and the French Republican calendar, use the CAL_FRENCH constant, as shown in Example 3-43.

Example 3-43. Using the French Republican calendar

```
<?php
// 13 Floréal XI
$jd = cal_to_jd(CAL_FRENCH, 8, 13, 11);
// $jd = 2379714

$french = cal_from_jd($jd, CAL_FRENCH);
/* $french is an array:
array(9) {
  ["date"]=>
  string(7) "8/13/11"
  ["month"]=>
  int(8)
  ["day"]=>
  int(13)
  ["year"]=>
  int(11)
  ["dow"]=>
  int(2)
  ["abbrevdayname"]=>
  string(3) "Tue"
  ["dayname"]=>
  string(7) "Tuesday"
  ["abbrevmonth"]=>
  string(7) "Floreal"
  ["monthname"]=>
  string(7) "Floreal"
}
*/

// May 3, 1803 - sale of Louisiana to the US
$gregorian = cal_from_jd($jd, CAL_GREGORIAN);
/* $gregorian is an array:
array(9) {
  ["date"]=>
```

```
    string(8) "5/3/1803"
    ["month"]=>
    int(5)
    ["day"]=>
    int(3)
    ["year"]=>
    int(1803)
    ["dow"]=>
    int(2)
    ["abbrevdayname"]=>
    string(3) "Tue"
    ["dayname"]=>
    string(7) "Tuesday"
    ["abbrevmonth"]=>
    string(3) "May"
    ["monthname"]=>
    string(3) "May"
}
*/
?>
```

The valid range for the French Republican calendar is September 1792 to September 1806, which is small, but since the calendar was only in use from October 1793 to January 1806, that's comprehensive enough. Note that the month names that cal_from_jd( ) returns do not have proper accents—they are, for example, Floreal instead of Floréal.

To convert between Julian days and the Jewish calendar, use the CAL_JEWISH constant, as shown in Example 3-44.

Example 3-44. Using the Jewish calendar
```
<?php
// 14 Adar 5761
$jd = cal_to_jd(CAL_JEWISH, 6, 14, 5761);
// $jd = 2451978

$jewish = cal_from_jd($jd, CAL_JEWISH);
/* $jewish is an array:
array(9) {
  ["date"]=>
  string(9) "6/14/5761"
  ["month"]=>
  int(6)
  ["day"]=>
  int(14)
  ["year"]=>
  int(5761)
  ["dow"]=>
  int(5)
  ["abbrevdayname"]=>
  string(3) "Fri"
  ["dayname"]=>
  string(6) "Friday"
  ["abbrevmonth"]=>
```

```
      string(5) "AdarI"
      ["monthname"]=>
      string(5) "AdarI"
}
*/

$gregorian = cal_from_jd($jd, CAL_GREGORIAN);
/* $gregorian is an array:
array(9) {
   ["date"]=>
   string(8) "3/9/2001"
   ["month"]=>
   int(3)
   ["day"]=>
   int(9)
   ["year"]=>
   int(2001)
   ["dow"]=>
   int(5)
   ["abbrevdayname"]=>
   string(3) "Fri"
   ["dayname"]=>
   string(6) "Friday"
   ["abbrevmonth"]=>
   string(3) "Mar"
   ["monthname"]=>
   string(5) "March"
}
*/
?>
```

The valid range for the Jewish calendar starts with 3761 BCE (year 1 on the Jewish calendar). Note that whether or not it falls within a leap year, the month Adar is always returned as AdarI. In leap years, Adar II is returned as AdarII.

See Also

Documentation for the calendar functions at *http://www.php.net/calendar*; the history of the Gregorian calendar is explained at *http://scienceworld.wolfram.com/astronomy/ GregorianCalendar.html*.

3.16 Using Dates Outside the Range of an Epoch Timestamp

Problem

You want to use dates that are outside the range of what a 32-bit epoch timestamp can handle: roughly before 1901 or after 2038.

Solution

Use the PEAR Date_Calc class, which can handle dates from January 1, 1 CE to December 31, 9999 CE. Example 3-45 prints formatted dates for two days in the 9th century CE.

Example 3-45. Using Date_Calc

```php
<?php
require_once 'Date/Calc.php';

// April 17, 1790
$date = Date_Calc::dateFormat( 17, 4, 1790, '%A %B %e, %Y');

print "Benjamin Franklin died on $date.";
?>
```

Example 3-45 prints:

```
Benjamin Franklin died on Saturday April 17, 1790.
```

Discussion

Because Date_Calc uses its own internal representation for dates, it's not subject to the limits of storing an epoch timestamp in a 32-bit integer. Its `dateFormat( )` method works similarly to `strftime( )`—it turns a format string into a formatted date and time string. Table 3-7 lists the formatting characters that `dateFormat( )` understands.

Table 3-7. Formatting characters for Date_Calc::dateFormat( )

Character	Description
%d	Day of month, with leading 0
%e	Day of month, no leading 0
%w	Day of week, no leading 0, Sunday is 0
%j	Day of year, with leading 0
%E	Day count according to internal Date_Calc epoch
%a	Weekday name, short
%A	Weekday name, full
%U	Week number of current year
%m	Month number, no leading 0, January is 1
%b	Month name, short
%B	Month name, long
%y	Year, 2-digit with leading 0
%Y	Year, 4-digit with leading 0
%n	Newline
%t	Tab

Character	Description
%%	%

Date_Calc makes it easy to work with a wide range of Gregorian calendar dates, but it does not have comprehensive knowledge of the religious, political, and cultural factors that have caused modification to the calendar over time.

See Also

The PEAR Date package at *http://pear.php.net/package/Date*. The tip of the calendar-changing-over-time-wackiness iceberg is explored at *http://en.wikipedia.org/wiki/Old_Style_and_New_Style_dates*.

3.17 Program: Calendar

The pc_calendar( ) function shown in Example 3-47 prints out a month's calendar, similar to the Unix *cal* program. Example 3-46 shows how you can use the function, including default styles for its layout.

Example 3-46. Using pc_calendar( )

```
<style type="text/css">
.prev { text-align: left; }
.next { text-align: right; }
.day, .month, .weekday { text-align: center; }
.today { background: yellow; }
.blank { }
</style>
<?php
// print the calendar for the current month if a month
// or year isn't in the query string
$month = isset($_GET['month']) ? intval($_GET['month']) : date('m');
$year = isset($_GET['year']) ? intval($_GET['year']) : date('y');
?>
```

The pc_calendar( ) function prints out a table with a month's calendar in it. It provides links to the previous and next month and highlights the current day, as shown in Example 3-47.

Example 3-47. pc_calendar( )

```
<?php
function pc_calendar($month,$year,$opts = '') {
    // set default options
    if (! is_array($opts)) { $opts = array(); }
    if (! isset($opts['id'])) { $opts['id'] = 'calendar'; }
    if (! isset($opts['month_link'])) {
        $opts['month_link'] =
            '<a href="'.$_SERVER['PHP_SELF'].'?month=%d&amp;year=%d">%s</a>';
    }
    $classes = array();
```

```php
    foreach (array('prev','month','next','weekday','blank','day','today') as $class) {
        if (isset($opts[$class.'_class'])) {
            $classes[$class] = htmlentities($opts[$class.'_class']);
        } else {
            $classes[$class] = $class;
        }
    }

    list($this_month,$this_year,$this_day) = split(',',strftime('%m,%Y,%d'));
    $day_highlight = (($this_month == $month) && ($this_year == $year));

    list($prev_month,$prev_year) =
        split(',',strftime('%m,%Y',mktime(0,0,0,$month-1,1,$year)));
    $prev_month_link = sprintf($opts['month_link'],$prev_month,$prev_year,'&laquo;');

    list($next_month,$next_year) =
        split(',',strftime('%m,%Y',mktime(0,0,0,$month+1,1,$year)));
    $next_month_link = sprintf($opts['month_link'],$next_month,$next_year,'&raquo;');

?>
<table id="<?php echo htmlentities($opts['id']) ?>">
        <tr>
                <td class="<?php echo $classes['prev'] ?>">
                        <?php print $prev_month_link ?>
                </td>
                <td class="<?php echo $classes['month'] ?>" colspan="5">
                <?php print strftime('%B %Y',mktime(0,0,0,$month,1,$year)); ?>
                </td>
                <td class="<?php echo $classes['next'] ?>">
                        <?php print $next_month_link ?>
                </td>
        </tr>
<?php
    $totaldays = date('t',mktime(0,0,0,$month,1,$year));

    // print out days of the week
    print '<tr>';
    $weekdays = array('Su','Mo','Tu','We','Th','Fr','Sa');
    while (list($k,$v) = each($weekdays)) {
        print '<td class="'.$classes['weekday'].'">'.$v.'</td>';
    }
    print '</tr><tr>';
    // align the first day of the month with the right week day
    $day_offset = date("w",mktime(0, 0, 0, $month, 1, $year));
    if ($day_offset > 0) {
        for ($i = 0; $i < $day_offset; $i++) {
            print '<td class="'.$classes['blank'].'"> </td>';
        }
    }
    $yesterday = time() - 86400;

    // print out the days
    for ($day = 1; $day <= $totaldays; $day++) {
        $day_secs = mktime(0,0,0,$month,$day,$year);
        if ($day_secs >= $yesterday) {
```

```
            if ($day_highlight && ($day == $this_day)) {
                print '<td class="' . $classes['today'] .'">' . $day . '</td>';
            } else {
                print '<td class="' . $classes['day'] .'">' . $day . '</td>';
            }
        } else {
            print '<td class="' . $classes['day'] .'">' . $day .'</td>';
        }
        $day_offset++;

        // start a new row each week //
        if ($day_offset == 7) {
            $day_offset = 0;
            if ($day < $totaldays) { print "</tr>\n<tr>"; }
        }
    }
    // fill in the last week with blanks //
    if ($day_offset > 0) { $day_offset = 7 - $day_offset; }
    if ($day_offset > 0) {
        for ($i = 0; $i < $day_offset; $i++) {
            print '<td class="'.$classes['blank'].'"> </td>';
        }
    }
    print '</tr></table>';
}
?>
```

The pc_calendar( ) function begins by checking options passed to it in $opts. You can pass a printf( )-style format string in $opts['month_link'] to change how the links to the previous and next months are printed as well as an id attribute for the table. The id defaults to calendar if not specified.

Additionally, you can pass in class names to use for various elements in the layout. The option names for these classes are prev_class, month_class, next_class, weekday_class, blank_class, day_class, and today_class. The default values are prev, month, next, weekday, blank, day, and today. Example 3-46 includes styles that provide a basic pleasant layout for the table, including highlighting the current day in yellow.

Next, the function sets $day_highlight to true if the month and year for the calendar match the current month and year. The links to the previous month and next month are put into $prev_month_link and $next_month_link using the format string in $opts['month_link'].

pc_calendar( ) then prints out the top of the HTML table that contains the calendar and a table row of weekday abbreviations. Using the day of the week returned from strftime('%w'), blank table cells are printed so the first day of the month is aligned with the appropriate day of the week. For example, if the first day of the month is a Tuesday, two blank cells have to be printed to occupy the slots under Sunday and Monday in the first row of the table.

After this preliminary information has been printed, pc_calendar( ) loops through all the days in the month. It prints a plain table cell for most days, but a table cell with a different background color for the current day. When `$day_offset` reaches 7, a week has completed, and a new table row needs to start.

Once a table cell has been printed for each day in the month, blank cells are added to fill out the last row of the table. For example, if the last day of the month is a Thursday, two cells are added to occupy the slots under Friday and Saturday. Last, the table is closed, and the calendar is complete.

CHAPTER 4

Arrays

4.0 Introduction

Arrays are lists: lists of people, lists of sizes, lists of books. To store a group of related items in a variable, use an array. Like a list on a piece of paper, the elements in array have an order. Usually, each new item comes after the last entry in the array, but just as you can wedge a new entry between a pair of lines already in a paper list, you can do the same with arrays in PHP.

In many languages, there is only one type of array: this is called a *numerical array* (or just an array). In a numerical array, if you want to find an entry, you need to know its position within the array, known as an *index*. Positions are identified by numbers: they start at 0 and work upward one by one.

In some languages, there is also another type of array: an *associative array*, also known as a *hash*. In an associative array, indexes aren't integers, but strings. So in a numerical array of U.S. presidents, "Abraham Lincoln" might have index 16; in the associative-array version, the index might be "Honest." However, while numerical arrays have a strict ordering imposed by their keys, associative arrays frequently make no guarantees about the key ordering. Elements are added in a certain order, but there's no way to determine the order later.

In a few languages, there are both numerical and associative arrays. But usually the numerical array $presidents and the associative array $presidents are distinct arrays. Each array type has a specific behavior, and you need to operate on it accordingly. PHP has both numerical and associative arrays, but they don't behave independently.

In PHP, numerical arrays *are* associative arrays, and associative arrays *are* numerical arrays. So which kind are they really? Both and neither. The line between them constantly blurs back and forth from one to another. At first, this can be disorienting, especially if you're used to rigid behavior, but soon you'll find this flexibility an asset.

To assign multiple values to an array in one step, use array( ):

```
$fruits = array('Apples', 'Bananas', 'Cantaloupes', 'Dates');
```

Now, the value of `$fruits[2]` is `'Cantaloupes'`.

`array( )` is very handy when you have a short list of known values. The same array is also produced by:

```
$fruits[0] = 'Apples';
$fruits[1] = 'Bananas';
$fruits[2] = 'Cantaloupes';
$fruits[3] = 'Dates';
```

and:

```
$fruits[] = 'Apples';
$fruits[] = 'Bananas';
$fruits[] = 'Cantaloupes';
$fruits[] = 'Dates';
```

Assigning a value to an array with an empty subscript is shorthand for adding a new element to the end of the array. So PHP looks up the length of `$fruits` and uses that as the position for the value you're assigning. This assumes, of course, that `$fruits` isn't set to a scalar value, such as 3, and isn't an object. PHP complains if you try to treat a non-array as an array; however, if this is the first time you're using this variable, PHP automatically converts it to an array and begins indexing at 0.

An identical feature is the function `array_push( )`, which pushes a new value on top of the array stack. However, the `$foo[ ]` notation is the more traditional PHP style; it's also faster. But sometimes, using `array_push( )` more accurately conveys the stack nature of what you're trying to do, especially when combined with `array_pop( )`, which removes the last element from an array and returns it.

So far, we've placed integers and strings only inside arrays. However, PHP allows you to assign any data type you want to an array element: booleans, integers, floating-point numbers, strings, objects, resources, `NULL`, and even other arrays. So you can pull arrays or objects directly from a database and place them into an array:

```
while ($row = mysql_fetch_row($r)) {
    $fruits[] = $row;
}

while ($obj = mysql_fetch_object($s)) {
    $vegetables[] = $obj;
}
```

The first `while` statement creates an array of arrays; the second creates an array of objects. See Recipe 4.2 for more on storing multiple elements per key.

To define an array using not integer keys but string keys, you can also use `array( )`, but specify the key/value pairs with `=>`:

```
$fruits = array('red' => 'Apples', 'yellow' => 'Bananas',
                'beige' => 'Cantaloupes', 'brown' => 'Dates');
```

Now, the value of `$fruits['beige']` is `'Cantaloupes'`. This is shorthand for:

```
$fruits['red'] = 'Apples';
$fruits['yellow'] = 'Bananas';
$fruits['beige'] = 'Cantaloupes';
$fruits['brown'] = 'Dates';
```

Each array can only hold one unique value for each key. Adding:

```
$fruits['red'] = 'Strawberry';
```

overwrites the value of `'Apples'`. However, you can always add another key at a later time:

```
$fruits['orange'] = 'Orange';
```

The more you program in PHP, the more you find yourself using associative arrays instead of numerical ones. Instead of creating a numeric array with string values, you can create an associative array and place your values as its keys. If you want, you can then store additional information in the element's value. There's no speed penalty for doing this, and PHP preserves the ordering. Plus, looking up or changing a value is easy because you already know the key.

The easiest way to cycle though an array and operate on all or some of the elements inside is to use `foreach`:

```
$fruits = array('red' => 'Apples', 'yellow' => 'Bananas',
                'beige' => 'Cantaloupes', 'brown' => 'Dates');

foreach ($fruits as $color => $fruit) {
    print "$fruit are $color.\n";
}
Apples are red.
Bananas are yellow.
Cantaloupes are beige.
Dates are brown.
```

Each time through the loop, PHP assigns the next key to `$color` and the key's value to `$fruit`. When there are no elements left in the array, the loop finishes.

To break an array apart into individual variables, use `list( )`:

```
$fruits = array('Apples', 'Bananas', 'Cantaloupes', 'Dates');

list($red, $yellow, $beige, $brown) = $fruits;
```

4.1 Specifying an Array Not Beginning at Element 0

Problem

You want to assign multiple elements to an array in one step, but you don't want the first index to be 0.

Solution

Instruct `array( )` to use a different index using the `=>` syntax:

```
$presidents = array(1 => 'Washington', 'Adams', 'Jefferson', 'Madison');
```

Discussion

Arrays in PHP—like most, but not all, computer languages—begin with the first entry located at index 0. Sometimes, however, the data you're storing makes more sense if the list begins at 1. (And we're not just talking to recovering Pascal programmers here.)

In the Solution, George Washington is the first president, not the zeroth, so if you wish to print a list of the presidents, it's simpler to do this:

```
foreach ($presidents as $number => $president) {
    print "$number: $president\n";
}
```

than this:

```
foreach ($presidents as $number => $president) {
    $number++;
    print "$number: $president\n";
}
```

The feature isn't restricted to the number 1; any integer works:

```
$reconstruction_presidents = array(16 => 'Lincoln', 'Johnson', 'Grant');
```

Also, you can use => multiple times in one call:

```
$whig_presidents = array(9 => 'Harrison', 'Tyler',* 12 => 'Taylor', 'Fillmore');
```

PHP even allows you to use negative numbers in the **array( )** call. (In fact, this method works for non-integer keys, too.) What you'll get is technically an associative array, although as we said, the line between numeric arrays and associative arrays is often blurred in PHP; this is just another one of these cases:

```
$us_leaders = array(-1 => 'George II', 'George III', 'Washington');
```

If Washington is the first U.S. leader, George III is the zeroth, and his grandfather George II is the negative-first.

Of course, you can mix and match numeric and string keys in one **array( )** definition, but it's confusing and very rarely needed:

```
$presidents = array(1 => 'Washington', 'Adams', 'Honest' => 'Lincoln', 'Jefferson');
```

This is equivalent to:

```
$presidents[1]         = 'Washington';   // Key is 1
$presidents[]          = 'Adams';        // Key is 1 + 1 => 2
$presidents['Honest']  = 'Lincoln';      // Key is 'Honest'
$presidents[]          = 'Jefferson';    // Key is 2 + 1 => 3
```

---

* John Tyler was elected as Harrison's vice president under the Whig Party platform but was expelled from the party shortly after assuming the presidency following the death of Harrison.

See Also

Documentation on `array( )` at *http://www.php.net/array*.

4.2 Storing Multiple Elements Per Key in an Array

Problem

You want to associate multiple elements with a single key.

Solution

Store the multiple elements in an array:

```
$fruits = array('red' => array('strawberry','apple'),
                'yellow' => array('banana'));
```

Or use an object:

```
while ($obj = mysql_fetch_object($r)) {
    $fruits[] = $obj;
}
```

Discussion

In PHP, keys are unique per array, so you can't associate more than one entry in a key without overwriting the old value. Instead, store your values in an anonymous array:

```
$fruits['red'][] = 'strawberry';
$fruits['red'][] = 'apple';
$fruits['yellow'][] = 'banana';
```

Or, if you're processing items in a loop:

```
while (list($color,$fruit) = mysql_fetch_array($r)) {
    $fruits[$color][] = $fruit;
}
```

To print the entries, loop through the array:

```
foreach ($fruits as $color=>$color_fruit) {
    // $color_fruit is an array
    foreach ($color_fruit as $fruit) {
        print "$fruit is colored $color.<br>";
    }
}
```

Or use the `pc_array_to_comma_string( )` function from Recipe 4.9.

```
foreach ($fruits as $color=>$color_fruit) {
    print "$color colored fruits include " .
        pc_array_to_comma_string($color_fruit) . "<br>";
}
```

In PHP 5.0.0 and above, you don't need `pc_array_range( )`: just pass an increment to `range( )` as a third argument:

```
$odd = range(1, 52, 2);
$even = range(2, 52, 2);
```

See Also

Recipe 4.9 for how to print arrays with commas.

4.3 Initializing an Array to a Range of Integers

Problem

You want to assign a series of consecutive integers to an array.

Solution

Use range($start, $stop):

```
$cards = range(1, 52);
```

Discussion

For increments other than 1, you can use:

```
function pc_array_range($start, $stop, $step) {
    $array = array();
    for ($i = $start; $i <= $stop; $i += $step) {
        $array[] = $i;
    }
    return $array;
}
```

So for odd numbers:

```
$odd = pc_array_range(1, 52, 2);
```

And for even numbers:

```
$even = pc_array_range(2, 52, 2);
```

In PHP 5.0.0 and above, you don't need pc_array_range( ): just pass an increment to range( ) as a third argument:

```
$odd = range(1, 52, 2);
$even = range(2, 52, 2);
```

See Also

Recipe 2.4 for how to operate on a series of integers; documentation on range( ) at *http://www.php.net/range*.

4.4 Iterating Through an Array

Problem

You want to cycle though an array and operate on all or some of the elements inside.

Solution

Use foreach:

```
foreach ($array as $value) {
    // Act on $value
}
```

Or to get an array's keys and values:

```
foreach ($array as $key => $value) {
    // Act II
}
```

Another technique is to use for:

```
for ($key = 0, $size = count($array); $key < $size; $key++) {
    // Act III
}
```

Finally, you can use each( ) in combination with list( ) and while:

```
reset($array) // reset internal pointer to beginning of array
while (list($key, $value) = each ($array)) {
    // Final Act
}
```

Discussion

A foreach loop is the most concise to iterate through an array:

```
// foreach with values
foreach ($items as $cost) {
    ...
}

// foreach with keys and values
foreach($items as $item => $cost) {
    ...
}
```

With foreach, PHP iterates over a copy of the array instead of the actual array. In contrast, when using each( ) and for, PHP iterates over the original array. So if you modify the array inside the loop, you may (or may not) get the behavior you expect.

If you want to modify the array, reference it directly:

```
reset($items);
while (list($item, $cost) = each($items)) {
    if (! in_stock($item)) {
```

```
        unset($items[$item]);              // address the array directly
    }
}
```

The variables returned by each( ) aren't aliases for the original values in the array: they're copies, so if you modify them, it's not reflected in the array. That's why you need to modify $items[$item] instead of $item.

When using each( ), PHP keeps track of where you are inside the loop. After completing a first pass through, to begin again at the start, call reset( ) to move the pointer back to the front of the array. Otherwise, each( ) returns false.

The for loop works only for arrays with consecutive integer keys. Unless you're modifying the size of your array, it's inefficient to recompute the count( ) of $items each time through the loop, so we always use a $size variable to hold the array's size:

```
for ($item = 0, $size = count($items); $item < $size; $item++) {
    ...
}
```

If you prefer to count efficiently with one variable, count backward:

```
for ($item = count($items) - 1; $item >= 0; $item--) {
    ...
}
```

The associative array version of the for loop is:

```
for (reset($array); $key = key($array); next($array) ) {
    ...
}
```

This fails if any element holds a string that evaluates to false, so a perfectly normal value such as 0 causes the loop to end early.

Finally, use array_map( ) to hand off each element to a function for processing:

```
// lowercase all words
$lc = array_map('strtolower', $words);
```

The first argument to array_map( ) is a function to modify an individual element, and the second is the array to be iterated through.

Generally, we find this function less flexible than the previous methods, but it is well-suited for the processing and merging of multiple arrays.

If you're unsure if the data you'll be processing is a scalar or an array, you need to protect against calling foreach with a non-array. One method is to use is_array( ):

```
if (is_array($items)) {
    // foreach loop code for array
} else {
    // code for scalar
}
```

Another method is to coerce all variables into array form using settype( ):

```
settype($items, 'array');
// loop code for arrays
```

This turns a scalar value into a one-element array and cleans up your code at the expense of a little overhead.

See Also

Documentation on `for` at *http://www.php.net/for*, `foreach` at *http://www.php.net/foreach*, `while` at *http://www.php.net/while*, `each()` at *http://www.php.net/each*, `reset()` at *http://www.php.net/reset*, and `array_map()` at *http://www.php.net/array-map*.

4.5 Deleting Elements from an Array

Problem

You want to remove one or more elements from an array.

Solution

To delete one element, use `unset()`:

```
unset($array[3]);
unset($array['foo']);
```

To delete multiple noncontiguous elements, also use `unset()`:

```
unset($array[3], $array[5]);
unset($array['foo'], $array['bar']);
```

To delete multiple contiguous elements, use `array_splice()`:

```
array_splice($array, $offset, $length);
```

Discussion

Using these functions removes all references to these elements from PHP. If you want to keep a key in the array, but with an empty value, assign the empty string to the element:

```
$array[3] = $array['foo'] = '';
```

Besides syntax, there's a logical difference between using `unset()` and assigning `''` to the element. The first says, "This doesn't exist anymore," while the second says, "This still exists, but its value is the empty string."

If you're dealing with numbers, assigning 0 may be a better alternative. So if a company stopped production of the model XL1000 sprocket, it would update its inventory with:

```
unset($products['XL1000']);
```

However, if the company temporarily ran out of XL1000 sprockets but was planning to receive a new shipment from the plant later this week, this is better:

```
$products['XL1000'] = 0;
```

If you unset( ) an element, PHP adjusts the array so that looping still works correctly.
It doesn't compact the array to fill in the missing holes. This is what we mean when we
say that all arrays are associative, even when they appear to be numeric. Here's an
example:

```
// create a "numeric" array
$animals = array('ant', 'bee', 'cat', 'dog', 'elk', 'fox');
print $animals[1];   // prints 'bee'
print $animals[2];   // prints 'cat'
count($animals);     // returns 6

// unset()
unset($animals[1]); // removes element $animals[1] = 'bee'
print $animals[1];   // prints '' and throws an E_NOTICE error
print $animals[2];   // still prints 'cat'
count($animals);     // returns 5, even though $array[5] is 'fox'

// add new element
$animals[] = 'gnu'; // add new element (not Unix)
print $animals[1];   // prints '', still empty
print $animals[6];   // prints 'gnu', this is where 'gnu' ended up
count($animals);     // returns 6

// assign ''
$animals[2] = '';    // zero out value
print $animals[2];   // prints ''
count($animals);     // returns 6, count does not decrease
```

To compact the array into a densely filled numeric array, use **array_values( )**:

```
$animals = array_values($animals);
```

Alternatively, **array_splice( )** automatically reindexes arrays to avoid leaving holes:

```
// create a "numeric" array
$animals = array('ant', 'bee', 'cat', 'dog', 'elk', 'fox');
array_splice($animals, 2, 2);
print_r($animals);
Array
(
    [0] => ant
    [1] => bee
    [2] => elk
    [3] => fox
)
```

This is useful if you're using the array as a queue and want to remove items from the
queue while still allowing random access. To safely remove the first or last element
from an array, use **array_shift( )** and **array_pop( )**, respectively.

However, if you find yourself often running into problems because of holes in arrays,
you may not be "thinking PHP." Look at the ways to iterate through the array in
Recipe 4.4 that don't involve using a **for** loop.

See Also

Recipe 4.4 for iteration techniques; documentation on unset( ) at *http://www.php.net/unset*, array_splice( ) at *http://www.php.net/array-splice*, and array_values( ) at *http://www.php.net/array-values*.

4.6 Changing Array Size

Problem

You want to modify the size of an array, either by making it larger or smaller than its current size.

Solution

Use array_pad( ) to make an array grow:

```
// start at three
$array = array('apple', 'banana', 'coconut');

// grow to five
$array = array_pad($array, 5, '');
```

Now, count($array) is 5, and the last two elements, $array[3] and $array[4], contain the empty string.

To reduce an array, you can use array_splice( ):

```
// no assignment to $array
array_splice($array, 2);
```

This removes all but the first two elements from $array.

Discussion

Arrays aren't a predeclared size in PHP, so you can resize them on the fly.

To pad an array, use array_pad( ). The first argument is the array to be padded. The next argument is the size and direction you want to pad. To pad to the right, use a positive integer; to pad to the left, use a negative one. The third argument is the value to be assigned to the newly created entries. The function returns a modified array and doesn't alter the original.

Here are some examples:

```
// make a four-element array with 'dates' to the right
$array = array('apple', 'banana', 'coconut');
$array = array_pad($array, 4, 'dates');
print_r($array);
Array
(
    [0] => apple
    [1] => banana
```

```
        [2] => coconut
        [3] => dates
)

// make a six-element array with 'zucchinis' to the left
$array = array_pad($array, -6, 'zucchini');
print_r($array);
Array
(
    [0] => zucchini
    [1] => zucchini
    [2] => apple
    [3] => banana
    [4] => coconut
    [5] => dates
)
```

Be careful: `array_pad($array, 4, 'dates')` makes sure an `$array` is *at least* four elements long; it doesn't add four *new* elements. In this case, if `$array` was already four elements or larger, `array_pad( )` would return an unaltered `$array`.

Also, if you declare a value for a fourth element, `$array[4]`:

```
$array = array('apple', 'banana', 'coconut');
$array[4] = 'dates';
```

you end up with a four-element array with indexes 0, 1, 2, and 4:

```
Array
(
    [0] => apple
    [1] => banana
    [2] => coconut
    [4] => dates
)
```

PHP essentially turns this into an associative array that happens to have integer keys.

The `array_splice( )` function, unlike `array_pad( )`, has the side effect of modifying the original array. It returns the spliced-out array. That's why you don't assign the return value to `$array`. However, like `array_pad( )`, you can splice from either the right or left. So calling `array_splice( )` with a value of -2 chops off the last two elements from the end:

```
// make a four-element array
$array = array('apple', 'banana', 'coconut', 'dates');

// shrink to three elements
array_splice($array, 3);

// remove last element, equivalent to array_pop()
array_splice($array, -1);

// only remaining fruits are apple and banana
print_r($array);
Array
```

```
(
    [0] => apple
    [1] => banana
)
```

See Also

Documentation on `array_pad( )` at *http://www.php.net/array-pad* and `array_splice( )` at *http://www.php.net/array-splice*.

4.7 Appending One Array to Another

Problem

You want to combine two arrays into one.

Solution

Use `array_merge( )`:

```
$garden = array_merge($fruits, $vegetables);
```

Discussion

The `array_merge( )` function works with both predefined arrays and arrays defined in place using `array( )`:

```
$p_languages = array('Perl', 'PHP');
$p_languages = array_merge($p_languages, array('Python'));
print_r($p_languages);
Array
(
    [0] => PHP
    [1] => Perl
    [2] => Python
)
```

Accordingly, merged arrays can be either preexisting arrays, as with `$p_languages`, or anonymous arrays, as with `array('Python')`.

You can't use `array_push( )`, because PHP won't automatically flatten out the array into a series of independent variables, and you'll end up with a nested array. Thus:

```
array_push($p_languages, array('Python'));
print_r($p_languages);
Array
(
    [0] => PHP
    [1] => Perl
    [2] => Array
        (
            [0] => Python
        )
```

```
)
```

Merging arrays with only numerical keys causes the arrays to get renumbered, so values aren't lost. Merging arrays with string keys causes the second array to overwrite the value of any duplicated keys. Arrays with both types of keys exhibit both types of behavior. For example:

```
$lc = array('a', 'b' => 'b'); // lower-case letters as values
$uc = array('A', 'b' => 'B'); // upper-case letters as values
$ac = array_merge($lc, $uc);  // all-cases?
print_r($ac);
Array
(
    [0] => a
    [b] => B
    [1] => A
)
```

The uppercase A has been renumbered from index 0 to index 1, to avoid a collision, and merged onto the end. The uppercase B has overwritten the lowercase b and replaced it in the original place within the array.

The + operator can also merge arrays. The array on the right overwrites any identically named keys found on the left. It doesn't do any reordering to prevent collisions. Using the previous example:

```
print_r($uc + $lc);
print_r($lc + $uc);
Array
(
    [0] => a
    [b] => b
)
Array
(
    [0] => A
    [b] => B
)
```

Since a and A both have a key of 0, and b and B both have a key of b, you end up with a total of only two elements in the merged arrays.

In the first case, $a + $b becomes just $b, and in the other, $b + $a becomes $a.

However, if you had two distinctly keyed arrays, this wouldn't be a problem, and the new array would be the union of the two arrays.

See Also

Documentation on array_merge( ) at *http://www.php.net/array-merge*.

4.8 Turning an Array into a String

Problem

You have an array, and you want to convert it into a nicely formatted string.

Solution

Use `join( )`:

```
// make a comma delimited list
$string = join(',', $array);
```

Or loop yourself:

```
$string = '';

foreach ($array as $key => $value) {
    $string .= ",$value";
}

$string = substr($string, 1); // remove leading ","
```

Discussion

If you can use `join( )`, do; it's faster than any PHP-based loop. However, `join( )` isn't very flexible. First, it places a delimiter only between elements, not around them. To wrap elements inside HTML bold tags and separate them with commas, do this:

```
$left  = '<b>';
$right = '</b>';

$html = $left . join("$right,$left", $html) . $right;
```

Second, `join( )` doesn't allow you to discriminate against values. If you want to include a subset of entries, you need to loop yourself:

```
$string = '';

foreach ($fields as $key => $value) {
    // don't include password
    if ('password' != $key) {
        $string .= ",<b>$value</b>";
    }
}

$string = substr($string, 1); // remove leading ","
```

Notice that a separator is always added to each value and then stripped off outside the loop. While it's somewhat wasteful to add something that will be subtracted later, it's far cleaner and efficient (in most cases) than attempting to embed logic inside of the loop. To wit:

```
$string = '';
foreach ($fields as $key => $value) {
```

```
    // don't include password
    if ('password' != $value) {
        if (!empty($string)) { $string .= ','; }
        $string .= "<b>$value</b>";
    }
}
```

Now you have to check `$string` every time you append a value. That's worse than the simple `substr()` call. Also, prepend the delimiter (in this case a comma) instead of appending it because it's faster to shorten a string from the front than the rear.

See Also

Recipe 4.9 for printing an array with commas; documentation on `join()` at *http://www.php.net/join* and `substr()` at *http://www.php.net/substr*.

4.9 Printing an Array with Commas

Problem

You want to print out an array with commas separating the elements and with an "and" before the last element if there are more than two elements in the array.

Solution

Use the `pc_array_to_comma_string()` function shown in Example 4-1, which returns the correct string.

Example 4-1. pc_array_to_comma_string()

```
function pc_array_to_comma_string($array) {

    switch (count($array)) {
    case 0:
        return '';

    case 1:
        return reset($array);

    case 2:
        return join(' and ', $array);

    default:
        $last = array_pop($array);
        return join(', ', $array) . ", and $last";
    }
}
```

Discussion

If you have a list of items to print, it's useful to print them in a grammatically correct fashion. It looks awkward to display text like this:

```
$thundercats = array('Lion-O', 'Panthro', 'Tygra', 'Cheetara', 'Snarf');
print 'ThunderCat good guys include ' . join(', ', $thundercats) . '.';
ThunderCat good guys include Lion-O, Panthro, Tygra, Cheetara, Snarf.
```

This implementation of this function isn't completely straightforward, since we want `pc_array_to_comma_string()` to work with all arrays, not just numeric ones beginning at 0. If restricted only to that subset, for an array of size one, you return `$array[0]`. But if the array doesn't begin at 0, `$array[0]` is empty. So you can use the fact that `reset()`, which resets an array's internal pointer, also returns the value of the first array element.

For similar reasons, you call `array_pop()` to grab the end element, instead of assuming it's located at `$array[count($array)-1]`. This allows you to use `join()` on `$array`.

Also note that the code for case 2 actually works correctly for case 1, too. And the default code works (though inefficiently) for case 2; however, the transitive property doesn't apply, so you can't use the default code on elements of size 1.

See Also

Recipe 4.8 for turning an array into a string; documentation on `join()` at *http://www.php.net/join*, `array_pop()` at *http://www.php.net/array-pop*, and `reset()` at *http://www.php.net/reset*.

4.10 Checking if a Key Is in an Array

Problem

You want to know if an array contains a certain key.

Solution

Use `array_key_exists()` to check for a key no matter what the associated value is:

```
if (array_key_exists('key', $array)) {
    /* there is a value for $array['key'] */
}
```

Use `isset()` to find a key whose associated value is anything but `null`:

```
if (isset($array['key'])) { /* there is a non-null value for 'key' in $array */ }
```

Discussion

The `array_key_exists()` function completely ignores array values—it just reports whether there is an element in the array with a particular key. `isset()`, however, behaves the same way on array keys as it does with other variables. A `null` value causes `isset()` to return false. See the Introduction to Chapter 5 for more information about the truth value of variables.

See Also

Documentation on isset( ) at *http://www.php.net/isset* and on array_key_exists( ) at *http://www.php.net/array_key_exists*.

4.11 Checking if an Element Is in an Array

Problem

You want to know if an array contains a certain value.

Solution

Use in_array( ):

```
if (in_array($value, $array)) {
    // an element has $value as its value in array $array
}
```

Discussion

Use in_array( ) to check if an element of an array holds a value:

```
$book_collection = array('Emma', 'Pride and Prejudice', 'Northhanger Abbey');
$book = 'Sense and Sensibility';

if (in_array($book, $book_collection) {
    echo 'Own it.';
} else {
    echo 'Need it.';
}
```

The default behavior of in_array( ) is to compare items using the == operator. To use the strict equality check, ===, pass true as the third parameter to in_array( ):

```
$array = array(1, '2', 'three');

in_array(0, $array);          // true!
in_array(0, $array, true);    // false
in_array(1, $array);          // true
in_array(1, $array, true);    // true
in_array(2, $array);          // true
in_array(2, $array, true);    // false
```

The first check, in_array(0, $array), evaluates to true because to compare the number 0 against the string three, PHP casts three to an integer. Since three isn't a numeric string, as is 2, it becomes 0. Therefore, in_array( ) thinks there's a match.

Consequently, when comparing numbers against data that may contain strings, it's safest to use a strict comparison.

If you find yourself calling in_array( ) multiple times on the same array, it may be better to use an associative array, with the original array elements as the keys in the new associative array. Looking up entries using in_array( ) takes linear time; with an associative array, it takes constant time.

If you can't create the associative array directly but need to convert from a traditional one with integer keys, use array_flip( ) to swap the keys and values of an array:

```
$book_collection = array('Emma',
                         'Pride and Prejudice',
                         'Northhanger Abbey');

// convert from numeric array to associative array
$book_collection = array_flip($book_collection);
$book = 'Sense and Sensibility';

if (isset($book_collection[$book])) {
    echo 'Own it.';
} else {
    echo 'Need it.';
}
```

Note that doing this condenses multiple keys with the same value into one element in the flipped array.

See Also

Recipe 4.12 for determining the position of a value in an array; documentation on in_array( ) at *http://www.php.net/in-array* and array_flip( ) at the following address: *http://www.php.net/array-flip*.

4.12 Finding the Position of a Value in an Array

Problem

You want to know if a value is in an array. If the value is in the array, you want to know its key.

Solution

Use array_search( ). It returns the key of the found value. If the value is not in the array, it returns false:

```
$position = array_search($value, $array);
if ($position !== false) {
    // the element in position $position has $value as its value in array $array
}
```

Discussion

Use in_array( ) to find if an array contains a value; use array_search( ) to discover where that value is located. However, because array_search( ) gracefully handles searches in which the value isn't found, it's better to use array_search( ) instead of in_array( ). The speed difference is minute, and the extra information is potentially useful:

```
$favorite_foods = array(1 => 'artichokes', 'bread', 'cauliflower', 'deviled eggs');
$food = 'cauliflower';
$position = array_search($food, $favorite_foods);

if ($position !== false) {
    echo "My #$position favorite food is $food";
} else {
    echo "Blech! I hate $food!";
}
```

Use the !== check against false because if your string is found in the array at position 0, the if evaluates to a logical false, which isn't what is meant or wanted.

If a value is in the array multiple times, array_search( ) is only guaranteed to return one of the instances, not the first instance.

See Also

Recipe 4.11 for checking whether an element is in an array; documentation on array_search( ) at *http://www.php.net/array-search*; for more sophisticated searching of arrays using regular expression, see preg_replace( ), which is found at *http://www.php.net/preg-replace* and Chapter 22.

4.13 Finding Elements That Pass a Certain Test

Problem

You want to locate entries in an array that meet certain requirements.

Solution

Use a foreach loop:

```
$movies = array(...);

foreach ($movies as $movie) {
    if ($movie['box_office_gross'] < 5000000) { $flops[] = $movie; }
}
```

Or array_filter( ):

```
$movies = array(...);

function flops($movie) {
    return ($movie['box_office_gross'] < 5000000) ? 1 : 0;
}

$flops = array_filter($movies, 'flops');
```

Discussion

The foreach loops are simple: you iterate through the data and append elements to the return array that match your criteria.

If you want only the first such element, exit the loop using break:

```
foreach ($movies as $movie) {
    if ($movie['box_office_gross'] > 200000000) { $blockbuster = $movie; break; }
}
```

You can also return directly from a function:

```
function blockbuster($movies) {
    foreach ($movies as $movie) {
        if ($movie['box_office_gross'] > 200000000) { return $movie; }
    }
}
```

With array_filter( ), however, you first create a callback function that returns true for values you want to keep and false for values you don't. Using array_filter( ), you then instruct PHP to process the array as you do in the foreach.

It's impossible to bail out early from array_filter( ), so foreach provides more flexibility and is simpler to understand. Also, it's one of the few cases in which the built-in PHP function doesn't clearly outperform user-level code.

See Also

Documentation on array_filter( ) at *http://www.php.net/array-filter*.

4.14 Finding the Largest or Smallest Valued Element in an Array

Problem

You have an array of elements, and you want to find the largest or smallest valued element. For example, you want to find the appropriate scale when creating a histogram.

Solution

To find the largest element, use max( ):

```
$largest = max($array);
```

To find the smallest element, use min( ):

```
$smallest = min($array);
```

Discussion

Normally, max( ) returns the larger of two elements, but if you pass it an array, it searches the entire array instead. Unfortunately, there's no way to find the index of the largest element using max( ). To do that, you must sort the array in reverse order to put the largest element in position 0:

```
arsort($array);
```

Now the value of the largest element is $array[0].

If you don't want to disturb the order of the original array, make a copy and sort the copy:

```
$copy = $array;
arsort($copy);
```

The same concept applies to min( ) but uses asort( ) instead of arsort( ).

See Also

Recipe 4.16 for sorting an array; documentation on max( ) at *http://www.php.net/max*, min( ) at *http://www.php.net/min*, arsort( ) at *http://www.php.net/arsort*, and asort( ) at *http://www.php.net/asort*.

4.15 Reversing an Array

Problem

You want to reverse the order of the elements in an array.

Solution

Use array_reverse( ):

```
$array = array('Zero', 'One', 'Two');
$reversed = array_reverse($array);
```

Discussion

The array_reverse( ) function reverses the elements in an array. However, it's often possible to avoid this operation. If you wish to reverse an array you've just sorted, modify the sort to do the inverse. If you want to reverse a list you're about to loop through and process, just invert the loop. Instead of:

```
for ($i = 0, $size = count($array); $i < $size; $i++) {
    ...
}
```

do the following:

```
for ($i = count($array) - 1; $i >=0 ; $i--) {
    ...
}
```

However, as always, use a `for` loop only on a tightly packed array.

Another alternative would be, if possible, to invert the order elements are placed into the array. For instance, if you're populating an array from a series of rows returned from a database, you should be able to modify the query to ORDER DESC. See your database manual for the exact syntax for your database.

See Also

Documentation on `array_reverse( )` at *http://www.php.net/array-reverse*.

4.16 Sorting an Array

Problem

You want to sort an array in a specific way.

Solution

To sort an array using the traditional definition of sort, use `sort( )`:

```
$states = array('Delaware', 'Pennsylvania', 'New Jersey');
sort($states);
```

To sort numerically, pass SORT_NUMERIC as the second argument to `sort( )`:

```
$scores = array(1, 10, 2, 20);
sort($scores, SORT_NUMERIC);
```

This resorts the numbers in ascending order (1, 2, 10, 20) instead of lexicographical order (1, 10, 2, 20).

Discussion

The `sort( )` function doesn't preserve the key/value association between elements; instead, entries are reindexed starting at 0 and going upward. (The one exception to this rule is a one-element array; its lone element doesn't have its index reset to 0. This is fixed as of PHP 4.2.3.)

To preserve the key/value links, use `asort( )`. The `asort( )` function is normally used for associative arrays, but it can also be useful when the indexes of the entries are meaningful:

```
$states = array(1 => 'Delaware', 'Pennsylvania', 'New Jersey');
asort($states);

while (list($rank, $state) = each($states)) {
    print "$state was the #$rank state to join the United States\n";
```

```
    }
```

Use `natsort( )` to sort the array using a natural sorting algorithm. Under natural sorting, you can mix strings and numbers inside your elements and still get the right answer:

```
$tests = array('test1.php', 'test10.php', 'test11.php', 'test2.php');
natsort($tests);
```

The elements are now ordered `'test1.php'`, `'test2.php'`, `'test10.php'`, and `'test11.php'`. With natural sorting, the number 10 comes after the number 2; the opposite occurs under traditional sorting. For case-insensitive natural sorting, use `natcasesort( )`.

To sort the array in reverse order, use `rsort( )` or `arsort( )`, which is like `rsort( )` but also preserves keys. There is no `natrsort( )` or `natcasersort( )`. You can also pass `SORT_NUMERIC` into these functions.

See Also

Recipe 4.17 for sorting with a custom comparison function and Recipe 4.18 for sorting multiple arrays; documentation on `sort( )` at *http://www.php.net/sort*, `asort( )` at *http://www.php.net/asort*, `natsort( )` at *http://www.php.net/natsort*, `natcasesort( )` at *http://www.php.net/natcasesort*, `rsort( )` at *http://www.php.net/rsort*, and `arsort( )` at *http://www.php.net/arsort*.

4.17 Sorting an Array by a Computable Field

Problem

You want to define your own sorting routine.

Solution

Use `usort( )` in combination with a custom comparison function:

```
// sort in reverse natural order
function natrsort($a, $b) {
    return strnatcmp($b, $a);
}

$tests = array('test1.php', 'test10.php', 'test11.php', 'test2.php');
usort($tests, 'natrsort');
```

Discussion

The comparison function must return a value greater that 0 if `$a > $b`, 0 if `$a == $b`, and a value less than 0 if `$a < $b`. To sort in reverse, do the opposite. The function in the Solution, `strnatcmp( )`, obeys those rules.

To reverse the sort, instead of multiplying the return value of `strnatcmp($a, $b)` by -1, switch the order of the arguments to `strnatcmp($b, $a)`.

The sort function doesn't need to be a wrapper for an existing sort. For instance, the `pc_date_sort( )` function, shown in Example 4-2, shows how to sort dates.

Example 4-2. pc_date_sort( )

```
// expects dates in the form of "MM/DD/YYYY"
function pc_date_sort($a, $b) {
    list($a_month, $a_day, $a_year) = explode('/', $a);
    list($b_month, $b_day, $b_year) = explode('/', $b);

    if ($a_year  > $b_year ) return  1;
    if ($a_year  < $b_year ) return -1;

    if ($a_month > $b_month) return  1;
    if ($a_month < $b_month) return -1;

    if ($a_day   > $b_day  ) return  1;
    if ($a_day   < $b_day  ) return -1;

    return 0;
}

$dates = array('12/14/2000', '08/10/2001', '08/07/1999');
usort($dates, 'pc_date_sort');
```

While sorting, `usort( )` frequently recomputes the sort function's return values each time it's needed to compare two elements, which slows the sort. To avoid unnecessary work, you can cache the comparison values, as shown in `pc_array_sort( )` in Example 4-3.

Example 4-3. pc_array_sort( )

```
function pc_array_sort($array, $map_func, $sort_func = '') {
    $mapped = array_map($map_func, $array);    // cache $map_func() values

    if ('' == $sort_func) {
        asort($mapped);                        // asort() is faster then usort()
    } else {
        uasort($mapped, $sort_func);           // need to preserve keys
    }

    while (list($key) = each($mapped)) {
        $sorted[] = $array[$key];              // use sorted keys
    }

    return $sorted;
}
```

To avoid unnecessary work, `pc_array_sort( )` uses a temporary array, `$mapped`, to cache the return values. It then sorts `$mapped`, using either the default sort order or a user-specified sorting routine. Importantly, it uses a sort that preserves the key/value relationship. By default, it uses **asort( )** because **asort( )** is faster than **uasort( )**. (Slowness in **uasort( )** is the whole reason for **pc_array_sort( )** after all.) Finally, it creates a sorted array, **$sorted**, using the sorted keys in **$mapped** to index the values in the original array.

For small arrays or simple sort functions, **usort( )** is faster, but as the number of computations grows, **pc_array_sort( )** surpasses **usort( )**. The following example sorts elements by their string lengths, a relatively quick custom sort:

```
function pc_u_length($a, $b) {
    $a = strlen($a);
    $b = strlen($b);

    if ($a == $b) return  0;
    if ($a  > $b) return  1;
                  return -1;
}

function pc_map_length($a) {
    return strlen($a);
}

$tests = array('one', 'two', 'three', 'four', 'five',
               'six', 'seven', 'eight', 'nine', 'ten');

// faster for < 5 elements using pc_u_length()
usort($tests, 'pc_u_length');

// faster for >= 5 elements using pc_map_length()
$tests = pc_array_sort($tests, 'pc_map_length');
```

Here, **pc_array_sort( )** is faster than **usort( )** once the array reaches five elements.

See Also

Recipe 4.16 for basic sorting and Recipe 4.18 for sorting multiple arrays; documentation on **usort( )** at *http://www.php.net/usort*, **asort( )** at *http://www.php.net/asort*, and **array_map( )** at *http://www.php.net/array-map*.

4.18 Sorting Multiple Arrays

Problem

You want to sort multiple arrays or an array with multiple dimensions.

Solution

Use **array_multisort( )**:

To sort multiple arrays simultaneously, pass multiple arrays to **array_multisort( )**:

```
$colors = array('Red', 'White', 'Blue');
$cities = array('Boston', 'New York', 'Chicago');
```

```
array_multisort($colors, $cities);
print_r($colors);
print_r($cities);
Array
(
    [0] => Blue
    [1] => Red
    [2] => White
)
Array
(
    [0] => Chicago
    [1] => Boston
    [2] => New York
)
```

To sort multiple dimensions within a single array, pass the specific array elements:

```
$stuff = array('colors' => array('Red', 'White', 'Blue'),
               'cities' => array('Boston', 'New York', 'Chicago'));

array_multisort($stuff['colors'], $stuff['cities']);
print_r($stuff);
Array
(
    [colors] => Array
        (
            [0] => Blue
            [1] => Red
            [2] => White
        )

    [cities] => Array
        (
            [0] => Chicago
            [1] => Boston
            [2] => New York
        )

)
```

To modify the sort type, as in sort( ), pass in SORT_REGULAR, SORT_NUMERIC, or SORT_STRING after the array. To modify the sort order, unlike in sort( ), pass in SORT_ASC or SORT_DESC after the array. You can also pass in both a sort type and a sort order after the array.

Discussion

The array_multisort( ) function can sort several arrays at once or a multidimensional array by one or more dimensions. The arrays are treated as columns of a table to be sorted by rows. The first array is the main one to sort by; all the items in the other arrays are reordered based on the sorted order of the first array. If items in the first array compare as equal, the sort order is determined by the second array, and so on.

The default sorting values are SORT_REGULAR and SORT_ASC, and they're reset after each array, so there's no reason to pass either of these two values, except for clarity:

```
$numbers = array(0, 1, 2, 3);
$letters = array('a', 'b', 'c', 'd');
array_multisort($numbers, SORT_NUMERIC, SORT_DESC,
                $letters, SORT_STRING , SORT_DESC);
```

This example reverses the arrays.

See Also

Recipe 4.16 for simple sorting and Recipe 4.17 for sorting with a custom function; documentation on array_multisort( ) at *http://www.php.net/array-multisort*.

4.19 Sorting an Array Using a Method Instead of a Function

Problem

You want to define a custom sorting routine to order an array. However, instead of using a function, you want to use an object method.

Solution

Pass in an array holding a class name and method in place of the function name:

```
usort($access_times, array('dates', 'compare'));
```

Discussion

As with a custom sort function, the object method needs to take two input arguments and return 1, 0, or −1, depending if the first parameter is larger than, equal to, or less than the second:

```
class pc_sort {
    // reverse-order string comparison
    function strrcmp($a, $b) {
        return strcmp($b, $a);
    }
}

usort($words, array('pc_sort', 'strrcmp'));
```

See Also

Chapter 7 for more on classes and objects; Recipe 4.17 for more on custom sorting of arrays.

4.20 Randomizing an Array

Problem

You want to scramble the elements of an array in a random order.

Solution

Use shuffle( ):

```
shuffle($array);
```

Discussion

It's suprisingly tricky to properly shuffle an array. In fact, up until PHP 4.3, PHP's shuffle( ) routine wasn't a truly random shuffle. It would mix elements around, but certain combinations were more likely than others.

Therefore, you should use PHP's shuffle( ) function whenever possible.

See Also

Documentation on shuffle( ) at *http://www.php.net/shuffle*.

4.21 Removing Duplicate Elements from an Array

Problem

You want to eliminate duplicates from an array.

Solution

If the array is already complete, use array_unique( ), which returns a new array that contains no duplicate values:

```
$unique = array_unique($array);
```

If you create the array while processing results, here is a technique for numerical arrays:

```
foreach ($_REQUEST['fruits'] as $fruit) {
    if (!in_array($array, $fruit)) { $array[] = $fruit; }
}
```

Here's one for associative arrays:

```
foreach ($_REQUEST['fruits'] as $fruit) {
    $array[$fruit] = $fruit;
}
```

Discussion

Once processing is completed, `array_unique( )` is the best way to eliminate duplicates. But if you're inside a loop, you can eliminate the duplicate entries from appearing by checking if they're already in the array.

An even faster method than using `in_array( )` is to create a hybrid array in which the key and the value for each element are the same. This eliminates the linear check of `in_array( )` but still allows you to take advantage of the array family of functions that operate over the values of an array instead of the keys.

In fact, it's faster to use the associative array method and then call `array_values( )` on the result (or, for that matter, `array_keys( )`, but `array_values( )` is slightly faster) than to create a numeric array directly with the overhead of `in_array( )`.

See Also

Documentation on `array_unique( )` at *http://www.php.net/array-unique*.

4.22 Applying a Function to Each Element in an Array

Problem

You want to apply a function or method to each element in an array. This allows you to transform the input data for the entire set all at once.

Solution

Use `array_walk( )`:

```
function escape_data(&$value, $key) {
    $value = htmlentities($value, ENT_QUOTES);
}

$names = array('firstname' => "Baba",
               'lastname'  => "O'Riley");

array_walk($names, 'escape_data');

foreach ($names as $name) {
    print "$name\n";
}

Baba
O&#039;Riley
```

For nested data, use `array_walk_recursive( )`:

```
function escape_data(&$value, $key) {
    $value = htmlentities($value, ENT_QUOTES);
}
```

```
$names = array('firstnames' => array("Baba", "Bill"),
               'lastnames'  => array("O'Riley", "O'Reilly"));

array_walk_recursive($names, 'escape_data');

foreach ($names as $nametypes) {
    foreach ($nametypes as $name) {
        print "$name\n";
    }
}

Baba
Bill
O&#039;Riley
O&#039;Reilly
```

Discussion

It's frequently useful to loop through all the elements of an array. One option is to foreach through the data. However, an alternative choice is the array_walk( ) function.

This function takes an array and the name of a callback function, which is the function that processes the elements of the array. The callback function takes two parameters, a value and a key. It can also take an optional third parameter, which is any additional data you wish to expose within the callback.

Here's an example that ensures all the data in the $names array is properly HTML encoded. The callback function, escape_data( ), takes the array values, passes them to htmlentities( ) to encode the key HTML entities, and assigns the result back to $value:

```
function escape_data(&$value, $key) {
    $value = htmlentities($value, ENT_QUOTES);
}

$names = array('firstname' => "Baba",
               'lastname'  => "O'Riley");

array_walk($names, 'escape_data');

foreach ($names as $name) {
    print "$name\n";
}

Baba
O&#039;Riley
```

Since array_walk operates in-place instead of returning a modified copy of the array, you must pass in values by reference when you want to modify the elements. In those cases, as in this example, there is an & before the parameter name. However, this is only necessary when you wish to alter the array.

When you have a series of nested arrays, use the array_walk_recursive( ) function:

```
function escape_data(&$value, $key) {
    $value = htmlentities($value, ENT_QUOTES);
}

$names = array('firstnames' => array("Baba", "Bill"),
               'lastnames'  => array("O'Riley", "O'Reilly"));

array_walk_recursive($names, 'escape_data');

foreach ($names as $nametypes) {
    foreach ($nametypes as $name) {
        print "$name\n";
    }
}

Baba
Bill
O&#039;Riley
O&#039;Reilly
```

The `array_walk_recursive( )` function only passes non-array elements to the callback, so you don't need to modify a callback when switching from `array_walk( )`.

See Also

Documentation on `array_walk( )` at *http://www.php.net/array-walk*, `array_walk_recursive( )` at *http://www.php.net/array_walk_recursive*, and `htmlentities( )` at *http://www.php.net/htmlentities*.

4.23 Finding the Union, Intersection, or Difference of Two Arrays

Problem

You have a pair of arrays, and you want to find their union (all the elements), intersection (elements in both, not just one), or difference (in one but not both).

Solution

To compute the union:

```
$union = array_unique(array_merge($a, $b));
```

To compute the intersection:

```
$intersection = array_intersect($a, $b);
```

To find the simple difference:

```
$difference = array_diff($a, $b);
```

And for the symmetric difference:

```
$difference = array_merge(array_diff($a, $b), array_diff($b, $a));
```

Discussion

Many necessary components for these calculations are built into PHP; it's just a matter of combining them in the proper sequence.

To find the union, you merge the two arrays to create one giant array with all of the values. But `array_merge( )` allows duplicate values when merging two numeric arrays, so you call `array_unique( )` to filter them out. This can leave gaps between entries because `array_unique( )` doesn't compact the array. It isn't a problem, however, as `foreach` and `each( )` handle sparsely filled arrays without a hitch.

The function to calculate the intersection is simply named `array_intersection( )` and requires no additional work on your part.

The `array_diff( )` function returns an array containing all the unique elements in `$old` that aren't in `$new`. This is known as the *simple difference*:

```
$old = array('To', 'be', 'or', 'not', 'to', 'be');
$new = array('To', 'be', 'or', 'whatever');
$difference = array_diff($old, $new);

$old = array('To', 'be', 'or', 'not', 'to', 'be');
$new = array('To', 'be', 'or', 'whatever');
$difference = array_diff($old, $new);
Array
(
    [3] => not
    [4] => to
)
```

The resulting array, `$difference` contains `'not'` and `'to'` because `array_diff( )` is case-sensitive. It doesn't contain `'whatever'` because it doesn't appear in `$old`.

To get a reverse difference, or in other words, to find the unique elements in `$new` that are lacking in `$old`, flip the arguments:

```
$old = array('To', 'be', 'or', 'not', 'to', 'be');
$new = array('To', 'be', 'or', 'whatever');
$reverse_diff = array_diff($new, $old);

$old = array('To', 'be', 'or', 'not', 'to', 'be');
$new = array('To', 'be', 'or', 'whatever');
$reverse_diff = array_diff($new, $old);
Array
(
    [3] => whatever
)
```

The `$reverse_diff` array contains only `'whatever'`.

If you want to apply a function or other filter to `array_diff( )`, roll your own diffing algorithm:

```
// implement case-insensitive diffing; diff -i

$seen = array();
foreach ($new as $n) {
    $seen[strtolower($n)]++;
}

foreach ($old as $o) {
    $o = strtolower($o);
    if (!$seen[$o]) { $diff[$o] = $o; }
}
```

The first `foreach` builds an associative array lookup table. You then loop through `$old` and, if you can't find an entry in your lookup, add the element to `$diff`.

It can be a little faster to combine `array_diff( )` with `array_map( )`:

```
$diff = array_diff(array_map('strtolower', $old), array_map('strtolower', $new));
```

The symmetric difference is what's in $a but not $b, and what's in $b but not $a:

```
$difference = array_merge(array_diff($a, $b), array_diff($b, $a));
```

Once stated, the algorithm is straightforward. You call `array_diff( )` twice and find the two differences. Then you merge them together into one array. There's no need to call `array_unique( )` since you've intentionally constructed these arrays to have nothing in common.

See Also

Documentation on `array_unique( )` at *http://www.php.net/array-unique*, `array_intersect( )` at *http://www.php.net/array-intersect*, `array_diff( )` at *http://www.php.net/array-diff*, `array_merge( )` at *http://www.php.net/array-merge*, and `array_map( )` at *http://www.php.net/array-map*.

4.24 Making an Object Act like an Array

Problem

You have an object, but you want to be able to treat it as an array. This allows you to combine the benefits from an object-oriented design with the familiar interface of an array.

Solution

Implement SPL's `ArrayAccess` interface:

```
class FakeArray implements ArrayAccess {

    private $elements;

    public function __construct() {
```

```
        $this->elements = array();
    }

    public function offsetExists($offset) {
        return isset($this->elements[$offset]);
    }

    public function offsetGet($offset) {
        return $this->elements[$offset];
    }

    public function offsetSet($offset, $value) {
        return $this->elements[$offset] = $value;
    }

    public function offsetUnset($offset) {
        unset($this->elements[$offset]);
    }
}

$array = new FakeArray;

// What's Opera, Doc?
$array['animal'] = 'wabbit';

// Be very quiet I'm hunting wabbits
if (isset($array['animal']) &&
    // Wabbit tracks!!!
    $array['animal'] == 'wabbit') {

    // Kill the wabbit, kill the wabbit, kill the wabbit
    unset($array['animal']);
    // Yo ho to oh! Yo ho to oh! Yo ho...
}

// What have I done?? I've killed the wabbit....
// Poor little bunny, poor little wabbit...
if (!isset($array['animal'])) {
    print "Well, what did you expect in an opera? A happy ending?\n";
}
Well, what did you expect in an opera? A happy ending?
```

Discussion

The `ArrayAccess` interface allows you to manipulate data in an object using the same set of conventions you use for arrays. This allows you to leverage the benefits of an object-oriented design, such as using a class hierarchy or implementing additional methods on the object, but still allow people to interact with the object using a familiar interface. Alternatively, it allows you create an "array" that stores its data in an external location, such as shared memory or a database.

An implementation of `ArrayAccess` requires four methods: `offsetExists( )`, which indicates whether an element is defined; `offsetGet( )`, which returns an element's value;

offsetSet( ), which sets an element to a new value; and offsetUnset( ), which removes an element and its value.

This example stores the data locally in an object property:

```
class FakeArray implements ArrayAccess {

    private $elements;

    public function __construct() {
        $this->elements = array();
    }

    public function offsetExists($offset) {
        return isset($this->elements[$offset]);
    }

    public function offsetGet($offset) {
        return $this->elements[$offset];
    }

    public function offsetSet($offset, $value) {
        return $this->elements[$offset] = $value;
    }

    public function offsetUnset($offset) {
        unset($this->elements[$offset]);
    }
}
```

The object constructor initializes the $elements property to a new array. This provides you with a place to store the keys and values of your array. That property is defined as private, so people can only access the data through one of the accessor methods defined as part of the interface.

The next four methods implement everything you need to manipulate an array. Since offsetExists( ) checks if an array element is set, the method returns the value of isset($this->elements[$offset]).

The offsetGet( ) and offsetSet( ) methods interact with the $elements property as you would normally use those features with an array.

Last, the offsetUnset( ) method simply calls unset( ) on the element. Unlike the other three methods, it does not return the value from its operation. That's because unset( ) is a statement, not a function, and doesn't return a value.

Now you can instantiate an instance of FakeArray and manipulate it like an array:

```
$array = new FakeArray;

// What's Opera, Doc?
$array['animal'] = 'wabbit';

// Be very quiet I'm hunting wabbits
if (isset($array['animal']) &&
```

```
    // Wabbit tracks!!!
    $array['animal'] == 'wabbit') {

        // Kill the wabbit, kill the wabbit, kill the wabbit
        unset($array['animal']);
        // Yo ho to oh! Yo ho to oh! Yo ho...
}

// What have I done?? I've killed the wabbit....
// Poor little bunny, poor little wabbit...
if (!isset($array['animal'])) {
    print "Well, what did you expect in an opera? A happy ending?\n";
}
Well, what did you expect in an opera? A happy ending?
```

Each operation calls one of your methods: assigning a value to $array['animal'] triggers offsetSet( ), checking isset($array['animal']) invokes offsetExists( ), offsetGet( ) comes into play when you do the comparison $array['animal'] == 'wabbit', and offsetUnset( ) is called for unset($array['animal']).

As you can see, after all this, the wabbit is "dead."

See Also

More on objects in Chapter 7; the ArrayAccess reference page at *http://www.php.net/ ~helly/php/ext/spl/interfaceArrayAccess.html*; and the Wikipedia entry on "What's Opera, Doc?" at *http://en.wikipedia.org/wiki/What%27s_Opera%2C_Doc.*

4.25 Program: Printing a Horizontally Columned HTML Table

Converting an array into a horizontally columned table places a fixed number of elements in a row. The first set goes in the opening table row, the second set goes in the next row, and so forth. Finally, you reach the final row, where you might need to optionally pad the row with empty table data cells.

The function pc_grid_horizontal( ), shown in Example 4-4, lets you specify an array and number of columns. It assumes your table width is 100%, but you can alter the $table_width variable to change this.

Example 4-4. pc_grid_horizontal( )

```
    function pc_grid_horizontal($array, $size) {

        // compute <td> width %ages
        $table_width = 100;
        $width = intval($table_width / $size);

        // define how our <tr> and <td> tags appear
        // sprintf() requires us to use %% to get literal %
        $tr = '<tr align="center">';
        $td = "<td width=\"$width%%\">%s</td>";

        // open table
```

```
$grid = "<table width=\"$table_width%%\">$tr";

// loop through entries and display in rows of size $sized
// $i keeps track of when we need a new table tow
$i = 0;
foreach ($array as $e) {
    $grid .= sprintf($td, $e);
    $i++;

    // end of a row
    // close it up and open a new one
    if (!($i % $size)) {
        $grid .= "</tr>$tr";
    }
}

// pad out remaining cells with blanks
while ($i % $size) {
    $grid .= sprintf($td, ' ');
    $i++;
}

// add </tr>, if necessary
$end_tr_len = strlen($tr) * -1;
if (substr($grid, $end_tr_len) != $tr) {
    $grid .= '</tr>';
} else {
    $grid = substr($grid, 0, $end_tr_len);
}

// close table
$grid .= '</table>';

return $grid;
}
```

The function begins by calculating the width of each <td> as a percentage of the total table size. Depending on the number of columns and the overall size, the sum of the <td> widths might not equal the <table> width, but this shouldn't affect the displayed HTML in a noticeable fashion. Next, define the <td> and <tr> tags, using printf-style formatting notation. To get the literal % needed for the <td> width percentage, use a double %%.

The meat of the function is the foreach loop through the array in which we append each <td> to the $grid. If you reach the end of a row, which happens when the total number of elements processed is a multiple of the number of elements in a row, you close and then reopen the <tr>.

Once you finish adding all the elements, you need to pad the final row with blank or empty <td> elements. Put a non-breaking space inside the data cell instead of leaving it empty to make the table render properly in the browser. Now, make sure there isn't an extra <tr> at the end of the grid, which occurs when the number of elements is an

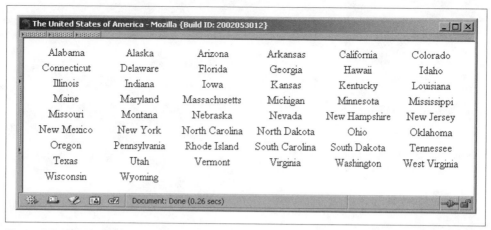

Figure 4-1. The United States of America

exact multiple of the width (in other words, if you didn't need to add padding cells). Finally, you can close the table.

For example, let's print the names of the 50 U.S. states in a six-column table:

```
// establish connection to database
$dsn = 'mysql://user:password@localhost/table';
$dbh = DB::connect($dsn);
if (DB::isError($dbh)) { die ($dbh->getMessage()); }

// query the database for the 50 states
$sql = "SELECT state FROM states";
$sth = $dbh->query($sql);

// load data into array from database
while ($row = $sth->fetchRow(DB_FETCHMODE_ASSOC)) {
  $states[] = $row['state'];
}

// generate the HTML table
$grid = pc_grid_horizontal($states, 6);

// and print it out
print $grid;
```

When rendered in a browser, it looks like Figure 4-1.

Because 50 doesn't divide evenly by 6, there are four extra padding cells in the last row.

Variables

5.0 Introduction

Along with conditional logic, variables are the core of what makes computer programs powerful and flexible. If you think of a variable as a bucket with a name that holds a value, PHP lets you have plain old buckets, buckets that contain the name of other buckets, buckets with numbers or strings in them, buckets holding arrays of other buckets, buckets full of objects, and just about any other variation on that analogy you can think of.

A variable is either set or unset. A variable with any value assigned to it, `true` or `false`, empty or nonempty, is set. The function `isset( )` returns `true` when passed a variable that's set. To turn a variable that's set into one that's unset, call `unset( )` on the variable or assign `null` to the variable. Scalars, arrays, and objects can all be passed to `unset( )`. You can also pass `unset( )` multiple variables to unset them all:

```
unset($vegetables);
unset($vegetables[12]);
unset($earth, $moon, $stars);
```

If a variable is present in the query string of a URL, even if it has no value assigned to it, it is set. Thus:

```
http://www.example.com/set.php?chimps=&monkeys=12
```

sets `$_GET['monkeys']` to `12` and `$_GET['chimps']` to the empty string.

All unset variables are also empty. Set variables may be empty or nonempty. Empty variables have values that evaluate to `false` as a boolean: the integer 0, the double 0.0, the empty string, the string `"0"`, the boolean `false`, an array with no elements, an object with no properties (in versions of PHP prior to PHP 5) and `NULL`. Everything else is nonempty. This includes the string `"00"`, and the string `" "`, containing just a space character.

Variables evaluate to either `true` or `false`. The values listed earlier that evaluate to `false` as a boolean are the complete set of what's `false` in PHP. Every other value is `true`. The distinction between empty and `false` is that emptiness is only possible for variables.

Constants and return values from functions can be `false`, but they can't be empty. For example, Example 5-1 shows a valid use of `empty( )` because `$first_name` is a variable.

Example 5-1. Correctly checking if a variable is empty
```
if (empty($first_name)) { .. }
```

On the other hand, the code in Example 5-2 returns parse errors because `0` (a constant) and the return value from `get_first_name( )` can't be empty.

Example 5-2. Incorrectly checking if a constant is empty
```
if (empty(0)) { .. }
if (empty(get_first_name())) { .. }
```

5.1 Avoiding == Versus = Confusion

Problem

You don't want to accidentally assign values when comparing a variable and a constant.

Solution

Use:
```
if (12 == $dwarves) { ... }
```
instead of:
```
if ($dwarves == 12) { ... }
```

Putting the constant on the left triggers a parse error with the assignment operator. In other words, PHP complains when you write:
```
if (12 = $dwarves) { ... }
```
but:
```
if ($dwarves = 12) { ... }
```

silently executes, assigning `12` to the variable `$dwarves`, and then executing the code inside the block. (`$dwarves = 12` evaluates to `12`, which is `true`.)

Discussion

Putting a constant on the left side of a comparison coerces the comparison to the type of the constant. This causes problems when you are comparing an integer with a variable that could be an integer or a string. `0 == $dwarves` is `true` when `$dwarves` is `0`, but it's also true when `$dwarves` is `sleepy`. Since an integer (`0`) is on the left side of the comparison, PHP converts what's on the right (the string `sleepy`) to an integer (`0`) before comparing. To avoid this, use the identity operator, `0 === $dwarves`, instead.

See Also

Documentation for = at *http://www.php.net/language.operators.assignment.php* and for == and === at *http://www.php.net/manual/language.operators.comparison.php*.

5.2 Establishing a Default Value

Problem

You want to assign a default value to a variable that doesn't already have a value. It often happens that you want a hardcoded default value for a variable that can be overridden from form input or through an environment variable.

Solution

Use `isset( )` to assign a default to a variable that may already have a value:

```
if (! isset($cars)) { $cars = $default_cars; }
```

Use the ternary (a ? b : c) operator to give a new variable a (possibly default) value:

```
$cars = isset($_REQUEST['cars']) ? $_REQUEST['cars'] : $default_cars;
```

Discussion

Using `isset( )` is essential when assigning default values. Without it, the nondefault value can't be 0 or anything else that evaluates to `false`. Consider this assignment:

```
$cars = $_REQUEST['cars'] ? $_REQUEST['cars'] : $default_cars;
```

If `$_REQUEST['cars']` is 0, `$cars` is set to `$default_cars` even though 0 may be a valid value for `$cars`.

An alternative syntax for checking arrays is the `array_key_exists( )` function:

```
$cars = array_key_exists('cars', $_REQUEST) ? $_REQUEST['cars'] : $default_cars;
```

The one difference between `isset( )` and `array_key_exists( )` is that when a key exists but its value is `null`, then `array_key_exists( )` returns `true`, while `isset( )` returns false:

```
$vehicles = array('cars' => null);
array_key_exists('cars', $vehicles); // true
isset($vehicles['cars']);            // false
```

You can use an array of defaults to set multiple default values easily. The keys in the defaults array are variable names, and the values in the array are the defaults for each variable:

```
$defaults = array('emperors'  => array('Rudolf II','Caligula'),
                  'vegetable' => 'celery',
                  'acres'     => 15);

foreach ($defaults as $k => $v) {
```

```
        if (! isset($GLOBALS[$k])) { $GLOBALS[$k] = $v; }
    }
```

Because the variables are set in the global namespace, the previous code doesn't work for setting function-private defaults. To do that, use variable variables:

```
    foreach ($defaults as $k => $v) {
        if (! isset($$k)) { $$k = $v; }
    }
```

In this example, the first time through the loop, `$k` is `emperors`, so `$$k` is `$emperors`.

See Also

Documentation on `isset( )` at *http://www.php.net/isset*.

5.3 Exchanging Values Without Using Temporary Variables

Problem

You want to exchange the values in two variables without using additional variables for storage.

Solution

To swap `$a` and `$b`:

```
    list($a,$b) = array($b,$a);
```

Discussion

PHP's `list( )` language construct lets you assign values from an array to individual variables. Its counterpart on the right side of the expression, `array( )`, lets you construct arrays from individual values. Assigning the array that `array( )` returns to the variables in the `list( )` lets you juggle the order of those values. This works with more than two values, as well:

```
    list($yesterday,$today,$tomorrow) = array($today,$tomorrow,$yesterday);
```

This method isn't faster than using temporary variables, so you should use it for clarity, but not speed.

See Also

Documentation on `list( )` at *http://www.php.net/list* and `array( )` at *http://www.php.net/array*.

5.4 Creating a Dynamic Variable Name

Problem

You want to construct a variable's name dynamically. For example, you want to use variable names that match the field names from a database query.

Solution

Use PHP's variable variable syntax by prepending a $ to a variable whose value is the variable name you want:

```
$animal = 'turtles';
$turtles = 103;
print $$animal;
```

```
103
```

Discussion

Placing two dollar signs before a variable name causes PHP to de-reference the right variable name to get a value. It then uses that value as the name of your "real" variable. For example:

```
$animal = 'turtles';
$turtles = 103;
print $$animal;
```

```
103
```

This prints 103. Because $animal = 'turtles', $$animal is $turtles, which equals 103.

Using curly braces, you can construct more complicated expressions that indicate variable names:

```
$stooges = array('Moe','Larry','Curly');
$stooge_moe = 'Moses Horwitz';
$stooge_larry = 'Louis Feinberg';
$stooge_curly = 'Jerome Horwitz';

foreach ($stooges as $s) {
  print "$s's real name was ${'stooge_'.strtolower($s)}.\n";
}
Moe's real name was Moses Horwitz.
Larry's real name was Louis Feinberg.
Curly's real name was Jerome Horwitz.
```

PHP evaluates the expression between the curly braces and uses it as a variable name. That expression can even have function calls in it, such as strtolower( ).

Variable variables are also useful when iterating through similarly named variables. Say you are querying a database table that has fields named title_1, title_2, etc. If you want to check if a title matches any of those values, the easiest way is to loop through them like this:

```
for ($i = 1; $i <= $n; $i++) {
    $t = "title_$i";
    if ($title == $$t) { /* match */ }
}
```

Of course, it would be more straightforward to store these values in an array, but if you are maintaining old code that uses this technique (and you can't change it), variable variables are helpful.

The curly brace syntax is also necessary in resolving ambiguity about array elements. The variable variable $$donkeys[12] could have two meanings. The first is "take what's in the 12th element of the $donkeys array and use that as a variable name." Write this as: ${$donkeys[12]}. The second is "use what's in the scalar $donkeys as an array name and look in the 12th element of that array." Write this as: ${$donkeys}[12].

You are not limited by two dollar signs. You can use three, or more, but in practice it's rare to see greater than two levels of indirection.

See Also

http://www.php.net/language.variables.variable for documentation on variable variables.

5.5 Using Static Variables

Problem

You want a local variable to retain its value between invocations of a function.

Solution

Declare the variable as static:

```
function track_times_called() {
    static $i = 0;
    $i++;
    return $i;
}
```

Discussion

Declaring a variable static causes its value to be remembered by a function. So, if there are subsequent calls to the function, you can access the value of the saved variable. The pc_check_the_count( ) function shown in Example 5-3 uses static variables to keep track of the strikes and balls for a baseball batter.

Example 5-3. pc_check_the_count( )

```php
<?php
function pc_check_the_count($pitch) {
    static $strikes = 0;
    static $balls   = 0;

    switch ($pitch) {
    case 'foul':
        if (2 == $strikes) break; // nothing happens if 2 strikes
        // otherwise, act like a strike
    case 'strike':
        $strikes++;
        break;
    case 'ball':
        $balls++;
        break;
    }

    if (3 == $strikes) {
        $strikes = $balls = 0;
        return 'strike out';
    }
    if (4 == $balls) {
        $strikes = $balls = 0;
        return 'walk';
    }
    return 'at bat';
}

$what_happened = pc_check_the_count($pitch);
?>
```

In pc_check_the_count( ), the logic of what happens to the batter depending on the pitch count is in the switch statement inside the function. You can instead return the number of strikes and balls, but this requires you to place the checks for striking out, walking, and staying at the plate in multiple places in the code.

While static variables retain their values between function calls, they do so only during one invocation of a script. A static variable accessed in one request doesn't keep its value for the next request to the same page.

See Also

Documentation on static variables at *http://www.php.net/language.variables.scope*.

5.6 Sharing Variables Between Processes

Problem

You want a way to share information between processes that provides fast access to the shared data.

Solution

Use one of the two bundled shared memory extensions, shmop or System V shared memory.

With shmop, you create a block and read and write to and from it, as shown in Example 5-4.

Example 5-4. Using the shmop shared memory functions

```php
<?php
// create key
$shmop_key = ftok(__FILE__, 'p');
// create 16384 byte shared memory block
$shmop_id = shmop_open($shmop_key, "c", 0600, 16384);
// retrieve the entire shared memory segment
$population = shmop_read($shmop_id, 0, 0);
// manipulate the data
$population += ($births + $immigrants - $deaths - $emigrants);
// store the value back in the shared memory segment
$shmop_bytes_written = shmop_write($shmop_id, $population, 0);
// check that it fit
if ($shmop_bytes_written != strlen($population)) {
    echo "Can't write the all of: $population\n";
}
// close the handle
shmop_close($shmop_id);
?>
```

With System V shared memory, you store the data in a shared memory segment, and guarantee exclusive access to the shared memory with a semaphore, as shown in Example 5-5.

Example 5-5. Using the System V shared memory functions

```php
<?php
$semaphore_id = 100;
$segment_id   = 200;
// get a handle to the semaphore associated with the shared memory
// segment we want
$sem = sem_get($semaphore_id,1,0600);
// ensure exclusive access to the semaphore
sem_acquire($sem) or die("Can't acquire semaphore");
// get a handle to our shared memory segment
$shm = shm_attach($segment_id,16384,0600);
// retrieve a value from the shared memory segment
$population = shm_get_var($shm,'population');
// manipulate the value
$population += ($births + $immigrants - $deaths - $emigrants);
// store the value back in the shared memory segment
shm_put_var($shm,'population',$population);
// release the handle to the shared memory segment
shm_detach($shm);
// release the semaphore so other processes can acquire it
```

```
sem_release($sem);
?>
```

Discussion

A shared memory segment is a slice of your machine's RAM that different processes (such as the multiple web server processes that handle requests) can access. These two extensions solve the similar problem of allowing you to save information between requests in a fast and efficient manner, but they take slightly different approaches and have slightly different interfaces as a result.

The shmop functions have an interface similar to the familiar file manipulation. You can open a segment, read in data, write to it, and close it. Like a file, there's no built-in segmentation of the data, it's all just a series of consecutive characters.

In Example 5-4, you first create the shared memory block. Unlike a file, you must pre-declare the maximum size. In this example, it's 16,384 bytes:

```
// create key
$shmop_key = ftok(__FILE__, 'p');
// create 16384 byte shared memory block
$shmop_id = shmop_open($shmop_key, "c", 0600, 16384);
```

Just as you distinguish files by using filenames, shmop segments are differentiated by keys. Unlike filenames, these keys aren't strings but integers, so they're not easy to remember. Therefore, it's best to use the ftok( ) function to convert a human-friendly name, in this case the filename in the form of __FILE__, to a format suitable for shmop_open( ). The ftok( ) function also takes a one-fscharacter "project identifier." This helps you avoid collisions in case you accidently reuse the same string. Here it's p, for PHP.

Once you have a key, pass it to shmop_create( ), along with the "flag" you want, the file permissions (in octal), and the block size. See Table 5-1 for a list of suitable flags.

These permissions work just like file permissions, so 0600 means that the user that created the block can read it and write to it. In this context, user doesn't just mean the process that created the semaphore but any process with the same user ID. Permissions of 0600 should be appropriate for most uses, in which web server processes run as the same user.

Table 5-1. shmop_open( ) flags

Flag	Description
a	Opens for read-only *access*.
c	*Creates* a new segment. If it already exists, opens it for read and write access.
w	Opens for read and *write* access.
n	Creates a *new* segment, but fails if one already exists. Useful to avoid race conditions.

Once you have a handle, you can read from the segment using `shmop_read( )` and manipulate the data:

```
// retrieve the entire shared memory segment
$population = shmop_read($shmop_id, 0, 0);
// manipulate the data
$population += ($births + $immigrants - $deaths - $emigrants);
```

This code reads in the entire segment. To read in a shorter amount, adjust the second and third parameters. The second parameter is the start, and the third is the length. As a shortcut, you can set the length to 0 to read to the end of the segment.

Once you have the adjusted data, store it back with `shmop_write( )` and release the handle with `shmop_close( )`:

```
// store the value back in the shared memory segment
$shmop_bytes_written = shmop_write($shmop_id, $population, 0);
// check that it fit
if ($shmop_bytes_written != strlen($population)) {
    echo "Can't write the all of: $population\n";
}
// close the handle
shmop_close($shmop_id);
```

Since shared memory segments are of a fixed length, if you're not careful, you can try to write more data than you have room. Check to see if this happened by comparing the value returned from `shmop_write( )` with the string length of your data. They should be the same. If `shmop_write( )` returned a smaller value, then it was only able to fit that many bytes in the segment before running out of space.

In constrast to shmop, the System V shared memory functions behave similar to an array. You access slices of the segment by specifying a key, such as `population`, and manipulate them directly. Depending on what you're storing, this direct access can be more convenient.

However, the interface is more complex as a result, and System V shared memory also requires you to do manage locking in the form of semaphore.

A semaphore makes sure that the different processes don't step on each other's toes when they access the shared memory segment. Before a process can use the segment, it needs to get control of the semaphore. When it's done with the segment, it releases the semaphore for another process to grab.

To get control of a semaphore, use `sem_get( )` to find the semaphore's ID. The first argument to `sem_get( )` is an integer semaphore key. You can make the key any integer you want, as long as all programs that need to access this particular semaphore use the same key. If a semaphore with the specified key doesn't already exist, it's created; the maximum number of processes that can access the semaphore is set to the second argument of `sem_get( )` (in this case, 1); and the semaphore's permissions are set to `sem_get( )`'s third argument (0600). Permissions here behave like they do with files and shmop. For example:

```
$semaphore_id = 100;
$segment_id   = 200;
// get a handle to the semaphore associated with the shared memory
// segment we want
$sem = sem_get($semaphore_id,1,0600);
// ensure exclusive access to the semaphore
sem_acquire($sem) or die("Can't acquire semaphore");
```

sem_get( ) returns an identifier that points to the underlying system semaphore. Use this ID to gain control of the semaphore with sem_acquire( ). This function waits until the semaphore can be acquired (perhaps waiting until other processes release the semaphore) and then returns true. It returns false on error. Errors include invalid permissions or not enough memory to create the semaphore. Once the semaphore is acquired, you can read from the shared memory segment:

```
// get a handle to our shared memory segment
$shm = shm_attach($segment_id,16384,0600);
// retrieve a value from the shared memory segment
$population = shm_get_var($shm,'population');
// manipulate the value
$population += ($births + $immigrants - $deaths - $emigrants);
```

First, establish a link to the particular shared memory segment with shm_attach( ). As with sem_get( ), the first argument to shm_attach( ) is an integer key. This time, however, it identifies the desired segment, not the semaphore. If the segment with the specified key doesn't exist, the other arguments create it. The second argument (16384) is the size in bytes of the segment, and the last argument (0600) is the permissions on the segment. shm_attach(200,16384,0600) creates a 16K shared memory segment that can be read from and written to only by the user who created it. The function returns the identifier you need to read from and write to the shared memory segment.

After attaching to the segment, pull variables out of it with shm_get_var($shm, 'population'). This looks in the shared memory segment identified by $shm and retrieves the value of the variable called population. You can store any type of variable in shared memory. Once the variable is retrieved, it can be operated on like other variables. shm_put_var($shm,'population',$population) puts the value of $population back into the shared memory segment as a variable called population.

You're now done with the shared memory statement. Detach from it with shm_detach( ) and release the semaphore with sem_release( ) so another process can use it:

```
// release the handle to the shared memory segment
shm_detach($shm);
// release the semaphore so other processes can acquire it
sem_release($sem);
```

Shared memory's chief advantage is that it's fast. But since it's stored in RAM, it can't hold too much data, and it doesn't persist when a machine is rebooted (unless you take special steps to write the information in shared memory to disk before shutdown and then load it into memory again at startup).

You cannot use System V shared memory under Windows, but the shmop functions work fine. Besides these two bundled extensions, another option is to use the APC extension, which beyond its main purpose of caching and optimization support for PHP, also provides a way to store data.

See Also

APC at *http://pecl.php.net/apc*; documentation on shmop at *http://www.php.net/ shmop* and System V shared memory and semaphore functions at *http://www.php.net/ sem*.

5.7 Encapsulating Complex Data Types in a String

Problem

You want a string representation of an array or object for storage in a file or database. This string should be easily reconstitutable into the original array or object.

Solution

Use serialize( ) to encode variables and their values into a textual form:

```
$pantry = array('sugar' => '2 lbs.','butter' => '3 sticks');
$fp = fopen('/tmp/pantry','w') or die ("Can't open pantry");
fputs($fp,serialize($pantry));
fclose($fp);
```

To recreate the variables, use unserialize( ):

```
$new_pantry = unserialize(file_get_contents('/tmp/pantry'));
```

Discussion

The serialized string that is reconstituted into $pantry looks like:

```
a:2:{s:5:"sugar";s:6:"2 lbs.";s:6:"butter";s:8:"3 sticks";}
```

This stores enough information to bring back all the values in the array, but the variable name itself isn't stored in the serialized representation.

When passing serialized data from page to page in a URL, call urlencode( ) on the data to make sure URL metacharacters are escaped in it:

```
$shopping_cart = array('Poppy Seed Bagel' => 2,
                       'Plain Bagel' => 1,
                       'Lox' => 4);
print '<a href="next.php?cart='.urlencode(serialize($shopping_cart)).'">Next</a>';
```

The magic_quotes_gpc and magic_quotes_runtime configuration settings affect data being passed to unserialize( ). If magic_quotes_gpc is on, data passed in URLs, POST variables, or cookies must be processed with stripslashes( ) before it's unserialized:

```
$new_cart = unserialize(stripslashes($cart)); // if magic_quotes_gpc is on
$new_cart = unserialize($cart);               // if magic_quotes_gpc is off
```

If `magic_quotes_runtime` is on, serialized data stored in a file must be processed with `addslashes( )` when writing and `stripslashes( )` when reading:

```
$fp = fopen('/tmp/cart','w');
fputs($fp,addslashes(serialize($a)));
fclose($fp);

// if magic_quotes_runtime is on
$new_cart = unserialize(stripslashes(file_get_contents('/tmp/cart')));
// if magic_quotes_runtime is off
$new_cart = unserialize(file_get_contents('/tmp/cart'));
```

Serialized data read from a database must also be processed with `stripslashes( )` when `magic_quotes_runtime` is on:

```
mysql_query(
    "INSERT INTO cart (id,data) VALUES (1,'".addslashes(serialize($cart))."')");

$r = mysql_query('SELECT data FROM cart WHERE id = 1');
$ob = mysql_fetch_object($r);
// if magic_quotes_runtime is on
$new_cart = unserialize(stripslashes($ob->data));
// if magic_quotes_runtime is off
$new_cart = unserialize($ob->data);
```

Serialized data going into a database always needs to have `addslashes( )` called on it (or, better yet, the database-appropriate escaping method) to ensure it's saved properly.

When you unserialize an object, PHP automatically invokes its `__wakeUp( )` method. This allows the object to reestablish any state that's not preserved across serialization, such as database connection. This can alter your environment, so be sure you know what you're unserializing. See Recipe 7.18 for more details.

See Also

Recipe 10.9 for information on escaping data for a database.

5.8 Dumping Variable Contents as Strings

Problem

You want to inspect the values stored in a variable. It may be a complicated nested array or object, so you can't just print it out or loop through it.

Solution

Use `print_r( )` or `var_dump( )`:

```
$array = array("name" => "frank", 12, array(3, 4));
```

```
print_r($array);
Array
(
    [name] => frank
    [0] => 12
    [1] => Array
        (
            [0] => 3
            [1] => 4
        )
)
var_dump($array);
array(3) {
  ["name"]=>
  string(5) "frank"
  [0]=>
  int(12)
  [1]=>
  array(2) {
    [0]=>
    int(3)
    [1]=>
    int(4)
  }
}
```

Discussion

The output of print_r( ) is more concise and easier to read. The output of var_dump( ), however, gives data types and lengths for each variable.

Since these functions recursively work their way through variables, if you have references within a variable pointing back to the variable itself, you can end up with an infinite loop. Both functions stop themselves from printing variable information forever, though. Once print_r( ) has seen a variable once, it prints *RECURSION* instead of printing information about the variable again and continues iterating through the rest of the information it has to print. var_dump( ) prints a variable twice before printing *RECURSION* and skipping it. Consider the arrays $user_1 and $user_2, which reference each other through their friend elements:

```
$user_1 = array('name' => 'Max Bialystock',
                'username' => 'max');

$user_2 = array('name' => 'Leo Bloom',
                'username' => 'leo');

// Max and Leo are friends
$user_2['friend'] = &$user_1;
$user_1['friend'] = &$user_2;

// Max and Leo have jobs
$user_1['job'] = 'Swindler';
$user_2['job'] = 'Accountant';
```

The output of print_r($user_2) is:

```
Array
(
    [name] => Leo Bloom
    [username] => leo
    [friend] => Array
        (
            [name] => Max Bialystock
            [username] => max
            [friend] => Array
                (
                    [name] => Leo Bloom
                    [username] => leo
                    [friend] => Array
 *RECURSION*
                    [job] => Accountant
                )

            [job] => Swindler
        )

    [job] => Accountant
)
```

When print_r( ) sees the reference to $user_1 the second time, it prints *RECURSION* instead of descending into the array. It then continues on its way, printing the remaining elements of $user_1 and $user_2.

Confronted with recursion, var_dump( ) behaves differently:

```
array(4) {
  ["name"]=>
  string(9) "Leo Bloom"
  ["username"]=>
  string(3) "leo"
  ["friend"]=>
  &array(4) {
    ["name"]=>
    string(14) "Max Bialystock"
    ["username"]=>
    string(3) "max"
    ["friend"]=>
    &array(4) {
      ["name"]=>
      string(9) "Leo Bloom"
      ["username"]=>
      string(3) "leo"
      ["friend"]=>
      &array(4) {
        ["name"]=>
        string(14) "Max Bialystock"
        ["username"]=>
        string(3) "max"
        ["friend"]=>
        &array(4) {
```

```
          ["name"]=>
          string(9) "Leo Bloom"
          ["username"]=>
          string(3) "leo"
          ["friend"]=>
          *RECURSION*
          ["job"]=>
          string(10) "Accountant"
        }
        ["job"]=>
        string(8) "Swindler"
      }
      ["job"]=>
      string(10) "Accountant"
    }
    ["job"]=>
    string(8) "Swindler"
  }
  ["job"]=>
  string(10) "Accountant"
}
```

It's not until the third appearance of the reference to $user_1 that var_dump( ) stops recursing.

Even though print_r( ) and var_dump( ) print their results instead of returning them, you can capture the data without printing it in one of two ways.

First, you can pass true as the second parameter to print_r( ):

```
$output = print_r($user, true);
```

This does not work with var_dump( ); however, you can use output buffering instead:

```
ob_start();
var_dump($user);
$dump = ob_get_contents();
ob_end_clean();
```

This puts the results of var_dump($user) in $dump.

See Also

Output buffering is discussed in Recipe 8.12; documentation on print_r( ) at *http://www.php.net/print-r* and var_dump( ) at *http://www.php.net/var-dump*.

Functions

6.0 Introduction

Functions help you create organized and reusable code. They allow you to abstract out details so your code becomes more flexible and more readable. Without functions, it is impossible to write easily maintainable programs because you're constantly updating identical blocks of code in multiple places and in multiple files.

With a function you pass a number of arguments in and get a value back:

```
// add two numbers together
function add($a, $b) {
    return $a + $b;
}

$total = add(2, 2);     // 4
```

Declare a function using the `function` keyword, followed by the name of the function and any parameters in parentheses. To invoke a function, simply use the function name, specifying argument values for any parameters to the function. If the function returns a value, you can assign the result of the function to a variable, as shown in the previous example.

You don't need to predeclare a function before you call it. PHP parses the entire file before it begins executing, so you can intermix function declarations and invocations. You can't, however, redefine a function in PHP. If PHP encounters a function with a name identical to one it's already found, it throws a fatal error and dies.

Sometimes, the standard procedure of passing in a fixed number of arguments and getting one value back doesn't quite fit a particular situation in your code. Maybe you don't know ahead of time exactly how many parameters your function needs to accept. Or you do know your parameters, but they're almost always the same values, so it's tedious to continue to repass them. Or you want to return more than one value from your function.

This chapter helps you use PHP to solve these types of problems. We begin by detailing different ways to pass arguments to a function. Recipes 6.1 through 6.5 cover passing arguments by value, reference, and as named parameters; assigning default parameter values; and functions with a variable number of parameters.

The four recipes after 6.5 are all about returning values from a function. Recipe 6.6 describes returning by reference; Recipe 6.7 covers returning more than one variable; Recipe 6.8 describes how to skip selected return values; and Recipe 6.9 talks about the best way to return and check for failure from a function. The final three recipes show how to call variable functions, deal with variable scoping problems, and dynamically create a function. If you want a variable to maintain its value between function invocations, see Recipe 5.5.

6.1 Accessing Function Parameters

Problem

You want to access the values passed to a function.

Solution

Use the names from the function prototype:

```
function commercial_sponsorship($letter, $number) {
    print "This episode of Sesame Street is brought to you by ";
    print "the letter $letter and number $number.\n";
}

commercial_sponsorship('G', 3);
commercial_sponsorship($another_letter, $another_number);
```

Discussion

Inside the function, it doesn't matter whether the values are passed in as strings, numbers, arrays, or another kind of variable. You can treat them all the same and refer to them using the names from the prototype.

Unless specified, all non-object values being passed into and out of a function are passed by value, not by reference. (By default, objects are passed by reference.) This means PHP makes a copy of the value and provides you with that copy to access and manipulate. Therefore, any changes you make to your copy don't alter the original value. Here's an example:

```
function add_one($number) {
    $number++;
}

$number = 1;
add_one($number);
print "$number\n";
1
```

If the variable was passed by reference, the value of $number would be 2.

In many languages, passing variables by reference has the additional benefit of being significantly faster than passing them by value. While the passing-by-reference is faster in PHP, the speed difference is marginal. For that reason, we suggest passing variables by reference only when actually necessary and never as a performance-enhancing trick.

See Also

Recipe 6.3 to pass values by reference and Recipe 6.6 to return values by reference.

6.2 Setting Default Values for Function Parameters

Problem

You want a parameter to have a default value if the function's caller doesn't pass it. For example, a function to draw a table might have a parameter for border width, which defaults to 1 if no width is given.

Solution

Assign the default value to the parameters inside the function prototype:

```
function wrap_html_tag($string, $tag = 'b') {
    return "<$tag>$string</$tag>";
}
```

Discussion

The example in the Solution sets the default tag value to b, for bold. For example:

```
$string = 'I am some HTML';
wrap_html_tag($string);
```

returns:

```
<b>I am some HTML</b>
```

This example:

```
wrap_html_tag($string, 'i');
```

returns:

```
<i>I am some HTML</i>
```

There are two important things to remember when assigning default values. First, all parameters with default values must appear after parameters without defaults. Otherwise, PHP can't tell which parameters are omitted and should take the default value and which arguments are overriding the default. So wrap_html_tag( ) can't be defined as:

```
function wrap_html_tag($tag = 'i', $string)
```

If you do this and pass wrap_html_tag( ) only a single argument, PHP assigns the value to $tag and issues a warning complaining of a missing second argument.

Second, the assigned value must be a constant, such as a string or a number. It can't be a variable. Again, using `wrap_html_tag( )`, such as our example, you can't do this:

```
$my_favorite_html_tag = 'i';

function wrap_html_tag($string, $tag = $my_favorite_html_tag) {
    ...
}
```

If you want to assign a default of nothing, one solution is to assign the empty string to your parameter:

```
function wrap_html_tag($string, $tag = '') {
    if (empty($tag)) return $string;
    return "<$tag>$string</$tag>";
}
```

This function returns the original string, if no value is passed in for the `$tag`. Or if a (nonempty) tag is passed in, it returns the string wrapped inside of tags.

Depending on circumstances, another option for the `$tag` default value is either 0 or NULL. In `wrap_html_tag( )`, you don't want to allow an empty-valued tag. However, in some cases, the empty string can be an acceptable option. For instance, `join( )` is often called on the empty string, after calling `file( )`, to place a file into a string. Also, as the following code shows, you can use a default message if no argument is provided but an empty message if the empty string is passed:

```
function pc_log_db_error($message = NULL) {
    if (is_null($message)) {
        $message = 'Couldn't connect to DB';
    }

    error_log("[DB] [$message]");
}
```

See Also

Recipe 6.5 on creating functions that take a variable number of arguments.

6.3 Passing Values by Reference

Problem

You want to pass a variable to a function and have it retain any changes made to its value inside the function.

Solution

To instruct a function to accept an argument passed by reference instead of value, prepend an & to the parameter name in the function prototype:

```
function wrap_html_tag(&$string, $tag = 'b') {
    $string = "<$tag>$string</$tag>";
}
```

Now there's no need to return the string because the original is modified in place.

Discussion

Passing a variable to a function by reference allows you to avoid the work of returning the variable and assigning the return value to the original variable. It is also useful when you want a function to return a boolean success value of true or false, but you still want to modify argument values with the function.

You can't switch between passing a parameter by value or reference; it's either one or the other. In other words, there's no way to tell PHP to optionally treat the variable as a reference or as a value.

Also, if a parameter is declared to accept a value by reference, you can't pass a constant string (or number, etc.), or PHP will die with a fatal error.

See Also

Recipe 6.6 on returning values by reference.

6.4 Using Named Parameters

Problem

You want to specify your arguments to a function by name, instead of simply their position in the function invocation.

Solution

Have the function use one parameter but make it an associative array:

```
function image($img) {
    $tag  = '<img src="' . $img['src'] . '" ';
    $tag .= 'alt="' . ($img['alt'] ? $img['alt'] : '') .'">';
    return $tag;
}

$image = image(array('src' => 'cow.png', 'alt' => 'cows say moo'));
$image = image(array('src' => 'pig.jpeg'));
```

Discussion

While using named parameters makes the code inside your functions more complex, it ensures the calling code is easier to read. Since a function lives in one place but is called in many, this makes for more understandable code.

When you use this technique, PHP doesn't complain if you accidentally misspell a parameter's name, so you need to be careful because the parser won't catch these types of mistakes. Also, you can't take advantage of PHP's ability to assign a default value for a parameter. Luckily, you can work around this deficit with some simple code at the top of the function:

```
function image($img) {
    if (! isset($img['src']))    { $img['src']    = 'cow.png';      }
    if (! isset($img['alt']))    { $img['alt']    = 'milk factory'; }
    if (! isset($img['height'])) { $img['height'] = 100;            }
    if (! isset($img['width']))  { $img['width']  = 50;             }
    ...
}
```

Using the isset( ) function, check to see if a value for each parameter is set; if not, assign a default value.

Alternatively, you can write a short function to handle this:

```
function pc_assign_defaults($array, $defaults) {
    $a = array();
    foreach ($defaults as $d => $v) {
        $a[$d] = isset($array[$d]) ? $array[$d] : $v;
    }

    return $a;
}
```

This function loops through a series of keys from an array of defaults and checks if a given array, $array, has a value set. If it doesn't, the function assigns a default value from $defaults. To use it in the previous snippet, replace the top lines with:

```
function image($img) {
    $defaults = array('src'    => 'cow.png',
                      'alt'    => 'milk factory',
                      'height' => 100,
                      'width'  => 50
                     );
    $img = pc_assign_defaults($img, $defaults);
    ...
}
```

This is nicer because it introduces more flexibility into the code. If you want to modify how defaults are assigned, you only need to change it inside pc_assign_defaults( ) and not in hundreds of lines of code inside various functions. Also, it's clearer to have an array of name/value pairs and one line that assigns the defaults instead of intermixing the two concepts in a series of almost identical repeated lines.

See Also

Recipe 6.5 on creating functions that accept a variable number of arguments.

6.5 Creating Functions That Take a Variable Number of Arguments

Problem

You want to define a function that takes a variable number of arguments.

Solution

Pass an array and place the variable arguments inside the array:

```
// find the "average" of a group of numbers
function mean($numbers) {
    // initialize to avoid warnings
    $sum = 0;

    // the number of elements in the array
    $size = count($numbers);

    // iterate through the array and add up the numbers
    for ($i = 0; $i < $size; $i++) {
        $sum += $numbers[$i];
    }

    // divide by the amount of numbers
    $average = $sum / $size;

    // return average
    return $average;
}

$mean = mean(array(96, 93, 97));
```

Discussion

There are two good solutions, depending on your coding style and preferences. The more traditional PHP method is the one described in the Solution. We prefer this method because using arrays in PHP is a frequent activity; therefore, all programmers are familiar with arrays and their behavior.

So while this method creates some additional overhead, bundling variables is commonplace. It's done in Recipe 6.4 to create named parameters and in Recipe 6.7 to return more than one value from a function. Also, inside the function, the syntax to access and manipulate the array involves basic commands such as `$array[$i]` and `count($array)`.

However, this can seem clunky, so PHP provides an alternative and allows you direct access to the argument list, as shown in Example 6-1.

Example 6-1. Accessing function parameters without using the argument list

```
// find the "average" of a group of numbers
function mean() {
    // initialize to avoid warnings
    $sum = 0;

    // the number of arguments passed to the function
    $size = func_num_args();

    // iterate through the arguments and add up the numbers
    for ($i = 0; $i < $size; $i++) {
        $sum += func_get_arg($i);
    }

    // divide by the amount of numbers
    $average = $sum / $size;

    // return average
    return $average;
}

$mean = mean(96, 93, 97);
```

This example uses a set of functions that return data based on the arguments passed to the function they are called from. First, func_num_args( ) returns an integer with the number of arguments passed into its invoking function—in this case, mean( ). From there, you can then call func_get_arg( ) to find the specific argument value for each position.

When you call mean(96, 93, 97), func_num_args( ) returns 3. The first argument is in position 0, so you iterate from 0 to 2, not 1 to 3. That's what happens inside the for loop where $i goes from 0 to less than $size. As you can see, this is the same logic used in Example 6-1 in which an array was passed. If you're worried about the potential overhead from using func_get_arg( ) inside a loop, don't be. This version is actually faster than the array passing method.

There is a third version of this function that uses func_get_args( ) to return an array containing all the values passed to the function. It ends up looking like a hybrid between the previous two functions, as shown in Example 6-2.

Example 6-2. Accessing function parameters without using the argument list

```
// find the "average" of a group of numbers
function mean() {
    // initialize to avoid warnings
    $sum = 0;

    // load the arguments into $numbers
    $numbers = func_get_args();

    // the number of elements in the array
    $size = count($numbers);
```

```
    // iterate through the array and add up the numbers
    for ($i = 0; $i < $size; $i++) {
        $sum += $numbers[$i];
    }

    // divide by the amount of numbers
    $average = $sum / $size;

    // return average
    return $average;
}

$mean = mean(96, 93, 97);
```

Here you have the dual advantages of not needing to place the numbers inside a temporary array when passing them into mean( ), but inside the function you can continue to treat them as if you did. Unfortunately, this method is slightly slower than the first two.

See Also

Recipe 6.7 on returning multiple values from a function; documentation on func_num_args( ) at *http://www.php.net/func-num-args*, func_get_arg( ) at *http://www.php.net/func-get-arg*, and func_get_args( ) at *http://www.php.net/func-get-args*.

6.6 Returning Values by Reference

Problem

You want to return a value by reference, not by value. This allows you to avoid making a duplicate copy of a variable.

Solution

The syntax for returning a variable by reference is similar to passing it by reference. However, instead of placing an & before the parameter, place it before the name of the function:

```
function &pc_array_find_value($needle, &$haystack) {
    foreach ($haystack as $key => $value) {
        if ($needle == $value) {
            return $haystack[$key];
        }
    }
}
```

Also, you must use the =& assignment operator instead of plain = when invoking the function:

```
$html =& pc_array_find_value('The Doors', $artists);
```

Discussion

Returning a reference from a function allows you to directly operate on the return value and have those changes directly reflected in the original variable.

For instance, Example 6-3 searches through an array looking for the first element that matches a value. It returns the first matching value. For instance, you need to search through a list of famous people from Minnesota looking for Prince, so you can update his name.

Example 6-3. Returning an array value from a function by reference

```
function &pc_array_find_value($needle, &$haystack) {
    foreach ($haystack as $key => $value) {
        if ($needle == $value) {
            return $haystack[$key];
        }
    }
}

$minnesota = array('Bob Dylan', 'F. Scott Fitzgerald', 'Prince', 'Charles Schultz');

$prince =& pc_array_find_value('Prince', $minnesota);

$prince = 'O(+>'; // The ASCII version of Prince's unpronounceable symbol

print_r($minnesota);
Array
(
    [0] => Bob Dylan
    [1] => F. Scott Fitzgerald
    [2] => O(+>
    [3] => Charles Schultz
)
```

Without the ability to return values by reference, you would need to return the array key and then re-reference the original array:

```
function pc_array_find_value($needle, &$haystack) {
    foreach ($haystack as $key => $value) {
        if ($needle == $value) {
            return $key;
        }
    }
}

$minnesota = array('Bob Dylan', 'F. Scott Fitzgerald', 'Prince', 'Charles Schultz');

$prince =& pc_array_find_value('Prince', $minnesota);

$minnesota[$prince] = 'O(+>'; // The ASCII version of Prince's unpronounceable symbol
```

When returning a reference from a function, you must return a reference to a variable, not a string. For example, this is not legal:

```
function &pc_array_find_value($needle, &$haystack) {
    foreach ($haystack as $key => $value) {
        if ($needle == $value) {
            $match = $haystack[$key];
        }
    }

    return "$match is found in position $key";
}
```

That's because `"$match is found in position $key"` is a string, and it doesn't make logical sense to return a reference to non-variables. As of PHP 5, you're warned when you do this.

Unlike passing values into functions, in which an argument is either passed by value or by reference, you can optionally choose not to assign a reference and just take the returned value. Just use = instead of =&, and PHP assigns the value instead of the reference.

See Also

Recipe 6.3 on passing values by reference.

6.7 Returning More Than One Value

Problem

You want to return more than one value from a function.

Solution

Return an array and use list( ) to separate elements:

```
function averages($stats) {
    ...
    return array($median, $mean, $mode);
}

list($median, $mean, $mode) = averages($stats);
```

Discussion

From a performance perspective, this isn't a great idea. There is a bit of overhead because PHP is forced to first create an array and then dispose of it. That's what is happening in this example:

```
function time_parts($time) {
    return explode(':', $time);
}

list($hour, $minute, $second) = time_parts('12:34:56');
```

You pass in a time string as you might see on a digital clock and call `explode( )` to break it apart as array elements. When `time_parts( )` returns, use `list( )` to take each element and store it in a scalar variable. Although this is a little inefficient, the other possible solutions are worse because they can lead to confusing code.

One alternative is to pass the values in by reference. However, this is somewhat clumsy and can be nonintuitive since it doesn't always make logical sense to pass the necessary variables into the function. For instance:

```
function time_parts($time, &$hour, &$minute, &$second) {
    list($hour, $minute, $second) = explode(':', $time);
}

time_parts('12:34:56', $hour, $minute, $second);
```

Without knowledge of the function prototype, there's no way to look at this and know `$hour`, `$minute`, and `$second` are, in essence, the return values of `time_parts( )`.

You can also use global variables, but this clutters the global namespace and also makes it difficult to easily see which variables are being silently modified in the function. For example:

```
function time_parts($time) {
    global $hour, $minute, $second;
    list($hour, $minute, $second) = explode(':', $time);
}

time_parts('12:34:56');
```

Again, here it's clear because the function is directly above the call, but if the function is in a different file or written by another person, it'd be more mysterious and thus open to creating a subtle bug.

Our advice is that if you modify a value inside a function, return that value and assign it to a variable unless you have a very good reason not to, such as significant performance issues. It's cleaner and easier to understand and maintain.

See Also

Recipe 6.3 on passing values by reference and Recipe 6.11 for information on variable scoping.

6.8 Skipping Selected Return Values

Problem

A function returns multiple values, but you only care about some of them.

Solution

Omit variables inside of `list( )`:

```
// Only care about minutes
function time_parts($time) {
    return explode(':', $time);
}

list(, $minute,) = time_parts('12:34:56');
```

Discussion

Even though it looks like there's a mistake in the code, the code in the Solution is valid PHP. This is most frequently seen when a programmer is iterating through an array using each( ), but cares only about the array values:

```
while (list(,$value) = each($array)) {
    process($value);
}
```

However, this is more clearly written using foreach:

```
foreach ($array as $value) {
    process($value);
}
```

To reduce confusion, don't use this feature; but if a function returns many values, and you only want one or two of them, this technique can come in handy. One example of this case is if you read in fields using fgetcsv( ), which returns an array holding the fields from the line. In that case, you can use the following:

```
while ($fields = fgetcsv($fh, 4096)) {
    print $fields[2] . "\n";  // the third field
}
```

If it's an internally written function and not built-in, you could also make the returning array have string keys, because it's hard to remember, for example, that array element 2 is associated with 'rank':

```
while ($fields = read_fields($filename)) {
    $rank = $fields['rank']; // the third field is now called rank
    print "$rank\n";
}
```

However, here's the most efficient method:

```
while (list(,,$rank,,) = fgetcsv($fh, 4096)) {
    print "$rank\n";           // directly assign $rank
}
```

Be careful you don't miscount the amount of commas; you'll end up with a bug.

See Also

Recipe 1.11 for more on reading files using fgetcsv( ).

6.9 Returning Failure

Problem

You want to indicate failure from a function.

Solution

Return `false`:

```
function lookup($name) {
    if (empty($name)) { return false; }
    ...
}

if (false !== lookup($name)) { /* act upon lookup */ } else { /* log an error */ }
```

Discussion

In PHP, non-true values aren't standardized and can easily cause errors. As a result, your functions should return the defined `false` keyword because this works best when checking a logical value.

Other possibilities are `''` or `0`. However, while all three evaluate to non-true inside an `if`, there's actually a difference among them. Also, sometimes a return value of `0` is a meaningful result, but you still want to be able to also return failure.

For example, `strpos()` returns the location of the first substring within a string. If the substring isn't found, `strpos()` returns `false`. If it is found, it returns an integer with the position. Therefore, to find a substring position, you might write:

```
if (strpos($string, $substring)) { /* found it! */ }
```

However, if `$substring` is found at the exact start of `$string`, the value returned is `0`. Unfortunately, inside the `if`, this evaluates to `false`, so the conditional is not executed. Here's the correct way to handle the return value of `strpos()`:

```
if (false !== strpos($string, $substring)) { /* found it! */ }
```

Also, `false` is always guaranteed to be false in the current version of PHP and forever more. Other values may not guarantee this. For example, in PHP 3, `empty('0')` was `true`, but it changed to `false` in PHP 4.

See Also

The introduction to Chapter 5 for more on the truth values of variables; documentation on `strpos()` at *http://www.php.net/strpos* and `empty()` at *http://www.php.net/empty*.

6.10 Calling Variable Functions

Problem

You want to call different functions depending on a variable's value.

Solution

Use `call_user_func( )`:

```
function get_file($filename) { return file_get_contents($filename); }

$function = 'get_file';
$filename = 'graphic.png';

// calls get_file('graphic.png')
call_user_func($function, $filename);
```

Use `call_user_func_array( )` when your functions accept differing argument counts:

```
function get_file($filename) { return file_get_contents($filename); }
function put_file($filename, $data) { return file_put_contents($filename, $data); }

if ($action == 'get') {
    $function = 'get_file';
    $args = array('graphic.png');
} elseif ($action == 'put') {
    $function = 'put_file';
    $args = array('graphic.png', $graphic);
}

// calls get_file('graphic.png')
// calls put_file('graphic.png', $graphic)
call_user_func_array($function, $args);
```

Discussion

The `call_user_func( )` and `call_user_func_array( )` functions are a little different from your standard PHP functions. Their first argument isn't a string to print, or a number to add, but the name of a function that's executed. The concept of passing a function name that the language invokes is known as a callback, or a callback function.

The prototype of `call_user_func_array( )` comes in quite handy when you're invoking a callback inside a function that can accept a variable number of arguments. In these cases, instead of embedding the logic inside your function, you can grab all the arguments directly using `func_get_args( )`:

```
// logging function that accepts printf-style formatting
// it prints a time stamp, the string, and a new line
function logf() {
    $date = date(DATE_RSS);
    $args = func_get_args();
```

```
        return print "$date: " . call_user_func_array('sprintf', $args) . "\n";
    }

    logf('<a href="%s">%s</a>','http://developer.ebay.com','eBay Developer Program');
```

**Sat, 23 Sep 2006 18:32:51 PDT: <a href="http://developer.ebay.com">
eBay Developer Program</a>**

The `logf( )` function has the same interface as the `printf` family: the first argument is a formatting specifier and the remaining arguments are data that's interpolated into the string based on the formatting codes. Since there could be any number of arguments following the formatting code, you cannot use `call_user_func( )`.

Instead, you grab all the arguments in an array using `func_get_args( )` and pass that array to `sprintf` using `call_user_func_array( )`.

In this particular example, you can also use `vsprintf( )`, which is a version of `sprintf( )` that, like `call_user_func_array( )`, accepts an array of arguments:

```
    // logging function that accepts printf-style formatting
    // it prints a time stamp, the string, and a new line
    function logf() {
        $date = date(DATE_RSS);
        $args = func_get_args();
        $format = array_shift($args);

        return print "$date: " . vsprintf($format, $args) . "\n";
    }
```

If you have more than two possibilities to call, use an associative array of function names:

```
    $dispatch = array(
        'add'      => 'do_add',
        'commit'   => 'do_commit',
        'checkout' => 'do_checkout',
        'update'   => 'do_update'
    );

    $cmd = (isset($_REQUEST['command']) ? $_REQUEST['command'] : '');

    if (array_key_exists($cmd, $dispatch)) {
        $function = $dispatch[$cmd];
        call_user_func($function); // call function
    } else {
        error_log("Unknown command $cmd");
    }
```

This code takes the command name from a request and executes that function. Note the check to see that the command is in a list of acceptable commands. This prevents your code from calling whatever function was passed in from a request, such as `phpinfo( )`. This makes your code more secure and allows you to easily log errors.

Another advantage is that you can map multiple commands to the same function, so you can have a long and a short name:

```
$dispatch = array(
    'add'      => 'do_add',
    'commit'   => 'do_commit',   'ci' => 'do_commit',
    'checkout' => 'do_checkout', 'co' => 'do_checkout',
    'update'   => 'do_update',    'up' => 'do_update'
);
```

See Also

Documentation on `array_key_exists()` at *http://www.php.net/array-key-exists*, `call_user_func()` at *http://www.php.net/call-user-func*, `call_user_func_array()` at *http://www.php.net/call-user-func-array*, and `isset()` at *http://www.php.net/isset*.

6.11 Accessing a Global Variable Inside a Function

Problem

You need to access a global variable inside a function.

Solution

Bring the global variable into local scope with the `global` keyword:

```
function eat_fruit($fruit) {
    global $chew_count;

    for ($i = $chew_count; $i > 0; $i--) {
        ...
    }
}
```

Or reference it directly in `$GLOBALS`:

```
function eat_fruit($fruit) {
    for ($i = $GLOBALS['chew_count']; $i > 0; $i--) {
        ...
    }
}
```

Discussion

If you use a number of global variables inside a function, the `global` keyword may make the syntax of the function easier to understand, especially if the global variables are interpolated in strings.

You can use the `global` keyword to bring multiple global variables into local scope by specifying the variables as a comma-separated list:

```
global $age,$gender,shoe_size;
```

You can also specify the names of global variables using variable variables:

```
$which_var = 'age';
global $$which_var; // refers to the global variable $age
```

However, if you call unset( ) on a variable brought into local scope using the global keyword, the variable is unset only within the function. To unset the variable in the global scope, you must call unset( ) on the element of the $GLOBALS array:

```
$food = 'pizza';
$drink = 'beer';

function party() {
    global $food, $drink;

    unset($food);              // eat pizza
    unset($GLOBALS['drink']); // drink beer
}

print "$food: $drink\n";
party();
print "$food: $drink\n";

pizza: beer
pizza:
```

You can see that $food stayed the same, while $drink was unset. Declaring a variable global inside a function is similar to assigning a reference of the global variable to the local one:

```
$food = &GLOBALS['food'];
```

See Also

Documentation on variable scope at *http://www.php.net/variables.scope* and variable references at *http://www.php.net/language.references*.

6.12 Creating Dynamic Functions

Problem

You want to create and define a function as your program is running.

Solution

Use create_function( ):

```
$add = create_function('$i,$j', 'return $i+$j;');

$add(1, 1); // returns 2
```

Discussion

The first parameter to create_function( ) is a string that contains the arguments for the function, and the second is the function body. Using create_function( ) is exceptionally slow, so if you can predefine the function, it's best to do so.

The most frequently used case of create_function( ) in action is to create custom sorting functions for usort( ) or array_walk( ):

```
// sort files in reverse natural order
usort($files, create_function('$a, $b', 'return strnatcmp($b, $a);'));
```

See Also

Recipe 4.17 for information on usort( ); documentation on create_function( ) at *http://www.php.net/create-function* and on usort( ) at *http://www.php.net/usort.*

Classes and Objects

7.0 Introduction

PHP 5 has significantly improved support for object-oriented programming (OOP). This is a major change and a key reason to upgrade your code from PHP 4. If you're a fan of OOP, you will be very happy with the tools PHP 5 provides you.

Early versions of PHP were strictly procedural: you could define functions, but not objects. PHP 3 introduced an extremely rudimentary form of objects, written as a late-night hack. Back in 1997, nobody expected the explosion in the number of PHP programmers, or that people would write large-scale programs in PHP. Therefore, these limitations weren't considered a problem.

Over the years, PHP gained additional object-oriented features; however, the development team never redesigned the core OO code to gracefully handle objects and classes. As a result, although PHP 4 improved overall performance, writing complex OO programs with it is still difficult, if not nearly impossible.

PHP 5 fixes these problems by using Zend Engine 2 (ZE2). ZE2 enables PHP to include more advanced object-oriented features, while still providing a high degree of backward compatibility to the millions of PHP scripts already written.

If you don't have experience with object-oriented programming outside of PHP, then you're in for a bit of a surprise. While some of the new features allow you to do things more easily, many features don't let you do anything new at all. In many ways, they *restrict* what you can do.

Even though it seems counterintuitive, these limitations actually help you quickly write safe code because they promote code reuse and data encapsulation. These key OO programming techniques are explained throughout the chapter. But first, here's an introduction to object-oriented programming, its vocabulary, and its concepts.

A class is a package containing two things: data and methods to access and modify that data. The data portion consists of variables; they're known as properties. The other part of a class is a set of functions that can use its properties—they're called methods.

When you define a class, you don't define an object that can be accessed and manipulated. Instead, you define a template for an object. From this blueprint, you create malleable objects through a process known as instantiation. A program can have multiple objects of the same class, just as a person can have more than one book or many pieces of fruit.

Classes also live in a defined hierarchy. Each class down the line is more specialized than the one above it. These specialized classes are called child classes, while the class they're modifying is called the parent class. For example, a parent class could be a building. Buildings can be further divided into residential and commercial. Residential buildings can be further subdivided into houses and apartment buildings, and so forth. The top-most parent class is also called the base class.

Both houses and apartment buildings have the same set of properties as all residential buildings, just as residential and commercial buildings share some things in common. When classes are used to express these parent-child relationships, the child class inherits the properties and methods defined in the parent class. This allows you to reuse the code from the parent class and requires you to write code only to adapt the new child to its specialized circumstances. This is called *inheritance* and is one of the major advantages of classes over functions. The process of defining a child class from a parent is known as subclassing or extending.

Objects play another role in PHP outside their traditional OO position. Since PHP can't use more than one namespace, the ability for a class to package multiple properties into a single object is extremely helpful. It allows clearly demarcated separate areas for variables.

Classes in PHP are easy to define and create:

```
class guest_book {
 public $comments;
 public $last_visitor;

 function update($comment, $visitor) {
 ...
 }

}
```

The `class` keyword defines a class, just as `function` defines a function. Properties are declared using the `public` keyword. Method declaration is identical to function definition.

The `new` keyword instantiates an object:

```
$gb = new guest_book;
```

Object instantiation is covered in more detail in Recipe 7.1.

Inside a class, you can optionally declare properties using `public`. There's no requirement to do so, but it is a useful way to reveal all the variables of the class. Since PHP doesn't force you to predeclare all your variables, it's possible to create one inside a class without PHP throwing an error or otherwise letting you know. This can cause the list of variables at the top of a class definition to be misleading, because it's not the same as the list of variables actually in the class.

In PHP 4, you declared a property using var instead of public. You can still use var, but public was added as a synonym because PHP 5 actually offers three different types of properties: public, protected, and private properties. Public properties are identical to properties in PHP 4, but the other two types behave differently. This is explained in more detail in Recipe 7.4.

Besides declaring a property, you can also assign it a value:

```
public $last_visitor = 'Donnan';
```

You can assign constant values only using this construct:

```
public $last_visitor = 'Donnan'; // okay
public $last_visitor = 9; // okay
public $last_visitor = array('Jesse'); // okay
public $last_visitor = pick_visitor(); // bad
public $last_visitor = 'Chris' . '9'; // bad
```

If you try to assign something else, PHP dies with a parse error.

To assign a non-constant value to a variable, do it from a method inside the class:

```
class guest_book {
  public $last_visitor;

  public function update($comment, $visitor) {
    if (!empty($comment)) {
      array_unshift($this->comments, $comment);
      $this->last_visitor = $visitor;
    }
  }
}
```

If the visitor left a comment, you add it to the beginning of the array of comments and set that person as the latest visitor to the guest book. The variable $this is a special variable that refers to the current object. So to access the $last_visitor property of an object from inside that object, refer to $this->last_visitor.

To assign nonconstant values to variables upon instantiation, assign them in the class constructor. The class constructor is a method automatically called when a new object is created, and it is named __construct( ), as shown in Example 7-1.

Example 7-1. Assigning values to properties within a class constructor

```
class guest_book {
  public $comments;
  public $last_visitor;

  public function __construct($user) {
    $dbh = mysqli_connect('localhost', 'username', 'password', 'sites');
    $user = mysqli_real_escape_string($dbh, $user);
```

```
    $sql = "SELECT comments, last_visitor FROM guest_books WHERE user='$user'";
    $r = mysqli_query($dbh, $sql);

    if ($obj = mysqli_fetch_object($dbh, $r)) {
      $this->comments = $obj->comments;
      $this->last_visitor = $obj->last_visitor;
    }
  }
}

$gb = new guest_book('stewart');
```

Constructors are covered in Recipe 7.2. Note that in PHP 4, constructors had the same name as the class. In this example, that would be guest_book.

Be careful not to mistakenly type $this->$size. This is legal, but it's not the same as $this->size. Instead, it accesses the property of the object whose name is the value stored in the $size variable. More often than not, $size is undefined, so $this->$size appears empty. For more on variable property names, see Recipe 5.4.

Besides using -> to access a method or member variable, you can also use ::. This syntax accesses static methods in a class. These methods are identical for every instance of a class, because they can't rely on instance-specific data. There's no $this in a static method. For example:

```
class convert {
// convert from Celsius to Fahrenheit
 public static function c2f($degrees) {
   return (1.8 * $degrees) + 32;
 }
}

$f = convert::c2f(100); // 212
```

To implement inheritance by extending an existing class, use the extends keyword:

```
class xhtml extends xml {
  // ...
}
```

Child classes inherit parent methods and can optionally choose to implement their own specific versions, as shown in Example 7-2.

Example 7-2. Overriding parent methods

```
class DB {
 public $result;

 function getResult() {
  return $this->result;
 }

 function query($sql) {
  error_log("query() must be overridden by a database-specific child");
  return false;
```

```
  }
 }

 class MySQL extends DB {
  function query($sql) {
   $this->result = mysql_query($sql);
  }
 }
```

The MySQLclass above inherits the getResult( )method unchanged from the parent DB class, but has its own MySQL-specific query( )method.

Preface the method name with parent:: to explicitly call a parent method, as shown in Example 7-3.

Example 7-3. Calling parent methods explicitly

```
 function escape($sql) {
  $safe_sql = mysql_real_escape_string($sql); // escape special characters
  $safe_sql = parent::escape($safe_sql); // parent method adds '' around $sql
  return $safe_sql;
 }
```

Recipe 7-14 covers accessing overridden methods.

7.1 Instantiating Objects

Problem

You want to create a new instance of an object.

Solution

Define the class, then use new to create an instance of the class:

```
 class user {
     function load_info($username) {
         // load profile from database
     }
 }

 $user = new user;
 $user->load_info($_GET['username']);
```

Discussion

You can instantiate multiple instances of the same object:

```
 $adam = new user;
 $adam->load_info('adam');

 $dave = new user;
 $dave->load_info('adam');
```

These are two independent objects that happen to have identical information. They're like identical twins; they may start off the same, but they go on to live separate lives.

See Also

Recipe 7.10 for more on copying and cloning objects; documentation on classes and objects at *http://www.php.net/oop*.

7.2 Defining Object Constructors

Problem

You want to define a method that is called when an object is instantiated. For example, you want to automatically load information from a database into an object upon creation.

Solution

Define a method named __construct( ):

```
class user {
    function __construct($username, $password) {
        ...
    }
}
```

Discussion

The method named __construct( ) (that's two underscores before the word con struct) acts as a constructor, as shown in Example 7-4.

Example 7-4. Defining an object constructor

```
class user {
  public $username;

  function __construct($username, $password) {
     if ($this->validate_user($username, $password)) {
        $this->username = $username;
     }
  }
}

$user = new user('Grif', 'Mistoffelees'); // using built-in constructor
```

In PHP 4, constructors had the same name as the class, as shown in Example 7-5.

Example 7-5. Defining object constructors in PHP 4

```
class user {
  function user($username, $password) {
     ...
```

```
        }
    }
```

For backward compatibilty, if PHP 5 does not find a method named __construct( ), but does find one with the same name as the class (the PHP 4 constructor naming convention), it will use that method as the class constructor.

Having a standard name for all constructors, such as what PHP 5 implements, makes it easier to call your parent's constructor (because you don't need to know the name of the parent class) and also doesn't require you to modify the constructor if you rename your class.

See Also

Recipe 7.14 for more on calling parent constructors; documentation on object constructors at *http://www.php.net/oop.constructor*.

7.3 Defining Object Destructors

Problem

You want to define a method that is called when an object is destroyed. For example, you want to automatically save information from a database into an object when it's deleted.

Solution

Objects are automatically destroyed when a script terminates. To force the destruction of an object, use unset( ), as shown in Example 7-6.

Example 7-6. Deleting an object

```
    $car = new car; // buy new car
    ...
    unset($car);     // car wreck
```

To make PHP call a method when an object is eliminated, define a method named __destruct( ), as shown in Example 7-7.

Example 7-7. Defining an object destructor

```
    class car {
        function __destruct() {
            // head to car dealer
        }
    }
```

Discussion

It's not normally necessary to manually clean up objects, but if you have a large loop, unset( ) can help keep memory usage from spiraling out of control.

PHP 5 supports object destructors. Destructors are like constructors, except that they're called when the object is deleted. Even if you don't delete the object yourself using `unset( )`, PHP still calls the destructor when it determines that the object is no longer used. This may be when the script ends, but it can be much earlier.

You use a destructor to clean up after an object. For instance, the `Database` destructor would disconnect from the database and free up the connection. Unlike constructors, you cannot pass information to a destructor, because you're never sure when it's going to be run.

Therefore, if your destructor needs any instance-specific information, store it as a property, as shown in Example 7-8.

Example 7-8. Accessing instance-specific data within a destructor

```
// Destructor
class Database {
    function __destruct() {
        db_close($this->handle); // close the database connection
    }
}
```

Destructors are executed before PHP terminates the request and finishes sending data. Therefore, you can print from them, write to a database, or even ping a remote server.

You cannot, however, assume that PHP will destroy objects in any particular order. Therefore, you should not reference another object in your destructor, as PHP may have already destroyed it. Doing so will not cause a crash, but it will cause your code to behave in an unpredictable (and buggy) manner.

There are no backward compatibility issues with destructors, because they aren't available in PHP 4. However, that doesn't mean people didn't try to recreate them using other language features. If you emulated destructors, you will want to port your code, because PHP 5's destructors are more efficient and easier to use.

See Also

Documentation on `unset( )` at *http://www.php.net/unset*.

7.4 Implementing Access Control

Problem

You want to assign a visibility to methods and properties so they can only be accessed within classes that have a specific relationship to the object.

Solution

Use the `public`, `protected`, and `private` keywords, as shown in Example 7-9.

Example 7-9. Class using access control

```php
class Person {
    public $name;      // accesible anywhere
    protected $age;    // accesible within the class and child classes
    private $salary;   // accesible only within this specific class

    public function __construct() {
    // ...
    }

    protected function set_age() {
    // ...
    }

    private function set_salary() {
    // ...
    }
}
```

Discussion

PHP allows you to enforce where you can access methods and properties. There are three levels of visibility:

- public
- protected
- private

Making a method or property `public` means anyone can call or edit it. This is the same behavior as versions of PHP before PHP 5.

You can also label a method or property as `protected`, which restricts access to only the current class and any child classes that extend that class.

The final visibility is `private`, which is the most restrictive. Properties and methods that are `private` can only be accessed within that specific class.

If you're unfamiliar with this concept, access control can seem like an odd thing. However, when you use access control, you can actually create more robust code because it promotes data encapsulation, a key tenet of OO programming.

Inevitably, whenever you write code, there's some part—the way you store the data, what parameters the functions take, how the database is organized—that doesn't work as well as it should. It's too slow, too awkward, or doesn't allow you to add new features, so you clean it up.

Fixing code is a good thing, unless you accidently break other parts of your system in the process. When a program is designed with a high degree of encapsulation, the underlying data structures and database tables are not accessed directly. Instead, you define a set of functions and route all your requests through these functions.

For example, you have a database table that stores names and email addresses. A program with poor encapsulation directly accesses the table whenever it needs to fetch a person's email address, as shown in Example 7-10.

Example 7-10. Selecting an email address

```
$name   = 'Rasmus Lerdorf';
$db     = mysqli_connect();
$result = mysqli_query($db, "SELECT email FROM users
                            WHERE name  LIKE '$name'");
$row    = mysqli_fetch_assoc($db, $r);
$email  = $row['email'];
```

A better encapsulated program uses a function instead, as shown in Example 7-11.

Example 7-11. Selecting an email address using a function

```
function getEmail($name) {
    $db = mysqli_connect();
    $result = mysqli_query($db, "SELECT email FROM users
                                WHERE name  LIKE '$name'");
    $row   = mysqli_fetch_assoc($db, $r);
    $email = $row['email'];
    return $email
}

$email = getEmail('Rasmus Lerdorf');
```

Using getEmail( ) has many benefits, including reducing the amount of code you need to write to fetch an email address. However, it also lets you safely alter your database schema because you only need to change the single query in getEmail( ) instead of searching through every line of every file, looking for places where you SELECT data from the users table.

It's hard to write a well-encapsulated program using functions, because the only way to signal to people "Don't touch this!" is through comments and programming conventions.

Objects allow you to wall off implementation internals from outside access. This prevents people from relying on code that may change and forces them to use your functions to reach the data. Functions of this type are known as accessors, because they allow access to otherwise protected information. When redesigning code, if you update the accessors to work as before, none of the code will break.

Marking something as protected or private signals that it may change in the future, so people shouldn't access it or they'll violate encapsulation.

This is more than a social convention. PHP actually prevents people from calling a private method or reading a private property outside of the class. Therefore, from an external perspective, these methods and properties might as well not exist because there's no way to access them.

In object-oriented programming, there is an implicit contract between the author and the users of the class. The users agree not to worry about the implementation details. The author agrees that as long as a person uses public methods they'll always work, even if the author redesigns the class.

When deciding between `protected` and `private`, both provide protection against usage outside of the class. Therefore, the decision to choose one visibility versus the other really comes down to a judgement call—do you expect someone will need to invoke that method in a child class?

Since it's hard to come up ahead of time with a complete list, it's best to lean toward using `protected` over `private` unless you're 110 percent sure that `private` is the right choice, and there's really no reason someone should ever need that method.

7.5 Preventing Changes to Classes and Methods

Problem

You want to prevent another developer from redefining specific methods within a child class, or even from subclassing the entire class itself.

Solution

Label the particular methods or class as `final`:

```
final public function connect($server, $username, $password) {
    // Method definition here
}
```

And:

```
final class MySQL {
    // Class definition here
}
```

Discussion

Inheritance is normally a good thing, but it can make sense to restrict it.

The best reason to declare a method `final` is that a real danger could arise if someone overrides it. For example, data corruption, a race condition, or a potential crash or deadlock from forgetting (or forgetting to release) a lock or a semaphore.

Another common reason to declare a method `final` is that the method is "perfect." When you believe there's no way to update the method to make it better, declare it using the `final` keyword. This prevents subclasses from ruining it by reimplementing the method in an inferior manner.

However, think hard before you choose `final` in this case. It's impossible to come up with all the reasons someone may need to override a method. If you're distributing a third-party library (such as a PEAR package), you will cause a real headache if you incorrectly mark a method as `final`.

Make a method final by placing the `final` keyword at the beginning of the method declaration, as shown in Example 7-12.

Example 7-12. Defining a final method

```
final public function connect($server, $username, $password) {
    // Method definition here
}
```

This prevents someone from subclassing the class and creating a different `connect( )` method.

To prevent subclassing of an entire class, don't mark each method `final`. Instead, make a final class as shown in Example 7-13.

Example 7-13. Defining a final class

```
final class MySQL {
    // Class definition here
}
```

A final class cannot be subclassed. This differs from a class in which every method is `final` because that class can be extended and provided with additional methods, even if you cannot alter any of the preexisting methods.

7.6 Defining Object Stringification

Problem

You want to control how PHP displays an object when you print it.

Solution

Implement a `__toString( )` method, as shown in Example 7-14.

Example 7-14. Defining a class's stringification

```
class Person {
    // Rest of class here

    public function __toString() {
        return "$this->name <$this->email>";
    }
}
```

Discussion

PHP provides objects with a way to control how they are converted to strings. This allows you to print an object in a friendly way without resorting to lots of additional code.

PHP calls an object's `__toString( )` method when you `echo` or `print` the object by itself, as shown in Example 7-15.

Example 7-15. Defining a class's stringification

```
class Person {
    protected $name;
    protected $email;

    public function setName($name) {
        $this->name = $name;
    }

    public function setEmail($email) {
        $this->email = $email;
    }

    public function __toString() {
        return "$this->name <$this->email>";
    }
}
```

You can write:

```
$rasmus = new Person;
$rasmus->setName('Rasmus Lerdorf');
$rasmus->setEmail('rasmus@php.net');
print $rasmus;
Rasmus Lerdorf <rasmus@php.net>
```

This causes PHP to invoke the `__toString( )` method behind the scenes and return the stringified version of the object.

Your method *must* return a string; otherwise, PHP will issue an error. While this seems obvious, you can sometimes get tripped up by PHP's auto-casting features, which do not apply here.

For example, it's easy to treat the string `'9'` and the integer `9` identically, since PHP generally switches seamlessly between the two depending on context, almost always to the correct result.

However, in this case, you cannot return integers from `__toString( )`. If you suspect you may be in a position to return a non-string value from this method, consider explicitly casting the results, as shown in Example 7-16.

Example 7-16. Casting the return value

```
class TextInput {
    // Rest of class here
```

```
    public function __toString() {
        return (string) $this->label;
    }
}
```

By casting `$this->label` to a string, you don't need to worry if someone decided to label that text input with a number.

The `__toString()` feature has a number of limitations in versions of PHP prior to PHP 5.2. For example, it does not work for interpolated or concatenated strings (see Example 7-17).

Example 7-17. Invoking __toString()

```
print  "PHP was created by $rasmus";
print  'PHP was created by '. $rasmus;
printf('PHP was created by %s', $rasmus);
```

The one exception is a dusty corner of PHP that uses `echo` and a comma (,) instead of period (.) to combine items, as shown in Example 7-18.

Example 7-18. Invoking object stringification and concateination

```
echo   'PHP was created by ', $rasmus;
PHP was created by Rasmus Lerdorf <rasmus@php.net>
```

Earlier version of PHP 5 will also *not* autoconvert objects to strings when you pass them to a function that requires a string argument. You should call `__toString()` on them instead (see Example 7-19).

Example 7-19. Invoking __toString() directly

```
print htmlentities($rasmus);                    // bad
print htmlentities($rasmus->__toString());     // good
```

This also applies when you:

- Place the object inside double quotes or a heredoc
- Concatenate with the object using dot (.)
- Cast the object to a string using `(string)` or `strval()`
- Treat the object as a string in `printf()` by indicating it should be formatted with `%s`

Therefore, if you're using `__toString()` heavily in your code, it's best to use PHP 5.2 or greater.

7.7 Specifying Interfaces

Problem

You want to ensure a class implements one or more methods with specific names, visibilities, and prototypes.

Solution

Define an interface and declare that your class will implement that interface:

```
interface Nameable {
    public function getName();
    public function setName($name);
}

class Book implements Nameable {
    private $name;

    public function getName() {
        return $this->name;
    }

    public function setName($name) {
        return $this->name = $name;
    }
}
```

The Nameable interface defines two methods necessary to name an object. Since books are nameable, the Book class says it implements the Nameable interface, and then defines the two methods in the class body.

Discussion

In object-oriented programming, objects must work together. Therefore, you should be able to require a class (or more than one class) to implement methods that are necessary for the class to interact properly in your system.

For instance, an e-commerce application needs to know a certain set of information about every item up for sale. These items may be represented as different classes: Book, CD, DVD, etc. However, at the very minimum you need to know that every item in your catalog has a name, regardless of its type. (You probably also want them to have a price and maybe even an ID, while you're at it.)

The mechanism for forcing classes to support the same set of methods is called an *interface*. Defining an interface is similar to defining a class (see Example 7-20).

Example 7-20. Defining an interface

```
interface Nameable {
    public function getName();
```

```
    public function setName($name);
}
```

Instead of using the keyword `class`, an interface uses the keyword `interface`. Inside the interface, define your method prototypes, but don't provide an implementation.

This creates an interface named `Nameable`. Any class that's `Nameable` must implement the two methods listed in the interface: `getName()` and `setName()`.

When a class supports all the methods in the interface, it's said to *implement the interface*. You agree to implement an interface in your class definition (see Example 7-21).

Example 7-21. Implementing an interface
```
class Book implements Nameable {
    private $name;

    public function getName() {
        return $this->name;
    }

    public function setName($name) {
        return $this->name = $name;
    }
}
```

Failing to implement all the methods listed in an interface, or implementing them with a different prototype, causes PHP to emit a fatal error.

A class can agree to implement as many interfaces as you want. For instance, you may want to have a `Listenable` interface that specifies how you can retrieve an audio clip for an item. In this case, the `CD` and `DVD` classes would also implement `Listenable`, whereas the `Book` class wouldn't. (Unless, of course, it is an audio book.)

When you use interfaces, it's important to declare your classes before you instantiate objects. Otherwise, when a class implements interfaces, PHP 5 can sometimes become confused. To avoid breaking existing applications, this requirement is not enforced, but it's best not to rely on this behavior.

To check if a class implements a specific interface, use `class_implements()`, as shown in Example 7-22.

Example 7-22. Checking if a class implements an interface
```
class Book implements Nameable {
    // .. Code here
}

$interfaces = class_implements('Book');
if (isset($interfaces['Nameable'])) {
    // Book implements Nameable
}
```

You can also use the Reflection classes, shown in Example 7-23.

Example 7-23. Checking if a class implements an interface using the Reflection classes

```
class Book implements Nameable {
// .. Code here
}
$rc = new ReflectionClass('Book');
if ($rc->implementsInterface('Nameable')) {
  print "Book implements Nameable\n";
}
```

See Also

Recipe 7.19 for more on the Reflection classes; documentation on `class_implements()` at *http://www.php.net/class_implements* and interfaces at *http://www.php.net/interfaces*.

7.8 Creating Abstract Base Classes

Problem

You want to create an "abstract" class, or, in other words, one that is not directly instantiable, but acts as a common base for children classes.

Solution

Label the class as `abstract`:

```
abstract class Database {
  // ...
}
```

Do this by placing the `abstract` keyword before the `class` definition.

You must also define at least one abstract method in your class. Do this by placing the `abstract` keyword in front of the method definition:

```
abstract class Database {
    abstract public function connect();
    abstract public function query();
    abstract public function fetch();
    abstract public function close();
}
```

Discussion

Abstact classes are best used when you have a series of objects that are related using the "is a" relationship. Therefore, it makes logical sense to have them descend from a common parent. However, while the children are tangible, the parent is abstract.

Take, for example, a `Database` class. A database is a real object, so it makes sense to have a `Database` class. However, although Oracle, MySQL, Postgres, MSSQL, and hundreds of other databases exist, you cannot download and install a generic database. You must choose a specific database.

PHP provides a way for you to create a class that cannot be instantiated. This class is known as an *abstract class*. For example, see the `Database` class in Example 7-24.

Example 7-24. Defining an abstract class

```
abstract class Database {
    abstract public function connect();
    abstract public function query();
    abstract public function fetch();
    abstract public function close();
}
```

Mark a class as abstract by placing the `abstract` keyword before `class`.

Abstract classes must contain at least one method that is also marked `abstract`. These methods are called *abstract methods*. `Database` contains four abstract methods: `connect()`, `query()`, `fetch()`, and `close()`. These four methods are the basic set of functionality necessary to use a database.

If a class contains an abstract method, the class must also be declared abstract. However, abstract classes can contain non-abstract methods (even though there are no regular methods in `Database`).

Abstract methods, like methods listed in an interface, are not implemented inside the abstract class. Instead, abstract methods are implemented in a child class that extends the abstract parent. For instance, you could use a `MySQL` class, as shown in Example 7-25.

Example 7-25. Implementing a class based on an abstract class

```
class MySQL extends Database {
    protected $dbh;
    protected $query;

    public function connect($server, $username, $password, $database) {
        $this->dbh = mysqli_connect($server, $username,
                                    $password, $database);
    }

    public function query($sql) {
        $this->query = mysqli_query($this->dbh, $sql);
    }

    public function fetch() {
        return mysqli_fetch_row($this->dbh, $this->query);
    }

    public function close() {
        mysqli_close($this->dbh);
    }
}
```

If a subclass fails to implement all the abstract methods in the parent class, then it itself is abstract and another class must come along and further subclass the child. You might do this if you want to create two MySQL classes: one that fetches information as objects and another that returns arrays.

There are two requirements for abstract methods:

- Abstract methods cannot be defined `private`, because they need to be inherited.
- Abstract methods cannot be defined `final`, because they need to be overridden.

Abstract classes and interfaces are similar concepts, but are not identical. For one, you can implement multiple interfaces, but extend only one abstract class. Additionally, in an interface you can only define method prototypes—you cannot implement them. An abstract class, in comparison, needs only one abstract method to be abstract, and can have many non-abstract methods and even properties.

You should also use abstract classes when the "is a" rule applies. For example, since you can say "MySQL is a Database," it makes sense for `Database` to be abstract class. In constrast, you cannot say, "Book is a Nameable" or "Book is a Name," so `Nameable` should be an interface.

7.9 Assigning Object References

Problem

You want to link two objects, so when you update one, you also update the other.

Solution

Use = to assign one object to another by reference:

```
$adam = new user;
$dave = $adam;
```

Discussion

When you do an object assignment using =, you don't create a new copy of an object, but a reference to the first. So, modifying one alters the other.

This is different from how PHP 5 treats other types of variables, where it does a copy-by-value. It is also different from PHP 4, where all variables are copied by value, regardless of their type.

So where you used to use =& in PHP 4 to make two objects point at each other, you can now use only =:

```
$adam = new user;
$adam->load_info('adam');

$dave = $adam;
```

Now $dave and $adam are two names for the exact same object.

See Also

Recipe 7.10 for more on cloning objects; documentation on references at *http://www.php.net/references*.

7.10 Cloning Objects

Problem

You want to copy an object.

Solution

Copy objects by reference using =:

```
$rasmus = $zeev;
```

Copy objects by value using `clone`:

```
$rasmus = clone $zeev;
```

Discussion

PHP 5 copies objects by reference instead of value. When you assign an existing object to a new variable, that new variable is just another name for the existing object. Accessing the object by the old or new name produces the same results.

To create an independent instance of a value with the same contents, otherwise known as copying by value, use the `clone` keyword. Otherwise, the second object is simply a reference to the first.

This cloning process copies every property in the first object to the second. This includes properties holding objects, so the cloned object may end up sharing object references with the original.

This is frequently not the desired behavior. For example, consider the aggregated version of `Person` that holds an `Address` object in Example 7-26.

Example 7-26. Using an aggregated class

```
class Address {
  protected $city;
  protected $country;

  public function setCity($city) { $this->city = $city; }
  public function getCity() { return $this->city; }
  public function setCountry($country) { $this->country = $country; }
  public function getCountry() { return $this-> country;}
}

class Person {
 protected $name;
```

```
    protected $address;

    public function __construct() { $this->address = new Address; }
    public function setName($name) { $this->name = $name; }
    public function getName() { return $this->name; }
    public function __call($method, $arguments) {
     if (method_exists($this->address, $method)) {
      return call_user_func_array( array($this->address, $method), $arguments);
     }
    }
   }
```

An aggregated class is one that embeds another class inside in a way that makes it easy to access both the original and embedded classes. The key point to remember is that the $address property holds an Address object.

With this class, Example 7-27 shows what happens when you clone an object.

Example 7-27. Cloning an aggregated class
```
    $rasmus = new Person;
    $rasmus->setName('Rasmus Lerdorf');
    $rasmus->setCity('Sunnyvale');

    $zeev = clone $rasmus;
    $zeev->setName('Zeev Suraski');
    $zeev->setCity('Tel Aviv');

    print $rasmus->getName() . ' lives in ' . $rasmus->getCity() . '.';
    print $zeev->getName() . ' lives in ' . $zeev->getCity() . '.';

    Rasmus Lerdorf lives in Tel Aviv.

    Zeev Suraski lives in Tel Aviv.
```

Interesting. Calling setName( ) worked correctly because the $name property is a string, so it's copied by value. However, since $address is an object, it's copied by reference, so getCity( ) doesn't produce the correct results, and you end up relocating Rasmus to Tel Aviv.

This type of object cloning is known as a shallow clone or a shallow copy. In contrast, a "deep clone" occurs when all objects involved are cloned. This is PHP 4's cloning method.

Control how PHP 5 clones an object by implementing a __clone( ) method in your class. When this method exists, PHP allows __clone( ) to override its default behavior, as shown in Example 7-28.

Example 7-28. Properly implementing cloning in aggregated classes
```
    class Person {
     // ... everything from before
     public function __clone() {
      $this->address = clone $this->address;
```

```
        }
    }
```

Inside of __clone( ), you're automatically presented with a shallow copy of the variable, stored in $this , the object that PHP provides when __clone( ) does not exist.

Since PHP has already copied all the properties, you only need to overwrite the ones you dislike. Here, $name is okay, but $address needs to be explicitly cloned.

Now the clone behaves correctly, as shown in Example 7-29.

Example 7-29. Cloning an aggregated class

```
$rasmus = new Person;
$rasmus->setName('Rasmus Lerdorf');
$rasmus->setCity('Sunnyvale');

$zeev = clone $rasmus;
$zeev->setName('Zeev Suraski');
$zeev->setCity('Tel Aviv');

print $rasmus->getName() . ' lives in ' . $rasmus->getCity() . '.';
print $zeev->getName() . ' lives in ' . $zeev->getCity() . '.';

Rasmus Lerdorf lives in Sunnyvale.

Zeev Suraski lives in Tel Aviv.
```

Using the clone operator on objects stored in properties causes PHP to check whether any of those objects contain a __clone( ) method. If one exists, PHP calls it. This repeats for any objects that are nested even further.

This process correctly clones the entire object and demonstrates why it's called a deep copy.

See Also

Recipe 7.9 for more on assigning objects by reference.

7.11 Overriding Property Accesses

Problem

You want handler functions to execute whenever you read and write object properties. This lets you write generalized code to handle property access in your class.

Solution

Use the magical methods __get( ) and __set( ) to intercept property requests.

To improve this abstraction, also implement __isset( ) and __unset( ) methods to make the class behave correctly when you check a property using isset( ) or delete it using unset( ).

Discussion

Property overloading allows you to seamlessly obscure from the user the actual location of your object's properties and the data structure you use to store them.

For example, the Person class shown in Example 7-30 stores variables in an array, $__data.

Example 7-30. Implementing magic accessor methods

```
class Person {
    private $__data = array();

    public function __get($property) {
        if (isset($this->__data[$property])) {
            return $this->__data[$property];
        } else {
            return false;
        }
    }

    public function __set($property, $value) {
        $this->__data[$property] = $value;
    }
}
```

Example 7-31 shows how to use the Person class.

Example 7-31. Using magic accessor methods

```
$johnwood = new Person;
$johnwood->email = 'jonathan@wopr.mil'; // sets $user->__data['email']
print $johnwood->email;                 // reads $user->__data['email']
jonathan@wopr.mil
```

When you set data, __set( ) rewrites the element inside of $__data. Likewise, use __get( ) to trap the call and return the correct array element.

Using these methods and an array as the alternate variable storage source makes it less painful to implement object encapsulation. Instead of writing a pair of accessor methods for every class property, you use __get( ) and __set( ).

With __get( ) and __set( ), you can use what appear to be public properties, such as $johnwood->name, without violating encapsulation. This is because the programmer isn't reading from and writing to those properties directly, but is instead being routed through accessor methods.

The __get( ) method takes the property name as its single parameter. Within the method, you check to see whether that property has a value inside $__data. If it does, the method returns that value; otherwise, it returns false.

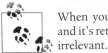 When you read $johnwood->name, you actually call __get('name') and it's returning $__data['name'], but for all external purposes that's irrelevant.

The __set( ) method takes two arguments: the property name and the new value. Otherwise, the logic inside the method is similar to __get( ).

Besides reducing the number of methods in your classes, these magical methods also make it easy to implement a centralized set of input and output validation.

Additionally, Example 7-32 shows how you can also enforce exactly what properties are legal and illegal for a given class.

Example 7-32. Enforcing property access using magic accessor methods

```
class Person {
    // list person and email as valid properties
    protected $__data = array('person', 'email');

    public function __get($property) {
        if (isset($this->__data[$property])) {
            return $this->__data[$property];
        } else {
            return false;
        }
    }

    // enforce the restriction of only setting
    // pre-defined properties
    public function __set($property, $value) {
        if (isset($this->__data[$property])) {
            return $this->__data[$property] = $value;
        } else {
            return false;
        }
    }
}
```

In this updated version of the code, you explicitly list the object's valid properties names when you define the $__data property. Then, inside __set( ), you use isset( ) to confirm that all property writes are going to allowable names.

Preventing rogue reads and writes is why the visibility of the $__data property isn't public, but protected. Otherwise, someone could do this:

```
$person = new Person;
$person->__data['fake_property'] = 'fake_data';
```

because the magical accessors aren't used for existing properties.

Pay attention to this important implementation detail. In particular, if you're expecting people to extend the class, they could introduce a property that conflicts with a property you're expecting to handle using __get( ) and __set( ). For that reason, the property in Example 7-32 is called $__data with two leading underscores.

You should consider prefixing all your "actual" properties in classes where you use magical accessors to prevent collisions between properties that should be handled using normal methods and ones that should be routed through __get( ) and __set( ).

There are three downsides to using __get( ) and __set( ). First, these methods only catch missing properties. If you define a property for your class, __get( ) and __set( ) are not invoked by PHP when that property is accessed.

This is the case even if the property you're trying to access isn't visible in the current scope (for instance, when you're reading a property that exists in the class but isn't accessible to you, because it's declared private). Doing this causes PHP to emit a fatal error:

```
PHP Fatal error:  Cannot access private property...
```

Second, these methods completely destroy any notion of property inheritance. If a parent object has a __get( ) method and you implement your own version of __get( ) in the child, your object won't function correctly because the parent's __get( ) method is never called.

You can work around this by calling parent::__get( ), but it is something you need to explicitly manage instead of "getting for free" as part of OO design.

The illusion is incomplete because it doesn't extend to the isset( ) and unset( ) methods. For instance, if you try to check if an overloaded property isset( ), you will not get an accurate answer, as PHP doesn't know to invoke __get( ).

You can fix this by implementing your own version of these methods in the class, called __isset( ) and __unset( ), shown in Example 7-33.

Example 7-33. Implementing magic methods for isset() and unset()

```php
class Person {
    // list person and email as valid properties
    protected $data = array('person', 'email');

    public function __get($property) {
        if (isset($this->data[$property])) {
            return $this->data[$property];
        } else {
            return false;
        }
    }

    // enforce the restriction of only setting
    // pre-defined properties
    public function __set($property, $value) {
        if (isset($this->data[$property])) {
            return $this->data[$property] = $value;
        } else {
            return false;
```

```
            }
        }

        public function __isset($property) {
            if (isset($this->data[$property])) {
                return true;
            } else {
                return false;
            }
        }

        public function __unset($property) {
            if (isset($this->data[$property])) {
                return unset($this->data[$property]);
            } else {
                return false;
            }
        }
    }
}
```

The __isset( ) method checks inside the $data element and returns true or false depending on the status of the property you're checking.

Likewise, __unset( ) passes back the value of unset( ) applied to the "real" property, or false if it's not set.

Implementing these two methods isn't required when using __get( ) and __set( ), but it's best to do so as it's hard to predict how you may use object properties. Failing to code these methods will lead to confusion when someone (perhaps even yourself) doesn't know (or forgets) that this class is using magic accessor methods.

However, the __isset( ) and __unset( ) methods are only available as of PHP 5.1.

Other reasons to consider not using magical accessors are:

- They're relatively slow. They're both slower than direct property access and explicitly writing accessor methods for all your properties.
- They make it impossible for the Reflection classes and tools such as phpDocumentor to automatically document your code.
- You cannot use them with static properties.

See Also

Documentation on magic methods found at *http://www.php.net/manual/en/language.oop5.magic.php*.

7.12 Calling Methods on an Object Returned by Another Method

Problem

You need to call a method on an object returned by another method.

Solution

Call the second method directly from the first:

```
$orange = $fruit->get('citrus')->peel();
```

Discussion

PHP is smart enough to first call `$fruit->get('citrus')` and then invoke the `peel()` method on what's returned.

This is an improvement over PHP 4, where you needed to use a temporary variable:

```
$orange = $fruit->get('citrus');
$orange->peel();
```

Another victory for PHP 5!

7.13 Aggregating Objects

Problem

You want to compose two or more objects together so that they appear to behave as a single object.

Solution

Aggregate the objects together and use the __call() magic method to intercept method invocations and route them accordingly:

```
class Address {
    protected $city;

    public function setCity($city) {
        $this->city = $city;
    }

    public function getCity() {
        return $this->city;
    }
}

class Person {
    protected $name;
```

```
    protected $address;

    public function __construct() {
        $this->address = new Address;
    }

    public function setName($name) {
        $this->name = $name;
    }

    public function getName() {
        return $this->name;
    }

    public function __call($method, $arguments) {
        if (method_exists($this->address, $method)) {
            return call_user_func_array(
                array($this->address, $method), $arguments);
        }
    }
}

$rasmus = new Person;
$rasmus->setName('Rasmus Lerdorf');
$rasmus->setCity('Sunnyvale');

print $rasmus->getName() . ' lives in ' . $rasmus->getCity() . '.';
Rasmus Lerdorf lives in Sunnyvale.
```

An instance of the `Address` object is created during the construction of every `Person`. When you invoke methods not defined in `Person`, the `__call()` method catches them and, when applicable, dispatches them using `call_user_func_array()`.

Discussion

In this recipe, you cannot say a `Person` "is an" `Address` or vice versa. Therefore, it doesn't make sense for one class to **extend** the other.

However, it makes sense for them to be separate classes so that they provide maximum flexibility and reuse, as well as reduced duplicated code. So you check if another rule —the "has a" rule—applies. Since a `Person` "has an" `Address`, it makes sense to aggregate the classes together.

With aggregation, one object acts as a container for one or more additional objects. This is another way of solving the problem of multiple inheritance because you can easily piece together an object out of smaller components.

For example, a `Person` object can contain an `Address` object. Clearly, `People` have addresses. However, addresses aren't unique to people; they also belong to businesses and other entities. Therefore, instead of hardcoding address information inside of `Person`, it makes sense to create a separate `Address` class that can be used by multiple classes.

Example 7-34 shows how this works in practice.

Example 7-34. Aggregating an address object

```php
class Address {
    protected $city;

    public function setCity($city) {
        $this->city = $city;
    }

    public function getCity() {
        return $this->city;
    }
}

class Person {
    protected $name;
    protected $address;

    public function __construct() {
        $this->address = new Address;
    }

    public function setName($name) {
        $this->name = $name;
    }

    public function getName() {
        return $this->name;
    }

    public function __call($method, $arguments) {
        if (method_exists($this->address, $method)) {
            return call_user_func_array(
                array($this->address, $method), $arguments);
        }
    }
}
```

The Address class stores a city and has two accessor methods to manipulate the data, setCity( ) and getCity( ).

Person has setName( ) and getName( ), similar to Address, but it also has two other methods: __construct( ) and __call( ).

Its constructor instantiates an Address object and stores it in a protected $address property. This allows methods inside Person to access $address, but prevents others from talking directly to the class.

Ideally, when you call a method that exists in Address, PHP would automatically execute it. This does not occur, since Person does not extend Address. You must write code to glue these calls to the appropriate methods yourself.

Wrapper methods are one option. For example:

```
    public function setCity($city) {
            $this->address->setCity($city);
    }
```

This setCity( ) method passes along its data to the setCity( ) method stored in $address. This is simple, but it is also tedious because you must write a wrapper for every method.

Using __call( ) lets you automate this process by centralizing these methods into a single place, as shown in Example 7-35.

Example 7-35. Centralizing method invocation using __call( )

```
    public function __call($method, $arguments) {
            if (method_exists($this->address, $method)) {
                return call_user_func_array(
                    array($this->address, $method), $arguments);
            }
    }
```

The __call( ) method captures any calls to undefined methods in a class. It is invoked with two arguments: the name of the method and an array holding the parameters passed to the method. The first argument lets you see which method was called, so you can determine whether it's appropriate to dispatch it to $address.

Here, you want to pass along the method if it's a valid method of the Address class. Check this using method_exists( ), providing the object as the first parameter and the method name as the second.

If the function returns true, you know this method is valid, so you can call it. Unfortunately, you're still left with the burden of unwrapping the arguments out of the $arguments array. That can be painful.

The seldom used and oddly named call_user_func_array( ) function solves this problem. This function lets you call a user function and pass along arguments in an array. Its first parameter is your function name, and the second is the array of arguments.

In this case, however, you want to call an object method instead of a function. There's a special syntax to cover this situation. Instead of passing the function name, you pass an array with two elements. The first element is the object, and the other is the method name.

This causes call_user_func_array( ) to invoke the method on your object. You must then return the result of call_user_func_array( ) back to the original caller, or your return values will be silently discarded.

Here's an example of Person that calls both a method defined in Person and one from Address:

```
    $rasmus = new Person;
    $rasmus->setName('Rasmus Lerdorf');
    $rasmus->setCity('Sunnyvale');
```

```
print $rasmus->getName() . ' lives in ' . $rasmus->getCity() . '.';
Rasmus Lerdorf lives in Sunnyvale.
```

Even though setCity( ) and getCity( ) aren't methods of Person, you have aggregated them into that class.

You can aggregate additional objects into a single class, and also be more selective as to which methods you expose to the outside user. This requires some basic filtering based on the method name.

See Also

Documentation on magic methods at *http://www.php.net/manual/en/language.oop5.magic.php.*

7.14 Accessing Overridden Methods

Problem

You want to access a method in the parent class that's been overridden in the child.

Solution

Prefix parent:: to the method name:

```
class shape {
    function draw() {
        // write to screen
    }
}

class circle extends shape {
    function draw($origin, $radius) {
        // validate data
        if ($radius > 0) {
            parent::draw();
            return true;
        }

        return false;
    }
}
```

Discussion

When you override a parent method by defining one in the child, the parent method isn't called unless you explicitly reference it.

In the Solution, we override the draw( ) method in the child class, circle, because you want to accept circle-specific parameters and validate the data. However, in this case, we still want to perform the generic shape::draw( ) action, which does the actual drawing, so we call parent::draw( ) inside your method if $radius is greater than 0.

Only code inside the class can use `parent::`. Calling `parent::draw( )` from outside the class gets you a parse error. For example, if `circle::draw( )` checked only the radius, but you also wanted to call `shape::draw( )`, this wouldn't work:[*]

```
$circle = new circle;
if ($circle->draw($origin, $radius)) {
    $circle->parent::draw();
}
```

This also applies to object constructors, so it's quite common to see the following:

```
class circle {
    function __construct($x, $y, $r) {
        // call shape's constructor first
        parent::__construct();
        // now do circle-specific stuff
    }
}
```

The simplicity of invoking a parent constructor is one advantage of PHP 5's consistent naming scheme for constructors, as you need to jump through all sorts of hoops to implement this in PHP 4 in a non-brittle way.fs

See Also

Recipe 7.2 for more on object constructors; documentation on class parents at *http:// www.php.net/keyword.parent* and on `get_parent_class( )` at *http://www.php.net/get-pa rent-class.*

7.15 Using Method Polymorphism

Problem

You want to execute different code depending on the number and type of arguments passed to a method.

Solution

PHP doesn't support method polymorphism as a built-in feature. However, you can emulate it using various type-checking functions. The following `combine( )` function uses `is_numeric( )`, `is_string( )`, `is_array( )`, and `is_bool( )`:

```
// combine() adds numbers, concatenates strings, merges arrays,
// and ANDs bitwise and boolean arguments
function combine($a, $b) {
    if (is_int($a) && is_int($b))     {
        return $a + $b;
    }
```

---

[*] In fact, it fails with the error unexpected `T_PAAMAYIM_NEKUDOTAYIM`, which is Hebrew for "double-colon."

```
        if (is_float($a) && is_float($b))   {
            return $a + $b;
        }

        if (is_string($a) && is_string($b)) {
            return "$a$b";
        }

        if (is_array($a) && is_array($b))   {
            return array_merge($a, $b);
        }

        if (is_bool($a) && is_bool($b))     {
            return $a & $b;
        }

        return false;
    }
```

Discussion

Because PHP doesn't allow you to declare a variable's type in a method prototype, it can't conditionally execute a different method based on the method's signature, as Java and C++ can. You can, instead, make one function and use a `switch` statement to manually recreate this feature.

For example, PHP lets you edit images using GD. It can be handy in an image class to be able to pass in either the location of the image (remote or local) or the handle PHP has assigned to an existing image stream. Example 7-36 shows a `pc_Image` class that does just that.

Example 7-36. pc_Image class

```
    class pc_Image {

        protected $handle;

        function ImageCreate($image) {
            if (is_string($image)) {
                // simple file type guessing

                // grab file suffix
                $info = pathinfo($image);
                $extension = strtolower($info['extension']);
                switch ($extension) {
                case 'jpg':
                case 'jpeg':
                    $this->handle = ImageCreateFromJPEG($image);
                    break;
                case 'png':
                    $this->handle = ImageCreateFromPNG($image);
                    break;
                default:
```

```
                die('Images must be JPEGs or PNGs.');
            }
        } elseif (is_resource($image)) {
            $this->handle = $image;
        } else {
            die('Variables must be strings or resources.');
        }
    }
}
```

In this case, any string passed in is treated as the location of a file, so we use
pathinfo( ) to grab the file extension. Once we know the extension, we try to guess
which ImageCreateFrom( ) function accurately opens the image and create a handle.

If it's not a string, we're dealing directly with a GD stream, which is a type of
resource. Since there's no conversion necessary, we assign the stream directly to
$handle. Of course, if you're using this class in a production environment, you'd be
more robust in your error handling.

Method polymorphism also encompasses methods with differing numbers of arguments. The code to find the number of arguments inside a method is identical to how
you process variable argument functions using func_num_args( ). This is discussed in
Recipe 6.5.

See Also

Recipe 6.5 for variable argument functions; documentation on is_string( ) at *http://
www.php.net/is-string*, is_resource( ) at *http://www.php.net/is-resource*, and
pathinfo( ) at *http://www.php.net/pathinfo*.

7.16 Defining Class Constants

Problem

You want to define constants on a per-class basis, not on a global basis.

Solution

Define them like class properties, but use the const label instead:

```
class Math {
    const pi = 3.14159; // universal
    const  e = 2.71828; // constants
}

$area = math::pi * $radius * $radius;
```

Discussion

PHP reuses its concept of global constants and applies them to classes. Essentially, these
are final properties.

Declare them using the const label:

```
class Math {
    const pi = 3.14159; // universal
    const  e = 2.71828; // constants
}

$area = math::pi * $radius * $radius;
```

Like static properties, you can access constants without first instantiating a new instance of your class, and they're accessed using the double colon (::) notation. Prefix the word self:: to the constant name to use it inside of a class.

Unlike properties, constants do not have a dollar sign ($) before them:

```
class Circle {
    const pi = 3.14159;
    protected $radius;

    public function __construct($radius) {
        $this->radius = $radius;
    }

    public function circumference() {
        return 2 * self::pi * $this->radius;
    }
}

$c = new circle(1);
print $c->circumference();
6.28318
```

This example creates a circle with a radius of 1 and then calls the circumference method to calculate its circumference. To use the class's pi constant, refer to it as circumference; otherwise, PHP tries to access circumference value of the global pi constant:

```
define('pi', 10); // global pi constant

class Circle {
    const pi = 3.14159; // class pi constant
    protected $radius;

    public function __construct($radius) {
        $this->radius = $radius;
    }

    public function circumference() {
        return 2 * pi * $this->radius;
    }

}

$c = new circle(1);
print $c->circumference();
20
```

Oops! PHP has used the value of 10 instead of 3.14159, so the new answer is 20 instead of 6.28318.

Although it's unlikely that you will accidentally redefine π (you'll probably use the built-in M_PI constant anyway), this can still slip you up.

You cannot assign the value of an expression to a constant, nor can they use information passed into your script:

```
// invalid
class permissions {
    const    read = 1 << 2;
    const    write = 1 << 1;
    const execute = 1 << 0;
}

// invalid and insecure
class database {
    const debug = $_REQUEST['debug'];
}
```

Neither the constants in permissions nor the debug constant in database are acceptable because they are not fixed. Even the first example, 1 << 2, where PHP does not need to read in external data, is not allowed.

Since you need to access constants using an explicit name, either self:: or the name of the class, you cannot dynamically calculate the class name during runtime. It must be declared beforehand. For example:

```
class Constants {
    const pi = 3.14159;

    // rest of class here
}

$class = 'Constants';

print $class::pi;
```

This produces a parse error, even though this type of construct is legal for non-constant expressions, such as $class->pi.

See Also

Documentation on class constants is available at *http://www.php.net/manual/en/ language.oop5.constants.php*.

7.17 Defining Static Properties and Methods

Problem

You want to define methods in an object, and be able to access them without instantiating a object.

Solution

Declare the method as `static`:

```php
class Format {
    public static function number($number, $decimals = 2,
                                  $decimal = ',', $thousands = '.') {
        return number_format($number, $decimals, $decimal, $thousands);
    }
}

print Format::number(1234.567);
1,234.57
```

Discussion

Occasionally, you want to define a collection of methods in an object, but you want to be able to invoke those methods without instantiating a object. In PHP 5, declaring a method `static` lets you call it directly:

```php
class Format {
    public static function number($number, $decimals = 2,
                                  $decimal = ',', $thousands = '.') {
        return number_format($number, $decimals, $decimal, $thousands);
    }
}

print Format::number(1234.567);
1,234.57
```

Since static methods don't require an object instance, use the class name instead of the object. Don't place a dollar sign ($) before the class name.

Static methods aren't referenced with an arrow (->), but with double colons (::)—this signals to PHP that the method is static. So in the example, the `number( )` method of the `Format` class is accessed using `Format::number( )`.

Number formatting doesn't depend on any other object properties or methods. Therefore, it makes sense to declare this method `static`. This way, for example, inside your shopping cart application, you can format the price of items in a pretty manner with just one line of code and still use an object instead of a global function.

Static methods do not operate on a specific instance of the class where they're defined. PHP does not "construct" a temporary object for you to use while you're inside the method. Therefore, you cannot refer to `$this` inside a static method, because there's no `$this` on which to operate. Calling a static method is just like calling a regular function.

PHP 5 also has a feature known as *static properties*. Every instance of a class shares these properties in common. Thus, static properties act as class-namespaced global variables.

One reason for using a static property is to share a database connection among multiple `Database` objects. For efficiency, you shouldn't create a new connection to your database every time you instantiate `Database`. Instead, negotiate a connection the first time and reuse that connection in each additional instance, as shown in Example 7-37.

Example 7-37. Sharing a static method across instances

```
class Database {
    private static $dbh = NULL;

    public function __construct($server, $username, $password) {
        if (self::$dbh == NULL) {
            self::$dbh = db_connect($server, $username, $password);
        } else {
            // reuse existing connection
        }
    }
}

$db  = new Database('db.example.com', 'web', 'jsd6w@2d');
// Do a bunch of queries

$db2 = new Database('db.example.com', 'web', 'jsd6w@2d');
// Do some additional queries
```

Static properties, like static methods, use the double colon notation. To refer to a static property inside of a class, use the special prefix of `self`. `self` is to static properties and methods as `$this` is to instantiated properties and methods.

The constructor uses `self::$dbh` to access the static `connection` property. When `$db` is instantiated, `dbh` is still set to `NULL`, so the constructor calls `db_connect( )` to negotiate a new connection with the database.

This does not occur when you create `$db2`, since `dbh` has been set to the database handle.

See Also

Documentation on the `static` keyword at *http://www.php.net/manual/en/language.oop5.static.php*.

7.18 Controlling Object Serialization

Problem

You want to control how an object behaves when you `serialize( )` and `unserialize( )` it. This is useful when you need to establish and close connections to remote resources, such as databases, files, and web services.

Solution

Define the magical methods `__sleep( )` and `__wakeUp( )`, as shown in Example 7-38.

Example 7-38. Controlling serialization using __sleep( ) and __wakeUp( )

```php
<?php
class LogFile {
    protected $filename;
    protected $handle;

    public function __construct($filename) {
        $this->filename = $filename;
        $this->open();
    }

    private function open() {
        $this->handle = fopen($this->filename, 'a');
    }

    public function __destruct($filename) {
        fclose($this->handle);
    }

    // called when object is serialized
    // should return an array of object properties to serialize
    public function __sleep() {
        return array('filename');
    }

    // called when object is unserialized
    public function __wakeUp() {
        $this->open();
    }
}
?>
```

Discussion

When you serialize an object in PHP, it preserves all your object properties. However, this does not include connections or handles that you hold to outside resources, such as databases, files, and web services.

These must be reestablished when you unserialize the object, or the object will not behave correctly. You can do this explicitly within your code, but it's better to abstract this away and let PHP handle everything behind the scenes.

Do this through the __sleep( ) and __wakeUp( ) magic methods. When you call serialize( ) on a object, PHP invokes __sleep( ); when you unserialize( ) it, it calls __wakeUp( ).

The LogFile class in Example 7-38 has five simple methods. The constructor takes a filename and saves it for future access. The open( ) method opens this file and stores the file handle, which is closed in the object's destructor.

The __sleep( ) method returns an array of properties to store during object serialization. Since file handles aren't preserved across serializations, it only returns array('filename') because that's all you need to store.

That's why when the object is reserialized, you need to reopen the file. This is handled inside of __wakeUp( ), which calls the same open( ) method used by the constructor. Since you cannot pass arguments to __wakeUp( ), it needs to get the filename from somewhere else. Fortunately, it's able to access object properties, which is why the filename is saved there.

It's important to realize that the same instance can be serialized multiple times in a single request, or even continued to be used after its serialized. Therefore, you shouldn't do anything in __sleep( ) that could prevent either of these two actions. The __sleep( ) method should only be used to exclude properties that shouldn't be serialized because they take up too much disk space, or are calculated based on other data and should be recalculated or otherwise made fresh during object unserialization.

That's why the call to fclose( ) appears in the destructor and not in __sleep( ).

See Also

Documentation on magic methods at *http://www.php.net/manual/en/ language.oop5.magic.php*; the unserialize( ) function at *http://www.php.net/unserial ize* and the serialize( ) function is found at *http://www.php.net/serialize*.

7.19 Introspecting Objects

Problem

You want to inspect an object to see what methods and properties it has, which lets you write code that works on any generic object, regardless of type.

Solution

Use the Reflection classes to probe an object for information.

For a quick overview of the class, call Reflection::export( ):

```
// learn about cars
Reflection::export(new ReflectionClass('car'));
```

Or probe for specific data:

```
$car = new ReflectionClass('car');
if ($car->hasMethod('retractTop')) {
    // car is a convertible
}
```

Discussion

It's rare to have an object and be unable to examine the actual code to see how it's described. Still, with the Reflection classes, you can programmatically extract information about both object-oriented features, such as classes, methods, and properties, but also non-OO features, such as functions and extensions.

This is useful for projects you want to apply to a whole range of different classes, such as creating automated class documentation, generic object debuggers, and state savers, like serialize( ).

To help show how the Reflection classes work, Example 7-39 contains an example Person class that uses many of PHP 5's OO features.

Example 7-39. Person class

```
class Person {
    public $name;
    protected $spouse;
    private $password;

    public function __construct($name) {
        $this->name = $name
    }

    public function getName() {
        return $name;
    }

    protected function setSpouse(Person $spouse) {
        if (!isset($this->spouse)) {
            $this->spouse = $spouse;
        }
    }

    private function setPassword($password) {
        $this->password = $password;
    }
}
```

For a quick overview of the class, call Reflection::export( ):

```
Reflection::export(new ReflectionClass('Person'));
Class [ <user> class Person ] {
  @@ /www/reflection.php 3-25

  - Constants [0] {
  }

  - Static properties [0] {
  }

  - Static methods [0] {
  }

  - Properties [3] {
    Property [ <default> public $name ]
    Property [ <default> protected $spouse ]
    Property [ <default> private $password ]
  }

  - Methods [4] {
```

```
Method [ <user> <ctor> public method _ _construct ] {
  @@ /www/reflection.php 8 - 10

  - Parameters [1] {
    Parameter #0 [ $name ]
  }
}

Method [ <user> public method getName ] {
  @@ /www/reflection.php 12 - 14
}

Method [ <user> protected method setSpouse ] {
  @@ /www/reflection.php 16 - 20

  - Parameters [1] {
    Parameter #0 [ Person or NULL $spouse ]
  }
}

Method [ <user> private method setPassword ] {
  @@ /www/reflection.php 22 - 24

  - Parameters [1] {
    Parameter #0 [ $password ]
  }
 }
 }
}
```

The `Reflection::export()` static method takes an instance of the `ReflectionClass` class and returns a copious amount of information. As you can see, it details the number of constants, static properties, static methods, properties, and methods in the class. Each item is broken down into component parts. For instance, all the entries contain visibility identifiers (`private`, `protected`, or `public`), and methods have a list of their parameters underneath their definition.

`Reflection::export()` not only reports the file where everything is defined, but even gives the line numbers! This lets you extract code from a file and place it in your documentation.

Example 7-40 shows a short command-line script that searches for the filename and starting line number of a method or function.

Example 7-40. Using reflection to locate function and method definitions

```php
<?php
if ($argc < 2) {
    print "$argv[0]: function/method, classes1.php [, ... classesN.php]\n";
    exit;
}

// Grab the function name
$function = $argv[1];
```

```
// Include the files
foreach (array_slice($argv, 2) as $filename) {
    include_once $filename;
}

try {
    if (strpos($function, '::')) {
        // It's a method
        list ($class, $method) = explode('::', $function);
        $reflect = new ReflectionMethod($class, $method);
    } else {
        // It's a function
        $reflect = new ReflectionFunction($function);
    }

    $file = $reflect->getFileName();
    $line = $reflect->getStartLine();

    printf ("%s | %s | %d\n", "$function()", $file, $line);
} catch (ReflectionException $e) {
    printf ("%s not found.\n", "$function()");
}

?>
```

Pass the function or method name as the first argument, and the include files as the remaining arguments. These files are then included, so make sure they don't print out anything.

The next step is to determine whether the first argument is a method or a function. Since methods are in the form class::method, you can use strpos( ) to tell them apart.

If it's a method, use explode( ) to separate the class from the method, passing both to ReflectionMethod. If it's a function, you can directly instantiate a ReflectionFunction without any difficulty.

Since ReflectionMethod extends ReflectionFunction, you can then call both getFileName( ) and getStartLine( ) of either class. This gathers the information that you need to print out, which is done via printf( ).

When you try to instantiate a ReflectionMethod or ReflectionFunction with the name of an undefined method, these classes throw a ReflectionException. Here, it's caught and an error message is displayed.

A more complex script that prints out the same type of information for all user-defined methods and functions appears in Recipe 7.23.

If you just need a quick view at an object instance, and don't want to fiddle with the Reflection classes, use either var_dump( ), var_export( ), or print_r( ) to print the object's values. Each of these three functions prints out information in a slightly different way; var_export( ) can optionally return the information, instead of displaying it.

See Also

Recipe 5.8 for more on printing variables; documentation on Reflection at *http://www.php.net/manual/en/language.oop5.reflection.php*, `var_dump( )` at *http://www.php.net/var-dump*, `var_export( )` at *http://www.php.net/var-export*, and `print_r( )` at *http://www.php.net/print-r*.

7.20 Checking if an Object Is an Instance of a Specific Class

Problem

You want to check if an object is an instance of a specific class.

Solution

To check that a value passed as a function argument is an instance of a specific class, specify the class name in your function prototype:

```
public function add(Person $person) {
        // add $person to address book
    }
}
```

In other contexts, use the `instanceof` operator:

```php
<?php
$media = get_something_from_catalog();
if ($media instanceof Book) {
  // do bookish things
} else if ($media instanceof DVD) {
  // watch the movie
}
?>
```

Discussion

One way of enforcing controls on your objects is by using *type hints*. A type hint is a way to tell PHP that an object passed to a function or method must be of a certain class.

To do this, specify a class name in your function and method prototypes. As of PHP 5.1, you can also require that an argument is an array, by using the keyword `array`. This only works for classes and arrays, though, not for any other variable types. You cannot, for example, specify strings or integers.

For example, to require the first argument to your `AddressBook` class's `add( )` method to be of type `Person`:

```
class AddressBook {

    public function add(Person $person) {
        // add $person to address book
```

```
        }
    }
```

Then, if you call **add( )** but pass a string, you get a fatal error:

```
$book = new AddressBook;

$person = 'Rasmus Lerdorf';

$book->add($person);
PHP Fatal error:  Argument 1 must be an object of class Person in...
```

Placing a type hint of **Person** in the first argument of your function declaration is equivalent to adding the following PHP code to the function:

```
public function add($person) {
        if (!($person instanceof Person)) {
                die("Argument 1 must be an instance of Person");
        }
    }
```

The **instanceof** operator checks whether an object is an instance of a particular class. This code makes sure **$person** is a **Person**.

PHP 4 does not have an **instanceof** operator. You need to use the **is_a( )** function, which is deprecated in PHP 5.

The **instanceof** operator also returns **true** with classes that are subclasses of the one you're comparing against. For instance:

```
class Person { /* ... */ }

class Kid extends Person { /* ... */ }

$kid = new Kid;

if ($kid instanceof Person) {
    print "Kids are people, too.\n";
}
```

Kids are people, too.

Last, you can use **instanceof** to see if a class has implemented a specific interface:

```
interface Nameable {
    public function getName();
    public function setName($name);
}

class Book implements Nameable {
    private $name;

    public function getName() {
        return $this->name;
    }

    public function setName($name) {
```

```
        return $this->name = $name;
    }
}

$book = new Book;
if ($book instanceof Book) {
    print "You can name a Book.\n";
}
```

You can name a Book

Type hinting has the side benefit of integrating API documentation directly into the class itself. If you see that a class constructor takes an Event type, you know exactly what to provide the method. Additionally, you know that the code and the "documentation" must always be in sync, because it's baked directly into the class definition.

You can also use type hinting in interface definitions, which lets you further specify all your interface details.

However, type hinting does come at the cost of less flexibility. There's no way to allow a parameter to accept more than one type of object, so this places some restrictions on how you design your object hierarchy.

Also, the penalty for violating a type hint is quite drastic—the script aborts with a fatal error. In a web context, you may want to have more control over how errors are handled and recover more gracefully from this kind of mistake. Implementing your own form of type checking inside of methods lets you print out an error page if you choose.

Last, unlike some languages, you cannot use type hinting for return values, so there's no way to mandate that a particular function always returns an object of a particular type.

See Also

Documentation on type hints at *http://www.php.net/manual/language.oop5.typehinting.php* and instanceof at *http://www.php.net/manual/language.operators.type.php*

7.21 Autoloading Class Files upon Object Instantiation

Problem

You don't want to include all your class definitions within every page. Instead, you want to dynamically load only the ones necessary in that page.

Solution

Use the __autoload( ) magic method:

```
function __autoload($class_name) {
    include "$class_name.php";
```

```
    }

    $person = new Person;
```

Discussion

When you normally attempt to instantiate a class that's not defined, PHP dies with a fatal error because it can't locate what you're looking for. Therefore, it's typical to load in all the potential classes for a page, regardless of whether they're actually invoked.

This has the side effect of increasing processing time, as PHP must parse every class, even the unused ones. One solution is to load missing code on the fly using the __autoload( ) method, which is invoked when you instantiate undefined classes.

For example, here's how you include all the classes used by your script:

```
function __autoload($class_name) {
    include "$class_name.php";
}

$person = new Person;
```

The __autoload( ) function receives the class name as its single parameter. This example appends a *.php* extension to that name and tries to include a file based on $class_name. So when you instantiate a new Person, it looks for *Person.php* in your include_path.

When __autoload( ) fails to successfully load a class definition for the object you're trying to instantiate, PHP fails with a fatal error, just as it does when it can't find a class definition without autoload.

If you adopt the PEAR-style naming convention of placing an underscore between words to reflect the file hierarchy, use the code in Example 7-41.

Example 7-41. Autoloading classes using PEAR naming conventions

```
function __autoload($package_name) {
    // split on underscore
    $folders = split('_', $package_name);
    // rejoin based on directory structure
    // use DIRECTORY_SEPARATOR constant to work on all platforms
    $path    = join(DIRECTORY_SEPARATOR, $folders);
    // append extension
    $path   .= '.php';

    include $path;
}
```

With the code in Example 7-41, you can do the following:

```
    $person = new Animals_Person;
```

If the class isn't defined, Animals_Person gets passed to __autoload( ). The function splits the class name on underscore (_) and joins it on DIRECTORY_SEPARATOR. This turns the string into Animals/Person on Unix machines (and Animals\Person on Windows).

Next, a *.php* extension is appended, and then the file *Animals/Person.php* is included for use.

While using __autoload( ) slightly increases processing time during the addition of a class, it is called only once per class. Multiple instances of the same class does not result in multiple calls to __autoload( ).

Before deploying __autoload( ), be sure to benchmark that the overhead of opening, reading, and closing the multiple files necessary isn't actually more of a performance penalty than the additional parsing time of the unused classes.

In particular if you're using an opcode cache, such as APC or Zend Accelerator, using __autoload( ) and include_once can hurt performance. For best results, you should include all your files at the top of the script and make sure you don't reinclude a file twice.

See Also

Documentation on autoloading is available at *http://www.php.net/manual/language.oop5.autoload.php*.

7.22 Instantiating an Object Dynamically

Problem

You want to instantiate an object, but you don't know the name of the class until your code is executed. For example, you want to localize your site by creating an object belonging to a specific language. However, until the page is requested, you don't know which language to select.

Solution

Use a variable for your class name:

```
$language = $_REQUEST['language'];
$valid_langs = array('en_US' => 'US English',
                     'en_UK' => 'British English',
                     'es_US' => 'US Spanish',
                     'fr_CA' => 'Canadian French');

if (isset($valid_langs[$language]) && class_exists($language)) {
    $lang = new $language;
}
```

Discussion

Sometimes you may not know the class name you want to instantiate at runtime, but you know part of it. For instance, to provide your class hierarchy a pseudonamespace, you may prefix a leading series of characters in front of all class names; this is why we often use pc_ to represent *PHP Cookbook* or PEAR uses Net_ before all networking classes.

However, while this is legal PHP:

```php
$class_name = 'Net_Ping';
$class = new $class_name;                // new Net_Ping
```

This is not:

```php
$partial_class_name = 'Ping';
$class = new "Net_$partial_class_name"; // new Net_Ping
```

This, however, is okay:

```php
$partial_class_name = 'Ping';
$class_prefix = 'Net_';

$class_name = "$class_prefix$partial_class_name";
$class = new $class_name;                // new Net_Ping
```

So you can't instantiate an object when its class name is defined using variable concatenation in the same step. However, because you can use simple variable names, the solution is to preconcatenate the class name.

See Also

Documentation on class_exists( ) at *http://www.php.net/class-exists*.

7.23 Program: whereis

While tools such as phpDocumentor provide quite detailed information about an entire series of classes, it can be useful to get a quick dump that lists all the functions and methods defined in a list of files.

The program in Example 7-42 loops through a list of files, includes them, and then uses the Reflection classes to gather information about them. Once the master list is compiled, the functions and methods are sorted alphabetically and printed out.

Example 7-42. whereis

```php
<?php
if ($argc < 2) {
    print "$argv[0]: classes1.php [, ...]\n";
    exit;
}

// Include the files
foreach (array_slice($argv, 1) as $filename) {
    include_once $filename;
}

// Get all the method and function information
// Start with the classes
$methods = array();
```

```php
foreach (get_declared_classes() as $class) {
    $r = new ReflectionClass($class);
    // Eliminate built-in classes
    if ($r->isUserDefined()) {
        foreach ($r->getMethods() as $method) {
            // Eliminate inherited methods
            if ($method->getDeclaringClass()->getName() == $class) {
                $signature = "$class::" . $method->getName();
                $methods[$signature] = $method;
            }
        }
    }
}

// Then add the functions
$functions = array();
$defined_functions = get_defined_functions();
foreach ($defined_functions['user'] as $function) {
    $functions[$function] = new ReflectionFunction($function);
}

// Sort methods alphabetically by class
function sort_methods($a, $b) {
    list ($a_class, $a_method) = explode('::', $a);
    list ($b_class, $b_method) = explode('::', $b);

    if ($cmp = strcasecmp($a_class, $b_class)) {
        return $cmp;
    }

    return strcasecmp($a_method, $b_method);
}
uksort($methods, 'sort_methods');

// Sort functions alphabetically
// This is less complicated, but don't forget to
// remove the method sorting function from the list
unset($functions['sort_methods']);
// Sort 'em
ksort($functions);

// Print out information
foreach (array_merge($functions, $methods) as $name => $reflect) {
    $file = $reflect->getFileName();
    $line = $reflect->getStartLine();

    printf ("%-25s | %-40s | %6d\n", "$name()", $file, $line);
}
?>
```

This code uses both the Reflection classes and also a couple of PHP functions, get_declared_classes( ) and get_declared_functions( ), that aren't part of the Reflection classes, but help with introspection.

It's important to filter out any built-in PHP classes and functions; otherwise, the report will be less about your code and more about your PHP installation. This is handled in two different ways. Since `get_declared_classes( )` doesn't distinguish between user and internal classes, the code calls `ReflectionClass::isUserDefined( )` to check. The `get_defined_function( )` call, on the other hand, actually computes this for you, putting the information in the `user` array element.

Since it's easier to scan the output of a sorted list, the script sorts the arrays of methods and functions. Since multiple classes can have the same method, you need to use a user-defined sorting method, `sort_methods( )`, which first compares two methods by their class names and then by their method names.

Once the data is sorted, it's a relatively easy task to loop though the merged arrays, gather up the filename and starting line numbers, and print out a report.

Here's the results of running the PEAR `HTTP` class through the script:

```
HTTP::Date()               | /usr/lib/php/HTTP.php    |    38
HTTP::head()               | /usr/lib/php/HTTP.php    |   144
HTTP::negotiateLanguage()  | /usr/lib/php/HTTP.php    |    77
HTTP::redirect()           | /usr/lib/php/HTTP.php    |   186
```

Web Basics

8.0 Introduction

Web programming is probably why you're reading this book. It's why the first version of PHP was written and what continues to make it so popular today. With PHP, it's easy to write dynamic web programs that do almost anything. Other chapters cover various PHP capabilities, like graphics, regular expressions, database access, and file I/O. These capabilities are all part of web programming, but this chapter focuses on some web-specific concepts and organizational topics that will make your web programming stronger.

Recipes 8.1, 8.2, and 8.3 show how to set, read, and delete cookies. A cookie is a small text string that the server instructs the browser to send along with requests the browser makes. Normally, HTTP requests aren't "stateful"; each request can't be connected to a previous one. A cookie, however, can link different requests by the same user. This makes it easier to build features such as shopping carts or to keep track of a user's search history.

Recipe 8.4 shows how to redirect users to a different web page than the one they requested. Discovering the features of a user's browser is shown in Recipe 8.5. Recipe 8.6 shows the details of constructing a URL that includes a get query string, including proper encoding of special characters and handling of HTML entities. Similarly, Recipe 8.7 provides information on reading the data submitted in the body of a post request. Recipe 8.8 discusses a common web formatting need: displaying rows of an HTML table such that alternating rows have different colors or styles.

The next three recipes demonstrate how to use authentication, which lets you protect your web pages with passwords. PHP's special features for dealing with HTTP Basic authentication are explained in Recipe 8.9. Sometimes it's a better idea to roll your own authentication method using cookies, as shown in Recipe 8.10.

The three following recipes deal with output control. Recipe 8.11 shows how to force output to be sent to the browser. Recipe 8.12 explains the output buffering functions. Output buffers enable you to capture output that would otherwise be printed or delay output until an entire page is processed. Automatic compression of output is shown in Recipe 8.13.

The next two recipes show how to interact with external variables: environment variables and PHP configuration settings. Recipes 8.14 and 8.15 discuss environment variables. If Apache is your web server, you can use the techniques in Recipe 8.16 to communicate with other Apache modules from within your PHP programs.

This chapter also includes two programs that demonstrate some of the concepts in the recipes. Recipe 8.17 validates user accounts by sending an email message with a customized link to each new user. If the user doesn't visit the link within a week of receiving the message, the account is deleted. Recipe 8.18 is a small example of a Wiki—a system that makes any page on your web site editable from within the web browser.

8.1 Setting Cookies

Problem

You want to set a cookie so that your web site can recognize subsequent requests from the same web browser.

Solution

Call setcookie( ) with a cookie name and value, as in Example 8-1.

Example 8-1. Setting a cookie

```
<?php
setcookie('flavor','chocolate chip');
?>
```

Discussion

Cookies are sent with the HTTP headers, so if you're not using output buffering, setcookie( ) must be called before any output is generated.

Pass additional arguments to setcookie( ) to control cookie behavior. The third argument to setcookie( ) is an expiration time, expressed as an epoch timestamp. For example, the cookie set in Example 8-2 expires at noon GMT on December 3, 2004.

Example 8-2. Setting an expiring cookie

```
<?php
setcookie('flavor','chocolate chip',1259841600);
?>
```

If the third argument to setcookie( ) is missing (or empty), the cookie expires when the browser is closed. Also, many systems can't handle a cookie expiration time greater than 2147483647, because that's the largest epoch timestamp that fits in a 32-bit integer, as discussed in the introduction to Chapter 3.

The fourth argument to setcookie( ) is a path. The cookie is sent back to the server only when pages whose path begin with the specified string are requested. For example, the cookie set in Example 8-3 is sent back only to pages whose path begins with */products/*.

Example 8-3. Setting a cookie with a path restriction

```
<?php
setcookie('flavor','chocolate chip','','/products/');
?>
```

The page that's setting the cookie in Example 8-3 doesn't have to have a URL whose path component begins with */products/*, but the cookie is sent back only to pages that do.

The fifth argument to setcookie( ) is a domain. The cookie is sent back to the server only when pages whose hostname ends with the specified domain are requested. For example, the first cookie in Example 8-4 is sent back to all hosts in the *example.com* domain, but the second cookie is sent only with requests to the host *jeannie.example.com*.

Example 8-4. Setting a cookie with a domain restriction

```
<?php
setcookie('flavor','chocolate chip','','','.example.com');
setcookie('flavor','chocolate chip','','','jeannie.example.com');
?>
```

If the first cookie's domain was just *example.com* instead of *.example.com*, it would be sent only to the single host *example.com* (and not *www.example.com* or *jeannie.example.com*). If a domain is not specified when setcookie( ) is called, then the browser sends back the cookie only with requests to the same hostname as the request in which the cookie was set.

The last optional argument to setcookie( ) is a flag that, if set to true, instructs the browser only to send the cookie over an SSL connection. This can be useful if the cookie contains sensitive information, but remember that the data in the cookie is stored as unencrypted plain text on the user's computer.

Different browsers handle cookies in slightly different ways, especially with regard to how strictly they match path and domain strings and how they determine priority between different cookies of the same name. The setcookie( ) page of the online manual has helpful clarifications of these differences.

See Also

Recipe 8.2 shows how to read cookie values; Recipe 8.3 shows how to delete cookies; Recipe 8.12 explains output buffering; documentation on setcookie( ) at *http://*

www.php.net/setcookie; an expanded cookie specification is detailed in RFC 2965 at
http://www.faqs.org/rfcs/rfc2965.html.

8.2 Reading Cookie Values

Problem

You want to read the value of a cookie that you've previously set.

Solution

Look in the `$_COOKIE` auto-global array, as shown in Example 8-5.

Example 8-5. Reading a cookie value

```php
<?php
if (isset($_COOKIE['flavor'])) {
    print "You ate a {$_COOKIE['flavor']} cookie.";
}
?>
```

Discussion

A cookie's value isn't available in `$_COOKIE` during the request in which the cookie is set. In other words, the `setcookie( )` function doesn't alter the value of `$_COOKIE`. On subsequent requests, however, each cookie sent back to the server is stored in `$_COOKIE`. If `register_globals` is on, cookie values are also assigned to global variables.

When a browser sends a cookie back to the server, it sends only the value. You can't access the cookie's domain, path, expiration time, or secure status through `$_COOKIE` because the browser doesn't send that to the server.

To print the names and values of all cookies sent in a particular request, loop through the `$_COOKIE` array, as in Example 8-6.

Example 8-6. Reading all cookie values

```php
<?php
foreach ($_COOKIE as $cookie_name => $cookie_value) {
    print "$cookie_name = $cookie_value <br/>";
}
?>
```

See Also

Recipe 8.1 shows how to set cookies; Recipe 8.3 shows how to delete cookies; Recipe 8.12 explains output buffering; Recipe 9.15 for information on `register_globals`.

8.3 Deleting Cookies

Problem

You want to delete a cookie so a browser doesn't send it back to the server. For example, you're using cookies to track whether a user is logged in to your web site, and a user logs out.

Solution

Call `setcookie( )` with no value for the cookie and an expiration time in the past, as in Example 8-7.

Example 8-7. Deleting a cookie

```
<?php
setcookie('flavor','',1);
?>
```

Discussion

It's a good idea to make the expiration time a long time in the past, in case your server and the user's computer have unsynchronized clocks. For example, if your server thinks it's 3:06 P.M. and a user's computer thinks it's 3:02 P.M., a cookie with an expiration time of 3:05 P.M. isn't deleted by that user's computer even though the time is in the past for the server.

The call to `setcookie( )` that deletes a cookie has to have the same arguments (except for value and time) that the call to `setcookie( )` that set the cookie did, so include the path, domain, and secure flag if necessary.

See Also

Recipe 8.1 shows how to set cookies; Recipe 8.2 shows how to read cookie values; Recipe 8.12 explains output buffering; documentation on `setcookie( )` at *http://www.php.net/setcookie*.

8.4 Redirecting to a Different Location

Problem

You want to automatically send a user to a new URL. For example, after successfully saving form data, you want to redirect a user to a page that confirms that the data has been saved.

Solution

Before any output is printed, use header( ) to send a Location header with the new URL, and then call exit( ) so that nothing else is printed. Example 8-8 shows how to do this.

Example 8-8. Redirecting to a different location

```php
<?php
header('Location: http://www.example.com/confirm.html');
exit();
?>
```

Discussion

If you want to pass variables to the new page, you can include them in the query string of the URL, as in Example 8-9.

Example 8-9. Redirecting with query string variables

```php
<?php
header('Location: http://www.example.com/?monkey=turtle');
exit();
?>
```

Redirect URLs should include the protocol and hostname. They shouldn't be just a pathname. Example 8-10 shows a good Location header and a bad one.

Example 8-10. Good and bad Location headers

```php
<?php
// Good Redirect
header('Location: http://www.example.com/catalog/food/pemmican.php');

// Bad Redirect
header('Location: /catalog/food/pemmican.php');
?>
```

The URL that you are redirecting a user to is retrieved with get. You can't redirect someone to retrieve a URL via post. With JavaScript, however, you can simulate a redirect via post by generating a form that gets submitted (via post) automatically. When a (JavaScript-enabled) browser receives the page in Example 8-11, it will immediately post the form that is included.

Example 8-11. Redirecting via a posted form

```html
<html>
  <body onload="document.getElementById('redirectForm').submit()">
    <form id='redirectForm' method='POST' action='/done.html'>
      <input type='hidden' name='status' value='complete'/>
      <input type='hidden' name='id' value='Ou812'/>
      <input type='submit' value='Please Click Here To Continue'/>
    </form>
  </body>
</html>
```

The form in Example 8-11 has an `id` of `redirectForm`, so the code in the `<body/>` element's `onload` attribute submits the form. The `onload` action does not execute if the browser has JavaScript disabled. In that situation, the user sees a `Please Click Here To Con tinue` button.

See Also

Documentation on `header( )` at *http://www.php.net/header*.

8.5 Detecting Different Browsers

Problem

You want to generate content based on the capabilities of a user's browser.

Solution

Use the object returned by `get_browser( )` to determine a browser's capabilities, as shown in Example 8-12.

Example 8-12. Getting browser information

```php
<?php
$browser = get_browser();
if ($browser->frames) {
    // print out a frame-based layout
} elseif ($browser->tables) {
    // print out a table-based layout
} else {
    // print out a boring layout
}
?>
```

Discussion

The `get_browser( )` function examines the environment variable (set by the web server) and compares it to browsers listed in an external browser capability file. Due to licensing issues, PHP isn't distributed with a browser capability file. The "Obtaining PHP" section of the PHP FAQ (*http://www.php.net/faq.obtaining*) lists *http://www.garykeith.com/browsers/downloads.asp* as a source for a browser capability file. Download the *php_browscap.ini* file from that site.

Once you download a browser capability file, you need to tell PHP where to find it by setting the `browscap` configuration directive to the pathname of the file. If you use PHP as a CGI, set the directive in the *php.ini* file, as in Example 8-13.

Example 8-13. Setting browscap in php.ini

```
browscap=/usr/local/lib/php_browscap.ini
```

Many of the capabilities get_browser( ) finds are shown in Table 8-1. For user-configurable capabilities such as javascript or cookies, though, get_browser( ) just tells you if the browser can support those functions. It doesn't tell you if the user has disabled the functions. If JavaScript is turned off in a JavaScript-capable browser or a user refuses to accept cookies when the browser prompts him, get_browser( ) still indicates that the browser supports those functions.

Table 8-1. Browser capability object properties

Property	Description
platform	Operating system the browser is running on (e.g., Windows, Macintosh, Unix, Win32, Linux, MacPPC)
version	Full browser version (e.g., 5.0, 3.5, 6.0b2)
majorver	Major browser version (e.g., 5, 3, 6)
minorver	Minor browser version (e.g., 0, 5, 02)
frames	1 if the browser supports frames
tables	1 if the browser supports tables
cookies	1 if the browser supports cookies
backgroundsounds	1 if the browser supports background sounds with <embed> or <bgsound>
vbscript	1 if the browser supports VBScript
javascript	1 if the browser supports JavaScript
javaapplets	1 if the browser can run Java applets
activexcontrols	1 if the browser can run ActiveX controls

See Also

Documentation on get_browser( ) at *http://www.php.net/get-browser*.

8.6 Building a Query String

Problem

You need to construct a link that includes name/value pairs in a query string.

Solution

Use the http_build_query( ) function, as in Example 8-14.

Example 8-14. Building a query string

```php
<?php
$vars = array('name' => 'Oscar the Grouch',
              'color' => 'green',
              'favorite_punctuation' => '#');
$query_string = http_build_query($vars);
```

```
$url = '/muppet/select.php?' . $query_string;
?>
```

Discussion

The URL built in Example 8-14 is:

```
/muppet/select.php?name=Oscar+the+Grouch&color=green&favorite_punctuation=%23
```

The query string has spaces encoded as +. Special characters such as # are hex encoded as %23 because the ASCII value of # is 35, which is 23 in hexadecimal.

Although the encoding that `http_build_query( )` does prevents any special characters in the variable names or values from disrupting the constructed URL, you may have problems if your variable names begin with the names of HTML entities. Consider this partial URL for retrieving information about a stereo system:

```
/stereo.php?speakers=12&cdplayer=52&amp=10
```

The HTML entity for ampersand (&) is & so a browser may interpret that URL as:

```
/stereo.php?speakers=12&cdplayer=52&=10
```

To prevent embedded entities from corrupting your URLs, you have three choices. The first is to choose variable names that can't be confused with entities, such as _amp instead of amp. The second is to convert characters with HTML entity equivalents to those entities before printing out the URL. Use `htmlentities( )`:

```
$url = '/muppet/select.php?' . htmlentities($query_string);
```

The resulting URL is:

```
/muppet/select.php?name=Oscar+the+Grouch&amp;color=green&amp;favorite_punctuation=%23
```

Your third choice is to change the argument separator from & to & by setting the configuration directive `arg_separator.input` to &. Then, `http_build_query( )` joins the different name=value pairs with &:

```
/muppet/select.php?name=Oscar+the+Grouch&amp;color=green&amp;favorite_punctuation=%23
```

See Also

Documentation on `http_build_query( )` at *http://www.php.net/http_build_query* and `htmlentities( )` at *http://www.php.net/htmlentities*.

8.7 Reading the Post Request Body

Problem

You want direct access to the body of a post request, not just the parsed data that PHP puts in $_POST for you. For example, you want to handle an XML document that's been posted as part of a web services request.

Solution

Read from the `php://input` stream, as in Example 8-15.

Example 8-15. Reading the post request body

```php
<?php
$body = file_get_contents('php://input');
?>
```

Discussion

The auto-global array `$_POST` is great when you just need access to submitted form variables, but it doesn't cut it when you need raw, uncut access to the whole request body. That's where the `php://input` stream comes in. Read the entire thing with `file_get_contents()`, or if you're expecting a large request body, read it in chunks with `fread()`.

If the configuration directive `always_populate_raw_post_data` is on, then raw post data is also put into the global variable `$HTTP_RAW_POST_DATA`. But to write maximally portable code, you should use `php://input` instead—that works even when `always_populate_raw_post_data` is turned off.

See Also

Documentation on `php://input` at *http://www.php.net/wrappers* and on `always_populate_raw_post_data` at *http://www.php.net/ini.core#ini.always-populate-raw-post-data*.

8.8 Generating HTML Tables with Alternating Row Styles

Problem

You want to display a table of information with alternating rows having different visual appearance. For example, you want to have even-numbered rows in a table have a white background and odd-numbered rows have a gray background.

Solution

Switch back and forth between two CSS styles as you generate the HTML for the table. Example 8-16 uses this technique with data retrieved from a database.

Example 8-16. Generating an HTML table with alternating row styles

```css
<style type="text/css">
.even-row {
    background: white;
}
.odd-row {
    background: gray;
```

```
  }
  </style>
  <table>
  <tr><th>Quantity</th><th>Ingredient</th></tr>
  <?php
  $styles = array('even-row','odd-row');
  $db = new PDO('sqlite:altrow.db');
  foreach ($db->query('SELECT quantity, ingredient FROM ingredients') as $i => $row) { ?>
  <tr class="<?php echo $styles[$i % 2]; ?>">
    <td><?php echo htmlentities($row['quantity']) ?></td>
    <td><?php echo htmlentities($row['ingredient']) ?></td></tr>
  <?php } ?>
  </table>
```

Discussion

The key to the concise code in Example 8-16 is the array of CSS class names in $styles and the use of %, PHP's "remainder" operator. The remainder operator returns the remainder after dividing two numbers. The remainder when dividing something by two (in this case, the row number in the result set—$i) is either 0 or 1. This provides a handy way to alternate between the first and second elements of the $styles array.

See Also

Documentation on PHP's arithmetic operators at *http://www.php.net/ language.operators.arithmetic.*

8.9 Using HTTP Basic or Digest Authentication

Problem

You want to use PHP to protect parts of your web site with passwords. Instead of storing the passwords in an external file and letting the web server handle the authentication, you want the password verification logic to be in a PHP program.

Solution

The $_SERVER['PHP_AUTH_USER'] and $_SERVER['PHP_AUTH_PW'] global variables contain the username and password supplied by the user, if any. To deny access to a page, send a WWW-Authenticate header identifying the authentication realm as part of a response with status code 401, as shown in Example 8-17.

Example 8-17. Enforcing Basic authentication

```
<?php
header('WWW-Authenticate: Basic realm="My Website"');
header('HTTP/1.0 401 Unauthorized');
echo "You need to enter a valid username and password.";
exit();
?>
```

Discussion

When a browser sees a 401 header, it pops up a dialog box for a username and password. Those authentication credentials (the username and password), if accepted by the server, are associated with the realm in the WWW-Authenticate header. Code that checks authentication credentials needs to be executed before any output is sent to the browser, since it might send headers. For example, you can use a function such as pc_validate( ), shown in Example 8-18.

Example 8-18. pc_validate( )

```php
<?php
function pc_validate($user,$pass) {
    /* replace with appropriate username and password checking,
       such as checking a database */
    $users = array('david' => 'fadj&32',
                   'adam'  => '8HEj838');

    if (isset($users[$user]) && ($users[$user] == $pass)) {
        return true;
    } else {
        return false;
    }
}
?>
```

Example 8-19 shows how to use pc_validate( ).

Example 8-19. Using a validation function

```php
<?php
if (! pc_validate($_SERVER['PHP_AUTH_USER'], $_SERVER['PHP_AUTH_PW'])) {
    header('WWW-Authenticate: Basic realm="My Website"');
    header('HTTP/1.0 401 Unauthorized');
    echo "You need to enter a valid username and password.";
    exit;
}
?>
```

Replace the contents of the pc_validate( ) function with appropriate logic to determine if a user entered the correct password. You can also change the realm string from "My Website" and the message that gets printed if a user hits "cancel" in her browser's authentication box from "You need to enter a valid username and password."

PHP 5.1.0 and later support Digest authentication in addition to Basic authentication. With Basic authentication, usernames and passwords are sent in the clear on the network, just minimally obscured by Base64 encoding. With Digest authentication, however, the password itself is never sent from the browser to the server. Instead, only a hash of the password with some other values is sent. This reduces the possibility that the network traffic could be captured and replayed by an attacker. The increased security provided by Digest authentication means that the code to implement is more

complicated than just a simple password comparison. Example 8-20 provides functions
that compute digest authentication as specified in RFC 2617.

Example 8-20. Using Digest authentication

```php
<?php

/* replace with appropriate username and password checking,
    such as checking a database */
$users = array('david' => 'fadj&32',
               'adam'  => '8HEj838');
$realm = 'My website';

$username = pc_validate_digest($realm, $users);

// Execution never reaches this point if invalid auth data is provided
print "Hello, " . htmlentities($username);

function pc_validate_digest($realm, $users) {
    // Fail if no digest has been provided by the client
    if (! isset($_SERVER['PHP_AUTH_DIGEST'])) {
        pc_send_digest($realm);
    }
    // Fail if digest can't be parsed
    $username = pc_parse_digest($_SERVER['PHP_AUTH_DIGEST'], $realm, $users);
    if ($username === false) {
        pc_send_digest($realm);
    }
    // Valid username was specified in the digest
    return $username;
}

function pc_send_digest($realm) {
    header('HTTP/1.0 401 Unauthorized');
    $nonce = md5(uniqid());
    $opaque = md5($realm);
    header("WWW-Authenticate: Digest realm=\"$realm\" qop=\"auth\" ".
           "nonce=\"$nonce\" opaque=\"$opaque\"");
    echo "You need to enter a valid username and password.";
    exit;
}

function pc_parse_digest($digest, $realm, $users) {
    // We need to find the following values in the digest header:
    // username, uri, qop, cnonce, nc, and response
    $digest_info = array();
    foreach (array('username','uri','nonce','cnonce','response') as $part) {
        // Delimiter can either be ' or " or nothing (for qop and nc)
        if (preg_match('/'.$part.'=([\'"]?)(.*?)\1/', $digest, $match)) {
            // The part was found, save it for calculation
            $digest_info[$part] = $match[2];
        } else {
            // If the part is missing, the digest can't be validated;
            return false;
        }
    }
```

```
        // Make sure the right qop has been provided
        if (preg_match('/qop=auth(,|$)/', $digest)) {
            $digest_info['qop'] = 'auth';
        } else {
            return false;
        }
        // Make sure a valid nonce count has been provided
        if (preg_match('/nc=([0-9a-f]{8})(,|$)/', $digest, $match)) {
            $digest_info['nc'] = $match[1];
        } else {
            return false;
        }

        // Now that all the necessary values have been slurped out of the
        // digest header, do the algorithmic computations necessary to
        // make sure that the right information was provided.
        //
        // These calculations are described in sections 3.2.2, 3.2.2.1,
        // and 3.2.2.2 of RFC 2617.
        // Algorithm is MD5
        $A1 = $digest_info['username'] . ':' . $realm . ':' . $users[$digest_info['username']];
        // qop is 'auth'
        $A2 = $_SERVER['REQUEST_METHOD'] . ':' . $digest_info['uri'];
        $request_digest = md5(implode(':', array(md5($A1), $digest_info['nonce'], $digest_info['nc'],
        $digest_info['cnonce'], $digest_info['qop'], md5($A2))));

        // Did what was sent match what we computed?
        if ($request_digest != $digest_info['response']) {
            return false;
        }

        // Everything's OK, return the username
        return $digest_info['username'];
    }
?>
```

If you're not using PHP 5.1.0 or later but are using PHP as an Apache module, you can use Digest authentication with code such as the HTTPDigest class by Paul James, which is available at *http://www.peej.co.uk/projects/phphttpdigest.html*.

Neither HTTP Basic nor Digest authentication can be used if you're running PHP as a CGI program. If you can't run PHP as a server module, you can use cookie authentication, discussed in Recipe 8.10.

Another issue with HTTP authentication is that it provides no simple way for a user to log out, other than to exit his browser. The PHP online manual has a few suggestions for log out methods that work with varying degrees of success with different server and browser combinations at *http://www.php.net/features.http-auth*.

There is a straightforward way, however, to force a user to log out after a fixed time interval: include a time calculation in the realm string. Browsers use the same username and password combination every time they're asked for credentials in the same realm.

By changing the realm name, the browser is forced to ask the user for new credentials. Example 8-21 uses Basic authentication and forces a log out every night at midnight.

Example 8-21. Forcing logout with Basic authentication

```php
<?php
if (! pc_validate($_SERVER['PHP_AUTH_USER'],$_SERVER['PHP_AUTH_PW'])) {
    $realm = 'My Website for '.date('Y-m-d');
    header('WWW-Authenticate: Basic realm="'.$realm.'"');
    header('HTTP/1.0 401 Unauthorized');
    echo "You need to enter a valid username and password.";
    exit;
}
?>
```

You can also have a user-specific timeout without changing the realm name by storing the time that a user logs in or accesses a protected page. The `pc_validate2( )` function in Example 8-22 stores login time in a database and forces a logout if it's been more than 15 minutes since the user last requested a protected page.

Example 8-22. pc_validate2( )

```php
<?php
function pc_validate2($user,$pass) {
    $safe_user = strtr(addslashes($user),array('_' => '\_', '%' => '\%'));
    $r = mysql_query("SELECT password,last_access
                      FROM users WHERE user LIKE '$safe_user'");

    if (mysql_numrows($r) == 1) {
        $ob = mysql_fetch_object($r);
        if ($ob->password == $pass) {
            $now = time();
            if (($now - $ob->last_access) > (15 * 60)) {
                return false;
            } else {
                // update the last access time
                mysql_query("UPDATE users SET last_access = NOW()
                             WHERE user LIKE '$safe_user'");
                return true;
            }
        }
    } else {
        return false;
    }
}
```

See Also

Recipe 8.10; the HTTP Authentication section of the PHP online manual at *http://www.php.net/features.http-auth*.

8.10 Using Cookie Authentication

Problem

You want more control over the user login procedure, such as presenting your own login form.

Solution

Store authentication status in a cookie or as part of a session. When a user logs in successfully, put her username in a cookie. Also include a hash of the username and a secret word so a user can't just make up an authentication cookie with a username in it, as shown in Example 8-23.

Example 8-23. Using cookie authentication

```php
<?php
$secret_word = 'if i ate spinach';
if (pc_validate($_POST['username'],$_POST['password'])) {
    setcookie('login',
              $_POST['username'].','.md5($_POST['username'].$secret_word));
}
?>
```

Discussion

When using cookie authentication, you have to display your own login form, such as the form in Example 8-24.

Example 8-24. Sample cookie authentication login form

```html
<form method="POST" action="login.php">
Username: <input type="text" name="username"> <br>
Password: <input type="password" name="password"> <br>
<input type="submit" value="Log In">
</form>
```

You can use the same pc_validate( ) function from Example 8-18 to verify the username and password. The only difference is that you pass it $_POST['username'] and $_POST['password'] as the credentials instead of $_SERVER['PHP_AUTH_USER'] and $_SERVER['PHP_AUTH_PW']. If the password checks out, send back a cookie that contains a username and a hash of the username, and a secret word. The hash prevents a user from faking a login just by sending a cookie with a username in it.

Once the user has logged in, a page just needs to verify that a valid login cookie was sent in order to do special things for that logged-in user. Example 8-25 shows one way to do this.

Example 8-25. Verifying a login cookie

```php
<?php
unset($username);
```

```
if ($_COOKIE['login']) {
    list($c_username,$cookie_hash) = split(',',$_COOKIE['login']);
    if (md5($c_username.$secret_word) == $cookie_hash) {
        $username = $c_username;
    } else {
        print "You have sent a bad cookie.";
    }
}

if ($username) {
    print "Welcome, $username.";
} else {
    print "Welcome, anonymous user.";
}
?>
```

If you use the built-in session support, you can add the username and hash to the session and avoid sending a separate cookie. When someone logs in, set an additional variable in the session instead of sending a cookie, as shown in Example 8-26.

Example 8-26. Storing login info in a session
```
<?php
if (pc_validate($_POST['username'],$_POST['password'])) {
    $_SESSION['login'] =
        $_POST['username'].','.md5($_POST['username'].$secret_word));
}
?>
```

The verification code, shown in Example 8-27, is almost the same; it just uses $_SESSION instead of $_COOKIE.

Example 8-27. Verifying session info
```
<?php
unset($username);
if (isset($_SESSION['login'])) {
    list($c_username,$cookie_hash) = explode(',',$_SESSION['login']);
    if (md5($c_username.$secret_word) == $cookie_hash) {
        $username = $c_username;
    } else {
        print "You have tampered with your session.";
    }
}
?>
```

Using cookie or session authentication instead of HTTP Basic authentication makes it much easier for users to log out: you just delete their login cookie or remove the login variable from their session. Another advantage of storing authentication information in a session is that you can link users' browsing activities while logged in to their browsing activities before they log in or after they log out. With HTTP Basic authentication, you have no way of tying the requests with a username to the requests that the same user made before they supplied a username. Looking for requests from the same IP address is error prone, especially if the user is behind a firewall or proxy server. If you are using sessions, you can modify the login procedure to log the connection between session ID and username using code such as that in Example 8-28.

Example 8-28. Connecting logged-out and logged-in usage

```php
<?php
if (pc_validate($_POST['username'],$_POST['password'])) {
    $_SESSION['login'] =
        $_POST['username'].','.md5($_POST['username'].$secret_word));
    error_log('Session id '.session_id().' log in as '.$_REQUEST['username']);
}
```

Example 8-28 writes a message to the error log, but it could just as easily record the information in a database that you could use in your analysis of site usage and traffic.

One danger of using session IDs is that sessions are hijackable. If Alice guesses Bob's session ID, she can masquerade as Bob to the web server. The session module has two optional configuration directives that help you make session IDs harder to guess. The `session.entropy_file` directive contains a path to a device or file that generates randomness, such as */dev/random* or */dev/urandom*. The `session.entropy_length` directive holds the number of bytes to be read from the entropy file when creating session IDs.

No matter how hard session IDs are to guess, they can also be stolen if they are sent in clear text between your server and a user's browser. HTTP Basic authentication also has this problem. Use SSL to guard against network sniffing, as described in Recipe 18.13.

See Also

Recipe 8.9; Recipe 20.9 discusses logging errors; Recipe 18.9 discusses verifying data with hashes; documentation on `setcookie()` at *http://www.php.net/setcookie* and on `md5()` at *http://www.php.net/md5*.

8.11 Flushing Output to the Browser

Problem

You want to force output to be sent to the browser. For example, before doing a slow database query, you want to give the user a status update.

Solution

Use `flush()`, as in Example 8-29.

Example 8-29. Flushing output to the browser

```php
<?php
print 'Finding identical snowflakes...';
flush();
```

```
$sth = $dbh->query(
    'SELECT shape,COUNT(*) AS c FROM snowflakes GROUP BY shape HAVING c > 1');
?>
```

Discussion

The flush( ) function sends all output that PHP has internally buffered to the web server, but the web server may have internal buffering of its own that delays when the data reaches the browser. Additionally, some browsers don't display data immediately upon receiving it, and some versions of Internet Explorer don't display a page until it has received at least 256 bytes. To force IE to display content, print blank spaces at the beginning of the page, as shown in Example 8-30.

Example 8-30. Forcing IE to display content immediately

```
<?php
print str_repeat(' ',300);
print 'Finding identical snowflakes...';
flush();
$sth = $dbh->query(
    'SELECT shape,COUNT(*) AS c FROM snowflakes GROUP BY shape HAVING c > 1');
?>
```

See Also

Recipe 23.13; documentation on flush( ) at *http://www.php.net/flush*.

8.12 Buffering Output to the Browser

Problem

You want to start generating output before you're finished sending headers or cookies.

Solution

Call ob_start( ) at the top of your page and ob_end_flush( ) at the bottom. You can then intermix commands that generate output and commands that send headers. The output won't be sent until ob_end_flush( ) is called. This is demonstrated in Example 8-31.

Example 8-31. Buffering output

```
<?php ob_start(); ?>

I haven't decided if I want to send a cookie yet.

<?php setcookie('heron','great blue'); ?>

Yes, sending that cookie was the right decision.

<?php ob_end_flush(); ?>
```

Discussion

You can pass ob_start( ) the name of a callback function to process the output buffer with that function. This is useful for postprocessing all the content in a page, such as hiding email addresses from address-harvesting robots. Such a callback is shown in Example 8-32.

Example 8-32. Using a callback with ob_start( )

```php
<?php
function mangle_email($s) {
    return preg_replace('/([^@\s]+)@([-a-z0-9]+\.)+[a-z]{2,}/is',
                        '<$1@...>',
                        $s);
}

ob_start('mangle_email');
?>

I would not like spam sent to ronald@example.com!

<?php ob_end_flush(); ?>
```

The mangle_email( ) function transforms the output to:

```
I would not like spam sent to <ronald@...>!
```

The output_buffering configuration directive turns output buffering on for all pages:

```
output_buffering = On
```

Similarly, output_handler sets an output buffer processing callback to be used on all pages:

```
output_handler=mangle_email
```

Setting an output_handler automatically sets output_buffering to on.

See Also

Documentation on ob_start( ) at *http://www.php.net/ob-start*, ob_end_flush( ) at *http://www.php.net/ob-end-flush*, and output buffering at *http://www.php.net/outcontrol*.

8.13 Compressing Web Output

Problem

You want to send compressed content to browsers that support automatic decompression.

Solution

Add this setting to your *php.ini* file:

```
zlib.output_compression=1
```

Discussion

Browsers tell the server that they can accept compressed responses with the `Accept-Encoding` header. If a browser sends `Accept-Encoding: gzip` or `Accept-Encoding: deflate`, and PHP is built with the *zlib* extension, the `zlib.output_compression` configuration directive tells PHP to compress the output with the appropriate algorithm before sending it back to the browser. The browser uncompresses the data before displaying it.

You can adjust the compression level with the `zlib.output_compression_level` configuration directive:

```
; minimal compression
zlib.output_compression_level=1

; maximal compression
zlib.output_compression_level=9
```

At higher compression levels, less data needs to be sent from the server to the browser, but more server CPU time must be used to compress the data.

See Also

Documentation on the *zlib* extension at *http://www.php.net/zlib*.

8.14 Reading Environment Variables

Problem

You want to get the value of an environment variable.

Solution

Read the value from the `$_ENV` auto-global array as shown in Example 8-33.

Example 8-33. Reading an environment variable
```
<?php
$name = $_ENV['USER'];
?>
```

Discussion

Environment variables are named values associated with a process. For instance, in Unix, you can check the value of `$_ENV['HOME']` to find the home directory of a user, as shown in Example 8-34.

Example 8-34. Reading another environment variable

```php
<?php
print $_ENV['HOME']; // user's home directory
?>
```

Early versions of PHP automatically created PHP variables for all environment variables by default. As of 4.1.0, *php.ini-recommended* disables this because of speed considerations; however, *php.ini-dist* continues to enable $_ENV for backward compatibility.

The $_ENV array is created only if the value of the variables_order configuration directive contains E. If $_ENV isn't available, use getenv( ) to retrieve an environment variable, as shown in Example 8-35.

Example 8-35. Using getenv( )

```php
<?php
$path = getenv('PATH');
?>
```

The getenv( ) function isn't available if you're running PHP as an ISAPI module.

See Also

Recipe 8.15 on setting environment variables; documentation on getenv( ) at *http://www.php.net/getenv*; information on environment variables in PHP at *http://www.php.net/reserved.variables.php#reserved.variables.environment*.

8.15 Setting Environment Variables

Problem

You want to set an environment variable in a script or in your server configuration. Setting environment variables in your server configuration on a host-by-host basis allows you to configure virtual hosts differently.

Solution

To set an environment variable in a script, use putenv( ), as in Example 8-36.

Example 8-36. Setting an environment variable

```php
<?php
putenv('ORACLE_SID=ORACLE'); // configure oci extension
?>
```

To set an environment variable in your Apache *httpd.conf* file, use SetEnv as shown in Example 8-37. Note that variables set this way show up in the PHP auto-global array $_SERVER, not $_ENV.

Example 8-37. Setting an environment variable in Apache configuration

```php
<?php
SetEnv DATABASE_PASSWORD password
?>
```

Discussion

An advantage of setting variables in *httpd.conf* is that you can set more restrictive read permissions on it than on your PHP scripts. Since PHP files need to be readable by the web server process, this generally allows other users on the system to view them. By storing passwords in *httpd.conf*, you can avoid placing a password in a publicly available file. Also, if you have multiple hostnames that map to the same document root, you can configure your scripts to behave differently based on the hostnames.

For example, you could have *members.example.com* and *guests.example.com*. The members version requires authentication and allows users additional access. The guests version provides a restricted set of options, but without authentication. Example 8-38 shows how this could work.

Example 8-38. Adjusting behavior based on an environment variable

```php
<?php
$version = $_SERVER['SITE_VERSION'];

// redirect to http://guest.example.com, if user fails to sign in correctly
if ('members' == $version) {
    if (!authenticate_user($_POST['username'], $_POST['password'])) {
        header('Location: http://guest.example.com/');
        exit;
    }
}
include_once "${version}_header"; // load custom header
```

See Also

Recipe 8.14 on getting the values of environment variables; documentation on putenv( ) at *http://www.php.net/putenv*; information on setting environment variables in Apache at *http://httpd.apache.org/docs/mod/mod_env.html*.

8.16 Communicating Within Apache

Problem

You want to communicate from PHP to other parts of the Apache request process. This includes setting variables in the *access_log*.

Solution

Use apache_note( ) as shown in Example 8-39.

Example 8-39. Communicating within Apache

```
<?php
// get value
$session = apache_note('session');

// set value
apache_note('session', $session);
?>
```

Discussion

When Apache processes a request from a client, it goes through a series of steps; PHP plays only one part in the entire chain. Apache also remaps URLs, authenticates users, logs requests, and more. While processing a request, each handler has access to a set of key/value pairs called the *notes table*. The `apache_note( )` function provides access to the notes table to retrieve information set by handlers earlier on in the process and leave information for handlers later on.

For example, if you use the session module to track users and preserve variables across requests, you can integrate this with your logfile analysis so you can determine the average number of page views per user. Use `apache_note( )` in combination with the logging module to write the session ID directly to the *access_log* for each request. First, add the session ID to the notes table with the code in Example 8-40.

Example 8-40. Adding the session ID to the notes table

```
<?php
// retrieve the session ID and add it to Apache's notes table
apache_note('session_id', session_id());
?>
```

Then, modify your *httpd.conf* file to add the string `%{session_id}n` to your `LogFormat`. The trailing n tells Apache to use a variable stored in its notes table by another module.

If PHP is built with the `--enable-memory-limit` configuration option, it stores the peak memory usage of each request in a note called `mod_php_memory_usage`. Add the memory usage information to a `LogFormat` with `%{mod_php_memory_usage}n`.

See Also

Documentation on `apache_note( )` at *http://www.php.net/apache-note*; information on logging in Apache at *http://httpd.apache.org/docs/mod/mod_log_config.html*.

8.17 Program: Web Site Account (De)activator

When users sign up for your web site, it's helpful to know that they've provided you with a correct email address. To validate the email address they provide, send an email to the address they supply when they sign up. If they don't visit a special URL included in the email after a few days, deactivate their account.

This system has three parts. The first is the *notify-user.php* program that sends an email to a new user and asks that user to visit a verification URL, shown in Example 8-42. The second, shown in Example 8-43, is the *verify-user.php* page that handles the verification URL and marks users as valid. The third is the *delete-user.php* program that deactivates accounts of users who don't visit the verification URL after a certain amount of time. This program is shown in Example 8-44.

Example 8-41 contains the SQL to create the table in which the user information is stored.

Example 8-41. SQL for user verification table

```
CREATE TABLE users (
  email VARCHAR(255) NOT NULL,
  created_on DATETIME NOT NULL,
  verify_string VARCHAR(16) NOT NULL,
  verified TINYINT UNSIGNED
);
```

What's in Example 8-41 is the minimum amount of information necessary for user verification. You probably want to store more information than this about your users. When creating a user's account, save information to the users table, and send the user an email telling him how to verify his account. The code in Example 8-42 assumes that the user's email address is stored in the variable $email.

Example 8-42. notify-user.php

```php
<?php
// Connect to the database
$db = new PDO('sqlite:users.db');

$email = 'david';

// generate verify_string
$verify_string = '';
for ($i = 0; $i < 16; $i++) {
    $verify_string .= chr(mt_rand(32,126));
}

// insert user into database
// This uses an SQLite-specific datetime() function
$sth = $db->prepare("INSERT INTO users " .
                    "(email, created_on, verify_string, verified) " .
                    "VALUES (?, datetime('now'), ?, 0)");
$sth->execute(array($email, $verify_string));

$verify_string = urlencode($verify_string);
$safe_email = urlencode($email);

$verify_url = "http://www.example.com/verify-user.php";

$mail_body=<<<_MAIL_
To $email:
```

```
Please click on the following link to verify your account creation:

$verify_url?email=$safe_email&verify_string=$verify_string

If you do not verify your account in the next seven days, it will be
deleted.
_MAIL_;

// mail($email,"User Verification",$mail_body);
print "$email, $mail_body";
```

The verification page that users are directed to when they follow the link in the email message updates the users table if the proper information has been provided, as shown in Example 8-43.

Example 8-43. verify-user.php

```php
<?php
// Connect to the database
$db = new PDO('sqlite:users.db');

$sth = $db->prepare('UPDATE users SET verified = 1 WHERE email = ? '.
                    ' AND verify_string = ? AND verified = 0');

$res = $sth->execute(array($_GET['email'], $_GET['verify_string']));
var_dump($res, $sth->rowCount());
if (! $res) {
    print "Please try again later due to a database error.";
} else {
    if ($sth->rowCount() == 1) {
        print "Thank you, your account is verified.";
    } else {
        print "Sorry, you could not be verified.";
    }
}
?>
```

The user's verification status is updated only if the email address and verify string provided match a row in the database that has not already been verified. The last step is the short program that deletes unverified users after the appropriate interval, as shown in Example 8-44.

Example 8-44. delete-user.php

```php
<?php
// Connect to the database
$db = new PDO('sqlite:users.db');

$window = '-7 days';

$sth = $db->prepare("DELETE FROM users WHERE verified = 0 AND ".
                    "created_on < datetime('now',?)");
$res = $sth->execute(array($window));

if ($res) {
```

```
      print "Deactivated " . $sth->rowCount() . " users.\n";
   } else {
      print "Can't delete users.\n";
   }
   ?>
```

Run the program in Example 8-44 once a day to scrub the users table of users that haven't been verified. If you want to change how long users have to verify themselves, adjust the value of $window, and update the text of the email message sent to users to reflect the new value.

8.18 Program: Tiny Wiki

The program in Example 8-45 puts together various concepts discussed in this chapter and implements a complete Wiki system—a web site whose pages are all user-editable. It follows a structure common among simple PHP programs of its type. The first part of the code defines various configuration settings. Then comes an if/else section that decides what to do (display a page, save page edits, etc.) based on the values of submitted form or URL variables. The remainder of the program consists of the functions invoked from that if/else section—functions to print the page header and footer, load saved page contents, and display a page-editing form.

The tiny Wiki relies on an external library, PHP Markdown by Michel Fortin, to handle translating from the handy and compact Markdown syntax to HTML. You can get PHP Markdown from *http://www.michelf.com/projects/php-markdown/*.

Example 8-45. Tiny Wiki

```php
<?php

// Use the Markdown function from
// http://www.michelf.com/projects/php-markdown/
// for Wiki-like text markup
require_once 'markdown.php';

// The directory where the Wiki pages will be stored
// Make sure the web server user can write to it
define('PAGEDIR',dirname(__FILE__) . '/pages');

// Get page name, or use default
$page = isset($_GET['page']) ? $_GET['page'] : 'Home';

// Figure out what to do: display an edit form, save an
// edit form, or display a page

// Display an edit form that's been asked for
if (isset($_GET['edit'])) {
    pageHeader($page);
    edit($page);
    pageFooter($page, false);
}
// Save a submitted edit form
```

```php
else if (isset($_POST['edit'])) {
    file_put_contents(pageToFile($_POST['page']), $_POST['contents']);
    // Redirect to the regular view of the just-edited page
    header('Location: http://'.$_SERVER['HTTP_HOST'] . $_SERVER['SCRIPT_NAME'] .
        '?page='.urlencode($_POST['page']));
    exit();
}
// Display a page
else {
    pageHeader($page);
    // If the page exists, display it and the footer with an "Edit" link
    if (is_readable(pageToFile($page))) {
        // Get the contents of the page from the file it's saved in
        $text = file_get_contents(pageToFile($page));
        // Convert Markdown syntax (using Markdown() from markdown.php)
        $text = Markdown($text);
        // Make bare [links] link to other wiki pages
        $text = wikiLinks($text);
        // Display the page
        echo $text;
        // Display the footer
        pageFooter($page, true);
    }
    // If the page doesn't exist, display an edit form
    // and the footer without an "Edit" link
    else {
        edit($page, true);
        pageFooter($page, false);
    }
}

// The page header -- pretty simple, just the title and the usual HTML
// pleasantries
function pageheader($page) { ?>
<html>
<head>
<title>Wiki: <?php echo htmlentities($page) ?></title>
</head>
<body>
<h1><?php echo htmlentities($page) ?></h1>
<hr/>
<?php
}

// The page footer -- a "last modified" timestamp, an optional
// "Edit" link, and a link back to the front page of the Wiki
function pageFooter($page, $displayEditLink) {
    $timestamp = @filemtime(pageToFile($page));
    if ($timestamp) {
        $lastModified = strftime('%c', $timestamp);
    } else {
        $lastModified = 'Never';
    }
    if ($displayEditLink) {
        $editLink = ' - <a href="?page='.urlencode($page).'&edit=true">Edit</a>';
```

```php
    } else {
        $editLink = '';
    }
?>
<hr/>
<em>Last Modified: <?php echo $lastModified ?></em>
<?php echo $editLink ?> - <a href="<?php echo $_SERVER['SCRIPT_NAME'] ?>">Home</a>
</body>
</html>
<?php
}


// Display an edit form. If the page already exists, include its current
// contents in the form
function edit($page, $isNew = false) {
    if ($isNew) {
        $contents = '';
?>
<p><b>This page doesn't exist yet.</b> To create it, enter its contents below
and click the <b>Save</b> button.</p>
    <?php } else {
        $contents = file_get_contents(pageToFile($page));
    }
?>
<form method='post' action='<?php echo htmlentities($_SERVER['SCRIPT_NAME']) ?>'>
<input type='hidden' name='edit' value='true'/>
<input type='hidden' name='page' value='<?php echo htmlentities($page) ?>'/>
<textarea name='contents' rows='20' cols='60'>
<?php echo htmlentities($contents) ?></textarea>
<br/>
<input type='submit' value='Save'/>
</form>
<?php
}


// Convert a submitted page to a filename. Using md5() prevents naughty
// characters in $page from causing security problems
function pageToFile($page) {
    return PAGEDIR.'/'.md5($page);
}


// Turn text such as [something] in a page into an HTML link to the
// Wiki page "something"
function wikiLinks($page) {
    if (preg_match_all('/\[([^\]]+?)\]/', $page, $matches, PREG_SET_ORDER)) {
        foreach ($matches as $match) {
            $page = str_replace($match[0], '<a href="'.$_SERVER['SCRIPT_NAME'].
'?page='.urlencode($match[1]).'">'.htmlentities($match[1]).'</a>', $page);
        }
    }
    return $page;
}
?>
```

CHAPTER 9

Form

9.0 Introduction

The genius of PHP is its seamless integration of form variables into your programs. It makes web programming smooth and simple, speeding the cycle from web form to PHP code to HTML output.

With that convenience, however, comes the responsibility to make sure that the user-provided information that flows so easily into your program contains appropriate content. External input can never be trusted, so it's imperative always to validate all incoming data. Recipes 9.2 through 9.9 show how to validate common kinds of information as well as providing general guidelines on arbitrary form validation you might need to do. Recipe 9.10 discusses escaping HTML entities to allow the safe display of user-entered data. Recipe 9.14 covers how to process files uploaded by a user.

HTTP is a "stateless" protocol—it has no built-in mechanism that helps you to save information from one page so you can access it in other pages. Recipes 9.11, 9.12, and 9.13 all show ways to work around the fundamental problem of figuring out which user is making which requests to your web server.

Whenever PHP processes a page, it checks for URL and form variables, uploaded files, applicable cookies, and web server and environment variables. These are then directly accessible in the following arrays: $_GET, $_POST, $_FILES, $_COOKIE, $_SERVER, and $_ENV. They hold, respectively, all variables set in the query string, in the body of a post request, by uploaded files, by cookies, by the web server, and by the environment in which the web server is running. There's also $_REQUEST, which is one giant array that contains the values from the other six arrays.

When placing elements inside of $_REQUEST, if two arrays both have a key with the same name, PHP breaks the tie by relying on the variables_order configuration directive. By default, variables_order is EGPCS (or GPCS, if you're using the *php.ini-recommended* configuration file). So PHP first adds environment variables to $_REQUEST and then adds query string, post, cookie, and web server variables to the array, in this order. For instance, since C comes after P in the default order, a cookie named username overwrites a posted variable named username. Note that the GPCS value from *php.ini-recommended* means that the $_ENV array doesn't get populated with environment variables.

While $_REQUEST can be convenient, it's usually a better idea to look in the more detailed array directly. That way, you know exactly what you're getting and don't have to be concerned that a change in variables_order affects the behavior of your program.

All of these arrays are *auto-global*. That means global inside of a function or class— they're always in scope.

Prior to PHP 4.1, these auto-global variables didn't exist. Instead, there were regular arrays named $HTTP_COOKIE_VARS, $HTTP_ENV_VARS, $HTTP_GET_VARS, $HTTP_POST_VARS, $HTTP_POST_FILES, and $HTTP_SERVER_VARS. These arrays are still available for legacy reasons, but the newer arrays are easier to work with. These older arrays are populated only if the track_vars configuration directive is on, but as of PHP 4.0.3, this feature is always enabled.

Finally, if the register_globals configuration directive is on, all these variables are also available as variables in the global namespace. So $_GET['password'] is also just $password. While convenient, this introduces major security problems because malicious users can easily set variables from the outside and overwrite trusted internal variables. Starting with PHP 4.2, register_globals defaults to off.

Example 9-1 is a basic form. The form asks the user to enter his first name. When the form is submitted the information is sent to *hello.php*.

Example 9-1. Basic HTML form

```
<form action="hello.php" method="post">
What is your first name?
<input type="text" name="first_name" />
<input type="submit" value="Say Hello" />
</form>
```

The name of the text input element inside the form is first_name. Also, the method of the form is post. This means that when the form is submitted, $_POST['first_name'] will hold whatever string the user typed in. (It could also be empty, of course, if he didn't type anything.)

Example 9-2 shows the contents of *hello.php*, which will display information from the form.

Example 9-2. Basic PHP form processing

```
<?php
echo 'Hello, ' . $_POST['first_name'] . '!';
?>
```

If you type Twinkle into the form in Example 9-1, Example 9-2 prints:

```
Hello, Twinkle!
```

Example 9-2 is so basic that it omits two important steps that should be in all PHP form-processing applications: data validation (to make sure what's typed into the form is acceptable to your program), and output escaping (to make sure that malicious users can't use your web site to attack others). Recipes 9.2 through 9.9 discuss data validation and Recipe 9.10 discusses output escaping.

9.1 Processing Form Input

Problem

You want to use the same HTML page to emit a form and then process the data entered into it. In other words, you're trying to avoid a proliferation of pages that each handle different steps in a transaction.

Solution

Use the `$_SERVER['REQUEST_METHOD']` variable to determine whether the request was submitted with the **get** or **post** method. If the **get** method was used, print the form. If the **post** method was used, process the form. Example 9-3 combines the form from Example 9-1 and the code from Example 9-2 into one program, deciding what to do based on `$_SERVER['REQUEST_METHOD']`.

Example 9-3. Deciding what to do based on request method

```php
<?php if ($_SERVER['REQUEST_METHOD'] == 'GET') { ?>
<form action="<?php echo $_SERVER['SCRIPT_NAME'] ?>" method="post">
What is your first name?
<input type="text" name="first_name" />
<input type="submit" value="Say Hello" />
</form>
<?php } else {
    echo 'Hello, ' . $_POST['first_name'] . '!';
}
?>
```

Discussion

Back in the hazy past, in the early days of the Web, when our ancestors scratched out forms, they usually made two files: a static HTML page with the form and a script that processed the form and returned a dynamically generated response to the user. This was a little unwieldy because *form.html* led to *form.cgi* and, if you changed one page, you needed to also remember to edit the other, or your script might break.

Usually, forms are easier to maintain when all parts live in the same file and context dictates which sections to display. The **get** method (what your browser uses when you just type in a URL or click on a link) means "Hey, server, give me something you've got." The **post** method (what your browser uses when you submit a form whose method attribute is set to **post**) means "Hey, server, here's some data that changes something." So the characteristic response to a get request is the HTML form, and the response to the post request is the results of processing that form. In Example 9-3, the "processing" is extremely simple—just printing a greeting. In more typical applications, the processing is more complicated—saving information to a database or sending an email message.

Note that although the XHTML specification requires that the method attribute of a <form/> element be lowercase (get or post), the HTTP specification requires that a web browser use all uppercase (GET or POST) when sending the request method to the server. The value in $_SERVER['REQUEST_METHOD'] is whatever the browser sends, so in practice it will always be uppercase.

One other technique also makes pages easier to maintain: don't hardcode the path to your page directly into the form action. This makes it impossible to rename or relocate your page without also editing it. Instead, use the $_SERVER['SCRIPT_NAME'] variable as the form action. This is set up by PHP on each request to contain the filename (relative to the document root) of the current script.

See Also

Recipe 9.11 for handling multipage forms.

9.2 Validating Form Input: Required Fields

Problem

You want to make sure a value has been supplied for a form element. For example, you want to make sure a text box hasn't been left blank.

Solution

Use strlen( ) to test the element in $_GET or $_POST, as in Example 9-4.

Example 9-4. Testing a required field

```php
<?php
if (! strlen($_POST['flavor'])) {
    print 'You must enter your favorite ice cream flavor.';
}
?>
```

Discussion

Different types of form elements cause different types of behavior in $_GET and $_POST when left empty. Blank text boxes, text areas, and file-upload boxes result in elements whose value is a zero-length string. Unchecked checkboxes and radio buttons don't produce any elements in $_GET or $_POST. Browsers generally force a selection in a drop-down menu that only allows one choice, but drop-down menus that allow multiple choices and have no choices selected act like checkboxes—they don't produce any elements in $_GET or $_POST.

What's worse, requests don't have to come from web browsers. Your PHP program may receive a request from another program, a curious hacker constructing requests by hand, or a malicious attacker building requests in an attempt to find holes in your system. To make your code as robust as possible, always check that a particular element exists in $_GET or $_POST before applying other validation strategies to the element. Additionally, if the validation strategy assumes that the element is an array of values (as in Example 9-15), ensure that the value really is an array by using is_array( ).

Example 9-5 uses isset( ), strlen( ), and is_array( ) for maximally strict form validation.

Example 9-5. Strict form validation

```php
<?php
// Making sure $_POST['flavor'] exists before checking its length
if (! (isset($_POST['flavor']) && strlen($_POST['flavor']))) {
    print 'You must enter your favorite ice cream flavor.';
}

// $_POST['color'] is optional, but if it's supplied, it must be
// more than 5 characters
if (isset($_POST['color']) && (strlen($_POST['color']) <=5 )) {
    print 'Color must be more than 5 characters.';
}

// Making sure $_POST['choices'] exists and is an array
if (! (isset($_POST['choices']) && is_array($_POST['choices']))) {
    print 'You must select some choices.';
}
?>
```

In a moment of weakness, you may be tempted to use empty( ) instead of strlen( ) to test if a value has been entered in a text box. Succumbing to such weakness leads to problems since the one character string 0 is false according to the rules of PHP's boolean calculations. That means if someone types 0 into the children text box, causing $_POST['children'] to contain 0, empty($_POST['children']) is true—which, from a form validation perspective, is wrong.

See Also

Recipe 9.5 for information about validating drop-down menus, Recipe 9.6 for information about validating radio buttons, and Recipe 9.7 for information about validating checkboxes.

9.3 Validating Form Input: Numbers

Problem

You want to make sure a number is entered in a form input box. For example, you don't want someone to be able to say that her age is "old enough" or "tangerine," but instead want values such as 13 or 56.

Solution

If you're looking for an integer larger than or equal to zero, use `ctype_digit()`, as shown in Example 9-6.

Example 9-6. Validating a number with ctype_digit()

```php
<?php
if (! ctype_digit($_POST['age'])) {
    print 'Your age must be a number bigger than or equal to zero.';
}
?>
```

If you're looking for a positive or negative integer, compare the submitted value to what you get when casting it to an integer and then back to a string, as in Example 9-7.

Example 9-7. Validating an integer with typecasting

```php
<?php
if ($_POST['rating'] != strval(intval($_POST['rating']))) {
    print 'Your rating must be an integer.';
}
?>
```

If you're looking for a positive or negative decimal number, compare the submitted value to what you get when casting it to a floating-point number and then back to a string, as in Example 9-8.

Example 9-8. Validating a decimal number with typecasting

```php
<?php
if ($_POST['temperature'] != strval(floatval($_POST['temperature']))) {
    print 'Your temperature must be a number.';
}
?>
```

Discussion

Number validation is one of those things in PHP that seems like it's simple, but is a little trickier than it first appears. A common impulse is to use the built-in `is_numeric()` function for number validation. Unfortunately, what `is_numeric()` thinks is "numeric" is more in line with how a computer behaves than a human. For example, `is_numeric( )` considers hexadecimal number strings such as `0xCAFE` and exponentially notated number strings such as `10e40` as numbers.

Something else to keep in mind when validating numbers (and all form input): values in `$_GET` and `$_POST` are always strings. That means that if someone submits a form with `06520` typed into a text box named `zip_code`, the value of `$_POST['zip_code']` is the five character string `06520`, not the integer 6,520.

So if what you need to validate is "this value consists only of digits," then `ctype_digit( )` is the way to go. It is the fastest way to validate a number. `ctype_digit( )`, like all the `ctype` functions, requires its input to be a string, but that's taken care of for you when validating form input, since all values in `$_GET` and `$_POST` are strings.

Before PHP 5.1, `ctype_digit( )` doesn't do what you expect if you give it an empty string (`ctype_digit('')` returns `true`), so be sure to check an input as described in Recipe 9.2 before passing it to `ctype_digit( )`. Also, a downside to `ctype_digit( )` (in all versions of PHP) is that it's not very flexible. All it knows about are digits. If you want to accept negative numbers or decimal numbers, it can't help you.

In those cases, turn to two of PHP's typecasting functions: `intval( )`, which "integerifies" a string, and `floatval( )`, which "floatifies" it. Each of these functions, when given a string, do their best to produce a number from what's in the string. If the string just contains a valid number, that's what you get back. For example, `intval('06520')` returns the integer 6520, `intval('-2853')` returns the integer −2853, `floatval('3.1415')` returns the floating-point number 3.1415, and `floatval('-473.20')` returns the floating-point number −473.2.

Where these functions come in handy in input validation, however, is how they treat strings that aren't valid numbers. Each returns as much number as it can find in the string, starting from the beginning and ignoring initial whitespace. That is, `intval('-6 weeks')` returns −6, `intval('30x bigger')` returns 30, `intval('3.1415')` returns 3, and `intval('21+up')` returns 21. `floatval( )` behaves similarly, but allows decimal points. For example, `floatval('127.128.129.130')` returns 127.128. When given a string with no valid number characters in it, both functions return 0.

This means that passing the user input through either `intval( )` or `floatval( )` works as a filter, leaving valid values unmodified, but changing invalid values to just their numerical essence. The resulting comparison with the original input succeeds if the value has passed through the filter without being modified—in other words, the comparison succeeds if the original input is a valid integer or decimal number.

It is necessary to convert what comes out of `intval( )` or `floatval( )` to a string with `strval( )` to make sure PHP does the comparison properly. When PHP compares two strings, the comparison behaves as you'd expect. (The result is `true` if the strings are the same, and `false` otherwise.) However, when PHP compares a string and a number (such as the result of `intval( )` or `floatval( )`), it attempts to convert the string to a number (using the rules outlined above). This would counteract the "filter" properties of intval( ) or floatval( ), so we need to prevent it from happening. Ensuring that two strings are compared accomplishes this.

If all of this typecasting has you feeling a bit queasy and you're a fan of regular expressions, feel free to use those instead. Example 9-9 shows regular expressions that validate an integer and a decimal number.

Example 9-9. Validating numbers with regular expressions

```php
<?php
// The pattern matches an optional - sign and then
// at least one digit
if (! preg_match('/^-?\d+$/'$_POST['rating'])) {
    print 'Your rating must be an integer.';
}

// The pattern matches an optional - sign and then
// Optional digits to go before a decimal point
// An optional decimal point
// And then at least one digit
if (! preg_match('/^-?\d*\.?\d+$/',$_POST['temperature'])) {
    print 'Your temperature must be a number.';
}
?>
```

It is a common refrain among performance-tuning purists that regular expressions should be avoided because they are comparatively slow. In this case, however, with such simple regular expressions, they are about equally efficient as the typecasting. If you're more comfortable with regular expressions, or you're using them in other validation contexts as well, they can be a handy choice. The regular expression also allows you to consider valid numbers, such as 782364.238723123, that cannot be stored as a PHP float without losing precision. This can be useful with data such as a longitude or latitude that you plan to store as a string. The regular expression also allows you to consider valid numbers, such as 782364.238723123, that cannot be stored as a PHP float without losing precision. This can be useful with data such as a longitude or latitude that you plan to store as a string. That said, the ctype_digit( ) function is much faster than either typecasting or a regular expression, so if that does what you need, use it.

See Also

Recipe 9.2 for information on validating required fields; documentation on ctype_digit( ) at *http://www.php.net/ctype_digit*.

9.4 Validating Form Input: Email Addresses

Problem

You want to know whether an email address a user has provided is valid.

Solution

Use the `is_valid_email_address()` function in Example 9-10. It tells you whether an email address is valid according to the rules in RFC 822.

Example 9-10. Validating an email address

```
function is_valid_email_address($email){
        $qtext = '[^\\x0d\\x22\\x5c\\x80-\\xff]';
        $dtext = '[^\\x0d\\x5b-\\x5d\\x80-\\xff]';
        $atom = '[^\\x00-\\x20\\x22\\x28\\x29\\x2c\\x2e\\x3a-\\x3c'.
                '\\x3e\\x40\\x5b-\\x5d\\x7f-\\xff]+';
        $quoted_pair = '\\x5c[\\x00-\\x7f]';
        $domain_literal = "\\x5b($dtext|$quoted_pair)*\\x5d";
        $quoted_string = "\\x22($qtext|$quoted_pair)*\\x22";
        $domain_ref = $atom;
        $sub_domain = "($domain_ref|$domain_literal)";
        $word = "($atom|$quoted_string)";
        $domain = "$sub_domain(\\x2e$sub_domain)*";
        $local_part = "$word(\\x2e$word)*";
        $addr_spec = "$local_part\\x40$domain";
        return preg_match("!^$addr_spec$!", $email) ? 1 : 0;
}

if (is_valid_email_address('cal@example.com')) {
    print 'cal@example.com is a valid e-mail address';
} else {
    print 'cal@example.com is not a valid e-mail address';
}
```

Discussion

RFC 822 defines the standards for a valid email address. The function in Example 9-10, by Cal Henderson, uses the grammar rules laid out in that RFC to build a regular expression. You can read more about how the function is constructed at *http://www.iamcal.com/publish/articles/php/parsing_email*. Cal has also written a function that validates according to the more complicated rules in RFC 2822. That function is available for download from *http://code.iamcal.com/php/rfc822/rfc822.phps*.

The function in Example 9-10 only checks that a particular address is syntactically correct. This is useful for preventing a user from accidentally telling you that her email address is `bingolover2261@example` instead of `bingolover2261@example.com`. What it doesn't tell you, however, is what happens if you send a message to that address. Furthermore, it doesn't let you know that the person providing the email address is in control of the address. For those sorts of validations, you need to send a confirmation message to the address. The confirmation message can ask the user to take some affirmative task (reply to the message, click on a link) to indicate they're the same person that entered the address on the form. Or, the confirmation message can tell the user what to do (reply to the message, click on a link), if she's *not* the same person that entered the address on the form. Recipe 8.17 demonstrates a system that sends an email message containing a link that the recipient must click on to confirm that she provided the address.

See Also

RFC 822 at *http://www.faqs.org/rfcs/rfc822.html*, RFC 2822 at *http://www.faqs.org/rfcs/rfc2822.html*, "Parsing Email Addresses in PHP" by Cal Henderson at *http://www.iamcal.com/publish/articles/php/parsing_email*, and the functions available for download at *http://code.iamcal.com/php/rfc822/*.

9.5 Validating Form Input: Drop-Down Menus

Problem

You want to make sure that a valid choice was selected from a drop-down menu generated by the HTML `<select/>` element.

Solution

Use an array of values to generate the menu. Then validate the input by checking that the value is in the array. Example 9-11 uses `in_array( )` to do the validation.

Example 9-11. Validating a drop-down menu with in_array( )

```
<?php
// Generating the menu
$choices = array('Eggs','Toast','Coffee');
echo "<select name='food'>\n";
foreach ($choices as $choice) {
    echo "<option>$choice</option>\n";
}
echo "</select>";

// Then, later, validating the menu
if (! in_array($_POST['food'], $choices)) {
    echo "You must select a valid choice.";
}
?>
```

The menu that Example 9-11 generates is:

```
<select name='food'>
<option>Eggs</option>
<option>Toast</option>
<option>Coffee</option>
</select>
```

To work with a menu that sets `value` attributes on each `<option/>` element, use `array_key_exists( )` to validate the input, as shown in Example 9-12.

Example 9-12. Validating a drop-down menu with array_key_exists()

```php
<?php
// Generating the menu
$choices = array('eggs' => 'Eggs Benedict',
                 'toast' => 'Buttered Toast with Jam',
                 'coffee' => 'Piping Hot Coffee');
echo "<select name='food'>\n";
foreach ($choices as $key => $choice) {
    echo "<option value='$key'>$choice</option>\n";
}
echo "</select>";

// Then, later, validating the menu
if (! array_key_exists($_POST['food'], $choices)) {
    echo "You must select a valid choice.";
}
?>
```

The menu that Example 9-12 generates is:

```
<select name='food'>
<option value='eggs'>Eggs Benedict</option>
<option value='toast'>Buttered Toast with Jam</option>
<option value='coffee'>Piping Hot Coffee</option>
</select>
```

Discussion

The methods in Example 9-11 and Example 9-12 differ in the kinds of menus that they generate. Example 9-11 has a `$choices` array with automatic numeric keys and outputs `<option/>` elements. Example 9-12 has a `$choices` array with explicit keys and outputs `<option/>` elements with `value` attributes drawn from those keys.

In either case, the validation strategy is the same: make sure that the value submitted for the form element is one of the allowed choices. For requests submitted by well-behaved browsers, this validation rule never fails—web browsers generally don't let you make up your choice for a drop-down menu. Remember, though, that there's nothing requiring that requests to your PHP program come from a well-behaved web browser. They could come from a buggy browser or from a bored 11-year-old with a copy of the HTTP specification in one hand and a command-line telnet client in the other. Because you always need to be mindful of malicious, hand-crafted HTTP requests, it's important to validate input even in circumstances where most users will never encounter an error.

See Also

Documentation on `in_array()` at *http://www.php.net/in_array* and on `array_key_exists()` at *http://www.php.net/array_key_exists*.

9.6 Validating Form Input: Radio Buttons

Problem

You want to make sure a valid radio button is selected from a group of radio buttons.

Solution

Use an array of values to generate the menu. Then validate the input by checking that the submitted value is in the array. Example 9-13 uses `array_key_exists( )` to do the validation.

Example 9-13. Validating a radio button

```php
<?php
// Generating the radio buttons
$choices = array('eggs' => 'Eggs Benedict',
                 'toast' => 'Buttered Toast with Jam',
                 'coffee' => 'Piping Hot Coffee');
foreach ($choices as $key => $choice) {
    echo "<input type='radio' name='food' value='$key'/> $choice \n";
}


// Then, later, validating the radio button submission
if (! array_key_exists($_POST['food'], $choices)) {
    echo "You must select a valid choice.";
}
?>
```

Discussion

The radio button validation in Example 9-13 is very similar to the drop-down menu validation in Example 9-12. They both follow the same pattern—define the data that describes the choices, generate the appropriate HTML, and then use the defined data to ensure that a valid value was submitted. The difference is in what HTML is generated.

Another difference between drop-down menus and radio buttons is how defaults are handled. When the HTML doesn't explicitly specify a default choice for a drop-down menu, the first choice in the menu is used. However, when the HTML doesn't explicitly specify a default choice for a set of radio buttons, no choice is used as a default.

To ensure that one of a set of radio buttons is chosen in a well-behaved web browser, give the default choice a `checked="checked"` attribute. In addition, to guard against missing values in hand-crafted malicious requests, use `isset( )` to ensure that something was submitted for the radio button, as described in Recipe 9.2.

See Also

Recipe 9.2 for information on validating required fields; documentation on array_key_exists( ) at *http://www.php.net/array_key_exists*.

9.7 Validating Form Input: Checkboxes

Problem

You want to make sure only valid checkboxes are checked.

Solution

For a single checkbox, ensure that if a value is supplied, it's the correct one. If a value isn't supplied for the checkbox, then the box wasn't checked. Example 9-14 figures out whether a checkbox was checked, unchecked, or had an invalid value submitted.

Example 9-14. Validating a single checkbox

```php
<?php
// Generating the checkbox
$value = 'yes';
echo "<input type='checkbox' name='subscribe' value='yes'/> Subscribe?";

// Then, later, validating the checkbox
if (isset($_POST['subscribe'])) {
    // A value was submitted and it's the right one
    if ($_POST['subscribe'] == $value) {
        $subscribed = true;
    } else {
        // A value was submitted and it's the wrong one
        $subscribed = false;
        print 'Invalid checkbox value submitted.';
    }
} else {
    // No value was submitted
    $subscribed = false;
}

if ($subscribed) {
    print 'You are subscribed.';
} else {
    print 'You are not subscribed';
}
```

For a group of checkboxes, use an array of values to generate the checkboxes. Then, use array_intersect( ) to ensure that the set of submitted values is contained within the set of acceptable values, as shown in Example 9-15.

Example 9-15. Validating a group of checkboxes

```php
<?php
// Generating the checkboxes
```

```
$choices = array('eggs'   => 'Eggs Benedict',
                 'toast'  => 'Buttered Toast with Jam',
                 'coffee' => 'Piping Hot Coffee');
foreach ($choices as $key => $choice) {
    echo "<input type='checkbox' name='food[]' value='$key'/> $choice \n";
}
?>

// Then, later, validating the radio button submission
if (array_intersect($_POST['food'], array_keys($choices)) != $_POST['food']) {
    echo "You must select only valid choices.";
}
?>
```

Discussion

For PHP to handle multiple checkbox values properly, the checkboxes' name attribute must end with [], as described in Recipe 9.17. Those multiple values are formatted in $_POST as an array. Since the checkbox name in Example 9-15 is food[], $_POST ['food'] holds the array of values from the checked boxes.

The array_intersect( ) function finds all of the elements in $_POST['food'] that are also in array_keys($choices). That is, it filters the submitted choices ($_POST['food']), only allowing through values that are acceptable—keys in the $choices array. If all of the values in $_POST['food'] are acceptable, then the result of array_intersect($_POST['food'], array_keys($choices)) is an unmodified copy of $_POST['food']. So if the result isn't equal to $_POST['food'], something invalid was submitted.

Checkboxes have the same issues with default values as do radio buttons. So just as with radio buttons, use the rules in Recipe 9.2 to determine that something was submitted for the checkbox before proceeding with further validation.

See Also

Recipe 9.2 for information about validating required fields; documentation on array_intersect( ) at *http://www.php.net/array_intersect*.

9.8 Validating Form Input: Dates and Times

Problem

You want to make sure that a date or time a user entered is valid. For example, you want to ensure that a user hasn't attempted to schedule an event for the 45th of August or provided a credit card that has already expired.

Solution

If your form provides month, day, and year as separate elements, plug those values into checkdate( ), as in Example 9-16. This tells you whether or not the month, day, and year are valid.

Example 9-16. Checking a particular date

```php
<?php
if (! checkdate($_POST['month'], $_POST['day'], $_POST['year'])) {
    print "The date you entered doesn't exist!";
}
?>
```

To check that a date is before or after a particular value, convert the user-supplied values to a timestamp, compute the timestamp for the threshhold date, and compare the two. Example 9-17 checks that the supplied credit card expiration month and year are after the current month.

Example 9-17. Checking credit card expiration

```php
<?php
// The beginning of the month in which the credit card expires
$expires = mktime(0, 0, 0, $_POST['month'], 1, $_POST['year']);
// The beginning of next month
// If date('n') + 1 == 13, mktime() does the right thing and uses
// January of the following year.
$nextMonth = mktime(0, 0, 0, date('n') + 1, 1);
if ($expires < $nextMonth) {
    print "Sorry, that credit card expires too soon.";
}
?>
```

Discussion

checkdate( ) is handy because it knows about leap year and how many days are in each month, saving you from tedious comparisons of each component of the date. For range validations—making sure a date or time is before, after, or between other dates or times —it's easiest to work with epoch timestamps.

See Also

Chapter 3 discusses the finer points of date and time handling.

9.9 Validating Form Input: Credit Cards

Problem

You want to make sure a user hasn't entered a bogus credit card number.

Solution

The `is_valid_credit_card( )` function in Example 9-18 tells you whether a provided credit card number is syntactically valid.

Example 9-18. Validating a credit card number

```php
<?php
function is_valid_credit_card($s) {
    // Remove non-digits and reverse
    $s = strrev(preg_replace('/[^\d]/','',$s));
    // compute checksum
    $sum = 0;
    for ($i = 0, $j = strlen($s); $i < $j; $i++) {
        // Use even digits as-is
        if (($i % 2) == 0) {
            $val = $s[$i];
        } else {
            // Double odd digits and subtract 9 if greater than 9
            $val = $s[$i] * 2;
            if ($val > 9) { $val -= 9; }
        }
        $sum += $val;
    }
    // Number is valid if sum is a multiple of ten
    return (($sum % 10) == 0);
}

if (! is_valid_credit_card($_POST['credit_card'])) {
    print 'Sorry, that card number is invalid.';
}

?>
```

Discussion

Credit cards use the *Luhn algorithm* to prevent against accidental error. This algorithm, which the `is_valid_credit_card( )` function in Example 9-18 uses, does some manipulations on the individual digits of the card number to tell whether the number is acceptable.

Validating a credit card is a bit like validating an email address. *Syntactic* validation—making sure the provided value is a sequence of characters that matches a standard—is relatively easy. *Semantic* validation, however, is trickier. The credit card number 4111 1111 1111 1111 sails through the function in Example 9-18 but isn't valid. It's a well-known test number that looks like a Visa card number. (And, as such, is handy for using in books when one needs an example.)

Just as strong email address validation requires external verification (usually by sending a message to the address with a confirmation link in it), credit card validation requires external validation by submitting the credit card number to a payment processor along with associated account info (card holder name and address) and making sure you get back an approval.

Syntactic validation is good protection against inadvertent user typos but, obviously, is not all you need to do when checking credit card numbers.

See Also

Recipe 9.4 for information about validating email addresses; *http://en.wikipedia.org/wiki/Luhn* for information about the Luhn algorithm.

9.10 Preventing Cross-Site Scripting

Problem

You want to securely display user-entered data on an HTML page. For example, you want to allow users to add comments to a blog post without worrying that HTML or JavaScript in a comment will cause problems.

Solution

Pass user input through `htmlentities( )` before displaying it, as in Example 9-19.

Example 9-19. Escaping HTML

```php
<?php
print 'The comment was: ';
print htmlentities($_POST['comment']);
?>
```

Discussion

PHP has a pair of functions to escape HTML entities. The most basic is `htmlspecialchars( )`, which escapes four characters: < > " and &. Depending on optional parameters, it can also translate ' instead of or in addition to ". For more complex encoding, use `htmlentities( )`; it expands on `htmlspecialchars( )` to encode any character that has an HTML entity. Example 9-20 shows `htmlspecialchars( ) in action`.

Example 9-20. Escaping HTML entities

```php
<?php
$html = "<a href='fletch.html'>Stew's favorite movie.</a>\n";
print htmlspecialchars($html);              // double-quotes
print htmlspecialchars($html, ENT_QUOTES);   // single- and double-quotes
print htmlspecialchars($html, ENT_NOQUOTES); // neither
```

Example 9-20 prints:

```
&lt;a href=&quot;fletch.html&quot;&gt;Stew's favorite movie.&lt;/a&gt;
&lt;a href=&quot;fletch.html&quot;&gt;Stew&#039;s favorite movie.&lt;/a&gt;
&lt;a href="fletch.html"&gt;Stew's favorite movie.&lt;/a&gt;
```

By default, both `htmlentities( )` and `htmlspecialchars( )` use the ISO-8859-1 character set. To use a different character set, pass the character set as a third argument. For example, to use UTF-8, call `htmlentities($string, ENT_QUOTES, 'UTF-8')`.

See Also

Recipes 18.4 and 19.13; documentation on `htmlentities( )` at *http://www.php.net/htmlentities* and `htmlspecialchars( )` at *http://www.php.net/htmlspecialchars*.

9.11 Working with Multipage Forms

Problem

You want to use a form that displays more than one page and preserves data from one page to the next. For example, your form is for a survey that has too many questions to put them all on one page.

Solution

Use session tracking to store form information for each stage as well as a variable to keep track of what stage to display. Example 9-21 displays a two-page form and then the collected results.

Example 9-21. Making a multipage form

```php
<?php
// Turn on sessions
session_start();

// Figure out what stage to use
if (($_SERVER['REQUEST_METHOD'] == 'GET') || (! isset($_POST['stage']))) {
    $stage = 1;
} else {
    $stage = (int) $_POST['stage'];
}

// Save any submitted data
if ($stage > 1) {
    foreach ($_POST as $key => $value) {
        $_SESSION[$key] = $value;
    }
}

if ($stage == 1) { ?>

<form action='<?php echo $_SERVER['SCRIPT_NAME'] ?>' method='post'>

Name: <input type='text' name='name'/> <br/>
Age:  <input type='text' name='age'/> </br/>

<input type='hidden' name='stage' value='<?php echo $stage + 1 ?>'/>
```

```
<input type='submit' value='Next'/>
</form>

<?php } else if ($stage == 2) { ?>

<form action='<?php echo $_SERVER['SCRIPT_NAME'] ?>' method='post'>

Favorite Color: <input type='text' name='color'/> <br/>
Favorite Food:  <input type='text' name='food'/> </br/>


<input type='hidden' name='stage' value='<?php echo $stage + 1 ?>'/>
<input type='submit' value='Done'/>
</form>

<?php } else if ($stage == 3) { ?>

    Hello <?php echo $_SESSION['name'] ?>.
    You are <?php echo $_SESSION['age'] ?> years old.
    Your favorite color is <?php echo $_SESSION['color'] ?>
    and your favorite food is <?php echo $_SESSION['food'] ?>.

<?php } ?>
```

Discussion

At the beginning of each stage in Example 9-21, all the submitted form variables are copied into $_SESSION. This makes them available on subsequent requests, including the code that runs in stage 3, which displays everything that's been saved.

PHP's sessions are perfect for this kind of task since all of the data in a session is stored on the server. This keeps each request small—no need to resubmit stuff that's been entered on a previous stage—and reduces the validation overhead. You only have to validate each piece of submitted data when it's submitted.

See Also

Recipe 11.1 for information about session handling.

9.12 Redisplaying Forms with Inline Error Messages

Problem

When there's a problem with data entered in a form, you want to print out error messages alongside the problem fields, instead of a generic error message at the top of the form. You also want to preserve the values the user entered in the form, so they don't have to redo the entire thing.

Solution

As you validate, keep track of form errors in an array keyed by element name. Then, when it's time to display the form, print the appropriate error message next to each element. To preserve user input, use the appropriate HTML idiom: a `value` attribute (with entity encoding) for most `<input/>` elements, a `checked='checked'` attribute for radio buttons and checkboxes, and a `selected='selected'` attribute on `<option/>` elements in drop-down menus. Example 9-22 displays and validates a form with a text box, a checkbox, and a drop-down menu.

Example 9-22. Redisplaying a form with error messages and preserved input

```php
<?php
// Set up some options for the drop-down menu
$flavors = array('Vanilla','Chocolate','Rhinoceros');

if ($_SERVER['REQUEST_METHOD'] == 'GET') {
    // Just display the form if the request is a GET
    display_form(array());
} else {
    // The request is a POST, so validate the form
    $errors = validate_form();
    if (count($errors)) {
        // If there were errors, redisplay the form with the errors
        display_form($errors);
    } else {
        // The form data was valid, so congratulate the user
        print 'The form is submitted!';
    }
}

function display_form($errors) {
    global $flavors;

    // Set up defaults
    $defaults['name'] = isset($_POST['name']) ? htmlentities($_POST['name']) : '';
    $defaults['age'] = isset($_POST['age']) ? "checked='checked'" : '';
    foreach ($flavors as $flavor) {
        if (isset($_POST['flavor']) && ($_POST['flavor'] == $flavor)) {
            $defaults['flavor'][$flavor] = "selected='selected'";
        } else {
            $defaults['flavor'][$flavor] = '';
        }
    }
    ?>

<form action='<?php echo $_SERVER['SCRIPT_NAME'] ?>' method='post'>
<dl>
<dt>Your Name:</dt>
<?php print_error('name', $errors) ?>
<dd><input type='text' name='name' value='<?php echo $defaults['name'] ?>'/></dd>
<dt>Are you over 18 years old?</dt>
<?php print_error('age', $errors) ?>
<dd><input type='checkbox' name='age' value='1' <?php echo $defaults['age'] ?>/> Yes</dd>
<dt>Your favorite ice cream flavor:</dt>
<?php print_error('flavor', $errors) ?>
<dd><select name='flavor'>
<?php foreach ($flavors as $flavor) {
    echo "<option {$defaults['flavor'][$flavor]}>$flavor</option>";
```

```
} ?>
</select></dd>
</dl>
<input type='submit' value='Send Info'/>
</form>
<?php }

// A helper function to make generating the HTML for an error message easier
function print_error($key, $errors) {
    if (isset($errors[$key])) {
        print "<dd class='error'>{$errors[$key]}</dd>";
    }
}

function validate_form() {
    global $flavors;

    // Start out with no errors
    $errors = array();

    // name is required and must be at least 3 characters
    if (! (isset($_POST['name']) && (strlen($_POST['name']) > 3))) {
        $errors['name'] = 'Enter a name of at least 3 letters';
    }
    if (isset($_POST['age']) && ($_POST['age'] != '1')) {
        $errors['age'] = 'Invalid age checkbox value.';
    }
    // flavor is optional but if submitted must be in $flavors
    if (isset($_POST['flavor']) && (! in_array($_POST['flavor'], $flavors))) {
        $errors['flavor'] = 'Choose a valid flavor.';
    }

    return $errors;
}
?>
```

Discussion

When a form is submitted with invalid data, it's more pleasant for the user if the form is redisplayed with error messages in appropriate places rather than a generic "the form is invalid" message at the top of the form. The validate_form( ) function in Example 9-22 builds up an array of error messages that display_form( ) uses to print the messages in the right places.

Extending Example 9-22 is a matter of expanding the checks in validate_form( ) to handle the appropriate validation needs of your form and including the correct HTML generation in display_form( ) so that the form includes the input elements you want.

See Also

Recipes 9.2 to 9.9 for various form validation strategies.

9.13 Guarding Against Multiple Submission of the Same Form

Problem

You want to prevent a user from submitting the same form more than once.

Solution

Include a hidden field in the form with a unique value. When validating the form, check if a form has already been submitted with that value. If it has, reject the submission. If it hasn't, process the form and record the value for later use. Additionally, use Java-Script to disable the form Submit button once the form has been submitted.

Example 9-23 uses the `uniqid( )` and `md5( )` functions to insert a unique ID field in a form. It also sets the form's `onsubmit` handler to a small bit of JavaScript that disables the submit button once the form's been submitted.

Example 9-23. Insert a unique ID into a form

```
<form method="post" action="<?php echo $_SERVER['SCRIPT_NAME'] ?>"
     onsubmit="document.getElementById('submit-button').disabled = true;">
<!-- insert all the normal form elements you need -->
<input type='hidden' name='token' value='<?php echo md5(uniqid()) ?>'/>
<input type='submit' value='Save Data' id='submit-button'/>
</form>
```

Example 9-24 checks the submitted token against saved data in an SQLite database to see if the form has already been submitted.

Example 9-24. Checking a form for resubmission

```
if ($_SERVER['REQUEST_METHOD'] == 'POST') {
    $db = new PDO('sqlite:/tmp/formjs.db');
    $db->beginTransaction();
    $sth = $db->prepare('SELECT * FROM forms WHERE token = ?');
    $sth->execute(array($_POST['token']));
    if (count($sth->fetchAll())) {
        print "This form has already been submitted!";
        $db->rollBack();
    } else {
        /* Validation code for the rest of the form goes here --
         * validate everything before inserting the token */
        $sth = $db->prepare('INSERT INTO forms (token) VALUES (?)');
        $sth->execute(array($_POST['token']));
        $db->commit();
        print "The form is submitted successfully.";
    }
}
?>
```

Discussion

For a variety of reasons, users often resubmit a form. Usually it's a slip-of-the-mouse: double-clicking the Submit button. They may hit their web browser's Back button to edit or recheck information, but then they re-hit Submit instead of Forward. It can be intentional: they're trying to stuff the ballot box for an online survey or sweepstakes. Our Solution prevents the non-malicious attack and can slow down the malicious user. It won't, however, eliminate all fraudulent use: more complicated work is required for that.

The Solution does prevent your database from being cluttered with too many copies of the same record. By generating a token that's placed in the form, you can uniquely identify that specific instance of the form, even when cookies are disabled. The uniqid( ) function generates an acceptable one-time token. The md5( ) function doesn't add any additional randomness to the token, but restricts the characters that could be in it. The results of uniqid( ) can be a mix of different letters and other characters. The results of md5( ) consist only of digits and the letters abcdef. For English-speaking users at least, this ensures that the token doesn't contain any naughty words.

It's tempting to avoid generating a random token and instead use a number one greater than the number of records already in your database table. There are (at least) two problems with this method. First, it creates a race condition. What happens when a second person starts the form before the first person has completed it? The second form will then have the same token as the first, and conflicts will occur. This can be worked around by creating a new blank record in the database when the form is requested, so the second person will get a number one higher than the first. However, this can lead to empty rows in the database if users opt not to complete the form.

The other reason not do this is because it makes it trivial to edit another record in the database by manually adjusting the ID to a different number. Depending on your security settings, a fake get or post submission allows the data to be altered without difficulty. A random token, however, can't be guessed merely by moving to a different integer.

See Also

Recipe 18.9 for more details on verifying data with hashes; documentation on uniqid( ) at *http://www.php.net/uniqid* and on md5( ) at *http://www.php.net/md5*.

9.14 Processing Uploaded Files

Problem

You want to process a file uploaded by a user. For example, you're building a photo-sharing web site and you want to store user-supplied photos.

Solution

Use the $_FILES array to get information about uploaded files. Example 9-25 saves an uploaded file to the */tmp* directory on the web server.

Example 9-25. Uploading a file

```php
<?php if ($_SERVER['REQUEST_METHOD'] == 'GET') { ?>
<form method="post" action="<?php echo $_SERVER['SCRIPT_NAME'] ?>"
      enctype="multipart/form-data">
<input type="file" name="document"/>
<input type="submit" value="Send File"/>
</form>
<?php } else {
    if (isset($_FILES['document']) &&
    ($_FILES['document']['error'] == UPLOAD_ERR_OK)) {
        $newPath = '/tmp/' . basename($_FILES['document']['name']);
        if (move_uploaded_file($_FILES['document']['tmp_name'], $newPath)) {
            print "File saved in $newPath";
        } else {
            print "Couldn't move file to $newPath";
        }
    } else {
        print "No valid file uploaded.";
    }
}
?>
```

Discussion

Starting in PHP 4.1, all uploaded files appear in the $_FILES auto-global array. For each file element in the form, an array is created in $_FILES whose key is the file element's name. For example, the form in Example 9-25 has a file element named document, so $_FILES['document'] contains the information about the uploaded file. Each of these per-file arrays has five elements:

name
> The name of the uploaded file. This is supplied by the browser so it could be a full pathname or just a filename.

type
> The MIME type of the file, as supplied by the browser.

size
> The size of the file in bytes, as calculated by the server.

tmp_name
> The location in which the file is temporarily stored on the server.

error
> An error code describing what (if anything) went wrong with the file upload. (This element is available in PHP 4.2.0 and later versions.)

If you're using a version of PHP earlier than 4.1, this information is in $HTTP_POST_FILES instead of $_FILES.

The possible values of the **error** element are:

UPLOAD_ERR_OK (0)
> Upload succeeded (no error).

UPLOAD_ERR_INI_SIZE (1)

    The size of the uploaded file is bigger than the value of the `upload_max_filesize` configuration directive.

UPLOAD_ERR_FORM_SIZE (2)

    The size of the uploaded file is bigger than the value of the form's `MAX_FILE_SIZE` element.

UPLOAD_ERR_PARTIAL (3)

    Only part of the file was uploaded.

UPLOAD_ERR_NO_FILE (4)

    There was no file uploaded.

UPLOAD_ERR_NO_TMP_DIR (6)

    The upload failed because there was no temporary directory to store the file (available in PHP 4.3.10, 5.0.3, and later).

UPLOAD_ERR_CANT_WRITE (7)

    PHP couldn't write the file to disk (available in PHP 5.1.0 and later).

For all of the `error` values, the listed constants are available in PHP 4.3.0 and later. In earlier versions of PHP, use the number in parentheses next to the constant instead.

The `is_uploaded_file( )` function confirms that the file you're about to process is a legitimate file resulting from a user upload. Always check the `tmp_name` value before processing it as any other file. This ensures that a malicious user can't trick your code into processing a system file as an upload.

You can also move the file to a permanent location; use `move_uploaded_file( )`, as in Example 9-25. It also does a check to make sure that the file being moved is really an uploaded file. Note that the value stored in `tmp_name` is the complete path to the file, not just the base name. Use `basename( )` to chop off the leading directories if needed.

Be sure to check that PHP has permission to read and write to both the directory in which temporary files are saved (set by the `upload_tmp_dir` configuration directive) and the location to which you're trying to copy the file. PHP is often running under a special username such as `nobody` or `apache`, instead of your personal username. Because of this, if you're running under `safe_mode`, copying a file to a new location will probably not allow you to access it again.

Processing files can be a subtle task because not all browsers submit the same information. It's important to do it correctly, however, or you open yourself up to security problems. You are, after all, allowing strangers to upload any file they choose to your machine; malicious people may see this as an opportunity to crack into or crash the computer.

As a result, PHP has a number of features that allow you to place restrictions on uploaded files, including the ability to completely turn off file uploads altogether. So if you're experiencing difficulty processing uploaded files, check that your file isn't being rejected because it seems to pose a security risk.

To do such a check, first make sure `file_uploads` is set to `On` inside your configuration file. Next, make sure your file size isn't larger than `upload_max_filesize`; this defaults to 2 MB, which stops someone from trying to crash the machine by filling up the hard drive with a giant file. Additionally, there's a `post_max_size` directive, which controls the maximum size of all the `post` data allowed in a single request; its initial setting is 8 MB.

From the perspective of browser differences and user error, if you don't see what you expect in `$_FILES`, make sure you add `enctype="multipart/form-data"` to the form's opening tag. PHP needs this to process the file information properly.

Also, if no file is selected for uploading, versions of PHP prior to 4.1 set `tmp_name` to `none`; newer versions set it to the empty string. PHP 4.2.1 allows files of length 0. To be sure a file was uploaded and isn't empty (although blank files may be what you want, depending on the circumstances), you need to make sure `tmp_name` is set and `size` is greater than 0. Last, not all browsers necessarily send the same MIME type for a file; what they send depends on their knowledge of different file types.

See Also

Documentation on handling file uploads at *http://www.php.net/features.file-upload* and on `basename( )` at *http://www.php.net/basename*.

9.15 Preventing Global Variable Injection

Problem

You want to access form input variables without allowing malicious users to set arbitrary global variables in your program.

Solution

Disable the `register_globals` configuration directive and access variables only from the `$_GET`, `$_POST`, and `$_COOKIE` arrays to make sure you know exactly where your variables are coming from.

To do this, make sure `register_globals = Off` appears in your *php.ini* file.

As of PHP 4.2, this is the default configuration.

Discussion

When `register_globals` is set to `on`, external variables, including those from forms and cookies, are imported directly into the global namespace. This is a great convenience, but it can also open up some security holes if you're not very diligent about checking your variables and where they're defined. Why? Because there may be a variable you use internally that isn't supposed to be accessible from the outside but has its value rewritten without your knowledge.

Example 9-26 contains a simple example: imagine you have a page in which a user enters a username and password. If they are validated, you return her user identification number and use that numerical identifier to look up and print out her personal information.

Example 9-26. Insecure register_globals code

```php
<?php
// assume magic_quotes_gpc is set to Off
$username = $dbh->quote($_GET['username']);
$password = $dbh->quote($_GET['password']);

$sth = $dbh->query("SELECT id FROM users WHERE username = $username AND
                    password = $password");

if (1 == $sth->numRows()) {
    $row = $sth->fetchRow(DB_FETCHMODE_OBJECT);
    $id = $row->id;
} else {
    "Print bad username and password";
}

if (!empty($id)) {
    $sth = $dbh->query("SELECT * FROM profile WHERE id = $id");
}
```

Normally, `$id` is set only by your program and is a result of a verified database lookup. However, if someone alters the query string, and passes in a value for `$id`, you'll have problems. With `register_globals` enabled, your script could still execute the second database query and return results even after a bad username and password lookup. Without `register_globals`, $id remains unset because only `$_REQUEST['id']` and `$_GET['id']` are set.

Of course, there are other ways to solve this problem, even when using `register_globals`. You can restructure your code not to allow such a loophole. One way to do this is in Example 9-27.

Example 9-27. Avoiding register_globals problems

```php
<?php
$sth = $dbh->query("SELECT id FROM users WHERE username = $username AND
                    password = $password");

if (1 == $sth->numRows()) {
    $row = $sth->fetchRow(DB_FETCHMODE_OBJECT);
    $id = $row->id;
    if (!empty($id)) {
        $sth = $dbh->query("SELECT * FROM profile WHERE id = $id");
    }
} else {
    "Print bad username and password";
}
```

In Example 9-27 $id has a value only when it's been explicitly set from a database call. Sometimes, however, it is difficult to do this because of how your program is laid out. Another solution is to manually unset( ) or initialize all variables at the top of your script. This removes the bad $id value before it gets a chance to affect your code. However, because PHP doesn't require variable initialization, it's possible to forget to do this in one place; a bug can then slip in without a warning from PHP.

See Also

Documentation on register_globals can be found at *http://www.php.net/ security.registerglobals.php*.

9.16 Handling Remote Variables with Periods in Their Names

Problem

You want to process a variable with a period in its name, but when a form is submitted, you can't find the variable in $_GET or $_POST.

Solution

Replace the period in the variable's name with an underscore. For example, if you have a form input element named hot.dog, you access it inside PHP as the variable $_GET ['hot_dog'] or $_POST['hot_dog'].

Discussion

During PHP's pimply adolescence when register_globals was on by default, a form variable named hot.dog couldn't become $hot.dog—periods aren't allowed in variable names. To work around that, the . was changed to _. While $_GET['hot.dog'] and $_POST['hot.dog'] don't have this problem, the translation still happens for legacy and consistency reasons, no matter your register_globals setting.

You usually run into this translation when there's an element of type image in a form that's used to submit the form. For example, a form element such as <input type="image" name="locations" src="locations.gif">, when clicked, submits the form. The x and y coordinates of the click are submitted as locations.x and locations.y. So in PHP, to find where a user clicked, you need to check $_POST['locations_x'] and $_POST['locations_y'].

See Also

Documentation on variables from outside PHP at *http://www.php.net/ language.variables.external*.

9.17 Using Form Elements with Multiple Options

Problem

You have form elements that let a user select multiple choices, such as a drop-down menu or a group of checkboxes, but PHP sees only one of the submitted values.

Solution

End the form element's name with a pair of square brackets ([]). Example 9-28 shows a properly named group of checkboxes.

Example 9-28. Naming a checkbox group

```
<input type="checkbox" name="boroughs[]" value="bronx"> The Bronx
<input type="checkbox" name="boroughs[]" value="brooklyn"> Brooklyn
<input type="checkbox" name="boroughs[]" value="manhattan"> Manhattan
<input type="checkbox" name="boroughs[]" value="queens"> Queens
<input type="checkbox" name="boroughs[]" value="statenisland"> Staten Island
```

Then, treat the submitted data as an array inside of $_GET or $_POST, as in Example 9-29.

Example 9-29. Handling a submitted checkbox group

```php
<?php
print 'I love ' . join(' and ', $_POST['boroughs']) . '!';
?>
```

Discussion

Putting [ ] at the end of the form element name tells PHP to treat the incoming data as an array instead of a scalar. When PHP sees more than one submitted value assigned to that variable, it keeps them all. If the first three boxes in Example 9-28 were checked, it's as if you'd written the code in Example 9-30 at the top of your program.

Example 9-30. Code equivalent of a multiple-value form element submission

```php
<?php
$_POST['boroughs'][] = "bronx";
$_POST['boroughs'][] = "brooklyn";
$_POST['boroughs'][] = "manhattan";
?>
```

A similar syntax also works with multidimensional arrays. For example, you can have a checkbox such as `<input type="checkbox" name="population[NY][NYC]" value="8008278">`. If checked, this form element sets $_POST['population']['NY']['NYC'] to 8008278.

See Also

The introduction to Chapter 4 for more on arrays.

9.18 Creating Drop-Down Menus Based on the Current Date

Problem

You want to create a series of drop-down menus that are based automatically on the current date.

Solution

Use date( ) to find the current time in the web server's time zone and loop through the days with mktime( ).

Example 9-31 generates <option/> values for today and the six days that follow. In this case, "today" is December 3, 2008.

Example 9-31. Generating date-based drop-down menu options

```php
<?php
list($hour, $minute, $second, $month, $day, $year) =
                              split(':', date('h:i:s:m:d:Y'));
// print out one week's worth of days
for ($i = 0; $i < 7; ++$i) {
    $timestamp = mktime($hour, $minute, $second, $month, $day + $i, $year);
    $date = date("D, F j, Y", $timestamp);
    print "<option value='$timestamp'>$date</option>\n";
}
?>
```

When run on December 3, 2008, Example 9-31 prints:

```
<option value='1228305600'>Wed, December 3, 2008</option>
<option value='1228392000'>Thu, December 4, 2008</option>
<option value='1228478400'>Fri, December 5, 2008</option>
<option value='1228564800'>Sat, December 6, 2008</option>
<option value='1228651200'>Sun, December 7, 2008</option>
<option value='1228737600'>Mon, December 8, 2008</option>
<option value='1228824000'>Tue, December 9, 2008</option>
```

Discussion

In Example 9-31 we set the value for each date as its Unix timestamp representation because we find this easier to handle inside our programs. Of course, you can use any format you find most useful and appropriate.

Don't be tempted to eliminate the calls to mktime( ); dates and times aren't as consistent as you'd hope. Depending on what you're doing, you might not get the results you want. Example 9-32 takes the shortcut of just incrementing the timestamp by the number of seconds in each day (60 seconds per minute × 60 minutes per hour × 24 hours per day = 86,400 seconds).

Example 9-32. Incorrectly generating date-based drop-down menu options

```php
<?php
$timestamp = mktime(0, 0, 0, 10, 30, 2008); // October 30, 2008
$one_day = 60 * 60 * 24; // number of seconds in a day

// print out one week's worth of days
for ($i = 0; $i < 7; ++$i) {
    $date = date("D, F j, Y", $timestamp);
    print "<option value='$timestamp'>$date</option>\n";
    $timestamp += $one_day;
}
?>
```

Example 9-32 prints:

```
<option value='1225339200'>Thu, October 30, 2008</option>
<option value='1225425600'>Fri, October 31, 2008</option>
<option value='1225512000'>Sat, November 1, 2008</option>
<option value='1225598400'>Sun, November 2, 2008</option>
<option value='1225684800'>Sun, November 2, 2008</option>
<option value='1225771200'>Mon, November 3, 2008</option>
<option value='1225857600'>Tue, November 4, 2008</option>
```

Example 9-32 should print out the month, day, and year for a seven-day period starting October 30, 2008. However, it doesn't work as expected.

Why are there two `Sun, November 2, 2008` in the list? The answer: daylight saving time. It's not true that the number of seconds in a day stays constant; in fact, it's almost guaranteed to change. Worst of all, if you're not near either of the changeover dates, you're liable to miss this bug during testing.

See Also

Chapter 3, particularly Recipe 3.12, but also Recipes 3.2, 3.3, 3.4, 3.5, 3.6, 3.11, and 3.14; documentation on `date()` at *http://www.php.net/date* and `mktime()` at *http://www.php.net/mktime*.

CHAPTER 10

Database Access

10.0 Introduction

Databases are central to many web applications. A database can hold almost any collection of information you may want to search and update, such as a user list, a product catalog, or recent headlines. One reason why PHP is such a great web programming language is its extensive database support. PHP can interact with (at last count) more than 20 different databases, some relational and some not. The relational databases it can talk to are Apache Derby, DB++, FrontBase, IBM Cloudscape, IBM DB2, Informix, Interbase, Ingres II, Microsoft SQL Server, mSQL, MySQL, MySQL MaxDB, Oracle, Ovrimos SQL Server, PostgreSQL, SQLite, and Sybase. The nonrelational databases it can talk to are dBase, filePro, HyperWave, Paradox, and the DBM family of flat-file databases. It also has ODBC support, so even if your favorite database isn't in the list, as long as it supports ODBC, you can use it with PHP.

DBM databases, discussed in Recipe 10.1, are simple, robust, and efficient flat files but limit the structure of your data to key/value pairs. If your data can be organized as a mapping of keys to values, DBM databases are a great choice.

PHP really shines, though, when paired with an SQL database. This combination is used for most of the recipes in this chapter. SQL databases can be complicated, but they are extremely powerful. To use PHP with a particular SQL database, PHP must be explicitly told to include support for that database when it is compiled. If PHP is built to support dynamic module loading, the database support can also be built as a dynamic module.

The SQL database examples in this chapter use PHP 5's PDO database access layer. With PDO, you use the same PHP functions no matter what database engine you're talking to. Although the syntax of the SQL may differ from database to database, the PHP code remains similar. In this regard, PDO offers data *access* abstraction, not total database abstraction. Other PHP libraries, such as PEAR DB (*http://pear.php.net/pack age/db*), ADODb (*http://adodb.sourceforge.net/*), and MDB2 (*http://pear.php.net/pack age/MDB2*) attempt to solve the total database abstraction problem—they hide different databases' implementation details such as date handling and column types behind a layer of code. While this sort of abstraction can save you some work if you're writing software that is intended to be used with lots of different types of databases, but it can cause other problems. When you write SQL focused on a particular type of database, you can take advantage of that database's features for maximum performance.

PHP 5 comes bundled with SQLite, a powerful database that doesn't require a separate server. It's a great choice when you have a moderate amount of traffic and don't want to deal with the hassles of running a database server. Recipe 10.2 discusses some of the ins and outs of SQLite. With PHP 4, you can use SQLite via the PECL SQLite extension (*http://pecl.php.net/package/SQLite*).

Many SQL examples in this chapter use a table of information about Zodiac signs. The table's structure is shown in Example 10-1. The data in the table is shown in Example 10-2.

Example 10-1. Sample table structure

```
CREATE TABLE zodiac (
    id INT UNSIGNED NOT NULL,
    sign CHAR(11),
    symbol CHAR(13),
    planet CHAR(7),
    element CHAR(5),
    start_month TINYINT,
    start_day TINYINT,
    end_month TINYINT,
    end_day TINYINT,
    PRIMARY KEY(id)
);
```

Example 10-2. Sample table data

```
INSERT INTO zodiac VALUES (1,'Aries','Ram','Mars','fire',3,21,4,19);
INSERT INTO zodiac VALUES (2,'Taurus','Bull','Venus','earth',4,20,5,20);
INSERT INTO zodiac VALUES (3,'Gemini','Twins','Mercury','air',5,21,6,21);
INSERT INTO zodiac VALUES (4,'Cancer','Crab','Moon','water',6,22,7,22);
INSERT INTO zodiac VALUES (5,'Leo','Lion','Sun','fire',7,23,8,22);
INSERT INTO zodiac VALUES (6,'Virgo','Virgin','Mercury','earth',8,23,9,22);
INSERT INTO zodiac VALUES (7,'Libra','Scales','Venus','air',9,23,10,23);
INSERT INTO zodiac VALUES (8,'Scorpio','Scorpion','Mars','water',10,24,11,21);
INSERT INTO zodiac VALUES (9,'Sagittarius','Archer','Jupiter','fire',11,22,12,21);
INSERT INTO zodiac VALUES (10,'Capricorn','Goat','Saturn','earth',12,22,1,19);
INSERT INTO zodiac VALUES (11,'Aquarius','Water Carrier','Uranus','air',1,20,2,18);
INSERT INTO zodiac VALUES (12,'Pisces','Fishes','Neptune','water',2,19,3,20);
```

Recipes 10.3 through 10.8 cover the basics of connecting to a database server, sending queries and getting the results back, as well as using queries that change the data in the database.

Typical PHP programs capture information from HTML form fields and store that information in the database. Some characters, such as the apostrophe and backslash, have special meaning in SQL, so you have to be careful if your form data contains those characters. PHP has a feature called "magic quotes" that attempts to make this easier.

When the configuration setting `magic_quotes_gpc` is on, variables coming from `get` requests, `post` requests, and cookies have single quotes, double quotes, backslashes, and nulls escaped with a backslash. You can also turn on `magic_quotes_runtime` to automatically escape quotes, backslashes, and nulls from external sources such as database queries or text files. For example, if `magic_quotes_runtime` is on and you read a file into an array with `file( )`, the special characters in that array are backslash-escaped.

Unfortunately, "magic quotes" usually turns out to be more like "annoying quotes." If you want to use submitted form data in any other context than just an SQL query (for example, displaying it in a page), then you need to undo the escaping so the page looks right. If you've run into a PHP web site in which backslashes seem to accumulate before single quotes in text fields, the culprit is almost certainly magic quotes. Recipe 10.7 explains PDO's *bound parameters* support, which is a better way to make sure that special characters in user input are properly escaped when the user input is incorporated into SQL queries. Recipe 10.9 discusses escaping special characters in queries in more detail. General debugging techniques you can use to handle errors resulting from database queries are covered in Recipe 10.10.

The remaining recipes cover database tasks that are more involved than just simple queries. Recipe 10.11 shows how to automatically generate unique ID values you can use as record identifiers. Recipe 10.12 covers building queries at runtime from a list of fields. This makes it easier to manage `INSERT` and `UPDATE` queries that involve a lot of columns. Recipe 10.13 demonstrates how to display links that let you page through a result set, displaying a few records on each page. To speed up your database access, you can cache queries and their results, as explained in Recipe 10.14.

Recipe 10.15 shows some techniques for managing access to a single database connection from various places in a large program. Last, Recipe 10.16 ties together some of the topics discussed in the chapter in a complete program that stores a threaded message board in a database.

10.1 Using DBM Databases

Problem

You have data that can be easily represented as key/value pairs, want to store it safely, and have very fast lookups based on those keys.

Solution

Use the DBA abstraction layer to access a DBM-style database, as shown in Example 10-3.

Example 10-3. Using a DBM database

```php
<?php
$dbh = dba_open('fish.db','c','gdbm') or die($php_errormsg);
```

```
// retrieve and change values
if (dba_exists('flounder',$dbh)) {
  $flounder_count = dba_fetch('flounder',$dbh);
  $flounder_count++;
  dba_replace('flounder',$flounder_count, $dbh);
  print "Updated the flounder count.";
} else {
  dba_insert('flounder',1, $dbh);
  print "Started the flounder count.";
}

// no more tilapia
dba_delete('tilapia',$dbh);

// what fish do we have?
for ($key = dba_firstkey($dbh);  $key !== false; $key = dba_nextkey($dbh)) {
   $value = dba_fetch($key, $dbh);
   print "$key: $value\n";
}

dba_close($dbh);
?>
```

Discussion

PHP can support a few different kinds of DBM backends: GDBM, NDBM, DB2, DB3, DBM, and CDB. The DBA abstraction layer lets you use the same functions on any DBM backend. All these backends store key/value pairs. You can iterate through all the keys in a database, retrieve the value associated with a particular key, and find if a particular key exists. Both the keys and the values are strings.

The program in Example 10-4 maintains a list of usernames and passwords in a DBM database. The username is the first command-line argument, and the password is the second argument. If the given username already exists in the database, the password is changed to the given password; otherwise, the user and password combination are added to the database.

Example 10-4. Tracking users and passwords with a DBM database

```
<?php
$user = $_SERVER['argv'][1];
$password = $_SERVER['argv'][2];

$data_file = '/tmp/users.db';

$dbh = dba_open($data_file,'c','gdbm') or die("Can't open db $data_file");

if (dba_exists($user,$dbh)) {
    print "User $user exists. Changing password.";
} else {
    print "Adding user $user.";
}
```

```
dba_replace($user,$password,$dbh) or die("Can't write to database $data_file");

dba_close($dbh);
?>
```

The dba_open( ) function returns a handle to a DBM file (or false on error). It takes
three arguments. The first is the filename of the DBM file. The second argument is the
mode for opening the file. A mode of r opens an existing database for read-only access,
and w opens an existing database for read-write access. The c mode opens a database
for read-write access and creates the database if it doesn't already exist. Last, n does
the same thing as c, but if the database already exists, n empties it. The third argument
to dba_open( ) is which DBM handler to use; this example uses 'gdbm'. To find what
DBM handlers are compiled into your PHP installation, look at the "DBA" section of
the output from phpinfo( ). The "Supported handlers" line gives you your choices.

To find if a key has been set in a DBM database, use dba_exists( ). It takes two arguments: a string key and a DBM filehandle. It looks for the key in the DBM file and
returns true if it finds the key (or false if it doesn't). The dba_replace( ) function takes
three arguments: a string key, a string value, and a DBM filehandle. It puts the key/
value pair into the DBM file. If an entry already exists with the given key, it overwrites
that entry with the new value.

To close a database, call dba_close( ). A DBM file opened with dba_open( ) is automatically closed at the end of a request, but you need to call dba_close( ) explicitly to close
persistent connections created with dba_open( ).

You can use dba_firstkey( ) and dba_nextkey( ) to iterate through all the keys in a DBM
file and dba_fetch( ) to retrieve the values associated with each key. The program in
Example 10-5 calculates the total length of all passwords in a DBM file.

Example 10-5. Calculating password length with DBM

```php
<?php
$data_file = '/tmp/users.db';
$total_length = 0;
if (! ($dbh = dba_open($data_file,'r','gdbm'))) {
    die("Can't open database $data_file");
}

$k = dba_firstkey($dbh);
while ($k) {
    $total_length += strlen(dba_fetch($k,$dbh));
    $k = dba_nextkey($dbh);
}

print "Total length of all passwords is $total_length characters.";

dba_close($dbh);
```

The dba_firstkey( ) function initializes $k to the first key in the DBM file. Each time
through the while loop, dba_fetch( ) retrieves the value associated with key $k and

$total_length is incremented by the length of the value (calculated with strlen( )). With dba_nextkey( ), $k is set to the next key in the file.

One way to store complex data in a DBM database is with serialize( ). Example 10-6 stores structured user information in a DBM database by serializing the structure before storing it and unserializing when retrieving it.

Example 10-6. Storing structured data in a DBM database

```
<?php
$dbh = dba_open('users.db','c','gdbm') or die($php_errormsg);

// read in and unserialize the data
if ($exists = dba_exists($_POST['username'], $dbh)) {
    $serialized_data = dba_fetch($_POST['username'], $dbh) or die($php_errormsg);
    $data = unserialize($serialized_data);
} else {
    $data = array();
}

// update values
if ($_POST['new_password']) {
    $data['password'] = $_POST['new_password'];
}
$data['last_access'] = time();

// write data back to file
if ($exists) {
    dba_replace($_POST['username'],serialize($data), $dbh);
} else {
    dba_insert($_POST['username'],serialize($data), $dbh);
}

dba_close($dbh);
?>
```

While Example 10-6 can store multiple users' data in the same file, you can't search for, for example, a user's last access time, without looping through each key in the file. If you need to do those kinds of searches, put your data in an SQL database.

Each DBM handler has different behavior in some areas. For example, GDBM provides internal locking. If one process has opened a GDBM file in read-write mode, other calls to dba_open( ) to open the same file in read-write mode will fail. For other DBM handlers, add an l to the mode you pass to dba_open( ) to lock the database with a separate .*lck* file or a d to lock the database file itself. Two DBA functions are also database-specific: dba_optimize( ) and dba_sync( ). The dba_optimize( ) function calls a handler-specific DBM file-optimization function. Currently, this is implemented only for GDBM, for which its gdbm_reorganize( ) function is called. The dba_sync( ) function calls a handler-specific DBM file synchronizing function. For DB2 and DB3, their sync( ) function is called. For GDBM, its gdbm_sync( ) function is called. Nothing happens for other DBM handlers.

Using a DBM database is a step up from a plain text file but it lacks most features of an SQL database. Your data structure is limited to key/value pairs, and locking robustness varies greatly depending on the DBM handler. Still, DBM handlers can be a good choice for heavily accessed read-only data.

See Also

Recipe 5.7 discusses serializing data; documentation on the DBA functions at *http://www.php.net/dba*; for more information on the DB2 and DB3 DBM handlers, see *http://www.sleepycat.com/products/bdb.html* (note that these handlers are not generally free for commercial use); for GDBM, check out *http://www.gnu.org/directory/gdbm.html* or *http://www.mit.edu:8001/afs/athena.mit.edu/project/gnu/doc/html/gdbm_toc.html*.

10.2 Using an SQLite Database

Problem

You want to use a relational database that doesn't involve a separate server process.

Solution

Use SQLite. This robust, powerful database program comes with PHP 5 and doesn't require running a separate server. An SQLite database is just a file. Example 10-7 creates an SQLite database, populates it with a table if it doesn't already exist, and then puts some data into the table.

Example 10-7. Creating an SQLite database

```
<?php
$db = new PDO('sqlite:/usr/local/zodiac');

// Create the table and insert the data atomically
$db->beginTransaction();
// Try to find a table named 'zodiac'
$q = $db->query("SELECT name FROM sqlite_master WHERE type = 'table'" .
                " AND name = 'zodiac'");
// If the query didn't return a row, then create the table
// and insert the data
if ($q->fetch() === false) {
    $db->exec(<<<_SQL_
CREATE TABLE zodiac (
  id INT UNSIGNED NOT NULL,
  sign CHAR(11),
  symbol CHAR(13),
  planet CHAR(7),
  element CHAR(5),
  start_month TINYINT,
  start_day TINYINT,
  end_month TINYINT,
  end_day TINYINT,
```

```
    PRIMARY KEY(id)
)
_SQL_
);

    // The individual SQL statements
    $sql=<<<_SQL_
INSERT INTO zodiac VALUES (1,'Aries','Ram','Mars','fire',3,21,4,19);
INSERT INTO zodiac VALUES (2,'Taurus','Bull','Venus','earth',4,20,5,20);
INSERT INTO zodiac VALUES (3,'Gemini','Twins','Mercury','air',5,21,6,21);
INSERT INTO zodiac VALUES (4,'Cancer','Crab','Moon','water',6,22,7,22);
INSERT INTO zodiac VALUES (5,'Leo','Lion','Sun','fire',7,23,8,22);
INSERT INTO zodiac VALUES (6,'Virgo','Virgin','Mercury','earth',8,23,9,22);
INSERT INTO zodiac VALUES (7,'Libra','Scales','Venus','air',9,23,10,23);
INSERT INTO zodiac VALUES (8,'Scorpio','Scorpion','Mars','water',10,24,11,21);
INSERT INTO zodiac VALUES (9,'Sagittarius','Archer','Jupiter','fire',11,22,12,21);
INSERT INTO zodiac VALUES (10,'Capricorn','Goat','Saturn','earth',12,22,1,19);
INSERT INTO zodiac VALUES (11,'Aquarius','Water Carrier','Uranus','air',1,20,2,18);
INSERT INTO zodiac VALUES (12,'Pisces','Fishes','Neptune','water',2,19,3,20);
_SQL_;

    // Chop up each line of SQL and execute it
    foreach (explode("\n",trim($sql)) as $q) {
        $db->exec(trim($q));
    }
    $db->commit();
} else {
    // Nothing happened, so end the transaction
    $db->rollback();
}
?>
```

Discussion

Because SQLite databases are just regular files, all the precautions and gotchas that apply to file access in PHP apply to SQLite databases. The user that your PHP process is running as must have permission to read from and write to the location where the SQLite database is. It is an extremely good idea to make this location somewhere outside your web server's document root. If the database file can be read directly by the web server, then a user who guesses its location can retrieve the entire thing, bypassing any restrictions you've built into the queries in your PHP programs.

In PHP, the `sqlite` extension provides regular SQLite access as well as a PDO driver for SQLite version 2. The `pdo_sqlite` extension provides a PDO driver for SQLite version 3. If you're starting from scratch, use the PDO driver for SQLite 3, since it's faster and has more features. If you already have an SQLite 2 database, consider using the PDO drivers to migrate to SQLite 3.

The `sqlite_master` table referenced in Example 10-7 is special system table that holds information about other tables—so it's useful in determining whether a particular table exists yet. Other databases have their own ways of providing this sort of system metadata.

See Also

Documentation on SQLite at *http://www.sqlite.org/docs.html* and on `sqlite_master` at *http://www.sqlite.org/faq.html#q9*.

10.3 Connecting to an SQL Database

Problem

You want access to a SQL database to store or retrieve information. Without a database, dynamic web sites aren't very dynamic.

Solution

Create a new `PDO` object with the appropriate connection string. Example 10-8 shows `PDO` object creation for a few different kinds of databases.

Example 10-8. Connecting with PDO

```php
<?php
// MySQL expects parameters in the string
$mysql = new PDO('mysql:host=db.example.com', $user, $password);
// Separate multiple parameters with ;
$mysql = new PDO('mysql:host=db.example.com;port=31075', $user, $password)
$mysql = new PDO('mysql:host=db.example.com;port=31075;dbname=food', $user, $password)
// Connect to a local MySQL Server
$mysql = new PDO('mysql:unix_socket=/tmp/mysql.sock', $user, $password)

// PostgreSQL also expects parameters in the string
$pgsql = new PDO('pgsql:host=db.example.com', $user, $password);
// But you separate multiple parameters with ' '
$pgsql = new PDO('pgsql:host=db.example.com port=31075', $user, $password)
$pgsql = new PDO('pgsql:host=db.example.com port=31075 dbname=food', $user, $password)
// You can put the user and password in the DSN if you like.
$pgsql = new PDO("pgsql:host=db.example.com port=31075 dbname=food user=$user password=$password");

// Oracle
// If a database name is defined in tnsnames.ora, just put that in the DSN
$oci = new PDO('oci:food', $user, $password)
// Otherwise, specify an Instant Client URI
$oci = new PDO('oci:dbname=//db.example.com:1521/food', $user, $password)

// Sybase (If PDO is using FreeTDS)
$sybase = new PDO('sybase:host=db.example.com;dbname=food', $user, $password)
// Microsoft SQL Server (If PDO is using MS SQL Server libraries)
$mssql = new PDO('mssql:host=db.example.com;dbname=food', $user, $password);
// DBLib (for other versions of DB-lib)
$dblib = new PDO('dblib:host=db.example.com;dbname=food', $user, $password);

// ODBC -- a predefined connection
$odbc = new PDO('odbc:DSN=food');
// ODBC -- an ad-hoc connection. Provide whatever the underlying driver needs
```

```
$odbc = new PDO('odbc:Driver={Microsoft Access Driver (*.mdb)};DBQ=
C:\\data\\food.mdb;Uid=Chef');

// SQLite just expects a filename -- no user or password
$sqlite = new PDO('sqlite:/usr/local/zodiac.db');
$sqlite = new PDO('sqlite:c:/data/zodiac.db');
// SQLite can also handle in-memory, temporary databases
$sqlite = new PDO('sqlite::memory:');
// SQLite v2 DSNs look similar to v3
$sqlite2 = new PDO('sqlite2:/usr/local/old-zodiac.db');
?>
```

Discussion

If all goes well, the PDO constructor returns a new object that can be used for querying the database. If there's a problem, a PDOException is thrown.

As you can see from Example 10-8, the format of the DSN is highly dependent on which kind of database you're attempting to connect to. In general, though, the first argument to the PDO constructor is a string that describes the location and name of the database you want and the second and third arguments are the username and password to connect to the database with. Note that to use a particular PDO backend, PHP must be built with support for that backend. Use the output from phpinfo( ) to determine what PDO backends your PHP setup has.

See Also

Recipe 10.4 for querying an SQL database; Recipe 10.6 for modifying an SQL database; documentation on PDO at *http://www.php.net/PDO*.

10.4 Querying an SQL Database

Problem

You want to retrieve some data from your database.

Solution

Use PDO::query( ) to send the SQL query to the database, and then a foreach loop to retrieve each row of the result, as shown in Example 10-9.

Example 10-9. Sending a query to the database

```
<?php
$st = $db->query('SELECT symbol,planet FROM zodiac');
foreach ($st->fetchAll() as $row) {
    print "{$row['symbol']} goes with {$row['planet']} <br/>\n";
}
?>
```

Discussion

The query( ) method returns a PDOStatement object. Its fetchAll( ) provides a concise way to do something with each row returned from a query.

The fetch( ) method returns a row at a time, as shown in Example 10-10.

Example 10-10. Fetching individual rows

```php
<?php
$rows = $db->query('SELECT symbol,planet FROM zodiac');
$firstRow = $rows->fetch();
print "The first results are that {$row['symbol']} goes with {$row['planet']}";
?>
```

Each call to fetch( ) returns the next row in the result set. When there are no more rows available, fetch( ) returns false.

By default, fetch( ) returns an array containing each column in the result set row *twice* —once with an index corresponding to the column name and once with a numerical index. That means that the $firstRow variable in Example 10-10 has four elements: $firstRow[0] is Ram, $firstRow[1] is Mars, $firstRow['symbol'] is Ram, and $firstRow ['planet'] is Mars.

To have fetch( ) return rows in a different format, pass a PDO::FETCH_* constant to query( ) as a second argument. You can also pass one of the constants as the first argument to fetch( ). The allowable constants and what they make fetch( ) return are listed in Table 10-1.

Table 10-1. PDO::FETCH_* constants

Constant	Row format
PDO::FETCH_BOTH	Array with both numeric and string (column names) keys. The default format.
PDO::FETCH_NUM	Array with numeric keys.
PDO::FETCH_ASSOC	Array with string (column names) keys.
PDO::FETCH_OBJ	Object of class stdClass with column names as property names.
PDO::FETCH_LAZY	Object of class PDORow with column names as property names. The properties aren't populated until accessed, so this is a good choice if your result row has a lot of columns. Note that if you store the returned object and fetch another row, the stored object is updated with values from the new row.

In addition to the choices in Table 10-1, there are additional ways a row can be structured. These other ways require more than just passing a constant to query( ) or fetch( ), however.

In combination with bindColumn( ), the PDO::FETCH_BOUND fetch mode lets you set up variables whose values get refreshed each time fetch( ) is called. Example 10-11 shows how this works.

Example 10-11. Binding result columns

```php
<?php
$row = $db->query('SELECT symbol,planet FROM zodiac',PDO::FETCH_BOUND);
// Put the value of the 'symbol' column in $symbol
$row->bindColumn('symbol', $symbol);
// Put the value of the second column ('planet') in $planet
$row->bindColumn(2, $planet);
while ($row->fetch()) {
    print "$symbol goes with $planet. <br/>\n";
}
?>
```

In Example 10-11, each time fetch( ) is called, $symbol and $planet are assigned new values. Note that you can use either a column name or number with bindColumn( ). Column numbers start at 1.

When used with query( ), the PDO::FETCH_INTO and PDO::FETCH_CLASS constants put re-sult rows into specialized objects of particular classes. To use these modes, first create a class that extends the built-in PDOStatement class. Example 10-12 extends PDOState ment with a method that reports the average length of all the column values and then sets up a query to use it.

Example 10-12. Extending PDOStatement

```php
<?php
class AvgStatement extends PDOStatement {
    public function avg() {
        $sum = 0;
        $vars = get_object_vars($this);
        // Remove PDOStatement's built-in 'queryString' variable
        unset($vars['queryString']);
        foreach ($vars as $var => $value) {
            $sum += strlen($value);
        }
        return $sum / count($vars);
    }
}
$row = new AvgStatement;
$results = $db->query('SELECT symbol,planet FROM zodiac',PDO::FETCH_INTO, $row);
// Each time fetch() is called, $row is repopulated
while ($results->fetch()) {
    print "$row->symbol belongs to $row->planet (Average: {$row->avg()}) <br/>\n";
}
?>
```

In Example 10-12, the second and third arguments to query( ) tell PDO "each time you fetch a new row, stuff the values into properties of the $row variable." Then, inside the while( ) loop, the properties of $row are available, as well as the newly defined avg( ) method.

PDO::FETCH_INTO is useful when you want to keep data around in the same object, such as whether you're displaying an odd- or even-numbered row, throughout all the calls to fetch( ). But when you want a new object for each row, use PDO::FETCH_CLASS. Pass it to query( ) like PDO::FETCH_INTO, but make the third argument to query( ) a class name, not an object instance. The class name you provide with PDO::FETCH_CLASS must extend PDOStatement.

See Also

Recipe 10.5 for other ways to retrieve data; Recipe 10.6 for modifying an SQL database; Recipe 10.7 for repeating queries efficiently; documentation on PDO at *http://www.php.net/PDO*.

10.5 Retrieving Rows Without a Loop

Problem

You want a concise way to execute a query and retrieve the data it returns.

Solution

Use fetchAll( ) to get all the results from a query at once, as shown in Example 10-13.

Example 10-13. Getting all results at once

```php
<?php
$st = $db->query('SELECT planet, element FROM zodiac');
$results = $st->fetchAll();
foreach ($results as $i => $result) {
    print "Planet $i is {$result['planet']} <br/>\n";
}
?>
```

Discussion

The fetchAll( ) method is useful when you need to do something that depends on all the rows a query returns, such as counting how many rows there are or handling rows out of order. Like fetch( ), fetchAll( ) defaults to representing each row as an array with both numeric and string keys and accepts the various PDO::FETCH_* constants to change that behavior.

fetchAll( ) also accepts a few other constants that affect the results it returns. To retrieve just a single column from the results, pass PDO::FETCH_COLUMN and a second argument, the index of the column you want. The first column is 0, not 1.

See Also

Recipe 10.4 for querying an SQL database and more information on fetch modes; Recipe 10.6 for modifying an SQL database; Recipe 10.7 for repeating queries efficiently; documentation on PDO at *http://www.php.net/PDO*.

10.6 Modifying Data in an SQL Database

Problem

You want to add, remove, or change data in an SQL database.

Solution

Use `PDO::exec( )` to send an `INSERT`, `DELETE`, or `UPDATE` command, as shown in Example 10-14.

Example 10-14. Using PDO::exec( )

```php
<?php
$db->exec("INSERT INTO family (id,name) VALUES (1,'Vito')");

$db->exec("DELETE FROM family WHERE name LIKE 'Fredo'");

$db->exec("UPDATE family SET is_naive = 1 WHERE name LIKE 'Kay'");
?>
```

You can also prepare a query with `PDO::prepare( )` and execute it with `PDOStatement::execute( )`, as shown in Example 10-15.

Example 10-15. Preparing and executing a query

```php
<?php
$st = $db->prepare('INSERT INTO family (id,name) VALUES (?,?)');
$st->execute(array(1,'Vito'));

$st = $db->prepare('DELETE FROM family WHERE name LIKE ?');
$st->execute(array('Fredo'));

$st = $db->prepare('UPDATE family SET is_naive = ? WHERE name LIKE ?');
$st->execute(array(1,'Kay');
?>
```

Discussion

The `exec( )` method sends to the database whatever it's passed. For `INSERT`, `UPDATE`, and `DELETE` queries, it returns the number of rows affected by the query.

The `prepare( )` and `execute( )` methods are especially useful for queries that you want to execute multiple times. Once you've prepared a query, you can execute it with new values without re-preparing it. Example 10-16 reuses the same prepared query three times.

Example 10-16. Reusing a prepared statement

```php
<?php
$st = $db->prepare('DELETE FROM family WHERE name LIKE ?');
$st->execute(array('Fredo'));
$st->execute(array('Sonny'));
```

```php
$st->execute(array('Luca Brasi'));
?>
```

See Also

Recipe 10.7 for information on repeating queries; documentation on `PDO::exec( )` at *http://www.php.net/PDO::exec*, on `PDO::prepare( )` at *http://www.php.net/PDO::pre pare*, and on `PDOStatement::execute( )` at *http://www.php.net/PDOStatement::execute*.

10.7 Repeating Queries Efficiently

Problem

You want to run the same query multiple times, substituting in different values each time.

Solution

Set up the query with `PDO::prepare( )` and then run it by calling `execute( )` on the prepared statement that `prepare( )` returns. The placeholders in the query passed to `prepare( )` are replaced with data by `execute( )`, as shown in Example 10-17.

Example 10-17. Running prepared statements

```php
<?php
// Prepare
$st = $db->prepare("SELECT sign FROM zodiac WHERE element LIKE ?");
// Execute once
$st->execute(array('fire'));
while ($row = $st->fetch()) {
    print $row[0] . "<br/>\n";
}
// Execute again
$st->execute(array('water'));
while ($row = $st->fetch()) {
    print $row[0] . "<br/>\n";
}
?>
```

Discussion

The values passed to `execute( )` are called *bound parameters*—each value is associated with (or "bound to") a placeholder in the query. Two great things about bound parameters are security and speed. With bound parameters, you don't have to worry about SQL injection attacks. PDO appropriately quotes and escapes each parameter so that special characters are neutralized. Also, upon `prepare( )`, many database backends do some parsing and optimizing of the query, so each call to `execute( )` is faster than calling `exec( )` or `query( )` with a fully formed query in a string you've built yourself.

In Example 10-17, the first execute( ) runs the query SELECT sign FROM zodiac WHERE element LIKE 'fire'. The second execute( ) runs SELECT sign FROM zodiac WHERE element LIKE 'water'.

Each time, execute( ) substitutes the value in its second argument for the ? placeholder. If there is more than one placeholder, put the arguments in the array in the order they should appear in the query. Example 10-18 shows prepare( ) and execute( ) with two placeholders.

Example 10-18. Multiple placeholders

```php
<?php
$st = $db->prepare(
    "SELECT sign FROM zodiac WHERE element LIKE ? OR planet LIKE ?");

// SELECT sign FROM zodiac WHERE element LIKE 'earth' OR planet LIKE 'Mars'
$st->execute(array('earth','Mars'));
?>
```

In addition to the ? placeholder style, PDO also supports named placeholders. If you've got a lot of placeholders in a query, this can make them easier to read. Instead of ?, put a placeholder name (which has to begin with a colon) in the query, and then use those placeholder names (without the colons) as keys in the parameter array you pass to execute( ). Example 10-19 shows named placeholders in action.

Example 10-19. Using named placeholders

```php
<?php
$st = $db->prepare(
    "SELECT sign FROM zodiac WHERE element LIKE :element OR planet LIKE :planet");
// SELECT sign FROM zodiac WHERE element LIKE 'earth' OR planet LIKE 'Mars'
$st->execute(array('planet' => 'Mars', 'element' => 'earth'));
$row = $st->fetch();
```

With named placeholders, your queries are easier to read and you can provide the values to execute( ) in any order. Note, though, that each placeholder name can only appear in a query once. If you want to provide the same value more than once in a query, use two different placeholder names and include the value twice in the array passed to execute( ).

Aside from ? and named placeholders, prepare( ) offers a third way to stuff values into queries: bindParam( ). This method automatically associates what's in a variable with a particular placeholder. Example 10-20 shows how to use bindParam( ).

Example 10-20. Using bindParam( )

```php
<?php
$pairs = array('Mars' => 'water',
               'Moon' => 'water',
               'Sun'  => 'fire');
$st = $db->prepare(
    "SELECT sign FROM zodiac WHERE element LIKE :element AND planet LIKE :planet");
$st->bindParam(':element', $element);
```

```
    $st->bindparam(':planet', $planet);
    foreach ($pairs as $planet => $element) {
        // No need to pass anything to execute() --
        // the values come from $element and $planet
        $st->execute();
        var_dump($st->fetch());
    }
    ?>
```

In Example 10-20, there's no need to pass any values to execute( ). The two calls to bindParam( ) tell PDO "whenever you execute $st, use whatever's in the $element variable for the :element placeholder and whatever's in the $planet variable for the :planet placeholder." The values in those variables when you call bindParam( ) don't matter—it's the values in those variables when execute( ) is called that counts. Since the foreach statement puts array keys in $planet and array values in $element, the keys and values from $pairs are substituted into the query.

If you use ? placeholders with prepare( ), provide a placeholder position as the first argument to bindParam( ) instead of a parameter name. Placeholder positions start at 1, not 0.

bindParam( ) takes its cue on how to deal with the provided value based on that value's PHP type. Force bindParam( ) to treat the value as a particular type by passing a type constant as a third argument. The type constants that bindParam( ) understands are listed in Table 10-2.

Table 10-2. PDO::PARAM_* constants

Constant	Type
PDO::PARAM_NULL	NULL
PDO::PARAM_BOOL	Boolean
PDO::PARAM_INT	Integer
PDO::PARAM_STR	String
PDO::PARAM_LOB	"Large Object"

The PDO::PARAM_LOB type is particularly handy because it treats the parameter as a stream. It makes for an efficient way to stuff the contents of files (or anything that can be represented by a stream, such as a remote URL) into a database table. Example 10-21 uses glob( ) to slurp the contents of all the files in a directory into a database table.

Example 10-21. Putting file contents into a database with PDO::PARAM_LOB

```
    <?php
    $st = $db->prepare('INSERT INTO files (path,contents) VALUES (:path,:contents)');
    $st->bindParam(':path',$path);
    $st->bindParam(':contents',$fp,PDO::PARAM_LOB);
    foreach (glob('c:/documents/*.*') as $path) {
        // Get a filehandle that PDO::PARAM_LOB can work with
```

```
        $fp = fopen($path,'r');
        $st->execute();
    }
    ?>
```

Using PDO::PARAM_LOB effectively depends on your underlying database. For example, with Oracle your query must create an empty LOB handle and be inside a transaction. The "Inserting an image into a database: Oracle" example of the PDO manpage at *http://www.php.net/PDO* shows the proper syntax to do this.

See Also

Documentation on PDO::prepare( ) at *http://www.php.net/PDO::prepare*, PDOStatement::execute( ) at *http://www.php.net/PDOStatement::execute*, on PDO::bindParam( ) at *http://www.php.net/PDO::bindParam*, and on PDO::PARAM_LOB in the "Large Objects" section of *http://www.php.net/PDO*.

10.8 Finding the Number of Rows Returned by a Query

Problem

You want to know how many rows a SELECT query returned, or you want to know how many rows were changed by an INSERT, UPDATE, or DELETE query.

Solution

If you're issuing an INSERT, UPDATE, or DELETE with PDO::exec( ), the return value from exec( ) is the number of modified rows.

If you're issuing an INSERT, UPDATE, or DELETE with PDO::prepare( ) and PDOStatement::execute( ), call PDOStatement::rowCount( ) to get the number of modified rows, as shown in Example 10-22.

Example 10-22. Counting rows with rowCount( )
```
<?php
$st = $db->prepare('DELETE FROM family WHERE name LIKE ?');
$st->execute(array('Fredo'));
print "Deleted rows: " . $st->rowCount();
$st->execute(array('Sonny'));
print "Deleted rows: " . $st->rowCount();
$st->execute(array('Luca Brasi'));
print "Deleted rows: " . $st->rowCount();
?>
```

If you're issuing a SELECT statement, the only foolproof way to find out how many rows are returned is to retrieve them all with fetchAll( ) and then count how many rows you have, as shown in Example 10-23.

Example 10-23. Counting rows from a SELECT

```php
<?php
$st = $db->query('SELECT symbol,planet FROM zodiac');
$all= $st->fetchAll(PDO::FETCH_COLUMN, 1);
print "Retrieved ". count($all) . " rows";
?>
```

Discussion

Although some database backends provide information to PDO about the number of rows retrieved by a SELECT so that rowCount( ) can work in those circumstances, not all do. So relying on that behavior isn't a good idea.

However, retrieving everything in a large result set can be inefficient. As an alternative, ask the database to calculate a result set size with the COUNT(*) function. Use the same WHERE clause as you would otherwise, but ask SELECT to return COUNT(*) instead of a list of fields.

See Also

Documentation on PDO::rowCount at *http://www.php.net/PDO::rowCount* and on PDO::exec( ) at *http://www.php.net/exec*.

10.9 Escaping Quotes

Problem

You need to make text or binary data safe for queries.

Solution

Write all your queries with placeholders so that prepare( ) and execute( ) can escape strings for you. Recipe 10.7 details the different ways to use placeholders.

If you need to apply escaping yourself, use the PDO::quote( ) method. The rare circumstance you might need to do this could be if you want to escape SQL wildcards coming from user input, as shown in Example 10-24.

Example 10-24. Manual quoting

```php
<?php
$safe = $db->quote($_GET['searchTerm']);
$safe = strtr($safe,array('_' => '\_', '%' => '\%'));
$st = $db->query("SELECT * FROM zodiac WHERE planet LIKE $safe");
?>
```

Discussion

The PDO::quote( ) method makes sure that text or binary data is appropriately quoted, but you may also need to quote the SQL wildcard characters % and _ to ensure that

SELECT statements using the LIKE operator return the right results. If $_GET['searchTerm'] is set to Melm% and Example 10-24 doesn't call strtr( ), its query returns rows with planet set to Melmac, Melmacko, Melmacedonia, or anything else beginning with Melm.

Because % is the SQL wildcard meaning "match any number of characters" (like * in shell globbing) and _ is the SQL wildcard meaning "match one character" (like ? in shell globbing), those need to be backslash-escaped as well.

strtr( ) must be called after PDO::quote( ). Otherwise, PDO::quote( ) would backslash-escape the backslashes strtr( ) adds. With PDO::quote( ) first, Melm_ is turned into Melm _, which is interpreted by the database to mean "the string M e l m followed by a literal underscore character." With PDO::quote( ) after strtr( ), Melm_ is turned into Melm_, which is interpreted by the database to mean "the string Melm followed by a literal backslash character, followed by the underscore wildcard." This is the same thing that would happen if we escaped the SQL wildcards and then used the resulting value as a bound parameter.

Quoting of placeholder values happens even if magic_quotes_gpc or magic_quotes_run time is turned on. Similarly, if you call PDO::quote( ) on a value when magic quotes are active, the value gets quoted anyway. For maximum portability, remove the magic quotes–supplied backslashes before you use a query with placeholders or call PDO::quote( ). Example 10-25 shows this check.

Example 10-25. Checking for magic quotes

```php
<?php
// The behavior of magic_quotes_sybase can also affect things
if (get_magic_quotes_gpc() && (! ini_get('magic_quotes_sybase'))) {
    $fruit = stripslashes($_GET['fruit']);
} else {
    $fruit = $_GET['fruit'];
}
$st = $db->prepare('UPDATE orchard SET trees = trees - 1 WHERE fruit = ?');
$st->execute(array($fruit));
?>
```

If you have any control over your server, turn magic quotes off and make your life a lot easier. However, if you're trying to write maximally portable code that could run in an environment you don't control, you need to look out for this problem.

See Also

Documentation on PDO::quote( ) at *http://www.php.net/PDO::quote* and on magic quotes at *http://www.php.net/manual/en/ref.info.php#ini.magic-quotes-gpc*.

10.10 Logging Debugging Information and Errors

Problem

You want access to information to help you debug database problems. For example, when a query fails, you want to see what error message the database returns.

Solution

Use PDO::errorCode( ) or PDOStatement::errorCode( ) after an operation to get an error code if the operation failed. The corresponding errorInfo( ) method returns more information about the error. Example 10-26 handles the error that results from trying to access a nonexistent table.

Example 10-26. Printing error information

```php
<?php
$st = $db->prepare('SELECT * FROM imaginary_table');
if (! $st) {
    $error = $db->errorInfo();
    print "Problem ({$error[2]})";
}
?>
```

Discussion

The errorCode( ) method returns a five-character error code. PDO uses the SQL 92 SQLSTATE error codes. By that standard, 00000 means "no error," so a call to errorCode( ) that returns 00000 indicates success.

The errorInfo( ) method returns a three-element array. The first element contains the five-character SQLSTATE code (the same thing that errorCode( ) returns). The second element is a database backend-specific error code. The third element is a database backend-specific error message.

Make sure to call errorCode( ) or errorInfo( ) on the same object on which you called the method that you're checking for an error. In Example 10-26, the prepare( ) method is called on the PDO object, so errorInfo( ) is called on the PDO object. If you want to check whether a fetch( ) called on a PDOStatement object succeeded, call errorCode( ) or errorInfo( ) on the PDOStatement object.

One exception to this rule is when creating a new PDO object. If that fails, PDO throws an exception. It does this because otherwise there'd be no object on which you could call errorCode( ) or errorInfo( ). The message in the exception details why the connection failed.

To have PDO throw exceptions *every* time it encounters an error, call setAttribute (PDO::ATTR_ERRMODE, PDO::ERRMODE_EXCEPTION) on your PDO object after it's created. This way, you can handle database problems uniformly instead of larding your code with repeated calls to `errorCode( )` and `errorInfo( )`. Example 10-27 performs a series of database operations wrapped inside a `try`/`catch` block.

Example 10-27. Catching database exceptions

```php
<?php
try {
    $db = new PDO('sqlite:/usr/local/zodiac.db');
    // Make all DB errors throw exceptions
    $db->setAttribute(PDO::ATTR_ERRMODE, PDO::ERRMODE_EXCEPTION);
    $st = $db->prepare('SELECT * FROM zodiac');
    $st->execute();
    while ($row = $st->fetch(PDO::FETCH_NUM)) {
        print implode(',',$row). "<br/>\n";
    }
} catch (Exception $e) {
    print "Database Problem: " . $e->getMessage();
}
?>
```

Handling PDO errors as exceptions is useful inside of transactions, too. If there's a problem with a query once the transaction's started, just roll back the transaction when handling the exception.

Similar to the exception error mode is the "warning" error mode. `setAttribute` `(PDO::ATTR_ERRMODE, PDO::ERRMODE_WARNING)` tells PDO to issue warnings when a database error is encountered. If you prefer to work with regular PHP errors instead of exceptions, this is the error mode for you. Set up a custom error handler with `set_error_handler( )` to handle `E_WARNING` level events and you can deal with your database problems in the error handler.

Whatever the error mode, PDO throws an exception if the initial `PDO` object creation fails. When using PDO, it's an extremely good idea to set up a default exception handler with `set_exception_handler( )`. Without a default exception handler, an uncaught exception causes the display of a complete stack trace if `display_errors` is on. If an exception is thrown when connecting to the database, this stack trace may contain sensitive information, including database connection credentials.

See Also

Documentation on `PDO::errorCode( )` at *http://www.php.net/PDO::errorCode*, on `PDO::errorInfo( )` at *http://www.php.net/PDO::errorInfo*, on `PDOStatement::errorCode( )` at *http://www.php.net/PDOStatement::errorCode*, on `PDOStatement::errorInfo( )` at *http://www.php.net/PDOStatement::errorInfo*, on `set_exception_handler( )` at *http://www.php.net/set_exception_handler*, and on `set_error_handler( )` at *http://www.php.net/set-error-handler*. A list of some SQL 92 SQLSTATE error codes that PDO knows about is available at *http://cvs.php.net/ viewcvs.cgi/php-src/ext/pdo/pdo_sqlstate.c?view=markup*, but some database backends may raise errors other than the ones listed.

10.11 Creating Unique Identifiers

Problem

You want to assign unique IDs to users, articles, or other objects as you add them to your database.

Solution

Use PHP's `uniqid()` function to generate an identifier. To restrict the set of characters in the identifier, pass it through `md5()`, which returns a string containing only numerals and the letters a through f. Example 10-28 creates identifiers using both techniques.

Example 10-28. Creating unique identifiers

```php
<?php
$st = $db->prepare('INSERT INTO users (id, name) VALUES (?,?)');
$st->execute(array(uniqid(), 'Jacob'));
$st->execute(array(md5(uniqid()), 'Ruby'));
?>
```

You can also use a database-specific method to have the database generate the ID. For example, SQLite 3 and MySQL support `AUTOINCREMENT` columns that automatically assign increasing integers to a column as rows are inserted.

Discussion

`uniqid()` uses the current time (in microseconds) and a random number to generate a string that is extremely difficult to guess. `md5()` computes a hash of whatever you give it. It doesn't add any randomness to the identifier, but restricts the characters that appear in it. The results of `md5()` don't contain any punctuation, so you don't have to worry about escaping issues. Plus, you can't spell any naughty words with just the first six letters of the alphabet (in English, at least).

If you'd rather give your database the responsibility of generating the unique identifier, use the appropriate syntax when creating a table. Example 10-29 shows how to create a table in SQLite with a column that gets an auto-incremented integer ID each time a new row is inserted.

Example 10-29. Creating an auto-increment column with SQLite

```php
<?php
// the type INTEGER PRIMARY KEY AUTOINCREMENT tells SQLite
// to assign ascending IDs
$db->exec(<<<_SQL_
  CREATE TABLE users (
    id  INTEGER PRIMARY KEY AUTOINCREMENT,
    name VARCHAR(255)
  )
_SQL_
```

```
);

// No need to insert a value for 'id' -- SQLite assigns it
$st = $db->prepare('INSERT INTO users (name) VALUES (?)');

// These rows are assigned 'id' values
foreach (array('Jacob','Ruby') as $name) {
    $st->execute(array($name));
}
?>
```

Example 10-30 shows the same thing for MySQL.

Example 10-30. Creating an auto-increment column with MySQL

```
<?php
// the AUTO_INCREMENT tells MySQL to assign ascending IDs
// that column must be the PRIMARY KEY
$db->exec(<<<_SQL_
  CREATE TABLE users (
    id  INT NOT NULL AUTO_INCREMENT,
    name VARCHAR(255),
    PRIMARY KEY(id)
  )
_SQL_
);

// No need to insert a value for 'id' -- MySQL assigns it
$st = $db->prepare('INSERT INTO users (name) VALUES (?)');

// These rows are assigned 'id' values
foreach (array('Jacob','Ruby') as $name) {
    $st->execute(array($name));
}
?>
```

When the database creates ID values automatically, the PDO::lastInsertId( ) method retrieves them. Call lastInsertId( ) on your PDO object to get the auto-generated ID of the last inserted row. Some database backends also let you pass a sequence name to lastInsertId( ) to get the last value from the sequence.

See Also

Documentation on uniqid( ) at *http://www.php.net/uniqid*, on md5( ) at *http://www.php.net/md5*, on PDO::lastInsertId( ) at *http://www.php.net/PDO::lastInsertId*, on SQLite and AUTOINCREMENT at *http://www.sqlite.org/faq.html#q1*, and on MySQL and is found AUTO_INCREMENT at *http://dev.mysql.com/doc/refman/5.0/en/example-auto-increment.html*.

10.12 Building Queries Programmatically

Problem

You want to construct an INSERT or UPDATE query from an array of field names. For example, you want to insert a new user into your database. Instead of hardcoding each field of user information (such as username, email address, postal address, birthdate, etc.), you put the field names in an array and use the array to build the query. This is easier to maintain, especially if you need to conditionally INSERT or UPDATE with the same set of fields.

Solution

To construct an UPDATE query, build an array of field/value pairs and then implode( ) together each element of that array, as shown in Example 10-31.

Example 10-31. Building an UPDATE query

```php
<?php
// A list of field names
$fields = array('symbol','planet','element');

$update_fields = array();
$update_values = array();
foreach ($fields as $field) {
    $update_fields[] = "$field = ?";
    // Assume the data is coming from a form
    $update_values[] = $_POST[$field];
}

$st = $db->prepare("UPDATE zodiac SET " .
                    implode(',', $update_fields) .
                    'WHERE sign = ?');

// Add 'sign' to the values array
$update_values[] = $_GET['sign'];

// Execute the query
$st->execute($update_values);
?>
```

For an INSERT query, do the same thing, although the SQL syntax is a little different, as Example 10-32 demonstrates.

Example 10-32. Building an INSERT query

```php
<?php
// A list of field names
$fields = array('symbol','planet','element');
$placeholders = array();
$values = array();
foreach ($fields as $field) {
```

```
        // One placeholder per field
        $placeholders[] = '?';
        // Assume the data is coming from a form
        $values[] = $_POST[$field];
    }

    $st = $db->prepare('INSERT INTO zodiac (' .
                        implode(',',$fields) .
                        ') VALUES (' .
                        implode(',', $placeholders) .
                        ')');
    // Execute the query
    $st->execute($values);
    ?>
```

Discussion

Placeholders make this sort of thing a breeze. Because they take care of escaping the provided data, you can easily stuff user-submitted data into programatically generated queries.

If you use sequence-generated integers as primary keys, you can combine the two query-construction techniques into one function. That function determines whether a record exists and then generates the correct query, including a new ID, as shown in the pc_build_query( ) function in Example 10-33.

Example 10-33. pc_build_query()

```
<?php
function pc_build_query($db,$key_field,$fields,$table) {
    $values = array();
    if (! empty($_POST[$key_field])) {
        $update_fields = array();
        foreach ($fields as $field) {
            $update_fields[] = "$field = ?";
            // Assume the data is coming from a form
            $values[] = $_POST[$field];
        }
        // Add the key field's value to the $values array
        $values[] = $_POST[$key_field];
        $st = $db->prepare("UPDATE $table SET " .
                    implode(',', $update_fields) .
                    "WHERE $key_field = ?");
    } else {
        // Start values off with a unique ID
        // If your DB is set to generate this value, use NULL instead
        $values[] = md5(uniqid());
        $placeholders = array('?');
        foreach ($fields as $field) {
            // One placeholder per field
            $placeholders[] = '?';
            // Assume the data is coming from a form
            $values[] = $_POST[$field];
        }
        $st = $db->prepare("INSERT INTO $table ($key_field," .
```

```
                          implode(',',$fields) . ') VALUES ('.
                          implode(',',$placeholders) .')');
        }
        $st->execute($values);
        return $st;
    }
?>
```

Using this function, you can make a simple page to edit all the information in the
zodiac table, shown in Example 10-34.

Example 10-34. A simple add/edit record page

```
<?php
$db = new PDO('sqlite:/usr/local/data/zodiac.db');
$db->setAttribute(PDO::ATTR_ERRMODE, PDO::ERRMODE_EXCEPTION);

$fields = array('sign','symbol','planet','element',
                'start_month','start_day','end_month','end_day');

$cmd = isset($_REQUEST['cmd']) ? $_REQUEST['cmd'] : 'show';

switch ($cmd) {
 case 'edit':
 try {
    $st = $db->prepare('SELECT ' . implode(',',$fields) .
                       ' FROM zodiac WHERE id = ?');
    $st->execute(array($_REQUEST['id']));
    $row = $st->fetch(PDO::FETCH_ASSOC);
 } catch (Exception $e) {
    $row = array();
 }
 case 'add':
    print '<form method="post" action="' .
          htmlentities($_SERVER['PHP_SELF']) . '">';
    print '<input type="hidden" name="cmd" value="save">';
    print '<table>';
    if ('edit' == $_REQUEST['cmd']) {
        printf('<input type="hidden" name="id" value="%d">',
               $_REQUEST['id']);
    }
    foreach ($fields as $field) {
        if ('edit' == $_REQUEST['cmd']) {
            $value = htmlentities($row[$field]);
        } else {
            $value = '';
        }
        printf('<tr><td>%s: </td><td><input type="text" name="%s" value="%s">',
               $field,$field,$value);
        printf('</td></tr>');
    }
    print '<tr><td></td><td><input type="submit" value="Save"></td></tr>';
    print '</table></form>';
    break;
 case 'save':
    try {
```

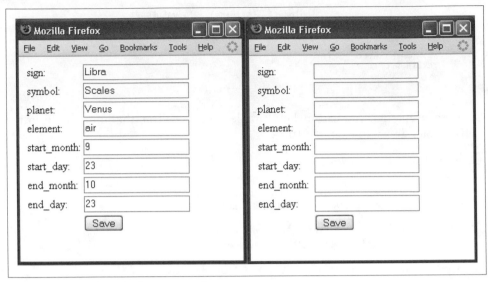

Figure 10-1. Adding and editing a record

```
        $st = pc_build_query($db,'id',$fields,'zodiac');
        print 'Added info.';
    } catch (Exception $e) {
        print "Couldn't add info: " . htmlentities($e->getMessage());
    }
        print '<hr>';
case 'show':
default:
        $self = htmlentities($_SERVER['PHP_SELF']);
        print '<ul>';
        foreach ($db->query('SELECT id,sign FROM zodiac') as $row) {
            printf('<li> <a href="%s?cmd=edit&id=%s">%s</a>',
                    $self,$row['id'],$row['sign']);
        }
        print '<hr><li> <a href="'.$self.'?cmd=add">Add New</a>';
        print '</ul>';
        break;
}?>
```

The switch statement controls what action the program takes based on the value of
$_REQUEST['cmd']. If $_REQUEST['cmd'] is add or edit, the program displays a form with
text boxes for each field in the $fields array, as shown in Figure 10-1. If
$_REQUEST['cmd'] is edit, values for the row with the supplied $id are loaded from the
database and displayed as defaults. If $_REQUEST['cmd'] is save, the program uses
pc_build_query( ) to generate an appropriate query to either INSERT or UPDATE the data
in the database. After saving (or if no $_REQUEST['cmd'] is specified), the program dis-
plays a list of all zodiac signs, as shown in Figure 10-2.

Whether pc_build_query( ) builds an INSERT or UPDATE statement is based on the presence of the request variable $_REQUEST['id'] (because id is passed in $key_field). If

Figure 10-2. Listing records

$_REQUEST['id'] is not empty, the function builds an UPDATE query to change the row with that ID. If $_REQUEST['id'] is empty (or it hasn't been set at all), the function generates a new ID and uses that new ID in an INSERT query that adds a row to the table. To have pc_build_query( ) respect a database's AUTOINCREMENT setting, start $values off with null instead of md5(uniqid( )).

See Also

Recipe 10.7 for information about placeholders, prepare( ), and execute( ); documentation on PDO::prepare( ) at *http://www.php.net/PDO::prepare* and on PDOStatement::execute( ) at *http://www.php.net/PDOStatement::execute( ).*

10.13 Making Paginated Links for a Series of Records

Problem

You want to display a large dataset a page at a time and provide links that move through the dataset.

Solution

Use database-appropriate syntax to grab just a section of all the rows that match your query. Example 10-35 shows how this works with SQLite.

Example 10-35. Paging with SQLite

```php
<?php
// Select 5 rows, starting after the first 3
foreach ($db->query('SELECT * FROM zodiac ' .
                    'ORDER BY sign LIMIT 5 ' .
                    'OFFSET 3') as $row) {
    // Do something with each row
}
?>
```

The `pc_indexed_links( )` and `pc_print_link( )` functions in this recipe assist with printing paging information. Example 10-36 shows them in action.

Example 10-36. Displaying paginated results

```php
<?php
$offset = isset($_GET['offset']) ? intval($_GET['offset']) : 1;
if (! $offset) { $offset = 1; }
$per_page = 5;
$total = $db->query('SELECT COUNT(*) FROM zodiac')->fetchColumn(0);

$limitedSQL = 'SELECT * FROM zodiac ORDER BY id ' .
              "LIMIT $per_page OFFSET " . ($offset-1);
$lastRowNumber = $offset - 1;

foreach ($db->query($limitedSQL) as $row) {
    $lastRowNumber++;
    print "{$row['sign']}, {$row['symbol']} ({$row['id']}) <br/>\n";
}

pc_indexed_links($total,$offset,$per_page);
print "<br/>";
print "(Displaying $offset - $lastRowNumber of $total)";
?>
```

Discussion

`pc_print_link( )` is shown in Example 10-37 and `pc_indexed_links( )` in Example 10-38.

Example 10-37. pc_print_link( )

```php
<?php
function pc_print_link($inactive,$text,$offset='') {
    if ($inactive) {
        print "<span class='inactive'>$text</span>";
    } else {
        print "<span class='active'>".
              "<a href='" . htmlentities($_SERVER['PHP_SELF']) .
              "?offset=$offset'>$text</a></span>";
    }
}
?>
```

Example 10-38. pc_indexed_links( )

```php
<?php
function pc_indexed_links($total,$offset,$per_page) {
    $separator = ' | ';

    // print "<<Prev" link
    pc_print_link($offset == 1, '<< Prev', $offset - $per_page);

    // print all groupings except last one
    for ($start = 1, $end = $per_page;
        $end < $total;
        $start += $per_page, $end += $per_page) {
            print $separator;
            pc_print_link($offset == $start, "$start-$end", $start);
    }

    /* print the last grouping -
     * at this point, $start points to the element at the beginning
     * of the last grouping
     */

    /* the text should only contain a range if there's more than
     * one element on the last page. For example, the last grouping
     * of 11 elements with 5 per page should just say "11", not "11-11"
     */
    $end = ($total > $start) ? "-$total" : '';

    print $separator;
    pc_print_link($offset == $start, "$start$end", $start);

    // print "Next>>" link
    print $separator;
    pc_print_link($offset == $start, 'Next >>',$offset + $per_page);
}
?>
```

To use these functions, retrieve the correct subset of the data using and then print it out. Call `pc_indexed_links( )` to display the indexed links.

After connecting to the database, you need to make sure `$offset` has an appropriate value. `$offset` is the beginning record in the result set that should be displayed. To start at the beginning of the result set, `$offset` should be 1. The variable `$per_page` is set to how many records to display on each page, and `$total` is the total number of records in the entire result set. For this example, all the zodiac records are displayed, so `$total` is set to the count of all the rows in the entire table.

The SQL query that retrieves information in the proper order is:

```php
<?php
$limitedSQL = 'SELECT * FROM zodiac ORDER BY id ' .
"LIMIT $per_page OFFSET " . ($offset-1);
?>
```

The `LIMIT` and `OFFSET` keywords are how you tell SQLite to return just a subset of all matching rows.

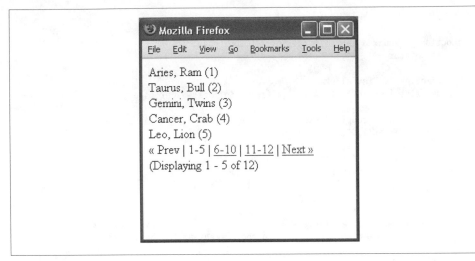

Figure 10-3. Paginated results with pc_indexed_links( )

The relevant rows are retrieved by `$db->query($limitedSQL)`, and then information is displayed from each row. After the rows, `pc_indexed_links( )` provides navigation links. The output when `$offset` is not set (or is 1) is shown in Figure 10-3.

In Figure 10-3, "6-10," "11-12," and "Next >>" are links to the same page with adjusted `$offset` arguments, while "<< Prev" and "1-5" are grayed out, because what they would link to is what's currently displayed.

See Also

A discussion of paging in the Solar framework at *http://paul-m-jones.com/blog/?p=185* and information on different database paging syntaxes at *http://troels.arvin.dk/db/rdbms/#select-limit-offset*.

10.14 Caching Queries and Results

Problem

You don't want to rerun potentially expensive database queries when the results haven't changed.

Solution

Use PEAR's `Cache_Lite` package. It makes it simple to cache arbitrary data. In this case, cache the results of a `SELECT` query and use the text of the query as a cache key. Example 10-39 shows how to cache query results with `Cache_Lite`.

Example 10-39. Caching query results

```php
<?php
require_once 'Cache/Lite.php';
```

```
$opts = array(
    // Where to put the cached data
    'cacheDir' => 'c:/tmp',
    // Let us store arrays in the cache
    'automaticSerialization' => true,
    // How long stuff lives in the cache
    'lifeTime' => 600 /* ten minutes */);

// Create the cache
$cache = new Cache_Lite($opts);

// Connect to the database
$db = new PDO('sqlite:c:/data/zodiac.db');

// Define our query and its parameters
$sql = 'SELECT * FROM zodiac WHERE planet = ?';
$params = array($_GET['planet']);

// Get the unique cache key
$key = cache_key($sql, $params);

// Try to get results from the cache
$results = $cache->get($key);

if ($results === false) {
    // No results found, so do the query and put the results in the cache
    $st = $db->prepare($sql);
    $st->execute($params);
    $results = $st->fetchAll();
    $cache->save($results);
}

// Whether from the cache or not, $results has our data
foreach ($results as $result) {
    print "$result[id]: $result[planet], $result[sign] <br/>\n";
}

function cache_key($sql, $params) {
    return md5($sql .
            implode('|',array_keys($params)) .
            implode('|',$params));
}
?>
```

Discussion

Cache_Lite is a generic, lightweight mechanism for caching arbitrary information. It uses files to store the information it's caching. The Cache_Lite constructor takes an array of options that control its behavior. The two most important ones in Example 10-39 are automaticSerialization, which makes it easier to store arrays in the cache, and cacheDir, which defines where the cache files go. Make sure cacheDir ends with a /.

The cache is just a mapping of keys to values. It's up to us to make sure that we supply a cache key that uniquely identifies the data we want to cache—in this case, the SQL query and the parameters bound to it. The cache_key function computes an appropriate key. After that, Example 10-39 just checks to see if the results are already in the cache. If not, it executes the query against the database and stuffs the results in the cache for next time.

Note that you can't put a PDO or PDOStatement object in the cache—you have to fetch results and then put the results in the cache.

By default, entries stay in the cache for one hour. You can adjust this by passing a different value (in seconds) as the lifeTime option when creating a new Cache_Lite object. Pass in null if you don't want data to automatically expire.

The cache isn't altered if you change the database with an INSERT, UPDATE, or DELETE query. If there are cached SELECT statements that refer to data no longer in the database, you need to explicitly remove everything from the cache with the Cache_Lite::clean( ) method. You can also remove an individual element from the cache by passing a cache key to Cache_Lite::remove( ).

The cache_key( ) function in Example 10-39 is case sensitive. This means that if the results of SELECT * FROM zodiac are in the cache, and you run the query SELECT * from zodiac, the results aren't found in the cache and the query is run again. Maintaining consistent capitalization, spacing, and field ordering when constructing your SQL queries results in more efficient cache usage.

See Also

Documentation on Cache_Lite found at *http://pear.php.net/manual/en/ package.caching.cache-lite.php*.

10.15 Accessing a Database Connection Anywhere in Your Program

Problem

You've got a program with lots of functions and classes in it, and you want to maintain a single database connection that's easily accessible from anywhere in the program.

Solution

Use a static class method that creates the connection if it doesn't exist and returns the connection (see Example 10-40).

Example 10-40. Creating a database connection in a static class method

```php
<?php
class DBCxn {
```

```php
    // What DSN to connect to?
    public static $dsn = 'sqlite:c:/data/zodiac.db';
    public static $user = null;
    public static $pass = null;
    public static $driverOpts = null;

    // Internal variable to hold the connection
    private static $db;
    // No cloning or instantiating allowed
    final private function __construct() { }
    final private function __clone() { }

    public static function get() {
        // Connect if not already connected
        if (is_null(self::$db)) {
            self::$db = new PDO(self::$dsn, self::$user, self::$pass,
                                self::$driverOpts);
        }
        // Return the connection
        return self::$db;
    }
}
?>
```

Discussion

The `DBCxn::get()` method defined in Example 10-40 accomplishes two things: you can call it from anywhere in your program without worrying about variable scope and it prevents more than one connection from being created in a program.

To change what kind of connection `DBCxn::get()` provides, just alter the `$dsn`, `$user`, `$pass`, and `$driverOpts` properties of the class. If you need to manage multiple different database connections during the same script execution, change `$dsn` and `$db` to an array and have `get()` accept an argument identifying which connection to use. Example 10-41 shows a version of `DBCxn` that provides access to three different databases.

Example 10-41. Handling connections to multiple databases

```php
<?php
class DBCxn {
    // What DSNs to connect to?
    public static $dsn =
        array('zodiac' => 'sqlite:c:/data/zodiac.db',
              'users' => array('mysql:host=db.example.com','monty','7f2iuh'),
              'stats' => array('oci:statistics', 'statsuser','statspass'));

    // Internal variable to hold the connection
    private static $db = array();
    // No cloning or instantiating allowed
    final private function __construct() { }
    final private function __clone() { }

    public static function get($key) {
```

```
        if (! isset(self::$dsn[$key])) {
            throw new Exception("Unknown DSN: $key");
        }
        // Connect if not already connected
        if (! isset(self::$db[$key])) {
            if (is_array(self::$dsn[$key])) {
                // The next two lines only work with PHP 5.1.3 and above
                $c = new ReflectionClass('PDO');
                self::$db[$key] = $c->newInstanceArgs(self::$dsn[$key]);
            } else {
                self::$db[$key] = new PDO(self::$dsn[$key]);
            }
        }
        // Return the connection
        return self::$db[$key];
    }
}
?>
```

In Example 10-41, you must pass a key to DBCxn::get( ) that identifies which entry in $dsn to use. The code inside get( ) is a little more complicated, too, because it has to handle variable numbers of arguments to the PDO constructor. Some databases, such as SQLite, just need one argument. Others may provide two, three, or four arguments. Example 10-41 uses the ReflectionClass::newInstanceArgs( ) method, added in PHP 5.1.3, to concisely call a constructor and provide arguments in an array. If you're using an earlier version of PHP, replace the calls to new ReflectionClass('PDO') and to newInstanceArgs( ) with the code in Example 10-42.

Example 10-42. Calling the PDO constructor with older PHP versions

```
<?php
$args = self::$dsn[$key];
$argCount = count($args);
if ($argCount == 1) {
    self::$db[$key] = new PDO($args[0]);
} else if ($argCount == 2) {
    self::$db[$key] = new PDO($args[0],$args[1]);
} else if ($argCount == 3) {
    self::$db[$key] = new PDO($args[0],$args[1],$args[2]);
} else if ($argCount == 4) {
    self::$db[$key] = new PDO($args[0],$args[1],$args[2],$args[3]);
}
?>
```

Example 10-42 checks for each possible count of arguments to provide to the PDO constructor and invokes the constructor accordingly.

See Also

Documentation on PDO::__construct( ) at *http://www.php.net/PDO::__construct* and on ReflectionClass::newInstanceArgs( ) can be found at *http://www.php.net/language.oop5.reflection*.

10.16 Program: Storing a Threaded Message Board

Storing and retrieving threaded messages requires extra care to display the threads in the correct order. Finding the children of each message and building the tree of message relationships can easily lead to a recursive web of queries. Users generally look at a list of messages and read individual messages far more often then they post messages. With a little extra processing when saving a new message to the database, the query that retrieves a list of messages to display is simpler and much more efficient.

Store messages in a table structured like this:

```
CREATE TABLE pc_message (
    id INT UNSIGNED NOT NULL,
    posted_on DATETIME NOT NULL,
    author CHAR(255),
    subject CHAR(255),
    body MEDIUMTEXT,
    thread_id INT UNSIGNED NOT NULL,
    parent_id INT UNSIGNED NOT NULL,
    level INT UNSIGNED NOT NULL,
    thread_pos INT UNSIGNED NOT NULL,
    PRIMARY KEY(id)
);
```

The primary key, id, is a unique integer that identifies a particular message. The time and date that a message is posted is stored in posted_on, and author, subject, and body are (surprise!) a message's author, subject, and body. The remaining four fields keep track of the threading relationships between messages. The integer thread_id identifies each thread. All messages in a particular thread have the same thread_id. If a message is a reply to another message, parent_id is the id of the replied-to message. level is how many replies into a thread a message is. The first message in a thread has level 0. A reply to that level message has level 1, and a reply to that level 1 message has level 2. Multiple messages in a thread can have the same level and the same parent_id. For example, if someone starts off a thread with a message about the merits of BeOS over CP/M, the angry replies to that message from CP/M's legions of fans all have level 1 and a parent_id equal to the id of the original message.

The last field, thread_pos, is what makes the easy display of messages possible. When displayed, all messages in a thread are ordered by their thread_pos value.

Here are the rules for calculating thread_pos:

- The first message in a thread has thread_pos = 0.

- For a new message N, if there are no messages in the thread with the same parent as N, N's thread_pos is one greater than its parent's thread_pos.

- For a new message N, if there are messages in the thread with the same parent as N, N's thread_pos is one greater than the biggest thread_pos of all the messages with the same parent as N.

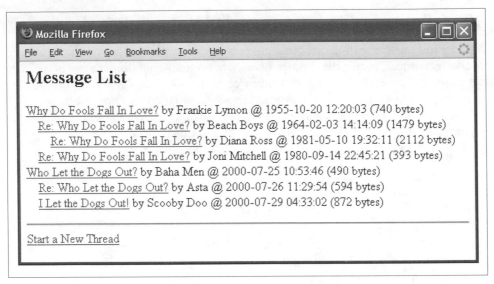

Figure 10-4. A threaded message board

- After new message N's `thread_pos` is determined, all messages in the same thread with a `thread_pos` value greater than or equal to N's have their `thread_pos` value incremented by 1 (to make room for N).

The message board program, *message.php*, shown in Example 10-43 saves messages and properly calculates `thread_pos`. Sample output is shown in Figure 10-4.

Example 10-43. message.php

```php
<?php

$board = new MessageBoard();
$board->go();

class MessageBoard {
    protected $db;
    protected $form_errors = array();
    protected $inTransaction = false;

    public function __construct() {
        set_exception_handler(array($this,'logAndDie'));
        $this->db = new PDO('sqlite:/usr/local/data/message.db');
        $this->db->setAttribute(PDO::ATTR_ERRMODE,PDO::ERRMODE_EXCEPTION);
    }

    public function go() {
        // The value of $_REQUEST['cmd'] tells us what to do
        $cmd = isset($_REQUEST['cmd']) ? $_REQUEST['cmd'] : 'show';
        switch ($cmd) {
            case 'read':            // read an individual message
                $this->read();
                break;
```

```
          case 'post':           // display the form to post a message
            $this->post();
            break;
          case 'save':           // save a posted message
            if ($this->valid()) { // if the message is valid,
                $this->save();    // then save it
                $this->show();    // and display the message list
            } else {
                $this->post();    // otherwise, redisplay the posting form
            }
            break;
          case 'show':           // show a message list by default
          default:
            $this->show();
            break;
        }
    }
}

// save() saves the message to the database
protected function save() {

    $parent_id = isset($_REQUEST['parent_id']) ?
                 intval($_REQUEST['parent_id']) : 0;

    // Make sure pc_message doesn't change while we're working with it.
    $this->db->beginTransaction();
    $this->inTransaction = true;

    // is this message a reply?
    if ($parent_id) {
        // get the thread, level, and thread_pos of the parent message
        $st = $this->db->prepare("SELECT thread_id,level,thread_pos
                            FROM pc_message WHERE id = ?");
        $st->execute(array($parent_id));
        $parent = $st->fetch();

        // a reply's level is one greater than its parent's
        $level = $parent['level'] + 1;

        /* what's the biggest thread_pos in this thread among messages
        with the same parent? */
        $st = $this->db->prepare('SELECT MAX(thread_pos) FROM pc_message
                WHERE thread_id = ? AND parent_id = ?');
        $st->execute(array($parent['thread_id'], $parent_id));
        $thread_pos = $st->fetchColumn(0);

        // are there existing replies to this parent?
        if ($thread_pos) {
            // this thread_pos goes after the biggest existing one
            $thread_pos++;
        } else {
            // this is the first reply, so put it right after the parent
            $thread_pos = $parent['thread_pos'] + 1;
        }
```

```
            /* increment the thread_pos of all messages in the thread that
            come after this one */
        $st = $this->db->prepare('UPDATE pc_message SET thread_pos = thread_pos + 1
                        WHERE thread_id = ? AND thread_pos >= ?');
        $st->execute(array($parent['thread_id'], $thread_pos));

            // the new message should be saved with the parent's thread_id
            $thread_id = $parent['thread_id'];
        } else {
            // the message is not a reply, so it's the start of a new thread
        $thread_id = $this->db->query('SELECT MAX(thread_id) + 1 FROM pc_message')
                        ->fetchColumn(0);
            $level = 0;
            $thread_pos = 0;
        }

        /* insert the message into the database. Using prepare() and execute()
        makes sure that all fields are properly quoted */
        $st = $this->db->prepare("INSERT INTO pc_message (id,thread_id,parent_id,
                        thread_pos,posted_on,level,author,subject,body)
                        VALUES (?,?,?,?,?,?,?,?,?)");

        $st->execute(array(null,$thread_id,$parent_id,$thread_pos,
                        date('c'),$level,$_REQUEST['author'],
                        $_REQUEST['subject'],$_REQUEST['body']));

        // Commit all the operations
        $this->db->commit();
        $this->inTransaction = false;
}

// show() displays a list of all messages
protected function show() {
    print '<h2>Message List</h2><p>';

    /* order the messages by their thread (thread_id) and their position
    within the thread (thread_pos) */
    $st = $this->db->query("SELECT id,author,subject,LENGTH(body) AS body_length,
                    posted_on,level FROM pc_message
                    ORDER BY thread_id,thread_pos");
    while ($row = $st->fetch()) {
        // indent messages with level > 0
        print str_repeat(' ',4 * $row['level']);
        // print out information about the message with a link to read it
        print "<a href='" . htmlentities($_SERVER['PHP_SELF']) .
        "?cmd=read&amp;id={$row['id']}'>" .
        htmlentities($row['subject']) . '</a> by ' .
        htmlentities($row['author']) . ' @ ' .
        htmlentities($row['posted_on']) .
        " ({$row['body_length']} bytes) <br/>";
    }

    // provide a way to post a non-reply message
    print "<hr/><a href='" .
        htmlentities($_SERVER['PHP_SELF']) .
```

```
            "?cmd=post'>Start a New Thread</a>";
    }

    // read() displays an individual message
    public function read() {

        /* make sure the message id we're passed is an integer and really
        represents a message */
        if (! isset($_REQUEST['id'])) {
            throw new Exception('No message ID supplied');
        }
        $id = intval($_REQUEST['id']);
        $st = $this->db->prepare("SELECT author,subject,body,posted_on
                                  FROM pc_message WHERE id = ?");
        $st->execute(array($id));
        $msg = $st->fetch();
        if (! $msg) {
            throw new Exception('Bad message ID');
        }

        /* don't display user-entered HTML, but display newlines as
        HTML line breaks */
        $body = nl2br(htmlentities($msg['body']));

        // display the message with links to reply and return to the message list
        $self = htmlentities($_SERVER['PHP_SELF']);
        $subject = htmlentities($msg['subject']);
        $author = htmlentities($msg['author']);
        print<<<_HTML_
<h2>$subject</h2>
<h3>by $author</h3>
<p>$body</p>
<hr/>
<a href="$self?cmd=post&parent_id=$id">Reply</a>
<br/>
<a href="$self?cmd=list">List Messages</a>
_HTML_;
    }

    // post() displays the form for posting a message
    public function post() {
        $safe =  array();
        foreach (array('author','subject','body') as $field) {
            // escape characters in default field values
            if (isset($_POST[$field])) {
                $safe[$field] = htmlentities($_POST[$field]);
            } else {
                $safe[$field] = '';
            }
            // make the error messages display in red
            if (isset($this->form_errors[$field])) {
                $this->form_errors[$field] = '<span style="color: red">' .
                    $this->form_errors[$field] . '</span><br/>';
            } else {
                $this->form_errors[$field] = '';
```

```
        }
    }

    // is this message a reply
    if (isset($_REQUEST['parent_id']) &&
        $parent_id = intval($_REQUEST['parent_id'])) {

        // send the parent_id along when the form is submitted
        $parent_field =
            sprintf('<input type="hidden" name="parent_id" value="%d" />',
                    $parent_id);

        // if no subject's been passed in, use the subject of the parent
        if (! strlen($safe['subject'])) {
            $st = $this->db->prepare('SELECT subject FROM pc_message WHERE id = ?');
            $st->execute(array($parent_id));
            $parent_subject = $st->fetchColumn(0);

            /* prefix 'Re: ' to the parent subject if it exists and
               doesn't already have a 'Re:' */
            $safe['subject'] = htmlentities($parent_subject);
            if ($parent_subject && (! preg_match('/^re:/i',$parent_subject))) {
                $safe['subject'] = "Re: {$safe['subject']}";
            }
        }
    } else {
        $parent_field = '';
    }


    // display the posting form, with errors and default values
    $self = htmlentities($_SERVER['PHP_SELF']);
    print<<<_HTML_
<form method="post" action="$self">
<table>
<tr>
 <td>Your Name:</td>
 <td>{$this->form_errors['author']}
    <input type="text" name="author" value="{$safe['author']}" />
</td>
<tr>
 <td>Subject:</td>
 <td>{$this->form_errors['subject']}
    <input type="text" name="subject" value="{$safe['subject']}" />
</td>
<tr>
 <td>Message:</td>
 <td>{$this->form_errors['body']}
    <textarea rows="4" cols="30" wrap="physical"
              name="body">{$safe['body']}</textarea>
</td>
<tr><td colspan="2"><input type="submit" value="Post Message" /></td></tr>
</table>
$parent_field
<input type="hidden" name="cmd" value="save" />
```

```
        </form>
        _HTML_;
            }

        // validate() makes sure something is entered in each field
        public function valid() {
            $this->form_errors = array();
            if (! (isset($_POST['author']) && strlen(trim($_POST['author'])))) {
                $this->form_errors['author'] = 'Please enter your name.';
            }
            if (! (isset($_POST['subject']) && strlen(trim($_POST['subject'])))) {
                $this->form_errors['subject'] = 'Please enter a message subject.';
            }
            if (! (isset($_POST['body']) && strlen(trim($_POST['body'])))) {
                $this->form_errors['body'] = 'Please enter a message body.';
            }

            return (count($this->form_errors) == 0);
        }

        public function logAndDie(Exception $e) {
            print 'ERROR: ' . htmlentities($e->getMessage());
            if ($this->db && $this->db->inTransaction) {
                $this->db->rollback();
            }
            exit();
        }
    }
}
?>
```

To properly handle concurrent usage, save( ) needs exclusive access to the msg table between the time it starts calculating the thread_pos of the new message and when it actually inserts the new message into the database. We've used PDO's beginTransaction( ) and commit( ) methods to accomplish this. Note that logAndDie( ), the exception handler, rolls back the transaction when appropriate if an error occured inside the transaction. Although PDO always calls rollback( ) at the end of a script if a transaction was started, explicitly including the call inside logAndDie( ) makes clearer what's happening to someone reading the code.

The level field can be used when displaying messages to limit what you retrieve from the database. If discussion threads become very deep, this can help prevent your pages from growing too large. Example 10-44 shows how to display just the first message in each thread and any replies to that first message.

Example 10-44. Limiting thread depth
```
<?php
$st = $this->db->query(
    "SELECT * FROM pc_message WHERE level <= 1 ORDER BY thread_id,thread_pos");
while ($row = $st->fetch()) {
    // display each message
}
?>
```

If you're interested in having a discussion group on your web site, you may want to use one of the existing PHP message board packages. A popular one is FUDForum (*http://fudforum.org/forum/*), and there are a number of others listed at *http://www.zend.com/apps.php?CID=261*.

CHAPTER 11

Sessions and Data Persistence

11.0 Introduction

As web applications have matured, the need for *statefulness* has become a common requirement. Stateful web applications, meaning applications that keep track of a particular visitor's information as he travels throughout a site, are now so common that they are taken for granted.

Given the prevalence of web applications that keep track of things for their visitors—such as shopping carts, online banking, personalized home page portals, and social networking community sites—it is hard to imagine the Internet we use every day without stateful applications.

HTTP, the protocol that web servers and clients use to talk to each other, is a stateless protocol by design. However, since PHP 4.0, developers who've built applications with PHP have had a convenient set of session management functions that have made the challenge of implementing statefulness much easier. This chapter focuses on several good practices to keep in mind while developing stateful applications.

Sessions are focused on maintaining visitor-specific state between requests. Some applications also require an equivalent type of lightweight storage of non-visitor-specific state for a period of time at the server-side level. This is known as data persistence.

Recipe 11.1 explains PHP's session module, which lets you easily associate persistent data with a user as he moves through your site. Recipes 11.2 and 11.3 explore session hijacking and session fixation vulnerabilities and how to avoid them.

Session data is stored in flat files in the server's */tmp* directory by default. Recipes 11.4 and 11.5 explain how to store session data in alternate locations, such as a database and shared memory, and discusses the pros and cons of these different approaches.

Recipe 11.6 demonstrates how to use shared memory for more than just session data storage, and Recipe 11.7 illustrates techniques for longer-term storage of summary information that has been gleaned from logfiles.

11.1 Using Session Tracking

Problem

You want to maintain information about a user as she moves through your site.

Solution

Use the sessions module. The `session_start()` function initializes a session, and accessing an element in the auto-global `$_SESSION` array tells PHP to keep track of the corresponding variable:

```php
<?php
session_start();
$_SESSION['visits']++;
print 'You have visited here '.$_SESSION['visits'].' times.';
?>
```

Discussion

The session function keep track of users by issuing them cookies with randomly generated session IDs.

By default, PHP stores session data in files in the */tmp* directory on your server. Each session is stored in its own file. To change the directory in which the files are saved, set the `session.save_path` configuration directive to the new directory in *php.ini* or with `ini_set()`. You can also call `session_save_path()` with the new directory to change directories, but you need to do this before starting the session or accessing any session variables.

To start a session automatically on each request, set `session.auto_start` to `1` in *php.ini*. With `session.auto_start`, there's no need to call `session_start()`.

With the `session.use_trans_sid` configuration directive turned on, if PHP detects that a user doesn't accept the session ID cookie, it automatically adds the session ID to URLs and forms.* For example, consider this code that prints a URL:

```php
<?php
print '<a href="train.php">Take the A Train</a>';
?>
```

If sessions are enabled, but a user doesn't accept cookies, what's sent to the browser is something like:

```php
<?php
<a href="train.php?PHPSESSID=2eb89f3344520d11969a79aea6bd2fdd">Take the A Train</a>
?>
```

In this example, the session name is `PHPSESSID` and the session name is `2eb89f3344520d11969a79aea6bd2fdd`. PHP adds those to the URL so they are passed along

---

* Before PHP 4.2.0, this behavior had to be explicitly enabled by building PHP with the `--enable-trans-sid` configuration setting.

to the next page. Forms are modified to include a hidden element that passes the session ID.

Due to a variety of security concerns relating to embedding session IDs in URLs, this behavior is disabled by default. To enable transparent session IDs in URLs, you need to turn on `session.use_trans_sid` in *php.ini* or through the use of `ini_set('session.use_trans_sid', true)` in your scripts before the session is started.

Although `session.use_trans_sid` is convenient, it can cause you some security-related headaches. Because URLs have session IDs in them, distribution of such a URL lets anybody who receives the URL act as the user to whom the session ID was given. A user that copies a URL from his web browser and pastes it into an email message sent to friends unwittingly allows all those friends (and anybody else to whom the message is forwarded) to visit your site and impersonate him.

What's worse, when a user clicks on a link on your site that takes him to another site, the user's browser passes along the session ID–containing URL as the referring URL to the external site. Even if the folks who run that external site don't maliciously mine these referrer URLs, referrer logs are often inadvertently exposed to search engines. Search for `PHPSESSID referer` on your favorite search engine, and you'll probably find some referrer logs with PHP session IDs embedded in them.

Separately, redirects with the `Location` header aren't automatically modified, so you have to add a session ID to them yourself using the `SID` constant:

```
$redirect_url = 'http://www.example.com/airplane.php';
if (defined('SID') && (!isset($_COOKIE[session_name()]))) {
    $redirect_url .= '?' . SID;
}

header("Location: $redirect_url");
```

The `session_name()` function returns the name of the cookie to the session ID is stored in, so this code appends the `SID` constant to `$redirect_url` if the constant is defined, and the session cookie isn't set.

See Also

Documentation on `session_start()` at *http://www.php.net/session-start* and `session_save_path()` at *http://www.php.net/session-save-path*. The session module has a number of configuration directives that help you do things like manage how long sessions can last and how they are cached. These options are detailed in the "Sessions" section of the online manual at *http://www.php.net/session*.

11.2 Preventing Session Hijacking

Problem

You want make sure an attacker can't access another user's session.

Solution

Allow passing of session IDs via cookies only, and generate an additional session token that is passed via URLs. Only requests that contain a valid session ID and a valid session token may access the session:

```php
<?php
ini_set('session.use_only_cookies', true);
session_start();

$salt     = 'YourSpecialValueHere';
$tokenstr = (str) date('W') . $salt;
$token    = md5($tokenstr);

if (!isset($_REQUEST['token']) || $_REQUEST['token'] != $token) {
    // prompt for login
    exit;
}

$_SESSION['token'] = $token;
output_add_rewrite_var('token', $token);
?>
```

If you're using a PHP version earlier than 4.3.0, output_add_rewrite_var( ) is not available. Instead, use the code in Example 11-1.

Example 11-1. Adding a session token to links

```php
<?php
ini_set('session.use_only_cookies', true);
session_start();

$salt     = 'YourSpecialValueHere';
$tokenstr = (str) date('W') . $salt;
$token    = md5($tokenstr);

if (!isset($_REQUEST['token']) || $_REQUEST['token'] != $token) {
    // prompt for login
    exit;
}

$_SESSION['token'] = $token;

ob_start('inject_session_token');

function inject_session_token($buffer)
{
    $hyperlink_pattern = "/<a[^>]+href=\"([^\"]+)/i";
    preg_match_all($hyperlink_pattern, $buffer, $matches);

    foreach ($matches[1] as $link) {
        if (strpos($link, '?') === false) {
            $newlink = $link . '?token=' . $_SESSION['token'];
        } else {
            $newlink = $link .= '&token=' . $_SESSION['token'];
        }
```

```
        $buffer = str_replace($link, $newlink, $buffer);
    }

    return $buffer;
}
```

The regular expression for matching hyperlinks in the `inject_session_token( )` function isn't bulletproof; it will not catch hyperlinks with `href` attributes quoted with single quotes.

Discussion

This example creates an auto-shifting token by joining the current week number together with a salt term of your choice. With this technique, tokens will be valid for a reasonable period of time without being fixed.

We then check for the token in the request, and if it's not found, we prompt for a new login.

If it is found, it needs to be added to generated links. `output_add_rewrite_var( )` does this easily. Without `output_add_rewrite_var( )`, we continue generating the page and declare an output buffer callback function that will make sure that any hyperlinks on the page are modified to contain the current token before the page is displayed.

Note that the `inject_session_token( )` function in the example does not address imagemaps, form submissions, or Ajax calls; make sure that you adjust any such functionality on a page to include the session token that's been generated and stored in the session.

See Also

Recipe 18.1 for more information on regenerating IDs to prevent session fixation.

11.3 Preventing Session Fixation

Problem

You want to make sure that your application is not vulnerable to session fixation attacks.

Solution

Require the use of session cookies without session identifiers appended to URLs, and generate a new session ID frequently:

```
ini_set('session.use_only_cookies', true);
session_start();
if (!isset($_SESSION['generated'])
    || $_SESSION['generated'] < (time() - 30)) {
    session_regenerate_id();
```

```
        $_SESSION['generated'] = time();
    }
```

Discussion

In this example, we start by setting PHP's session behavior to use cookies only. This overrides PHP's default behavior of transparently appending values such as `?PHPSESSID=12345678` to any URL on a page whenever a visitor's session is started if he doesn't have cookies enabled in his browser.

Once the session is started, we set a value that will keep track of the last time a session ID was generated. By requiring a new one to be generated on a regular basis—every 30 seconds in this example—the opportunity for an attacker to obtain a valid session ID is dramatically reduced.

These two approaches combine to virtually eliminate the risk of session fixation. An attacker has a hard time obtaining a valid session ID because it changes so often, and since sessions IDs can only be passed in cookies, a URL-based attack is not possible. Finally, since we enabled the `session.use_only_cookies` setting, no session cookies will be left lying around in browser histories or in server referrer logs.

See Also

"Session Fixation Vulnerability in Web-based Applications," *http://www.acros.si/ papers/session_fixation.pdf*; Recipe 18.1 for information about regenerating session IDs on privilege escalation.

11.4 Storing Sessions in a Database

Problem

You want to store session data in a database instead of in files. If multiple web servers all have access to the same database, the session data is then mirrored across all the web servers.

Solution

Use a class or a set of functions in conjunction with the `session_set_save_handler( )` function to define database-aware routines for session management. For example, use PEAR's `HTTP_Session` package for convenient database session storage:

```php
<?php
require_once 'HTTP/Session/Container/DB.php';

$s = new HTTP_Session_Container_DB('mysql://user:password@localhost/db');
ini_get('session.auto_start') or session_start();
?>
```

Discussion

One of the most powerful aspects of the session module is its abstraction of how sessions get saved. The `session_set_save_handler()` function tells PHP to use different functions for the various session operations such as saving a session and reading session data.

The PEAR `HTTP_Session` package provides classes that take advantage of PEAR's `DB`, `MDB`, and `MDB2` database abstraction packages to store session data in a database. If the database is shared between multiple web servers, users' session information is portable across all those web servers. So if you have a bunch of web servers behind a load balancer, you don't need any fancy tricks to ensure that a user's session data is accurate no matter which web server she gets sent to.

To use `HTTP_Session_Container_DB`, pass a data source name (DSN) to the class when you instantiate it. The session data is stored in a table called `sessiondata` whose structure is:

```
CREATE TABLE sessiondata
(
  id CHAR(32) NOT NULL,
  data MEDIUMBLOB,
  expiry INT UNSIGNED NOT NULL,
  PRIMARY KEY (id)
);
```

If you want the table name to be different than `sessiondata`, you can set a new table name with an options array when instantiating the `HTTP_Session_Container_DB` class:

```php
<?php
require_once 'HTTP/Session/Container/DB.php';

$options = array(
  'table' => 'php_session',
  'dsn'   => 'mysql://user:password@localhost/db'
);
$s = new HTTP_Session_Container_DB($options);
ini_get('session.auto_start') or session_start();
?>
```

To customize an aspect of how the container classes provided by `HTTP_Session` manipulate session data, you can modify the behavior by extending one of the container classes. This is better than writing a completely new session handler class.

See Also

Documentation on `session_set_save_handler()` at *http://www.php.net/session-set-save-handler*; information on installing PEAR packages, such as `HTTP_Session`, is covered in Recipe 26.4.

11.5 Storing Sessions in Shared Memory

Problem

You want to store session data in shared memory to maximize performance.

Solution

Use the `pc_Shm_Session` class shown in Example 11-2. For example:

```php
<?php
$s = new pc_Shm_Session();
ini_get('session.auto_start') or session_start();
?>
```

Discussion

As discussed in Recipe 11.4, the session module allows users to define their own session handling methods. While this flexibility is most commonly used to store session data in a database, you may find that performance suffers with the overhead of the database connection and the subsequent queries. If sharing session data across a bunch of web servers is not a concern, you can boost session handling performance by storing that data in shared memory.

Before deciding to use shared memory for session storage, make sure that you can spare the amount of memory that your traffic plus your average session data size will consume. The performance boost of shared memory session storage won't matter if your site's sessions consume all available memory on your system!

To store session data in shared memory, you need to have the shared memory functions explicitly enabled by building PHP with `--enable-shmop`. You will also need the `pc_Shm` class shown in Example 11-2, as well as the `pc_Shm_Session` class shown in Example 11-3.

Example 11-2. pc_Shm class

```php
class pc_Shm {

  var $tmp;
  var $size;
  var $shm;
  var $keyfile;

  function pc_Shm($tmp = '') {
    if (!function_exists('shmop_open')) {
      trigger_error('pc_Shm: shmop extension is required.', E_USER_ERROR);
      return;
    }

    if ($tmp != '' && is_dir($tmp) && is_writable($tmp)) {
      $this->tmp = $tmp;
```

```php
    } else {
      $this->tmp = '/tmp';
    }

    // default to 16k
    $this->size = 16384;

    return true;
  }

  function __construct($tmp = '') {
    return $this->pc_Shm($tmp);
  }

  function setSize($size) {
    if (ctype_digit($size)) {
      $this->size = $size;
    }
  }

  function open($id) {
    $key = $this->_getKey($id);
    $shm = shmop_open($key, 'c', 0644, $this->size);
    if (!$shm) {
      trigger_error('pc_Shm: could not create shared memory segment', E_USER_ERROR);
      return false;
    }
    $this->shm = $shm;
    return true;
  }

  function write($data) {
    $written = shmop_write($this->shm, $data, 0);
    if ($written != strlen($data)) {
      trigger_error('pc_Shm: could not write entire length of data', E_USER_ERROR);
      return false;
    }
    return true;
  }

  function read() {
    $data = shmop_read($this->shm, 0, $this->size);
    if (!$data) {
      trigger_error('pc_Shm: could not read from shared memory block', E_USER_ERROR);
      return false;
    }
    return $data;
  }

  function delete() {
    if (shmop_delete($this->shm)) {
      if (file_exists($this->tmp . DIRECTORY_SEPARATOR . $this->keyfile)) {
        unlink($this->tmp . DIRECTORY_SEPARATOR . $this->keyfile);
      }
    }
```

```
    return true;
  }

  function close() {
    return shmop_close($this->shm);
  }

  function fetch($id) {
    $this->open($id);
    $data = $this->read();
    $this->close();
    return $data;
  }

  function save($id, $data) {
    $this->open($id);
    $result = $this->write($data);
    if (! (bool) $result) {
      return false;
    } else {
      $this->close();
      return $result;
    }
  }

  function _getKey($id) {
    $this->keyfile = 'pcshm_' . $id;
    if (!file_exists($this->tmp . DIRECTORY_SEPARATOR . $this->keyfile)) {
      touch($this->tmp . DIRECTORY_SEPARATOR . $this->keyfile);
    }
    return ftok($this->tmp . DIRECTORY_SEPARATOR . $this->keyfile, 'R');
  }
}
```

The pc_Shm class provides an object-oriented wrapper around PHP's shmop functions.
The pc_Shm::_getKey( ) method provides a convenient way to transparently calculate a
memory address, which is often the biggest obstacle for people getting familiar with
the shmop functions. By abstracting the memory address, reading and writing from
shared memory is as easy as manipulating a value in an associative array.

pc_Shm creates 16k memory blocks by default. To adjust the size of the blocks used,
pass a value in bytes to the pc_Shm::setSize( ) method.

With pc_Shm defined, pc_Shm_Session has what it needs to easily provide custom methods for session_set_save_handler( ). Example 11-3 shows the pc_Shm_Session class.

Example 11-3. pc_Shm_Session class

```
class pc_Shm_Session {

  var $shm;

  function pc_Shm_Session($tmp = '') {
    if (!function_exists('shmop_open')) {
      trigger_error("pc_Shm_Session: shmop extension is required.",E_USER_ERROR);
```

```
    return;
  }

  if (! session_set_save_handler(array(&$this, '_open'),
                    array(&$this, '_close'),
                    array(&$this, '_read'),
                    array(&$this, '_write'),
                    array(&$this, '_destroy'),
                    array(&$this, '_gc'))) {
    trigger_error('pc_Shm_Session: session_set_save_handler() failed', E_USER_ERROR);
    return;
  }

  $this->shm = new pc_Shm();

  return true;
}

function __construct() {
  return $this->pc_Shm_Session();
}

function setSize($size) {
  if (ctype_digit($size)) {
    $this->shm->setSize($size);
  }
}

function _open() {
  return true;
}

function _close() {
  return true;
}

function _read($id) {
  $this->shm->open($id);
  $data = $this->shm->read();
  $this->shm->close();
  return $data;
}

function _write($id, $data) {
  $this->shm->open($id);
  $this->shm->write($data);
  $this->shm->close();
  return true;

}

function _destroy($id) {
  $this->shm->open($id);
  $this->shm->delete();
  $this->shm->close();
```

```
    }

    function _gc($maxlifetime) {
      $d = dir($this->tmp);
      while (false !== ($entry = $d->read())) {
        if (substr($entry, 0, 6) == 'pcshm_') {
          $tmpfile = $this->tmp . DIRECTORY_SEPARATOR . $entry;
          $id = substr($entry, 6);
          $fmtime = filemtime($tmpfile);
          $age = now() - $fmtime;
          if ($age >= $maxlifetime) {
            $this->shm->open($id);
            $this->shm->delete();
            $this->shm->close();
          }
        }
      }
      $d->close();
      return true;
    }

}
```

Versions of Microsoft Windows prior to Windows 2000 do not support shared memory. Also, when using PHP in a Windows server environment, shmop functions will only work if PHP is running as a web server module, such those provided by Apache or IIS. CLI and CGI interfaces to PHP do not support shmop functions under Windows.

It's possible that you may not need to use these classes at all. If your web server can be configured to mount a ramdisk partition such as /dev/shm, using shared memory for session storage may be as simple as:

```php
<?php
ini_set('session.save_path', '/dev/shm');
ini_get('session.auto_start') or session_start();
?>
```

See Also

Documentation on session_set_save_handler( ) at *http://www.php.net/session-set-save-handler*; documentation on shmop functions at *http://www.php.net/shmop*. Information on configuring ramdisks on Linux-based systems is available at *http://www.linuxhq.com/kernel/file/Documentation/ramdisk.txt*.

11.6 Storing Arbitrary Data in Shared Memory

Problem

You want a chunk of data to be available to all web server processes through shared memory.

Solution

Use the `pc_Shm` class shown in Example 11-2. For example, to store a string in shared memory, used the `pc_Shm::save( )` method, which accepts a key/value pair:

```php
<?php
$shm = new pc_Shm();
$secret_code = 'land shark';
$shm->save('mysecret', $secret_code);
?>
```

Another process can then access that data from shared memory with the `pc_Shm::fetch( )` method:

```php
<?php
$shm = new pc_Shm();
print $shm->fetch('mysecret');
?>
```

Discussion

Occasionally there are times when you want to cache a value or set of values in shared memory for rapid retrieval. If your web server is busy with disk I/O, it may make sense to leverage the shmop functions to achieve greater performance with storage and retrieval of information in that cache.

The `pc_Shm` class has two convenient methods, `pc_Shm::fetch( )` and `pc_Shm::save( )`, which abstract away the need to set memory addresses or explictly open and close the shared memory segments.

It's important to remember that, unlike setting a key/value pair in a regular PHP array, the shmop functions need to allocate a specific amount of space that the data stored there is *expected* to consume. The `pc_Shm` class allocates 16k for each value by default. If data you need to store is larger than 16k, you need to increase the amount of space the shmop functions should reserve. For example:

```php
<?php
$shm = new pc_Shm();
$shm->setSize(24576); // 24k
$shm->save('longstring', 'Lorem ipsum pri eu simul nominati...');
?>
```

See Also

Recipe 11.5 and Recipe 5.6; the Memcache section of the PHP online manual at *http://www.php.net/memcache*. Memcache is a very fast and efficient alternative to the shmop functions. More information about memcache can be found at *http://www.danga.com/memcached/*. Also, the PECL apc module (*http://pecl.php.net/apc*) offers functions for storing data in shared memory.

11.7 Caching Calculated Results in Summary Tables

Problem

You need to collect statistics from log tables that are too large to efficiently query in real time.

Solution

Create a table that stores summary data from the complete log table, and query the summary table to generate reports in nearly real time.

Discussion

Let's say that you are logging search queries that web site visitors use on search engines like Google and Yahoo! to find your web site, and tracking those queries in MySQL. Your search term tracking log table has this structure:

```
CREATE TABLE searches
(
    searchterm    VARCHAR(255) NOT NULL,  # search term determined from HTTP_REFERER
                                           parsing
    dt            DATETIME NOT NULL,       # request date
    source        VARCHAR(15) NOT NULL     # site where search was performed
);
```

If you are fortunate enough to be logging thousands or tens of thousands of visits from the major search engines per hour, the searches table could grow to an unmanageable size over a period of several months.

You may wish to generate reports that illustrate trends of search terms that have driven traffic to your web site over time from each major search engine so that you can determine which search engine to purchase advertising with.

Create a summary table that reflects what your report needs to display, and then query the full dataset hourly and store the result in the summary table for speedy retrieval during report generation. Your summary table would have this structure:

```
CREATE TABLE searchsummary
(
    searchterm    VARCHAR(255) NOT NULL,   # search term
    source        VARCHAR(15) NOT NULL,    # site where search was performed
    sdate         DATE NOT NULL,           # date search performed
    searches      INT UNSIGNED NOT NULL,   # number of searches
    PRIMARY KEY (searchterm, source, sdate)
);
```

Your report generation script can then use PDO to query the searchsummary table, and if results are not available, collect them from the searches table and cache the result in searchsummary:

```
$st = $db->prepare('SELECT COUNT(*)
```

```
                            FROM
                                searchsummary
                            WHERE
                                sdate = ?');
    $st->execute(array(date('Y-m-d', strtotime('yesterday'))));

    $row = $st->fetch();

    // no matches in cache
    if ($row[0] == 0) {
        $st2 = $db->prepare('SELECT
                                searchterm,
                                source,
                                FROM_DAYS(TO_DAYS(dt)) AS sdate,
                                COUNT(*) as searches
                            WHERE
                                TO_DAYS(dt) = ?');
        $st2->execute(array(date('Y-m-d', strtotime('yesterday'))));

        $stInsert = $db->prepare('INSERT INTO searchsummary
                                (searchterm,source,sdate,searches)
                                VALUES (?,?,?,?)');
        while ($row->fetch(PDO::FETCH_NUM)) {
            $stInsert->execute($row);
        }
    }
}
?>
```

Using this technique, your script will only incur the overhead of querying the full log table once, and all subsequent requests will retrieve a single row of summary data per search term.

See Also

Recipe 10.7 for information about PDO::prepare( ) and PDOStatement::execute( ).

CHAPTER 12

XML

12.0 Introduction

XML has gained popularity as a data-exchange and message-passing format. As web services become more widespread, XML plays an even more important role in a developer's life. With the help of a few extensions, PHP lets you read and write XML for every occasion.

XML provides developers with a structured way to mark up data with tags arranged in a tree-like hierarchy. One perspective on XML is to treat it as CSV on steroids. You can use XML to store records broken into a series of fields. But instead of merely separating each field with a comma, you can include a field name, a type, and attributes alongside the data.

Another view of XML is as a document representation language. For instance, this book was written using XML. The book is divided into chapters; each chapter into recipes; and each recipe into Problem, Solution, and Discussion sections. Within any individual section, we further subdivide the text into paragraphs, tables, figures, and examples. An article on a web page can similarly be divided into the page title and headline, the authors of the piece, the story itself, and any sidebars, related links, and additional content.

XML content looks similar to HTML. Both use tags bracketed by < and > for marking up text. But XML is both stricter and looser than HTML. It's stricter because all container tags must be properly closed. No opening elements are allowed without a corresponding closing tag. It's looser because you're not forced to use a set list of tags, such as `<a>`, `<img>`, and `<h1>`. Instead, you have the freedom to choose a set of tag names that best describe your data.

Other key differences between XML and HTML are case sensitivity, attribute quoting, and whitespace. In HTML, `<B>` and `<b>` are the same bold tag; in XML, they're two different tags. In HTML, you can often omit quotation marks around attributes; XML, however, requires them. So you must always write:

```
<element attribute="value">
```

Additionally, HTML parsers generally ignore whitespace, so a run of 20 consecutive spaces is treated the same as one space. XML parsers preserve whitespace, unless explicitly instructed otherwise. Because all elements must be closed, empty elements must end with />. For instance, in HTML, the line break is <br>, while in XHTML, which is HTML that validates as XML, it's written as <br />.*

There is another restriction on XML documents. When XML documents are parsed into a tree of elements, the outermost element is known as the *root element*. Just as a tree has only one trunk, an XML document must have exactly one root element. In the previous book example, this means chapters must be bundled inside a book tag. If you want to place multiple books inside a document, you need to package them inside a bookcase or another container. This limitation applies only to the document root. Again, just like trees can have multiple branches off of the trunk, it's legal to store multiple books inside a bookcase.

This chapter doesn't aim to teach you XML; for an introduction to XML, see *Learning XML* by Erik T. Ray (O'Reilly). A solid nuts-and-bolts guide to all aspects of XML is *XML in a Nutshell* by Elliotte Rusty Harold and W. Scott Means (O'Reilly).

Now that we've covered the rules, here's an example: if you are a librarian and want to convert your card catalog to XML, start with this basic set of XML tags:

```
<book>
    <title>PHP Cookbook</title>
    <author>Sklar, David and Trachtenberg, Adam</author>
    <subject>PHP</subject>
</book>
```

From there, you can add new elements or modify existing ones. For example, <author> can be divided into first and last name, or you can allow for multiple records so two authors aren't placed in one field.

PHP 5 has a completely new set of XML extensions that address major problems in PHP 4's XML extensions. While PHP 4 allows you to manipulate XML, its XML tools are only superficially related. Each tool covers one part of the XML experience, but they weren't designed to work together, and PHP 4 support for the more advanced XML features is often patchy. Not so in PHP 5. The new XML extensions:

- Work together as a unified whole
- Are standardized on a single XML library: libxml2
- Fully comply with W3C specifications
- Efficiently process data
- Provide you with the right XML tool for your job

Additionally, following the PHP tenet that creating web applications should be easy, there's a new XML extension that makes it simple to read and alter XML documents.

---

* This is why nl2br( ) outputs <br />; its output is XML compatible.

The aptly named SimpleXML extension allows you to interact with the information in an XML document as though these pieces of information are arrays and objects, iterating through them with foreach loops and editing them in place merely by assigning new values to variables.

The first two recipes in this chapter cover parsing XML. Recipe 12.1 shows how to write XML without additional tools. To use the DOM extension to write XML in a standardized fashion, see Recipe 12.2.

The complement to writing XML is parsing XML. That's the subject of the next three recipes. They're divided based upon the complexity and size of the XML document you're trying to parse. Recipe 12.3 covers how to parse basic XML documents. If you need more sophisticated XML parsing tools, move onto Recipe 12.4. When your XML documents are extremely large and memory intensive, turn to Recipe 12.5. If this is your first time using XML, and you're unsure which recipe is right for you, try them in order, as the code becomes increasingly complex as your requirements go up.

XPath is the topic of Recipe 12.6. It's a W3C standard for extracting specific information from XML documents. We like to think of it as regular expressions for XML. XPath is one of the most useful, yet unused parts of the XML family of specifications. If you process XML on a regular basis, you should be familiar with XPath.

With XSLT, you can take an XSL stylesheet and turn XML into viewable output. By separating content from presentation, you can make one stylesheet for web browsers, another for PDAs, and a third for cell phones, all without changing the content itself. This is the subject of Recipe 12.7.

After introducing XSLT, the two recipes that follow show how to pass information back and forth between PHP and XSLT. Recipe 12.8 tells how to send data from PHP to an XSLT stylesheet; Recipe 12.9 shows how to call out to PHP from within an XSLT stylesheet.

As long as your XML document abides by the structural rules of XML, it is known as *well-formed*. However, unlike HTML, which has a specific set of elements and attributes that much appear in set places, XML has no such restrictions.

Yet, in some cases, such as XHTML, the XML version of HTML, it's useful to make sure your XML documents abide by a specification. This allows tools, such as web browsers, RSS readers, or your own scripts, to easily process the input. When an XML document follows all the rules set out by a specification, then it is known as *valid*. Recipe 12.10 covers how to validate an XML document.

One of PHP 5's major limitations is its handling of character sets and document encodings. PHP strings are not associated with a particular encoding, but all the XML extensions require UTF-8 input and emit UTF-8 output. Therefore, if you use a character set incompatible with UTF-8, you must manually convert your data both before sending it into an XML extension and after you receive it back. Recipe 12.11 explores the best ways to handle this process.

The chapter concludes with a number of recipes dedicated to reading and writing a number of common types of XML documents, specifically RSS and Atom. These are the two most popular data syndication formats, and are useful for exchanging many types of data, including blog posts, podcasts, and even mapping information.

PHP Cookbook also covers all the popular types of web services: REST, XML-RPC, and SOAP. This topic is so important, it gets two dedicated chapters of its own. Chapter 14 describes how to consume web services, while Chapter 15 tells how to can implement web services of your very own.

12.1 Generating XML as a String

Problem

You want to generate XML. For instance, you want to provide an XML version of your data for another program to parse.

Solution

Loop through your data and print it out surrounded by the correct XML tags:

```php
<?php
header('Content-Type: text/xml');
print '<?xml version="1.0"?>' . "\n";
print "<shows>\n";

$shows = array(array('name'     => 'Simpsons',
                     'channel'  => 'FOX',
                     'start'    => '8:00 PM',
                     'duration' => '30'),

               array('name'     => 'Law & Order',
                     'channel'  => 'NBC',
                     'start'    => '8:00 PM',
                     'duration' => '60'));

foreach ($shows as $show) {
    print "   <show>\n";
    foreach($show as $tag => $data) {
        print "      <$tag>" . htmlspecialchars($data) . "</$tag>\n";
    }
    print "   </show>\n";
}

print "</shows>\n";
?>
```

Discussion

Printing out XML manually mostly involves lots of foreach loops as you iterate through arrays. However, there are a few tricky details. First, you need to call header( ) to set the correct Content-Type header for the document. Since you're sending XML instead of HTML, it should be text/xml.

Next, depending on your settings for the short_open_tag configuration directive, trying to print the XML declaration may accidentally turn on PHP processing. Since the <? of <?xml version="1.0"?> is the short PHP open tag, to print the declaration to the browser you need to either disable the directive or print the line from within PHP. We do the latter in the Solution.

Last, entities must be escaped. For example, the & in the show Law & Order needs to be &. Call htmlspecialchars( ) to escape your data.

The output from the example in the Solution is shown in Example 12-1.

Example 12-1. Tonight's TV listings

```
<?xml version="1.0"?>
<shows>
    <show>
        <name>Simpsons</name>
        <channel>FOX</channel>
        <start>8:00 PM</start>
        <duration>30</duration>
    </show>
    <show>
        <name>Law &amp; Order</name>
        <channel>NBC</channel>
        <start>8:00 PM</start>
        <duration>60</duration>
    </show>
</shows>
```

See Also

Recipe 12.2 for generating XML using DOM; documentation on htmlspecialchars( ) at *http://www.php.net/htmlspecialchars*.

12.2 Generating XML with the DOM

Problem

You want to generate XML but want to do it in an organized way instead of using print and loops.

Solution

Use the DOM extension to create a DOMDocument object. After building up the document, call DOMDocument::save( ) or DOMDocument::saveXML( ) to generate a well-formed XML document:

```php
<?php
// create a new document
```

```php
$dom = new DOMDocument('1.0');

// create the root element, <book>, and append it to the document
$book = $dom->appendChild($dom->createElement('book'));

// create the title element and append it to $book
$title = $book->appendChild($dom->createElement('title'));

// set the text and the cover attribute for $title
$title->appendChild($dom->createTextNode('PHP Cookbook'));
$title->setAttribute('cover', 'soft');

// create and append author elements to $book
$sklar = $book->appendChild($dom->createElement('author'));
// create and append the text for each element
$sklar->appendChild($dom->createTextNode('Sklar'));

$trachtenberg = $book->appendChild($dom->createElement('author'));
$trachtenberg->appendChild($dom->createTextNode('Trachtenberg'));

// print a nicely formatted version of the DOM document as XML
$dom->formatOutput = true;
echo $dom->saveXML();
?>

<?xml version="1.0"?>
<book>
  <title cover="soft">PHP Cookbook</title>
  <author>Sklar</author>
  <author>Trachtenberg</author>
</book>
```

Discussion

The DOM methods follow a pattern. You create an object as either an element or a text node, add and set any attributes you want, and then append it to the tree in the spot it belongs.

Before creating elements, create a new document, passing the XML version as the sole argument:

```php
$dom = new DOMDocument('1.0');
```

Now create new elements belonging to the document. Despite being associated with a specific document, nodes don't join the document tree until appended:

```php
$book_element = $dom->createElement('book');
$book = $dom->appendChild($book_element);
```

Here a new book element is created and assigned to the object $book_element. To create the document root, append $book_element as a child of the $dom document. The result, $book, refers to the specific element and its location within the DOM object.

All nodes are created by calling a method on $dom. Once a node is created, it can be appended to any element in the tree. The element from which we call the appendChild( ) method determines the location in the tree where the node is placed. In the previous case, $book_element is appended to $dom. The element appended to $dom is the top-level node, or the *root node*.

You can also append a new child element to $book. Since $book is a child of $dom, the new element is, by extension, a grandchild of $dom:

```
$title_element = $dom->createElement('title');
$title = $book->appendChild($title_element);
```

By calling $book->appendChild( ), this code places the $title_element element under the $book element.

To add the text inside the <title></title> tags, create a text node using createTextNode( ) and append it to $title:

```
$text_node = $dom->createTextNode('PHP Cookbook');
$title->appendChild($text_node);
```

Since $title is already added to the document, there's no need to re-append it to $book.

The order in which you append children to nodes isn't important. The following four lines, which first append the text node to $title_element and then to $book, are equivalent to the previous code:

```
$title_element = $dom->createElement('title');
$text_node = $dom->createTextNode('PHP Cookbook');

$title_element->appendChild($text_node);
$book->appendChild($title_element);
```

To add an attribute, call setAttribute( ) upon a node, passing the attribute name and value as arguments:

```
$title->setAttribute('cover', 'soft');
```

If you print the title element now, it looks like this:

```
<title cover="soft">PHP Cookbook</title>
```

Once you're finished, you can output the document as a string or to a file:

```
// put the string representation of the XML document in $books
$books = $dom->saveXML();

// write the XML document to books.xml
$dom->save('books.xml');
```

By default, these methods generate XML output in one long line without any whitespace, including indentations and line breaks. To fix this, set the formatOutput attribute of your DOMDocument to true:

```
// print a nicely formatted version of the DOM document as XML
$dom->formatOutput = true;
```

This causes the DOM extension to generate XML like this:

```
<?xml version="1.0"?>
<book>
  <title cover="soft">PHP Cookbook</title>
</book>
```

See Also

Recipe 12.1 for writing XML without DOM; Recipe 12.4 for parsing XML with DOM; documentation on `DOMDocument` at *http://www.php.net/function.dom-domdocument-construct.php* and the DOM functions in general at *http://www.php.net/dom*; more information about the underlying libxml2 C library at *http://xmlsoft.org/*.

12.3 Parsing Basic XML Documents

Problem

You want to parse a basic XML document that follows a known schema, and you don't need access to more esoteric XML features, such as processing instructions.

Solution

Use the SimpleXML extension. Here's how to read XML from a file:

```
<?php
$sx = simplexml_load_file('address-book.xml');

foreach ($sx->person as $person) {
    $firstname_text_value = $person->firstname;
    $lastname_text_value = $person->lastname;

    print "$firstname_text_value $lastname_text_value\n";
}
?>
David Sklar
Adam Trachtenberg
```

Discussion

SimpleXML has been described as "the mostest bestest thing ever." While it's hard to live up to such grand praise, SimpleXML does do a remarkable job of making it—dare we say—simple to interact with XML. When you want to read a configuration file written in XML, parse an RSS feed, or process the result of a REST request, SimpleXML excels at these tasks. It doesn't work well for more complex XML-related jobs, such as reading a document where you don't know the format ahead of time or when you need to access processing instructions or comments.

SimpleXML turns elements into object properties. The text between the tags is assigned to the property. If more than one element with the same name lives in the same place (such as multiple `<people>`s), then they're placed inside a list.

Element attributes become array elements, where the array key is the attribute name and the key's value is the attribute's value.

To access a single value, reference it directly using object method notation. Let's use this XML fragment as example:

```
<firstname>David</firstname>
```

If you have this in a SimpleXML object, `$firstname`, here's all you need to do to access `David`:

```
$firstname
```

SimpleXML assumes that when you have a node that contains only text, you're interested in the text. Therefore, `print $firstname` does what you expect it to: it prints `David`.

Iteration methods, like `foreach`, are the best choice for cycling through multiple elements. Code for this is shown in later examples.

Attributes are stored as array elements. For example, this prints out the `id` attribute for the first `person` element:

```
<?php
$ab = simplexml_load_file('address-book.xml');

// the id attribute of the first person
print $ab->person['id'] . "\n";
?>
```

which gives you:

```
1
```

Example 12-2 contains a more complete example based on this simple address book in XML. It's used in the code examples that follow.

Example 12-2. Simple address book in XML

```
<?xml version="1.0"?>
<address-book>
    <person id="1">
        <!--David Sklar-->
        <firstname>David</firstname>
        <lastname>Sklar</lastname>
        <city>New York</city>
        <state>NY</state>
        <email>sklar@php.net</email>
    </person>

    <person id="2">
        <!--Adam Trachtenberg-->
        <firstname>Adam</firstname>
        <lastname>Trachtenberg</lastname>
        <city>San Francisco</city>
        <state>CA</state>
        <email>amt@php.net</email>
```

```
        </person>
    </address-book>
```

Example 12-3 shows how you use SimpleXML to pull out all the first and last names.

Example 12-3. Using SimpleXML to extract data
```
$sx = simplexml_load_file('address-book.xml');

foreach ($sx->person as $person) {
    $firstname_text_value = $person->firstname;
    $lastname_text_value = $person->lastname;

    print "$firstname_text_value $lastname_text_value\n";
}
```
David Sklar
Adam Trachtenberg

When you use SimpleXML, you can directly iterate over elements using `foreach`. Here, the iteration occurs over `$sx->person`, which holds all the `person` nodes.

You can also directly print SimpleXML objects, as shown in Example 12-4.

Example 12-4. Printing SimpleXML objects
```
<?php
foreach ($sx->person as $person) {
    print "$person->firstname $person->lastname\n";
}
?>
```
David Sklar
Adam Trachtenberg

PHP interpolates SimpleXML objects inside of quoted strings and retrieves the text stored in them.

See Also

Recipe 12.4 for parsing complex XML documents; Recipe 12.5 for parsing large XML documents; documentation on SimpleXML at *http://www.php.net/simplexml*; more information about the underlying libxml2 C library at *http://xmlsoft.org/*.

12.4 Parsing Complex XML Documents

Problem

You have a complex XML document, such as one where you need to introspect the document to determine its schema, or you need to use more esoteric XML features, such as processing instructions or comments.

Solution

Use the DOM extension. It provides a complete interface to all aspects of the XML specification.

```php
<?php
$dom = new DOMDocument;
$dom->load('address-book.xml');

foreach ($dom->getElementsByTagname('person') as $person) {
    $firstname = $person->getElementsByTagname('firstname');
    $firstname_text_value = $firstname->item(0)->firstChild->nodeValue;

    $lastname = $person->getElementsByTagname('lastname');
    $lastname_text_value = $lastname->item(0)->firstChild->nodeValue;

    print "$firstname_text_value $lastname_text_value\n";
}
?>
```

David Sklar
Adam Trachtenberg

Discussion

The W3C's DOM provides a platform- and language-neutral method that specifies the structure and content of a document. Using the DOM, you can read an XML document into a tree of nodes and then maneuver through the tree to locate information about a particular element or elements that match your criteria. This is called *tree-based parsing*.

Additionally, you can modify the structure by creating, editing, and deleting nodes. In fact, you can use the DOM functions to author a new XML document from scratch; see Recipe 12.2.

One of the major advantages of the DOM is that by following the W3C's specification, many languages implement DOM functions in a similar manner. Therefore, the work of translating logic and instructions from one application to another is considerably simplified. PHP 5 comes with a new series of DOM methods that are in stricter compliance with the DOM standard than previous versions of PHP.

The DOM is large and complex. For more information, read the specification at *http://www.w3.org/DOM/* or pick up a copy of *XML in a Nutshell*.

DOM functions in PHP are object oriented. To move from one node to another, access properties such as `$node->childNodes`, which contains an array of node objects, and `$node->parentNode`, which contains the parent node object. Therefore, to process a node, check its type and call a corresponding method, as shown in Example 12-5.

Example 12-5. Parsing a DOM object

```php
<?php
// $node is the DOM parsed node <book cover="soft">PHP Cookbook</book>
$type = $node->nodeType;
```

```
    switch($type) {
    case XML_ELEMENT_NODE:
        // I'm a tag. I have a tagname property.
        print $node->tagName;  // prints the tagname property: "book"
        break;
    case XML_ATTRIBUTE_NODE:
        // I'm an attribute. I have a name and a value property.
        print $node->name;  // prints the name property: "cover"
        print $node->value; // prints the value property: "soft"
        break;
    case XML_TEXT_NODE:
        // I'm a piece of text inside an element.
        // I have a name and a content property.
        print $node->nodeName;  // prints the name property: "#text"
        print $node->nodeValue; // prints the text content: "PHP Cookbook"
        break;
    default:
        // another type
        break;
    }
    ?>
```

To automatically search through a DOM tree for specific elements, use
getElementsByTagname( ). Example 12-6 shows how to do so with multiple book records.

Example 12-6. Card catalog in XML

```
<books>
    <book>
        <title>PHP Cookbook</title>
        <author>Sklar</author>
        <author>Trachtenberg</author>
        <subject>PHP</subject>
    </book>
    <book>
        <title>Perl Cookbook</title>
        <author>Christiansen</author>
        <author>Torkington</author>
        <subject>Perl</subject>
    </book>
</books>
```

Example 12-7 shows how to find all authors.

Example 12-7. Printing all authors using DOM

```
// find and print all authors
$authors = $dom->getElementsByTagname('author');

// loop through author elements
foreach ($authors as $author) {
    // childNodes holds the author values
    $text_nodes = $author->childNodes;
```

```
        foreach ($text_nodes as $text) {
            print $text->nodeValue . "\n";
        }
    }

Sklar
Trachtenberg
Christiansen
Torkington
```

The getElementsByTagname( ) method returns an array of element node objects. By looping through each element's children, you can get to the text node associated with that element. From there, you can pull out the node values, which in this case are the names of the book authors, such as Sklar and Trachtenberg.

See Also

Recipe 12.3 for parsing simple XML documents; Recipe 12.5 for parsing large XML documents; documentation on DOM at *http://www.php.net/dom*; more information about the underlying libxml2 C library at *http://xmlsoft.org/*.

12.5 Parsing Large XML Documents

Problem

You want to parse a large XML document. This document is so large that it's impractical to use SimpleXML or DOM because you cannot hold the entire document in memory. Instead, you must load the document in one section at a time.

Solution

Use the XMLReader extension:

```
<?php
$reader = new XMLReader();
$reader->open('card-catalog.xml');

/* Loop through document */
while ($reader->read()) {
    /* If you're at an element named 'author' */
    if ($reader->nodeType == XMLREADER::ELEMENT && $reader->localName == 'author') {
        /* Move to the text node and print it out */
        $reader->read();
        print $reader->value . "\n";
    }
}
?>
```

Discussion

There are two major types of XML parsers: ones that hold the entire document in memory at once, and ones that hold only a small portion of the document in memory at any given time.

The first kind are called tree-based parsers, since they store the document into a data structure known as a tree. The SimpleXML and DOM extensions, from Recipes 12.3 and 12.4, are tree-based parsers. Using a tree-based parser is easier for you, but requires PHP to use more RAM. With most XML documents, this isn't a problem. However, when your XML document is quite large, then this can cause major performance issues.

The other kind of XML parser is a stream-based parser. Stream-based parsers don't store the entire document in memory; instead, they read in one node at a time and allow you to interact with it in real time. Once you move onto the next node, the old one is thrown away—unless you explicitly store it yourself for later use. This makes stream-based parsers faster and less memory consuming, but you may have to write more code to process the document.

The easiest way to process XML data using a stream-based parser is using the XMLReader extension. This extension is based on the C# XmlTextReader API. If you're familiar with the SAX (Simple API for XML) interface from PHP 4, it's still available in PHP 5, but the XMLReader extension is more intuitive, feature-rich, and faster.

XMLReader is enabled by default as of PHP 5.1. If you're running PHP 5.0.x, grab the extension from PECL at *http://pecl.php.net/package/xmlReader* and install it yourself.

Begin by creating a new instance of the XMLReader class and specifying the location of your XML data:

```php
<?php
// Create a new XMLReader object
$reader = new XMLReader();

// Load from a file or URL
$reader->open('document.xml');

// Or, load from a PHP variable
$reader->XML($document);
?>
```

Most of the time, you'll use the XMLReader::open( ) method to pull in data from an external source, but you can also load it from an existing PHP variable with XMLReader::XML( ).

Once the object is configured, you begin processing the data. At the start, you're positioned at the top of the document. You can maneuver through the document using a combination of the two navigation methods XMLReader provides: XMLReader::read( ) and XMLReader::next( ). The first method reads in the piece of XML data that immediately follows the current position. The second method moves to the next sibling element after the current position.

For example, look at the XML in Example 12-8.

Example 12-8. Card catalog in XML

```
<books>
    <book isbn="1565926811">
        <title>PHP Cookbook</title>
        <author>Sklar</author>
        <author>Trachtenberg</author>
        <subject>PHP</subject>
    </book>
    <book isbn="0596003137">
        <title>Perl Cookbook</title>
        <author>Christiansen</author>
        <author>Torkington</author>
        <subject>Perl</subject>
    </book>
</books>
```

When the object is positioned at the first `<book>` element, the `read( )` method moves you to the next element underneath `<book>`. (This is technically the whitespace between `<book>` and `<title>`.) In comparison, `next( )` moves you to the next `<book>` element and skips the entire *PHP Cookbook* subtree.

These methods return `true` when they're able to successfully move to another node, and `false` when they cannot. So, it's typical to use them inside a `while` loop, as such:

```
/* Loop through document */
while ($reader->read()) {
    /* Process XML */
}
```

This causes the object to read in the entire XML document one piece at a time. Inside the `while( )`, examine `$reader` and process it accordingly.

A common aspect to check is the node type. This lets you know if you've reached an element (and then check the name of that element), a closing element, an attribute, a piece of text, some whitespace, or any other part of an XML document. Do this by referencing the `nodeType` attribute:

```
/* Loop through document */
while ($reader->read()) {
    /* If you're at an element named 'author' */
    if ($reader->nodeType == XMLREADER::ELEMENT && $reader->localName == 'author') {
        /* Process author element */
    }
}
```

This code checks if the node is an element and, if so, that its name is `author`. For a complete list of possible values stored in `nodeType`, check out Table 12-1.

Table 12-1. *XMLReader node type values*

Node type	Description
XMLReader::NONE	No node type
XMLReader::ELEMENT	Start element
XMLReader::ATTRIBUTE	Attribute node
XMLReader::TEXT	Text node
XMLReader::CDATA	CDATA node
XMLReader::ENTITY_REF	Entity Reference node
XMLReader::ENTITY	Entity Declaration node
XMLReader::PI	Processing Instruction node
XMLReader::COMMENT	Comment node
XMLReader::DOC	Document node
XMLReader::DOC_TYPE	Document Type node
XMLReader::DOC_FRAGMENT	Document Fragment node
XMLReader::NOTATION	Notation node
XMLReader::WHITESPACE	Whitespace node
XMLReader::SIGNIFICANT_WHITESPACE	Significant Whitespace node
XMLReader::END_ELEMENT	End Element
XMLReader::END_ENTITY	End Entity
XMLReader::XML_DECLARATION	XML Declaration node

From there, you can decide how to handle that element and the data it contains. For example, printing out all the author names in the card catalog:

```
$reader = new XMLReader();
$reader->open('card-catalog.xml');

/* Loop through document */
while ($reader->read()) {
    /* If you're at an element named 'author' */
    if ($reader->nodeType == XMLREADER::ELEMENT && $reader->localName == 'author') {
        /* Move to the text node and print it out */
        $reader->read();
        print $reader->value . "\n";
    }
}

Sklar
Trachtenberg
Christiansen
Torkington
```

Once you've reached the <author> element, call $reader->read( ) to advance to the text *inside* it. From there, you can find the author names inside of $reader->value.

The `XMLReader::value` attribute provides you access with a node's value. This only applies to nodes where this is a meaningful concept, such as text nodes or CDATA nodes. In all other cases, such as element nodes, this attribute is set to the empty string.

Table 12-2 contains a complete listing of XMLReader object properties, including `value`.

Table 12-2. XMLReader node type values

Name	Type	Description
attributeCount	int	Number of node attributes
baseURI	string	Base URI of the node
depth	int	Tree depth of the node, starting at 0
hasAttributes	bool	If the node has attributes
hasValue	bool	If the node has a text value
isDefault	bool	If the attribute value is defaulted from DTD
isEmptyElement	bool	If the node is an empty element tag
localName	string	Local name of the node
name	string	Qualified name of the node
namespaceURI	string	URI of the namespace associated with the node
nodeType	int	Node type of the node
prefix	string	Namespace prefix associated with the node
value	string	Text value of the node
xmlLang	string	xml:lang scope of the node

There's one remaining major piece of XMLReader functionality: attributes. XMLReader has a special set of methods to access attribute data when it's on top of an element node, including the following: `moveToAttribute( )`, `moveToFirstAttribute( )`, and `moveToNextAttribute( )`.

The `moveToAttribute( )` method lets you specify an attribute name. For example, here's code using the card catalog XML to print out all the ISBN numbers:

```php
<?php
$reader = new XMLReader();
$reader->XML($catalog);

/* Loop through document */
while ($reader->read()) {
    /* If you're at an element named 'book' */
    if ($reader->nodeType == XMLREADER::ELEMENT && $reader->localName == 'book') {
        $reader->moveToAttribute('isbn');
        print $reader->value . "\n";
    }
}
?>
```

Once you've found the <book> element, call `moveToAttribute('isbn')` to advance to the isbn attribute, so you can read its value and print it out.

In the examples in this recipe, we print out information on all books. However, it's easy to modify them to retrieve data only for one specific book. For example, this code combines pieces of the examples to print out all the data for *Perl Cookbook* in an efficient fashion:

```php
<?php
$reader = new XMLReader();
$reader->XML($catalog);

// Perl Cookbook ISBN is 0596003137
// Use array to make it easy to add additional ISBNs
$isbns = array('0596003137' => true);

/* Loop through document to find first <book> */
while ($reader->read()) {
    /* If you're at an element named 'book' */
    if ($reader->nodeType == XMLREADER::ELEMENT &&
        $reader->localName == 'book') {
        break;
    }
}

/* Loop through <book>s to find right ISBNs */
do {
    if ($reader->moveToAttribute('isbn') &&
        isset($isbns[$reader->value])) {
        while ($reader->read()) {
            switch ($reader->nodeType) {
            case XMLREADER::ELEMENT:
                print $reader->localName . ": ";
                break;
            case XMLREADER::TEXT:
                print $reader->value . "\n";
                break;
            case XMLREADER::END_ELEMENT;
                if ($reader->localName == 'book') {
                    break 2;
                }
            }
        }
    }
} while ($reader->next());
?>

title: Perl Cookbook
author: Christiansen
author: Torkington
subject: Perl
```

The first while( ) iterates sequentially until it finds the first <book> element.

Having lined yourself up correctly, you then break out of the loop and start checking ISBN numbers. That's handled inside a do... while( ) loop that uses $reader->next( ) to move down the <book> list. You cannot use a regular while( ) here or you'll skip over the first <book>. Also, this is a perfect example of when to use $reader->next( ) instead of $reader->read( ).

If the ISBN matches a value in $isbns, then you want to process the data inside the current <book>. This is handled using yet another while( ) and a switch( ).

There are three different switch( ) cases: an opening element, element text, and a closing element. If you're opening an element, you print out the element's name and a colon. If you're text, you print out the textual data. And if you're closing an element, you check to see whether you're closing the <book>. If so, then you've reached the end of the data for that particular book, and you need to return to the do... while( ) loop. This is handled using a break 2;; while jumps back two levels, instead of the usual one level.

See Also

Recipe 12.3 for parsing simple XML documents; Recipe 12.4 for parsing complex XML documents; documentation on XMLReader at *http://www.php.net/xmlreader*; more information about the underlying libxml2 C library's XMLReader functions at *http://xmlsoft.org/xmlreader.html*.

12.6 Extracting Information Using XPath

Problem

You want to make sophisticated queries of your XML data without parsing the document node by node.

Solution

Use XPath.

XPath is available in SimpleXML:

```php
<?php
$s = simplexml_load_file('address-book.xml');
$emails = $s->xpath('/address-book/person/email');

foreach ($emails as $email) {
    // do something with $email
}
?>
```

And in DOM:

```php
<?php
$dom = new DOMDocument;
```

```
$dom->load('address-book.xml');
$xpath = new DOMXPath($dom);
$email = $xpath->query('/address-book/person/email');

foreach ($emails as $email) {
    // do something with $email
}
?>
```

Discussion

Except for the simplest documents, it's rarely easy to access the data you want one element at a time. As your XML files become increasingly complex and your parsing desires grow, using XPath is easier than filtering the data inside a `foreach`.

PHP has an XPath class that takes a DOM object as its constructor. You can then search the object and receive DOM nodes in reply. SimpleXML also supports XPath, and it's easier to use because it's integrated into the SimpleXML object.

DOM supports XPath queries, but you do not perform the query directly on the DOM object itself. Instead, you create a `DOMXPath` object, as shown in Example 12-9.

Example 12-9. Using XPath and DOM

```
$dom = new DOMDocument;
$dom->load('address-book.xml');
$xpath = new DOMXPath($dom);
$email = $xpath->query('/address-book/person/email');
```

Instantiate `DOMXPath` by passing in a `DOMDocument` to the constructor. To execute the XPath query, call `query( )` with the query text as your argument. This returns an iterable DOM node list of matching nodes (see Example 12-10).

Example 12-10. Using XPath with DOM in a basic example

```
$dom = new DOMDocument;
$dom->load('address-book.xml');
$xpath = new DOMXPath($dom);
$emails = $xpath->query('/address-book/person/email');

foreach ($emails as $e) {
    $email = $e->firstChild->nodeValue;
    // do something with $email
}
```

After creating a new `DOMXPath` object, query this object using `DOMXPath::query( )`, passing the XPath query as the first parameter (in this example, it's `/people/person/email`). This function returns a node list of matching DOM nodes.

By default, `DOMXPath::query( )` operates on the entire XML document. Search a subsection of the tree by passing in the subtree as a final parameter to `query( )`. For instance, to gather all the first and last names of people in the address book, retrieve all the `people` nodes and query each node individually, as shown in Example 12-11.

Example 12-11. Using XPath with DOM in a more complicated example

```
$dom = new DOMDocument;
$dom->load('address-book.xml');
$xpath = new DOMXPath($dom);
$person = $xpath->query('/address-book/person');

foreach ($person as $p) {
    $fn = $xpath->query('firstname', $p);
    $firstname = $fn->item(0)->firstChild->nodeValue;

    $ln = $xpath->query('lastname', $p);
    $lastname = $ln->item(0)->firstChild->nodeValue;

    print "$firstname $lastname\n";
}

David Sklar
Adam Trachtenberg
```

Inside the `foreach`, call `DOMXPath::query( )` to retrieve the `firstname` and `lastname` nodes. Now, in addition to the XPath query, also pass `$p` to the method. This makes the search local to the node.

In contrast to DOM, all SimpleXML objects have an integrated `xpath( )` method. Calling this method queries the current object using XPath and returns a SimpleXML object containing the matching nodes, so you don't need to instantiate another object to use XPath. The method's one argument is your XPath query.

Use Example 12-12 to find all the matching email addresses in the sample address book.

Example 12-12. Using XPath and SimpleXML in a basic example

```
$s = simplexml_load_file('address-book.xml');
$emails = $s->xpath('/address-book/person/email');

foreach ($emails as $email) {
    // do something with $email
}
```

This is shorter because there's no need to dereference the `firstNode` or to take the `nodeValue`.

SimpleXML handles the more complicated example, too. Since `xpath( )` returns SimpleXML objects, you can query them directly, as in Example 12-13.

Example 12-13. Using XPath with SimpleXML in a more complicated example

```
$s = simplexml_load_file('address-book.xml');
$people = $s->xpath('/address-book/person');

foreach($people as $p) {
    list($firstname) = $p->xpath('firstname');
    list($lastname) = $p->xpath('lastname');
```

```
        print "$firstname $lastname\n";
    }

    David Sklar
    Adam Trachtenberg
```

Since the inner XPath queries return only one element, use list to grab it from the array.

See Also

Documentation on DOM XPath at *http://www.php.net/function.dom-domxpath-construct.php*; the offical XPath specification at *http://www.w3.org/TR/xpath*; the XPath chapter from *XML in a Nutshell* at *http://www.oreilly.com/catalog/xmlnut/chapter/ch09.html*.

12.7 Transforming XML with XSLT

Problem

You have an XML document and an XSL stylesheet. You want to transform the document using XSLT and capture the results. This lets you apply stylesheets to your data and create different versions of your content for different media.

Solution

Use PHP's XSLT extension:

```
// Load XSL template
$xsl = newDOMDocument;
$xsl->load('stylesheet.xsl');

// Create new XSLTProcessor
$xslt = new XSLTProcessor();
// Load stylesheet
$xslt->importStylesheet($xsl);

// Load XML input file
$xml = new DOMDocument;
$xml->load('data.xml');

// Transform to string
$results = $xslt->transformToXML($xml);

// Transform to a file
$results = $xslt->transformToURI($xml, 'results.txt');

// Transform to DOM object
$results = $xslt->transformToDoc($xml);
```

The transformed text is stored in $results.

Discussion

XML documents describe the content of data, but they don't contain any information about how that data should be displayed. However, when XML content is coupled with a stylesheet described using XSL (eXtensible Stylesheet Language), the content is displayed according to specific visual rules.

The glue between XML and XSL is XSLT (eXtensible Stylesheet Language Transformations). These transformations apply the series of rules enumerated in the stylesheet to your XML data. So just as PHP parses your code and combines it with user input to create a dynamic page, an XSLT program uses XSL and XML to output a new page that contains more XML, HTML, or any other format you can describe.

There are a few XSLT programs available, each with different features and limitations. PHP 5 supports only the libxslt processor. This is a different processor than PHP 4 used.

Using XSLT in PHP 5 involves two main steps: preparing the XSLT object and then triggering the actual transformation for each XML file.

To begin, load in the stylesheet using DOM. Then, instantiate a new `XSLTProcessor` object, and import the XSLT document by passing in your newly created DOM object to the `importStylesheet( )` method, as shown in Example 12-14.

Example 12-14. Configuring the XSLT processor

```
// Load XSL template
$xsl = newDOMDocument;
$xsl->load('stylesheet.xsl');

// Create new XSLTProcessor
$xslt = new XSLTProcessor();
// Load stylesheet
$xslt->importStylesheet($xsl);
```

Now the transformer is up and running. You can transform any DOM object in one of three ways: into a string, into a file, or back into another DOM object, as shown in Example 12-15.

Example 12-15. Transforming the XML data

```
// Load XML input file
$xml = new DOMDocument;
$xml->load('data.xml');

// Transform to string
$results = $xslt->transformToXML($xml);

// Transform to a file
$results = $xslt->transformToURI($xml, 'results.txt');

// Transform to DOM object
$results = $xslt->transformToDoc($xml);
```

When you call transformToXML( ) or transformToDoc( ), the extension returns the result string or object. In contrast, transformToURI( ) returns the number of bytes written to the file, not the actual document.

These methods return false when they fail, so to accurately check for failure, write:

```
if (false === ($results = $xslt->transformToXML($xml))) {
    // an error occurred
}
```

Using === prevents a return value of 0 from being confused with an actual error.

See Also

Documentation on XSL functions at *http://www.php.net/xsl*; *XSLT* by Doug Tidwell (O'Reilly).

12.8 Setting XSLT Parameters from PHP

Problem

You want to set parameters in your XSLT stylesheet from PHP.

Solution

Use the XSLTProcessor::setParameter( ) method:

```
// This could also come from $_GET['city'];
$city = 'San Francisco';

$dom  = new DOMDocument
$dom->load('address-book.xml');
$xsl  = new DOMDocument
$xsl->load('stylesheet.xsl');

$xslt = new XSLTProcessor();
$xslt->importStylesheet($xsl);
$xslt->setParameter(NULL, 'city', $city);
print $xslt->transformToXML($dom);
```

This code sets the XSLT city parameter to the value stored in the PHP variable $city.

Discussion

You can pass data from PHP into your XSLT stylesheet with the setParameter( ) method. This allows you to do things such as filter data in your stylesheet based on user input.

For example, the program in Example 12-16 allows you to find people based on their city.

Example 12-16. Setting XSLT parameters from PHP

```
// This could also come from $_GET['city'];
$city = 'San Francisco';

$dom  = new DOMDocument
$dom->load('address-book.xml');
$xsl  = new DOMDocument
$xsl->load('stylesheet.xsl');

$xslt = new XSLTProcessor();
$xslt->importStylesheet($xsl);
$xslt->setParameter(NULL, 'city', $city);
print $xslt->transformToXML($dom);
```

The program uses the following stylesheet:

```
<?xml version="1.0" ?>
<xsl:stylesheet version="1.0"
  xmlns:xsl="http://www.w3.org/1999/XSL/Transform">

<xsl:template match="@*|node()">
  <xsl:copy>
    <xsl:apply-templates select="@*|node()"/>
  </xsl:copy>
</xsl:template>

<xsl:template match="/address-book/person">
  <xsl:if test="city=$city">
    <xsl:copy>
      <xsl:apply-templates select="@*|node()"/>
    </xsl:copy>
  </xsl:if>
</xsl:template>
</xsl:stylesheet>
```

The program and stylesheet combine to produce the following results:

```
<?xml version="1.0"?>
<address-book>


    <person id="2">
        <!--Adam Trachtenberg-->
        <firstname>Adam</firstname>
        <lastname>Trachtenberg</lastname>
        <city>San Francisco</city>
        <state>CA</state>
        <email>amt@php.net</email>
    </person>
</address-book>
```

The PHP script does a standard XSLT transformation, except that it calls `$xslt->setParameter(NULL, 'city', $city)`. The first argument is the parameter's namespace, the second is the parameter's name, and the third is the parameter's value.

Here, the value stored in the PHP variable $city—in this case, San Francisco—is assigned to the XSLT parameter city, which does not live under a namespace. This is equal to placing the following in an XSLT file:

```
<xsl:param name="city">San Francisco</xsl:param>
```

You usually access a parameter inside a stylesheet like you do a PHP variable, by placing a dollar sign ($) in front of its name. The stylesheet example creates a template that matches /address-book/person nodes.

Inside the template, you test whether city=$city; in other words, is the city child of the current node equal to the value of the city parameter? If there's a match, the children are copied along; otherwise, the records are eliminated.

In this case, city is set to San Francisco, so David's record is removed and Adam's remains.

See Also

Documentation on XSLTProcessor::setParameter at *http://www.php.net/manual/function.xsl-xsltprocessor-set-parameter.php*; *XSLT* by Doug Tidwell (O'Reilly).

12.9 Calling PHP Functions from XSLT Stylesheets

Problem

You want to call PHP functions from within an XSLT stylesheet.

Solution

Invoke the XSLTProcessor::registerPHPFunctions() method to enable this functionality:

```
$xslt = new XSLTProcessor();
$xslt->registerPHPFunctions();
```

And use the function() or functionString() function within your stylesheet:

```
<?xml version="1.0" ?>
<xsl:stylesheet version="1.0"
    xmlns:xsl="http://www.w3.org/1999/XSL/Transform"
    xmlns:php="http://php.net/xsl"
    xsl:extension-element-prefixes="php">

<xsl:template match="/">
    <xsl:value-of select="php:function('strftime', '%c')" />
</xsl:template>

</xsl:stylesheet>
```

Discussion

XSLT parameters are great when you need to communicate from PHP to XSLT. However, they're not very useful when you require the reverse. You can't use parameters to extract information from the stylesheet during the transformation. Ideally, you could call PHP functions from a stylesheet and pass information back to PHP.

Fortunately, there's a method that implements this functionality: `registerPHPFunctions( )`. Here's how it's enabled:

```
$xslt = new XSLTProcessor();
$xslt->registerPHPFunctions();
```

This allows you to call any PHP function from your stylesheets. It's not available by default because it presents a security risk if you're processing stylesheets controlled by other people.

Both built-in and user-defined functions work. Inside your stylesheet, you must define a namespace and call the `function( )` or `functionString( )` methods, as shown in Example 12-17.

Example 12-17. Calling PHP from an XSL stylesheet

```
<?xml version="1.0" ?>
<xsl:stylesheet version="1.0"
    xmlns:xsl="http://www.w3.org/1999/XSL/Transform"
    xmlns:php="http://php.net/xsl"
    xsl:extension-element-prefixes="php">

<xsl:template match="/">
    <xsl:value-of select="php:function('strftime', '%c')" />
</xsl:template>

</xsl:stylesheet>
```

At the top of the stylesheet, define the namespace for PHP: `http://php.net/xsl`. This example sets the namespace prefix to `php`. Also, set the `extension-element-prefixes` value to `php` so XSLT knows these are functions.

To call a PHP function, reference `php:function( )`. The first parameter is the function name; additional parameters are the function arguments. In this case, the function name is `strftime` and the one argument is `%c`. This causes `strftime` to return the current date and time.

Example 12-18 uses this stylesheet, stored as *stylesheet.xsl*, to process a single-element XML document.

Example 12-18. Transforming XML with XSLT and PHP functions

```
$dom  = new DOMDocument;
$dom->loadXML('<blank/>');
$xsl  = new DOMDocument
$xsl->load('stylesheet.xsl');
```

```
$xslt = new XSLTProcessor();
$xslt->importStylesheet($xsl);
$xslt->registerPHPFunctions();
print $xslt->transformToXML($dom);
```

Mon Jul 22 19:10:21 2004

This works like standard XSLT processing, but there's an additional call to
`registerPHPFunctions()` to activate PHP function support.

You can also return DOM objects. Example 12-19 takes the XML address book and
mangles all the email addresses to turn the hostname portion into three dots. Everything
else in the document is left untouched.

Example 12-19. Spam protecting email addresses

```
function mangle_email($nodes) {
    return preg_replace('/([^@\s]+)@([-a-z0-9]+\.)+[a-z]{2,}/is',
                        '$1@...',
                        $nodes[0]->nodeValue);
}

$dom  = new DOMDocument;
$dom->load('address-book.xml');
$xsl  = new DOMDocument
$xsl->load('stylesheet.xsl');

$xslt = new XSLTProcessor();
$xslt->importStylesheet($xsl);
$xslt->registerPhpFunctions();
print $xslt->transformToXML($dom);
```

Inside your stylesheet, create a special template for `/address-book/person/email` elements, as shown in Example 12-20.

Example 12-20. XSL stylesheet to spam protect email address

```
<?xml version="1.0" ?>
<xsl:stylesheet version="1.0"
  xmlns:xsl="http://www.w3.org/1999/XSL/Transform"
  xmlns:php="http://php.net/xsl"
  xsl:extension-element-prefixes="php">

<xsl:template match="@*|node()">
  <xsl:copy>
    <xsl:apply-templates select="@*|node()"/>
  </xsl:copy>
</xsl:template>


<xsl:template match="/address-book/person/email">
  <xsl:copy>
    <xsl:value-of select="php:function('mangle_email', node())" />
  </xsl:copy>
```

```
    </xsl:template>
  </xsl:stylesheet>
```

The first template ensures that the elements aren't modified, while the second passes the current node to PHP for mangling. In the second template, the `mangle_email()` function is passed the current node, represented in XPath as `node()`, instead of a string. Be sure not to place the node inside quotation marks, or you'll pass the literal text `node()`.

Nodes becomes DOM objects inside PHP and always arrive in an array. In this case, `mangle_email()` knows there's always only one object and it's a `DOMText` object, so the email address is located in `$nodes[0]->nodeValue`.

When you know that you're only interested in the text portion of a node, use the `functionString()` function. This function converts nodes to PHP strings, which allows you to omit the array access and `nodeValue` dereference:

```
function mangle_email($email) {
    return preg_replace('/([^@\s]+)@([-a-z0-9]+\.)+[a-z]{2,}/is',
                        '$1@...',
                        $email);
}

// all other code is the same as before
```

The new stylesheet template for `/address-book/person/email` is:

```
<xsl:template match="/address-book/person/email">
  <xsl:copy>
    <xsl:value-of
      select="php:functionString('mangle_email', node())" />
  </xsl:copy>
</xsl:template>
```

The `mangle_email()` function now processes `$email` instead of `$nodes[0]->nodeValue` because the template now calls the `functionString()` function.

The `function()` and `functionString()` methods are incredibly useful, but using them undermines the premise of XSL as a language-neutral transformation engine. When you call PHP from XSLT, you cannot easily reuse your stylesheets in projects that use Java, Perl, and other languages, because they cannot call PHP. Therefore, you should consider the trade-off between convenience and portability before using this feature.

See Also

Documentation on `XSLTProcessor::registerPHPFunctions()` at *http://www.php.net/ manual/function.xsl-xsltprocessor-register-php-functions.php*; *XSLT* by Doug Tidwell (O'Reilly).

12.10 Validating XML Documents

Problem

You want to make sure your XML document abides by a schema, such as XML Schema, RelaxNG, and DTDs.

Solution

Use the DOM extension.

With existing DOM objects, call `DOMDocument::schemaValidate()` or `DOMDocument::relaxNGValidate()`:

```
$file = 'address-book.xml';
$schema = 'address-book.xsd';
$ab = new DOMDocument
$ab->load($file);

if ($ab->schemaValidate($schema)) {
    print "$file is valid.\n";
} else {
    print "$file is invalid.\n";
}
```

If your XML document specifies a DTD at the top, call `DOMDocument::validate()` to validate it against the DTD.

With XML in a string, call `DOMDocument::schemaValidateSource()` or `DOMDocument::relaxNGValidateSource()`:

```
$xml = '<person><firstname>Adam</firstname></person>';
$schema = 'address-book.xsd';
$ab = new DOMDocument
$ab->&gt;load($file);

if ($ab->&gt;schemaValidateSource($schema)) {
    print "XML is valid.\n";
} else {
    print "XML is invalid.\n";
}
```

Discussion

Schemas are a way of defining a specification for your XML documents. While the goal is the same, there are multiple ways to encode a schema, each with a different syntax.

Some popular formats are DTDs (Document Type Definitions), XML Schema, and RelaxNG. DTDs have been around longer, but they are not written in XML and have other issues, so they can be difficult to work with. XML Schema and RelaxNG are more recent schemas and attempt to solve some of the issues surrounding DTDs.

PHP 5 uses the libxml2 library to provide its validation support. Therefore, it lets you validate files against all three types. It is most flexible when you're using XML Schema and RelaxNG, but its XML Schema support is incomplete. You shouldn't run into issues in most XML Schema documents; however, you may find that libxml2 cannot handle some complex schemas or schemas that use more esoteric features.

Within PHP, the DOM extension supports DTD, XML Schema, and RelaxNG validation, while SimpleXML provides only an XML Schema validator.

Validating any file using DOM is a similar process, regardless of the underlying schema format. To validate, call a validation method on a DOM object (see Example 12-21). It returns **true** if the file passes. If there's an error, it returns **false** and prints a message to the error log. There is no method for "capturing" the error message.

Example 12-21. Validating an XML document

```
$file = 'address-book.xml';
$schema = 'address-book.xsd';
$ab = new DOMDocument
$ab->load($file);

if ($ab->schemaValidate($schema)) {
    print "$file is valid.\n";
} else {
    print "$file is invalid.\n";
}
```

If the schema is stored in a string, use DOMDocument::schemaValidateSource( ) instead of schemaValidate( ).

Table 12-3 lists all the validation methods.

Table 12-3. DOM schema validation methods

Method name	Schema type	Data location
schemaValidate	XML Schema	File
schemaValidateSource	XML Schema	String
relaxNGValidate	RelaxNG	File
relaxNGValidateSource	RelaxNG	String
validate	DTD	N/A

All of the validation methods behave in a similar manner, so you only need to switch the method name in the previous example to switch to a different validation scheme.

Both XML Schema and RelaxNG support validation against files and strings. You can validate a DOM object only against the DTD defined at the top of the XML document.

See Also

The XML Schema specification at *http://www.w3.org/XML/Schema*; the Relax NG specification at *http://www.relaxng.org/*.

12.11 Handling Content Encoding

Problem

PHP XML extensions use UTF-8, but your data is in a different content encoding.

Solution

Use the `iconv` library to convert it before passing it into an XML extension:

```
$utf_8 = iconv('ISO-8859-1', 'UTF-8', $iso_8859_1);
```

Then convert it back when you are finished:

```
$iso_8859_1 = iconv('UTF-8', 'ISO-8859-1', $utf_8);
```

Discussion

Character encoding is a major PHP 5 weakness. Fortunately, Unicode support is the major driver behind PHP 6. Since PHP 6 is still under development, in the meantime, you can run into problems if you're trying to use XML extensions with arbitrary encoded data.

For simplicity, the XML extensions all exclusively use the UTF-8 character encoding. That means they all expect data in UTF-8 and output all data in UTF-8. If your data is ASCII, then you don't need to worry, UTF-8 is a superset of ASCII. However, if you're using other encodings, then you will run into trouble sooner or later.

To work around this issue, use the `iconv` extension to manually encode data back and forth between your character sets and UTF-8. For example, to convert from ISO-8859-1 to UTF-8:

```
$utf_8 = iconv('ISO-8859-1', 'UTF-8', $iso_8859_1);
```

The `iconv` function supports two special modifiers for the destination encoding: `//TRANSLIT` and `//IGNORE`. The first option tells `iconv` that whenever it cannot exactly duplicate a character in the destination encoding, it should try to approximate it using a series of other characters. The other option makes `iconv` silently ignore any unconvertible characters.

For example, the string `$geb` holds the text `Gödel, Escher, Bach`. A straight conversion to ASCII produces an error:

```
echo iconv('UTF-8', 'ASCII', $geb);
PHP Notice:  iconv(): Detected an illegal character in input string...
```

Enabling the `//IGNORE` feature allows the conversion to occur:

```
echo iconv('UTF-8', 'ASCII//IGNORE', $geb);
```

However, the output isn't nice, because the ö is missing:

```
Gdel, Escher, Bach
```

The best solution is to use `//TRANSLIT`:

```
echo iconv('UTF-8', 'ASCII//TRANSLIT', $geb);
```

This produces a better-looking string:

```
G"odel, Escher, Bach
```

However, be careful when you use `//TRANSLIT`, as it can increase the number of characters. For example, the single character ö becomes two characters: " and o.

See Also

More information about working with UTF-8 text is in Recipe 19.13; documentation on iconv at *http://www.php.net/iconv*; the GNU libiconv home page at *http://www.gnu.org/software/libiconv/*.

12.12 Reading RSS and Atom Feeds

Problem

You want to retrieve RSS and Atom feeds and look at the items. This allows you to incorporate newsfeeds from multiple web sites into your application.

Solution

Use the MagpieRSS parser. Here's an example that reads the RSS feed for the *php.announce* mailing list:

```php
<?php
require 'rss_fetch.inc';

$feed = 'http://news.php.net/group.php?group=php.announce&format=rss';

$rss = fetch_rss( $feed );

print "<ul>\n";
foreach ($rss->items as $item) {
    print '<li><a href="' . $item['link'] . '">' . $item['title'] . "</a></li>\n";
}
print "</ul>\n";
?>
```

Discussion

RSS (RDF Site Summary) is an easy-to-use headline or article syndication format written in XML.[†] Many news web sites, such as the New York Times and the Washington Post, provide RSS feeds that update whenever new stories are published. Weblogs have also embraced RSS and having an RSS feed for your blog is a standard feature. The PHP web site also publishes RSS feeds for most PHP mailing lists.

[†] RDF stands for Resource Definition Framework. RSS also stands for Rich Site Summary.

Atom is a similar XML syndication format. It extends many of the concepts in RSS, including a way to read and write Atom data. It also attempts to provide a more well-defined syntax for syndication than RSS, as the RSS specification doesn't always clearly enumerate exactly what is or isn't permissible in a feed.

Using MagpieRSS, retrieving and parsing RSS and Atom feeds are simple:

```php
<?php
$feed = 'http://news.php.net/group.php?group=php.announce&format=rss';

$rss = fetch_rss($feed);
?>
```

This example reads in the RSS feed for the *php.announce* mailing list. The feed is then parsed by fetch_rss( ) and stored internally within $rss.

While this feed is RSS 0.93, there's no need to specify this to MagpieRSS. Its fetch_rss( ) function detects the syndication format, including Atom, and formats the document accordingly.

Each RSS item is then retrieved as an associative array using the items property:

```php
<?php
print "<ul>\n";

foreach ($rss->items as $item) {
    print '<li><a href="' . $item['link'] . '">' . $item['title'] . "</a></li>\n";
}

print "</ul>\n";
?>
```

This foreach loop creates an unordered list of items with the item title linking back to the URL associated with the complete article, as shown in Figure 12-1. Besides the required title and link fields, an item can have an optional description field that contains a brief write-up about the item.

Each channel also has an entry with information about the feed, as shown in Figure 12-2. To retrieve that data, call access the channel attribute:

```php
<?php
$feed = 'http://news.php.net/group.php?group=php.announce&format=rss';
$rss = fetch_rss($feed);


print "<ul>\n";

foreach ($rss->channel as $key => $value) {
    print "<li>$key: $value</li>\n";
}

print "</ul>\n";
?>
```

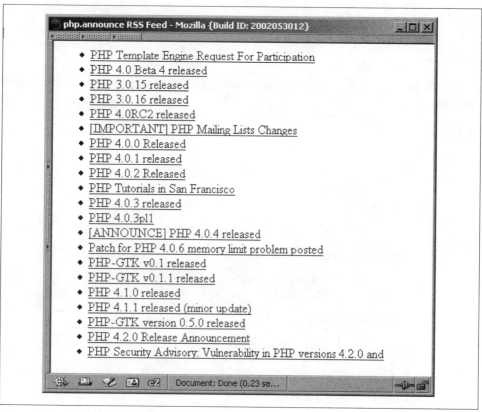

Figure 12-1. php.announce RSS feed

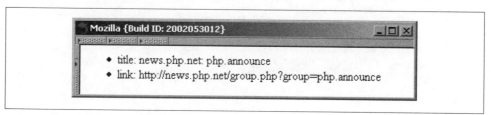

Figure 12-2. php.announce RSS channel information

See Also

The Magpie RSS home page at *http://magpierss.sourceforge.net/*; more information on RSS at *http://en.wikipedia.org/wiki/RSS_(protocol)*.

12.13 Writing RSS Feeds

Problem

You want to generate RSS feeds from your data. This will allow you to syndicate your content.

Solution

Use this class:

```php
<?php
class rss2 extends DOMDocument {
    private $channel;

    public function __construct($title, $link, $description) {
        parent::__construct();
        $this->formatOutput = true;

        $root = $this->appendChild($this->createElement('rss'));
        $root->setAttribute('version', '2.0');

        $channel= $root->appendChild($this->createElement('channel'));

        $channel->appendChild($this->createElement('title', $title));
        $channel->appendChild($this->createElement('link', $link));
        $channel->appendChild($this->createElement('description', $description));

        $this->channel = $channel;
    }

    public function addItem($title, $link, $description) {
        $item = $this->createElement('item');
        $item->appendChild($this->createElement('title', $title));
        $item->appendChild($this->createElement('link', $link));
        $item->appendChild($this->createElement('description', $description));

        $this->channel->appendChild($item);
    }
}

$rss = new rss2('Channel Title', 'http://www.example.org',
                'Channel Description');

$rss->addItem('Item 1', 'http://www.example.org/item1',
              'Item 1 Description');
$rss->addItem('Item 2', 'http://www.example.org/item2',
              'Item 2 Description');

print $rss->saveXML();
?>


<?xml version="1.0"?>
```

```
<rss version="2.0">
  <channel>
    <title>Channel Title</title>
    <link>http://www.example.org</link>
    <description>Channel Description</description>
    <item>
      <title>Item 1</title>
      <link>http://www.example.org/item1</link>
      <description>Item 1 Description</description>
    </item>
    <item>
      <title>Item 2</title>
      <link>http://www.example.org/item2</link>
      <description>Item 2 Description</description>
    </item>
  </channel>
</rss>
```

Discussion

RSS is XML, so you can leverage all the XML generation features of the DOM extension. The code in the Solution extends the DOMDocument class to build up a DOM tree by creating elements and appending them in the appropriate structure.

The class constructor sets up the <rss> and <channel> elements. It takes three arguments: the channel title, link, and description:

```
public function __construct($title, $link, $description) {
    parent::__construct();
    $this->formatOutput = true;

    $root = $this->appendChild($this->createElement('rss'));
    $root->setAttribute('version', '2.0');

    $channel= $root->appendChild($this->createElement('channel'));

    $channel->appendChild($this->createElement('title', $title));
    $channel->appendChild($this->createElement('link', $link));
    $channel->appendChild($this->createElement('description', $description));

    $this->channel = $channel;
}
```

Inside the method, you call parent::__construct( ) method to invoke the actual DOMDocument::__construct( ). Now you can begin building up the document.

First, set the formatOutput attribute to true. This adds indention and carriage returns to the output, so it's easy to read.

From there, create the document's root element, rss, and set its version attribute to 2.0, since this is an RSS 2.0 feed.

All the actual data lives inside a channel element underneath the rss node, so the next step is to make that element and also to set its title, link, and description child elements.

That data comes from the arguments passed to the constructor. It's set using a handy feature of the createElement( ) method, which lets you specify both an element's name and a text node with data in one call. This is a PHP 5 extension to the DOM specification.

Last, the channel element is saved for easy access later on.

With the main content defined, use the addItem( ) method to add item entries:

```php
public function addItem($title, $link, $description) {
    $item = $this->createElement('item');
    $item->appendChild($this->createElement('title', $title));
    $item->appendChild($this->createElement('link', $link));
    $item->appendChild($this->createElement('description', $description));

    $this->channel->appendChild($item);
}
```

Since item elements contain the same data as the channel, this code is almost identical to what appears in the constructor.

While a title, link, and description are required elements of the channel, they are actually optional in the item. The only requirement of an item is that it contains *either* a title or a description. That's it.

For simplicity, this code requires all three elements. Likewise, it doesn't provide a way to add in additional channel or item elements, such as the date the item was published or a GUID that uniquely identifies the item.

But 43 lines later, the basic RSS 2.0 class is finished. Use it like this:

```php
$rss = new rss2('Channel Title', 'http://www.example.org',
                'Channel Description');

$rss->addItem('Item 1', 'http://www.example.org/item1',
              'Item 1 Description');
$rss->addItem('Item 2', 'http://www.example.org/item2',
              'Item 2 Description');

print $rss->saveXML();

<?xml version="1.0"?>
<rss version="2.0">
  <channel>
    <title>Channel Title</title>
    <link>http://www.example.org</link>
    <description>Channel Description</description>
    <item>
      <title>Item 1</title>
      <link>http://www.example.org/item1</link>
      <description>Item 1 Description</description>
    </item>
    <item>
      <title>Item 2</title>
      <link>http://www.example.org/item2</link>
```

```
            <description>Item 2 Description</description>
        </item>
    </channel>
</rss>
```

Create a new instance of the rss2 class and pass along the channel data. Then call its addItem( ) method to add individual items to the channel. Once you're finished, you can convert the class to XML by using the parent DOMDocument::saveXML( ) method.

12.14 Writing Atom Feeds

Problem

You want to generate Atom feeds from your data. This will allow you to syndicate your content.

Solution

Use this class:

```
class atom1 extends DOMDocument {
    private $ns;

    public function __construct($title, $href, $name, $id) {
        parent::__construct();
        $this->formatOutput = true;

        $this->ns = 'http://www.w3.org/2005/Atom';

        $root = $this->appendChild($this->createElementNS($this->ns, 'feed'));

        $root->appendChild($this->createElementNS($this->ns, 'title', $title));
        $link = $root->appendChild($this->createElementNS($this->ns, 'link'));
        $link->setAttribute('href', $href);
        $root->appendChild($this->createElementNS($this->ns, 'updated',
            date('Y-m-d\\TH:i:sP')));
        $author = $root->appendChild($this->createElementNS($this->ns, 'author'));
        $author->appendChild($this->createElementNS($this->ns, 'name', $name));
        $root->appendChild($this->createElementNS($this->ns, 'id', $id));
    }

    public function addEntry($title, $link, $summary) {
        $entry = $this->createElementNS($this->ns, 'entry');
        $entry->appendChild($this->createElementNS($this->ns, 'title', $title));
        $entry->appendChild($this->createElementNS($this->ns, 'link', $link));

        $id = uniqid('http://example.org/atom/entry/ids/');
        $entry->appendChild($this->createElementNS($this->ns, 'id', $id));

        $entry->appendChild($this->createElementNS($this->ns, 'updated',
            date(DATE_ATOM)));
        $entry->appendChild($this->createElementNS($this->ns, 'summary',
$summary));
```

```
        $this->documentElement->appendChild($entry);
    }
}

$atom = new atom1('Channel Title', 'http://www.example.org',
                 'John Quincy Atom', 'http://example.org/atom/feed/ids/1');

$atom->addEntry('Item 1', 'http://www.example.org/item1',
               'Item 1 Description', 'http://example.org/atom/entry/ids/1');

$atom->addEntry('Item 2', 'http://www.example.org/item2',
               'Item 2 Description', 'http://example.org/atom/entry/ids/2');

print $atom->saveXML();

<?xml version="1.0"?>
<feed xmlns="http://www.w3.org/2005/Atom">
  <title>Channel Title</title>
  <link href="http://www.example.org"/>
  <updated>2006-10-23T22:33:59-07:00</updated>
  <author>
    <name>John Quincy Atom</name>
  </author>
  <id>http://example.org/atom/feed/ids/1</id>
  <entry>
    <title>Item 1</title>
    <link>http://www.example.org/item1</link>
    <id>http://example.org/atom/entry/ids/1</id>
    <updated>2006-10-23T20:23:32-07:00</updated>
    <summary>Item 1 Description</summary>
  </entry>
  <entry>
    <title>Item 2</title>
    <link>http://www.example.org/item2</link>
    <id>http://example.org/atom/entry/ids/2</id>
    <updated>2006-10-23T21:53:44-07:00</updated>
    <summary>Item 2 Description</summary>
  </entry>
</feed>
```

Discussion

The atom1 class is structured similar to the rss2 class from Recipe 12.13. Read its Discussion for a more detailed explanation of the overall code structure and DOM extension behavior. This recipe covers the differences between RSS and Atom and how the class is updated to handle them.

The Atom Specification is more complex than RSS. It requires you to place elements inside a namespace and also forces the generation of unique identifiers for a feed and individual items, along with the last updated times for those entries.

Also, while its general structure is similar to RSS, it uses different terminology. The root element is now a feed and an item is now an entry. You don't need a feed description, but you do need an author. And inside the entries, the description is a summary.

Last, there is no concept of a channel. Both feed data and entries are located directly under the document element.

Here's the updated constructor:

```php
public function __construct($title, $href, $name, $id) {
    parent::__construct();
    $this->formatOutput = true;

    $this->ns = 'http://www.w3.org/2005/Atom';

    $root = $this->appendChild($this->createElementNS($this->ns, 'feed'));

    $root->appendChild(
        $this->createElementNS($this->ns, 'title', $title));
    $link = $root->appendChild(
        $this->createElementNS($this->ns, 'link'));
    $link->setAttribute('href', $href);
    $root->appendChild($this->createElementNS(
        $this->ns, 'updated', date(DATE_ATOM)));
    $author = $root->appendChild(
        $this->createElementNS($this->ns, 'author'));
    $author->appendChild(
        $this->createElementNS($this->ns, 'name', $name));
    $root->appendChild(
        $this->createElementNS($this->ns, 'id', $id'));
}
```

All Atom elements live under the http://www.w3.org/2005/Atom XML namespace. Therefore, all atom1 methods use DOMDocument::createElementNS( ), which is the namespace version of DOMDocument::createElement( ). The Atom namespace is stored in atom1::ns, so it's easy to access.

The constructor now takes four arguments: title, link, author name, and feed ID. The title and id are defined similar to RSS channel elements. However, the link is actually set as the href attribute of the link element, and the name is a child of the author element.

Additionally, there is an updated element, which is set to the last update time. In this case, it's set to the current time and formatted using PHP's built-in DATE_ATOM constant formatting specification. This is only available as of PHP 5.1.1; if you're using an earlier version of PHP, substitute the string Y-m-d\\TH:i:sP.

The addItem( ) method is renamed to addEntry( ) to be consistent with the Atom specification:

```php
public function addEntry($title, $link, $summary, $id) {
    $entry = $this->createElementNS($this->ns, 'entry');
    $entry->appendChild(
        $this->createElementNS($this->ns, 'title', $title));
```

```
$entry->appendChild(
    $this->createElementNS($this->ns, 'link', $link));
$entry->appendChild(
    $this->createElementNS($this->ns, 'id', $id));
$entry->appendChild(
    $this->createElementNS($this->ns, 'updated', date(DATE_ATOM)));
$entry->appendChild(
    $this->createElementNS($this->ns, 'summary', $summary));

$this->documentElement->appendChild($entry);
}
```

It behaves very similar to its counterpart, with the few additions of new elements, such as id and updated.

Everything comes together like this:

```
$atom = new atom1('Channel Title', 'http://www.example.org',
                  'John Quincy Atom', 'http://example.org/atom/feed/ids/1');

$atom->addEntry('Item 1', 'http://www.example.org/item1',
                'Item 1 Description', 'http://example.org/atom/entry/ids/1');

$atom->addEntry('Item 2', 'http://www.example.org/item2',
                'Item 2 Description', 'http://example.org/atom/entry/ids/2');

print $atom->saveXML();

<?xml version="1.0"?>
<feed xmlns="http://www.w3.org/2005/Atom">
  <title>Channel Title</title>
  <link href="http://www.example.org"/>
  <updated>2006-10-23T22:33:59-07:00</updated>
  <author>
    <name>John Quincy Atom</name>
  </author>
  <id>http://example.org/atom/feed/ids/1</id>
  <entry>
    <title>Item 1</title>
    <link>http://www.example.org/item1</link>
    <id>http://example.org/atom/entry/ids/1</id>
    <updated>2006-10-23T20:23:32-07:00</updated>
    <summary>Item 1 Description</summary>
  </entry>
  <entry>
    <title>Item 2</title>
    <link>http://www.example.org/item2</link>
    <id>http://example.org/atom/entry/ids/2</id>
    <updated>2006-10-23T21:53:44-07:00</updated>
    <summary>Item 2 Description</summary>
  </entry>
</feed>
```

Like the rss2 class, atom1 implements only a small subset of the full specification. It's enough to generate a valid feed, but if you need to do more, then you will need to extend the class.

See Also

The Atom home page *http://www.atomenabled.org/*; the Atom Wiki at *http://www.intertwingly.net/wiki/pie/*; more information on Atom at *http://en.wikipedia.org/wiki/Atom_(standard)*.

CHAPTER 13

Web Automation

13.0 Introduction

Most of the time, PHP is part of a web server, sending content to browsers. Even when you run it from the command line, it usually performs a task and then prints some output. PHP can also be useful, however, playing the role of a web client, retrieving URLs and then operating on the content. Most recipes in this chapter cover retrieving URLs and processing the results, although there are a few other tasks in here as well, such as cleaning up URLs and some JavaScript-related operations.

There are many ways retrieve a remote URL in PHP. Choosing one method over another depends on your needs for simplicity, control, and portability. The three methods discussed in this chapter are standard file functions, the cURL extension, and the HTTP_Request class from PEAR. These three methods can generally do everything you need and at least one of them should be available to you whatever your server configuration or ability to install custom extensions. Other ways to retrieve remote URLs include the pecl_http extension (*http://pecl.php.net/package/pecl_http*), which, while still in development, offers some promising features, and using the fsockopen( ) function to open a socket over which you send an HTTP request that you construct piece by piece.

Using a standard file function such as file_get_contents( ) is simple and convenient. It automatically follows redirects, so if you use this function to retrieve the directory *http://www.example.com/people* and the server redirects you to *http://www.example.com/people/*, you'll get the contents of the directory index page, not a message telling you that the URL has moved. Standard file functions also work with both HTTP and FTP. The downside to this method is that it requires the allow_url_fopen configuration directive to be turned on.

The cURL extension is a powerful jack-of-all-request-trades. It relies on the popular libcurl (*http://curl.haxx.se/*) to provide a fast, configurable mechanism for handling a wide variety of network requests. If this extension is available on your server, we recommend you use it.

If `allow_url_fopen` is turned off and cURL is not available, the PEAR HTTP_Request module saves the day. Like all PEAR modules, it's plain PHP, so if you can save a PHP file on your server, you can use it. HTTP_Request supports just about anything you'd like to do when requesting a remote URL, including modifying request headers and body, using an arbitrary method, and retrieving response headers.

Recipes 13.1 through 13.7 explain how to make various kinds of HTTP requests, tweaking headers, method, body, and timing. Recipe 13.8 helps you go behind the scenes of an HTTP request to examine the headers in a request and response. If a request you're making from a program isn't giving you the results you're looking for, examining the headers often provides clues as to what's wrong.

Once you've retrieved the contents of a web page into a program, use Recipes 13.9 through 13.14 to help you manipulate those page contents. Recipe 13.9 demonstrates how to mark up certain words in a page with blocks of color. This technique is useful for highlighting search terms, for example. Recipe 13.11 provides a function to find all the links in a page. This is an essential building block for a web spider or a link checker. Converting between plain text and HTML is covered in Recipes 13.12 and 13.13. Recipe 13.14 shows how to remove all HTML and PHP tags from a web page.

Recipes 13.15 and 13.16 discuss how PHP and JavaScript can work together. Recipe 13.15 explores using PHP to respond to requests made by JavaScript, in which you have to be concerned about caching and using alternate content types. Recipe 13.16 provides a full-fledged example of PHP–JavaScript integration using the popular and powerful Dojo toolkit.

Two sample programs use the link extractor from Recipe 13.11. The program in Recipe 13.17 scans the links in a page and reports which are still valid, which have been moved, and which no longer work. The program in Recipe 13.18 reports on the freshness of links. It tells you when a linked-to page was last modified and if it's been moved.

13.1 Fetching a URL with the Get Method

Problem

You want to retrieve the contents of a URL. For example, you want to include part of one web page in another page's content.

Solution

Provide the URL to `file_get_contents( )`, as shown in Example 13-1.

Example 13-1. Fetching a URL with file_get_contents( )

```
<?php
$page = file_get_contents('http://www.example.com/robots.txt');
?>
```

Or you can use the cURL extension, as shown in Example 13-2.

Example 13-2. Fetching a URL with cURL

```php
<?php
$c = curl_init('http://www.example.com/robots.txt');
curl_setopt($c, CURLOPT_RETURNTRANSFER, true);
$page = curl_exec($c);
curl_close($c);
?>
```

You can also use the `HTTP_Request` class from PEAR, as shown in Example 13-3.

Example 13-3. Fetching a URL with HTTP_Request

```php
<?php
require_once 'HTTP/Request.php';
$r = new HTTP_Request('http://www.example.com/robots.txt');
$r->sendRequest();
$page = $r->getResponseBody();
?>
```

Discussion

`file_get_contents( )`, like all PHP file-handling functions, uses PHP's *streams* feature. This means that it can handle local files as well as a variety of network resources, including HTTP URLs. There's a catch, though—the `allow_url_fopen` configuration setting must be turned on (which it usually is).

This makes for extremely easy retrieval of remote documents. As Example 13-4 shows, you can use the same technique to grab a remote XML document.

Example 13-4. Fetching a remote XML document

```php
<?php
$url = 'http://rss.news.yahoo.com/rss/oddlyenough';
$rss = simplexml_load_file($url);
print '<ul>';
foreach ($rss->channel->item as $item) {
    print '<li><a href="' .
          htmlentities($item->link) .
          '">' .
          htmlentities($item->title) .
          '</a></li>';
}
print '</ul>';
?>
```

To retrieve a page that includes query string variables, use `http_build_query( )` to create the query string. It accepts an array of key/value pairs and returns a single string with everything properly escaped. You're still responsible for the ? in the URL that sets off the query string. Example 13-5 demonstrates `http_build_query( )`.

Example 13-5. Building a query string with http_build_query()

```php
<?php
$vars = array('page' => 4, 'search' => 'this & that');
```

```php
$qs = http_build_query($vars);
$url = 'http://www.example.com/search.php?' . $qs;
$page = file_get_contents($url);
?>
```

To retrieve a protected page, put the username and password in the URL. In Example 13-6, the username is david, and the password is hax0r.

Example 13-6. Retrieving a protected page

```php
<?php
$url = 'http://david:hax0r@www.example.com/secrets.php';
$page = file_get_contents($url);
?>
```

Example 13-7 shows how to retrieve a protected page with cURL.

Example 13-7. Retrieving a protected page with cURL

```php
<?php
$c = curl_init('http://www.example.com/secrets.php');
curl_setopt($c, CURLOPT_RETURNTRANSFER, true);
curl_setopt($c, CURLOPT_USERPWD, 'david:hax0r');
$page = curl_exec($c);
curl_close($c);
?>
```

Example 13-8 shows how to retrieve a protected page with HTTP_Request.

Example 13-8. Retrieving a protected page with HTTP_Request

```php
<?php
$r = new HTTP_Request('http://www.example.com/secrets.php');
$r->setBasicAuth('david','hax0r');
$r->sendRequest();
$page = $r->getResponseBody();
```

PHP's http stream wrapper automatically follows redirects. Since PHP 5.0.0, file_get_contents( ) and fopen( ) support a *stream context* argument that allows for specifying options about how the stream is retrieved. In PHP 5.1.0 and later, one of those options is max_redirects—the maximum number of redirects to follow. Example 13-9 sets max_redirects to 1, which turns off redirect following.

Example 13-9. Not following redirects

```php
<?php
$url = 'http://www.example.com/redirector.php';
// Define the options
$options = array('max_redirects' => 1 );
// Create a context with options for the http stream
$context = stream_context_create(array('http' => $options));
// Pass the options to file_get_contents. The second
// argument is whether to use the include path, which
// we don't want here.
print file_get_contents($url, false, $context);
```

The `max_redirects` stream wrapper option really indicates not how many redirects should be followed, but the maximum number of requests that should be made when following the redirect chain. That is, a value of 1 tells PHP to make at most 1 request —follow no redirects. A value of 2 tells PHP to make at most 2 requests—follow no more than 1 redirect. (A value of 0, however, behaves like a value of 1—PHP makes just 1 request.)

If the redirect chain would have PHP make more requests than are allowed by `max_redi rects`, PHP issues a warning.

cURL only follows redirects when the `CURLOPT_FOLLOWLOCATION` option is set, as shown in Example 13-10.

Example 13-10. Following redirects with cURL

```php
<?php
$c = curl_init('http://www.example.com/redirector.php');
curl_setopt($c, CURLOPT_RETURNTRANSFER, true);
curl_setopt($c, CURLOPT_FOLLOWLOCATION, true);
$page = curl_exec($c);
curl_close($c);
?>
```

To set a maximum number of redirects that cURL should follow, set `CURLOPT_FOLLOWLOCATION` to `true` and then set the `CURLOPT_MAXREDIRS` option to that maximum number.

`HTTP_Request` does not follow redirects, but another PEAR module, `HTTP_Client`, can. `HTTP_Client` wraps around `HTTP_Request` and provides additional capabilities. Example 13-11 shows how to use `HTTP_Client` to follow redirects.

Example 13-11. Following redirects with HTTP_Client

```php
<?php
require_once 'HTTP/Client.php';

// Create a client
$client = new HTTP_Client();
// Issue a GET request
$client->get($url);
// Get the response
$response = $client->currentResponse();
// $response is an array with three elements:
// code, headers, and body
print $response['body'];
?>
```

cURL can do a few different things with the page it retrieves. As you've seen in previous examples, if `CURLOPT_RETURNTRANSFER` is set, `curl_exec( )` returns the body of the page requested. If `CURLOPT_RETURNTRANSFER` is not set, `curl_exec( )` prints the response body.

To write the retrieved page to a file, open a file handle for writing with fopen( ) and set the CURLOPT_FILE option to that file handle. Example 13-12 uses cURL to copy a remote web page to a local file.

Example 13-12. Writing a response body to a file with cURL

```php
<?php
$fh = fopen('local-copy-of-files.html','w') or die($php_errormsg);
$c = curl_init('http://www.example.com/files.html');
curl_setopt($c, CURLOPT_FILE, $fh);
curl_exec($c);
curl_close($c);
?>
```

To pass the cURL resource and the contents of the retrieved page to a function, set the CURLOPT_WRITEFUNCTION option to a callback for that function (either a string function name or an array of object name or instance and method name). The "write function" must return the number of bytes it was passed. Note that with large responses, the write function might get called more than once as cURL processes the response in chunks. Example 13-13 uses a cURL write function to save page contents in a database.

Example 13-13. Saving a page to a database table with cURL

```php
<?php
class PageSaver {
    protected $db;
    protected $page ='';

    public function __construct() {
        $this->db = new PDO('sqlite:./pages.db');
    }

    public function write($curl, $data) {
        $this->page .= $data;
        return strlen($data);
    }

    public function save($curl) {
        $info = curl_getinfo($curl);
        $st = $this->db->prepare('INSERT INTO pages '.
                        '(url,page) VALUES (?,?)');
        $st->execute(array($info['url'], $this->page));
    }
}

// Create the saver instance
$pageSaver = new PageSaver();
// Create the cURL resources
$c = curl_init('http://www.sklar.com/');
// Set the write function
curl_setopt($c, CURLOPT_WRITEFUNCTION, array($pageSaver,'write'));
// Execute the request
curl_exec($c);
```

```
// Save the accumulate data
$pageSaver->save($c);
```

See Also

Recipe 13.2 for fetching a URL with the POST method; documentation on `file_get_contents()` at *http://www.php.net/file_get_contents*, `simplexml_load_file()` at *http://www.php.net/simplexml_load_file*, `stream_context_create()` at *http://www.php.net/stream_context_create*, `curl_init()` at *http://www.php.net/curl-init*, `curl_setopt()` at *http://www.php.net/curl-setopt*, `curl_exec()` at *http://www.php.net/curl-exec*, `curl_getinfo()` at *http://www.php.net/curl_getinfo*, and `curl_close()` at *http://www.php.net/curl-close*; the PEAR `HTTP_Request` class at *http://pear.php.net/package/HTTP_Request*; and the PEAR `HTTP_Client` class at *http://pear.php.net/package/HTTP_Client*.

13.2 Fetching a URL with the Post Method

Problem

You want to retrieve a URL with the post method, not the default get method. For example, you want to submit a form.

Solution

Set the `method` and `content` stream context options when using the `http` stream, as in Example 13-14.

Example 13-14. Using POST with the http stream

```php
<?php
$url = 'http://www.example.com/submit.php';
// The submitted form data, encoded as query-string-style
// name-value pairs
$body = 'monkey=uncle&rhino=aunt';
$options = array('method' => 'POST', 'content' => $body);
// Create the stream context
$context = stream_context_create(array('http' => $options));
// Pass the context to file_get_contents()
print file_get_contents($url, false, $context);
?>
```

With cURL, set the `CURLOPT_POST` and `CURLOPT_POSTFIELDS` options, as in Example 13-15.

Example 13-15. Using POST with cURL

```php
<?php
$url = 'http://www.example.com/submit.php';
// The submitted form data, encoded as query-string-style
// name-value pairs
```

```
$body = 'monkey=uncle&rhino=aunt';
$c = curl_init($url);
curl_setopt($c, CURLOPT_POST, true);
curl_setopt($c, CURLOPT_POSTFIELDS, $body);
curl_setopt($c, CURLOPT_RETURNTRANSFER, true);
$page = curl_exec($c);
curl_close($c);
?>
```

Example 13-16 shows how to post with HTTP_Request: pass HTTP_REQUEST_METHOD_POST to the constructor and call addPostData( ) once for each name/value pair in the data to submit.

Example 13-16. Using POST with HTTP_Request

```
<?php
require 'HTTP/Request.php';
$url = 'http://www.example.com/submit.php';
$r = new HTTP_Request($url);
$r->setMethod(HTTP_REQUEST_METHOD_POST);
$r->addPostData('monkey','uncle');
$r->addPostData('rhino','aunt');
$r->sendRequest();
$page = $r->getResponseBody();
?>
```

Discussion

Sending a post method request requires special handling of any arguments. In a get request, these arguments are in the query string, but in a post request, they go in the request body. Additionally, the request needs a Content-Length header that tells the server the size of the content to expect in the request body.

Although they each have different mechanisms by which you specify the request method and the body content, each of the examples in the Solution automatically add the proper Content-Length header for you.

If you use a stream context to send a post request, make sure to set the method option to post—case matters.

Retrieving a URL with post instead of get is especially useful if the get query string is very long, more than 200 characters or so. The HTTP 1.1 specification in RFC 2616 doesn't place a maximum length on URLs, so behavior varies among different web and proxy servers. If you retrieve URLs with get and receive unexpected results or results with status code 414 ("Request-URI Too Long"), convert the request to a post request.

See Also

Recipe 13.1 for fetching a URL with the get method; documentation on curl_setopt( ) at *http://www.php.net/curl-setopt* and on stream options at *http://www.php.net/wrappers.http*; the PEAR HTTP_Request class at *http://pear.php.net/pack*

age/HTTP_Request; RFC 2616 is available at *http://www.w3.org/Protocols/rfc2616/ rfc2616.html*.

13.3 Fetching a URL with Cookies

Problem

You want to retrieve a page that requires a cookie to be sent with the request for the page.

Solution

Use the `CURLOPT_COOKIE` option with cURL, as shown in Example 13-17.

Example 13-17. Sending cookies with cURL

```
<?php
$c = curl_init('http://www.example.com/needs-cookies.php');
curl_setopt($c, CURLOPT_COOKIE, 'user=ellen; activity=swimming');
curl_setopt($c, CURLOPT_RETURNTRANSFER, true);
$page = curl_exec($c);
curl_close($c);
?>
```

With HTTP_Request, use the `addHeader()` method to add a `Cookie` header, as shown in Example 13-18.

Example 13-18. Sending cookies with HTTP_Request

```
<?php
require 'HTTP/Request.php';
$r = new HTTP_Request('http://www.example.com/needs-cookies.php');
$r->addHeader('Cookie','user=ellen; activity=swimming');
$r->sendRequest();
$page = $r->getResponseBody();
?>
```

Discussion

Cookies are sent to the server in the `Cookie` request header. The cURL extension has a cookie-specific option, but with HTTP_Request, you have to add the `Cookie` header just as with other request headers. Multiple cookie values are sent in a semicolon-delimited list. The examples in the Solution send two cookies: one named `user` with value `ellen` and one named `activity` with value `swimming`.

To request a page that sets cookies and then make subsequent requests that include those newly set cookies, use cURL's "cookie jar" feature. On the first request, set `CURLOPT_COOKIEJAR` to the name of a file to store the cookies in. On subsequent requests, set `CURLOPT_COOKIEFILE` to the same filename, and cURL reads the cookies from the file and sends them along with the request. This is especially useful for a sequence of requests in which the first request logs into a site that sets session or authentication cookies, and then the rest of the requests need to include those cookies to be valid. Example 13-19 shows such a sequence of requests.

Example 13-19. Tracking cookies with cURL's cookie jar

```php
<?php
// A temporary file to hold the cookies
$cookie_jar = tempnam('/tmp','cookie');

// log in
$c = curl_init('https://bank.example.com/login.php?user=donald&password=b1gmoney$');
curl_setopt($c, CURLOPT_RETURNTRANSFER, true);
curl_setopt($c, CURLOPT_COOKIEJAR, $cookie_jar);
$page = curl_exec($c);
curl_close($c);

// retrieve account balance
$c = curl_init('http://bank.example.com/balance.php?account=checking');
curl_setopt($c, CURLOPT_RETURNTRANSFER, true);
curl_setopt($c, CURLOPT_COOKIEFILE, $cookie_jar);
$page = curl_exec($c);
curl_close($c);

// make a deposit
$c = curl_init('http://bank.example.com/deposit.php');
curl_setopt($c, CURLOPT_POST, true);
curl_setopt($c, CURLOPT_POSTFIELDS, 'account=checking&amount=122.44');
curl_setopt($c, CURLOPT_RETURNTRANSFER, true);
curl_setopt($c, CURLOPT_COOKIEFILE, $cookie_jar);
$page = curl_exec($c);
curl_close($c);

// remove the cookie jar
unlink($cookie_jar) or die("Can't unlink $cookie_jar");
?>
```

Be careful where you store the cookie jar. It needs to be in a place your web server has write access to, but if other users can read the file, they may be able to poach the authentication credentials stored in the cookies.

`HTTP_Client` offers a similar cookie-tracking feature. You don't have to do anything special to enable it. If you make multiple requests with the same `HTTP_Client` object, cookies are automatically preserved from one request to the next.

See Also

Documentation on `curl_setopt()` at *http://www.php.net/curl-setopt*; the PEAR `HTTP_Request` class at *http://pear.php.net/package/HTTP_Request*, the PEAR `HTTP_Cli ent` class at *http://pear.php.net/package/HTTP_Client*; "Persistent Client State - HTTP Cookies" at *http://wp.netscape.com/newsref/std/cookie_spec.html* and "HTTP Cookies:

Standards, Privacy, and Politics" by David M. Kristol at *http://arxiv.org/abs/cs.SE/0105018*.

13.4 Fetching a URL with Arbitrary Headers

Problem

You want to retrieve a URL that requires specific headers to be sent with the request for the page.

Solution

Set the `header` stream context option when using the `http` stream as in Example 13-20. The header value must be a single string. Separate multiple headers with a carriage return and newline (\r\n inside a double-quoted string).

Example 13-20. Sending a header with the http stream

```
<?php
$url = 'http://www.example.com/special-header.php';
$header = "X-Factor: 12\r\nMy-Header: Bob";
$options = array('header' => $header);
// Create the stream context
$context = stream_context_create(array('http' => $options));
// Pass the context to file_get_contents()
print file_get_contents($url, false, $context);
?>
```

With cURL, set the `CURLOPT_HTTPHEADER` option to an array of headers to send, as shown in Example 13-21.

Example 13-21. Sending a header with cURL

```
<?php
$c = curl_init('http://www.example.com/special-header.php');
curl_setopt($c, CURLOPT_RETURNTRANSFER, true);
curl_setopt($c, CURLOPT_HTTPHEADER, array('X-Factor: 12', 'My-Header: Bob'));
$page = curl_exec($c);
curl_close($c);
?>
```

With `HTTP_Request`, use the `addHeader( )` method, as shown in Example 13-22.

Example 13-22. Sending a header with HTTP_Request

```
<?php
require 'HTTP/Request.php';

$r = new HTTP_Request('http://www.example.com/special-header.php');
$r->addHeader('X-Factor',12);
$r->addHeader('My-Header','Bob');
$r->sendRequest();
```

```
$page = $r->getResponseBody();
?>
```

Discussion

cURL has special options for setting the `Referer` and `User-Agent` request headers—
`CURLOPT_REFERER` and `CURLOPT_USERAGENT`. Example 13-23 uses each of these options.

Example 13-23. Setting Referer and User-Agent with cURL

```
<?php
$c = curl_init('http://www.example.com/submit.php');
curl_setopt($c, CURLOPT_RETURNTRANSFER, true);
curl_setopt($c, CURLOPT_REFERER, 'http://www.example.com/form.php');
curl_setopt($c, CURLOPT_USERAGENT, 'cURL via PHP');
$page = curl_exec($c);
curl_close($c);
?>
```

See Also

Documentation on on the `http` stream wrapper at *http://www.php.net/wrappers.http*,
on `curl_setopt( )` at *http://www.php.net/curl-setopt*, and on the PEAR `HTTP_Request`
class at *http://pear.php.net/package/HTTP_Request*. The mailing-list message at *http://
lists.w3.org/Archives/Public/ietf-http-wg-old/1996MayAug/0734.html* explains the am-
bitious and revolutionary goals behind spelling "Referer" with one "r."

13.5 Fetching a URL with an Arbitrary Method

Problem

You want to retrieve a URL using a method more exotic than `get` or `post`, such as `put`
or `delete`.

Solution

Just as when using `post`, set the `method` and `content` stream context options when using
the `http` stream, as in Example 13-24.

Example 13-24. Using put with the http stream

```
<?php
$url = 'http://www.example.com/put.php';
// The request body, in arbitrary format
$body = '<menu>
 <dish type="appetizer">Chicken Soup</dish>
 <dish type="main course">Fried Monkey Brains</dish>
</menu>';
$options = array('method' => 'PUT', 'content' => $body);
// Create the stream context
$context = stream_context_create(array('http' => $options));
```

```
// Pass the context to file_get_contents()
print file_get_contents($url, false, $context);
?>
```

With cURL, set the `CURLOPT_CUSTOMREQUEST` option to the method name. To include a request body, set `CURLOPT_POSTFIELDS` to the the body, as in Example 13-25.

Example 13-25. Using put with cURL

```
<?php
// The request body, in arbitrary format
$body = '<menu>
 <dish type="appetizer">Chicken Soup</dish>
 <dish type="main course">Fried Monkey Brains</dish>
</menu>';
$c = curl_init($url);
curl_setopt($c, CURLOPT_CUSTOMREQUEST, 'PUT');
curl_setopt($c, CURLOPT_POSTFIELDS, $body);
curl_setopt($c, CURLOPT_RETURNTRANSFER, true);
$page = curl_exec($c);
curl_close($c);
?>
```

Example 13-26 shows how to put with `HTTP_Request`: pass `HTTP_REQUEST_METHOD_PUT` to the constructor and call `setBody( )` with the contents of the request body.

Example 13-26. Using put with HTTP_Request

```
<?php
require 'HTTP/Request.php';
$url = 'http://www.example.com/put.php';
$body = '<menu>
 <dish type="appetizer">Chicken Soup</dish>
 <dish type="main course">Fried Monkey Brains</dish>
</menu>';
$r = new HTTP_Request($url);
$r->setMethod(HTTP_REQUEST_METHOD_PUT);
$r->setBody($body);
$page = $r->getResponseBody();
?>
```

Discussion

As REST-style web services APIs grow more common, so do HTTP requests using lesser lights of the request-method pantheon, such as put and delete.

The put method is often used for uploading the contents of a particular file. cURL has three special options to help with this: `CURLOPT_PUT`, `CURLOPT_INFILE`, and `CURLOPT_INFI LESIZE`. To upload a file with put and cURL, set `CURLOPT_PUT` to true, `CURLOPT_INFILE` a filehandle opened to the file that should be uploaded, and `CURLOPT_INFILESIZE` to the size of that file. Example 13-27 uploads a file with put.

Example 13-27. Uploading a file with cURL and put

```
<?php
$url = 'http://www.example.com/upload.php';
```

```php
$filename = '/usr/local/data/pictures/piggy.jpg';
$fp = fopen($filename,'r');
$c = curl_init($url);
curl_setopt($c, CURLOPT_PUT, true);
curl_setopt($c, CURLOPT_INFILE, $fp);
curl_setopt($c, CURLOPT_INFILESIZE, filesize($filename));
curl_setopt($c, CURLOPT_RETURNTRANSFER, true);
$page = curl_exec($c);
print $page;
curl_close($c);
?>
```

See Also

Documentation on `curl_setopt( )` at *http://www.php.net/curl-setopt* and on stream options at *http://www.php.net/wrappers.http*; the PEAR `HTTP_Request` class at *http://pear.php.net/package/HTTP_Request*; Section 5.1.1 of RFC 2616, which discusses request methods, is available at *http://www.w3.org/Protocols/rfc2616/rfc2616-sec5.html#sec5.1.1*.

13.6 Fetching a URL with a Timeout

Problem

You want to fetch a remote URL, but don't want to wait around too long if the remote server is busy or slow.

Solution

With the `http` stream, set the `default_socket_timeout` configuration option. Example 13-28 waits no more than 15 seconds to establish the connection with the remote server.

Example 13-28. Setting a timeout with the http stream

```php
<?php
// 15 second timeout
ini_set('default_socket_timeout', 15);
$page = file_get_contents('http://slow.example.com/');
```

Note that changing `default_socket_timeout` affects all new sockets or remote connections created in a particular script execution.

With cURL, set the `CURLOPT_CONNECTTIMEOUT` option, as shown in Example 13-29.

Example 13-29. Setting a timeout with cURL

```php
<?php
$c = curl_init('http://slow.example.com/');
curl_setopt($c, CURLOPT_RETURNTRANSFER, true);
```

```
curl_setopt($c, CURLOPT_CONNECTTIMEOUT, 15);
$page = curl_exec($c);
curl_close($c);
?>
```

With `HTTP_Request`, set the `timeout` element in a parameter array passed to the `HTTP_Request` constructor, as shown in Example 13-30.

Example 13-30. Setting a timeout with HTTP_Request

```
<?php
require_once 'HTTP/Request.php';
$opts = array('timeout' => 15);
$req = new HTTP_Request('http://slow.example.com/', $opts);
$req->sendRequest();
?>
```

Discussion

Remote servers are fickle beasts. Even the most most robust, enterprise-class, mission-critical service can experience an outage. Alternatively, a remote service you depend on can be up and running, but be unable to handle your requests because of network problems between your server and the remote server. Limiting the amount of time that PHP waits to connect to a remote server is a good idea if using data from remote sources is part of your page construction process.

All of the techniques outlined in the Solution limit the amount of time PHP waits to connect to a remote server. Once the connection is made, though, all bets are off in terms of response time. If you're truly concerned about speedy responses, additionally set a limit on how long PHP waits to receive data from the already connected socket. For a stream connection, use the `stream_set_timeout( )` function. This function needs to be passed a stream resource, so you have to open a stream with `fopen( )`—no `file_get_contents( )` here. Example 13-31 limits the read timeout to 20 seconds.

Example 13-31. Setting the read timeout with the http stream

```
<?php
$url = 'http://slow.example.com';
$stream = fopen($url, 'r');
stream_set_timeout($stream, 20);
$response_body = stream_get_contents($stream);
?>
```

With cURL, set the `CURLOPT_TIMEOUT` to the maximum amount of time `curl_exec( )` should operate. This includes both the connection timeout and the time to read the entire response body.

With HTTP_Request, add a `readTimeout` value to the parameter array you pass to the constructor. This value must be a two-element array of seconds and microseconds. Example 13-32 sets the read timeout to 20 seconds.

Example 13-32. Setting a read timeout with HTTP_Request

```php
<?php
require_once 'HTTP/Request.php';
$opts = array('readTimeout' => array(20,0));
$req = new HTTP_Request('http://slow.example.com/', $opts);
$req->sendRequest();
?>
```

Although setting connection and read timeouts can improve performance, it can also lead to garbled responses. Your script could read just a partial response before a timeout expires. If you've set timeouts, be sure to validate the entire response that you've received. Alternatively, in situations where fast page generation is crucial, retrieve external data in a separate process and write it to a local cache. This way, your pages can use the cache without fear of timeouts or partial responses.

See Also

Documentation on `curl_setopt( )` at *http://www.php.net/curl-setopt*, on `stream_set_timeout( )` at *http://www.php.net/stream_set_timeout*, on `default_socket_timeout` at *http://www.php.net/filesystem*, and on the PEAR `HTTP_Request` class at *http://pear.php.net/package/HTTP_Request*.

13.7 Fetching an HTTPS URL

Problem

You want to retrieve a secure URL.

Solution

Use any of the techniques described in Recipes 13.1 or 13.2, providing a URL that begins with `https`.

Discussion

As long as PHP has been built with an SSL library such as OpenSSL, all of the functions that can retrieve regular URLs can retrieve secure URLs. Look for the "openssl" section in the output of `phpinfo( )` to see if your PHP setup has SSL support.

See Also

Recipes 13.1 and 13.2 for retrieving URLs, the OpenSSL Project at *http://www.openssl.org/*.

13.8 Debugging the Raw HTTP Exchange

Problem

You want to analyze the HTTP request a browser makes to your server and the corresponding HTTP response. For example, your server doesn't supply the expected response to a particular request so you want to see exactly what the components of the request are.

Solution

For simple requests, connect to the web server with Telnet and type in the request headers. A sample exchange is shown in Example 13-33.

Example 13-33. Sending a request with Telnet

```
% telnet www.example.com 80
Trying 10.3.75.31...
Connected to www.example.com (10.3.75.31).
Escape character is '^]'.
GET / HTTP/1.0
Host: www.example.com

HTTP/1.1 200 OK
Date: Sun, 03 Dec 2006 02:54:01 GMT
Server: Apache/2.2.2 (Unix)
Last-Modified: Fri, 20 Oct 2006 20:16:24 GMT
ETag: "1348010-2c-4c23b600"
Accept-Ranges: bytes
Content-Length: 44
Connection: close
Content-Type: text/html

[ the body of the response ]
```

Discussion

When you type in request headers, the web server doesn't know that it's just you typing and not a web browser submitting a request. However, some web servers have timeouts on how long they'll wait for a request, so it can be useful to pretype the request and then just paste it into Telnet. The first line of the request contains the request method (get), a space and the path of the file you want (/), and then a space and the protocol you're using (HTTP/1.0). The next line, the Host header, tells the server which virtual host to use if many are sharing the same IP address. A blank line tells the server that the request is over; it then spits back its response: first headers, then a blank line, and then the body of the response. The Netcat program (*http://netcat.sourceforge.net/*) is also useful for this sort of task.

Pasting text into Telnet can get tedious, and it's even harder to make requests with the post method that way. If you make a request with HTTP_Request, you can retrieve the response headers and the response body with the getResponseHeader( ) and getResponseBody( ) methods, as shown in Example 13-34.

Example 13-34. Getting response headers with HTTP_Request

```php
<?php
require 'HTTP/Request.php';
$r = new HTTP_Request('http://www.example.com/submit.php');
$r->setMethod(HTTP_REQUEST_METHOD_POST);
$r->addPostData('monkey','uncle');
$r->sendRequest();

$response_headers = $r->getResponseHeader();
$response_body    = $r->getResponseBody();
?>
```

To retrieve a specific response header, pass the header name to getResponseHeader( ). The header name must be all lowercase. Without an argument, getResponseHeader( ) returns an array containing all the response headers. HTTP_Request doesn't save the outgoing request in a variable, but you can reconstruct it by calling the _buildRequest( ) method, as shown in Example 13-35.

Example 13-35. Getting request headers with HTTP_Request

```php
<?php
require 'HTTP/Request.php';

$r = new HTTP_Request('http://www.example.com/submit.php');
$r->setMethod(HTTP_REQUEST_METHOD_POST);
$r->addPostData('monkey','uncle');

print $r->_buildRequest();
?>
```

The request that Example 13-35 is something like:

```
POST /submit.php HTTP/1.1
User-Agent: PEAR HTTP_Request class ( http://pear.php.net/ )
Content-Type: application/x-www-form-urlencoded
Connection: close
Host: www.example.com
Content-Length: 12

monkey=uncle
```

Accessing response headers with the http stream is possible, but you have to use a function such as fopen( ) that gives you a stream resource. One piece of the metadata you get when passing that stream resource to stream_get_meta_data( ) after the request has been made is the set of response headers. Example 13-36 demonstrates how to access response headers with a stream resource.

Example 13-36. Getting response headers with the http stream

```php
<?php
$url = 'http://www.example.com/submit.php';
```

```php
$stream = fopen($url, 'r');
$metadata = stream_get_meta_data($stream);
// The headers are stored in the 'wrapper_data'
foreach ($metadata['wrapper_data'] as $header) {
    print $header . "\n";
}
// The body can be retrieved with
// stream_get_contents()
$response_body = stream_get_contents($stream);
?>
```

stream_get_meta_data( ) returns an array of information about the stream. The wrapper_data element of that array contains wrapper-specific data. For the http wrapper, that means the response headers, one per subarray element. Example 13-36 prints something like:

```
HTTP/1.1 200 OK
Date: Sun, 07 May 2006 18:24:37 GMT
Server: Apache/2.2.2 (Unix)
Last-Modified: Sun, 07 May 2006 01:58:12 GMT
ETag: "1348011-7-16167500"
Accept-Ranges: bytes
Content-Length: 7
Connection: close
Content-Type: text/plain
```

The fopen( ) function accepts an optional stream context. Pass it as the fourth argument to fopen( ) if you want to use one. (The second argument is the mode and the third argument is the optional flag indicating whether to use include_path in looking for a file.)

With cURL, include response headers in the output from curl_exec( ) by setting the CURLOPT_HEADER option, as shown in Example 13-37.

Example 13-37. Getting response headers with cURL

```php
<?php
$c = curl_init('http://www.example.com/submit.php');
curl_setopt($c, CURLOPT_HEADER, true);
curl_setopt($c, CURLOPT_POST, true);
curl_setopt($c, CURLOPT_POSTFIELDS, 'monkey=uncle&rhino=aunt');
curl_setopt($c, CURLOPT_RETURNTRANSFER, true);
$response_headers_and_page = curl_exec($c);
curl_close($c);
?>
```

To write the response headers directly to a file, open a filehandle with fopen( ) and set CURLOPT_WRITEHEADER to that filehandle, as shown in Example 13-38.

Example 13-38. Writing response headers to a file with cURL

```php
<?php
$fh = fopen('/tmp/curl-response-headers.txt','w') or die($php_errormsg);
$c = curl_init('http://www.example.com/submit.php');
curl_setopt($c, CURLOPT_POST, true);
```

```
curl_setopt($c, CURLOPT_POSTFIELDS, 'monkey=uncle&rhino=aunt');
curl_setopt($c, CURLOPT_RETURNTRANSFER, true);
curl_setopt($c, CURLOPT_WRITEHEADER, $fh);
$page = curl_exec($c);
curl_close($c);
fclose($fh) or die($php_errormsg);
?>
```

cURL's `CURLOPT_VERBOSE` option causes `curl_exec( )` and `curl_close( )` to print out debugging information to standard error, including the contents of the request, as shown in Example 13-39.

Example 13-39. Verbose output from cURL

```
$c = curl_init('http://www.example.com/submit.php');
curl_setopt($c, CURLOPT_VERBOSE, true);
curl_setopt($c, CURLOPT_POST, true);
curl_setopt($c, CURLOPT_POSTFIELDS, 'monkey=uncle&rhino=aunt');
curl_setopt($c, CURLOPT_RETURNTRANSFER, true);
$page = curl_exec($c);
curl_close($c);
```

Example 13-39 prints something like:

```
* Connected to www.example.com (10.1.1.1)
> POST /submit.php HTTP/1.1
Host: www.example.com
Pragma: no-cache
Accept: image/gif, image/x-xbitmap, image/jpeg, image/pjpeg, */*
Content-Length: 23
Content-Type: application/x-www-form-urlencoded

monkey=uncle&rhino=aunt* Connection #0 left intact
* Closing connection #0
```

Because cURL prints the debugging information to standard error and not standard output, it can't be captured with output buffering. You can, however, open a filehandle for writing and set `CURLOUT_STDERR` to that filehandle to divert the debugging information to a file. This is shown in Example 13-40.

Example 13-40. Writing cURL verbose output to a file

```
<?php
$fh = fopen('/tmp/curl.out','w') or die($php_errormsg);
$c = curl_init('http://www.example.com/submit.php');
curl_setopt($c, CURLOPT_VERBOSE, true);
curl_setopt($c, CURLOPT_POST, true);
curl_setopt($c, CURLOPT_POSTFIELDS, 'monkey=uncle&rhino=aunt');
curl_setopt($c, CURLOPT_RETURNTRANSFER, true);
curl_setopt($c, CURLOPT_STDERR, $fh);
$page = curl_exec($c);
curl_close($c);
fclose($fh) or die($php_errormsg);
?>
```

Another way to access response headers with cURL is to write a "header function." This is similar to a cURL "write function" except it is called to handle response headers instead of the response body. Example 13-41 defines a HeaderSaver class whose header( ) method can be used as a header function to accumulate response headers.

Example 13-41. Using a cURL header function

```php
<?php

class HeaderSaver {
    public $headers = array();
    public $code = null;

    public function header($curl, $data){
        if (is_null($this->code) &&
            preg_match('@^HTTP/\d\.\d (\d+) @',$data,$matches)) {
            $this->code = $matches[1];
        } else {
            // Remove the trailing newline
            $trimmed = rtrim($data);
            if (strlen($trimmed)) {
                // If this line begins with a space or tab, it's a
                // continuation of the previous header
                if (($trimmed[0] == ' ') || ($trimmed[0] == "\t")) {
                    // Collapse the leading whitespace into one space
                    $trimmed = preg_replace('@^[ \t]+@',' ', $trimmed);
                    $this->headers[count($this->headers)-1] .= $trimmed;
                }
                // Otherwise, it's a new header
                else {
                    $this->headers[] = $trimmed;
                }
            }
        }
        return strlen($data);
    }

}

$h = new HeaderSaver();
$c = curl_init('http://www.example.com/plankton.php');
// Register the header function
curl_setopt($c, CURLOPT_HEADERFUNCTION, array($h,'header'));
curl_setopt($c, CURLOPT_RETURNTRANSFER, true);
$page = curl_exec($c);
// Now $h is populated with data
print 'The response code was: ' . $h->code . "\n";
print "The response headers were: \n";
foreach ($h->headers as $header) {
    print "  $header\n";
}
```

The HTTP 1.1 standard specifies that headers can span multiple lines by putting at least one space or tab character at the beginning of the additional lines of the header.

The header arrays returned by `stream_get_meta_data( )` and `HTTP_Request::getResponseHeader( )` do not properly handle multiline headers, though. The additional lines in a header are treated as separate headers. The code in Example 13-41, however, correctly combines the additional lines in multiline headers.

See Also

Documentation on `curl_setopt( )` at *http://www.php.net/curl-setopt*, on `stream_get_meta_data( )` at *http://www.php.net/stream_get_meta_data*, on `fopen( )` at *http://www.php.net/fopen*, and on the PEAR `HTTP_Request` class at *http://pear.php.net/package/HTTP_Request*; the syntax of an HTTP request is defined in RFC 2616 and available at *http://www.w3.org/Protocols/rfc2616/rfc2616.html*. The rules about multiline message headers are in Section 4.2: *http://www.w3.org/Protocols/rfc2616/rfc2616-sec4.html#sec4.2*. The `netcat` program is available from the GNU Netcat project at *http://netcat.sourceforge.net/*.

13.9 Marking Up a Web Page

Problem

You want to display a web page—for example, a search result—with certain words highlighted.

Solution

Build an array replacement for each word you want to highlight. Then, chop up the page into "HTML elements" and "text between HTML elements" and apply the replacements to just the text between HTML elements. Example 13-42 applies highlighting in the HTML in `$body` to the words found in `$words`.

Example 13-42. Marking up a web page

```
$body = '
<p>I like pickles and herring.</p>

<a href="pickle.php"><img src="pickle.jpg"/>A pickle picture</a>

I have a herringbone-patterned toaster cozy.

<herring>Herring is not a real HTML element!</herring>
';

$words = array('pickle','herring');
$replacements = array();
foreach ($words as $i => $word) {
    $replacements[] = "<span class='word-$i'>$word</span>";
}

// Split up the page into chunks delimited by a
```

```
    // reasonable approximation of what an HTML element
    // looks like.
    $parts = preg_split("{(<(?:\"[^\"]*\"|'[^']*'|[^'\"]>])*>)}",
                        $body,
                        -1,  // Unlimited number of chunks
                        PREG_SPLIT_DELIM_CAPTURE);
    foreach ($parts as $i => $part) {
        // Skip if this part is an HTML element
        if (isset($part[0]) && ($part[0] == '<')) { continue; }
        // Wrap the words with <span/>s
        $parts[$i] = str_replace($words, $replacements, $part);
    }

    // Reconstruct the body
    $body = implode('',$parts);

    print $body;
    ?>
```

Discussion

Example 13-42 prints:

```
<p>I like <span class='word-0'>pickle</span>s and <span class='word-1'>herring</span>.
</p>

<a href="pickle.php"><img src="pickle.jpg"/>A <span class='word-0'>pickle</span>
picture</a>

I have a <span class='word-1'>herring</span>bone-patterned toaster cozy.

<herring>Herring is not a real HTML element!</herring>
```

Each of the words in $words (pickle and herring) has been wrapped with a <span/> that has a specific class attribute. Use a CSS stylesheet to attach particular display attributes to these classes, such as a bright yellow background or a border.

The regular expression in Example 13-42 chops up $body into a series of chunks delimited by HTML elements. This lets us just replace the text between HTML elements and leaves HTML elements or attributes alone whose values might contain a search term. The regular expression does a pretty good job of matching HTML elements, but if you have some particularly crazy, malformed markup with mismatched or unescaped quotes, it might get confused.

Because str_replace() is case sensitive, only strings that exactly match words in $words are replaced. The last Herring in Example 13-42 doesn't get highlighted because it begins with a capital letter. To do case-insensitive matching, we need to switch from str_replace() to regular expressions. (We can't use str_ireplace() because the replacement has to preserve the case of what matched.) Example 13-43 shows the altered code that uses regular expressions to do the replacement.

Example 13-43. Marking up a web page with regular expressions
```
    <?php
    $body = '
```

```
<p>I like pickles and herring.</p>

<a href="pickle.php"><img src="pickle.jpg"/>A pickle picture</a>

I have a herringbone-patterned toaster cozy.

<herring>Herring is not a real HTML element!</herring>
';

$words = array('pickle','herring');
$patterns = array();
$replacements = array();
foreach ($words as $i => $word) {
    $patterns[] = '/' . preg_quote($word) .'/i';
    $replacements[] = "<span class='word-$i'>\\0</span>";
}

// Split up the page into chunks delimited by a
// reasonable approximation of what an HTML element
// looks like.
$parts = preg_split("{(<(?:\"[^\"]*\"|'[^']*'|[^'\">])*>)}",
                    $body,
                    -1,  // Unlimited number of chunks
                    PREG_SPLIT_DELIM_CAPTURE);
foreach ($parts as $i => $part) {
    // Skip if this part is an HTML element
    if (isset($part[0]) && ($part[0] == '<')) { continue; }
    // Wrap the words with <span/>s
    $parts[$i] = preg_replace($patterns, $replacements, $part);
}

// Reconstruct the body
$body = implode('',$parts);

print $body;
?>
```

The two differences in Example 13-43 are that it builds a $patterns array in the loop at the top and it uses the preg_replace( ) (with the $patterns array) instead of str_replace( ). The i at the end of each element in $patterns makes the match case insensitive. The \\0 in the replacement preserves the case in the replacement with the case of what it matched.

Switching to regular expressions also makes it easy to prevent substring matching. In both Example 13-42 and Example 13-43, the herring in herringbone gets highlighted. To prevent this, change $patterns[] = '/' . preg_quote($word) .'/i'; in Example 13-43 to $patterns[] = '/\b' . preg_quote($word) .'\b/i';. The additional \b items in the pattern tell preg_replace( ) only to match a word if it stands on its own.

See Also

Documentation on `str_replace()` at *http://www.php.net/str_replace*, on `str_ireplace()` at *http://www.php.net/str_ireplace*, on `preg_replace()` at *http://www.php.net/preg_replace*, and on `preg_split()` at *http://www.php.net/preg_split*.

13.10 Cleaning Up Broken or Nonstandard HTML

Problem

You've got some HTML with malformed syntax that you'd like to clean up. This makes it easier to parse and ensures that the pages you produce are standards compliant.

Solution

Use PHP's Tidy extension. It relies on the popular, powerful, HTML Tidy library to turn frightening piles of tag soup into well-formed, standards-compliant HTML or XHTML. Example 13-44 shows how to repair a file.

Example 13-44. Repairing an HTML file with Tidy

```php
<?php
$fixed = tidy_repair_file('bad.html');
file_put_contents('good.html', $fixed);
?>
```

Discussion

The HTML Tidy library has a large number of rules and features built up over time that creatively handle a wide variety of HTML abominations. Fortunately, you don't have to care about what all those rules are to reap the benefits of Tidy. Just pass a filename to `tidy_repair_file()` and you get back a cleaned-up version. For example, if *bad.html* contains:

```html
<img src="monkey.jpg">

<b>I <em>love</b> monkeys</em>.
```

then Example 13-44 writes the following out to *good.html*:

```html
<!DOCTYPE html PUBLIC "-//W3C//DTD HTML 3.2//EN">
<html>
<head>
<title></title>
</head>
<body>
<img src="monkey.jpg"> <b>I <em>love</em> monkeys</b>.
</body>
</html>
```

Tidy has a large number of configuration options that affect the output it produces. You can read about them at *http://tidy.sourceforge.net/docs/quickref.html*. Pass configuration to `tidy_repair_file()` by providing a second argument that is an array of configuration options and values. Example 13-45 uses the `output-xhtml` option, which tells Tidy to produce valid XHTML.

Example 13-45. Production of XHTML with Tidy

```
<?php
$config = array('output-xhtml' => true);
$fixed = tidy_repair_file('bad.html', $config);
file_put_contents('good.xhtml', $fixed);
?>
```

Example 13-45 writes the following to *good.xhtml*:

```
<!DOCTYPE html PUBLIC "-//W3C//DTD XHTML 1.0 Transitional//EN"
    "http://www.w3.org/TR/xhtml1/DTD/xhtml1-transitional.dtd">
<html xmlns="http://www.w3.org/1999/xhtml">
<head>
<title></title>
</head>
<body>
<img src="monkey.jpg" /> <b>I <em>love</em> monkeys</b>.
</body>
</html>
```

If your source HTML is in a string instead of a file, use `tidy_repair_string()`. It expects a first argument that contains HTML, not a filename.

See Also

Documentation on `tidy_repair_file()` at *http://www.php.net/tidy_repair_file*, on `tidy_repair_string()` at *http://www.php.net/tidy_repair_string*, and on Tidy configuration options at *http://tidy.sourceforge.net/docs/quickref.html*.

13.11 Extracting Links from an HTML File

Problem

You need to extract the URLs that are specified inside an HTML document.

Solution

Use Tidy to convert the document to XHTML, then use an XPath query to find all the links, as shown in Example 13-46.

Example 13-46. Extracting links with Tidy and XPath

```
<?php
$doc = new DOMDocument();
$opts = array('output-xml' => true,
                // Prevent DOMDocument from being confused about entities
                'numeric-entities' => true);
```

```
$doc->loadXML(tidy_repair_file('linklist.html',$opts));
$xpath = new DOMXPath($doc);
// Tell $xpath about the XHTML namespace
$xpath->registerNamespace('xhtml','http://www.w3.org/1999/xhtml');
foreach ($xpath->query('//xhtml:a/@href') as $node) {
    $link = $node->nodeValue;
    print $link . "\n";
}
```

If Tidy isn't available, use the `pc_link_extractor()` function shown in Example 13-47.

Example 13-47. Extracting links without Tidy

```
<?php
$html = file_get_contents('linklist.html');
$links = pc_link_extractor($html);
foreach ($links as $link) {
    print $link[0] . "\n";
}

function pc_link_extractor($html) {
    $links = array();
    preg_match_all('/<a\s+.*?href=[\"\']?([^\"\' >]*)[\"\']?[^>]*>(.*?)<\/a>/i',
                   $html,$matches,PREG_SET_ORDER);
    foreach($matches as $match) {
        $links[] = array($match[1],$match[2]);
    }
    return $links;
}
```

Discussion

The XHTML document that Tidy generates when the `output-xhtml` option is turned on may contain entities other than the four that are defined by the base XML specification (`&lt; &gt; &amp; &quot;`). Turning on the `numeric-entities` option prevents those other entities from appearing in the generated XHTML document. Their presence would cause `DOMDocument` to complain about undefined entities. An alternative is to leave out the `numeric-entities` option but set `$doc->resolveExternals` to `true`. This tells `DOMDocument` to fetch any Document Type Definition referenced in the file it's loading and use that to resolve the entities. Tidy generates XML with an appropriate DTD in it. The downside of this approach is that the DTD URL points to a resource on an external web server, so your program would have to download that resource each time it runs.

XHTML is an XML application—a defined XML vocabulary for expressing HTML. As such, all of its elements (the familiar `<a/>`, `<h1/>`, and so on) live in a namespace. The URI for that namespace is *http://www.w3.org/1999/xhtml*. For XPath queries to work properly, the namespace has to be attached to a prefix (that's what the `registerNamespace()` method does) and then used in the XPath query.

The `pc_link_extractor()` function is a useful alternative if Tidy isn't available. Its regular expression won't work on all links, such as those that are constructed with some hexadecimal escapes, but it should function on the majority of reasonably well-formed HTML. The function returns an array. Each element of that array is itself a two-element array. The first element is the target of the link, and the second element is the link anchor—text that is linked.

The XPath expression in Example 13-46 only grabs links, not anchors. Example 13-48 shows an alternative that produces both links and anchors.

Example 13-48. Extracting links and anchors with Tidy and XPath

```php
<?php
$doc = new DOMDocument();
$opts = array('output-xhtml'=>true,
              // Prevent DOMDocument from being confused about entities
              'numeric-entities' => true);
$doc->loadXML(tidy_repair_file('linklist.html',$opts));
$xpath = new DOMXPath($doc);
// Tell $xpath about the XHTML namespace
$xpath->registerNamespace('xhtml','http://www.w3.org/1999/xhtml');
foreach ($xpath->query('//xhtml:a') as $node) {
    $anchor = trim($node->textContent);
    $link = $node->getAttribute('href');
    print "$anchor -> $link \n";
}
```

In Example 13-48, the XPath query finds all the `<a/>` element nodes. The `textContent` property of the node holds the anchor text and the link is in the `href` attribute.

See Also

Documentation on on `DOMDocument` at *http://www.php.net/DOM*, on `DOMXPath::query()` at *http://www.php.net/DOM_DOMXPath::query*, on `DOMXPath::registerNamespace()` at *http://www.php.net/DOM_DOMXPath::registerNamespace*, on `tidy_repair_file()` at *http://www.php.net/tidy_repair_file*, and on `preg_match_all()` at *http://www.php.net/preg_match_all*; Recipe 13.10 has more information about Tidy; *http://www.w3.org/TR/xpath* describes XPath; *http://www.w3.org/TR/xhtml1/* details XHTML.

13.12 Converting Plain Text to HTML

Problem

You want to turn plain text into reasonably formatted HTML.

Solution

First, encode entities with `htmlentities()`. Then, transform the text into various HTML structures. The `pc_text2html()` function shown in Example 13-49 has basic transformations for links and paragraph breaks.

Example 13-49. pc_text2html()

```php
<?php
function pc_text2html($s) {
  $s = htmlentities($s);
  $grafs = split("\n\n",$s);
  for ($i = 0, $j = count($grafs); $i < $j; $i++) {
    // Link to what seem to be http or ftp URLs
    $grafs[$i] = preg_replace('/((ht|f)tp:\/\/[^\s&]+)/',
                              '<a href="$1">$1</a>',$grafs[$i]);

    // Link to email addresses
    $grafs[$i] = preg_replace('/[^@\s]+@([-a-z0-9]+\.)+[a-z]{2,}/i',
          '<a href="mailto:$1">$1</a>',$grafs[$i]);

    // Begin with a new paragraph
    $grafs[$i] = '<p>'.$grafs[$i].'</p>';
  }
  return implode("\n\n",$grafs);
}
?>
```

Discussion

The more you know about what the plain text looks like, the better your HTML conversion can be. For example, if emphasis is indicated with *asterisks* or /slashes/ around words, you can add rules that take care of that, as shown in Example 13-50.

Example 13-50. More text-to-HTML rules

```php
<?php
$grafs[$i] = preg_replace('/(\A|\s)\*([^*]+)\*(\s|\z)/',
                          '$1<b>$2</b>$3',$grafs[$i]);
$grafs[$i] = preg_replace('{(\A|\s)/([^/]+)/(\s|\z)}',
                          '$1<i>$2</i>$3',$grafs[$i]);
?>
```

See Also

Documentation on `preg_replace( )` at *http://www.php.net/preg_replace*.

13.13 Converting HTML to Plain Text

Problem

You need to convert HTML to readable, formatted plain text.

Solution

Use the `html2text` class available from *http://www.chuggnutt.com/html2text.php*. Example 13-51 shows it in action.

Example 13-51. Converting HTML to plain text

```
<?php
require_once 'class.html2text.inc';
$html = file_get_contents('http://www.example.com/article.html');
$converter = new html2text($html);
$plain_text = $converter->get_text();
?>
```

Discussion

The `html2text` class has a large number of formatting rules built in so your generated plain text has some visual layout for headings, paragraphs, and so on. It also includes a list of all the links in the HTML at the bottom of the text it generates.

See Also

http://www.chuggnutt.com/html2text.php for more information on `html2text` and links to download it.

13.14 Removing HTML and PHP Tags

Problem

You want to remove HTML and PHP tags from a string or file. For example, you want to make sure there is no HTML in a string before printing it or PHP in a string before passing it to `eval( )`.

Solution

Use `strip_tags( )` to remove HTML and PHP tags from a string, as shown in Example 13-52.

Example 13-52. Removing HTML and PHP tags

```
<?php

$html = '<a href="http://www.oreilly.com">I <b>love computer books.</b></a>
         <?php echo "Hello!" ?>';
print strip_tags($html);
?>
```

Example 13-52 prints:

```
I love computer books.
```

To strip tags from a stream as you read it, use the `string.strip_tags` stream filter, as shown in Example 13-53.

Example 13-53. Removing HTML and PHP tags from a stream

```
<?php
$stream = fopen('elephant.html','r');
```

```
stream_filter_append($stream, 'string.strip_tags');
print stream_get_contents($stream);
?>
```

Discussion

Both strip_tags( ) and the string.strip_tags filter can be told not to remove certain
tags. Provide a string containing of allowable tags to strip_tags( ) as a second argument. The tag specification is case insensitive, and for pairs of tags, you only have to
specify the opening tag. For example, to remove all but <b></b><i></i> tags from
$html, call strip_tags($html,'<b><i>').

With the string.strip_tags filter, pass a similar string as a fourth argument to
stream_filter_append( ). The third argument to stream_filter_append( ) controls
whether the filter is applied on reading (STREAM_FILTER_READ), writing
(STREAM_FILTER_WRITE), or both (STREAM_FILTER_ALL). Example 13-54 does what Example 13-53 does, but allows <b></b><i></i> tags.

Example 13-54. Removing some HTML and PHP tags from a stream

```
<?php
$stream = fopen('elephant.html','r');
stream_filter_append($stream, 'string.strip_tags',STREAM_FILTER_READ,'<b><i>');
print stream_get_contents($stream);
?>
```

stream_filter_append( ) also accepts an array of tag names instead of a string:
array('b','i') instead of '<b><i>'.

Whether with strip_tags( ) or the stream filter, attributes are not removed from allowed tags. This means that an attribute that changes display (such as style) or executes
JavaScript (any event handler) is preserved. If you are displaying "stripped" text of
arbitrary origin in a web browser to a user, this could result in cross-site scripting attacks.

See Also

Documentation on strip_tags( ) at *http://www.php.net/strip-tags*, on
stream_filter_append( ) at *http://www.php.net/stream_filter_append*, and stream filters
at *http://www.php.net/filters*. The PEAR package HTML_Safe attempts to remove un-
safe content from HTML and is available at *http://pear.php.net/package/HTML_Safe*.
Recipe 18.4 has more details on cross-site scripting.

13.15 Responding to an Ajax Request

Problem

You're using JavaScript to make in-page requests with XMLHTTPRequest and need to send
data in reply to one of those requests.

Solution

Set an appropriate `Content-Type` header and then emit properly formatted data. Example 13-55 sends a small XML document as a response.

Example 13-55. Sending an XML response

```
<?php header('Content-Type: text/xml'); ?>
<menu>
 <dish type="appetizer">Chicken Soup</dish>
 <dish type="main course">Fried Monkey Brains</dish>
</menu>
```

Example 13-56 uses the PEAR Services_JSON package to send a JSON response.

Example 13-56. Sending a JSON response

```
<?php
require_once 'Services/JSON.php';
$menu = array();
$menu[] = array('type' => 'appetizer',
                'dish' => 'Chicken Soup');
$menu[] = array('type' => 'main course',
                'dish' => 'Fried Monkey Brains');
header('Content-Type: application/json');
$json = new Services_JSON();
print $json->encode($menu);
?>
```

Example 13-57 uses the PECL `json` extension (which is bundled with PHP 5.2 and later) to send a JSON response.

Example 13-57. Sending a JSON response with PECL json

```
<?php
$menu = array();
$menu[] = array('type' => 'appetizer',
                'dish' => 'Chicken Soup');
$menu[] = array('type' => 'main course,'
                'dish' => 'Fried Monkey Brains');
header('Content-Type: application/json');
print json_encode($menu);
?>
```

Discussion

From a purely PHP perspective, sending a response to an `XMLHTTPRequest`-based request is no different than any other response. You send any necessary headers and then spit out some text. What's different, however, is what those headers are and, usually, what the text looks like.

JSON is a particularly useful format for these sorts of responses, because it's super easy to deal with the JSON-formatted data from within JavaScript. The output from Example 13-56 looks like this:

```
[{"type":"appetizer","dish":"Chicken Soup"},
 {"type":"main course","dish":"Fried Monkey Brains"}]
```

This encodes a two-element JavaScript array of hashes. The PEAR Services_JSON module is an easy way to turn PHP data structures (scalars, arrays, and objects) into JSON strings and vice versa. Since it's a PEAR module, you can use it even if you don't have access to your *php.ini* file or can't install binary extensions. If you can install your own extensions, consider using the PECL json extension instead for a big speed boost. Its json_encode() and json_decode() functions turn PHP data structures to JSON strings and back again.

With these types of responses, it's also important to pay attention to caching. Different browsers have a creative variety of caching strategies when it comes to requests made from within JavaScript. If your responses are sending dynamic data (which they usually are), then you probably don't want them to be cached. The two tools in your anti-caching toolbox are headers and URL poisoning. Example 13-58 shows the full complement of anti-caching headers you can issue from PHP to prevent a browser from caching a response.

Example 13-58. Anti-caching headers

```php
<?php
header("Expires: 0");
header("Last-Modified: " . gmdate("D, d M Y H:i:s") . " GMT");
header("Cache-Control: no-store, no-cache, must-revalidate");
// Add some IE-specific options
header("Cache-Control: post-check=0, pre-check=0", false);
// For HTTP/1.0
header("Pragma: no-cache");
?>
```

The other anti-caching tool, URL poisoning, requires cooperation from the JavaScript that is making the request. It adds a name/value pair to the query string of each request it makes using an arbitrary value. This makes the request URL different each time the request is made, preventing any misbehaving caches from getting in the way. The JavaScript Math.random() function is useful for generating these values.

See Also

Documentation on on header() at *http://www.php.net/header*. Read more about XMLHTTPRequest at *http://en.wikipedia.org/wiki/XMLHttpRequest*, JSON at *http://www.json.org*, Services_JSON at *http://pear.php.net/pepr/pepr-proposal-show.php?id=198*, and the PECL json extension at *http://pecl.php.net/package/json*. Michael Radwin's "HTTP Caching and Cache-Busting for Content Publishers" (*http://public.yahoo.com/~radwin/talks/http-caching-apachecon2005.htm*) is a good introduction to HTTP caching. Section 13 of RFC 2616 (*http://www.w3.org/Protocols/rfc2616/rfc2616-sec13.html#sec13*) has the gory details on HTTP caching.

13.16 Integrating with JavaScript

Problem

You want part of your page to update with server-side data without reloading the whole page. For example, you want to populate a list with search results.

Solution

Use a JavaScript toolkit such as Dojo to wire up the client side of things so that a particular user action (such as clicking a button) fires off a request to the server. Write appropriate PHP code to generate a response containing the right data. Then, use your JavaScript toolkit to put the results in the page correctly.

Example 13-59 shows a simple HTML document that loads Dojo and the code in Example 13-60. Example 13-60 is the JavaScript glue that sends a request off to the server when the Search button is clicked and makes sure the results end up on the page in the right place when they come back. Example 13-61 is the PHP code that does the searching and sends back a JSON-formatted response.

Example 13-59. Basic HTML for JavaScript integration

```html
<!-- Load Dojo -->
<script type="text/javascript" src="/dojo.js"></script>
<!-- Load our JavaScript -->
<script type="text/javascript" src="/search.js"></script>

<!-- Some input elements -->
<input type="text" id="q" />
<input type="button" id="go" value="Search"/>
<hr/>
<!-- Where the output goes -->
<div id="output"></div>
```

Example 13-60. JavaScript integration glue

```javascript
// When the page loads, run this code
dojo.addOnLoad(function() {
    // Call the search() function when the 'go' button is clicked
    dojo.event.connect(dojo.byId('go'), 'onclick', 'search');
});

function search() {
    // What's in the text box?
    var q = dojo.byId('q').value;
    // Send request to the server
    // The url should be to wherever you save the search page
    dojo.io.bind({ 'url': '/search.php',
                   'content': { 'q': q },
                   // Type of the response
                   'mimetype': 'text/json',
                   // Function to call when the response comes
                   'load': showResults });
```

```
    }

    // Handle the results
    function showResults(type, results, evt) {
        var html = '';
        // If we got some results...
        if (results.length > 0) {
            html = '<ul>';
            // Build a list of them
            for (var i in results) {
                html += '<li>' + dojo.string.escapeXml(results[i]) + '</li>';
            }
            html += '</ul>';
        } else {
            html = 'No results.';
        }
        // Put the result HTML in the page
        dojo.byId('output').innerHTML = html;
    }
```

Example 13-61. PHP to generate a response for JavaScript

```php
<?php
// Initialize JSON
require_once 'Services/JSON.php';
$json = new Services_JSON();

$results = array();
$q = isset($_GET['q']) ? $_GET['q'] : '';

// Connect to the database from Chapter 10
$db = new PDO('sqlite:/usr/local/data/zodiac.db');

// Do the query
$st = $db->prepare('SELECT symbol FROM zodiac WHERE planet LIKE ? ');
$st->execute(array($q.'%'));

// Build an array of results
while ($row = $st->fetch()) {
    $results[] = $row['symbol'];
}

// Splorp out all the anti-caching stuff
header("Expires: 0");
header("Last-Modified: " . gmdate("D, d M Y H:i:s") . " GMT");
header("Cache-Control: no-store, no-cache, must-revalidate");
// Add some IE-specific options
header("Cache-Control: post-check=0, pre-check=0", false);
// For HTTP/1.0
header("Pragma: no-cache");

// The response is JSON
header('Content-Type: application/json');

// Output the JSON data
```

```
print $json->encode($results);
?>
```

Discussion

The HTML in Example 13-59 is pretty minimal by design. All that's there are a few elements and calls to load external scripts. Separating JavaScript from HTML is good development practice—similar to segregating your presentation logic and your business logic on the server side. The first `<script/>` tag in Example 13-59 should point to wherever you've installed Dojo. The second should point to wherever you've put the code in Example 13-60. That handful of JavaScript functions provides the bridge between the HTML elements in Example 13-59 and the server-side code in Example 13-61. The first call to `dojo.addOnLoad()` tells the web browser, "When the page is finished loading, run the JavaScript code that tells the web browser, "When the go button is clicked, run the `search()` function."

A lot of JavaScript programming is *event based*—along the lines of setting up rules like "when such-and-such happens, run this function." A web page studded with JavaScript does not have a strictly procedural flow from start to finish. Instead, it presents the user with lots of possibilities—clicking buttons, typing stuff in text boxes, clicking on links, and so on. Your JavaScript code usually sets up various *event handlers*—functions that run in response to clicking, typing, and other events.

In Example 13-60, the `search()` function uses Dojo's `dojo.io.bind()` function to send a request back to the server, passing whatever's in the text box as the `q` query string parameter. The other arguments to `dojo.io.bind()` indicate that a JSON response is expected, and when the request arrives, it should be passed to the `showResults()` function.

The `showResults()` function, in turn, takes those results and builds an HTML list out of them. Once the list has been built up, it sets the content of the `output <div/>` to contain that HTML.

Example 13-61 is the familiar part of this triumvirate. It's very similar to any "search the database for some stuff based on user input" PHP script, except for how it returns results. Instead of printing HTML, it uses the techniques described in Recipe 13.15 to send back an uncacheable JSON response.

Writing applications that rely on JavaScript-based client-side activity requires a different programming paradigm than your typical PHP application. Instead of thinking about how to generate entire dynamic pages, you have to think about how to generate bits of dynamic data that client-side logic can display or manipulate in convenient ways. A toolkit such as Dojo gives you a robust platform on which to build such applications. It abstracts away many of the messy practicalities of JavaScript programming—cross-browser incompatibilities, the guts of asynchronous I/O, and other housekeeping.

There are PHP-centric JavaScript toolkits available, such as PEAR's HTML_Ajax and xajax. They aim to let you write PHP functions and methods and then call them easily from JavaScript, taking care of the tedious glue of mapping particular JavaScript functions to particular PHP functions. While these toolkits provide PHP-focused convenience, they do so at the cost of JavaScript-focused robustness. While either HTML_Ajax or xajax can be useful and convenient in quickly tying some server-side PHP code to client-side logic, they are not built to handle applications that are designed from the ground up as client focused.

That said, comfortably intersecting PHP and JavaScript is a problem for which many folks are actively developing solutions. Easier paths undoubtedly will emerge after these words are written.

See Also

Recipe 13.15 details sending JSON responses. Dojo is at *http://www.dojotoolkit.org/*, xajax at *http://www.xajaxproject.org/*, and HTML_Ajax at *http://pear.php.net/package/HTML_Ajax*. "Getting Rich with PHP" (*http://talks.php.net/show/tek06*) explores the performance implications of responding to lots of JavaScript-based requests. Other JavaScript toolkits include script.aculo.us (*http://script.aculo.us/*), Prototype (*http://prototype.conio.net/*), and the Yahoo! User Interface Library (*http://developer.yahoo.com/yui/index.html*).

13.17 Program: Finding Stale Links

The *stale-links.php* program in Example 13-62 produces a list of links in a page and their status. It tells you if the links are okay, if they've been moved somewhere else, or if they're bad. Run the program by passing it a URL to scan for links:

```
% php stale-links.php http://www.oreilly.com
http://www.oreilly.com/: OK
http://oreillynet.com/: OK
http://www.oreilly.com/store/: OK
http://safari.oreilly.com: OK
http://conferences.oreillynet.com/: OK
http://www.oreillylearning.com: OK
http://academic.oreilly.com: MOVED: http://academic.oreilly.com/index.csp
http://www.oreilly.com/about/: OK
...
```

The *stale-links.php* program uses the cURL extension to retrieve web pages (see Example 13-62). First, it retrieves the URL specified on the command line. Once a page has been retrieved, the program uses the XPath technique from Recipe 13.11 to get a list of links in the page. Then, after prepending a base URL to each link if necessary, the link is retrieved. Because we need just the headers of these responses, we use the HEAD method instead of GET by setting the `CURLOPT_NOBODY` option. Setting `CURLOPT_HEADER` tells `curl_exec( )` to include the response headers in the string it returns. Based on the response code, the status of the link is printed, along with its new location if it's been moved.

Example 13-62. stale-links.php

```php
<?php

if (! isset($_SERVER['argv'][1])) {
    die("No URL provided.\n");
}

$url = $_SERVER['argv'][1];

// Load the page
list($page,$pageInfo) = load_with_curl($url);

if (! strlen($page)) {
    die("No page retrieved from $url");
}

// Convert to XML for easy parsing
$opts = array('output-xhtml' => true,
              'numeric-entities' => true);
$xml = tidy_repair_string($page, $opts);
$doc = new DOMDocument();
$doc->loadXML($xml);
$xpath = new DOMXPath($doc);
$xpath->registerNamespace('xhtml','http://www.w3.org/1999/xhtml');

// Compute the Base URL for relative links
$baseURL = '';
// Check if there is a <base href=""/> in the page
$nodeList = $xpath->query('//xhtml:base/@href');
if ($nodeList->length == 1) {
    $baseURL = $nodeList->item(0)->nodeValue;
}
// No <base href=""/>, so build the Base URL from $url
else {
    $URLParts = parse_url($pageInfo['url']);
    if (! (isset($URLParts['path']) && strlen($URLParts['path']))) {
        $basePath = '';
    } else {
        $basePath = preg_replace('#/[^/]*$#','',$URLParts['path']);
    }
    if (isset($URLParts['username']) || isset($URLParts['password'])) {
        $auth = isset($URLParts['username']) ? $URLParts['username'] : '';
        $auth .= ':';
        $auth .= isset($URLParts['password']) ? $URLParts['password'] : '';
        $auth .= '@';
    } else {
        $auth = '';
    }
    $baseURL = $URLParts['scheme'] . '://' .
               $auth . $URLParts['host'] .
               $basePath;
}

// Keep track of the links we visit so we don't visit each more than once
$seenLinks = array();
```

```
// Grab all links
$links = $xpath->query('//xhtml:a/@href');

foreach ($links as $node) {
    $link = $node->nodeValue;
    // resolve relative links
    if (! preg_match('#^(http|https|mailto):#', $link)) {
        if (((strlen($link) == 0)) || ($link[0] != '/')) {
            $link = '/' . $link;
        }
        $link = $baseURL . $link;
    }
    // Skip this link if we've seen it already
    if (isset($seenLinks[$link])) {
        continue;
    }
    // Mark this link as seen
    $seenLinks[$link] = true;
    // Print the link we're visiting
    print $link.': ';
    flush();

    list($linkHeaders, $linkInfo) = load_with_curl($link, 'HEAD');
    // Decide what to do based on the response code
    // 2xx response codes mean the page is OK
    if (($linkInfo['http_code'] >= 200) && ($linkInfo['http_code'] < 300)) {
        $status = 'OK';
    }
    // 3xx response codes mean redirection
    else if (($linkInfo['http_code'] >= 300) && ($linkInfo['http_code'] < 400)) {
        $status = 'MOVED';
        if (preg_match('/^Location: (.*)$/m',$linkHeaders,$match)) {
            $status .= ': ' . trim($match[1]);
        }
    }
    // Other response codes mean errors
    else {
        $status = "ERROR: {$linkInfo['http_code']}";
    }
    // Print what we know about the link
    print "$status\n";
}

function load_with_curl($url, $method = 'GET') {
    $c = curl_init($url);
    curl_setopt($c, CURLOPT_RETURNTRANSFER, true);
    if ($method == 'GET') {
        curl_setopt($c,CURLOPT_FOLLOWLOCATION, true);
    }
    else if ($method == 'HEAD') {
        curl_setopt($c, CURLOPT_NOBODY, true);
        curl_setopt($c, CURLOPT_HEADER, true);
    }
    $response = curl_exec($c);
```

```
        return array($response, curl_getinfo($c));
    }
    ?>
```

13.18 Program: Finding Fresh Links

Example 13-63 is a modification of the program in Example 13-62 that produces a list
of links and their last-modified time. If the server on which a URL lives doesn't provide
a last-modified time, the program reports the URL's last-modified time as the time the
URL was requested. If the program can't retrieve the URL successfully, it prints out the
status code it got when it tried to retrieve the URL. Run the program by passing it a
URL to scan for links:

```
% php fresh-links.php http://www.oreilly.com
https://epoch.oreilly.com/account/default.orm: MOVED: https://epoch.oreilly.com/
lib/p_sso.orm?d=account
https://epoch.oreilly.com/shop/cart.orm: OK
http://www.oreilly.com/: OK; Last Modified: Mon, 08 May 2006 22:11:04 GMT
http://oreillynet.com/: OK
http://www.oreilly.com/store/: OK
http://safari.oreilly.com: OK
http://conferences.oreillynet.com/: OK
http://www.oreillylearning.com: OK
http://academic.oreilly.com: MOVED: http://academic.oreilly.com/index.csp
...
```

This output is from a run of the program at about 11:48 P.M. GMT on May 8, 2006.
Most links aren't accompanied by a last modified time—this means the server didn't
provide one, so the page is probably dynamic. The link to *http://www.oreilly.com/*
shows that page being about 90 minutes old. The link to *http://academic.oreilly.com*
shows that it has been moved elsewhere, as reported by the output of *stale-links.php* in
Recipe 13.17.

The program to find fresh links is conceptually almost identical to the program to find
stale links. It uses the same techniques to pull links out of a page; however, it uses the
HTTP_Request class instead of cURL to retrieve URLs. The code to get the base URL
specified on the command line is inside a loop so that it can follow any redirects that
are provided and easily return the final URL in a redirect chain.

Once a page has been retrieved, each linked URL is retrieved with the head method.
Instead of just printing out a new location for moved links, however, it prints out a
formatted version of the Last-Modified header if it's available.

Example 13-63. fresh-links.php

```
    <?php
    error_reporting(E_ALL);
    require_once 'HTTP/Request.php';

    if (! isset($_SERVER['argv'][1])) {
        die("No URL provided.\n");
    }
```

```
$url = $_SERVER['argv'][1];

// Load the page
$r = load_with_http_request($url);

if (! strlen($r->getResponseBody())) {
    die("No page retrieved from $url");
}

// Convert to XML for easy parsing
$opts = array('output-xhtml' => true,
              'numeric-entities' => true);
$xml = tidy_repair_string($r->getResponseBody(), $opts);
$doc = new DOMDocument();
$doc->loadXML($xml);
$xpath = new DOMXPath($doc);
$xpath->registerNamespace('xhtml','http://www.w3.org/1999/xhtml');

// Compute the Base URL for relative links.
$baseURL = '';
// Check if there is a <base href=""/> in the page
$nodeList = $xpath->query('//xhtml:base/@href');
if ($nodeList->length == 1) {
    $baseURL = $nodeList->item(0)->nodeValue;
}
// No <base href=""/>, so build the Base URL from $url
else {
    $URLParts = parse_url($r->_url->getURL());
    if (! (isset($URLParts['path']) && strlen($URLParts['path']))) {
        $basePath = '';
    } else {
        $basePath = preg_replace('#/[^/]*$#','',$URLParts['path']);
    }
    if (isset($URLParts['username']) || isset($URLParts['password'])) {
        $auth = isset($URLParts['username']) ? $URLParts['username'] : '';
        $auth .= ':';
        $auth .= isset($URLParts['password']) ? $URLParts['password'] : '';
        $auth .= '@';
    } else {
        $auth = '';
    }
    $baseURL = $URLParts['scheme'] . '://' .
               $auth . $URLParts['host'] .
               $basePath;
}

// Keep track of the links we visit so we don't visit each more than once
$seenLinks = array();

// Grab all links
$links = $xpath->query('//xhtml:a/@href');

foreach ($links as $node) {
    $link = $node->nodeValue;
```

```
    // Resolve relative links
    if (! preg_match('#^(http|https|mailto):#', $link)) {
        if (((strlen($link) == 0)) || ($link[0] != '/')) {
            $link = '/' . $link;
        }
        $link = $baseURL . $link;
    }
    // Skip this link if we've seen it already
    if (isset($seenLinks[$link])) {
        continue;
    }
    // Mark this link as seen
    $seenLinks[$link] = true;
    // Print the link we're visiting
    print $link.': ';
    flush();

    $r = load_with_http_request($link, 'HEAD');
    // Decide what to do based on the response code
    // 2xx response codes mean the page is OK

    if (($r->getResponseCode() >= 200) && ($r->getResponseCode() < 300)) {
        $status = 'OK';
    }
    // 3xx response codes mean redirection
    else if (($r->getResponseCode() >= 300) && ($r->getResponseCode() < 400)) {
        $status = 'MOVED';
        if (strlen($location = $r->getResponseHeader('location'))) {
            $status .= ": $location";
        }
    }
    // Other response codes mean errors
    else {
        $status = "ERROR: {$r->getResponseCode()}";
    }
    if (strlen($lastModified = $r->getResponseHeader('last-modified'))) {
        $status .= "; Last Modified: $lastModified";
    }
    // Print what we know about the link
    print "$status\n";
}

function load_with_http_request($url, $method = 'GET') {
    if ($method == 'GET') {
        $done = false; $max_redirects = 10;
        while ((! $done) && ($max_redirects > 0)) {
            $r = new HTTP_Request($url);
            $r->sendRequest();
            $responseCode = $r->getResponseCode();
            if (($responseCode >= 300) && ($responseCode < 400) &&
                strlen($location = $r->getResponseHeader('location'))) {
                    $url = $location;
                    $max_redirects--;
            } else {
                $done = true;
```

```
            }
        }
    } else {
        $r = new HTTP_Request($url);
        $r->setMethod(HTTP_REQUEST_METHOD_HEAD);
        $r->sendRequest();
    }
    return $r;
}
?>
```

CHAPTER 14

Consuming Web Services

14.0 Introduction

Web services allow you to exchange information over HTTP using XML. When you want to find out the weather forecast for New York City, the current stock price of IBM, or the cost of a flat screen TV on eBay, you can write a short script to gather that data in a format you can easily manipulate. From a developer's perspective, it's as if you're calling a local function that returns a value.

The key behind web services is platform-independent communication. Your PHP script running on Linux can talk to someone else's IIS server on a Windows box using ASP without any communication problems. Likewise, you can talk to a box running Solaris, Apache, and JSP using the same sets of tools and interfaces.

There are two major types of web services: REST and SOAP. A REST request is relatively straightforward, as they involve making an HTTP request of a server and processing an XML document that's returned as the response. Since most developers are familiar with HTTP and XML, the learning curve for REST is short and shallow.

The one downside to REST is that beyond these two conventions, there's not much in terms of standards as to how data should be passed in or returned. Every site is free to use what it feels is the best. While this is not a problem for small services, if not designed properly, this can cause complexity when a service grows.

Still, REST is a very popular format and its simplicity is a key factor in its success. Recipe 14.1 covers making REST requests.

The other popular web services format is SOAP, which is a W3C standard for passing messages across the network and calling functions on remote computers. SOAP provides developers with many options; however, this flexibility comes at a price. SOAP is quite complex, and the full specification is large and growing.

Ideally, SOAP should make things simpler. Communication between services is handled by a client and server that automatically serialize data types from one language to another. Therefore, you can pass and retrieve complex data structures back and forth without needing to worry about interoperability woes.

When this occurs, things are absolutely great and everything just works. However, because of the abstraction layer that SOAP places over communication, it can be difficult to debug when you run into a problem. Since you're not familiar with the underlying XML, it can take a while to get up to speed just to diagnose the issue.

PHP 5 bundles a SOAP extension, ext/soap. Right now, this extension implements most, but not all, of SOAP 1.2. Overall, this implementation is as good or better than other PHP SOAP toolkits, but it's possible that you'll find an area or two that are deal breakers.

It's enabled by default as of PHP 5.1, but you can enable SOAP support on earlier versions by adding `--enable-soap` to your PHP configure line. The only external library you need is `libxml2`, which is the same requirement for any of PHP 5's XML extensions.

SOAP is the subject of Recipes 14.2 to 14.11.

Complete details on SOAP are available on the W3 web site at *http://www.w3.org/2000/xp/Group/* and in *Programming Web Services with SOAP* by James Snell, Doug Tidwell, and Pavel Kulchenko (O'Reilly).

Beyond REST and SOAP, there's one other web services format that's relatively common, XML-RPC. XML-RPC is similar in spirit to SOAP, as it also converts native data into a language-netural format that you can pass into functions and receive replies. However, XML-RPC is far less complex than SOAP.

This is a great benefit when everything you need to do fits within the feature set of XML-RPC, but will cause issues when you try to break out of the box. The XML-RPC specification is not being actively worked on, so if you can't make it work, you'll need to switch to using REST or SOAP instead.

XML-RPC is the subject of Recipes 14.12 and 14.13.

14.1 Calling a REST Method

Problem

You want to make a REST request.

Solution

Use `file_get_contents( )`:

```php
<?php
$base = 'http://music.example.org/search.php';
$params = array('composer' => 'beethoven',
                'instrument' => 'cello');

$url = $base . '?' . http_build_query($params);

$response = file_get_contents($url);
?>
```

Or use cURL:

```php
<?php
$base = 'http://music.example.org/search.php';
$params = array('composer' => 'beethoven',
                'instrument' => 'cello');

$url = $base . '?' . http_build_query($params);

$c = curl_init($url);
curl_setopt($c, CURLOPT_RETURNTRANSFER, true);
$response = curl_exec($c);
curl_close($c);
?>
```

Discussion

REST is a style of web services in which you make requests using HTTP methods such as get and post, and the method type tells the server what action it should take. For example, get tells the server you want to retrieve existing data, whereas post means you want to update existing data. The server then replies with the results in an XML document that you can process.

The brilliance of REST is in its simplicity and use of existing standards. PHP's been letting you make HTTP requests and process XML documents for years, so everything you need to make and process REST requests is old hat.

There are many ways to execute HTTP requests in PHP, including file_get_contents( ), the cURL extension, and PEAR packages. The ins and outs of these options are covered in the beginning of Chapter 13.

Once you've retrieved the XML document, use any of PHP's XML extensions to process it. Given the nature of REST documents, and that you're usually familiar with the schema of the response, the SimpleXML extension is often the best choice. It's covered in Recipe 12.3. However, there are times when you may want to use other extensions, such as DOM, XMLReader, or even XSLT. These are covered throughout Chapter 12.

See Also

Chapter 13 goes into detail on retrieving remote URLs; Recipe 15.1 for more on serving REST requests.

14.2 Calling a SOAP Method with WSDL

Problem

You want to send a SOAP request. Creating a SOAP client allows you to gather information from SOAP servers, regardless of their operating system and middleware software.

Solution

Use the ext/soap extension. Here's client code that finds current stock quotes:

```php
<?php
$wsdl_url =
    'http://services.xmethods.net/soap/urn:xmethods-delayed-quotes.wsdl';

$client = new SOAPClient($wsdl_url);

$quote = $client->getQuote('EBAY'); // eBay, Inc.
print $quote;
?>
31.49
```

Discussion

There are a handful of SOAP implementations for PHP. If you're using PHP 5, it's highly recommended to use the bundled ext/soap extension. While this extension is not compatible with PHP 4, it has many advantages over PEAR::SOAP and NuSOAP, the two main PHP SOAP extensions that are PHP 4 compatible. In particular, ext/soap is:

- Written in C, not PHP, so it's fast and efficient.
- Bundled with PHP as of PHP 5, and enabled by default as of PHP 5.1.
- Compatible with many parts of the SOAP specifications.
- Written to take advantage of PHP 5 features, including exceptions.

To make a SOAP request, you instantiate a new **SOAPClient** object and pass the constructor the location of the web services' WSDL:

```php
$client = new SOAPClient('http://api.example.com/service.wsdl');
```

WSDL (Web Services Description Language) is an XML vocabulary that lets the implementor create a file that defines what methods and arguments his web service supports. This file is then placed on the Web for others to read.

WSDL is not particularly friendly for humans, but it's great for machines. When you point the SOAP extension at a WSDL file, the extension automatically creates an object for the web service, and you can manipulate this object as you would a PHP class.

The object even knows what parameters each method takes and each parameter's type. This is important because, unlike PHP, SOAP is strictly typed. You cannot provide a string 1 when SOAP wants an integer 1. WSDL allows the SOAP extension to coerce PHP variables into the appropriate types without any action on your part.

Therefore, whenever possible, you want to know the location of the server's WSDL file. This makes it much easier to make SOAP requests. Example 14-1 shows how to make a query using WSDL.

Example 14-1. SOAP client using WSDL

```php
<?php
$wsdl_url =
```

```
        'http://services.xmethods.net/soap/urn:xmethods-delayed-quotes.wsdl';

$client = new SOAPClient($wsdl_url);

$quote = $client->getQuote('EBAY'); // eBay, Inc.
print $quote;
?>
31.49
```

From XMethods's web site, you know that the WSDL file for this service is at *http://services.xmethods.net/soap/urn:xmethods-delayed-quotes.wsdl*.

You now instantiate a new SOAPClient object by passing $wsdl_url, the location of the WSDL file, to the constructor. This returns a client object, $client, that you use to make SOAP requests.

The constructor creates a SOAP client, but you still need to make the actual query itself, which is called getQuote( ). It takes one argument, the stock ticker. Pass your stock ticker, in this case EBAY, directly to the method.

When you call $client->getQuote(10001), the SOAP extension converts the PHP string EBAY to a SOAP message written in XML and sends an HTTP request to the XMethods server. After XMethods receives and processes your query, it replies with a SOAP message of its own. The SOAP extension listens for this response and parses the XML into a PHP object, which is then returned by the method and stored in $quote.

The $quote variable now holds the current stock price of the EBAY stock. Right now it's trading at $31.49 a share.

See Also

Recipe 14.3 for making SOAP requests without WSDL; Recipe 15.2 for more on SOAP servers; the ext/soap documentation at *http://www.php.net/soap*; *Programming Web Services with SOAP* by Doug Tidwell, James Snell, and Pavel Kulchenko (O'Reilly).

14.3 Calling a SOAP Method Without WSDL

Problem

You want to send a SOAP request to a service that does not expose a WSDL file, so you must specify the information usually provided there yourself.

Solution

Pass a null value for the location of the WSDL, and the main service settings, such as location and namespace URI, in the options array:

```
<?php
$opts = array('location' => 'http://64.124.140.30:9090/soap',
              'uri'      => 'urn:xmethods-delayed-quotes',
```

```
$client = new SOAPClient(null, $opts);
?>
```

Make requests using the __soapCall( ) method, passing the method name as the first parameter, and an array of method arguments as the second:

```
$quote = $client->__soapCall('getQuote', array('EBAY')); // eBay, Inc.

print $quote;
31.49
```

Discussion

Since you're not using WSDL, pass null as the first argument to SOAPClient. This tells the SOAP extension that you're passing the details about the web service in the second parameter of options.

This information is stored as an array. At a minimum, you must provide two entries: the URL where the SOAP server is located and the namespace URI that identifies the service. For example:

```
<?php
$opts = array('location' => 'http://64.124.140.30:9090/soap',
              'uri'      => 'urn:xmethods-delayed-quotes',
$client = new SOAPClient(null, $opts);
?>
```

The server's URL is the location element; here, the server is at *http://64.124.140.30:9090/soap*. The server's namespace is set using the uri element. This is urn:xmethods-delayed-quotes.

Now you have a SOAP client, but with a non-WSDL-based client, you can't directly invoke SOAP methods on the $client object. Instead, you reference the __soapCall( ) method, passing the method name as your first argument and an array of parameters as the second:

```
<?php
$quote = $client->__soapCall('getQuote', array('EBAY')); // eBay, Inc.

print $quote;
?>
31.49
```

Since the SOAP client no longer knows how many parameters to expect, you must bundle your parameters to __soapCall( ) inside of an array. Therefore, the stock quote is now passed as array('EBAY') instead of 'EBAY'.

This code is more complex than the WSDL solution, and it even takes advantage of some default SOAP settings assumed by SOAPClient. This interface for calling SOAP methods is also less elegant.

However, this is the only way to pass or read additional information, such as SOAP headers.

See Also

Recipe 14.2 for making SOAP requests with WSDL; Recipe 15.2 for more on SOAP servers; the ext/soap documentation at *http://www.php.net/soap*; *Programming Web Services with SOAP*, by Doug Tidwell, James Snell, and Pavel Kulchenko (O'Reilly).

14.4 Debugging SOAP Requests

Problem

Your SOAP request is not working as expected, but you're not sure why.

Solution

Enable the `trace` option when you create the `SOAPClient`:

```php
<?php
$opts = array('trace' => true);
$client = new SOAPClient($wsdl_url, $opts);
?>
```

Now you can access data sent across the wire:

```php
<?php
$response = $client->getQuote('EBAY');

// going...
print $client->__getRequestHeaders() . "\n";
print $client->__getRequest() . "\n";

// and coming...
print $client->__getReponseHeaders() . "\n";
print $client->__getRequest() . "\n";
?>
```

Discussion

SOAP requests can be difficult to debug. When all else fails, it can be necessary to visually inspect the actual HTTP and XML data being sent back and across forth the wire.

This can be tricky when the data is secured over SSL or you don't control the server. In these cases, it's easiest to ask the ext/soap extension to give you a complete accounting of everything sent and received.

First, you must enable the `trace` option. This tells the extension to store this information for later retrieval:

```php
<?php
$opts = array('trace' => true);
$client = new SOAPClient($wsdl_url, $opts);
?>
```

Now whenever you make a request, the most recent request data is available through four functions: two handle the outgoing request from PHP, and another handling the incoming response from the server:

```php
<?php
$response = $client->getQuote('EBAY');

// going...
print $client->__getRequestHeaders() . "\n";
print $client->__getRequest() . "\n";

// and coming...
print $client->__getReponseHeaders() . "\n";
print $client->__getRequest() . "\n";
?>
```

Now you can inspect the data to see what appears to be the problem. Usually, the SOAP envelope contains the wrong XML. It's well-formed; it's just not laid out how the SOAP server expects it.

At this level, it can be very helpful to have a few sample SOAP requests and replies that you know are valid. You can then attempt to reconstruct those requests using ext/soap one section at a time.

Debugging at this level can require an understanding of HTTP, XML, XML namespaces, XML Schema, SOAP, and WSDL. In particular, you may end up with two XML documents that are semantically equivalent, but appear different due to XML namespaces, prefixes, and default namespaces. If you are absolutely positive two documents are similar, but one is not working, you may want to use cURL to explicitly post the two different XML files to the server.

14.5 Using Complex SOAP Types

Problem

You need to pass data structures more complicated than strings, integers, and other simple types. Instead, you need to pass arrays and objects.

Solution

Pass the data as an associative array:

```php
$args = array('ticker' => array('EBAY', 'YHOO', 'GOOG'));

$client->getQuotes($args);
```

Discussion

It can be tricky figuring out how to map PHP data structures into the XML that's described in the WSDL—especially since the premise of SOAP is that general consumers of a SOAP service shouldn't be worrying about the underlying XML.

The ext/soap extension does a pretty good job of doing the right thing of properly converting data. However, sometimes you need to get down and dirty and read the WSDL yourself, or see if the service publishes a few SOAP examples that reveal the XML that it's expecting.

As a rule of thumb, when you're expected to pass multiple elements of the same name at the same level, such as:

```
<ticker>EBAY</ticker>
<ticker>YHOO</ticker>
<ticker>GOOG</ticker>
```

You should define an array containing a key of `ticker` and a value of another array. This array should contain the data that needs to get wrapped around `<ticker>` tags.

See Also

Recipe 14.6 for setting SOAP types.

14.6 Setting SOAP Types

Problem

You need to explicitly set an XML Schema type, but there's no way to tell ext/soap how to set that value through a normal PHP data structure.

Solution

Create a `SOAPVar` and pass the type and namespace in the constructor:

```
$ns = 'https://adwords.google.com/api/adwords/v2';
$job = new SOAPVar($data, SOAP_ENC_OBJECT, 'CustomReportJob', $ns);
$response = $client->scheduleReportJob(array('job' => $job));
```

This creates XML that looks like:

```
<ns1:job xsi:type="ns1:CustomReportJob">
...
</ns1:job>
```

Where the `ns1` namespace prefix is `https://adwords.google.com/api/adwords/v2`.

Discussion

The SOAP extension exposes a number of classes to help you create the data that you pass into SOAP clients. These are rarely necessary when you're using a WSDL file. However, sometimes it's unavoidable.

One such case is when you must set an XML Schema type attribute. SOAP uses XML Schema as its behind-the-scenes way of encoding data using XML. One feature of XML Schema is the ability to define the type of structure. Normally, this is one of the built-in XML Schema types, such as a string, integer, or object. However, you can extend XML Schema to create custom types.

When a service requires a custom type, you must set it using the SOAPVar class. This class takes six parameters. The first four are most important here. They are the data to be sent, the general class of XML Schema type, the name of the value assigned to the xsi:type attribute, and the namespace that value lives in.

For example, here's a piece of code that creates a CustomReportJob for the Google AdWords reporting web services:

```
$ns = 'https://adwords.google.com/api/adwords/v2';
$job = new SOAPVar($data, SOAP_ENC_OBJECT, 'CustomReportJob', $ns);
$response = $client->scheduleReportJob(array('job' => $job));
```

You can ignore the specific details as to what information is actually being passed into the service (it's stored in $data), or that it's an object (so you pass in SOAP_ENC_OBJECT as the second parameter). They're important, but not relevant to the XML Schema type.

For that, you must look at the third and fourth parameters to the SOAPVar constructor: 'CustomReportJob' and $ns.

In this example, you're creating a job of type CustomReportJob that lives under the XML namespace https://adwords.google.com/api/adwords/v2, which is the value of $ns.

Now when ext/soap serializes the data into XML, it adds the necessary attribute:

```
<ns1:job xsi:type="ns1:CustomReportJob">
...
</ns1:job>
```

Depending on the number of XML namespaces your code is using, you may or may not get the same prefix of ns1. The specific prefix string doesn't matter, what *does* matter is that your prefix is mapped to https://adwords.google.com/api/adwords/v2 in the SOAP-Envelope element, as it is here:

```
<SOAP-ENV:Envelope
    xmlns:SOAP-ENV="http://schemas.xmlsoap.org/soap/envelope/"
    xmlns:ns1="https://adwords.google.com/api/adwords/v2"
    xmlns:xsi="http://www.w3.org/2001/XMLSchema-instance">
```

See Also

Recipe 14.5 for using complex SOAP types.

14.7 Using SOAP Headers

Problem

You need to create a SOAP header and pass it along with your request. This is often a place where a service requires authentication credentials or other information not directly related to the request.

Solution

Use the `SOAPHeader` class to create the header.

To use the same headers for all requests to a service, call `__setSoapHeaders( )`:

```
$client = new SOAPClient('http://www.example.com/service.wsdl');

$username = new SOAPHeader('urn:service-namespace', 'Username', 'elvis');
$password = new SOAPHeader('urn:service-namespace', 'Password', 'the-king');

$headers = array($username, $password);

$client->__setSoapHeaders($headers);
```

You can also pass in headers on a per-call basis as the fourth argument to `__soapCall( )`:

```
$client = new SOAPClient('http://www.example.com/service.wsdl');

$username = new SOAPHeader('urn:service-namespace', 'Username', 'elvis');
$password = new SOAPHeader('urn:service-namespace', 'Password', 'the-king');

$headers = array($username, $password);

$client->__soapCall($function, $args, $options, $headers);
```

This creates XML that looks like this:

```
<SOAP-ENV:Header>
    <ns2:Username>elvis</ns2:Username>
    <ns2:Password>the-king</ns2:Password>
</SOAP-ENV:Header>
```

The namespace prefix may vary, but it will be mapped to the `urn:service-namespace` namespace URI.

Discussion

The SOAP envelope is divided into two parts, a SOAP header and a SOAP body. This division is similar to how HTTP has a header and a body. Most of the time you only need to access the body, but sometimes you also need to set headers, too.

The ext/soap extension does an excellent job making it simple to pass in data that's part of the SOAP body. However, while it supports everything you need to create SOAP headers, it doesn't make it easy.

Depending on the design of the SOAP headers, it can be of varying difficulty to create what you need. When all you need is data wrapped around elements, create SOAP Header objects and package them in an array:

```
$client = new SOAPClient('http://www.example.com/service.wsdl');

$username = new SOAPHeader('urn:service-namespace', 'Username', 'elivs');
$password = new SOAPHeader('urn:service-namespace', 'Password', 'the-king');

$headers = array($username, $password);
```

These headers can then be added on all requests for a particular SOAP client instance or on a per-call basis:

```
$client = new SOAPClient('http://www.example.com/service.wsdl');

// Use __setSoapHeaders() to add header to *all* requests
$client->__setSoapHeaders($headers);

// Or do it on a per-call basis
$client->__soapCall($function, $args, $options, $headers);
```

This adds the following XML to your request:

```
<SOAP-ENV:Header>
    <ns2:Username>elivs</ns2:Username>
    <ns2:Password>the-king</ns2:Password>
</SOAP-ENV:Header>
```

In your case, the namespace prefix may be something other than ns2, but it will be mapped to the urn:service-namespace namespace URI.

See Also

Recipe 15.6 for processing SOAP headers and Recipe 15.7 for sending SOAP headers from a SOAP server.

14.8 Using Authentication with SOAP

Problem

You need to authenticate your SOAP requests using HTTP Basic Authentication.

Solution

Pass a username and password in via the options array by setting the login and pass word keys:

```
$options = array('login'    => 'elvis',
                 'password' => 'the-king');

$client = new SOAPClient('http://www.example.com/service.wsdl',
                         $options);
```

Discussion

There are a number of ways to handle authentication within SOAP requests. A few popular ways are HTTP Basic Authentication, placing data inside the SOAP header, and using the WS-* specifications, including WS-Security.

To make ext/soap add HTTP Basic Authentication credentials to every request, pass your username and password in as options when you create the SOAP client:

```php
<?php
$options = array('login' => 'elvis',
                 'password' => 'the-king');

$client = new SOAPClient('http://www.example.com/service.wsdl',
                         $options);
?>
```

Now every request will have an additional HTTP header of `Authorization`.

If your service requires data set in the SOAP request header, see Recipe 14.7 for details on handling that.

As of this writing, you cannot use any XML Security specifications with ext/soap. However, Rob Richards is working on it. For more information, check out *http://www.cdatazone.org/index.php?/archives/9-WSSE-and-extsoap.html*.

See Also

Recipe 15.8 for handling SOAP authentication in a SOAP server.

14.9 Redefining an Endpoint

Problem

The WSDL file defines an endpoint for the service, but you need to change it to another URL. This happens when the service has testing and production sites, or requires you to pass additional query arguments as part of the URL.

Solution

If you want the same endpoint for all requests, specify a new `location` to the constructor in the options array:

```php
<?php
$options = array('location' => 'http://www.example.com/testing-endpoint');

$client = new SOAPClient('http://www.example.com/service.wsdl',
                         $options);
?>
```

If it changes from request to request, use the `__soapCall( )` method to pass a request-specific `location`:

```php
<?php
$client = new SOAPClient('http://www.example.com/service.wsdl');

$method = 'getTemp';
$args = array('94114');
$options = array('location' => 'http://www.example.com/endpoint?method=getTemp');

$request = $client->__soapCall($method, $args, $options);
?>
```

Discussion

In most cases, you never need to modify the endpoint specified in the WSDL. Most services have a singular fixed endpoint, so they put it in their WSDL and you're done.

However, some sites require you to modify the endpoint location depending on a number of conditions. For example, they have both testing and production sites. This is not an issue with read-only services, but when you can both read and write to a site, it's important to have a sandbox environment where you can test your code.

For simplicity, the site may only publish a single WSDL file that targets the production server by default, and require you to switch it to point at the testing server during development. In these cases, it's easiest to specify the new location as a one-time configuration option in the SOAPClient constructor:

```php
<?php
$options = array('location' => 'http://www.example.com/testing-endpoint');

$client = new SOAPClient('http://www.example.com/service.wsdl',
                         $options);
?>
```

The SOAPClient object takes an array of options as its second parameter. When you set the location element, it will override what's in the WSDL and use that URL as the location for all requests.

This method works best when you need to hit against the same URL for all requests. However, sometimes the endpoint can vary from request to request. For example, you may need to put the method name or other information within the URL itself.

Placing data in the URL allows the service to more efficiently route the request because it doesn't need to parse the XML document before dispatching it. For example, a large web service could have one pool of machines to handle searches and another pool of machines to handle updates. It can process requests faster if it can hand off the SOAP request directly to the proper pool simply by examining the URL.

This requires you to modify each request on a one-off basis. Therefore, you cannot use SOAPClient's method overriding abstraction. Instead, you need to use the __soapCall( ) method directly, passing the method name, arguments, and options:

```php
<?php
$client = new SOAPClient('http://www.example.com/service.wsdl');
```

```
$method = 'getTemp';
$args = array('94114');
$options = array('location' => 'http://www.example.com/endpoint?method=getTemp');

$request = $client->__soapCall($method, $args, $options);
?>
```

This code is equivalent to:

```
<?php
$client = new SOAPClient('http://www.example.com/service.wsdl');

$request = $client->getTemp('94114');
?>
```

However, it also changes the endpoint URL to point at *http://www.example.com/end point?method=getTemp* instead of the WSDL default.

To preserve the simple calling convention, subclass SOAPClient for your service and provide a custom __call( ) method:

```
<?php
class TemperatureService extends SOAPClient {
    public function __call($method, $args) {

        // Modify endpoint to include method name
        // Assumes consistent naming convention
        $location = "http://www.example.com/endpoint?method={$method}";
        $options = array('location' => $location);

        return $this->__soapCall($function, $args, array('location' => $location));
    }
}

$client = new TemperatureService('http://www.example.com/service.wsdl');

$request = $client->getTemp('94114');
?>
```

14.10 Catching SOAP Faults

Problem

You want to handle a SOAP server returning an error in the form of a SOAP fault. This allows you to fail gracefully when there's a problem with your request or the service.

Solution

Wrap your code inside a try/catch block and check for a SOAPFault:

```
<?php
try {
    $wsdl_url =
        'http://www.example.com/TemperatureService.wsdl';
```

```php
    $client = new SOAPClient($wsdl_url);

    $temp = $client->getTemp('New York'); // This should be a Zip Code
    print $temp;
} catch (SOAPFault $exception) {
    print $exception;
}
?>
```

Or configure your SOAPClient not to use exceptions, and check the return value of
is_soap_fault( ):

```php
<?php
$wsdl_url =
    'http://www.example.com/TemperatureService.wsdl';

// Disable exceptions
$opts = array('exceptions' => 0);
$client = new SOAPClient($wsdl_url, $opts);

$temp = $client->getTemp('New York'); // This should be a zip code
if (is_soap_fault($temp)) {
    print $exception;
} else {
    print $temp;
}
?>
```

Discussion

When a SOAP server generates an error, it returns a SOAP fault. This can be a mistake
on your part, such as calling a method that doesn't exist or passing the incorrect number
(or type) of parameters, or it can be a server error. For instance, the service lacks tem-
perature information for a particular zip code, but for reasons external to your SOAP
request.

The SOAP extension transforms SOAP faults into PHP exceptions, as shown in Example 14-2.

Example 14-2. Detecting SOAP faults with exceptions

```php
<?php
try {
    $wsdl_url =
        'http://www.example.com/TemperatureService.wsdl';

    $client = new SOAPClient($wsdl_url);

    $temp = $client->getTemp('New York'); // This should be a zip code
    print $temp;
} catch (SOAPFault $exception) {
    print $exception;
}
?>
```

```
SOAPFault exception: [SOAP-ENV:Server] Zip Code New York is unknown.
  in /www/www.example.com/soap.php:8
Stack trace:
#0 /www/www.example.com/soap.php(8): SOAPClient->getTemp('getTemp', Array)
#1 {main}
```

Since the server requires a zip code but Example 14-2 passed New York, the server returned a SOAP fault. Printing the exception gives you, among other debugging information, the error Zip Code New York is unknown.

If you dislike exceptions, make SOAP handle faults via a return code by setting the exceptions configuration setting to 0. This is done in Example 14-3.

Example 14-3. Detecting SOAP faults without exceptions

```
<?php
$wsdl_url =
    'http://www.example.com/TemperatureService.wsdl';

// Disable exceptions
$opts = array('exceptions' => 0);
$client = new SOAPClient($wsdl_url, $opts);

$temp = $client->&gt;getTemp('New York'); // This should be a Zip Code
if (is_soap_fault($temp)) {
    print $exception;
} else {
    print $temp;
}
?>
SOAPFault exception: [SOAP-ENV:Server] Zip Code New York is unknown.
  in /www/www.example.com/soap.php:8
#0 {main}
```

To alter the default settings for a SOAPClient object, pass in an array as the second argument to the constructor. This is the same array that you use to specify information about non-WSDL servers.

When exceptions are disabled, $temp contains either the valid response or a SOAP fault. Check is_soap_fault( ) to discover if there's an error.

See Also

Recipe 15.5 for throwing SOAP faults from a SOAP server.

14.11 Mapping XML Schema Data Types to PHP Classes

Problem

You want to automatically convert a SOAP object to a PHP object.

Solution

Define a PHP class and tell the `SOAPClient` to map a SOAP object to it using the `class map` option:

```
class PHPStockType {}; // stub class

$opts = array('classmap' => array('StockType' => 'PHPStockType'));
$client = new SOAPClient($wsdl_url, $opts);
```

Now any `StockType` structure will be converted to a `PHPStockType`.

Discussion

Class mapping can be very helpful in making SOAP objects easier to use. In particular, look to see where you can define a `__toString()` method to control how an object displays. It can also be useful to implement the `IteratorAggregate` and the `ArrayAccess` interfaces.

For example, a stock quote object may return a large amount of data about a stock: the current price, the 52-week high and low prices, the ticker symbol, etc. However, the key piece of data is the current price, so you may want to implement code such as this:

```php
<?php
class PHPStockType {
    public function __toString() {
        return (string) $this->currentPrice;
    }
}
?>
```

All the other data is still available, but when you print out the object, you get the most important value.

14.12 Calling an XML-RPC Method

Problem

You want to be an XML-RPC client and make requests of a server. XML-RPC lets PHP make function calls to web servers, even if they don't use PHP. The retrieved data is then automatically converted to PHP variables for use in your application.

Solution

Use PHP's built-in XML-RPC extension with some helper functions. PHP bundles the *xmlrpc-epi* extension. Unfortunately, xmlrpc-epi does not have any native C functions for taking an XML-RPC-formatted string and making a request. However, the folks behind xmlrpc-epi have a series of helper functions written in PHP available for download at *http://xmlrpc-epi.sourceforge.net/*. The only file used here is the one named *utils.php*, which is located in *sample/utils*. To install it, just copy that file to a location where PHP can find it in its `include_path`.

Here's client code that calls a function on an XML-RPC server that returns state names:

```php
<?php
// this is the default file name from the package
// kept here to avoid confusion over the file name
require 'utils.php';

// server settings
$host = 'betty.userland.com';
$port = 80;
$uri = '/RPC2';

// request settings
// pass in a number from 1-50; get the nth state in alphabetical order
// 1 is Alabama, 50 is Wyoming
$method = 'examples.getStateName';
$args = array(32); // data to be passed

// make associative array out of these variables
$request = compact('host', 'port', 'uri', 'method', 'args');

// this function makes the XML-RPC request
$result = xu_rpc_http_concise($request);

print "I love $result!\n";
?>
```

Discussion

XML-RPC, a format created by Userland Software, allows you to make a request to a web server using HTTP. The request itself is a specially formatted XML document. As a client, you build up an XML request to send that fits with the XML-RPC specification. You then send it to the server, and the server replies with an XML document. You then parse the XML to find the results. In the Solution, the XML-RPC server returns a state name, so the code prints:

```
I love New York!
```

Unlike earlier implementations of XML-RPC, which were coded in PHP, the current bundled extension is written in C, so there is a significant speed increase in processing time. To enable this extension while configuring PHP, add `--with-xmlrpc`.

The server settings tell PHP which web site to contact to make the request. The `$host` is the hostname of the machine; `$port` is the port the web server is running on, which is usually port 80; and `$uri` is the pathname to the XML-RPC server you wish to contact. This request is equivalent to *http://betty.userland.com:80/RPC2*. If no port is given, the function defaults to port 80, and the default URI is the web server root, /.

The request settings are the function to call and the data to pass to the function. The method `examples.getStateName` takes an integer from 1 to 50 and returns a string with the name of the U.S. state, in alphabetical order. In XML-RPC, method names can have periods, while in PHP, they cannot. If they could, the PHP equivalent to passing 32 as the argument to the XML-RPC call to examples.getStateName is calling a function named examples.getStateName( ):

```
examples.getStateName(32);
```

In XML-RPC, it looks like this:

```
<?xml version='1.0' encoding="iso-8859-1" ?>
<methodCall>
<methodName>examples.getStateName</methodName>
<params><param><value>
   <int>32</int>
  </value>
 </param>
</params>
</methodCall>
```

The server settings and request information go into a single associative array that is passed to xu_rpc_http_concise( ). As a shortcut, call compact( ), which is identical to:

```
$request = array('host'   => $host,
                 'port'   => $port,
                 'uri'    => $uri,
                 'method' => $method,
                 'args'   => $args);
```

The xu_rpc_http_concise( ) function makes the XML-RPC call and returns the results. Since the return value is a string, you can print $results directly. If the XML-RPC call returns multiple values, xu_rpc_http_concise( ) returns an array.

There are 10 different parameters that can be passed in the array to xu_rpc_http_concise( ), but the only one that's required is host. The parameters are shown in Table 14-1.

Table 14-1. Parameters for xu_rpc_http_concise( )

Name	Description
host	Server hostname
uri	Server URI (default /)
port	Server port (default 80)
method	Name of method to call
args	Arguments to pass to method
debug	Debug level (0 to 2: 0 is none, 2 is lots)
timeout	Number of seconds before timing out the request; a value of 0 means never timeout
user	Username for Basic HTTP Authentication, if necessary
pass	Password for Basic HTTP Authentication, if necessary
secure	Use SSL for encrypted transmissions; requires PHP to be built with SSL support (pass any true value)

See Also

Recipe 15.9 for more on XML-RPC servers; PHP helper functions for use with the xmlrpc-epi extension at *http://xmlrpc-epi.sourceforge.net/*; *Programming Web Services with XML-RPC* by Simon St.Laurent, Joe Johnston, and Edd Dumbill (O'Reilly); more on XML-RPC at *http://www.xml-rpc.com*.

14.13 Using Authentication with XML-RPC

Problem

You need to pass a username and password along with your XML-RPC request.

Solution

Set the user and pass options and call the xu_rpc_http_concise( ) method:

```php
<?php
require 'utils.php';

// ... other request parameters set here
$user = 'elvis';
$pass = 'the-king';

// make associative array out of these variables
$request = compact('host', 'port', 'uri', 'method', 'args', 'user', 'pass');

// this function makes the XML-RPC request
$result = xu_rpc_http_concise($request);
?>
```

Discussion

The XML-RPC library does not support HTTP Basic Authentication out of the box. However, the *utils.php* file mentioned in Recipe 14.12, will create the correct HTTP header for you when you pass in user and pass elements to xu_rpc_http_concise( ). For instance:

```php
<?php
require 'utils.php';

// ... other request parameters set here
$user = 'elvis';
$pass = 'the-king';

// make associative array out of these variables
$request = compact('host', 'port', 'uri', 'method', 'args', 'user', 'pass');

// this function makes the XML-RPC request
$result = xu_rpc_http_concise($request);
?>
```

In this code, the user is `elvis` and the pass is `the-king`. These variables are turned into an associative array, `$request`, along with the other necessary request data. (The other data is omitted for clarity.)

When you pass this information to `xu_rpc_http_concise( )`, the helper function will base64-encode the data and construct the header for you.

Assuming you have the correct credentials, the rest of the transaction should operate exactly the same as nonauthenticated requests.

CHAPTER 15

Building Web Services

15.0 Introduction

This chapter covers building web services. If you're unfamiliar with the fundamental concepts of web services, including REST, SOAP, and XML-RPC, jump back a chapter and read through Chapter 14. It provides the building blocks for the web services servers described here.

Recipe 15.1 covers building a REST method. With a REST server, you accept an HTTP request, process the incoming data, and reply, usually with XML.

From there, the chapter moves to SOAP. Recipes 15.2 and 15.3 show how to serve a SOAP method with and without input arguments.

Recipe 15.4 breaks the bad news that PHP cannot automatically generate WSDL files from PHP classes, while Recipe 15.5 shows how to throw SOAP faults.

SOAP headers are the topic of the next two recipes. First, in Recipe 15.6, you learn how to process a SOAP header. Then, Recipe 15.7 shows how to generate a SOAP header.

The SOAP portion concludes with a discussion on how to combine authentication with SOAP in Recipe 15.8.

The chapter concludes with a Recipe 15.9, a recipe on serving XML-RPC requests.

15.1 Serving a REST Method

Problem

You want to expose a server via REST. This allows people to make HTTP requests and receive XML in response.

Solution

The most basic REST server is a page that accepts query arguments and returns XML:

```php
<?php
// data
$music_database = <<<_MUSIC_
<?xml version="1.0" encoding="utf-8" ?>
<music>
    <album id="1">
        <name>Revolver</name>
        <artist>The Beatles</artist>
    </album>
    <!-- 941 more albums here -->
    <album id="943">
        <name>Miles And Coltrane</name>
        <artist>Miles Davis</artist>
        <artist>John Coltrane</artist>
    </album>
</music>
_MUSIC_;

// load data
$s = simplexml_load_string($music_database);

// query data
$artist = addslashes($_GET['artist']);
$query = "/music/album[artist = '$artist']";
$albums = $s->xpath($query);

// display query results as XML
print "<?xml version=\"1.0\" encoding=\"utf-8\" ?>\n";
print "<music>\n\t";
foreach ($albums as $a) {
    print $a->asXML();
}
print "\n</music>";
?>
```

When this page is stored at *http://api.example.org/music*, an HTTP GET request to *http://api.example.org/music?artist=The+Beatles* returns:

```xml
<?xml version="1.0" encoding="utf-8" ?>
<music>
    <album id="1">
        <name>Revolver</name>
        <artist>The Beatles</artist>
    </album>
</music>
```

Discussion

At its most basic level, serving a REST request is no different than processing an HTML form. The key difference is that you're replying with XML instead of HTML.

Input parameters come in as query parameters, so PHP parses them into $_GET. You then process the values in $_GET to determine the correct query for your data, which you use to retrieve the proper records to return.

For instance, Example 15-1 uses code that queries an XML document using XPath for all the albums put out by the artist passed in via the `artist` get variable.

Example 15-1. Implementing a REST query server

```php
<?php
// data
$music_database = <<<_MUSIC_
<?xml version="1.0" encoding="utf-8" ?>
<music>
    <album id="1">
        <name>Revolver</name>
        <artist>The Beatles</artist>
    </album>
    <!-- 941 more albums here -->
    <album id="943">
        <name>Miles And Coltrane</name>
        <artist>Miles Davis</artist>
        <artist>John Coltrane</artist>
    </album>
</music>
_MUSIC_;

// load data
$s = simplexml_load_string($music_database);

// query data
$artist = addslashes($_GET['artist']);
$query = "/music/album[artist = '$artist']";
$albums = $s->xpath($query);

// display query results as XML
print "<?xml version=\"1.0\" encoding=\"utf-8\" ?>\n";
print "<music>\n\t";
foreach ($albums as $a) {
    print $a->asXML();
}
print "\n</music>";
?>
```

For simplicity, Example 15-1 uses XML as the data source and XPath as the query language. This eliminates the need to convert the results to XML. It's likely that you will query a database using SQL. That's okay! For the purposes of REST, the particular backend system is irrelevant.

The important part is outputting your results as XML. In this case, since the data started as XML, you can wrap it inside a root element and echo it without any conversion:

```php
<?php
// display query results as XML
print "<?xml version=\"1.0\" encoding=\"utf-8\" ?>\n";
print "<music>\n\t";
foreach ($albums as $a) {
    print $a->asXML();
}
```

```
    print "\n</music>";
    ?>
```

This gives you:

```
<?xml version="1.0" encoding="utf-8" ?>
<music>
    <album id="1">
        <name>Revolver</name>
        <artist>The Beatles</artist>
    </album>
</music>
```

Now your work is done and it's up to the REST client to process the XML you returned, using the XML-processing tool of its choice. In PHP 5, this is frequently SimpleXML.

It's useful to publish a data schema for your REST responses. This lets people know what to expect from your replies and lets them validate the data to ensure its properly formatted. XML Schema and RelaxNG are two good choices for your schema.

REST isn't restricted to read-only operations, such as search. REST supports reading and writing data, including adding, updating, and deleting records.

There are two popular ways to expose this complete set of features:

1. Accepting an additional parameter on the query string.
2. Using HTTP verbs, such as post and put.

Both options are relatively straightforward to implement. This first is marginally easier, on both you and REST clients, but limits the size of the data you can accept and has potentially negative side effects.

When you use get for everything, it's very easy for people to construct requests because they can use just standard URLs with a query string. This is a familiar operation and people can even test their code by replicating their requests through the location bars on their web browsers.

However, many web servers place a limit on the size of the URLs they can process. People often need to pass large amounts of data when they add a new record. There's no such limitation on the size of post data. Therefore, get is not a good choice for adding or updating records.

Additionally, according to the HTTP specification, get requests are not supposed to alter backend data. You should design your site so that when a person makes two identical get requests, she gets two identical replies.

When you allow people to add, update, or delete records via get, you're violating this principle of HTTP. While this is normally not a problem, it can bite you when you're not looking. For instance, automated scripts, such as the Google spider, try to index your pages. If you expose destructive operations as URLs in the href attribute inside of HTML anchor tags, the spider may follow them, and delete information from your database in the process.

The initial release of the Google Web Accelerator caused problems on some web sites that used query-string-less URLs for delete operations. A discussion of the issue is at *http://radar.oreilly.com/archives/2005/05/google_web_acce_1.html*.

Still, adding another **get** parameter is straightforward and requires minimal edits, as shown in Example 15-2.

Example 15-2. Implementing a REST server with multiple operations

```php
<?php
// Add more action specific logic inside switch()
switch ($_GET['action']) {
case 'search':
    $action = 'search';
    break;
case 'add':
    $action = 'add';
    break;
case 'update':
    $action = 'update';
    break;
case 'delete':
    $action = 'delete';
    break;
default:
    // invalid action
    exit();
}

// Music Database XML document moved to file
$s = simplexml_load_string('music_database.xml');

if ($action == 'search') {
    $artist = $_GET['artist'];
    $query = "/music/album[artist = '$artist']";
    $albums = $s->xpath($query);

    // Display results here
} elseif ($action == 'add') {
    $artist = $_GET['artist'];
    $album = $_GET['album'];

    // Insert new node from input data
}

// ... other actions here
?>
```

At the top of the page, check `$_GET['action']` for a valid set of actions, and set the `$action` variable when you find one.

Then, load in the data source (which is where the XML flat file is less of a good choice, since you don't get locking out of the box like you do with databases).

Now you can perform your operation. For a search, query your data and print it out, just like in Example 15-1.

For an addition, you should update the data store, and then reply with a brief message saying everything succeeded. For example:

```
<?xml version="1.0" encoding="UTF-8"?>
<response code="200">Album added</response>
```

Alternatively, if there's a failure, send an error message:

```
<?xml version="1.0" encoding="UTF-8"?>
<response code="400">Invalid request</response>
```

While most people use this method of checking an action query parameter to decide what action to take, your other option is to use HTTP verbs, such as get, post, put, and delete. This is more "true" REST style, and allows you to not only comfortably process larger requests, but is also safer because it's far less likely that your data will be accidentally deleted.

Table 15-1 shows the general link between between SQL commands and HTTP verbs.

Table 15-1. SQL commands, HTTP verbs, and REST actions

SQL	REST
CREATE	POST
SELECT	GET
UPDATE	PUT
DELETE	DELETE

To use HTTP verbs, check the value of `$_SERVER['REQUEST_METHOD']` instead of `$_GET['action']`, as shown in Example 15-3.

Example 15-3. Implementing a REST server that uses HTTP verbs

```php
<?php
// Add more action specific logic inside switch()

// Convert to UPPER CASE
$request_method = strtoupper($_SERVER['REQUEST_METHOD']);

switch ($request_method) {
case 'GET':
    $action = 'search';
    break;
case 'POST':
    $action = 'add';
    break;
case 'PUT':
    $action = 'update';
    break;
case 'DELETE':
    $action = 'delete';
```

```
        break;
    default:
        // invalid action
        exit();
}

// ... other actions here
?>
```

Beyond switching to use the REQUEST_METHOD at the top of Example 15-3, you must also update your code to check the HTTP verb names of get, post, put, and delete. And you must now use $_POST instead of $_GET when the verb isn't get.

Remember that $_SERVER['REQUEST_METHOD'] is just as secure as $_GET['action'], which is to say not secure at all. Both of these values are easy to set, so if you're exposing sensitive data or allowing operations that can destroy data, make sure that the person making the request has permission to do so.

See Also

Recipe 14.1 for how to call REST methods; Recipe 9.1 for more on checking the value of the REQUEST_METHOD.

15.2 Serving a SOAP Method

Problem

You want to create a SOAP server to respond to SOAP requests.

Solution

Use ext/soap's SOAPServer class. Here's a server that returns the current date and time:

```
<?php
class pc_SOAP_return_time {
    public function return_time() {
        return date('Ymd\THis');
    }
}

$server = new SOAPServer(null, array('uri'=>'urn:pc_SOAP_return_time'));
$server->setClass('pc_SOAP_return_time');
$server->handle();
?>
```

Discussion

There are three steps to creating a SOAP server with ext/soap's SOAPServer class:

1. Create a class to process SOAP methods.

2. Create an instance of a SOAP server and associate the processing class with the instance.

3. Instruct the SOAP server to process the request and reply to the SOAP client.

The ext/soap SOAPServer class can use functions or classes to handle SOAP requests. Example 15-4 shows the pc_SOAP_return_time class, which has one method, return_time( ).

Example 15-4. pc_SOAP_return_time class

```
<?php
class pc_SOAP_return_time {
    public function return_time() {
        return date('Ymd\THis');
    }
}
?>
```

Once the class is defined, instantiate a SOAPServer object. If you have a WSDL file for your service, pass it as your first argument; otherwise, as in this case, pass null. The second argument contains your configuration options. Here, there's only uri, which specifies the SOAP server namespace. In Example 15-5, it's urn:pc_SOAP_return_time.

Example 15-5. Instantiating SOAPServer

```
<?php
$server = new SOAPServer(null, array('uri'=>'urn:pc_SOAP_return_time'));
?>
```

When ext/soap processes a SOAP request, it doesn't pay attention to the name of your PHP class, such as pc_SOAP_return_time. What really matters is the XML namespace, which you've just set as urn:pc_SOAP_return_time.

Next, call SOAPServer::setClass( ) with a class name. When a SOAP server receives a request for a method, it will try to call a class method with the same name:

```
<?php
$server->setClass('pc_SOAP_return_time');
$server->handle();
?>
```

Last, tell the server to respond to the request by calling SOAPServer::handle( ). The SOAPServer automatically processes the $GLOBALS['HTTP_RAW_POST_DATA'] variable, which is where PHP stores POST data.

If your SOAP request comes from another source, say an email message, you can pass that data to SOAPServer::handle( ):

```
<?php
$server->handle($soap_message_from_someplace_else);
?>
```

In both cases, the SOAPServer takes care of parsing the SOAP data and routing everything accordingly.

To call this procedure using an ext/soap client, use the code in Example 15-6.

Example 15-6. Getting the time using SOAP

```php
<?php
$opts = array('location' => 'http://api.example.org/getTime',
              'uri' => 'urn:pc_SOAP_return_time');

$client = new SOAPClient(null, $opts);

$result = $client->__soapCall('return_time', array());

print "The local time is $result.\n";
?>
```

This prints:

```
The local time is 20060816T083225.
```

Instead of binding an entire class, you can also associate an individual function:

```php
<?php
function return_time() {
    return date('Ymd\THis');
}

$server = new SOAPServer(null, array('uri'=>'urn:pc_SOAP_return_time'));
$server->addfunction('return_time');
$server->handle();
?>
```

You can call `SOAPServer::addFunction( )` with an array of function names to bind more than one function:

```php
<?php
$server = new SOAPServer(null, array('uri'=>'urn:pc_SOAP_return_time'));

// array of functions to expose
$functions = array('return_time', 'return_date');
$server->addfunction($functions);
?>
```

Another option is to bind all functions:

```php
<?php
$server = new SOAPServer(null, array('uri'=>'urn:pc_SOAP_return_time'));

// add *all* functions
$server->addfunction(SOAP_FUNCTIONS_ALL);
?>
```

This is *strongly* discouraged, as it's a giant security risk. You may accidentally include a function with secret information, which is then exposed since you're using `SOAP_FUNCTIONS_ALL`. You should *always* explicitly enumerate the functions you wish to expose on an opt-in basis.

If the method isn't labeled as `public` or isn't defined at all, such as `set_time`, the server replies with a SOAP fault, with a `faultstring` of `Function 'set_time' doesn't exist` and a `faultcode` of `SOAP-ENV:Server`.

To change this behavior, bind a class with a `__call( )` method:

```php
<?php
class pc_SOAP_Process_All_Methods {

    // Handle any undefined methods here
    public function __call($name, $args) {
        // ...
    }
}

$server = new SOAPServer(null, array('uri'=>'urn:pc_SOAP_Process_All_Methods'));
$server->setClass('pc_SOAP_Process_All_Methods');
$server->handle();
?>
```

If you build PHP with the zlib extension, `SOAPServer` will automatically support gzipped and compressed requests. It will uncompress the data before processing it.

See Also

Recipe 14.2 for calling a SOAP method; Recipe 15.3 for accepting arguments in a SOAP method; Recipe 15.5 for throwing SOAP faults; documentation on ext/soap at *http://www.php.net/soap*.

15.3 Accepting Arguments in a SOAP Method

Problem

You want your SOAP method to accept parameters.

Solution

Update the method prototype to include arguments:

```php
<?php
class pc_SOAP_return_time {
    public function return_time($tz = '') {
        // set the time zone based on the input
        if ($tz) { $my_tz = date_default_timezone_set($tz); }
        // get the new timestamp
        $date = date('Ymd\THis');
        // reset the time zone to default
        if ($tz) { date_default_timezone_set(ini_get('date.timezone')); }
        // return the timestamp
        return $date;
    }
}
```

```php
$server = new SOAPServer(null,array('uri'=>'urn:pc_SOAP_return_time'));
$server->setClass('pc_SOAP_return_time');
$server->handle();
?>
```

Discussion

The basics of serving SOAP requests are covered in Recipe 15.2. This recipe extends that example to demonstrate how to accept method arguments.

Read in parameters by altering the method prototype to include parameter names. Then modify the client request to include data for the additional arguments. Example 15-7 modifies the SOAP procedure to accept an optional time zone argument.

Example 15-7. Processing SOAP methods with parameters

```php
<?php
class pc_SOAP_return_time {
    public function return_time($tz = '') {
        // set the time zone based on the input
        if ($tz) { $my_tz = date_default_timezone_set($tz); }
        // get the new timestamp
        $date = date('Ymd\THis');
        // reset the time zone to default
        if ($tz) { date_default_timezone_set(ini_get('date.timezone')); }
        // return the timestamp
        return $date;
    }
}

$server = new SOAPServer(null,array('uri'=>'urn:pc_SOAP_return_time'));
$server->setClass('pc_SOAP_return_time');
$server->handle();
?>
```

The SOAP client can now pass in a tz option. Here it's Europe/Oslo:

```php
<?php
$opts = array('location' => 'http://api.example.org/getTime',
              'uri' => 'urn:pc_SOAP_return_time');

$client = new SOAPClient(null, $opts);

$result = $client->__soapCall('return_time', array('tz' => 'Europe/Oslo'));

print "The local time is $result.\n";
?>
```

With the new setting, the server returns a time nine hours ahead of the previous one:

```
The local time is 20060816T173225.
```

You can pass strings, numbers, arrays, and objects to a SOAP method. The ext/soap extension converts them from XML to native PHP data types.

See Also

Recipe 15.2 for processing SOAP requests without parameters.

15.4 Generating WSDL Automatically

Problem

You want to expose a set of methods via a SOAP web service. You want to automatically generate a WSDL file that describes this service.

Solution

The ext/soap extension does not support WSDL generation. However, there are a few other PHP scripts that you can use.

Discussion

Given the nature of SOAP, it's vital to provide clients with a WSDL file they can use to configure themselves for your server. Unfortunately, ext/soap does not support WSDL generation.

Therefore, you must either generate WSDL by hand from scratch, modify an existing document that supports a similar set of operations, or use an unofficial script, such as:

WSDL_Gen, by George Schlossnagle
> *http://www.schlossnagle.org/~george/blog/index.php?/archives/234-WSDLGeneration.html*

wsdl-writer, by Katy Coe based on code by David Griffin
> *http://www.djkaty.com/drupal/php-wsdl*

Web service helper, by David Kingma
> *http://jool.nl/new/*

None of these scripts supports the entire SOAP and WSDL specifications, and each one uses a slightly different syntax to accomplish its goal. You should investigate all of them to see if they do what you need and fit your programming styles.

See Also

The WSDL specification at *http://www.w3.org/TR/wsdl*.

15.5 Throwing SOAP Faults

Problem

You want to generate a SOAP fault, which is the mechanism SOAP uses to indicate errors.

Solution

Call the `SOAPServer::fault()` method:

```php
<?php
class pc_SOAP_return_time {
    public function return_time() {
        $date = date('Ymd\THis');
        if ($date === false) {
            $GLOBALS['server']->fault(1, 'Bad dates.');
        }
        return $date;
    }
}

$server = new SOAPServer(null,array('uri'=>'urn:pc_SOAP_return_time'));
$server->setClass('pc_SOAP_return_time');

?>
```

Or throw a `SOAPFault`:

```php
<?php
class pc_SOAP_return_time {
    public function return_time() {
        $date = date('Ymd\THis');
        if ($date === false) {
            throw new SOAPFault(1, 'Bad dates.');
        }
        return $date;
    }
}

$server = new SOAPServer(null,array('uri'=>'urn:pc_SOAP_return_time'));
$server->setClass('pc_SOAP_return_time');

?>
```

You can also `return` a `SOAPFault` instead of throwing it.

Discussion

The SOAP specification has a standard way of indicating errors: SOAP faults. SOAP faults are very similar to the OO concept of exceptions. In fact, ext/soap allows you to treat SOAP faults, from both a SOAP server and SOAP client perspective, in a very similar manner to how PHP handles exceptions.

While you can indicate SOAP faults in a number of ways, the easiest is to `throw` an instance of the `SOAPFault` class, passing an error code and an error string to the constructor, as shown in Example 15-8.

Example 15-8. Throwing a SOAP fault

```php
<?php
class pc_SOAP_return_time {
```

```
        public function return_time() {
            $date = date('Ymd\THis');
            if ($date === false) {
                throw new SOAPFault(1, 'Bad dates.');
            }
            return $date;
        }
    }

    $server = new SOAPServer(null, array('uri'=>'urn:pc_SOAP_return_time'));
    $server->setClass('pc_SOAP_return_time');

    $server->handle();
    }
    ?>
```

In Example 15-8, you throw a SOAPFault when date( ) returns false. The error code is 1, and in a moment of Indiana Jones–inspired whimsy, the error message is Bad dates..

These two values are mapped to the SOAP 1.1 specification's faultcode and fault string elements, respectively. At the time of this writing, there is not support for SOAP 1.2–style SOAP faults.

Normally, the error code is used to allow a program to process the error, while the error message is used to let a human understand what occurred—usually through a logfile or by printing it out.

Unlike HTTP and status codes, there is no convention for SOAP error codes. For example, the 500 block is not reserved for server errors. You have the freedom to make up whatever set of codes you want.

However, the SOAP extension will automatically set the HTTP status code to 500 when you issue a SOAP fault. This is required by the SOAP specification. You cannot use an HTTP status code other than 500.

Besides throwing a SOAPFault, you can also return one from your method, or invoke the SOAPServer::fault( ) method. These all generate the same SOAP fault data, so it's a matter of personal preference or coding situation.

Instead of using SOAPFault directly, you can also subclass it and use that class instead. This allows you to implement an integrated logging system, for example:

```
<?php
class pc_My_SOAPFault extends SOAPFault {
    public function __construct($code, $string) {
        parent::__construct($code, $string);
        error_log($this);
    }
}
?>
```

SOAP faults are automatically generated when you do something that generates an error, such as calling an undefined function.

See Also

Recipe 14.10 for catching SOAP faults in a SOAP client.

15.6 Processing a SOAP Header

Problem

You want to be able to read a SOAP header passed in from a SOAP in your SOAP server.

Solution

Bind a function or method with the same name as the SOAP header:

```
class pc_SOAP_return_time {
    public function set_timezone($tz) {
        date_default_timezone_set($tz);
    }

    public function return_time() {
        return date('Ymd\THis');
    }
}
```

When ext/soap gets a SOAP header named `set_timezone`, it calls the `set_timezone( )` method. Data placed inside the `set_timezone` element is passed as an argument.

SOAP headers are processed before the SOAP body.

Discussion

Like HTTP, SOAP lets you define both a SOAP header and a SOAP body element. While you must define a SOAP body, SOAP headers are optional. A SOAP header usually contains information such as authentication credentials or other data that's applicable to all requests you make to the service, instead of being specifically related to that particular method you're invoking.

When ext/soap sees a client request with a SOAP header, it will first try to invoke a function with that name. When that function ends, it will then invoke the function specified in the SOAP body. This allows you to take care of any pre-request work based on SOAP header data. For example, if there are authentication credentials in the header, you can validate the user or throw a SOAP fault if he's unauthorized.

Example 15-9 shows a version of the `return_time` SOAP server from Example 15-7 that lets you modify the time zone by setting a SOAP header instead of passing it as an optional parameter.

Example 15-9. Processing a SOAP header

```
<?php
class pc_SOAP_return_time {
```

```
        public function set_timezone($tz) {
            date_default_timezone_set($tz);
        }

        public function return_time() {
            return date('Ymd\THis');
        }
    }

    $server = new SOAPServer(null, array('uri'=>'urn:pc_SOAP_return_time'));
    $server->setClass('pc_SOAP_return_time');

    $server->handle();
    ?>
```

Example 15-9 supports two methods: set_timezone( ) and return_time( ). In practice, the first method is supposed to be invoked via a SOAP header and the second from the SOAP body, but ext/soap doesn't really distinguish between the two in a programmatic fashion.

However, when ext/soap sees a SOAP header, it will try to call the method with that before processing the body. Therefore, now you can pass a SOAP header named set_timezone to set the time zone to one other than the web server default. The header should contain the name of the time zone as data.

Then, after setting the time zone, the SOAP server will examine the SOAP body. When it finds the usual return_time request, it returns the date. However, the altered time zone value will still persist, so the date is shifted accordingly.

Example 15-10 shows how you call this from PHP.

Example 15-10. Getting the time using SOAP and setting the time zone using a SOAP header

```
    <?php
    $opts = array('location' => 'http://api.example.org/getTime',
                  'uri' => 'urn:pc_SOAP_return_time');

    $client = new SOAPClient(null, $opts);

    $set_timezone = new SOAPVar('Europe/Oslo', XSD_STRING);
    $tz = new SOAPHeader('urn:pc_SOAP_return_time', 'set_timezone', $set_timezone);

    $result = $client->__soapCall('return_time', array(), array(), array($tz));

    print "The local time is $result.\n";
    ?>
```

After creating a SOAPClient for the service, you create the SOAPHeader. This SOAPHeader element lives in the urn:pc_SOAP_return_time XML namespace and is named set_time zone. The ext/soap extension doesn't actually use the XML namespace value, (this may differ on other SOAP servers), but the header name is important, as that controls which method the SOAPServer invokes.

The third argument to the SOAPHeader constructor, $set_timezone, is the data contained inside the SOAP header. In Example 15-10, it's a SOAPVar.

The SOAPVar class is a low-level class used for creating SOAP variables, such as strings and arrays. When you are sending data in the SOAP body, you rarely need to use this class. However, due to limitations in ext/soap, it comes in handy when dealing with SOAP headers.

While building parts of the SOAP request using SOAPVar is cumbersome, it does give you complete control over what's sent. This code creates a string with a value of Europe/Oslo. The XSD_STRING constant is one of many XML Schema and SOAP constants registered by the ext/soap extension. See the SOAP page in the PHP manual at *http://www.php.net/soap* for the complete list.

The request in Example 15-10 serializes as:

```
<?xml version="1.0" encoding="UTF-8"?>
<SOAP-ENV:Envelope
    xmlns:SOAP-ENV="http://schemas.xmlsoap.org/soap/envelope/"
    xmlns:ns1="urn:pc_SOAP_return_time"
    xmlns:xsd="http://www.w3.org/2001/XMLSchema"
    xmlns:xsi="http://www.w3.org/2001/XMLSchema-instance"
    xmlns:SOAP-ENC="http://schemas.xmlsoap.org/soap/encoding/"
    SOAP-ENV:encodingStyle="http://schemas.xmlsoap.org/soap/encoding/">

    <SOAP-ENV:Header>
        <ns1:set_timezone>Europe/Oslo</ns1:set_timezone>
    </SOAP-ENV:Header>

    <SOAP-ENV:Body>
        <ns1:return_time/>
    </SOAP-ENV:Body>

</SOAP-ENV:Envelope>
```

If the SOAP client specifies a header, but you lack a method to process it, ext/soap will skip the method and move directly to the body. However, if the header's mustUnderstand attribute is flagged as true, then the SOAPServer will issue a SOAP fault with a fault code of SOAP-ENV:MustUnderstand and a fault string of Header not understood.

See Also

Recipe 15.7 for generating a SOAP header; Recipe 14.7 for using a a SOAP header; documentation on SOAPHeader at the following address: *http://www.php.net/manual/function.soap-soapheader-construct.php*.

15.7 Generating a SOAP Header

Problem

You want to emit a SOAP header from your SOAP server.

Solution

Call the addSoapHeader( ) method:

```php
<?php
class pc_SOAP_return_time {
    public function return_time() {
        $tz = date_default_timezone_get();
        $header = new SoapHeader('urn:pc_SOAP_return_time', 'get_timezone', $tz)
        $GLOBALS['server']->addSoapHeader($header);

        return date('Ymd\THis');
    }
}

$server = new SOAPServer(null, array('uri'=>'urn:pc_SOAP_return_time'));
$server->setClass('pc_SOAP_return_time');

$server->handle();
?>
```

This adds the following XML to the SOAP response:

```
<SOAP-ENV:Header><ns1:get_timezone>America/Los Angeles</ns1:get_timezone>
</SOAP-ENV:Header>
```

Discussion

It's typical to process SOAP headers sent by a SOAP client. That's the subject of Recipe 15.6. However, you can also create new SOAP headers from within your SOAP server and send them back to the client.

This breaks down into two steps:

1. Creating a new instance of SOAPHeader.
2. Adding that header to the reply using SOAPServer::addHeader( ).

Example 15-11 shows how that's implemented in PHP.

Example 15-11. Sending a SOAP header from a SOAP server

```php
<?php
class pc_SOAP_return_time {
    public function return_time() {
        $tz = date_default_timezone_get();
        $header = new SoapHeader('urn:pc_SOAP_return_time', 'get_timezone', $tz)
        $GLOBALS['server']->addSoapHeader($header);

        return date('Ymd\THis');
    }
}

$server = new SOAPServer(null, array('uri'=>'urn:pc_SOAP_return_time'));
$server->setClass('pc_SOAP_return_time');
```

```
$server->handle();
?>
```

In Example 15-11, the pc_SOAP_return_time( ) method creates a new SOAP header named get_timezone that contains the default time zone.

This header is then added to the reply by calling $GLOBALS['server']->addSoapHeader ($header);. Since there's no easy way to access the $server object from within the scope of the method, you access it directly through the $GLOBALS array.

Now, when ext/soap responds, it will embed the SOAP header in its reply. For example:

```
<SOAP-ENV:Header><ns1:get_timezone>America/Los Angeles</ns1:get_timezone>
</SOAP-ENV:Header>
```

It's then up to the SOAP client to decide how to process this header. You can access it using SOAPClient by passing a fifth argument to __soapCall( ):

```
$result = $client->__soapCall('return_time', array(), array(), array(), $output);
print_r($output);


Array
(
    [timezone] => America/Los_Angeles
)
```

See Also

Recipe 15.6 for processing a SOAP header; Recipe 14.7 for using a a SOAP header; documentation on SOAPHeader at the following address: *http://www.php.net/manual/ function.soap-soapheader-construct.php.*

15.8 Using Authentication with SOAP

Problem

You want to authenticate SOAP requests. This allows you to restrict services to only trusted clients.

Solution

Authenticate using HTTP Basic authentication:

```
<?php
// Your authentication logic
// Which is probably decoupled from your SOAP Server
function pc_authenticate_user($username, password) {
    // authenticate user
    $is_valid = true; // Implement your lookup here

    if ($is_valid) {
        return true;
```

```php
        } else {
            return false;
        }
    }


    class pc_SOAP_return_time {
        public function __construct() {
            // Throw SOAP fault for invalid username and password combo
            if (! pc_authenticate_user($_SERVER['PHP_AUTH_USER'],
                                        $_SERVER['PHP_AUTH_PW'])) {

                throw new SOAPFault("Incorrect username and password combination.", 401);
            }
        }

        // Rest of SOAP Server methods here...
    }

    $server = new SOAPServer(null,array('uri'=>"urn:pc_SOAP_return_time"));
    $server->setClass("pc_SOAP_return_time");

    $server->handle();
    ?>
```

Or use a SOAP header:

```php
    <?php
    // Your authentication logic
    // Which is probably decoupled from your SOAP Server
    function pc_authenticate_user($username, password) {
        // authenticate user
        $is_valid = true; // Implement your lookup here

        if ($is_valid) {
            return true;
        } else {
            return false;
        }
    }


    class pc_SOAP_return_time {
        public function authenticate_user($args) {
            // Throw SOAP fault for invalid username and password combo
            if (! pc_authenticate_user($args->username,
                                        $args->password)) {

                throw new SOAPFault("Incorrect username and password combination.", 401);
            }
        }

        // Rest of SOAP Server methods here...
    }

    $server = new SOAPServer(null, array('uri'=>'urn:pc_SOAP_return_time'));
```

```
$server->setClass('pc_SOAP_return_time');

$server->handle();
?>
```

Discussion

Compared to the standard authentication in the rest of your applications, SOAP authentication isn't too complicated. There are two easy ways of integrating it into your SOAP server: using HTTP Basic authentication or processing a custom SOAP header.

If you're unfamiliar with these concepts, you should first read Recipe 8.9 for a review of HTTP Basic and Digest authentication and Recipe 15.6 for information on SOAP headers and how to handle them.

Example 15-12 shows how it's done using HTTP Basic authentication.

Example 15-12. Authenticating using HTTP Basic authentication and a SOAP server

```php
<?php
// Your authentication logic
// Which is probably decoupled from your SOAP Server
function pc_authenticate_user($username, password) {
    // authenticate user
    $is_valid = true; // Implement your lookup here

    if ($is_valid) {
        return true;
    } else {
        return false;
    }
}


class pc_SOAP_return_time {
    public function __construct() {
        // Throw SOAP fault for invalid username and password combo
        if (! pc_authenticate_user($_SERVER['PHP_AUTH_USER'],
                                   $_SERVER['PHP_AUTH_PW'])) {

            throw new SOAPFault("Incorrect username and password combination.", 401);
        }
    }

    // Rest of SOAP Server methods here...
}

$server = new SOAPServer(null, array('uri'=>'urn:pc_SOAP_return_time'));
$server->setClass('pc_SOAP_return_time');

$server->handle();
?>
```

Example 15-12 defines pc_authenticate_user( ). This function isn't SOAP specific, it's your standard code to handle user authentication. In this example, it's a separate function to emphasize its decoupled nature. However, you could also define this as a `private` method inside of `pc_SOAP_return_time` if you wanted to have it save state or access other object properties.

By defining a constructor for `pc_SOAP_return_time`, you force the SOAP server to execute that code before it handles any SOAP headers or the SOAP body. Inside of `__construct( )`, call out to `pc_authenticate_user`, passing the variables where PHP stores HTTP Basic Authentication credentials, `$_SERVER['PHP_AUTH_USER']` and `$_SERVER['PHP_AUTH_PW']`.

If the authentication fails, throw a SOAP fault. Remember, you must send an HTTP Status Code of **500** on SOAP faults, so PHP will not return **401**.

You can pass HTTP Basic authentication credentials like this:

```php
<?php
$opts = array('location' => 'http://api.example.org/getTime',
              'uri' => 'urn:pc_SOAP_return_time',
              'login' => 'elvis',
              'password' => 'the-king',

$client = new SOAPClient(null, $opts);

$result = $client->__soapCall('return_time');
?>
```

The `SOAPClient` accepts the `login` and `password` options. These should be set to the proper username and password and ext/soap will do the rest to send them using HTTP Basic authentication.

The other option is to use not HTTP Basic authentication, but pass the username and password in a custom SOAP header. This allows you additional control over what information you gather and lets you extend into using a protocol other than HTTP.

The downside is that HTTP Basic authentication is a familiar concept, so people will need to learn how to construct your custom header.

Example 15-13 outlines the basic setup.

Example 15-13. Authenticating using a SOAP header and a SOAP server

```php
<?php
// Your authentication logic
// Which is probably decoupled from your SOAP Server
function pc_authenticate_user($username, password) {
    // authenticate user
    $is_valid = true; // Implement your lookup here

    if ($is_valid) {
        return true;
    } else {
        return false;
    }
}
```

```
class pc_SOAP_return_time {
    private $authenticated;

    public function __construct() {
        $this->authenticated = false;
    }

    public function authenticate_user($args) {
        // Throw SOAP fault for invalid username and password combo
        if (! pc_authenticate_user($args->username,
                                   $args->password)) {

            throw new SOAPFault("Incorrect username and password combination.", 401);
        }

        $this->authenticated = true;
    }

    // Rest of SOAP Server methods here...
    public function soap_method() {
        if ($this->authenticated) {
            // Method body here...
        } else {
            throw new SOAPFault("Must pass authenticate_user Header.", 401);
        }
    }

}

$server = new SOAPServer(null, array('uri'=>'urn:pc_SOAP_return_time'));
$server->setClass('pc_SOAP_return_time');

$server->handle();
?>
```

The pc_authenticate_user( ) function is identical, as there's no need for that low-level system to change merely because you altered the interface for passing the username and password.

However, instead of implementing the authentication check inside of the constructor, you place it inside a method named after your authentication header. Since there's no way to force ext/soap to require a SOAP header, use this method to set the authenticated property to true.

Then, make sure each of your SOAP body methods wraps the "real" code inside an if ($this->authenticated) check. If the SOAP client failed to pass the credentials, throw a SOAP fault.

Here's how you pass the credentials using SOAPClient:

```
<?php
$opts = array('location' => 'http://api.example.org/getTime',
              'uri' => 'urn:pc_SOAP_return_time');
```

```
$client = new SOAPClient(null, $opts);

class SOAPAuth {
    public $username;
    public $password;

    public function __construct($username, $password) {
        $this->username = $username;
        $this->password = $password;
    }
}

$auth = new SOAPAuth('elvis', 'the-king');
$header = new SOAPHeader('urn:example.org/auth', 'authenticate_user', $auth);
$result = $client->__soapCall('return_time', array(), array(), array($header));
?>
```

The easiest way to create a SOAP header with both `username` and `password` variables is to create a simple class with properties with those names and then pass an instance of that class to `SOAPHeader`.

The entire SOAP header is then sent as the fourth argument in your `__soapCall( )`.

See Also

Recipe 14.8 for using authentication in a SOAP client; Recipe 8.9 for information on HTTP Basic and Digest authentication in general.

15.9 Serving an XML-RPC Method

Problem

You want to create an XML-RPC server and respond to XML-RPC requests. This allows any XML-RPC-enabled client to ask your server questions and you to reply with data.

Solution

Use PHP's XML-RPC extension. Here is a PHP version of the Userland XML-RPC demonstration application that returns an ISO 8601 string with the current date and time:

```
// this is the function exposed as "get_time()"
function return_time($method, $args) {
    return date('Ymd\THis');
}

$server = xmlrpc_server_create() or die("Can't create server");
xmlrpc_server_register_method($server, 'return_time', 'get_time')
    or die("Can't register method.");

$request = $GLOBALS['HTTP_RAW_POST_DATA'];
```

```
$options = array('output_type' => 'xml', 'version' => 'xmlrpc');

print xmlrpc_server_call_method($server, $request, NULL, $options)
    or die("Can't call method");

xmlrpc_server_destroy($server);
```

Discussion

Since the bundled XML-RPC extension xmlrpc-epi is written in C, it processes XML-RPC requests in a speedy and efficient fashion. Add --with-xmlrpc to your configure string to enable this extension during compile time. For more on XML-RPC, see Recipe 14.12.

The Solution begins with a definition of the PHP function to associate with the XML-RPC method. The name of the function is return_time( ). This is later linked with the get_time( ) XML-RPC method:

```
function return_time($method, $args) {
    return date('Ymd\THis');
}
```

The function returns an ISO 8601–formatted string with the current date and time. Escape the T inside the call to date( ) because the specification requires a literal T to divide the date part and the time part. At August 21, 2002 at 3:03:51 P.M., the return value is 20020821T150351.

The function is automatically called with two parameters: the name of the XML-RPC method the server is responding to and an array of method arguments passed by the XML-RPC client to the server. In this example, the server ignores both variables.

Next, create the XML-RPC server and register the get_time( ) method:

```
$server = xmlrpc_server_create() or die("Can't create server");
xmlrpc_server_register_method($server, 'return_time', 'get_time');
```

Create a new server and assign it to $server and then call xmlrpc_server_register_method( ) with three parameters. The first is the newly created server, the second is the name of the method to register, and the third is the name of the PHP function to handle the request.

Now that everything is configured, tell the XML-RPC server to dispatch the method for processing and print the results to the client:

```
$request = $GLOBALS['HTTP_RAW_POST_DATA'];
$options = array('output_type' => 'xml', 'version' => 'xmlrpc');

print xmlrpc_server_call_method($server, $request, NULL, $options);
```

The client request comes in as POST data. PHP converts HTTP POST data to variables, but this is XML-RPC data, so the server needs to access the unparsed data, which is stored in $GLOBALS['HTTP_RAW_POST_DATA']. In this example, the request XML looks like this:

```
<?xml version="1.0" encoding="iso-8859-1"?>
<methodCall>
<methodName>get_time</methodName>
<params/></methodCall>
```

Thus, the server is responding to the get_time( ) method, and it expects no parameters.

You must also configure the response options to output the results in XML and interpret the request as XML-RPC. These two variables are then passed to xmlrpc_server_call_method( ) along with the XML-RPC server, $server. The third parameter to this function is for any user data you wish to provide; in this case, there is none, so pass NULL.

The xmlrpc_server_call_method( ) function decodes the variables, calls the correct function to handle the method, and encodes the response into XML-RPC. To reply to the client, all you need to do is print out what xmlrpc_server_call_method( ) returns.

Finally, clean up with a call to xmlrpc_server_destroy( ):

```
xmlrpc_server_destroy($server);
```

Using the XML-RPC client code from Recipe 14.12, you can make a request and find the time, as follows:

```
require 'utils.php';

$output = array('output_type' => 'xml', 'version' => 'xmlrpc');
$result = xu_rpc_http_concise(array(
                        'method'  => 'get_time',
                        'host'    => 'clock.example.com',
                        'port'    => 80,
                        'uri'     => '/time-xmlrpc.php',
                        'output'  => $output));

print "The local time is $result.\n";

The local time is 20020821T162615.
```

It is legal to associate multiple methods with a single XML-RPC server. You can also associate multiple methods with the same PHP function. For example, you can create a server that replies to two methods: get_gmtime( ) and get_time( ). The first method, get_gmtime( ), is similar to get_time( ), but it replies with the current time in GMT. To handle this, you can extend get_time( ) to take an optional parameter, which is the name of a time zone to use when computing the current time.

Here's how to change the return_time( ) function to handle both methods:

```
function return_time($method, $args) {
    if ('get_gmtime' == $method) {
        $tz = 'GMT';
    } elseif (!empty($args[0])) {
        $tz = $args[0];
    } else {
        // use local time zone
        $tz = '';
```

```
        }

    if ($tz) { putenv("TZ=$tz"); }
    $date = date('Ymd\THis');
    if ($tz) { putenv('TZ=EST5EDT'); } // change EST5EDT to your server's zone

    return $date;
}
```

This function uses both the $method and $args parameters. At the top of the function, we check if the request is for get_gmtime. If so, the time zone is set to GMT. If it isn't, see if an alternate time zone is specified as an argument by checking $args[0]. If neither check is true, keep the current time zone.

To configure the server to handle the new method, add only one new line:

```
    xmlrpc_server_register_method($server, 'return_time', 'get_gmtime');
```

This maps get_gmtime( ) to return_time( ).

Here's an example of a client in action. The first request is for get_time( ) with no parameters; the second calls get_time( ) with a time zone of PST8PDT, which is three hours behind the server; the last request is for the new get_gmtime( ) method, which is four hours ahead of the server's time zone:

```
    require 'utils.php';

    $output = array('output_type' => 'xml', 'version' => 'xmlrpc');

    // get_time()
    $result = xu_rpc_http_concise(array(
                            'method'  => 'get_time',
                            'host'    => 'clock.example.com',
                            'port'    => 80,
                            'uri'     => '/time.php',
                            'output'  => $output));

    print "The local time is $result.\n";

    // get_time('PST8PDT')
    $result = xu_rpc_http_concise(array(
                            'method'  => 'get_time',
                            'args'    => array('PST8PDT'),
                            'host'    => 'clock.example.com',
                            'port'    => 80,
                            'uri'     => '/time.php',
                            'output'  => $output));

    print "The time in PST8PDT is $result.\n";

    // get_gmtime()
    $result = xu_rpc_http_concise(array(
                            'method'  => 'get_gmtime',
                            'host'    => 'clock.example.com',
                            'port'    => 80,
                            'uri'     => '/time.php',
```

```
                              'output'  => $output));

    print "The time in GMT is $result.\n";

    The local time is 20020821T162615.
    The time in PST8PDT is 20020821T132615.
    The time in GMT is 20020821T202615.
```

See Also

Recipe 14.12 for more information about XML-RPC clients; documentation on `xmlrpc_server_create()` can be found at *http://www.php.net/xmlrpc-server-create*, `xmlrpc_server_register_method()` at *http://www.php.net/xmlrpc-server-register-meth od*, `xmlrpc_server_call_method()` at *http://www.php.net/xmlrpc-server-call-method*, and `xmlrpc_server_destroy()` at *http://www.php.net/xmlrpc-server-destroy*; *Programming Web Services with XML-RPC* by Simon St.Laurent, Joe Johnston, and Edd Dumbill (O'Reilly); more on XML-RPC at *http://www.xml-rpc.com*; the original current time XML-RPC server at *http://www.xmlrpc.com/currentTime*.

CHAPTER 16

Internet Services

16.0 Introduction

Before there was HTTP, there was FTP, NNTP, IMAP, POP3, and a whole alphabet soup of other protocols. Many people quickly embraced web browsers because the browser provided an integrated program that let them check their email, read newsgroups, transfer files, and view documents without worrying about the details surrounding the underlying means of communication. PHP provides functions, both natively and through PEAR, to use these other protocols. With them, you can use PHP to create web frontend applications that perform all sorts of network-enabled tasks, such as looking up domain names or sending web-based email. While PHP simplifies these jobs, it is important to understand the strengths and limitations of each protocol.

Recipes 16.1 to 16.3 cover the most popular feature of all: email. Recipe 16.1 shows how to send basic email messages. Recipe 16.2 describes MIME-encoded email, which enables you to send plain text and HTML-formatted messages. The IMAP and POP3 protocols, which are used to read mailboxes, are discussed in Recipe 16.3.

The next two recipes discuss how to read newsgroups with NNTP. Newsgroups are similar to mailing lists, but instead of every person on the list receiving an email message, people can access a news server and view just the messages they're interested in. Newsgroups also allow threaded discussions, so its easy to trace a conversation through the archives. Recipe 16.4 discusses posting messages, while Recipe 16.5 covers retrieving messages.

Recipe 16.6 covers how to exchange files using FTP (file transfer protocol), which is a method for sending and receiving files across the Internet. FTP servers can require users to log in with a password or allow anonymous usage.

Searching LDAP servers is the topic of Recipe 16.7, while Recipe 16.8 discusses how to authenticate users against an LDAP server. LDAP servers are used as address books and as centralized stores for user information. They're optimized for information retrieval and can be configured to replicate their data to ensure high reliability and quick response times.

The chapter concludes with recipes on networking. Recipe 16.9 covers DNS lookups, both from domain name to IP and vice versa. Recipe 16.10 tells how to check if a host is up and accessible with PEAR's ping module.

Other parts of the book deal with some network protocols as well. HTTP is covered in detail in Chapter 13. Those recipes discuss how to fetch URLs in a variety of different ways. Protocols that combine HTTP and XML are covered in Chapters 14 and 15. Those two chapters discuss consuming and serving web services, including the REST, SOAP, and XML-RPC protocols.

16.1 Sending Mail

Problem

You want to send an email message. This can be in direct response to a user's action, such as signing up for your site, or a recurring event at a set time, such as a weekly newsletter.

Solution

Use PEAR's `Mail` class:

```
require 'Mail.php';

$to = 'adam@example.com';

$headers['From'] = 'webmaster@example.com';
$headers['Subject'] = 'New Version of PHP Released!';

$body = 'Go to http://www.php.net and download it today!';

$message =& Mail::factory('mail');
$message->send($to, $headers, $body);
```

If you can't use PEAR's `Mail` class, use PHP's built-in `mail( )` function:

```
$to = 'adam@example.com';
$subject = 'New Version of PHP Released!';
$body = 'Go to http://www.php.net and download it today!';

mail($to, $subject, $body);
```

Discussion

PEAR's `Mail` class allows you to send mail three ways. You indicate the method to use when instantiating a mail object with `Mail::factory( )`.

- To send mail using an external program such as *sendmail* or *qmail*, pass `sendmail`.
- To use an SMTP server, pass `smtp`.

- To use the built-in `mail( )` function, pass `mail`. This tells `Mail` to apply the settings from your *php.ini*.

To use `sendmail` or `smtp`, you have to pass a second parameter indicating your settings. To use `sendmail`, specify a `sendmail_path` and `sendmail_args`:

```
$params['sendmail_path'] = '/usr/sbin/sendmail';
$params['sendmail_args'] = '-oi -t';

$message =& Mail::factory('sendmail', $params);
```

One good value for `sendmail_path` is */usr/lib/sendmail*. Unfortunately, *sendmail* tends to jump around from system to system, so it can be hard to track down. If you can't find it, try */usr/sbin/sendmail* or ask your system administrator.

Two useful flags to pass *sendmail* are `-oi` and `-t`. The `-oi` flag tells *sendmail* not to think a single dot (.) on a line is the end of the message. The `-t` flag makes *sendmail* parse the file for `To:` and other header lines.

If you prefer *qmail*, try using */var/qmail/bin/qmail-inject* or */var/qmail/bin/sendmail*.

If you're running Windows, you may want to use an SMTP server because most Windows machines don't have copies of *sendmail* installed. To do so, pass `smtp`:

```
$params['host'] = 'smtp.example.com';

$message =& Mail::factory('smtp', $params);
```

In `smtp` mode, you can pass five optional parameters. The `host` is the SMTP server hostname; it defaults to `localhost`. The `port` is the connection port; it defaults to `25`. To enable SMTP authentication, set `auth` to `true`. To allow the server to validate you, set `username` and `password`. SMTP functionality isn't restricted to Windows; it also works on Unix servers.

If you don't have PEAR's `Mail` class, you can use the built-in `mail( )` function. The program `mail( )` uses to send mail is specified in the `sendmail_path` configuration variable in your *php.ini* file. If you're running Windows, set the `SMTP` variable to the hostname of your SMTP server. Your `From` address comes from the `sendmail_from` variable.

Here's an example that uses `mail( )`:

```
$to = 'adam@example.com';
$subject = 'New Version of PHP Released!';
$body = 'Go to http://www.php.net and download it today!';

mail($to, $subject, $body);
```

The first parameter is the recipient's email address, the second is the message subject, and the last is the message body. You can also add extra headers with an optional fourth parameter. For example, here's how to add `Reply-To` and `Organization` headers:

```
$to = 'adam@example.com';
$subject = 'New Version of PHP Released!';
```

```
$body = 'Go to http://www.php.net and download it today!';
$header = "Reply-To: webmaster@example.com\r\n"
         ."Organization: The PHP Group";

mail($to, $subject, $body, $header);
```

Separate each header with \r\n, but don't add \r\n following the last header.

Regardless of which method you choose, it's a good idea to write a wrapper function to assist you in sending mail. Forcing all your mail through this function makes it easy to add logging and other checks to every message sent:

```
function pc_mail($to, $headers, $body) {
    $message =& Mail::factory('mail');

    $message->send($to, $headers, $body);
    error_log("[MAIL][TO: $to]");
}
```

Here a message is written to the error log, recording the recipient of each message that's sent. This provides a timestamp that allows you to more easily track complaints that someone is trying to use the site to send spam. Another option is to create a list of "do not send" email addresses, which prevent those people from ever receiving another message from your site. You can also validate all recipient email addresses, which reduces the number of bounced messages.

See Also

Recipe 9.4 for a regular expression to validate email addresses; Recipe 16.2 for sending MIME email; Recipe 16.3 for more on retrieving mail; documentation on `mail( )` at *http://www.php.net/mail*; the PEAR `Mail` class at *http://pear.php.net/package-info.php? package=Mail*; RFC 822 at *http://www.faqs.org/rfcs/rfc822.html*; O'Reilly publishes two books on sendmail: *sendmail* by Bryan Costales with Eric Allman and *sendmail Desktop Reference* by Bryan Costales and Eric Allman.

16.2 Sending MIME Mail

Problem

You want to send MIME email. For example, you want to send multipart messages with both plain text and HTML portions and have MIME-aware mail readers automatically display the correct portion.

Solution

Use the `Mail_mime` class in PEAR:

```
require 'Mail.php';
require 'Mail/mime.php';
```

```
$to = 'adam@example.com, sklar@example.com';

$headers['From'] = 'webmaster@example.com';
$headers['Subject'] = 'New Version of PHP Released!';

// create MIME object
$mime = new Mail_mime;

// add body parts
$text = 'Text version of email';
$mime->setTXTBody($text);

$html = '<html><body>HTML version of email</body></html>';
$mime->setHTMLBody($html);

$file = '/path/to/file.png';
$mime->addAttachment($file, 'image/png');

// get MIME formatted message headers and body
$body = $mime->get();
$headers = $mime->headers($headers);

$message =& Mail::factory('mail');
$message->send($to, $headers, $body);
```

Discussion

PEAR's `Mail_mime` class provides an object-oriented interface to all the behind-the-scenes details involved in creating an email message that contains both text and HTML parts. The class is similar to PEAR's `Mail` class, but instead of defining the body as a string of text, you create a `Mail_mime` object and call its methods to add parts to the body:

```
// create MIME object
$mime = new Mail_mime;

// add body parts
$text = 'Text version of email';
$mime->setTXTBody($text);

$html = '<html><body>HTML version of email</body></html>';
$mime->setHTMLBody($html);

$file = '/path/to/file.txt';
$mime->addAttachment($file, 'text/plain');

// get MIME formatted message headers and body
$body = $mime->get();
$headers = $mime->headers($headers);
```

The `Mail_mime::setTXTBody( )` and `Mail_mime::setHTMLBody( )` methods add the plain text and HTML body parts, respectively. Here, we pass in variables, but you can also pass a filename for `Mail_mime` to read. To use this option, pass **true** as the second parameter:

```
$text = '/path/to/email.txt';
$mime->setTXTBody($text, true);
```

To add an attachment to the message, such as a graphic or an archive, call
`Mail_mime::addAttachment( )`:

```
$file = '/path/to/file.png';
$mime->addAttachment($file,'image/png');
```

Pass the function to the location to the file and its MIME type.

Once the message is complete, do the final preparation and send it out:

```
// get MIME formatted message headers and body
$body = $mime->get();
$headers = $mime->headers($headers);

$message =& Mail::factory('mail');
$message->send($to, $headers, $body);
```

First, you have the `Mail_mime` object provide properly formatted headers and body. You
then use the parent `Mail` class to format the message and send it out with
`Mail_mime::send( )` .

See Also

Recipe 16.1 for sending regular email; Recipe 16.3 for more on retrieving mail; the
PEAR `Mail_Mime` class at *http://pear.php.net/package-info.php?package=Mail_Mime*.

16.3 Reading Mail with IMAP or POP3

Problem

You want to read mail using IMAP or POP3, which allows you to create a web-based
email client.

Solution

Use PHP's IMAP extension, which speaks both IMAP and POP3:

```
// open IMAP connection
$mail = imap_open('{mail.server.com:143}',         'username', 'password');
// or, open POP3 connection
$mail = imap_open('{mail.server.com:110/pop3}', 'username', 'password');

// grab a list of all the mail headers
$headers = imap_headers($mail);

// grab a header object for the last message in the mailbox
$last = imap_num_msg($mail);
$header = imap_header($mail, $last);

// grab the body for the same message
```

```
$body = imap_body($mail, $last);

// close the connection
imap_close($mail);
```

Discussion

The underlying library PHP uses to support IMAP and POP3 offers a seemingly un-ending number of features that allow you to essentially write an entire mail client. With all those features, however, comes complexity. In fact, there are currently 63 different functions in PHP beginning with the word imap, and that doesn't take into account that some also speak POP3 and NNTP.

However, the basics of talking with a mail server are straightforward. Like many features in PHP, you begin by opening the connection and grabbing a handle:

```
$mail = imap_open('{mail.server.com:143}', 'username', 'password');
```

This opens an IMAP connection to the server named *mail.server.com* on port 143. It also passes along a username and password as the second and third arguments.

To open a POP3 connection instead, append /pop3 to the end of the server and port. Since POP3 usually runs on port 110, add :110 after the server name:

```
$mail = imap_open('{mail.server.com:110/pop3}', 'username', 'password');
```

To encrypt your connection with SSL, add /ssl on to the end, just as you did with pop3. You also need to make sure your PHP installation is built with the --with-imap-ssl configuration option in addition to --with-imap. Also, you need to build the system IMAP library itself with SSL support. If you're using a self-signed certificate and wish to prevent an attempted validation, also add /novalidate-cert. Finally, most SSL connections talk on either port 993 or 995. All these options can come in any order, so the following is perfectly legal:

```
$mail = imap_open('{mail.server.com:993/novalidate-cert/pop3/ssl}',
                  'username', 'password');
```

Surrounding a variable with curly braces inside of a double-quoted string, such as {$var}, is a way to tell PHP exactly which variable to interpolate. Therefore, to use interpolated variables in this first parameter to imap_open( ), escape the opening {:

```
$server = 'mail.server.com';
$port = 993;

$mail = imap_open("\{$server:$port}", 'username', 'password');
```

Once you've opened a connection, you can ask the mail server a variety of questions. To get a listing of all the messages in your inbox, use imap_headers( ):

```
$headers = imap_headers($mail);
```

This returns an array in which each element is a formatted string corresponding to a message:

```
A    189) 5-Aug-2007 Beth Hondl          an invitation (1992 chars)
```

Alternatively, to retrieve a specific message, use `imap_header( )` and `imap_body( )` to pull the header object and body string:

```
$header = imap_header($message_number);
$body   = imap_body($message_number);
```

The `imap_header( )` function returns an object with many fields. Useful ones include `subject`, `fromaddress`, and `udate`. All the fields are listed in Table 16-2 in Recipe 16.5.

The `body` element is just a string, but if the message is a multipart message, such as one that contains both an HTML and a plain text version, `$body` holds both parts and the MIME lines describing them:

```
------=_Part_1046_3914492.1008372096119
Content-Type: text/plain; charset=us-ascii
Content-Transfer-Encoding: 7bit

Plain-Text Message

------=_Part_1046_3914492.1008372096119
Content-Type: text/html
Content-Transfer-Encoding: 7bit

<html>HTML Message</html>
------=_Part_1046_3914492.1008372096119--
```

To avoid this occurrence, use `imap_fetchstructure( )` in combination with `imap_fetchbody( )` to discover how the body is formatted and to extract just the parts you want:

```
// pull the plain text for message $n
$st = imap_fetchstructure($mail, $n);
if (!empty($st->parts)) {
    for ($i = 0, $j = count($st->parts); $i < $j; $i++) {
        $part = $st->parts[$i];
        if ($part->subtype == 'PLAIN') {
            $body = imap_fetchbody($mail, $n, $i+1);
        }
    }
} else {
    $body = imap_body($mail, $n));
}
```

If a message has multiple parts, `$st->parts` holds an array of objects describing them. The `part` property holds an integer describing the main body MIME type. Table 16-1 lists which numbers go with which MIME types. The `subtype` property holds the MIME subtype and tells if the part is `plain`, `html`, `png`, or another type, such as `octet-stream`.

Table 16-1. IMAP MIME type values

Number	MIME type	PHP constant	Description	Examples
0	text	TYPETEXT	Unformatted text	Plain text, HTML, XML

Number	MIME type	PHP constant	Description	Examples
1	multipart	TYPEMULTIPART	Multipart message	Mixed, form data, signed
2	message	TYPEMESSAGE	Encapsulated message	News, HTTP
3	application	TYPEAPPLICATION	Application data	Octet stream, PDF, Zip
4	audio	TYPEAUDIO	Music file	MP3, RealAudio
5	image	TYPEIMAGE	Graphic image	GIF, JPEG, PNG
6	video	TYPEVIDEO	Video clip	MPEG, Quicktime
7	other	TYPEOTHER	Everything else	VRML models

See Also

Recipes 16.1 and 16.2 for more on sending mail; documentation on imap_open( ) at
http://www.php.net/imap_open, imap_header( ) at *http://www.php.net/imap-header*,
imap-body( ) at *http://www.php.net/imap-body*, and IMAP in general at *http://www.php.net/imap*.

16.4 Posting Messages to Usenet Newsgroups

Problem

You want to post a message to a Usenet newsgroup, such as *comp.lang.php*.

Solution

Use imap_mail_compose( ) to format the message, and then write the message to the
server using sockets:

```
$headers['from'] = 'adam@example.com';
$headers['subject'] = 'New Version of PHP Released!';
$headers['custom_headers'][] = 'Newsgroups: comp.lang.php';

$body[0]['type'] = TYPETEXT;
$body[0]['subtype'] = 'plain';
$body[0]['contents.data'] = 'Go to http://www.php.net and download it today!';

$post = imap_mail_compose($headers, $body);

$server = 'nntp.example.com';
$port = 119;

$sh = fsockopen($server, $port) or die ("Can't connect to $server.");
fputs($sh, "POST\r\n");
fputs($sh, $post);
fputs($sh, ".\r\n");
fclose($sh);
```

Discussion

No built-in PHP functions can post a message to a newsgroup. Therefore, you must open a direct socket connection to the news server and send the commands to post the message. However, you can use imap_mail_compose( ) to format a post and create the headers and body for the message. Every message must have three headers: the From: address, the message Subject:, and the name of the newsgroup:

```
$headers['from'] = 'adam@example.com';
$headers['subject'] = 'New Version of PHP Released!';
$headers['custom_headers'][] = 'Newsgroups: comp.lang.php';
```

Create an array, $headers, to hold the message headers. You can directly assign the values for the From: and Subject: headers, but you can't do so for the Newsgroups: header. Because imap_mail_compose( ) is most frequently used to create email messages, the Newsgroups: header is not a predefined header. To work around this, you must instead add it with the custom_headers array element.

There is a different syntax for custom_headers. Instead of placing the lowercase header name as the element name and the header value as the array value, place the entire header as an array value. Between the header name and value, add a colon followed by a space. Be sure to correctly spell Newsgroups: with a capital N and final s.

The message body can contain multiple parts. As a result, the body parameter passed to imap_mail_compose( ) is an array of arrays. In the Solution, there was only one part, so you directly assign values to $body[0]:

```
$body[0]['type'] = TYPETEXT;
$body[0]['subtype'] = 'plain';
$body[0]['contents.data'] = 'Go to http://www.php.net and download it today!';
```

Each message part needs a MIME type and subtype. This message is ASCII, so the type is TYPETEXT, and the subtype is plain. Refer back to Table 16-1 in Recipe 16.3 for a listing of IMAP MIME type constants and what they represent. The contents.data field holds the message body.

To convert these arrays into a formatted string, call imap_mail_compose($body, $headers). It returns a post that looks like this:

```
From: adam@example.com
Subject: New Version of PHP Released!
MIME-Version: 1.0
Content-Type: TEXT/plain; CHARSET=US-ASCII
Newsgroups: comp.lang.php

Go to http://www.php.net and download it today!
```

Armed with a post the news server will accept, call fsockopen( ) to open a connection:

```
$server = 'nntp.example.com';
$port = 119;

$sh = fsockopen($server, $port) or die ("Can't connect to $server.");
```

The first parameter to fsockopen( ) is the hostname of the server, and the second is the port to use. If you don't know the name of your news server, try the hostnames *news*, *nntp*, or *news-server* in your domain: for example, *news.example.com*, *nntp.example.com*, or *news-server.example.com*. If none of these work, ask your system administrator. Traditionally, all news servers use port 119.

Once connected, you send the message:

```
fputs($sh, "POST\r\n");
fputs($sh, imap_mail_compose($headers, $body));
fputs($sh, ".\r\n");
```

The first line tells the news server that you want to post a message. The second is the message itself. To signal the end of the message, place a period on a line by itself. Every line must have both a carriage return and a newline at the end. Close the connection by calling fclose($sh).

Every message on the server is given a unique name, known as a Message-ID. If you want to reply to a message, take the Message-ID of the original message and use it as the value for a References header:

```
// retrieved when reading original message
$message_id = '<20030410020818.33915.php@news.example.com>';

$headers['custom_headers'][] = "References: $message_id";
```

See Also

Recipe 16.5 for more on reading newsgroups; documentation on imap_mail_compose( ) at *http://www.php.net/imap-mail-compose*, fsockopen( ) at *http://www.php.net/fsockopen*, fputs( ) at *http://www.php.net/fputs*, and fclose( ) at *http://www.php.net/fclose*; RFC 977 at *http://www.faqs.org/rfcs/rfc977.html*.

16.5 Reading Usenet News Messages

Problem

You want to read Usenet news messages using NNTP to talk to a news server.

Solution

Use PHP's IMAP extension. It also speaks NNTP:

```
// open a connection to the nntp server
$server = '{news.php.net/nntp:119}';
$group = 'php.general'; // main PHP mailing list
$nntp = imap_open("$server$group", '', '', OP_ANONYMOUS);

// get header
$header = imap_header($nntp, $msg);
```

```
// pull out fields
$subj  = $header->subject;
$from  = $header->from;
$email = $from[0]->mailbox."@".$from[0]->host;
$name  = $from[0]->personal;
$date  = date('m/d/Y h:i A', $header->udate);

// get body
$body  = nl2br(htmlspecialchars(imap_fetchbody($nntp,$msg,1)));

// close connection
imap_close($nntp);
```

Discussion

Reading news from a news server requires you to connect to the server and specify a group you're interested in reading:

```
// open a connection to the nntp server
$server = "{news.php.net/nntp:119}";
$group = "php.general";
$nntp = imap_open("$server$group",'','',OP_ANONYMOUS);
```

The function `imap_open( )` takes four parameters. The first specifies the news server to use and the newsgroup to read. The server here is *news.php.net*, the news server that mirrors all the PHP mailing lists. Add */nntp* to let the IMAP extension know you're reading news instead of mail, and specify 119 as a port; that's typically the port reserved for NNTP (Network News Transport Protocol), which is used to communicate with news servers, just as HTTP communicates with web servers. The group is *php.general*, the main mailing list of the PHP community.

The middle two arguments to `imap_open( )` are a username and password, in case you need to provide verification of your identity. Because *news.php.net* is open to all readers, leave them blank. Finally, pass the flag `OP_ANONYMOUS`, which tells IMAP you're an anonymous reader; it will not then keep a record of you in a special *.newsrc* file.

Once you're connected, you usually want to either get a general listing of recent messages or all the details about one specific message. Here's some code that displays recent messages:

```
// read and display posting index
$last = imap_num_msg($nntp);
$n = 10; // display last 10 messages

// table header
print <<<EOH
<table>
<tr>
    <th align="left">Subject</th>
    <th align="left">Sender</th>
    <th align="left">Date</th>
</tr>
EOH;
```

```
    // the messages
    for ($i = $last-$n+1; $i <= $last; $i++) {
        $header = imap_header($nntp, $i);

        if (! $header->Size) { continue; }

        $subj  = $header->subject;
        $from  = $header->from;
        $email = $from[0]->mailbox."@".$from[0]->host;
        $name  = $from[0]->personal ? $from[0]->personal : $email;
        $date  = date('m/d/Y h:i A', $header->udate);

    print <<<EOM
<tr>
    <td><a href="$_SERVER[PHP_SELF]"?msg=$i\">$subj</a></td>
    <td><a href="mailto:$email">$name</a></td>
    <td>$date</td>
</tr>
EOM;
        }

    // table footer
    echo "</table>\n";
```

To browse a listing of posts, you need to specify what you want by number. The first post ever to a group gets number 1, and the most recent post is the number returned from `imap_num_msg( )`. So to get the last $n messages, loop from `$last-$n+1` to `$last`.

Inside the loop, call `imap_header( )` to pull out the header information about a post. The header contains all the metainformation but not the actual text of the message; that's stored in the body. Because the header is usually much smaller than the body, this allows you to quickly retrieve data for many posts without taking too much time.

Now pass `imap_header( )` two parameters: the server connection handle and the message number. It returns an object with many properties, which are listed in Table 16-2.

Table 16-2. imap_header( ) fields from an NNTP server

Name	Description	Type	Example
date or Date	RFC 822–formatted date: date ('r')	String	Fri, 16 Aug 2002 01:52:24 -0400
subject or Subject	Message subject	String	Re: PHP Cookbook Revisions
message_id	A unique ID identifying the message	String	<20030410020818. 33915.php@news.example.com>
newsgroups	The name of the group the message was posted to	String	php.general
toaddress	The address the message was sent to	String	php-general@lists.php.net

Name	Description	Type	Example
to	Parsed version of toaddress field	Object	mailbox: "php-general", host: "lists-php.net"
fromaddress	The address that sent the message	String	Ralph Josephs <ralph@example.net>
from	Parsed version of fromad dress field	Object	personal: "Ralph Josephs", mailbox: "ralph", host: "example.net"
reply_toaddress	The address you should reply to, if you're trying to contact the author	String	rjosephs@example.net
reply_to	Parsed version of reply_toad dress field	Object	Mailbox: "rjosephs", host: "example.net"
senderaddress	The person who sent the message; almost always identical to the from field, but if the from field doesn't uniquely identify who sent the message, this field does	String	Ralph Josephs <ralph@example.net>
sender	Parsed version of senderad dress field	Object	Personal: "Ralph Josephs", mailbox: "ralph", host: "example.net"
Recent	If the message is recent, or new since the last time the user checked for mail	String	Y or N
Unseen	If the message is unseen	String	Y or " "
Flagged	If the message is marked	String	Y or " "
Answered	If a reply has been sent to this message	String	Y or " "
Deleted	If the message is deleted	String	Y or " "
Draft	If the message is a draft	String	Y or " "
Size	Size of the message in bytes	String	1345
udate	Unix timestamp of message date	Int	1013480645
Mesgno	The number of the message in the group	String	34943

Some of the more useful fields are: size, subject, the from list, and udate. The size property is the size of the message in bytes; if it's 0, the message was either deleted or otherwise removed. The subject field is the subject of the post. The from list is more complicated. It's an array of objects; each element in the array holds an object with three properties: personal, mailbox, and host. The personal field is the name of the poster: Homer Simpson. The mailbox field is the part of the email address before the @ sign: homer. The host is the part of the email address after the @ sign:

thesimpsons.com. Usually, there's just one element in the from list array, because a message usually has just one sender.

Pull the $header->from object into $from because PHP can't directly access $header->from[0]->personal due to the array in the middle. Then combine $from[0]->mailbox and $from[0]->host to form the poster's email address. Use the ternary operator to assign the personal field as the poster's name, if one is supplied; otherwise, make it the email address.

The udate field is the posting time as an Unix timestamp. Use date( ) to convert it from seconds to a more human-friendly format.

You can also view a specific posting as follows:

```
// read and display a single message
$header = imap_header($nntp, $msg);

$subj  = $header->subject;
$from  = $header->from;
$email = $from[0]->mailbox."@".$from[0]->host;
$name  = $from[0]->personal;
$date  = date('m/d/Y h:i A', $header->udate);
$body  = nl2br(htmlspecialchars(imap_fetchbody($nntp,$msg,1)));

print <<<EOM
<table>
<tr>
    <th align=left>From:</th>
    <td>$name &lt;<a href="mailto:$email">$email</a>&gt;</td>
</tr>
<tr>
    <th align=left>Subject:</th>
    <td>$subj</td>
</tr>
<tr>
    <th align=left>Date:</th>
    <td>$date</td>
</tr>
<tr>
    <td colspan="2">$body</td>
</tr>
</table>
EOM;
```

The code to grab a single message is similar to one that grabs a sequence of message headers. The main difference is that you define a $body variable that's the result of three chained functions. Innermost, you call imap_fetchbody( ) to return the message body; it takes the same parameters as imap_header( ). You pass that to htmlspecialchars( ) to escape any HTML that may interfere with yours. That result then is passed to nl2br( ) , which converts all the carriage returns to XHTML <br /> tags; the message should now look correct on a web page.

To disconnect from the IMAP server and close the stream, pass the IMAP connection handle to `imap_close( )`:

```
// close connection when finished
imap_close($nntp);
```

See Also

Recipe 16.4 for more on posting to newsgroups; documentation on `imap_open( )` at *http://www.php.net/imap-open*, `imap_header( )` at *http://www.php.net/imap-header*, `imap_body( )` at *http://www.php.net/imap-body*, and IMAP in general at *http://www.php.net/imap*; code to read newsgroups in PHP without using IMAP at *http://cvs.php.net/cvs.php/php-news-web*; RFC 977 at *http://www.faqs.org/rfcs/rfc977.html*.

16.6 Getting and Putting Files with FTP

Problem

You want to transfer files using FTP.

Solution

Use PHP's built-in FTP functions:

```
$c = ftp_connect('ftp.example.com')    or die("Can't connect");
ftp_login($c, $username, $password)    or die("Can't login");
ftp_put($c, $remote, $local, FTP_ASCII) or die("Can't transfer");
ftp_close($c);                         or die("Can't close");
```

You can also use the cURL extension:

```
$c = curl_init("ftp://$username:$password@ftp.example.com/$remote");
// $local is the location to store file on local machine
$fh = fopen($local, 'w') or die($php_errormsg);
curl_setopt($c, CURLOPT_FILE, $fh);
curl_exec($c);
curl_close($c);
```

Discussion

FTP is a method of exchanging files between one computer and another. Unlike with HTTP servers, it's easy to set up an FTP server to both send and receive files.

Using the built-in FTP functions doesn't require additional libraries, but you must specifically enable them with `--enable-ftp`. Because these functions are specialized to FTP, they're simple to use when transferring files.

All FTP transactions begin with establishing a connection from your computer, the local client, to another computer, the remote server:

```
$c = ftp_connect('ftp.example.com')    or die("Can't connect");
```

Once connected, you need to send your username and password; the remote server can then authenticate you and allow you to enter:

```
ftp_login($c, $username, $password)     or die("Can't login");
```

Some FTP servers support a feature known as anonymous FTP. Under anonymous FTP, users can log in without an account on the remote system. When you use anonymous FTP, your username is anonymous, and your password is your email address.

Here's how to transfer files with ftp_put( ) and ftp_get( ):

```
ftp_put($c, $remote, $local,  FTP_ASCII) or die("Can't transfer");
ftp_get($c, $local,  $remote, FTP_ASCII) or die("Can't transfer");
```

The ftp_put( ) function takes a file on your computer and copies it to the remote server; ftp_get( ) copies a file on the remote server to your computer. In the previous code, $remote is the pathname to the remote file, and $local points at the file on your computer.

There are two final parameters passed to these functions. The FTP_ASCII parameter, used here, transfers the file as if it were ASCII text. Under this option, line-feed endings are automatically converted as you move from one operating system to another. The other option is FTP_BINARY, which is used for non–plain text files, so no line-feed conversions take place.

Use ftp_fget( ) and ftp_fput( ) to download or upload a file to an existing open file pointer (opened using fopen( )) instead of to a location on the filesystem. For example, here's how to retrieve a file and write it to the existing file pointer, $fp:

```
$fp = fopen($file, 'w');
ftp_fget($c, $fp, $remote, FTP_ASCII)   or die("Can't transfer");
```

Finally, to disconnect from the remote host, call ftp_close( ) to log out:

```
ftp_close($c);                          or die("Can't close");
```

To adjust the amount of seconds the connection takes to time out, use ftp_set_option( ) :

```
// Up the time out value to two minutes:
set_time_limit(120)
$c = ftp_connect('ftp.example.com');
ftp_set_option($c, FTP_TIMEOUT_SEC, 120);
```

The default value is 90 seconds; however, the default max_execution_time of a PHP script is 30 seconds. So if your connection times out too early, be sure to check both values.

To use the cURL extension, you must download cURL from *http://curl.haxx.se/* and set the --with-curl configuration option when building PHP. To use cURL, start by creating a cURL handle with curl_init( ), and then specify what you want to do using curl_setopt( ). The curl_setopt( ) function takes three parameters: a cURL resource, the name of a cURL constant to modify, and a value to assign to the second parameter. In the Solution, the CURLOPT_FILE constant is used:

```
$c = curl_init("ftp://$username:$password@ftp.example.com/$remote");
// $local is the location to store file on local client
$fh = fopen($local, 'w') or die($php_errormsg);
curl_setopt($c, CURLOPT_FILE, $fh);
curl_exec($c);
curl_close($c);
```

You pass the URL to use to curl_init( ). Because the URL begins with ftp://, cURL
knows to use the FTP protocol. Instead of a separate call to log on to the remote server,
you embed the username and password directly into the URL. Next, you set the location
to store the file on your server. Now you open a file named $local for writing and pass
the filehandle to curl_setopt( ) as the value for CURLOPT_FILE. When cURL transfers the
file, it automatically writes to the filehandle. Once everything is configured, you call
curl_exec( ) to initiate the transaction and then curl_close( ) to close the connection.

See Also

Documentation on the FTP extension at *http://www.php.net/ftp* and cURL at *http://
www.php.net/curl*; RFC 959 at *http://www.faqs.org/rfcs/rfc969.html*.

16.7 Looking Up Addresses with LDAP

Problem

You want to query an LDAP server for address information.

Solution

Use PHP's LDAP extension:

```
$ds = ldap_connect('ldap.example.com')                    or die($php_errormsg);
ldap_bind($ds)                                            or die($php_errormsg);
$sr = ldap_search($ds, 'o=Example Inc.', c=US', 'sn=*')   or die($php_errormsg);
$e  = ldap_get_entries($ds, $sr)                          or die($php_errormsg);

for ($i=0; $i < $e['count']; $i++) {
    echo $info[$i]['cn'][0] . ' (' . $info[$i]['mail'][0] . ')<br>';
}

ldap_close($ds)                                           or die($php_errormsg);
```

Discussion

A (LDAP) server stores directory information, such as names and addresses, and allows
you to query it for results. In many ways, it's like a database, except that it's optimized
for storing information about people.

In addition, instead of the flat structure provided by a database, an LDAP server allows
you to organize people in a hierarchical fashion. For example, employees may be divided into marketing, technical, and operations divisions, or they can be split regionally

into North America, Europe, and Asia. This makes it easy to find all employees of a particular subset of a company.

When using LDAP, the address repository is called as a *data source*. Each entry in the repository has a globally unique identifier, known as a *distinguished name*. The distinguished name includes both a person's name, but also the company information. For instance, John Q. Smith, who works at Example Inc., a U.S. company, has a distinguished name of `cn=John Q. Smith, o=Example Inc., c=US`. In LDAP, `cn` stands for common name, `o` for organization, and `c` for country.

You must enable PHP's LDAP support with `--with-ldap`. You can download an LDAP server from *http://www.openldap.org*. This recipe assumes basic knowledge about LDAP. For more information, read the articles on the O'Reilly Network at *http://www.onlamp.com/topics/apache/ldap*.

Communicating with an LDAP server requires four steps: connecting, authenticating, searching records, and logging off. Besides searching, you can also add, alter, and delete records.

The opening transactions require you to connect to a specific LDAP server and then authenticate yourself in a process known as *binding*:

```
$ds = ldap_connect('ldap.example.com')          or die($php_errormsg);
ldap_bind($ds)                                   or die($php_errormsg);
```

Passing only the connection handle, `$ds`, to `ldap_bind( )` does an anonymous bind. To bind with a specific username and password, pass them as the second and third parameters, like so:

```
ldap_bind($ds, $username, $password)             or die($php_errormsg);
```

Once logged in, you can request information. Because the information is arranged in a hierarchy, you need to indicate the base distinguished name as the second parameter. Finally, you pass in the search criteria. For example, here's how to find all people with a surname of `Jones` at company `Example Inc.` located in the country `US`:

```
$sr = ldap_search($ds, 'o=Example Inc., c=US', 'sn=Jones') or die($php_errormsg);
$e  = ldap_get_entries($ds, $sr)                 or die($php_errormsg);
```

Once `ldap_search( )` returns results, use `ldap_get_entries( )` to retrieve the specific data records. Then iterate through the array of entries, `$e`:

```
for ($i=0; $i < $e['count']; $i++) {
    echo $e[$i]['cn'][0] . ' (' . $e[$i]['mail'][0] . ')<br>';
}
```

Instead of doing `count($e)`, use the precomputed record size located in `$e['count']`. Inside the loop, print the first common name and email address for each record. For example:

```
David Sklar (sklar@example.com)
Adam Trachtenberg (adam@example.com)
```

The `ldap_search( )` function searches the entire tree equal to and below the distin-guished name base. To restrict the results to a specific level, use `ldap_list( )`. Because the search takes place over a smaller set of records, `ldap_list( )` can be significantly faster than `ldap_search( )`.

See Also

Recipe 16.8 for authenticating users with LDAP; documentation on LDAP at *http://www.php.net/ldap*; RFC 2251 at *http://www.faqs.org/rfcs/rfc2251.html*.

16.8 Using LDAP for User Authentication

Problem

You want to restrict parts of your site to authenticated users. Instead of verifying people against a database or using HTTP Basic Authorization, you want to use an LDAP server. Holding all user information in an LDAP server makes centralized user administration easier.

Solution

Use PEAR's `Auth` class, which supports LDAP authentication:

```
$options = array('host'    => 'ldap.example.com',
                 'port'    => '389',
                 'base'    => 'o=Example Inc., c=US',
                 'userattr' => 'uid');

$auth = new Auth('LDAP', $options);

// begin validation
// print login screen for anonymous users
$auth->start();

if ($auth->getAuth()) {
    // content for validated users
} else {
    // content for anonymous users
}

// log users out
$auth->logout();
```

Discussion

LDAP servers are designed for address storage, lookup, and retrieval, and so are better to use than standard databases like MySQL or Oracle. LDAP servers are very fast, you can easily implement access control by granting different permissions to different groups of users, and many different programs can query the server. For example, most email clients can use an LDAP server as an address book, so if you address a message to "John Smith," the server replies with John's email address, *jsmith@example.com*.

PEAR's `Auth` class allows you to validate users against files, databases, and LDAP servers. The first parameter is the type of authentication to use, and the second is an array of information on how to validate users. For example:

```
$options = array('host'     => 'ldap.example.com',
                 'port'     => '389',
                 'base'     => 'o=Example Inc., c=US',
                 'userattr' => 'uid');

$auth = new Auth('LDAP', $options);
```

This creates a new `Auth` object that validates against an LDAP server located at *ldap.example.com* and communicates over port 389. The base directory name is o=Example Inc., c=US, and usernames are checked against the uid attribute. The uid field stands for user identifier. This is normally a username for a web site or a login name for a general account. If your server doesn't store uid attributes for each user, you can substitute the cn attribute. The common name field holds a user's full name, such as "John Q. Smith."

The `Auth::auth()` method also takes an optional third parameter—the name of a function that displays the sign-in form. This form can be formatted however you wish; the only requirement is that the form input fields must be called `username` and `password`. Also, the form must submit the data using POST:

```
$options = array('host'     => 'ldap.example.com',
                 'port'     => '389',
                 'base'     => 'o=Example Inc., c=US',
                 'userattr' => 'uid');

function pc_auth_ldap_signin() {
    print<<<_HTML_
<form method="post" action="$_SERVER[PHP_SELF]">
Name: <input name="username" type="text"><br />
Password: <input name="password" type="password"><br />
<input type="submit" value="Sign In">
</form>
_HTML_;
}

$auth = new Auth('LDAP', $options, 'pc_auth_ldap_signin');
```

Once the `Auth` object is instantiated, authenticate a user by calling `Auth::start()`:

```
$auth->start();
```

If the user is already signed in, nothing happens. If the user is anonymous, the sign-in form is printed. To validate a user, `Auth::start()` connects to the LDAP server, does an anonymous bind, and searches for an address in which the user attribute specified in the constructor matches the username passed in by the form:

```
$options['userattr'] = $_POST['username']
```

If `Auth::start( )` finds exactly one person that fits this criteria, it retrieves the designated name for the user, and attempts to do an authenticated bind, using the designated name and password from the form as the login credentials. The LDAP server then compares the password to the `userPassword` attribute associated with the designated name. If it matches, the user is authenticated.

You can call `Auth::getAuth( )` to return a boolean value describing a user's status:

```
if ($auth->getAuth()) {
    print 'Welcome member! Nice to see you again.';
} else {
    print 'Welcome guest. First time visiting?';
}
```

The `Auth` class uses the built-in session module to track users, so once validated, a person remains authenticated until the session expires, or you explicitly log him out with:

```
$auth->logout();
```

See Also

Recipe 16.7 for searching LDAP servers; PEAR's `Auth` class at *http://pear.php.net/pack age-info.php?package=Auth*.

16.9 Performing DNS Lookups

Problem

You want to look up a domain name or an IP address.

Solution

Use `gethostbyname( )` and `gethostbyaddr( )`:

```
$ip   = gethostbyname('www.example.com'); // 192.0.34.72
$host = gethostbyaddr('192.0.34.72'); // www.example.com
```

Discussion

You can't trust the name returned by `gethostbyaddr( )`. A DNS server with authority for a particular IP address can return any hostname at all. Usually, administrators set up DNS servers to reply with a correct hostname, but a malicious user may configure her DNS server to reply with incorrect hostnames. One way to combat this trickery is to call `gethostbyname( )` on the hostname returned from `gethostbyaddr( )` and make sure the name resolves to the original IP address.

If either function can't successfully look up the IP address or the domain name, it doesn't return `false`, but instead returns the argument passed to it. To check for failure, do this:

```
if ($host == ($ip = gethostbyname($host))) {
    // failure
}
```

This assigns the return value of gethostbyname( ) to $ip and also checks that $ip is not equal to the original $host.

Sometimes a single hostname can map to multiple IP addresses. To find all hosts, use gethostbynamel( ):

```
$hosts = gethostbynamel('www.yahoo.com');
print_r($hosts);

$hosts = gethostbynamel('www.yahoo.com');
print_r($hosts);
Array
(
    [0] => 64.58.76.176
    [1] => 64.58.76.224
    [2] => 64.58.76.177
    [3] => 64.58.76.227
    [4] => 64.58.76.179
    [5] => 64.58.76.225
    [6] => 64.58.76.178
    [7] => 64.58.76.229
    [8] => 64.58.76.223
)
```

In contrast to gethostbyname( ) and gethostbyaddr( ), gethostbynamel( ) returns an array, not a string.

You can also do more complicated DNS-related tasks. For instance, you can get the MX records using getmxrr( ):

```
getmxrr('yahoo.com', $hosts, $weight);
for ($i = 0; $i < count($hosts); $i++) {
    echo "$weight[$i] $hosts[$i]\n";
}

getmxrr('yahoo.com', $hosts, $weight);
for ($i = 0; $i < count($hosts); $i++) {
    echo "$weight[$i] $hosts[$i]\n";
}
5 mx4.mail.yahoo.com
1 mx2.mail.yahoo.com
1 mx1.mail.yahoo.com
```

To perform zone transfers, dynamic DNS updates, and more, see PEAR's Net_DNS package.

See Also

Documentation on gethostbyname( ) at *http://www.php.net/gethostbyname*, gethostbyaddr( ) *http://www.php.net/gethostbyaddr*, gethostbynamel( ) at *http://www.php.net/gethostbynamel*, and getmxrr( ) at *http://www.php.net/getmxrr*; PEAR's

Net_DNS package at *http://pear.php.net/package-info.php?package=Net_DNS*; *DNS and BIND* by Paul Albitz and Cricket Liu (O'Reilly).

16.10 Checking if a Host Is Alive

Problem

You want to ping a host to see if it is still up and accessible from your location.

Solution

Use PEAR's Net_Ping package:

```
require 'Net/Ping.php';

$ping = new Net_Ping;
if ($ping->checkhost('www.oreilly.com')) {
    print 'Reachable';
} else {
    print 'Unreachable';
}

$data = $ping->ping('www.oreilly.com');
```

Discussion

The *ping* program tries to send a message from your machine to another. If everything goes well, you get a series of statistics chronicling the transaction. An error means that *ping* can't reach the host for some reason.

On error, Net_Ping::checkhost( ) returns false, and Net_Ping::ping( ) returns the constant PING_HOST_NOT_FOUND. If there's a problem running the *ping* program (because Net_Ping is really just a wrapper for the program), PING_FAILED is returned.

If everything is okay, you receive an array similar to this:

```
$results = $ping->ping('www.oreilly.com');

foreach($results as $result) { print "$result\n"; }

$results = $ping->ping('www.oreilly.com');

foreach($results as $result) { print "$result\n"; }
PING www.oreilly.com (209.204.146.22) from 192.168.123.101 :
    32(60) bytes of data.
40 bytes from www.oreilly.com (209.204.146.22): icmp_seq=0 ttl=239
    time=96.704 msec
40 bytes from www.oreilly.com (209.204.146.22): icmp_seq=1 ttl=239
    time=86.567 msec
40 bytes from www.oreilly.com (209.204.146.22): icmp_seq=2 ttl=239
    time=86.563 msec
40 bytes from www.oreilly.com (209.204.146.22): icmp_seq=3 ttl=239
    time=136.565 msec
```

```
40 bytes from www.oreilly.com (209.204.146.22): icmp_seq=4 ttl=239
    time=86.627 msec

 -- - www.oreilly.com ping statistics  -- -
5 packets transmitted, 5 packets received, 0% packet loss
round-trip min/avg/max/mdev = 86.563/98.605/136.565/19.381 ms
```

Net_Ping doesn't do any parsing of the data to pull apart the information, such as the packet loss percentage or the average round-trip time. However, you can parse it yourself:

```
$results = $ping->ping('www.oreilly.com');

// grab last line of array; equivalent to non-destructive array_pop()
// or $results[count($results) - 1]
$round_trip = end($results);
preg_match_all('#[ /]([.\d]+)#', $round_trip, $times);

// pull out the data
list($min,$avg,$max,$mdev) = $times[1];
// or print it out
foreach($times[1] as $time) { print "$time\n"; }

$results = $ping->ping('www.oreilly.com');

// grab last line of array; equivalent to non-destructive array_pop()
// or $results[count($results) - 1]
$round_trip = end($results);
preg_match_all('#[ /]([.\d]+)#', $round_trip, $times);

// pull out the data
list($min,$avg,$max,$mdev) = $times[1];
// or print it out
foreach($times[1] as $time) { print "$time\n"; }
83.229
91.230
103.223
7.485
```

This regular expression searches for either a space or a slash. It then captures a sequence of one or more numbers and a decimal point. To avoid escaping /, we use the # non-standard character as your delimiter.

See Also

PEAR's Net_Ping package at *http://pear.php.net/package-info.php?package=Net_Ping*.

16.11 Getting Information About a Domain Name

Problem

You want to look up contact information or other details about a domain name.

Solution

Use PEAR's `Net_Whois` class:

```
require 'Net/Whois.php';
$server = 'whois.networksolutions.com';
$query  = 'example.org';
$data = Net_Whois::query($server, $query);
```

Discussion

The `Net_Whois::query( )` method returns a large text string whose contents reinforce how hard it can be to parse different Whois results:

```
Registrant:
Internet Assigned Numbers Authority (EXAMPLE2-DOM)
    4676 Admiralty Way, Suite 330
    Marina del Rey, CA 90292
    US

    Domain Name: EXAMPLE.ORG

    Administrative Contact, Technical Contact, Billing Contact:
        Internet Assigned Numbers Authority  (IANA)  iana@IANA.ORG
        4676 Admiralty Way, Suite 330
        Marina del Rey, CA 90292
        US
        310-823-9358
        Fax- 310-823-8649

    Record last updated on 07-Jan-2002.
    Record expires on 01-Sep-2009.
    Record created on 31-Aug-1995.
    Database last updated on 6-Apr-2002 02:56:00 EST.

    Domain servers in listed order:

    A.IANA-SERVERS.NET              192.0.34.43
    B.IANA-SERVERS.NET              193.0.0.236
```

For instance, if you want to parse out the names and IP addresses of the domain name servers, use this:

```
preg_match_all('/^\s*([\S]+)\s+([\d.]+)\s*$/m', $data, $dns,
               PREG_SET_ORDER);

foreach ($dns as $server) {
    print "$server[1] : $server[2]\n";
}
```

You must set `$server` to the correct Whois server for a domain to get information about that domain. If you don't know the server to use, query *whois.internic.net*:

```
require 'Net/Whois.php';

print Net_Whois::query('whois.internic.net','example.org');
```

```
require 'Net/Whois.php';

print Net_Whois::query('whois.internic.net','example.org');
[whois.internic.net]

Whois Server Version 1.3

Domain names in the .com, .net, and .org domains can now be registered
with many different competing registrars. Go to http://www.internic.net
for detailed information.

   Domain Name: EXAMPLE.ORG
   Registrar: NETWORK SOLUTIONS, INC.
   Whois Server: whois.networksolutions.com
   Referral URL: http://www.networksolutions.com
   Name Server: A.IANA-SERVERS.NET
   Name Server: B.IANA-SERVERS.NET
   Updated Date: 19-aug-2002


>>> Last update of whois database: Wed, 21 Aug 2002 04:56:56 EDT <<<

The Registry database contains ONLY .COM, .NET, .ORG, .EDU domains and
Registrars.
```

The Whois Server: line says that the correct server to ask for information about *example.org* is *whois.networksolutions.com*.

See Also

PEAR's Net_Whois class at *http://pear.php.net/package-info.php?package=Net_Whois*.

CHAPTER 17

Graphics

17.0 Introduction

With the assistance of the GD library, you can use PHP to create applications that use dynamic images to display stock quotes, reveal poll results, monitor system performance, and even create games. However, it's not like using Photoshop or GIMP; you can't draw a line by moving your mouse. Instead, you need to precisely specify a shape's type, size, and position.

GD has an existing API, and PHP tries to follows its syntax and function-naming conventions. So if you're familiar with GD from other languages, such as C or Perl, you can easily use GD with PHP. If GD is new to you, it may take a few minutes to figure it out, but soon you'll be drawing like Picasso.

The feature set of GD varies greatly depending on which version of GD you're running and which features were enabled during configuration. GD can support GIFs, JPEGs, PNGs, and WBMPs. GD reads in PNGs and JPEGs with almost no loss in quality. Also, GD supports PNG alpha channels, which allow you to specify a transparency level for each pixel.

Besides supporting multiple file formats, GD lets you draw pixels, lines, rectangles, polygons, arcs, ellipses, and circles in any color you want. Recipe 17.1 covers straight shapes, while Recipe 17.2 covers the curved ones. To fill shapes with a pattern instead of a solid color, see Recipe 17.3.

You can also draw text using a variety of font types, including built-in, TrueType, and PostScript Type 1 fonts. Recipe 17.4 shows the ins and outs of the three main text-drawing functions, and Recipe 17.5 shows how to center text within a canvas. These two recipes form the basis for Recipe 17.6, which combines an image template with real-time data to create dynamic images. GD also lets you make transparent GIFs and PNGs. Setting a color as transparent and using transparencies in patterns are discussed in Recipe 17.7.

To extract image metadata from digital photos and other images that store information using the EXIF standard, read Recipe 17.8.

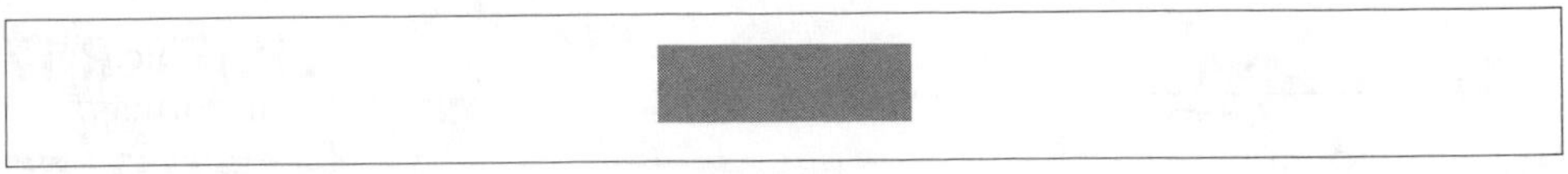

Figure 17-1. A gray rectangle on a white background

Recipe 17.9 moves away from GD and shows how to securely serve images by restricting user access. Last, there's an example application taking poll results and producing a dynamic bar graph showing what percentage of users voted for each answer.

All these features work with the version of GD bundled with PHP 5.1. If you have an earlier version, you should not have a problem. However, if a particular recipe needs a specific version of GD, it's noted in the recipe.

GD is available for download from the official GD site at *http://www.boutell.com/gd/*. The GD section of the online PHP Manual at *http://www.php.net/image* also lists the location of the additional libraries necessary to provide support for JPEGs and Type 1 fonts. However, the PHP team has recently taken over development of the GD library, so expect that it will be increasingly easy to use PHP and GD.

There are two easy ways to see which version, if any, of GD is installed on your server and how it's configured. One way is to call phpinfo( ). You should see --with-gd at the top under "Configure Command"; further down the page there is also a section titled "gd" that has more information about which version of GD is installed and what features are enabled. The other option is to check the return value of function_exists('imagecreate'). If it returns true, GD is installed. The imagetypes( ) function returns a bit field indicating which graphics formats are available. See *http://www.php.net/imagetypes* for more on how to use this function. If you want to use a feature that isn't enabled, you need to rebuild PHP yourself or get your ISP to do so.

The basic image generation process has three steps: creating the image, adding graphics and text to the canvas, and displaying or saving the image. For example:

```
$image = ImageCreate(200, 50);
$background_color = ImageColorAllocate($image, 255, 255, 255); // white
$gray            = ImageColorAllocate($image, 204, 204, 204); // gray

ImageFilledRectangle($image, 50, 10, 150, 40, $gray);

header('Content-type: image/png');
ImagePNG($image);
```

The output of this code, which prints a gray rectangle on a white background, is shown in Figure 17-1.

To begin, you create an image canvas. The ImageCreate( ) function doesn't return an actual image. Instead, it provides you with a handle to an image; it's not an actual graphic until you specifically tell PHP to write the image out. Using ImageCreate( ), you can juggle multiple images at the same time.

The parameters passed to ImageCreate( ) are the width and height of the graphic in pixels. In this case, it's 200 pixels across and 50 pixels high. Instead of creating a new

image, you can also edit existing images. To open a graphic, call
ImageCreateFromPNG( ) or a similarly named function to open a different file format. The
filename is the only argument, and files can live locally or on remote servers:

```
// open a PNG from the local machine
$graph = ImageCreateFromPNG('/path/to/graph.png');

// open a JPEG from a remote server
$icon  = ImageCreateFromJPEG('http://www.example.com/images/icon.jpeg');
```

Once you have an editable canvas, you get access to drawing colors by calling
ImageColorAllocate( ) :

```
$background_color = ImageColorAllocate($image, 255, 255, 255); // white
$gray             = ImageColorAllocate($image, 204, 204, 204); // gray
```

The ImageColorAllocate( ) function takes an image handle to allocate the color to three
integers. The three integers each range from 0 to 255 and specify the red, green, and
blue components of the color. This is the same RGB color combination that is used in
HTML to set a font or background color. So white is 255, 255, 255; black is 0, 0, 0;
and everything else is somewhere in between.

The first call to ImageAllocateColor( ) sets the background color. Additional calls allocate colors for drawing lines, shapes, or text. Therefore, set the background color to
255, 255, 255 and then grab a gray pen with ImageAllocateColor($image, 204, 204,
204). It may seem odd that the background color is determined by the order
ImageAllocateColor( ) is called and not by a separate function. But that's how things
work in GD, so PHP respects the convention.

Call ImageFilledRectangle( ) to place a box onto the canvas. ImageFilledRectangle( )
takes many parameters: the image to draw on, the x and y coordinates of the upper left
corner of the rectangle, the x and y coordinates of the lower right corner of the rectangle,
and finally, the color to use to draw the shape. Tell ImageFilledRectangle( ) to draw a
rectangle on $image, starting at (50,10) and going to (150,40), in the color gray:

```
ImageFilledRectangle($image, 50, 10, 150, 40, $gray);
```

Unlike a Cartesian graph, (0,0) is not in the lower left corner; instead, it's in the upper
left corner. So the vertical coordinate of the spot 10 pixels from the top of a 50-pixel-
high canvas is 10 because it's 10 pixels down from the top of the canvas. It's not 40,
because you measure from the top down, not the bottom up. And it's not −10, because
down is considered the positive direction, not the negative one.

Now that the image is all ready to go, you can serve it up. First, send a Content-Type
header to let the browser know what type of image you're sending. In this case, display
a PNG. Next, have PHP write the PNG image out using ImagePNG( ). Once the image is
sent, your task is over:

```
header('Content-Type: image/png');
ImagePNG($image);
```

To write the image to disk instead of sending it to the browser, provide a second argument to ImagePNG( ) with where to save the file:

```
ImagePng($image, '/path/to/your/new/image.png');
```

Since the file isn't going to the browser, there's no need to call header( ). Make sure to specify a path and an image name, and be sure PHP has permission to write to that location.

PHP cleans up the image when the script ends, but if you wish to manually deallocate the memory used by the image, calling ImageDestroy($image) forces PHP to get rid of the image immediately.

17.1 Drawing Lines, Rectangles, and Polygons

Problem

You want to draw a line, rectangle, or polygon. You also want to be able to control if the rectangle or polygon is open or filled in. For example, you want to be able to draw bar charts or create graphs of stock quotes.

Solution

To draw a line, use ImageLine( ):

```
ImageLine($image, $x1, $y1, $x2, $y2, $color);
```

To draw an open rectangle, use ImageRectangle( ):

```
ImageRectangle($image, $x1, $y1, $x2, $y2, $color);
```

To draw a solid rectangle, use ImageFilledRectangle( ):

```
ImageFilledRectangle($image, $x1, $y1, $x2, $y2, $color);
```

To draw an open polygon, use ImagePolygon( ):

```
$points = array($x1, $y1, $x2, $y2, $x3, $y3);
ImagePolygon($image, $points, count($points)/2, $color);
```

To draw a filled polygon, use ImageFilledPolygon( ):

```
$points = array($x1, $y1, $x2, $y2, $x3, $y3);
ImageFilledPolygon($image, $points, count($points)/2, $color);
```

Discussion

The prototypes for all five functions in the Solution are similar. The first parameter is the canvas to draw on. The next set of parameters are the x and y coordinates to specify where GD should draw the shape. In ImageLine( ), the four coordinates are the endpoints of the line, and in ImageRectangle( ), they're the opposite corners of the rectangle. For example, ImageLine($image, 0, 0, 100, 100, $color) produces a diagonal line. Pass-

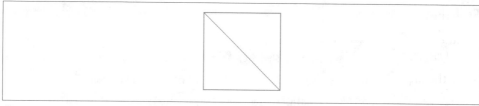

Figure 17-2. A diagonal line and a square

ing the same parameters to ImageRectangle( ) produces a rectangle with corners at (0,0), (100,0), (0,100), and (100,100). Both shapes are shown in Figure 17-2.

The ImagePolygon( ) function is slightly different because it can accept a variable number of vertices. Therefore, the second parameter is an array of x and y coordinates. The function starts at the first set of points and draws lines from vertex to vertex before finally completing the figure by connecting back to the original point. You must have a minimum of three vertices in your polygon (for a total of six elements in the array). The third parameter is the number of vertices in the shape; since that's always half of the number of elements in the array of points, a flexible value for this is count($points) / 2 because it allows you to update the array of vertices without breaking the call to ImageLine( ).

Last, all the functions take a final parameter that specifies the drawing color. This is usually a value returned from ImageColorAllocate( ) but can also be the constants IMG_COLOR_STYLED or IMG_COLOR_STYLEDBRUSHED, if you want to draw nonsolid lines, as discussed in Recipe 17.3.

These functions all draw open shapes. To get GD to fill the region with the drawing color, use ImageFilledRectangle( ) and ImageFilledPolygon( ) with the identical set of arguments as their unfilled cousins.

See Also

Recipe 17.2 for more on drawing other types of shapes; Recipe 17.3 for more on drawing with styles and brushes; documentation on ImageLine( ) at *http://www.php.net/image line*, ImageRectangle( ) at *http://www.php.net/imagerectangle*, ImagePolygon( ) at *http://www.php.net/imagepolygon*, and ImageColorAllocate( ) at *http://www.php.net/imageco lorallocate*.

17.2 Drawing Arcs, Ellipses, and Circles

Problem

You want to draw open or filled curves. For example, you want to draw a pie chart showing the results of a user poll.

Solution

To draw an arc, use `ImageArc( )`:

```
ImageArc($image, $x, $y, $width, $height, $start, $end, $color);
```

To draw an ellipse, use `ImageArc( )` and set `$start` to 0 and `$end` to 360:

```
ImageArc($image, $x, $y, $width, $height, 0, 360, $color);
```

To draw a circle, use `ImageArc( )`, set `$start` to 0, set `$end` to 360, and use the same value for both `$width` and `$height`:

```
ImageArc($image, $x, $y, $diameter, $diameter, 0, 360, $color);
```

Discussion

Because the `ImageArc( )` function is highly flexible, you can easily create common curves such as ellipses and circles by passing it the right values. Like many GD functions, the first parameter is the canvas. The next two parameters are the x and y coordinates for the center position of the arc. After that comes the arc width and height. Since a circle is an arc with the same width and height, to draw a circle, set both numbers to the diameter of the circle.

The sixth and seventh parameters are the starting and ending angles, in degrees. A value of 0 is at three o'clock. The arc then moves clockwise, so 90 is at six o'clock, 180 is at nine o'clock, and 270 is at the top of the hour. (Be careful—this behavior is not consistent among all GD functions. For example, when you rotate text, you turn in a counterclockwise direction.) Since the arc's center is located at (`$x,$y`), if you draw a semicircle from 0 to 180, it doesn't start at (`$x,$y`); instead, it begins at (`$x+($diameter/2),$y`).

As usual, the last parameter is the arc color.

For example, this draws an open black circle with a diameter of 100 pixels centered on the canvas, as shown in the left half of Figure 17-3:

```
$image = ImageCreate(100,100);
$bg = ImageColorAllocate($image, 255, 255, 255);
$black = ImageColorAllocate($image, 0, 0, 0);
ImageArc($image, 50, 50, 100, 100, 0, 360, $black);
```

To produce a solid ellipse or circle, call `ImageFillToBorder( )`:

```
ImageArc($image, $x, $y, $diameter, $diameter, 0, 360, $color);
ImageFillToBorder($image, $x, $y, $color, $color);
```

The `ImageFillToBorder( )` function floods a region beginning at (`$x,$y`) with the color specified as the last parameter until it hits the edge of the canvas or runs into a line with the same color as the third parameter.

Incorporating this into the earlier example gives:

```
$image = ImageCreate(100,100);
$bg = ImageColorAllocate($image, 255, 255, 255);
```

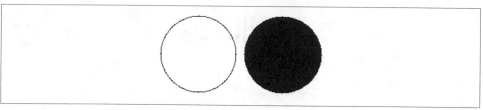

Figure 17-3. An open black circle and a filled black circle

```
$black = ImageColorAllocate($image, 0, 0, 0);
ImageArc($image, 50, 50, 100, 100, 0, 360, $black);
ImageFillToBorder($image, 50, 50, $black, $black);
```

The output is shown in the right half of Figure 17-3.

If you're running GD 2.x, you can call `ImageFilledArc( )` and pass in a final parameter that describes the fill style. GD 2.x also supports specific `ImageEllipse( )` and `ImageFilledEllipse( )` functions.

See Also

Recipe 17.2 for more on drawing other types of shapes; Recipe 17.3 for more on drawing with styles and brushes; documentation on `ImageArc( )` at *http://www.php.net/image arc*, `ImageFilledArc( )` at *http://www.php.net/imagefilledarc*, and `ImageFillToBorder( )` at *http://www.php.net/imagefilltoborder*.

17.3 Drawing with Patterned Lines

Problem

You want to draw shapes using line styles other than the default, a solid line.

Solution

To draw shapes with a patterned line, use `ImageSetStyle( )` and pass in `IMG_COLOR_STYLED` as the image color:

```
$black = ImageColorAllocate($image,   0,   0,   0);
$white = ImageColorAllocate($image, 255, 255, 255);

// make a two-pixel thick black and white dashed line
$style = array($black, $black, $white, $white);
ImageSetStyle($image, $style);

ImageLine($image, 0, 0, 50, 50, IMG_COLOR_STYLED);
ImageFilledRectangle($image, 50, 50, 100, 100, IMG_COLOR_STYLED);
```

Figure 17-4. Three squares with alternating white and black pixels

Discussion

The line pattern is defined by an array of colors. Each element in the array is another pixel in the brush. It's often useful to repeat the same color in successive elements, as this increases the size of the stripes in the pattern.

For instance, here is code for a square drawn with alternating white and black pixels, as shown in the left side of Figure 17-4:

```
$style = array($white, $black);
ImageSetStyle($image, $style);
ImageFilledRectangle($image, 0, 0, 49, 49, IMG_COLOR_STYLED);
```

This is the same square, but drawn with a style of five white pixels followed by five black ones, as shown in the middle of Figure 17-4:

```
$style = array($white, $white, $white, $white, $white,
               $black, $black, $black, $black, $black);
ImageSetStyle($image, $style);
ImageFilledRectangle($image, 0, 0, 49, 49, IMG_COLOR_STYLED);
```

The patterns look completely different, even though both styles are just white and black pixels.

If the brush doesn't fit an integer number of times in the shape, it wraps around. In the previous examples, the square is 50 pixels wide. Since the first brush is 2 pixels long, it fits exactly 25 times; the second brush is 10 pixels, so it fits 5 times. But if you make the square 45 by 45 and use the second brush, you don't get straight lines as you did previously, as shown in the right side of Figure 17-4:

```
ImageFilledRectangle($image, 0, 0, 44, 44, IMG_COLOR_STYLED);
```

See Also

Recipes 17.1 and 17.2 for more on drawing shapes; documentation on ImageSetStyle( ) at *http://www.php.net/imagesetstyle*.

17.4 Drawing Text

Problem

You want to draw text as a graphic. This allows you to make dynamic buttons or hit counters.

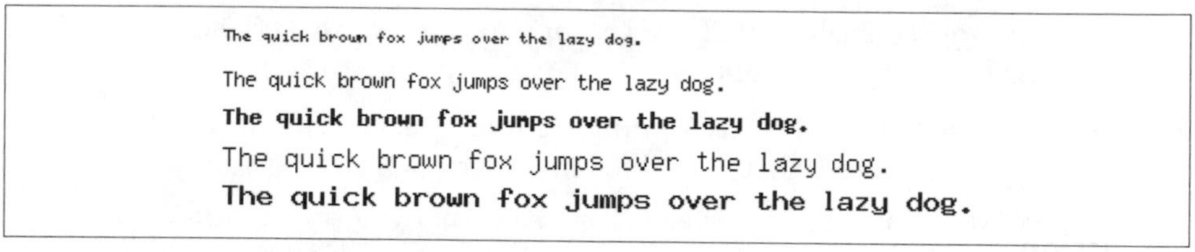

The quick brown fox jumps over the lazy dog.

The quick brown fox jumps over the lazy dog.

The quick brown fox jumps over the lazy dog.

The quick brown fox jumps over the lazy dog.

The quick brown fox jumps over the lazy dog.

Figure 17-5. Built-in GD font sizes

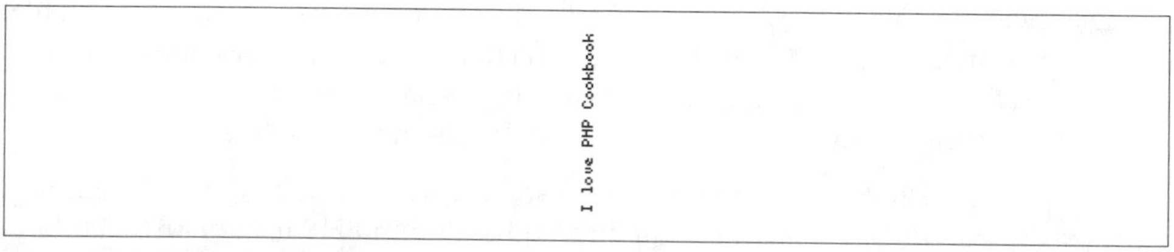

Figure 17-6. Vertical text

Solution

For built-in GD fonts, use ImageString( ):

```
ImageString($image, 1, $x, $y, 'I love PHP Cookbook', $text_color);
```

For TrueType fonts, use ImageTTFText( ):

```
ImageTTFText($image, $size, 0, $x, $y, $text_color, '/path/to/font.ttf',
             'I love PHP Cookbook');
```

For PostScript Type 1 fonts, use ImagePSLoadFont( ) and ImagePSText( ):

```
$font = ImagePSLoadFont('/path/to/font.pfb');
ImagePSText($image, 'I love PHP Cookbook', $font, $size,
            $text_color, $background_color, $x, $y);
```

Discussion

Call ImageString( ) to place text onto the canvas. Like other GD drawing functions, ImageString( ) needs many inputs: the image to draw on, the font number, the x and y coordinates of the upper right position of the first characters, the text string to display, and finally, the color to use to draw the string.

With ImageString( ), there are five possible font choices, from 1 to 5. Font number 1 is the smallest, while font 5 is the largest, as shown in Figure 17-5. Anything above or below that range generates a size equivalent to the closest legal number.

To draw text vertically instead of horizontally, use the function ImageStringUp( ) instead. Figure 17-6 shows the output:

```
ImageStringUp($image, 1, $x, $y, 'I love PHP Cookbook', $text_color);
```

To use TrueType fonts, you must also install the FreeType library and configure PHP during installation to use FreeType. The FreeType main site is *http://*

www.freetype.org. To enable FreeType 1.x support, use `--with-ttf` and for FreeType 2.x, pass `--with-freetype-dir=DIR`.

Like `ImageString( )`, `ImageTTFText( )` prints a string to a canvas, but it takes slightly different options and needs them in a different order:

```
ImageTTFText($image, $size, $angle, $x, $y, $text_color, '/path/to/font.ttf',
            $text);
```

The `$size` argument is the font size in pixels; `$angle` is an angle of rotation, in degrees going counterclockwise; and */path/to/font.ttf* is the pathname to the TrueType font file. Unlike `ImageString( )`, `($x,$y)` are the lower left coordinates of the baseline for the first character. (The baseline is where the bottom of most characters sit. Characters such as "g" and "j" extend below the baseline; "a" and "z" sit on the baseline.)

PostScript Type 1 fonts require *t1lib* to be installed, which can be downloaded from *ftp://sunsite.unc.edu/pub/Linux/libs/graphics/* and built into PHP using `--with-t1lib`.

Again, the syntax for printing text is similar but not the same:

```
$font = ImagePSLoadFont('/path/to/font.pfb');
ImagePSText($image, $text, $font, $size, $text_color, $background_color, $x, $y);
ImagePSFreeFont($font);
```

First, PostScript font names can't be directly passed into `ImagePSText( )`. Instead, they must be loaded using `ImagePSLoadFont( )`. On success, the function returns a font resource usable with `ImagePSText( )`. In addition, besides specifying a text color, you also pass a background color to be used in antialiasing calculations. The `($x,$y)` positioning is akin to the how the TrueType library does it. Last, when you're done with a font, you can release it from memory by calling `ImagePSFreeFont( )`.

Besides the mandatory arguments listed above, `ImagePSText( )` also accepts four optional ones, in this order: `space`, `tightness`, `angle`, and `antialias_steps`. You must include all four or none of the four (i.e., you can't pass one, two, or three of these arguments). The first controls the size of a physical space (i.e., what's generated by hitting the Space bar); the second is the tightness of the distance between letters; the third is a rotation angle, in degrees, counterclockwise; and the last is an antialiasing value. This number must be either 4 or 16. For better-looking, but more computationally expensive graphics, use 16 instead of 4.

By default, `space`, `tightness`, and `angle` are all 0. A positive number adds more space between words and letters or rotates the graphic counterclockwise. A negative number tightens words and letters or rotates in the opposite direction. The following example has the output shown in Figure 17-7:

```
// normal image
ImagePSText($image, $text, $font, $size, $black, $white, $x, $y,
            0, 0, 0, 4);

// extra space between words
ImagePSText($image, $text, $font, $size, $black, $white, $x, $y + 30,
            100, 0, 0, 4);
```

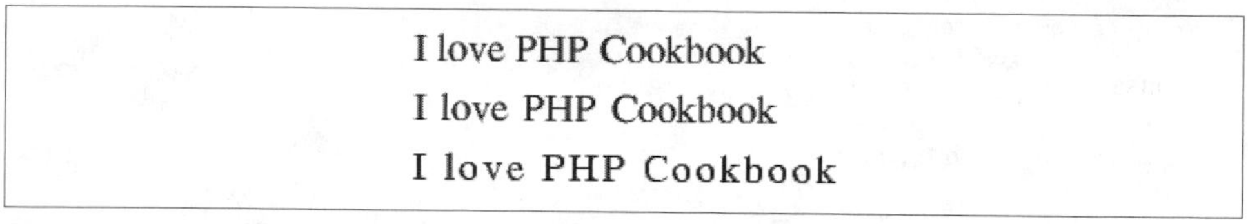

```
I love PHP Cookbook

I love PHP Cookbook

I love PHP Cookbook
```

Figure 17-7. Words with extra space and tightness

```
// extra space between letters
ImagePSText($image, $text, $font, $size, $black, $white, $x, $y + 60,
            0, 100, 0, 4);
```

See Also

Recipe 17.5 for drawing centered text; documentation on `ImageString( )` at *http://www.php.net/imagestring*, `ImageStringUp( )` at *http://www.php.net/imagestringup*, `ImageTTFText( )` at *http://www.php.net/imagettftext*, `ImagePSText( )` at *http://www.php.net/imagepstext*, and `ImagePSLoadFont( )` at *http://www.php.net/imagepsloadfont*.

17.5 Drawing Centered Text

Problem

You want to draw text in the center of an image.

Solution

Find the size of the image and the bounding box of the text. Using those coordinates, compute the correct spot to draw the text.

For built-in GD fonts, use the `pc_ImageStringCenter( )` function, shown in Example 17-1.

Example 17-1. pc_ImageStringCenter( )

```
function pc_ImageStringCenter($image, $text, $font) {

    // font sizes
    $width  = array(1 => 5, 6, 7, 8, 9);
    $height = array(1 => 6, 8, 13, 15, 15);

    // find the size of the image
    $xi = ImageSX($image);
    $yi = ImageSY($image);

    // find the size of the text
    $xr = $width[$font] * strlen($text);
    $yr = $height[$font];
```

```
      // compute centering
      $x = intval(($xi - $xr) / 2);
      $y = intval(($yi - $yr) / 2);

      return array($x, $y);
   }
```

For example:

```
   list($x, $y) = pc_ImageStringCenter($image, $text, $font);
   ImageString($image, $font, $x, $y, $text, $fore);
```

For PostScript fonts, use the **pc_ImagePSCenter( )** function, shown in Example 17-2.

Example 17-2. pc_ImagePSCenter( )

```
   function pc_ImagePSCenter($image, $text, $font, $size, $space = 0,
                             $tightness = 0, $angle = 0) {

      // find the size of the image
      $xi = ImageSX($image);
      $yi = ImageSY($image);

      // find the size of the text
      list($xl, $yl, $xr, $yr) = ImagePSBBox($text, $font, $size,
                                     $space, $tightness, $angle);

      // compute centering
      $x = intval(($xi - $xr) / 2);
      $y = intval(($yi + $yr) / 2);

      return array($x, $y);
   }
```

For example:

```
   list($x, $y) = pc_ImagePSCenter($image, $text, $font, $size);
   ImagePSText($image, $text, $font, $size, $fore, $back, $x, $y);
```

For TrueType fonts, use the **pc_ImageTTFCenter( )** function shown in Example 17-3.

Example 17-3. pc_ImageTTFCenter( )

```
   function pc_ImageTTFCenter($image, $text, $font, $size) {

      // find the size of the image
      $xi = ImageSX($image);
      $yi = ImageSY($image);

      // find the size of the text
      $box = ImageTTFBBox($size, $angle, $font, $text);

      $xr = abs(max($box[2], $box[4]));
      $yr = abs(max($box[5], $box[7]));

      // compute centering
      $x = intval(($xi - $xr) / 2);
```

```
        $y = intval(($yi + $yr) / 2);

        return array($x, $y);
    }
```

For example:

```
    list($x, $y) = pc_ImageTTFCenter($image, $text, $font, $size);
    ImageTTFText($image, $size, $angle, $x, $y, $fore, $font, $text);
```

Discussion

All three solution functions return the x and y coordinates for drawing. Of course,
depending on font type, size, and settings, the method used to compute these coordinates differs.

For PostScript Type 1 fonts, pass `pc_ImagePSCenter()` an image allocated from
`ImageCreate()` (or one of its friends) and a number of parameters to specify how to
draw the text. The first three parameters are required: the text to be drawn, the font,
and the font size. The next three are optional: the space in a font, the tightness between
letters, and an angle for rotation in degrees.

Inside the function, use `ImageSX()` and `ImageSY()` to find the size of the canvas; they
return the width and height of the graphic. Then call `ImagePSBBox()`. It returns four
integers: the x and y coordinates of the lower-leftmost location the text and the x and
y coordinates of the upper-rightmost location. Because the coordinates are relative to
the baseline of the text, it's typical for these not to be 0. For instance, a lowercase "g"
hangs below the bottom of the rest of the letters; so in that case, the lower left y value
is negative.

Armed with these six values, you can now calculate the correct centering values. Because coordinates of the canvas have (0,0) in the upper left corner, but `ImagePSText()`
wants the lower left corner, the formula for finding $x and $y isn't the same. For $x,
take the difference between the size of the canvas and the text. This gives the amount
of whitespace that surrounds the text. Then divide that number by two to find the
number of pixels you should leave to the left of the text. For $y, do the same, but add
$yi and $yr. By adding these numbers, you can find the coordinate of the far side of the
box, which is what is needed here because of the inverted way the y coordinate is entered
in GD.

Intentionally ignore the lower left coordinates in making these calculations. Because
the bulk of the text sits above the baseline, adding the descending pixels into the centering algorithm actually worsens the code; it appears offcenter to the eye.

To center text, put it together like this:

```
    function pc_ImagePSCenter($image, $text, $font, $size, $space = 0,
                             $tightness = 0, $angle = 0) {

        // find the size of the image
        $xi = ImageSX($image);
```

```
    $yi = ImageSY($image);

    // find the size of the text
    list($xl, $yl, $xr, $yr) = ImagePSBBox($text, $font, $size,
                                    $space, $tightness, $angle);

    // compute centering
    $x = intval(($xi - $xr) / 2);
    $y = intval(($yi + $yr) / 2);

    return array($x, $y);
}

$image = ImageCreate(500,500);
$text = 'PHP Cookbook Rules!';
$font = ImagePSLoadFont('/path/to/font.pfb');
$size = 20;
$black = ImageColorAllocate($image, 0, 0, 0);
$white = ImageColorAllocate($image, 255, 255, 255);

list($x, $y) = pc_ImagePSCenter($image, $text, $font, $size);
ImagePSText($image, $text, $font, $size, $white, $black, $x, $y);
ImagePSFreeFont($font);

header('Content-type: image/png');
ImagePng($image);

ImageDestroy($image);
```

Unfortunately, this example doesn't work for GD's built-in fonts or for TrueType fonts. There's no function to return the size of a string using the built-in fonts, and ImageTTFBBox( ) returns eight values instead of four. With a few modifications, however, you can accommodate these differences.

Because the built-in fonts are fixed width, you can easily measure the size of a character to create a function that returns the size of the text based on its length. Table 17-1 isn't 100 percent accurate, but it should return results within one or two pixels, which should be good enough for most cases.

Table 17-1. GD built-in font character sizes

Font number	Width	Height
1	5	6
2	6	8
3	7	13
4	8	15
5	9	15

Inside pc_ImageStringCenter( ), calculate the length of the string as an integral multiple based on its length; the height is just one character high. Note that ImageString( ) takes

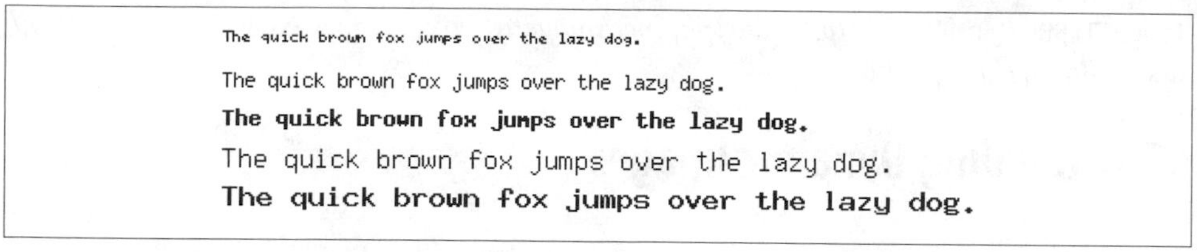

The quick brown fox jumps over the lazy dog.

The quick brown fox jumps over the lazy dog.

The quick brown fox jumps over the lazy dog.

The quick brown fox jumps over the lazy dog.

The quick brown fox jumps over the lazy dog.

Figure 17-8. Centered GD built-in fonts

its y coordinate as the uppermost part of the text, so you should switch the sign back to a minus when you compute $y.

Here is an example using all five fonts that centers text horizontally:

```
$text = 'The quick brown fox jumps over the lazy dog.';
for ($font = 1, $y = 5; $font <= 5; $font++, $y += 20) {
    list($x, $y) = pc_ImageStringCenter($image, $text, $font);
    ImageString($image, $font, $x, $y, $text, $color);
}
```

The output is shown in Figure 17-8.

For TrueType fonts, you need to use ImageTTFBBox( ) or the more modern ImageFtBBox( ). (The function with TTF in the name is for FreeType version 1.x; the one with Ft is for FreeType 2.x.) It returns eight numbers: the (x,y) coordinates of the four corners of the text starting in the lower left and moving around counterclockwise. So the second two coordinates are for the lower right spot, and so on.

To make pc_ImageTTFCenter( ), begin with pc_ImagePSCenter( ) and swap this line:

```
// find the size of the text
list($xl, $yl, $xr, $yr) = ImagePSBBox($text, $font, $size,
                                $space, $tightness, $angle);
```

with these:

```
// find the size of the text
$box = ImageTTFBBox($size, $angle, $font, $text);

$xr = abs(max($box[2], $box[4]));
$yr = abs(max($box[5], $box[7]));
```

Here's an example of pc_ImageTTFCenter( ) in use:

```
list($x, $y) = pc_ImageTTFCenter($image, $text, $font, $size);
ImageTTFText($image, $size, $angle, $x, $y, $white, $black,
            '/path/to/font.ttf', $text);
```

See Also

Recipe 17.4 for more on drawing text; Recipe 17.5 for more on centering text; documentation on ImageSX( ) at *http://www.php.net/imagesx*, ImageSY( ) at *http://www.php.net/imagesy*, ImagePSBBox( ) at *http://www.php.net/imagepsbbox*,

ImageTTFBBox() at *http://www.php.net/imagettfbbox*, ImageFtBBox() at *http://www.php.net/imageftbbox*.

17.6 Building Dynamic Images

Problem

You want to create an image based on an existing image template and dynamic data (typically text). For instance, you want to create a hit counter.

Solution

Load the template image, find the correct position to properly center your text, add the text to the canvas, and send the image to the browser:

```
// Configuration settings
$image    = ImageCreateFromPNG('button.png');
$text     = $_GET['text'];
$font     = ImagePSLoadFont('Times');
$size     = 24;
$color    = ImageColorAllocate($image,   0,   0,   0); // black
$bg_color = ImageColorAllocate($image, 255, 255, 255); // white

// Print-centered text
list($x, $y) = pc_ImagePSCenter($image, $text, $font, $size);
ImagePSText($image, $text, $font, $size, $color, $bg_color, $x, $y);

// Send image
header('Content-type: image/png');
ImagePNG($image);

// Clean up
ImagePSFreeFont($font);
ImageDestroy($image);
```

Discussion

Building dynamic images with GD is easy; all you need to do is combine a few recipes together. At the top of the code in the Solution, you load in an image from a stock template button; it acts as the background on which you overlay the text. We define the text to come directly from the query string. Alternatively, you can pull the string from a database (in the case of access counters) or a remote server (stock quotes or weather report icons).

After that, continue with the other settings: loading a font and specifying its size, color, and background color. Before printing the text, however, you need to compute its position; pc_ImagePSCenter() from Recipe 17.5 nicely solves this task. Last, serve the image, and deallocate the font and image from memory.

For example, the following code generates a page of HTML and image tags using dynamic buttons, as shown in Figure 17-9:

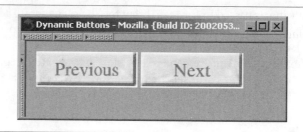

Figure 17-9. Sample button page

```php
<?php
if (isset($_GET['button'])) {

    // Configuration settings
    $image     = ImageCreateFromPNG('button.png');
    $text      = $_GET['button'];        // dynamically generated text
    $font      = ImagePSLoadFont('Times');
    $size      = 24;
    $color     = ImageColorAllocate($image,   0,   0,   0); // black
    $bg_color  = ImageColorAllocate($image, 255, 255, 255); // white

    // Print centered text
    list($x, $y) = pc_ImagePSCenter($image, $text, $font, $size);
    ImagePSText($image, $text, $font, $size, $color, $bg_color, $x, $y);

    // Send image
    header('Content-type: image/png');
    ImagePNG($image);

    // Clean up
    ImagePSFreeFont($font);
    ImageDestroy($image);

    $url = htmlentities($_SERVER['PHP_SELF']);

} else {
?>
<html>
<head>
    <title>Sample Button Page</title>
</head>
<body>
    <img src="<?php echo $url; ?>?button=Previous"
        alt="Previous" width="132" height="46">
    <img src="<?php echo $url; ?>?button=Next"
        alt="Next"     width="132" height="46">
</body>
</html>
<?php
}
?>
```

In this script, if a value is passed in for $_GET['button'], you generate a button and send out the PNG. If $_GET['button'] isn't set, you print a basic HTML page with two embedded calls back to the script with requests for button images one for a Previous button and one for a Next button. A more general solution is to create a separate *button.php* page that returns only graphics and set the image source to point at that page.

See Also

Recipe 17.4 for more on drawing text; Recipe 17.5 for more on centering text; Chapter 9, "Graphics," in *Programming PHP*, Second Edition, by Rasmus Lerdorf, Kevin Tatroe, and Peter MacIntyre (O'Reilly).

17.7 Getting and Setting a Transparent Color

Problem

You want to set one color in an image as transparent. When the image is overlayed on a background, the background shows through the transparent section of the image.

Solution

Use ImageColorTransparent( ):

```
$color = ImageColorAllocate($image, $red, $green, $blue);
ImageColorTransparent($image, $color);
```

Discussion

Both GIFs and PNGs support transparencies; JPEGs, however, do not. To refer to the transparent color within GD, use the constant IMG_COLOR_TRANSPARENT. For example, here's how to make a dashed line that alternates between black and transparent:

```
// make a two-pixel thick black and white dashed line
$style = array($black, $black, IMG_COLOR_TRANSPARENT, IMG_COLOR_TRANSPARENT);
ImageSetStyle($image, $style);
```

To find the current transparency setting, take the return value of ImageColorTransparent( ) and pass it to ImageColorsForIndex( ):

```
$transparent = ImageColorsForIndex($image, ImageColorTransparent($image));
print_r($transparent);

$transparent = ImageColorsForIndex($image, ImageColorTransparent($image));
print_r($transparent);
Array
(
    [red] => 255
    [green] => 255
    [blue] => 255
)
```

The `ImageColorsForIndex( )` function returns an array with the red, green, and blue values. In this case, the transparent color is white.

See Also

Documentation on `ImageColorTransparent( )` at *http://www.php.net/imagecolortrans parent* and on `ImageColorsForIndex( )` at *http://www.php.net/imagecolorsforindex*.

17.8 Reading EXIF Data

Problem

You want to extract metainformation from an image file. This lets you find out when the photo was taken, the image size, and the MIME type.

Solution

Use the `exif_read_data( )` function:

```
$exif = exif_read_data('/beth-and-seth.jpeg');

print_r($exif);
Array
(
    [FileName] => beth-and-seth.jpg
    [FileDateTime] => 1096055414
    [FileSize] => 182080
    [FileType] => 2
    [MimeType] => image/jpeg
    [SectionsFound] => APP12
    [COMPUTED] => Array
        (
            [html] => width="642" height="855"
            [Height] => 855
            [Width] => 642
            [IsColor] => 1
        )

    [Company] => Ducky
    [Info] =>
)
```

Discussion

The Exchangeable Image File Format (EXIF) is a standard for embedding metadata inside of pictures. Most digital cameras use EXIF, so it's an increasingly popular way of providing rich data in photo galleries such as Flickr.

PHP has a number of EXIF functions. They don't require external libraries, but must be enabled by passing the `--enable-exif` configuration flag.

The easiest way to extract data is through the exif_read_data( ) method. It returns an array of metadata, including the creation date of the photo, the MIME type (which you can use to help serve up the image), and the image dimensions:

```
$exif = exif_read_data('/beth-and-seth.jpeg');

print_r($exif);
Array
(
    [FileName] => beth-and-seth.jpg
    [FileDateTime] => 1096055414
    [FileSize] => 182080
    [FileType] => 2
    [MimeType] => image/jpeg
    [SectionsFound] => APP12
    [COMPUTED] => Array
        (
            [html] => width="642" height="855"
            [Height] => 855
            [Width] => 642
            [IsColor] => 1
        )

    [Company] => Ducky
    [Info] =>
)
```

Use the html value to directly embed within an <img> source tag.

You can also use the EXIF functions to retrieve a thumbnail image associated with the picture. To access this, call exif_thumbnail( ):

```
$thumb = exif_thumbnail('beth-and-seth.jpeg', $width, $height, $type);
```

The exif_thumbnail( ) function takes four parameters. The first is the filename. The last three are variables passed by reference where the width, height, and image type will be stored. The function returns the thumbnail image as a binary string, or false on failure.

To serve up the image directly, use the image_type_to_mime_type( ) to get the correct MIME type. Pass that along as an HTTP header and then display the image:

```
$thumb = exif_thumbnail('beth-and-seth.jpeg', $width, $height, $type);

if ($thumb != false) {
    $mime = image_type_to_mime_type($type);
    header("Content-type: $mime");
    print $image;
}
```

Alternatively, you can create an <img> link:

```
$file = 'beth-and-seth.jpeg';
$thumb = exif_thumbnail($file, $width, $height, $type);

if ($thumb != false) {
```

```
        $img = "<img src=\"$file\" alt=\"Beth and Seth\"
                    width=\"$width\" height=\"$height\" />
        print $img;
}
```

See Also

Documentation on `exif_read_data( )` at *http://www.php.net/exif-read-data* and on
`exif_thumbnail( )` at *http://www.php.net/exif-thumbnail*.

17.9 Serving Images Securely

Problem

You want to control who can view a set of images.

Solution

Don't keep the images in your document root, but store them elsewhere. To deliver a
file, manually open it and send it to the browser:

```
header('Content-Type: image/png');
readfile('/path/to/graphic.png');
```

Discussion

The first line in the Solution sends the `Content-Type` header to the browser, so the
browser knows what type of object is coming and displays it accordingly. The second
opens a file off a disk (or from a remote URL) for reading, reads it in, dumps it directly
to the browser, and closes the file.

The typical way to serve up an image is to use an `<img>` tag and set the `src` attribute to
point to a file on your web site. If you want to protect those images, you probably
should use some form of password authentication. Two methods are HTTP Basic and
Digest Authentication, which are covered in Recipe 8.9.

The typical way, however, may not always be the best. First, what happens if you want
to restrict the files people can view, but you don't want to make things complex by
using usernames and passwords? One option is to link only to the files; if users can't
click on the link, they can't view the file. They might, however, bookmark old files, or
they may also try and guess other filenames based on your naming scheme and manually
enter the URL into the browser.

If your content is embargoed, you don't want people to be able to guess your naming
scheme and view images. When information is embargoed, a select group of people,
usually reporters, are given a preview release, so they can write stories about the topic
or be ready to distribute it the moment the embargo is lifted. You can fix this by making
sure only legal content is under the document root, but this requires a lot of file shuffling

back and forth from directory to directory. Instead, you can keep all the files in one constant place, and deliver only files that pass a check inside your code.

For example, let's say you have a contract with a publishing corporation to redistribute one of their comics on your web site. However, they don't want you to create a virtual archive, so you agree to let your users view only the last two weeks' worth of strips. For everything else, they'll need to go to the official site. Also, you may get comics in advance of their publication date, but you don't want to let people get a free preview; you want them to keep coming back to your site on a daily basis.

Here's the solution. Files arrive named by date, so it's easy to identify which files belong to which day. Now, to lock out strips outside the rolling 14-day window, use code like this:

```php
// display a comic if it's less than 14 days old and not in the future

// calculate the current date
list($now_m,$now_d,$now_y) = explode(',',date('m,d,Y'));
$now = mktime(0,0,0,$now_m,$now_d,$now_y);

// two-hour boundary on either side to account for dst
$min_ok = $now - 14*86400 - 7200; // 14 days ago
$max_ok = $now + 7200;            // today

$mo = (int) $_GET['mo'];
$dy = (int) $_GET['dy'];
$yr = (int) $_GET['yr'];

// find the time stamp of the requested comic
$asked_for = mktime(0,0,0,$mo,$dy,$yr);

// compare the dates
if (($min_ok > $asked_for) || ($max_ok < $asked_for)) {
    echo 'You are not allowed to view the comic for that day.';
} else {
    header('Content-type: image/png');
    readfile("/www/comics/{$mo}{$dy}{$yr}.png");
}
```

See Also

Recipe 23.5 for more on reading files.

17.10 Program: Generating Bar Charts from Poll Results

When displaying the results of a poll, it can be more effective to generate a colorful bar chart instead of just printing the results as text. The function shown in Example 17-4 uses GD to create an image that displays the cumulative responses to a poll question.

Example 17-4. Graphical bar charts

```php
function pc_bar_chart($question, $answers) {
```

```
    // define colors to draw the bars
    $colors = array(array(255,102,0), array(0,153,0),
                    array(51,51,204), array(255,0,51),
                    array(255,255,0), array(102,255,255),
                    array(153,0,204));

    $total = array_sum($answers['votes']);

    // define some spacing values and other magic numbers
    $padding = 5;
    $line_width = 20;
    $scale = $line_width * 7.5;
    $bar_height = 10;

    $x = $y = $padding;

    // allocate a large palette for drawing, since you don't know
    // the image length ahead of time
    $image = ImageCreate(150, 500);
    $bg_color = ImageColorAllocate($image, 224, 224, 224);
    $black = ImageColorAllocate($image, 0, 0, 0);

    // print the question
    $wrapped = explode("\n", wordwrap($question, $line_width));
    foreach ($wrapped as $line) {
        ImageString($image, 3, $x, $y , $line, $black);
        $y += 12;
    }

    $y += $padding;

    // print the answers
    for ($i = 0; $i < count($answers['answer']); $i++) {

        // format percentage
        $percent = sprintf('%1.1f', 100*$answers['votes'][$i]/$total);
        $bar = sprintf('%d', $scale*$answers['votes'][$i]/$total);

        // grab color
        $c = $i % count($colors); // handle cases with more bars than colors
        $text_color = ImageColorAllocate($image, $colors[$c][0],
                                $colors[$c][1], $colors[$c][2]);

        // draw bar and percentage numbers
        ImageFilledRectangle($image, $x, $y, $x + $bar,
                              $y + $bar_height, $text_color);
        ImageString($image, 3, $x + $bar + $padding, $y,
                    "$percent%", $black);

        $y += 12;

        // print answer
        $wrapped = explode("\n", wordwrap($answers['answer'][$i], $line_width));
        foreach ($wrapped as $line) {
            ImageString($image, 2, $x, $y, $line, $black);
```

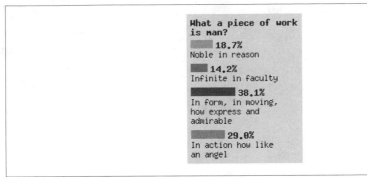

Figure 17-10. Graphical bar chart of poll results

```
            $y += 12;
        }

        $y += 7;
    }

    // crop image by copying it
    $chart = ImageCreate(150, $y);
    ImageCopy($chart, $image, 0, 0, 0, 0, 150, $y);

    // deliver image
    header ('Content-type: image/png');
    ImagePNG($chart);

    // clean up
    ImageDestroy($image);
    ImageDestroy($chart);
}
```

To call this program, create an array holding two parallel arrays: $answers['answer']
and $answer['votes']. Element $i of each array holds the answer text and the total
number of votes for answer $i. Figure 17-10 shows this sample output:

```
// Act II. Scene II.
$question = 'What a piece of work is man?';

$answers['answer'][] = 'Noble in reason';
$answers['votes'][]  = 29;

$answers['answer'][] = 'Infinite in faculty';
$answers['votes'][]  = 22;

$answers['answer'][] = 'In form, in moving, how express and admirable';
$answers['votes'][]  = 59;

$answers['answer'][] = 'In action how like an angel';
$answers['votes'][]  = 45;

pc_bar_chart($question, $answers);
```

Here the answers are manually assigned, but for a real poll, this data could be pulled from a database instead.

This program is a good start, but because it uses the built-in GD fonts, there are a lot of magic numbers embedded in the program corresponding to the font height and width. Also, the amount of space between each answer is hardcoded. If you modify this to handle more advanced fonts, such as PostScript or TrueType, you'll need to update the algorithms that control those numbers.

At the top of the function, a bunch of RGB combinations are defined; they are used as the colors to draw the bars. A variety of constants are broken out, such as `$line_width`, which is the maximum number of characters per line. The `$bar_height` variable determines how high the bars should be, and `$scale` scales the length of the bar as a function of the longest possible line. `$padding` is used to push the results five pixels away from the edge of the canvas.

You then make a very large canvas to draw the chart; later, you will crop the canvas down to size, but it can be difficult to know ahead of time how large our total size will be. The default background color of the bar chart is (224, 224, 224), a light gray.

In order to restrict the width of the chart to a reasonable size, we use `wordwrap()` to break our `$question` down to size and `explode()` it on `\n`. This gives us an array of correctly sized lines, which you loop on to print out one line at a time.

After printing the question, move on to the answers. First, we format the results numbers with `sprintf()`. To format the total percentage of votes for an answer as a floating-point number with one decimal point, use `%1.1f`. To find the length of the bar corresponding to that number, you compute a similar number, but instead of multiplying it by 100, multiply by a magic number, `$scale`, and return an integer.

The text color is pulled from the `$colors` array of RGB triplets. Then, call `ImageFilledRectangle()` to draw the bar and `ImageString()` to draw the percentage text to the right of the bar. After adding some padding, print the answer using the same algorithm used to print the question.

When all the answers have been printed, the total size of the bar chart is stored in `$y`. Now you can correctly crop the graphic to size, but there's no `ImageCrop()` function. To work around this, make a new canvas of the appropriate size and `ImageCopy()` over the part of the original canvas you want to keep. Then, serve the correctly sized image as a PNG using `ImagePNG()`, and clean up with two calls to `ImageDestroy()`.

As mentioned at the beginning of this section, this is just a quick-and-dirty function to print bar charts. It works and solves some problems, such a wrapped lines, but isn't 100 percent perfect. For instance, it's not very customizable. Many settings are baked directly into the code. Still, it shows how to put together a variety of GD functions to create a useful graphical application.

CHAPTER 18

Security and Encryption

18.0 Introduction

Web application security is an important topic that's gaining more attention from both the developers who create web applications, and the attackers who try to exploit them. As a PHP developer, your applications are sure to be the target of many attacks, and you need to be prepared.

A large number of web application vulnerabilities are due to a misplaced trust in data provided by third parties. Such data is known as input, and it should be considered *tainted* until proven otherwise. If you display tainted data to your users, you create *cross-site scripting* (XSS) vulnerabilities. Recipe 18.4 explains how to avoid these by escaping your output. If you use tainted data in your SQL queries, you can create *SQL injection* vulnerabilities. Recipe 18.5 shows you how to eliminate these.

When using data provided by third parties, including the data provided by your users, it is important to first verify that it is valid. This process is known as *filtering*, and Recipe 18.3 shows you how to guarantee that all input is filtered.

Not all security problems can be solved by filtering input and escaping output. Session fixation, an attack discussed in Recipe 18.1, causes a victim to use a session identifier chosen by an attacker. Cross-site request forgeries, a type of attack discussed in Recipe 18.2, cause a victim to send a request of an attacker's choosing.

Closely related to security is encryption, a powerful tool that can help boost your application's security. Just like any other tool, however, it must be used properly.

Encryption scrambles data. Some data scrambling can't be unscrambled without unreasonable amounts of processing. This is called *one-way encryption* or *hashing*. Other encryption methods work in two directions: data is encrypted, and then it's decrypted.

PHP supplies tools to encrypt and secure your data. Some tools, such as the md5( ) function, are part of PHP's base set of functions, and some are extensions that need to be explicitly included when PHP is compiled (e.g., *mcrypt*, *mhash*, and cURL).

Recipe 18.7 discusses using md5( ). It is most widely used for encrypting passwords.

mcrypt is a more full-featured encryption library that offers different algorithms and encryption modes. Because it supports different kinds of encryption, *mcrypt* is especially helpful when you need to exchange encrypted data with other systems or with programs not written in PHP. *mcrypt* is discussed in detail in Recipe 18.10.

PHP gives you the tools to protect your data with robust encryption, but encryption is just part of the large and often complex security picture. Your encrypted data can be unlocked with a key, so protecting that key is very important. If your encryption keys are accessible to unauthorized users (because they're stored in a file accessible via your web server or because they're stored in a file accessible by other users in a shared hosting environment, for example), your data is at risk, no matter how secure your chosen encryption algorithm is.

Sensitive data needs to be protected not only on the server, but also when it's traveling over the network between the server and your users. Data sent over regular HTTP is visible to anyone with access to the network at any point between your server and a user. Recipe 18.13 discusses how to use SSL to prevent network snoopers from observing data as it passes by. For a complete discussion on securing PHP applications, read *PHP Security* (O'Reilly) by Chris Shiflett.

18.1 Preventing Session Fixation

Problem

You need to ensure that a user's session identifier cannot be provided by a third party, such as an attacker who seeks to hijack the user's session.

Solution

Regenerate the session identifier with `session_regenerate_id( )` whenever there is a change in the user's privilege, such as after a successful login:

```php
<?php

session_regenerate_id();
$_SESSION['logged_in'] = true;

?>
```

Discussion

Sessions allow you to create variables that persist between requests. In order for sessions to work, each of the users' requests must include a session identifier that uniquely identifies a session.

By default, PHP accepts a session identifier sent in either a cookie or in the URL. An attacker can trick a victim into following a link to your application that includes an embedded session identifier:

```
<a href="http://example.org/login.php?PHPSESSID=1234">Click Here!</a>
```

A user who follows this link will resume the session identified as **1234**. Therefore, the attacker now knows the user's session identifier and can attempt to hijack the user's session by presenting the same session identifier.

If the user never logs in or performs any action that differentiates the user from among the other users of your application, the attacker gains nothing by hijacking the session. Therefore, by ensuring that the session identifier is regenerated whenever there is a change in privilege level, you effectively eliminate session fixation attacks. PHP takes care of updating the session data store and propagating the new session identifier, so you must only call this one function as appropriate.

See Also

Recipe 11.2 for more information about session options that can help to prevent hijacking and fixation. Recipe 11.3 shows a time-based session ID regeneration scheme.

18.2 Protecting Against Form Spoofing

Problem

You want to be sure that a form submission is valid and intentional.

Solution

Add a hidden form field with a one-time token, and store this token in the user's session:

```php
<?php

session_start();

$_SESSION['token'] = md5(uniqid(mt_rand(), true));

?>

<form action="buy.php" method="POST">
<input type="hidden" name="token" value="<?php echo $_SESSION['token']; ?>" />
<p>Stock Symbol: <input type="text" name="symbol" /></p>
<p>Quantity: <input type="text" name="quantity" /></p>
<p><input type="submit" value="Buy Stocks" /></p>
</form>
```

When you receive a request that represents a form submission, check the tokens to be sure they match:

```php
<?php

session_start();

if ($_POST['token'] != $_SESSION['token'] ||
    !isset($_SESSION['token'])) {
```

```
    /* Prompt user for password. */
} else {
    /* Continue. */
}

?>
```

Discussion

This technique protects against a group of attacks known as cross-site request forgeries (CSRF). These attacks all cause a victim to send requests to a target site without the victim's knowledge. Typically, the victim has an established level of privilege with the target site, so these attacks allow an attacker to perform actions that the attacker cannot otherwise perform.

Adding a token to your forms in this way does not prevent a user from forging his own request from himself, but this is not something you can prevent, nor is it something to be concerned with. If you filter input as discussed in Recipe 18.3, you force requests to abide by your rules. The technique shown in this recipe helps to make sure the request is intentional.

18.3 Ensuring Input Is Filtered

Problem

You need to be sure that all input is filtered before being used.

Solution

Initialize an empty array in which to store filtered data. After you've proven that something is valid, store it in this array:

```
<?php

/* Initialize an array for filtered data. */
$clean = array();

/* Allow alphabetic names. */
if (ctype_alpha($_POST['name'])) {
    $clean['name'] = $_POST['name'];
} else {
    /* Error */
}

?>
```

Discussion

By using a strict naming convention, you can more easily keep up with what input has been filtered. Always initializing $clean to an empty array ensures that data cannot be injected into the array; you must explicitly add it.

Once you adopt a technique such as the use of `$clean`, it is important that you only use data from this array in your business logic.

See Also

Recipes 9.2 to 9.9 discuss form input validation for different types of data in detail.

18.4 Avoiding Cross-Site Scripting

Problem

You need to safely avoid cross-site scripting (XSS) attacks in your PHP applications.

Solution

Escape all HTML output with `htmlentities( )`, being sure to indicate the correct character encoding:

```php
<?php

/* Note the character encoding. */
header('Content-Type: text/html; charset=UTF-8');

/* Initialize an array for escaped data. */
$html = array();

/* Escape the filtered data. */
$html['username'] = htmlentities($clean['username'], ENT_QUOTES, 'UTF-8');

echo "<p>Welcome back, {$html['username']}.</p>";

?>
```

Discussion

The `htmlentities( )` function replaces each character with its HTML entity, if it has one. For example, > is replaced with >. Although the immediate effect is that the data is modified, the purpose of the escaping is to preserve the data in a different context. Whenever a browser renders > as HTML, it appears on the screen as >.

XSS attacks try to take advantage of a situation where data provided by a third party is included in the HTML without being escaped properly. A clever attacker can provide code that can be very dangerous to your users when interpreted by their browsers. By using `htmlentities( )`, you can be sure that such third-party data is displayed properly and not interpreted.

See Also

Recipe 9.10 discusses cross-site scripting prevention in the context of submitted form data.

18.5 Eliminating SQL Injection

Problem

You need to eliminate SQL injection vulnerabilities in your PHP applications.

Solution

Use a database library such as PDO that performs the proper escaping for your database:

```php
<?php

$db = new PDO('mysql:host=localhost;dbname=users',
              $_SERVER['DB_USER'],
              $_SERVER['DB_PASSWORD']);

$statement = $db->prepare("INSERT
                           INTO   users (username, password)
                           VALUES (:username, :password)");

$statement->bindParam(':username', $clean['username']);
$statement->bindParam(':password', $clean['password']);

$statement->execute();

$db = NULL;

?>
```

Discussion

Using bound parameters ensures your data never enters a context where it is considered to be anything except raw data, so no value can possibly modify the format of the SQL query.

If you do not have access to PDO, you can use a database library written in PHP, such as PEAR::DB, that offers a similar feature:

```php
<?php

$st = $db->query('INSERT
          INTO   users (username, password)
          VALUES (?, ?)',
          array($clean['username'], $clean['password']));

?>
```

Although this method still intermingles your data with the SQL query, PEAR::DB ensures that the data is quoted and escaped properly, so there is no practical risk of SQL injection.

See Also

Chapter 10 for more information about PDO, particularly Recipes 10.4 and 10.7; documentation on PDO at *http://www.php.net/pdo*; on PEAR::DB at *http://pear.php.net/manual/en/package.database.db.php*.

18.6 Keeping Passwords Out of Your Site Files

Problem

You need to use a password to connect to a database, for example. You don't want to put the password in the PHP files you use on your site in case those files are exposed.

Solution

Store the password in an environment variable in a file that the web server loads when starting up. Then, just reference the environment variable in your code:

```php
<?php

mysql_connect('localhost', $_SERVER['DB_USER'], $_SERVER['DB_PASSWORD']);

?>
```

Discussion

While this technique removes passwords from the source code of your pages, it makes them available in other places that need to be protected. Most importantly, make sure that there are no publicly viewable pages that call phpinfo( ). Because phpinfo( ) displays all of the environment variables, it exposes any passwords you store there. Also, make sure not to expose the contents of $_SERVER in other ways, such as with the print_r( ) function.

Next, especially if you are using a shared host, make sure the environment variables are set in such a way that they are only available to your virtual host, not to all users. With Apache, you can do this by setting the variables in a separate file from the main configuration file:

```
SetEnv  DB_USER     "susannah"
SetEnv  DB_PASSWORD "y23a!t@ce8"
```

Inside the <VirtualHost> directive for the site in the main configuration file (httpd.conf), include this separate file as follows:

```
Include "/usr/local/apache/database-passwords"
```

Make sure that this separate file containing the password (e.g., */usr/local/apache/database-passwords*) is not readable by any user other than the one that controls the appropriate virtual host. When Apache starts up and is reading in configuration files, it's usually running as root, so it is able to read the included file. A child process that handles requests typically runs as an unprivileged user, so rogue scripts cannot read the protected file.

See Also

Documentation on Apache's Include directive at *http://httpd.apache.org/docs/mod/core.html#include*.

18.7 Storing Passwords

Problem

You need to keep track of users' passwords, so they can log in to your web site.

Solution

When a user signs up or registers, encrypt the chosen password with md5( ) and store the encrypted password in your database of users. For best results, use a salt:

```php
<?php

/* Initialize an array for filtered data. */
$clean = array();

/* Define a salt. */
define('SALT', 'flyingturtle');

/* Encrypt the password. */
$encrypted_password = md5(SALT . $_POST['password']);

/* Allow alphanumeric usernames. */
if (ctype_alnum($_POST['username'])) {
    $clean['username'] = $_POST['username'];
} else {
    /* Error */
}

/* Store user in the database. */
$st = $db->prepare('INSERT
            INTO    users (username, password)
            VALUES (?, ?)');
$st->execute(array($clean['username'], $encrypted_password));

?>
```

Then, when that user attempts to log in to your web site, encrypt the supplied password with `md5( )` and compare it to the stored encrypted password. If the two encrypted values match, the user has supplied the correct password:

```php
<?php

/* Initialize an array for filtered data. */
$clean = array();

/* Define a salt. */
define('SALT', 'flyingturtle');

/* Allow alphanumeric usernames. */
if (ctype_alnum($_POST['username'])) {
    $clean['username'] = $_POST['username'];
} else {
    /* Error */
}

$encrypted_password = $db->getOne('SELECT password
                                   FROM   users
                                   WHERE  username = ?',
                                   array($clean['username']));

if (md5(SALT . $_POST['password']) == $encrypted_password) {
    /* Login succeeds. */
} else {
    /* Login fails. */
}

?>
```

Discussion

Storing encrypted passwords prevents users' accounts from becoming compromised if an unauthorized person gets a peek at your username and password database (although such unauthorized peeks may foreshadow other security problems).

Using a salt as demonstrated helps protect against the presence of rainbow tables. Rainbow tables are collections of strings along with the encrypted version of those strings. For example, *http://md5.rednoize.com/* is a rainbow table lookup facility for MD5. If you enter a query such as 6b34fe24ac2ff8103f6fce1f0da2ef57 (the MD5 of chris), you can see how easily plain MD5s can be broken. By using a salt, the effectiveness of such a tool is significantly reduced.

Because MD5 is a one-way algorithm, your stored passwords are somewhat more secure. This also means that you can't get at the plain text of users' passwords, even if you need to. For example, if a user forgets his password, you won't be able to tell him what it is. The best you can do is reset the password to a new value and then tell the user the new password. A method for dealing with lost passwords is covered in Recipe 18.8.

See Also

Recipe 18.11 for information on storing encrypted data; documentation on `md5()` at
http://php.net/md5.

18.8 Dealing with Lost Passwords

Problem

You want to issue a password to a user who has lost her password.

Solution

Generate a new password and send it to the user's email address (which you should
have on file):

```php
<?php

/* Generate new password. */
$new_password = '';

for ($i = 0; $i < 8; $i++) {
    $new_password .= chr(mt_rand(33, 126));
}

/* Define a salt. */
define('SALT', 'flyingturtle');

/* Encrypt new password. */
$encrypted_password = md5(SALT . $new_password);

/* Save new encrypted password to the database. */
$st = $db->prepare('UPDATE users
            SET    password = ?
            WHERE  username = ?');

$st->execute(array($encrypted_password, $clean['username']));

/* Email new plain text password to user. */
mail($clean['email'], 'New Password', "Your new password is: $new_password");

?>
```

Discussion

If a user forgets her password, and you store encrypted passwords as recommended in
Recipe 18.7, you can't provide the forgotten password. The one-way nature of `md5()`
prevents you from retrieving the plain-text password.

Instead, generate a new password and send that to her email address. If you send the
new password to an address you don't already have on file for that user, you don't have

a way to verify that the new address really belongs to the user. It may be an attacker attempting to impersonate the real user.

Because the email containing the new password isn't encrypted, the code in the Solution doesn't include the username in the email message to reduce the chances that an attacker that eavesdrops on the email message can steal the password. To avoid disclosing a new password by email at all, let a user authenticate herself without a password by answering one or more personal questions (the answers to which you have on file). These questions can be "What was the name of your first pet?" or "What's your mother's maiden name?"—anything a malicious attacker is unlikely to know. If the user provides the correct answers to your questions, you can let her choose a new password.

One way to compromise between security and readability is to generate a password for a user out of actual words interrupted by some numbers:

```php
<?php

$words = array('mother', 'basset', 'detain', 'sudden', 'fellow', 'logged',
               'remove', 'snails', 'direct', 'serves', 'daring', 'chirps',
               'reward', 'snakes', 'uphold', 'wiring', 'nurses', 'regent',
               'ornate', 'dogmas', 'mended', 'hinges', 'verbal', 'grimes',
               'ritual', 'drying', 'chests', 'newark', 'winged', 'hobbit');

$word_count = count($words);

$password = sprintf('%s%02d%s',
                    $words[mt_rand(0,$word_count - 1)],
                    mt_rand(0,99),
                    $words[mt_rand(0,$word_count - 1)]);

echo $password;

?>
```

This code produces passwords that are two six-letter words with two numbers between them, like `mother43hobbit` or `verbal68nurses`. The passwords are long, but remembering them is made easier by the words in them.

See Also

Recipe 18.7 for information about storing encrypted passwords.

18.9 Verifying Data with Hashes

Problem

You want to make sure users don't alter data you've sent them in a cookie or form element.

Solution

Along with the data, send an MD5 hash of the data that uses a salt. When you receive the data back, compute the MD5 hash of the received value with the same salt. If they don't match, the user has altered the data.

Here's how to generate an MD5 hash in a hidden form field:

```php
<?php

/* Define a salt. */
define('SALT', 'flyingturtle');

$id = 1337;
$idcheck = md5(SALT . $id);

?>

<input type="hidden" name="id" value="<?php echo $id; ?>" />
<input type="hidden" name="idcheck" value="<?php echo $idcheck; ?>" />
```

Here's how to verify the hidden form field data when it's submitted:

```php
<?php

/* Initialize an array for filtered data. */
$clean = array();

/* Define a salt. */
define('SALT', 'flyingturtle');

if (md5(SALT . $_POST['id']) == $_POST['idcheck']) {
    $clean['id'] = $_POST['id'];
} else {
    /* Error */
}

?>
```

Discussion

When processing the submitted form data, compute the MD5 hash of the submitted value of $_POST['id'] with the same salt. If it matches $_POST['idcheck'], the value of $_POST['id'] has not been altered by the user. If the values don't match, you know that the value of $_POST['id'] you received is not the same as the one you sent.

To use an MD5 hash with a cookie, add it to the cookie value with implode( ):

```php
<?php

/* Define a salt. */
define('SALT', 'flyingturtle');

$name = 'Ellen';
```

```php
$namecheck = md5(SALT . $name);

setcookie('name', implode('|',array($name, $namecheck)));

?>
```

Parse the hash from the cookie value with `explode( )`:

```php
<?php

/* Define a salt. */
define('SALT', 'flyingturtle');

list($cookie_value, $cookie_check) = explode('|', $_COOKIE['name'], 2);

if (md5(SALT . $cookie_value) == $cookie_hash) {
    $clean['name'] = $cookie_value;
} else {
    /* Error */
}

?>
```

Using a data verification hash in a form or cookie obviously depends on the salt used in hash computation. If a malicious user discovers your salt, the hash offers no protection. Besides guarding the salt zealously, changing it frequently is a good idea. For an additional layer of protection, use different salts, choosing the specific salt to use in the hash based on some property of the `$id` value (10 different words selected by `$id%10`, for example). That way, the damage is slightly mitigated if one of the words is compromised.

If you have the *mhash* module installed, you're not limited to MD5 hashes. *mhash* supports a number of different hash algorithms. For more information about *mhash*, see the *mhash* material in the online PHP manual or the *mhash* home page at *http://mhash.sourceforge.net/*.

See Also

Recipe 18.9 for an example of using hashes with hidden form variables; documentation on `md5( )` at *http://www.php.net/md5* and the *mhash* extension at *http://www.php.net/mhash*.

18.10 Encrypting and Decrypting Data

Problem

You want to encrypt and decrypt data using one of a variety of popular algorithms.

Solution

Use PHP's *mcrypt* extension:

```php
<?php

$algorithm = MCRYPT_BLOWFISH;
$key = 'That golden key that opens the palace of eternity.';
$data = 'The chicken escapes at dawn. Send help with Mr. Blue.';
$mode = MCRYPT_MODE_CBC;

$iv = mcrypt_create_iv(mcrypt_get_iv_size($algorithm, $mode),
                       MCRYPT_DEV_URANDOM);

$encrypted_data = mcrypt_encrypt($algorithm, $key, $data, $mode, $iv);
$plain_text = base64_encode($encrypted_data);
echo $plain_text . "\n";

$encrypted_data = base64_decode($plain_text);
$decoded = mcrypt_decrypt($algorithm, $key, $encrypted_data, $mode, $iv);
echo $decoded . "\n";

?>
```
NNB9WnuCYjyd3Y7vUh7XDfWFCWnQYOBsMehHNmBHbGOdJ3cM+yghABb/XyrJ+w3xz9tms74/a7O=
The chicken escapes at dawn. Send help with Mr. Blue.

Discussion

The *mcrypt* extension is an interface with *mcrypt*, a library that implements many different encryption algorithms. The data is encrypted and decrypted by mcrypt_encrypt( ) and mcrypt_decrypt( ), respectively. They each take five arguments. The first is the algorithm to use. To find which algorithms *mcrypt* supports on your system, call mcrypt_list_algorithms( ). The full list of *mcrypt* algorithms is shown in Table 18-1. The second argument is the encryption key; the third argument is the data to encrypt or decrypt. The fourth argument is the mode for the encryption or decryption (a list of supported modes is returned by mcrypt_list_modes( )). The fifth argument is an initialization vector (IV), used by some modes as part of the encryption or decryption process.

Table 18-1 lists all the possible *mcrypt* algorithms, including the constant value used to indicate the algorithm, the key and block sizes in bits, and whether the algorithm is supported by *libmcrypt* 2.2.x and 2.4.x.

Table 18-1. mcrypt algorithm constants

Algorithm constant	Description	Key size	Block size	2.2.x	2.4.x
MCRYPT_3DES	Triple DES	168 (112 effective)	64	Yes	Yes
MCRYPT_TRIPLEDES	Triple DES	168 (112 effective)	64	No	Yes
MCRYPT_3WAY	3way (Joan Daemen)	96	96	Yes	No
MCRYPT_THREEWAY	3way	96	96	Yes	Yes
MCRYPT_BLOWFISH	Blowfish (Bruce Schneier)	Up to 448	64	No	Yes
MCRYPT_BLOWFISH_COMPAT	Blowfish with compatibility to other implementations	Up to 448	64	No	Yes

Algorithm constant	Description	Key size	Block size	2.2.x	2.4.x
MCRYPT_BLOWFISH_128	Blowfish	128	64	Yes	No
MCRYPT_BLOWFISH_192	Blowfish	192	64	Yes	—
MCRYPT_BLOWFISH_256	Blowfish	256	64	Yes	No
MCRYPT_BLOWFISH_448	Blowfish	448	64	Yes	No
MCRYPT_CAST_128	CAST (Carlisle Adams and Stafford Tavares)	128	64	Yes	Yes
MCRYPT_CAST_256	CAST	256	128	Yes	Yes
MCRYPT_CRYPT	One-rotor Unix crypt	104	8	—	Yes
MCRYPT_ENIGNA	One-rotor Unix crypt	104	8	No	Yes
MCRYPT_DES	U.S. Data Encryption Standard	56	64	Yes	Yes
MCRYPT_GOST	Soviet Gosudarstvennyi Standard ("Government Standard")	256	64	Yes	Yes
MCRYPT_IDEA	International Data Encryption Algorithm	128	64	Yes	Yes
MCRYPT_LOKI97	LOKI97 (Lawrie Brown, Josef Pieprzyk)	128, 192, or 256	64	Yes	Yes
MCRYPT_MARS	MARS (IBM)	128–448	128	No	Yes
MCRYPT_PANAMA	PANAMA (Joan Daemen, Craig Clapp)	-	Stream	No	Yes
MCRYPT_RC2	Rivest Cipher 2	8–1024	64	No	Yes
MCRYPT_RC2_1024	Rivest Cipher 2	1024	64	Yes	No
MCRYPT_RC2_128	Rivest Cipher 2	128	64	Yes	No
MCRYPT_RC2_256	Rivest Cipher 2	256	64	Yes	No
MCRYPT_RC4	Rivest Cipher 4	Up to 2048	Stream	Yes	No
MCRYPT_ARCFOUR	Non-trademarked RC4 compatible	Up to 2048	Stream	No	Yes
MCRYPT_ARCFOUR_IV	Arcfour with Initialization Vector	Up to 2048	Stream	No	Yes
MCRYPT_RC6	Rivest Cipher 6	128, 192, or 256	128	No	Yes
MCRYPT_RC6_128	Rivest Cipher 6	128	128	Yes	No
MCRYPT_RC6_192	Rivest Cipher 6	192	128	Yes	No
MCRYPT_RC6_256	Rivest Cipher 6	256	128	Yes	No
MCRYPT_RIJNDAEL_128	Rijndael (Joan Daemen, Vincent Rijmen)	128	128	Yes	Yes
MCRYPT_RIJNDAEL_192	Rijndael	192	192	Yes	Yes
MCRYPT_RIJNDAEL_256	Rijndael	256	256	Yes	Yes
MCRYPT_SAFERPLUS	SAFER+ (based on SAFER)	128, 192, or 256	128	Yes	Yes

Algorithm constant	Description	Key size	Block size	2.2.x	2.4.x
MCRYPT_SAFER_128	Secure And Fast Encryption Routine with strengthened key schedule	128	64	Yes	Yes
MCRYPT_SAFER_64	Secure And Fast Encryption Routine with strengthened key	64	64	Yes	Yes
MCRYPT_SERPENT	Serpent (Ross Anderson, Eli Biham, Lars Knudsen)	128, 192, or 256	128	No	Yes
MCRYPT_SERPENT_128	Serpent	128	128	Yes	No
MCRYPT_SERPENT_192	Serpent	192	128	Yes	No
MCRYPT_SERPENT_256	Serpent	256	128	Yes	No
MCRYPT_SKIPJACK	U.S. NSA Clipper Escrowed Encryption Standard	80	64	No	Yes
MCRYPT_TWOFISH	Twofish (Counterpane Systems)	128, 192, or 256	128	No	Yes
MCRYPT_TWOFISH_128	Twofish	128	128	Yes	No
MCRYPT_TWOFISH_192	Twofish	192	128	Yes	No
MCRYPT_TWOFISH_256	Twofish	256	128	Yes	No
MCRYPT_WAKE	Word Auto Key Encryption (David Wheeler)	256	32	No	Yes
MCRYPT_XTEA	Extended Tiny Encryption Algorithm (David Wheeler, Roger Needham)	128	64	Yes	Yes

Except for the data to encrypt or decrypt, all the other arguments must be the same when encrypting and decrypting. If you're using a mode that requires an initialization vector, it's OK to pass the initialization vector in the clear with the encrypted text.

The different modes are appropriate in different circumstances. Cipher Block Chaining (CBC) mode encrypts the data in blocks, and uses the encrypted value of each block (as well as the key) to compute the encrypted value of the next block. The initialization vector affects the encrypted value of the first block. Cipher Feedback (CFB) and Output Feedback (OFB) also use an initialization vector, but they encrypt data in units smaller than the block size. Note that OFB mode has security problems if you encrypt data in smaller units than its block size. Electronic Code Book (ECB) mode encrypts data in discrete blocks that don't depend on each other. ECB mode doesn't use an initialization vector. It is also less secure than other modes for repeated use, because the same plain text with a given key always produces the same cipher text. Constants to set each mode are listed in Table 18-2.

Table 18-2. mcrypt mode constants

Mode constant	Description
MCRYPT_MODE_ECB	Electronic Code Book mode
MCRYPT_MODE_CBC	Cipher Block Chaining mode
MCRYPT_MODE_CFB	Cipher Feedback mode
MCRYPT_MODE_OFB	Output Feedback mode with 8 bits of feedback
MCRYPT_MODE_NOFB	Output Feedback mode with *n* bits of feedback, where *n* is the block size of the algorithm used (*libmcrypt* 2.4 and higher only)
MCRYPT_MODE_STREAM	Stream Cipher mode, for algorithms such as RC4 and WAKE (*libmcrypt* 2.4 and higher only)

Different algorithms have different block sizes. You can retrieve the block size for a particular algorithm with mcrypt_get_block_size( ). Similarly, the initialization vector size is determined by the algorithm and the mode. mcrypt_create_iv( ) and mcrypt_get_iv_size( ) make it easy to create an appropriate random initialization vector:

```php
<?php

$iv = mcrypt_create_iv(mcrypt_get_iv_size($algorithm, $mode), MCRYPT_DEV_URANDOM);

?>
```

The first argument to mcrypt_create_iv( ) is the size of the vector, and the second is a source of randomness. You have three choices for the source of randomness: MCRYPT_DEV_RANDOM reads from the pseudodevice */dev/random*, MCRYPT_DEV_URANDOM reads from the pseudodevice */dev/urandom*, and MCRYPT_RAND uses an internal random number generator. Not all operating systems support random-generating pseudodevices. Make sure to call srand( ) before using MCRYPT_RAND in order to get a nonrepeating random number stream.

The code and examples in this recipe are compatible with *mcrypt* 2.4. PHP's mcrypt interface supports both *mcrypt* 2.2 and *mcrypt* 2.4, but there are differences between the two. With *mcrypt* 2.2, PHP supports only the following *mcrypt* functions: mcrypt_ecb( ), mcrypt_cbc( ), mcrypt_cfb( ), mcrypt_ofb( ), mcrypt_get_key_size( ), mcrypt_get_block_size( ), mcrypt_get_cipher_name( ), and mcrypt_create_iv( ). To encrypt or decrypt data with *mcrypt* 2.2, call the appropriate mcrypt_*MODE*( ) function, based on what mode you want to use, and pass it an argument that instructs it to encrypt or decrypt. The following code is the *mcrypt* 2.2–compatible version of the code in the Solution:

```php
<?php

$algorithm = MCRYPT_BLOWFISH;
$key  = 'That golden key that opens the palace of eternity.';
$data = 'The chicken escapes at dawn. Send help with Mr. Blue.';

$iv = mcrypt_create_iv(mcrypt_get_block_size($algorithm),
```

```
                    MCRYPT_DEV_URANDOM);

    $encrypted_data = mcrypt_cbc($algorithm, $key, $data, MCRYPT_ENCRYPT, $iv);
    $plain_text = base64_encode($encrypted_data);
    echo $plain_text . "\n";

    $encrypted_data = base64_decode($plain_text);
    $decoded = mcrypt_cbc($algorithm, $key, base64_decode($plain_text), MCRYPT_DECRYPT, $iv);
    echo $decoded . "\n";

    ?>
```

See Also

Documentation on the *mcrypt* extension at *http://www.php.net/mcrypt*; the *mcrypt* library is available at *http://mcrypt.hellug.gr/*; choosing an appropriate algorithm and using it securely requires care and planning: for more information about *mcrypt* and the cipher algorithms it uses, see the online PHP manual section on *mcrypt*, the *mcrypt* home page, and the manual pages for */dev/random* and */dev/urandom*; good books about cryptography include *Applied Cryptography* by Bruce Schneier (Wiley) and *Cryptography: Theory and Practice* by Douglas R. Stinson (Chapman & Hall).

18.11 Storing Encrypted Data in a File or Database

Problem

You want to store encrypted data that needs to be retrieved and decrypted later by your web server.

Solution

Store the additional information required to decrypt the data (such as algorithm, cipher mode, and initialization vector) along with the encrypted information, but not the key:

```
    <?php

    /* Encrypt the data. */
    $algorithm = MCRYPT_BLOWFISH;
    $mode = MCRYPT_MODE_CBC;
    $iv = mcrypt_create_iv(mcrypt_get_iv_size($algorithm, $mode), MCRYPT_DEV_URANDOM);
    $ciphertext = mcrypt_encrypt($algorithm, $_POST['key'], $_POST['data'], $mode, $iv);

    /* Store the encrypted data. */
    $st = $db->prepare('INSERT
                INTO  noc_list (algorithm, mode, iv, data)
                VALUES (?, ?, ?, ?)');
    $st->execute(array($algorithm, $mode, $iv, $ciphertext));

    ?>
```

To decrypt the data, retrieve a key from the user and use it with the saved data:

```php
<?php

$row = $db->query('SELECT *
                   FROM   noc_list
                   WHERE  id = 27')->fetch();
$plaintext = mcrypt_decrypt($row->algorithm,
                            $_POST['key'],
                            $row['data'],
                            $row['mode'],
                            $row['iv']);

?>
```

Discussion

The *save-crypt.php* script shown in Example 18-1 stores encrypted data to a file.

Example 18-1. save-crypt.php

```php
<?php

function show_form() {
    $html = array();
    $html['action'] = htmlentities($_SERVER['PHP_SELF'], ENT_QUOTES, 'UTF-8');

    print<<<FORM
<form method="POST" action="{$html['action']}">
<textarea name="data" rows="10" cols="40">Enter data to be encrypted here.</textarea>
<br />
Encryption Key: <input type="text" name="key" />
<br />
<input name="submit" type="submit" value="Save" />
</form>
FORM;
}

function save_form() {
    $algorithm  = MCRYPT_BLOWFISH;
    $mode = MCRYPT_MODE_CBC;

    /* Encrypt data. */
    $iv = mcrypt_create_iv(mcrypt_get_iv_size($algorithm, $mode), MCRYPT_DEV_URANDOM);
    $ciphertext = mcrypt_encrypt($algorithm,
                                 $_POST['key'],
                                 $_POST['data'],
                                 $mode,
                                 $iv);

    /* Save encrypted data. */
    $filename = tempnam('/tmp','enc') or exit($php_errormsg);
    $file = fopen($filename, 'w') or exit($php_errormsg);
    if (FALSE === fwrite($file, $iv.$ciphertext)) {
        fclose($file);
        exit($php_errormsg);
    }
```

```php
        fclose($file) or exit($php_errormsg);

        return $filename;
    }

    if (isset($_POST['submit'])) {
        $file = save_form();
        echo "Encrypted data saved to file: $file";
    } else {
        show_form();
    }

    ?>
```

Example 18-2 shows the corresponding program, *get-crypt.php*, that accepts a filename and key and produces the decrypted data.

Example 18-2. get-crypt.php

```php
    <?php

    function show_form() {
        $html = array();
        $html['action'] = htmlentities($_SERVER['PHP_SELF'], ENT_QUOTES, 'UTF-8');

        print<<<FORM
    <form method="POST" action="{$html['action']}">
    Encrypted File: <input type="text" name="file" />
    <br />
    Encryption Key: <input type="text" name="key" />
    <br />
    <input name="submit" type="submit" value="Display" />
    </form>
    FORM;

    function display() {
        $algorithm  = MCRYPT_BLOWFISH;
        $mode = MCRYPT_MODE_CBC;

        $file = fopen($_POST['file'], 'r') or exit($php_errormsg);
        $iv = fread($file, mcrypt_get_iv_size($algorithm, $mode));
        $ciphertext = fread($file, filesize($_POST['file']));
        fclose($fh);

        $plaintext = mcrypt_decrypt($algorithm, $_POST['key'], $ciphertext, $mode, $iv);
        echo "<pre>$plaintext</pre>";
    }

    if (isset($_POST['submit'])) {
        display();
    } else {
        show_form();
    }

    ?>
```

These two programs have their encryption algorithm and mode hardcoded in them, so there's no need to store this information in the file. The file consists of the initialization vector immediately followed by the encrypted data. There's no need for a delimiter after the initialization vector (IV), because `mcrypt_get_iv_size( )` returns exactly how many bytes the decryption program needs to read to get the whole IV. Everything after that in the file is encrypted data.

Encrypting files using the method in this recipe offers protection if an attacker gains access to the server on which the files are stored. Without the appropriate key or tremendous amounts of computing power, the attacker won't be able to read the files. However, the security that these encrypted file provides is undercut if the data to be encrypted and the encryption keys travel between your server and your users' web browsers in the clear. Someone who can intercept or monitor network traffic can see data before it even gets encrypted. To prevent this kind of eavesdropping, use SSL.

An additional risk when your web server encrypts data as in this recipe comes from how the data is visible before it's encrypted and written to a file. Someone with root or administrator access to the server can look in the memory the web server process is using and snoop on the unencrypted data and the key. If the operating system swaps the memory image of the web server process to disk, the unencrypted data might also be accessible in this swap file. This kind of attack can be difficult to pull off but can be devastating. Once the encrypted data is in a file, it's unreadable even to an attacker with root access to the web server, but if the attacker can peek at the unencrypted data before it's in that file, the encryption offers little protection.

See Also

Recipe 18.13 discusses SSL and protecting data as it moves over the network; documentation on `mcrypt_encrypt( )` at *http://www.php.net/mcrypt-encrypt*, `mcrypt_decrypt( )` at *http://www.php.net/mcrypt-decrypt*, `mcrypt_create_iv( )` at *http://www.php.net/mcrypt-create-iv*, and `mcrypt_get_iv_size( )` at *http://www.php.net/mcrypt-get-iv-size*.

18.12 Sharing Encrypted Data with Another Web Site

Problem

You want to exchange data securely with another web site.

Solution

If the other web site is pulling the data from your site, put the data up on a password-protected page. You can also make the data available in encrypted form, with or without a password. If you need to push the data to another web site, submit the potentially encrypted data via `post` to a password-protected URL.

Discussion

The following page requires a username and password and then encrypts and displays the contents of a file containing yesterday's account activity:

```php
<?php

$user = 'bank';
$password = 'fas8uj3';

if ($_SERVER['PHP_AUTH_USER'] != $user ||
    $_SERVER['PHP_AUTH_PW'] != $password) {
    header('WWW-Authenticate: Basic realm="Secure Transfer"');
    header('HTTP/1.0 401 Unauthorized');
    echo "You must supply a valid username and password for access.";
    exit;
}

header('Content-type: text/plain; charset=UTF-8');
$filename = strftime('/usr/local/account-activity.%Y-%m-%d', time() - 86400);
$data = implode('', file($filename));

$algorithm = MCRYPT_BLOWFISH;
$mode = MCRYPT_MODE_CBC;
$key  = "There are many ways to butter your toast.";

/* Encrypt data. */
$iv = mcrypt_create_iv(mcrypt_get_iv_size($algorithm, $mode), MCRYPT_DEV_URANDOM);
$ciphertext = mcrypt_encrypt($algorithm, $key, $data, $mode, $iv);

echo base64_encode($iv.$ciphertext);

?>
```

Here's the corresponding code to retrieve the encrypted page and decrypt the information:

```php
<?php

$user = 'bank';
$password = 'fas8uj3';
$algorithm = MCRYPT_BLOWFISH;
$mode = MCRYPT_MODE_CBC;
$key  = "There are many ways to butter your toast.";

$file = fopen("http://$user:$password@bank.example.com/accounts.php", 'r')
        or exit($php_errormsg);
$data = '';

while (!feof($file)) {
    $data .= fgets($file, 1048576);
}

fclose($file) or exit($php_errormsg);
$binary_data = base64_decode($data);
$iv_size = mcrypt_get_iv_size($algorithm, $mode);
```

```php
$iv = substr($binary_data, 0, $iv_size);
$ciphertext = substr($binary_data, $iv_size, strlen($binary_data));

echo mcrypt_decrypt($algorithm, $key, $ciphertext, $mode, $iv);

?>
```

The retrieval program does all the steps of the encryption program, but in reverse. It retrieves the Base64-encoded encrypted data, supplying a username and password. Then, it decodes the data with Base64 and separates out the initialization vector. Last, it decrypts the data and prints it out.

In the previous examples, the username and password are still sent over the network in clear text, unless the connections happen over SSL. However, if you're using SSL, it's probably not necessary to encrypt the contents of the file. We included both password-prompting and file encryption in these examples to show how it can be done.

There's one circumstance, however, in which both password protection and file encryption is helpful: if the file isn't automatically decrypted when it's retrieved. An automated program can retrieve the encrypted file and put it, still encrypted, in a place that can be accessed later. The decryption key thus doesn't need to be stored in the retrieval program.

See Also

Recipe 18.13 discusses SSL and protecting data as it moves over the network; documentation on mcrypt_encrypt( ) at *http://php.net/mcrypt-encrypt* and mcrypt_decrypt( ) at *http://php.net/mcrypt-decrypt*.

18.13 Detecting SSL

Problem

You want to know if a request arrived over SSL.

Solution

Test the value of $_SERVER['HTTPS']:

```php
<?php

if ('on' == $_SERVER['HTTPS']) {
  echo 'The secret ingredient in Coca-Cola is Soylent Green.';
} else {
  echo 'Coca-Cola contains many delicious natural and artificial flavors.';
}

?>
```

Discussion

SSL operates on a lower level than HTTP. The web server and a browser negotiate an appropriately secure connection, based on their capabilities, and the HTTP messages can pass over that secure connection. To an attacker intercepting the traffic, it's just a stream of nonsense bytes that can't be read.

Different web servers have different requirements to use SSL, so check your server's documentation for specific details. No changes have to be made to PHP to work over SSL.

In addition to altering code based on `$_SERVER['HTTPS']`, you can also set cookies to be exchanged only over SSL connections. If the last argument to `setcookie()` is `TRUE`, the browser sends the cookie back to the server only over a secure connection:

```php
<?php

/* Set an SSL-only cookie named "sslonly" with value "yes" that expires at the
   end of the current browser session. */

setcookie('sslonly', 'yes', '', '/', 'example.org', true);

?>
```

Although the browser sends these cookies back to the server only over an SSL connection, the server sends them to the browser (when you call `setcookie()` in your page) whether or not the request for the page that sets the cookie is over SSL. If you're putting sensitive data in the cookie, make sure that you set the cookie only in an SSL request as well. Also, keep in mind that the cookie data is unencrypted on the user's computer.

See Also

Documentation on `setcookie()` at *http://php.net/setcookie*.

18.14 Encrypting Email with GPG

Problem

You want to send encrypted email messages. For example, you take orders on your web site and need to send an email to your factory with order details for processing. By encrypting the email message, you prevent sensitive data such as credit card numbers from passing over the network in the clear.

Solution

Encrypt the body of the email message with GNU Privacy Guard (GPG) before sending it:

```php
<?php
```

```
$message_body = escapeshellarg($message_body);
$gpg_path    = '/usr/local/bin/gpg';
$sender      = 'web@example.com';
$recipient   = 'ordertaker@example.com';
$home_dir    = '/home/web';
$user_env    = 'web';

$cmd = "echo $message_body | HOME=$home_dir USER=$user_env $gpg_path " .
       '--quiet --no-secmem-warning --encrypt --sign --armor ' .
       "--recipient $recipient --local-user $sender";

$message_body = `$cmd`;

mail($recipient, 'Web Site Order', $message_body);

?>
```

The email message can be decrypted by GPG, Pretty Good Privacy (PGP), or an email client plug-in that supports either program.

Discussion

PGP is a popular public key encryption program; GPG is an open source program based on PGP. Because PGP is encumbered by a variety of patent and control issues, it's often easier to use GPG.

The code in the Solution invokes */usr/local/bin/gpg* to encrypt the message in $message_body. It uses the private key belonging to $sender and the public key belonging to $recipient. This means that only $recipient can decrypt the email message and when he does, he knows the message came from $sender.

Setting the HOME and USER environment variables tells GPG where to look for its keyring: *$HOME/.gnupg/secring.gpg*. The --quiet and --no-secmem-warning options suppress warnings GPG would otherwise generate. The --encrypt and --sign options tell GPG to both encrypt and sign the message. Encrypting the message obscures it to anyone other than the recipient. Signing it adds information so that the recipient knows who generated the message and when it was generated. The --armor option produces plaintext output instead of binary, so the encrypted message is suitable for emailing.

Normally, private keys are protected with a passphrase. If a private key protected by a passphrase is copied by an attacker, the attacker can't encrypt messages with the private key unless she also knows the passphrase. GPG prompts for the passphrase when encrypting a message. In this recipe, however, we don't want the private key of $sender to have a passphrase. If it did, the web site couldn't send new order email messages without a human typing in the passphrase each time. Storing the passphrase in a file and providing it to GPG each time you encrypt offers no additional security over not having a passphrase in the first place.

The downside of using a key without a passphrase for encryption is that an attacker who obtains the secret key can send fake order emails to your order processor. This is a manageable risk. Since orders can be submitted via a web site in the first place, there is already a place where false information can be injected into the order process. Any procedures for catching bad orders can also be triggered by these potential fake emails. Also, once the key theft is discovered, and the problem that enabled the theft is fixed, switching to a new private key easily disables the attacker.

See Also

The GNU Privacy Guard home page at *http://gnupg.org/* and the MIT PGP distribution site at *http://web.mit.edu/network/pgp.html*.

CHAPTER 19

Internationalization and Localization

19.0 Introduction

While everyone who programs in PHP has to learn some English eventually to get a handle on its function names and language constructs, PHP can create applications that speak just about any language. Some applications need to be used by speakers of many different languages. Taking an application written for French speakers and making it useful for German speakers is made easier by PHP's support for internationalization and localization.

Internationalization (often abbreviated I18N[*]) is the process of taking an application designed for just one locale and restructuring it so that it can be used in many different locales. Localization (often abbreviated L10N[†]) is the process of adding support for a new locale to an internationalized application.

A locale is a group of settings that describe text formatting and language customs in a particular area of the world. The settings are divided into six categories:

LC_COLLATE
> These settings control text sorting: which letters go before and after others in alphabetical order.

LC_CTYPE
> These settings control mapping between uppercase and lowercase letters as well as which characters fall into the different character classes, such as alphanumeric characters.

LC_MONETARY
> These settings describe the preferred format of currency information, such as what character to use as a decimal point and how to indicate negative amounts.

LC_NUMERIC
> These settings describe the preferred format of numeric information, such as how to group numbers and what character is used as a thousands separator.

[*] The word "internationalization" has 18 letters between the first "i" and the last "n."
[†] The word "localization" has 10 letters between the first "l" and the "n."

LC_TIME

> These settings describe the preferred format of time and date information, such as names of months and days and whether to use 24- or 12-hour time.

LC_MESSAGES

> This category contains text messages used by applications that need to display information in multiple languages.

There is also a metacategory, LC_ALL, that encompasses all the categories.

A locale name generally has three components. The first, an abbreviation that indicates a language, is mandatory. For example, "en" for English or "pt" for Portuguese. Next, after an underscore, comes an optional country specifier, to distinguish between different countries that speak different versions of the same language. For example, "en_US" for U.S. English and "en_UK" for British English, or "pt_BR" for Brazilian Portuguese and "pt_PT" for Portuguese Portuguese. Last, after a period, comes an optional character set specifier. For example, "zh_TW.Big5" for Taiwanese Chinese using the Big5 character set. While most locale names follow these conventions, some don't. One difficulty in using locales is that they can be arbitrarily named. Finding and setting a locale is discussed in Recipes 19.1 through 19.3.

Different techniques are necessary for correct localization of plain text, dates and times, and currency. Localization can also be applied to external entities your program uses, such as images and included files. Localizing these kinds of content is covered in Recipes 19.4 through 19.8.

Systems for dealing with large amounts of localization data are discussed in Recipes 19.9 and 19.10. Recipe 19.9 shows some simple ways to manage the data, and Recipe 19.10 introduces GNU *gettext*, a full-featured set of tools that provide localization support.

Recipes 19.11 through 19.13 discuss how to make sure your programs work well with a variety of character encodings so they can handle strings such as à l'Opéra-Théâtre, поленика, and 優之良品. One way to do this is to have all text your programs process be encoded as UTF-8. This encoding scheme can handle the Western characters in the familiar ISO-8859-1 encoding as well as characters for other writing systems around the world. These recipes focus on using UTF-8 to provide a seamless, language-independent experience for your users.

PHP 6, still in development when these words are being written, has greatly enhanced support for Unicode, including more efficient operations on multibyte strings and a completely revamped locale system. Andrei Zmievski's "PHP 6 and Unicode" talk, available at *http://www.gravitonic.com/talks/*, has an overview of the Unicode-related changes coming in PHP 6.

19.1 Listing Available Locales

Problem

You want to know what locales your system supports.

Solution

Use the *locale* program to list available locales; *locale -a* prints the locales your system supports.

Discussion

On Linux and Solaris systems, you can find `locale` at */usr/bin/locale*. On Windows XP, locales are listed in the "Standards and Formats" drop-down menu in the "Regional Options" tab of the "Regional and Language Options" section of the Control Panel.

Your mileage varies on other operating systems. BSD, for example, includes locale support but has no *locale* program to list locales. BSD locales are often stored in */usr/share/locale*, so looking in that directory may yield a list of usable locales.

While the locale system helps with many localization tasks, its lack of standardization can be frustrating. Systems aren't guaranteed to have the same locales or even use the same names for equivalent locales.

See Also

Your system's *locale(1)* manpage. A list of language strings that Windows understands as locale names is at *http://msdn.microsoft.com/library/default.asp?url=/library/en-us/vclib/html/_crt_language_strings.asphttp://msdn.microsoft.com/library/default.asp?url=/library/en-us/vclib/html/_crt_language_strings.asp*. A list of country/region strings that Windows understands as locale names is at *http://msdn.microsoft.com/library/default.asp?url=/library/en-us/vclib/html/_crt_country_strings.asp*.

19.2 Using a Particular Locale

Problem

You want PHP to use the settings of a particular locale.

Solution

Call `setlocale( )` with the appropriate category and locale. Here's how to use the `es_MX` (Mexican Spanish) locale for all categories:

```
setlocale(LC_ALL,'es_MX');
```

Here's how to use the `de_AT` (Austrian German) locale for time and date formatting:

```
setlocale(LC_TIME,'de_AT');
```

On Windows, the equivalent locale names are Spanish_Mexico and German_Austria.

Discussion

To find the current locale without changing it, call setlocale( ) with 0 for the locale, as in Example 19-1.

Example 19-1. Getting the current locale
```
<?php
print setlocale(LC_ALL,0);
?>
```

Many systems also support a set of aliases for common locales, listed in a file such as */usr/share/locale/locale.alias*. This file is a series of lines including:

```
russian       ru_RU.ISO-8859-5
slovak        sk_SK.ISO-8859-2
slovene       sl_SI.ISO-8859-2
slovenian     sl_SI.ISO-8859-2
spanish       es_ES.ISO-8859-1
swedish       sv_SE.ISO-8859-1
```

The first column of each line is an alias; the second column shows the locale and character set the alias points to. You can use the alias in calls to setlocale( ) instead of the corresponding string the alias points to. For example, you can do setlocale (LC_ALL,'swedish'); instead of setlocale(LC_ALL,'sv_SE.ISO-8859-1');.

Call setlocale( ) to change the locale on Windows as well. As described in Recipe 19.1, however, the locale names are different. If PHP is running in a multithreaded environment, changing the locale can have unexpected results. A call to setlocale( ) changes the locale for all threads in the current process. This means that when one thread changes the locale, it is immediately changed in other threads' running scripts. If you need to use setlocale( ), consider using a single-threaded server setup.

See Also

Recipe 19.3 shows how to set a default locale; documentation on setlocale( ) at *http://www.php.net/setlocale*.

19.3 Setting the Default Locale

Problem

You want to set a locale that all your PHP programs can use.

Solution

At the beginning of a file loaded by the `auto_prepend_file` configuration directive, call `setlocale( )` to set your desired locale, as in Example 19-2.

Example 19-2. Setting a default locale

```
<?php
setlocale(LC_ALL,'es_US');
?>
```

To use whatever default is set by the system environment variables, pass `null` as the locale to `setlocale( )`, as in Example 19-3.

Example 19-3. Setting a default locale based on system environment

```
<?php
setlocale(LC_ALL,null);
?>
```

Discussion

Even if you set up appropriate environment variables before you start your web server or PHP binary, PHP doesn't change its locale until you call `setlocale( )`. After setting environment variable LC_ALL to es_US, for example, PHP still runs in the default C locale.

See Also

Recipe 19.2 shows how to use a particular locale; documentation on `setlocale( )` at *http://www.php.net/setlocale* and `auto_prepend_file` at *http://www.php.net/manual/en/configuration.directives.php#ini.auto-prepend-file*.

19.4 Localizing Text Messages

Problem

You want to display text messages in a locale-appropriate language.

Solution

Maintain a message catalog of words and phrases and retrieve the appropriate string from the message catalog before printing it. Example 19-4 shows a simple message catalog with some foods in American and British English and a function to retrieve words from the catalog.

Example 19-4. A simple message catalog

```
<?php
$messages = array ('en_US' =>
            array(
              'My favorite foods are' => 'My favorite foods are',
```

```
                    'french fries'  => 'french fries',
                    'candy'         => 'candy',
                    'potato chips'  => 'potato chips',
                    'eggplant'      => 'eggplant'
                 ),
               'en_UK' =>
                 array(
                   'My favorite foods are' => 'My favourite foods are',
                   'french fries' => 'chips',
                   'candy'        => 'sweets',
                   'potato chips' => 'crisps',
                   'eggplant'     => 'aubergine'
                 )
               );

    function msg($s) {
        global $LANG, $messages;
        if (isset($messages[$LANG][$s])) {
            return $messages[$LANG][$s];
        } else {
            error_log("l10n error: LANG: $lang, message: '$s'");
        }
    }
    ?>
```

Discussion

Example 19-5 uses the message catalog to print out a list of foods.

Example 19-5. Using the message catalog

```
<?php
$LANG = 'en_UK';
print msg('My favorite foods are').":\n";
print msg('french fries')."\n";
print msg('potato chips')."\n";
print msg('candy')."\n";
?>
```

Example 19-5 prints:

```
My favourite foods are:
chips
crisps
sweets
```

To have Example 19-5 output in American English instead of British English, just set
$LANG to en_US.

You can combine the msg( ) message retrieval function with sprintf( ) to store phrases
that require values to be substituted into them. For example, consider the English sentence "I am 12 years old." In Spanish, the corresponding phrase is "Tengo 12 años."
The Spanish phrase can't be built by stitching together translations of "I am," the nu-
meral 12, and "years old." Instead, store them in the message catalogs as sprintf( )-
style format strings, as in Example 19-6.

Example 19-6. A sprintf()-style message catalog

```php
<?php
$messages = array ('en_US' => array('I am X years old.' => 'I am %d years old.'),
                   'es_US' => array('I am X years old.' => 'Tengo %d años.')
            );
?>
```

Example 19-7 passes the results of msg( ) to sprintf( ) as a format string.

Example 19-7. Using a sprintf()-style message catalog

```php
<?php
$LANG = 'es_US';
print sprintf(msg('I am X years old.'),12);
?>
```

Example 19-7 prints:

```
Tengo 12 años.
```

For phrases that require the substituted values to be in a different order in a different language, sprintf( ) supports changing the order of the arguments. This is shown in Example 19-8.

Example 19-8. Changing message catalog argument order

```php
<?php
$messages = array ('en_US' =>
                       array('I am X years and Y months old.' =>
                             'I am %d years and %d months old.'),
                   'es_US' =>
                       array('I am X years and Y months old.' =>
                             'Tengo %2$d meses y %1$d años.')
            );
?>
```

With either language, call sprintf( ) with the same order of arguments (i.e., first years, then months), as in Example 19-9.

Example 19-9. Using a message catalog with variable argument order

```php
<?php
$LANG = 'es_US';
print sprintf(msg('I am X years and Y months old.'),12,7);
$LANG = 'es_US';
print sprintf(msg('I am X years and Y months old.'),12,7);
?>
```

Example 19-9 prints:

```
I am 12 years and 7 months old.
Tengo 7 meses y 12 años.
```

In the format string, %2$ tells sprintf( ) to use the second argument, and %1$ tells it to use the first.

These phrases can also be stored as a function's return value instead of as a string in an array. Storing the phrases as functions removes the need to use `sprintf( )`. Example 19-10 shows some functions that return entire sentences.

Example 19-10. Message catalog functions

```php
<?php
// English version
function i_am_X_years_old($age) {
 return "I am $age years old.";
}

// Spanish version
function i_am_X_years_old($age) {
 return "Tengo $age años.";
}
?>
```

If some parts of the message catalog belong in an array, and some parts belong in functions, an object is a helpful container for a language's message catalog. Example 19-11 contains a base object and two simple message catalogs.

Example 19-11. Message catalog objects

```php
class pc_MC_Base {
    public $messages;
    public $lang;

    public function msg($s) {
      if (isset($this->messages[$s])) {
        return $this->messages[$s];
      } else {
        error_log("l10n error: LANG: $this->lang, message: '$s'");
      }
    }

}

class pc_MC_es_US extends pc_MC_Base {
    public $lang = 'es_US';
    public $messages = array ('chicken' => 'pollo',
                              'cow'     => 'vaca',
                              'horse'   => 'caballo'
                             );

    public function i_am_X_years_old($age) {
      return "Tengo $age años";
    }
}

class pc_MC_en_US extends pc_MC_Base {
    public $lang = 'en_US';
    public $messages = array ('chicken' => 'chicken',
                              'cow'     => 'cow',
                              'horse'   => 'horse'
```

```
    );
    public function i_am_X_years_old($age) {
      return "I am $age years old.";
    }
  }
  ?>
```

Each message catalog object extends the pc_MC_Base class to get the msg( ) method, and then defines its own messages (in its constructor) and its own functions that return phrases. Example 19-12 uses the message catalog object to print text in Spanish.

Example 19-12. Using a message catalog object

```
  <?php
  $MC = new pc_MC_es_US;

  print $MC->msg('cow');
  print $MC->i_am_X_years_old(15);
  ?>
```

To print the same text in English, $MC just needs to be instantiated as a pc_MC_en_US object instead of a pc_MC_es_US object. The rest of the code remains unchanged.

See Also

The introduction to Chapter 7 discusses object inheritance; documentation on sprintf( ) at *http://www.php.net/sprintf*.

19.5 Localizing Dates and Times

Problem

You want to display dates and times in a locale-specific manner.

Solution

Use strftime( )'s %c format string: print strftime('%c');. This format string displays a full time-and-date stamp in a locale-appropriate manner.

You can also store strftime( ) format strings as messages in your message catalog and pass the results to strftime( ), as in Example 19-13.

Example 19-13. Using a message catalog with strftime()

```
  <?php
  $MC = new pc_MC_es_US;
  print strftime($MC->msg('%Y-%m-%d'));
  ?>
```

Discussion

The `%c` format string tells `strftime( )` to return the preferred date and time representation for the current locale. It produces different results depending on the locale:

```
Sat May 13 13:53:31 2006       // in the default C locale
Sam 13 Mai 2006 13:53:31 EDT   // in the de_AT locale
sam 13 mai 2006 13:53:31 EDT   // in the fr_FR locale
```

The formatted time string that `%c` produces, while locale appropriate, isn't very flexible. If you just want the time, for example, you must pass a different format string to `strftime( )`. But these format strings themselves vary in different locales. In some locales, displaying an hour from 1 to 12 with an A.M./P.M. designation may be appropriate, while in others the hour should range from 0 to 23. To display appropriate time strings for a locale, add elements to the locale's `$messages` array for each time format you want. The key for a particular time format, such as `%H:%M`, is always the same in each locale. The value, however, can vary, such as `%H:%M` for 24-hour locales or `%I:%M%P` for 12-hour locales. Then, look up the appropriate format string and pass it to `strftime( )`, as shown in Example 19-14.

Example 19-14. Using time formatting with a message catalog

```php
<?php
$MC = new pc_MC_es_US;

print strftime($MC->msg('%H:%M'));
?>
```

Note that changing the locale doesn't change the time zone; it changes only the formatting of the displayed result.

See Also

Recipe 3.4 discusses the format strings that `strftime( )` accepts; Recipe 3.11 covers changing time zones in your program; documentation on `strftime( )` at *http://www.php.net/strftime*.

19.6 Localizing Currency Values

Problem

You want to display currency amounts in a locale-specific format.

Solution

Use the `money_format( )` function to produce an appropriately formatted string. Example 19-15 shows a few of the format characters that `money_format( )` understands.

Example 19-15. Formatting with money_format( )

```php
<?php
$income = 5549.3;
$debit  = -25.95;

$formats = array('%i', // international
                 '%n', // national
                 '%+n', // + and -
                 '%(n', // () for negative
                 );

setlocale(LC_ALL, 'en_US');
foreach ($formats as $format ) {
    print "$income @ $format = " .
        money_format($format,$income) .
        "\n";
    print "$debit @ $format = " .
        money_format($format,$debit) .
        "\n";
}
?>
```

Example 19-15 prints:

```
5549.3 @ %i = USD 5,549.30
-25.95 @ %i = -USD 25.95
5549.3 @ %n = $5,549.30
-25.95 @ %n = -$25.95
5549.3 @ %+n = $5,549.30
-25.95 @ %+n = -$25.95
5549.3 @ %(n = $5,549.30
-25.95 @ %(n = ($25.95)
```

money_format( ) is not available on Windows or before PHP 4.3.0. If you can't use money_format( ), use the pc_format_currency( ) function, shown in Example 19-17, to produce an appropriately formatted string. Example 19-16 shows pc_format_currency( ) in action.

Example 19-16. Using pc_format_currency( )

```php
<?php
setlocale(LC_ALL,'turkish');
print pc_format_currency(-12345678.45);
?>
```

Example 19-16 prints:

```
-12.345.678,45 TL
```

Discussion

money_format( ) is similar to sprintf( ) or strftime( )—you give it a formatting string and a value. Special sequences in the formatting string indicate how the value is formatted. Just as sprintf( ) requires the components of a format sequence to be in a particular order—percent sign, padding, type indicator, and so on—`money_format( )` requires that each format sequence be in a particular order: percent sign, flags, width, left precision, right precision, conversion character. Only the percent sign and the conversion character are mandatory. Table 19-1 lists the format characters that `money_format( )` understands.

Table 19-1. Format characters for money_format( )

Category	Format character	Description
Flag	=c	Use the single character c as a fill character. The default is space.
Flag	^	Don't use grouping characters.
Flag	+	Use locale-specified + and - characters to format positive and negative numbers. This is the default if neither the + or (flag is used.
Flag	(	Surround negative numbers with (and).
Flag	!	Don't use the currency symbol in the output string.
Flag	-	Left-justify all fields. If this is not present, fields are right justified.
Width	*width*	Make the minimum field width *width*. Default minimum field with is 0.
Left precision	#*precision*	If there are less than *precision* digits to the left of the decimal point, then the fill character is used to pad the width.
Right precision	.*precision*	The digits to the right of the decimal point are rounded to *precision* places before being formatted. If *precision* is 0, then neither a decimal point nor digits to the right of it are printed. The default is locale specific.
Conversion character	i	Use the international currency format. This usually means that a three-character code such as USD is used for the currency symbol.
Conversion character	n	Use the national currency format. This usually means that a locale-appropriate value, such as $, is used for the currency symbol.
Conversion character	%	A literal %.

Because `money_format( )` relies on the `strfmon( )` system function, it is only available when that system function is available. Windows does not provide the `strfmon( )` system function.

The `pc_format_currency( )` function, shown in Example 19-17, gets the currency formatting information from `localeconv( )` and then uses `number_format( )` and some logic to construct the correct string.

Example 19-17. pc_format_currency

```
<?php
function pc_format_currency($amt) {
    // get locale-specific currency formatting information
    $a = localeconv();

    // compute sign of $amt and then remove it
    if ($amt < 0) { $sign = -1; } else { $sign = 1; }
    $amt = abs($amt);
```

```
// format $amt with appropriate grouping, decimal point, and fractional digits
$amt = number_format($amt,$a['frac_digits'],$a['mon_decimal_point'],
                    $a['mon_thousands_sep']);

// figure out where to put the currency symbol and positive or negative signs
$currency_symbol = $a['currency_symbol'];
// is $amt >= 0 ?
if (1 == $sign) {
    $sign_symbol  = 'positive_sign';
    $cs_precedes  = 'p_cs_precedes';
    $sign_posn    = 'p_sign_posn';
    $sep_by_space = 'p_sep_by_space';
} else {
    $sign_symbol  = 'negative_sign';
    $cs_precedes  = 'n_cs_precedes';
    $sign_posn    = 'n_sign_posn';
    $sep_by_space = 'n_sep_by_space';
}
if ($a[$cs_precedes]) {
    if (3 == $a[$sign_posn]) {
        $currency_symbol = $a[$sign_symbol].$currency_symbol;
    } elseif (4 == $a[$sign_posn]) {
        $currency_symbol .= $a[$sign_symbol];
    }
    // currency symbol in front
    if ($a[$sep_by_space]) {
        $amt = $currency_symbol.' '.$amt;
    } else {
        $amt = $currency_symbol.$amt;
    }
} else {
    // currency symbol after amount
    if ($a[$sep_by_space]) {
        $amt .= ' '.$currency_symbol;
    } else {
        $amt .= $currency_symbol;
    }
}
if (0 == $a[$sign_posn]) {
    $amt = "($amt)";
} elseif (1 == $a[$sign_posn]) {
    $amt = $a[$sign_symbol].$amt;
} elseif (2 == $a[$sign_posn]) {
    $amt .= $a[$sign_symbol];
}
return $amt;
}
?>
```

The code in pc_format_currency( ) that puts the currency symbol and sign in the correct place is almost identical for positive and negative amounts; it just uses different elements of the array returned by localeconv( ). The relevant elements of the array returned by localeconv( ) are shown in Table 19-2.

Table 19-2. *Currency-related information from localeconv( )*

Array element	Description
currency_symbol	Local currency symbol
mon_decimal_point	Monetary decimal point character
mon_thousands_sep	Monetary thousands separator
positive_sign	Sign for positive values
negative_sign	Sign for negative values
frac_digits	Number of fractional digits
p_cs_precedes	1 if currency_symbol should precede a positive value, 0 if it should follow
p_sep_by_space	1 if a space should separate the currency symbol from a positive value, 0 if not
n_cs_precedes	1 if currency_symbol should precede a negative value, 0 if it should follow
n_sep_by_space	1 if a space should separate currency_symbol from a negative value, 0 if not
p_sign_posn	Positive sign position: • 0 if parentheses should surround the quantity and currency_symbol • 1 if the sign string should precede the quantity and currency_symbol • 2 if the sign string should follow the quantity and currency_symbol • 3 if the sign string should immediately precede currency_symbol • 4 if the sign string should immediately follow currency_symbol
n_sign_posn	Negative sign position: same possible values as p_sign_posn

See Also

Recipe 2.10 also discusses money_format( ); documentation on money_format( ) at *http://www.php.net/money_format*, on localeconv( ) at *http://www.php.net/localeconv*, and on number_format( ) at *http://www.php.net/number-format*.

19.7 Localizing Images

Problem

You want to display images that have text in them and have that text in a locale-appropriate language.

Solution

Make an image directory for each locale you want to support, as well as a global image directory for images that have no locale-specific information in them. Create copies of each locale-specific image in the appropriate locale-specific directory. Make sure that the images have the same filename in the different directories. Instead of printing out image URLs directly, use a wrapper function similar to the msg( ) function in Recipe 19.4 that prints out locale-specific text.

Discussion

The `img()` wrapper function in Example 19-18 looks for a locale-specific version of an image first, then a global one. If neither are present, it prints a message to the error log.

Example 19-18. Finding locale-specific images

```php
<?php
$image_base_path = '/usr/local/www/images';
$image_base_url  = '/images';

function img($f) {
    global $LANG;
    global $image_base_path;
    global $image_base_url;

    if (is_readable("$image_base_path/$LANG/$f")) {
        return "$image_base_url/$LANG/$f";
    } elseif (is_readable("$image_base_path/global/$f")) {
        return "$image_base_url/global/$f";
    } else {
        error_log("l10n error: LANG: $lang, image: '$f'");
    }
}
```

The `img()` function needs to know both the path to the image file in the filesystem (`$image_base_path`) and the path to the image from the base URL of your site (*/images*). It uses the first to test if the file can be read and the second to construct an appropriate URL for the image.

A localized image must have the same filename in each localization directory. For example, an image that says "New!" on a yellow starburst should be called *new.gif* in both the *images/en_US* directory and the *images/es_US* directory, even though the file *images/es_US/new.gif* is a picture of a yellow starburst with "¡Nuevo!" on it.

Don't forget that the `alt` text you display in your image tags also needs to be localized. Example 19-19 prints a complete localized `<img/>` element.

Example 19-19. A localized <img> element

```php
<?php
print '<img src="' . img('cancel.png') . '" ' .
      'alt="' . msg('Cancel') . '"/>';
?>
```

If the localized versions of a particular image have varied dimensions, store image height and width in the message catalog as well. Example 19-20 prints a localized `<img/>` element with `height` and `width` attributes.

Example 19-20. A localized <img/> element with height and width

```php
<?php
print '<img src="' . img('cancel.png') . '" ' .
      'alt="' . msg('Cancel') . '" ' .
```

```
                'height="' . msg('img-cancel-height') . '" ' .
                'width="' . msg('img-cancel-width') . '"/>';
    ?>
```

The localized messages for img-cancel-height and img-cancel-width are not text strings, but integers that describe the dimensions of the *cancel.png* image in each locale.

See Also

Recipe 19.4 discusses locale-specific message catalogs.

19.8 Localizing Included Files

Problem

You want to include locale-specific files in your pages.

Solution

Modify include_path once you've determined the appropriate locale, as shown in Example 19-21.

Example 19-21. Modifying include_path for localization

```
<?php
$base = '/usr/local/php-include';
$LANG = 'en_US';

$include_path = ini_get('include_path');
ini_set('include_path',"$base/$LANG:$base/global:$include_path");
?>
```

Discussion

In Example 19-21, the $base variable holds the name of the base directory for your included localized files. Files that are not locale-specific go in the *global* subdirectory of $base, and locale-specific files go in a subdirectory named after their locale (e.g., *en_US*). Prepending the locale-specific directory and then the global directory to the include path makes them the first two places PHP looks when you include a file. Putting the locale-specific directory first ensures that nonlocalized information is loaded only if localized information isn't available.

This technique is similar to what the img( ) function does in the Recipe 19.7. Here, however, you can take advantage of PHP's include_path feature to have the directory searching happen automatically. For maximum utility, reset include_path as early as possible in your code, preferably at the top of a file loaded via auto_prepend_file on every request.

See Also

Documentation on `include_path` at *http://www.php.net/manual/en/ configuration.directives.php#ini.include-path* and `auto_prepend_file` at *http:// www.php.net/manual/en/configuration.directives.php#ini.auto-prepend-file*.

19.9 Managing Localization Resources

Problem

You need to keep track of your various message catalogs and images.

Solution

Two techniques simplify the management of your localization resources. The first is making the new language of an object—for example, Canadian English—extend from a similar existing language, such as American English. You only have to change the words and phrases in the new object that differ from the original language.

The second technique: to track what phrases still need to be translated in new languages, put stubs in the new language object that have the same value as in your base language. By finding which values are the same in the base language and the new language, you can then generate a list of words and phrases to translate.

Discussion

The *catalog-compare.php* program shown in Example 19-22 prints out messages that are the same in two catalogs, as well as messages that are missing from one catalog but present in another.

Example 19-22. catalog-compare.php

```php
<?php

if (! (isset($_SERVER['argv'][1]) && isset($_SERVER['argv'][2]))) {
    die("Specify two locales to compare.");
}

$base = 'pc_MC_'.$_SERVER['argv'][1];
$other = 'pc_MC_'.$_SERVER['argv'][2];

require_once 'pc_MC_Base.php';
require_once "$base.php";
require_once "$other.php";

$base_obj = new $base;
$other_obj = new $other;

/* Check for messages in the other class that
 * are the same as the base class or are in
 * the base class but missing from the other class */
```

```
foreach ($base_obj->messages as $k => $v) {
    if (isset($other_obj->messages[$k])) {
        if ($v == $other_obj->messages[$k]) {
            print "SAME: $k\n";
        }
    } else {
        print "MISSING: $k\n";
    }
}

/* Check for messages in the other class but missing
 * from the base class */
foreach ($other_obj->messages as $k => $v) {
    if (! isset($base_obj->messages[$k])) {
        print "MISSING (BASE): $k\n";
    }
}
```

To use this program, put each message catalog object in a file with the same name as the object (e.g., the pc_MC_en_US class should be in a file named *pc_MC_en_US.php*, and the pc_MC_es_US class should be in a file named *pc_MC_es_US.php*). You then call the program with the two locale names as arguments on the command line:

```
% php catalog-compare.php en_US es_US
```

In a web context, it can be useful to use a different locale and message catalog on a per-request basis. The locale to use may come from the browser (in an Accept-Language header), or it may be explicitly set by the server (different virtual hosts may be set up to display the same content in different languages). If the same code needs to select a message catalog on a per-request basis, the message catalog class can be instantiated as in Example 19-23.

Example 19-23. Instantiating message catalogs

```php
<?php
// $locale comes from headers or virtual host name
$classname = "pc_MC_$locale";

require_once 'pc_MC_Base.php';
require_once $classname.'.php';

$MC = new $classname;
?>
```

See Also

Recipe 19.4 for a discussion of message catalogs; Recipe 7.19 for information on finding the methods and properties of an object.

19.10 Using gettext

Problem

You want a comprehensive system to create, manage, and deploy message catalogs.

Solution

Use PHP's *gettext* extension, which allows you to use GNU's *gettext* utilities. Example 19-24 uses the *gettext* functions to print messages from a custom message catalog.

Example 19-24. Using gettext

```php
<?php
// Define the directories where the "animals" catalog can be found
bindtextdomain('animals','/home/translator/custom/locale');
// Use the 'animals' catalog as a default
textdomain('animals');


$languages = array('en_US','fr_FR','de_DE');
foreach ($languages as $language) {
    // Change to the appropriate locale
    setlocale(LC_ALL, $language);
    // And get a localized string
    print gettext('Monkey');
    print "\n";
}
?>
```

Example 19-24 prints:

```
Monkey
Singe
Affe
```

Discussion

gettext is a set of tools that makes it easier for your application to produce multilingual messages. Compiling PHP with the `--with-gettext` option enables functions to retrieve the appropriate text from *gettext*-format message catalogs, and there are a number of external tools to edit the message catalogs.

With *gettext*, messages are divided into domains, and all messages for a particular domain are stored in the same file. `bindtextdomain( )` tells *gettext* where to find the message catalog for a particular domain. A call to:

```
bindtextdomain('animals','/home/translator/custom/locale')
```

indicates that the message catalog for the `animals` domain in the `en_US` locale is in the file */home/translator/custom/locale/en_US/LC_MESSAGES/animals.mo*.

The `textdomain('animals')` function sets the default domain to `animals`. Calling `gettext()` retrieves a message from the default domain. There are other functions, such as `dgettext()`, that let you retrieve a message from a different domain. When `gettext()` (or `dgettext()`) is called, it returns the appropriate message for the current locale. If there's no message in the catalog for the current locale that corresponds to the argument passed to it, `gettext()` (or `dgettext()`) returns just its argument. As a result, if you haven't translated all your messages, your code prints out in English (or whatever your base language is) for those untranslated messages.

Setting the default domain with `textdomain()` makes each subsequent retrieval of a message from that domain more concise, because you just have to call `gettext('Good morning')` instead of `dgettext('domain','Good morning')`. However, if even `gettext('Good morning')` is too much typing, you can take advantage of an undocumented function alias: `_()` for `gettext()`. Instead of `gettext('Good morning')`, use `_('Good morning')`.

The *gettext* web site has helpful and detailed information for managing the information flow between programmers and translators and how to efficiently use *gettext*. It also includes information on other tools you can use to manage your message catalogs, such as a special GNU Emacs mode.

A downside to *gettext* that you should be aware of: it's not thread safe. If you use *gettext* in a multithreaded web server, you may run into problems where changing settings in one thread affects other threads.

See Also

Documentation on *gettext* at *http://www.php.net/gettext*; the *gettext* library at *http://www.gnu.org/software/gettext/gettext.html*. "Gettext," by Joao Prado Maia (*http://www.onlamp.com/pub/a/php/2002/06/13/php.html*) explores how to use GNU utilities such as `xgettext` and `msgfmt` to generate and maintain your own message catalogs.

19.11 Setting the Character Encoding of Outgoing Data

Problem

You want to make sure that browsers correctly handle the UTF-8-encoded text that your programs emit.

Solution

Set PHP's `default_encoding` configuration directive to `utf-8`. This ensures that the `Content-Type` header PHP emits on HTML responses includes the `charset=utf-8` piece, which tells web browsers to interpret the page contents as UTF-8 encoded.

Discussion

Setting `default_encoding` gives web browsers a heads-up that your page contents should be interpreted as UTF-8 encoded. However, you still have the responsibility to make sure that the page contents really are properly UTF-8 encoded by using string functions appropriately. Recipe 19.13 details how to do that.

If you can't change the `default_encoding` configuration directive, send the proper `Content-Type` header yourself with the `header()` function, as shown in Example 19-25.

Example 19-25. Setting character encoding

```php
<?php
header('Content-Type: text/html;charset=utf-8');
?>
```

See Also

Recipe 19.13 for information on generating UTF-8-encoded text.

19.12 Setting the Character Encoding of Incoming Data

Problem

You want to make sure that data flowing into your program has a consistent character encoding so you can handle it properly. For example, you want to treat all incoming submitted form data as UTF-8.

Solution

You can't guarantee that browsers will respect the instructions you give them with regard to character encoding, but there are a number of things you can do that make well-behaved browsers generally follow the rules.

First, follow the instructions in Recipe 19.11 so that your programs tell browsers that they are emitting UTF-8-encoded text. A `Content-Type` header with a `charset` is a good hint to a browser that submitted forms should be encoded using the character encoding the header specifies.

Second, include an `accept-charset="utf-8"` attribute in `<form/>` elements that you output. Although it's not supported by all web browsers, it instructs the browser to encode the user-entered data in the form as UTF-8 before sending it to the server.

Discussion

In general, browsers send back form data with the same encoding that was used to generate the page containing the form. So if you standardize on UTF-8 output, you can be reasonably sure that you're always getting UTF-8 input. The `accept-charset`

<form/> attribute is part of the HTML 4.0 specification, but is not implemented every-where.

See Also

Recipe 19.11 for information about sending UTF-8-encoded output; the `accept-charset <form/>` attribute is described at *http://www.w3.org/TR/REC-html40/interact/forms.html#adef-accept-charset*.

19.13 Manipulating UTF-8 Text

Problem

You want to work with UTF-8-encoded text in your programs. For example, you want to properly calculate the length of multibyte strings and make sure that all text is output as proper UTF-8-encoded characters.

Solution

Use a combination of PHP functions for the variety of tasks that UTF-8 compliance demands.

If the `mbstring` extension is available, use its string functions for UTF-8-aware string manipulation. Example 19-26 uses the `mb_strlen()` function to compute the number of characters in each of two UTF-8-encoded strings.

Example 19-26. Using mb_strlen( )

```php
<?php
// Set the encoding properly
mb_internal_encoding('UTF-8');
// ö is two bytes
$name = 'Kurt Gödel';
// Each of these Hangul characters is three bytes
$dinner = '불고기';

$name_len_bytes = strlen($name);
$name_len_chars = mb_strlen($name);

$dinner_len_bytes = strlen($dinner);
$dinner_len_chars = mb_strlen($dinner);

print "$name is $name_len_bytes bytes and $name_len_chars chars\n";
print "$dinner is $dinner_len_bytes bytes and $dinner_len_chars chars\n";
?>
```

Example 19-26 prints:

```
Kurt Gödel is 11 bytes and 10 chars
불고기 is 9 bytes and 3 chars
```

The `iconv` extension, which is available by default in PHP 5, also offers a few multibyte-aware string manipulation functions, as shown in Example 19-27.

Example 19-27. Using iconv

```php
<?php
// Set the encoding properly
iconv_set_encoding('internal_encoding','UTF-8');
// ö is two bytes
$name = 'Kurt Gödel';
// Each of these Hangul characters is three bytes
$dinner = '불고기';

$name_len_bytes = strlen($name);
$name_len_chars = iconv_strlen($name);

$dinner_len_bytes = strlen($dinner);
$dinner_len_chars = iconv_strlen($dinner);

print "$name is $name_len_bytes bytes and $name_len_chars chars\n";
print "$dinner is $dinner_len_bytes bytes and $dinner_len_chars chars\n <br/>";

print "The seventh character of $name is " . iconv_substr($name,6,1) . "\n";
print "The last two characters of $dinner are " . iconv_substr($dinner,-2);
?>
```

Use the optional third argument to functions such as `htmlentities()` and `htmlspecialchars()` that instructs them to treat input as UTF-8 encoded, as shown in Example 19-28.

Example 19-28. UTF-8 HTML encoding

```php
<?php
$encoded_name = htmlspecialchars($_POST['name'], ENT_QUOTES, 'UTF-8');
$encoded_dinner = htmlentities($_POST['dinner'], ENT_QUOTES, 'UTF-8');
?>
```

Discussion

Eternal vigilance is the price of proper character encoding, at least until PHP 6 is released. If you've followed the instructions in Recipes 19.11 and 19.12, data coming into your program should be UTF-8 encoded and browsers will properly handle data coming out of your program as UTF-8 encoded. This leaves you with two responsibilities: to operate on strings in a UTF-8-aware manner and to generate text that is UTF-8 encoded.

Fulfilling the first responsibility is made easier once you have adopted the fundamental credo of internationalization awareness: a character is not a byte. The PHP-specific correlary to this axiom is that PHP's string functions only know about bytes, not characters. For example, the `strlen()` function counts the number of bytes in a string, not the number of characters. In the prelapsarian days of ISO-8859-1 encoding, this wasn't a problem—each of the 256 characters in the character set took up one byte. A UTF-8-encoded character, on the other hand, uses between one and four bytes. The `mbstring` and `iconv` extensions provide alternatives for some string functions that operate on a character-by-character basis, not a byte-by-byte basis. These functions are listed in Table 19-3.

Table 19-3. Character-Based Functions

Regular function	mbstring function	iconv function
strlen( )	mb_strlen( )	iconv_strlen( )
strpos( )	mb_strpos( )	iconv_strpos( )
strrpos( )	mb_strrpos( )	iconv_strrpos( )
substr( )	mb_substr( )	iconv_substr( )
strtolower( )	mb_strtolower( )	-
strtoupper( )	mb_strtoupper( )	-
substr_count( )	mb_substr_count( )	-
ereg( )	mb_ereg( )	-
eregi( )	mb_eregi( )	-
ereg_replace( )	mb_ereg_replace( )	-
eregi_replace( )	mb_eregi_replace( )	-
split( )	mb_split( )	-
mail( )	mb_send_mail( )	-

For `mbstring` to work properly, it needs to be told to use the UTF-8 encoding scheme. As in Example 19-26, you can do this in script with the `mb_internal_encoding( )` function. Or to set this value system-wide, set the `mbstring.internal_encoding` configuration directive to `UTF-8`.

`iconv` has similar needs. Use the `iconv_set_encoding( )` function as in Example 19-27 or set the `iconv.internal_encoding` configuration directive.

`mbstring` provides alternatives for the ereg family of regular expression functions. However, you can always use UTF-8 strings with the PCRE (`preg_*( )`) regular expression functions. The u modifier tells a preg function that the pattern string is UTF-8 encoded and enables the use of various Unicode properties in patterns. Example 19-29 uses the "lowercase letter" Unicode property to count the number of lowercase letters in each of two strings.

Example 19-29. UTF-8 regular expression matching

```php
<?php
$name = 'Kurt Gödel';
$dinner = '불고기';

$name_lower = preg_match_all('/\p{Ll}/u',$name,$match);
$dinner_lower = preg_match_all('/\p{Ll}/u',$dinner,$match);

print "There are $name_lower lowercase letters in $name. \n";
```

```
print "There are $dinner_lower lowercase letters in $dinner. \n";
?>
```

Example 19-29 prints:

```
There are 7 lowercase letters in Kurt Gödel.
There are 3 lowercase letters in 불고기.
```

Other functions help you translate between other character encodings and UTF-8. The
`utf8_encode( )` and `utf8_decode( )` functions move strings between the ISO-8859-1 encoding and UTF-8. Because ISO-8859-1 is the default encoding in many situations,
these functions are a handy way to bring non-UTF-8-aware data into compliance. For
example, the dictionaries that the pspell extension uses often have their entries encoded
in ISO-8859-1. In Example 19-30, the `utf8_encode( )` function is necessary to turn the
output of `pspell_suggest( )` into a proper UTF-8-encoded string.

Example 19-30. Applying UTF-8 encoding to ISO-8859-1 strings

```
<?php
$lang = isset($_GET['lang']) ? $_GET['lang'] : 'en';
$word = isset($_GET['word']) ? $_GET['word'] : 'asparagus';

$ps = pspell_new($lang);
$check = pspell_check($ps, $word);

print htmlspecialchars($word,ENT_QUOTES,'UTF-8');
print $check ? ' is ' : ' is not ';
print ' found in the dictionary.';
print '<hr/>';

if (! $check) {
    $suggestions = pspell_suggest($ps, $word);
    if (count($suggestions)) {
        print 'Suggestions: <ul>';
        foreach ($suggestions as $suggestion) {
            $utf8suggestion = utf8_encode($suggestion);
            $safesuggestion = htmlspecialchars($utf8suggestion,
                                        ENT_QUOTES,'UTF-8');
            print "<li>$safesuggestion</li>";
        }
        print '</ul>';
    }
}
?>
```

It may ease the cognitive burden of proper character encoding to think of it as a task
similar to HTML entity encoding. In each case, text must be processed so that it is
appropriately formatted for a particular context. With entity encoding, that usually
means running data retrieved from an external source through `htmlentities( )` or
`htmlspecialchars( )`. With character encoding, it means turning everything into UTF-8
before you process it, using a character-aware function for string operations, and ensuring strings are UTF-8 encoded before outputting them.

See Also

Recipes 19.11 and 19.12 for setting up your programs for receiving and sending UTF-8-encoded strings; documentation on `mbstring` at *http://www.php.net/mbstring*, on `iconv` at *http://www.php.net/iconv*, on `htmlentities( )` at *http://www.php.net/htmlenti ties*, on `htmlspecialchars( )` at *http://www.php.net/htmlspecialchars*, on PCRE pattern syntax at *http://www.php.net/reference.pcre.pattern.syntax*, on `utf8_encode( )` at *http:// www.php.net/utf8_encode*, and on `utf8_decode( )` at *http://www.php.net/utf8_decode*.

Good background resources on managing PHP and character set issues include:

- "An Overview on Globalizing Oracle PHP Applications" by Peter Linsley (*http://www.oracle.com/technology/tech/php/pdf/ globalizing_oracle_php_applications.pdf*)
- Character Sets/Character Encoding Issues on the PHP WACT Wiki (*http://www.phpwact.org/php/i18n/charsets*)
- "Characters vs. Bytes" by Tim Bray (*http://www.tbray.org/ongoing/When/200x/ 2003/04/26/UTF*)
- "A Tutorial on Character Code Issues" by Jukka Korpela (*http://www.cs.tut.fi/ ~jkorpela/chars.html*)

CHAPTER 20

Error Handling, Debugging, and Testing

20.0 Introduction

The name *programmer* for those who spend their time developing web applications is misleading: the vast majority of time one spends "programming" is actually spent *debugging*. Whether you're fixing typos or refactoring chunks of code that are performing poorly in a heavily loaded production environment, odds are you'll spend a large amount of your career debugging and testing, and debugging and testing again. And again, and again, and again.

The raucous party that is a frantic, all-night debugging session was probably omitted from your job description—who would sign up for that kind of fun? The fact is that errors, bugs, debugging, and testing are a part of the programmer's life. If you face this head on with good practices and techniques, you can minimize the time you spend debugging and maximize the time you spend on the good stuff.

Unfortunately, many developers don't spend much time building error handling, debugging, and testing skills; don't make the same mistake. If you employ what's affectionately known as pessimistic programming, you'll begin to plan for things to go wrong—and your application will be prepared to handle it gracefully during those moments.

Recipes 20.1 through 20.11 deal with errors: finding the source of errors, determining what was going on when an error occurred, hiding errors from end users, and logging errors so you can conduct informed debugging sessions after the error occurs.

Recipe 20.12 explores the use of Xdebug, an open source PHP extension that allows for line-by-line debugging in real time, along with a robust set of code-profiling features.

Recipes 20.13, 20.14, and 20.15 explore the world of unit testing in PHP, and show you how to turn your fixed bugs into a test suite that can help you ensure that once a bug is fixed, it stays fixed.

Recipe 20.16 introduces you to XAMPP, an easy way to set up a testing environment on your local computer, so that you can work in a sandbox environment without fear of breaking a production web site while you're trying to determine what's gone wrong.

Developing good debugging and testing habits is the thing that many developers put off for the longest time. Don't wait until the next project to start learning good practices; if you do, you may never get to it.

20.1 Finding and Fixing Parse Errors

Problem

Your PHP script fails to run due fatal parse errors, and you want to find the problem quickly and continue coding.

Solution

Check the line that the PHP interpreter reports as having a problem. If that line is OK, work your way backward in the program until you find the problematic line.

Or use a PHP-aware development environment that will alert you to syntax errors as you code, and that can also help track down parse errors when they occur.

Discussion

Like most programming languages, the PHP interpreter is very picky about the way scripts are written. When things aren't written exactly as they they should be, the PHP interpreter will halt parsing and let you know that things aren't right. This is called a parse error.

Take this flawed program:

```php
<?php
if isset($user_firstname) {
  print "Howdy, $user_firstname!";
} else {
  print "Howdy!";
}
?>
```

Save that to a file called howdy.php and run it, and PHP will display this error message:

```
Parse error: syntax error, unexpected T_ISSET, expecting '(' in
/var/www/howdy.php on line 2
```

Based on this message, we know that there's a problem on line 2—specifically, a syntax error; something about an unexpected T_ISSET.

When PHP parses scripts to convert them into a format that the computer can understand, it breaks each line down into chunks called *tokens*. There are dozens of tokens that PHP recognizes, and it knows the rules about what tokens are allowed to appear

---

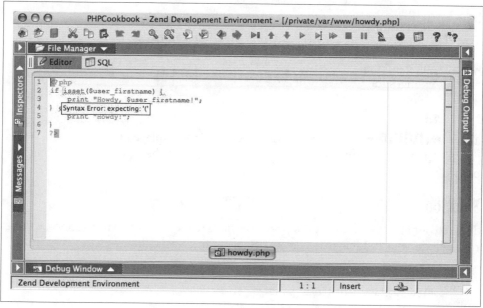

Figure 20-1. Zend Studio 5 sees the parse error before it happens

in what order in a line of PHP code. In the parse error above, the bit about an unexpected `T_ISSET` means that a `T_ISSET` token was encountered by the PHP interpreter where it's not supposed to be.

Reading a little further through the parse error, it's suddenly clear that PHP interpreter was expecting a `'('` where it found the `T_ISSET` token. Looking back at line 2 of the program, sure enough, the open parenthesis is missing after the `if` and before the `isset( )` function.

Some PHP-aware editing tools can alert you to these problems before you get to the stage of running the code and getting the parse error in the first place. Figure 20-1 shows our buggy program in Zend Studio 5, complete with advance warning of the parse error in our future.

It's not always as easy as going directly to the line that the parse error tells you to go to. Sometimes an error several lines prior to the one reported causes a problem that may not *seem* like a problem when it is encountered, but *is* a problem within the context of what is on the line that the parse error is referring to.

If you have difficulty finding the source of the error and don't have access to a debugging tool to help you root out the cause of the error, remember that when all else fails, commenting is your friend. Start by commenting out blocks of code before the line referred to in the parse error, and then rerunning the offending script. Through the process of elimination, you will eventually find the line causing the problem.

See Also

The PHP parser token cheatsheet at *http://www.php.net/tokens*.

20.2 Creating Your Own Exception Classes

Problem

You want control over how (or if) error messages are displayed to users, even though you're using several third-party libraries that each have their own views on handling errors.

Solution

Take advantage of PHP 5's support for exceptions to create your own exception handler that will do *your* bidding when errors occur in third-party libraries:

```php
class CustomException extends Exception
{
  public function __construct($message, $code = 0) {
    // make sure everything is assigned properly
    parent::__construct($message, $code);

    // log what we know
    $msg = "-----------------------------------------------\n";
    $msg .= __CLASS__ . ": [{$this->code}]: {$this->message}\n";
    $msg .= $this->getTraceAsString() . "\n";
    error_log($msg);
  }

  // overload the __toString() method to suppress any "normal" output
  public function __toString() {
    return $this->printMessage();
  }

  // map error codes to output messages or templates
  public function printMessage() {

    $usermsg = '';
    $code = $this->getCode();

    switch ($code) {
      case SOME_DEFINED_ERROR_CODE:
        $usermsg = 'Ooops! Sorry about that.';
        break;
      case OTHER_DEFINED_ERROR_CODE:
        $usermsg = "Drat!";
        break;
      default:
        $usermsg = file_get_contents('/templates/general_error.html');
        break;
    }
    return $usermsg;
```

```
    }

    // static exception_handler for default exception handling
    public static function exception_handler($exception) {
      throw new CustomException($exception);
    }

}

// make sure to catch every exception
set_exception_handler('CustomException', 'exception_handler');

try {
  $obj = new CoolThirdPartyPackage();
} catch (CustomException $e) {
  echo $e;
}
```

Discussion

PHP 5 introduced the concept of exceptions to PHP. Exceptions are a common construct in many other languages; they're used to deal gracefully with unforeseen error conditions. This is particularly useful when including third-party library code in your scripts when you're not 100 percent confident how that code will behave in unpredictable circumstances, such as loss of database connectivity, an unresponsive remote API server, or similar acts of randomness.

Exceptions provide your scripts with a **try/catch** structure you used to create a sandboxed section of your script where things can go horribly wrong without hurting anything else:

```
try {
  // do something
  $obj = new CoolThing();
} catch (CustomException $e) {
  // at this point, the CoolThing wasn't cool
  print $e;
}
```

So why use a custom exception, when PHP 5 already provides a perfectly functional exception class? The default exception class doesn't exactly fulfill the *graceful* part of handling unpredictable results. It just prints out an error message not much different from regular errors. If you want truly flexible handling of these unfortunate events, a custom exception handler allows you to do what you have determined is the most appropriate given the condition.

In the **CustomException** above, there are two objectives. The first is to log everything you can about what happened; the second is to be as cool as possible from the user's perspective.

The __construct() method sets up the exception by calling the parent's constructor (the constructor of the default exception class) to ensure that all possible values are set for use by our custom exception's methods.

Then, you immediately log what you can, using an error_log() call that you can replace with a custom error logger of your choice. In keeping with the goal of handling this error gracefully, make sure that your error logger is capable of logging this error without causing another one. For example, if the error you're about to log is related to failed database connectivity, it's probably a good idea if you don't try to log this error to an error log table on that same database server.

From there, the CustomException class is written to expect the calling code to print out the error. However, that is not required behavior. You could just as easily have a try/catch block like this:

```
try {
    // do something
    $obj = new CoolThing();
} catch (CustomException $e) {
    // at this point, the CoolThing wasn't cool
    $e->redirectToOhNoPage();
}
```

The segment catch (CustomException $e) means that an instance of the CustomException class will be instantiated and assigned to the variable $e. From there, $e is just an object that has some predefined values and methods relating to the problem that caused the exception, but is otherwise a regular object that can be as simple or as complicated as you want it to be.

One primary difference between a standard error handler and exceptions is the concept of *recovery*. The use case shown in this recipe thus far has a good correlation with the set_error_handler() usage from PHP 4 you may already be familiar with. The idea is that your custom handler can contain a clean-up routine that checks the state of the application at the time that the custom exception is caught, cleans up as best as it can, and dies gracefully.

Exceptions can also be used to easily recover from an error in the midst of an application's flow. For example, a try block can have multiple catch blocks that are somewhat neater than a bunch of if/else/else/else blocks:

```
try {
    // do something
    $obj = new CoolThing();
} catch (PossibleException $e) {
    // we thought this could possibly happen
    print "<!-- caught exception $e! -->";
    $obj = new PlanB();
} catch (AnotherPossibleException $e) {
    // we knew about this possibility as well
    print "<!-- aha! caught exception $e -->";
    $obj = new PlanC();
} catch (CustomException $e) {
```

```
        // if all else fails, go to clean-up
        $e->cleanUp();
        $e->bailOut();
    }
```

In this example, we're able to use the **try/catch** structure to check for exception conditions without stepping out of the flow of this chunk of code, unless all else truly fails. If we were unable to recover in any of the ways we knew how to in line with the flow of the application, we still have the option of bailing out to a catchall custom exception. We can even throw a new exception inside the catch blocks in order to influence the order in which exceptions bubble up to a **try/catch** block that may be wrapping the chunk of code currently executing.

See Also

Recipe 20.9 for more on logging errors; documentation on exceptions at *http://www.php.net/exceptions*.

20.3 Printing a Stack Trace

Problem

You want to know what's happening at a specific point in your program, and what happened leading up to that point.

Solution

Use debug_print_backtrace( ):

```
function stooges() {
  print "woo woo woo!\n";
  larry();
}

function larry() {
  curly();
}

function curly() {
  moe();
}

function moe() {
  debug_print_backtrace();
}

stooges();
```

This will print:

```
woo woo woo!
#0  moe() called at [backtrace.php:14]
```

```
#1   curly() called at [backtrace.php:10]
#2   larry() called at [backtrace.php:6]
#3   stooges() called at [backtrace.php:21]
```

Discussion

The `debug_backtrace()` function was introduced in PHP 4.3.0, followed by the handy `debug_print_backtrace()` function in PHP 5.0.0. This combination allows you to quickly get a sense of what has been been going on in your application immediately before you called a particular function.

The more complicated your application, the more information you can expect to have returned from the backtrace functions. For debugging larger codebases, you may achieve bug-hunting success more quickly using a full debugging extension, such as Xdebug, or an integrated development environment (IDE), such as PHPEdit or Zend Studio, that supports setting breakpoints, stepping in and out of blocks of code, watching the evolution of variables, and more.

If all you need is a little more information than you can get from sprinkling `print 'Here I am on line ' . __LINE__;` statements throughout your code, `debug_backtrace()` and/or `debug_print_backtrace()` will suit your needs well.

If you're still using PHP 4 and want the PHP 5–only `debug_print_backtrace()` function, you can use PEAR's `PHP_Compat` compatibility package. `PHP_Compat` provides an implementation of `debug_print_backtrace()` that is identical to the native PHP 5 function.

See Also

Documentation on `debug_backtrace()` at *http://www.php.net/debug-backtrace* and on `debug_print_backtrace()` at *http://www.php.net/debug-print-backtrace*; the PEAR `PHP_Compat` package at *http://pear.php.net/package/PHP_Compat*; Zend Studio IDE at *http://www.zend.com/products/zend_studio*; PHPEdit IDE at *http://www.waterproof.fr/products/PHPEdit/*.

20.4 Reading Configuration Variables

Problem

You want to get the value of a PHP configuration setting.

Solution

Use `ini_get()`:

```
// find out the include path:
$include_path = ini_get('include_path');
```

Discussion

To get all the configuration variable values in one step, call `ini_get_all( )`. It returns the variables in an associative array, and each array element is itself an associative array. The second array has three elements: a global value for the setting, a local value, and an access code:

```
// put all configuration variables in an associative array
$vars = ini_get_all();
print_r($vars['include_path']);
Array
(
    [global_value] => .:/usr/local/lib/php/
    [local_value] => .:/usr/local/lib/php/
    [access] => 7
)
```

The `global_value` is the value set from the *php.ini* file; the `local_value` is adjusted to account for any changes made in the web server's configuration file, any relevant *.htaccess* files, and the current script. The value of `access` is a numeric constant representing the places where this value can be altered. Table 20-1 explains the values for `access`. Note that the name `access` is a little misleading in this respect, as the value of the setting can always be checked, but not always adjusted.

Table 20-1. Access values

Value	PHP constant	Meaning
1	PHP_INI_USER	Any script, using ini_set( )
2	PHP_INI_PERDIR	Directory level, using .htaccess
4	PHP_INI_SYSTEM	System level, using php.ini or httpd.conf
7	PHP_INI_ALL	Everywhere: scripts, directories, and the system

A value of 6 means the setting can be changed in both the directory and system level, as 2 + 4 = 6. In practice, there are no variables modifiable only in `PHP_INI_USER` or `PHP_INI_PERDIR`, and all variables are modifiable in `PHP_INI_SYSTEM`, so everything has a value of 4, 6, or 7.

You can also get variables belonging to a specific extension by passing the extension name to `ini_get_all( )`:

```
// return just the session module specific variables
$session = ini_get_all('session');
```

By convention, the variables for an extension are prefixed with the extension name and a period. So all the session variables begin with `session.` and all the Java variables begin with `java.`, for example.

Since `ini_get( )` returns the current value for a configuration directive, if you want to check the original value from the *php.ini* file, use `get_cfg_var( )`:

```
$original = get_cfg_var('sendmail_from'); // have we changed our address?
```

The value returned by `get_cfg_var( )` is the same as what appears in the `global_value` element of the array returned by `ini_get_all( )`.

See Also

Recipe 20.5 on setting configuration variables; documentation on `ini_get( )` at *http://www.php.net/ini-get*, `ini_get_all( )` at *http://www.php.net/ini-get-all*, and `get_cfg_var( )` at *http://www.php.net/get-cfg-var*; a complete list of configuration variables, their defaults, and when they can be modified at *http://www.php.net/manual/en/ini.php*.ch20_configuration

20.5 Setting Configuration Variables

Problem

You want to change the value of a PHP configuration setting.

Solution

Use `ini_set( )`:

```
// add a directory to the include path
ini_set('include_path', ini_get('include_path') . ':/home/fezzik/php');
```

Discussion

Configuration variables are not permanently changed by `ini_set( )`. The new value lasts only for the duration of the request in which `ini_set( )` is called. To make a persistent modification, alter the values stored in the *php.ini* file.

It isn't meaningful to alter certain variables, such as `asp_tags`, because by the time you call `ini_set( )` to modify the setting, it's too late to change the behavior the setting affects. If a variable can't be changed, `ini_set( )` returns `false`.

However, it is useful to alter configuration variables in certain pages. For example, if you're running a script from the command line, set `html_errors` to `off`.

To reset a variable back to its original setting, use `ini_restore( )`:

```
ini_restore('sendmail_from'); // go back to the default value
```

See Also

Recipe 20.4 on getting values of configuration variables; documentation on `ini_set( )` at *http://www.php.net/ini-set* and `ini_restore( )` at *http://www.php.net/ini-restore*.

20.6 Hiding Error Messages from Users

Problem

You don't want PHP error messages visible to users.

Solution

Set the following values in your *php.ini* or web server configuration file:

```
display_errors =off
log_errors     =on
```

You may also set these values using `ini_set( )` if you do have access to edit your server's *php.ini* file.

```
ini_set('display_errors', 'off');
ini_set('log_errors', 'on');
```

These settings tell PHP not to display errors as HTML to the browser but to put them in the server's error log.

Discussion

When `log_errors` is set to `on`, error messages are written to the server's error log. If you want PHP errors to be written to a separate file, set the `error_log` configuration directive with the name of that file:

```
error_log   = /var/log/php.error.log
```

or:

```
ini_set('error_log', '/var/log/php.error.log');
```

If `error_log` is set to `syslog`, PHP error messages are sent to the system logger using *syslog(3)* on Unix and to the Event Log on Windows.

There are lots of error messages you want to show your users, such as telling them they've filled in a form incorrectly, but you should shield your users from internal errors that may reflect a problem with your code. There are two reasons for this. First, these errors appear unprofessional (to expert users) and confusing (to novice users). If something goes wrong when saving form input to a database, check the return code from the database query and display a message to your users apologizing and asking them to come back later. Showing them a cryptic error message straight from PHP doesn't inspire confidence in your web site.

Second, displaying these errors to users is a security risk. Depending on your database and the type of error, the error message may contain information about how to log in to your database or server and how it is structured. Malicious users can use this information to mount an attack on your web site.

For example, if your database server is down, and you attempt to connect to it with `mysql_connect( )`, PHP generates the following warning:

```
<br>
<b>Warning</b>:  Can't connect to MySQL server on 'db.example.com' (111) in
<b>/www/docroot/example.php</b> on line <b>3</b><br>
```

If this warning message is sent to a user's browser, he learns that your database server is called *db.example.com* and can focus his cracking efforts on it.

See Also

Recipe 20.9 for how to log errors; Recipe 20.5 for more about setting configuration values with `ini_set( )`; documentation on PHP configuration directives at *http://www.php.net/configuration*.

20.7 Tuning Error Handling

Problem

You want to alter the error-logging sensitivity on a particular page. This lets you control what types of errors are reported.

Solution

To adjust the types of errors PHP complains about, use `error_reporting( )`:

```
error_reporting(E_ALL);                // everything
error_reporting(E_ERROR | E_PARSE);    // only major problems
error_reporting(E_ALL & ~E_NOTICE);    // everything but notices
```

Discussion

Every error generated has an error type associated with it. For example, if you try to `array_pop( )` a string, PHP complains that "This argument needs to be an array," since you can only pop arrays. The error type associated with this message is `E_NOTICE`, a nonfatal runtime problem.

By default, the error reporting level is `E_ALL & ~E_NOTICE`, which means all error types except notices. The `&` is a logical `AND`, and the `~` is a logical `NOT`. However, the *php.ini-recommended* configuration file sets the error reporting level to `E_ALL`, which is all error types.

PHP 5 introduced a new error level, `E_STRICT`. Enabling `E_STRICT` during development has the benefit of PHP alerting you of ways your code could be improved. You will receive warnings about the use of deprecated functions, along with tips to nudge you in the direction of the latest and greatest suggested methods of coding. `E_STRICT` is the only error level not included in `E_ALL`; for maximum coverage during development, set the error reporting level to `E_ALL | E_STRICT`.

Error messages flagged as notices are runtime problems that are less serious than warnings. They're not necessarily wrong, but they indicate a potential problem. One example of an E_NOTICE is "Undefined variable," which occurs if you try to use a variable without previously assigning it a value:

```
// Generates an E_NOTICE
foreach ($array as $value) {
    $html .= $value;
}

// Doesn't generate any error message
$html = '';
foreach ($array as $value) {
    $html .= $value;
}
```

In the first case, the first time through the foreach, $html is undefined. So when you append to it, PHP lets you know you're appending to an undefined variable. In the second case, the empty string is assigned to $html above the loop to avoid the E_NOTICE. The previous two code snippets generate identical code because the default value of a variable is the empty string. The E_NOTICE can be helpful because, for example, you may have misspelled a variable name:

```
foreach ($array as $value) {
    $hmtl .= $value; // oops! that should be $html
}

$html = ''
foreach ($array as $value) {
    $hmtl .= $value; // oops! that should be $html
}
```

A custom error-handling function can parse errors based on their type and take an appropriate action. A complete list of error types is shown in Table 20-2.

Table 20-2. Error types

Value	Constant	Description	Catchable
1	E_ERROR	Nonrecoverable error	No
2	E_WARNING	Recoverable error	Yes
4	E_PARSE	Parser error	No
8	E_NOTICE	Possible error	Yes
16	E_CORE_ERROR	Like E_ERROR but generated by the PHP core	No
32	E_CORE_WARNING	Like E_WARNING but generated by the PHP core	No
64	E_COMPILE_ERROR	Like E_ERROR but generated by the Zend Engine	No
128	E_COMPILE_WARNING	Like E_WARNING but generated by the Zend Engine	No
256	E_USER_ERROR	Like E_ERROR but triggered by calling trigger_error( )	Yes
512	E_USER_WARNING	Like E_WARNING but triggered by calling trigger_error( )	Yes

Value	Constant	Description	Catchable
1024	E_USER_NOTICE	Like E_NOTICE but triggered by calling `trigger_error( )`	Yes
2047	E_ALL	Everything except E_STRICT	N/A
2048	E_STRICT	Runtime notices in which PHP suggests changes to improve code quality (since PHP 5)	N/A

Errors labeled catchable can be processed by the function registered using `set_error_handler( )`. The others indicate such a serious problem that they're not safe to be handled by users, and PHP must take care of them.

See Also

Recipe 20.8 shows how to set up a custom error handler; documentation on `error_reporting( )` at *http://www.php.net/error-reporting* and `set_error_handler( )` at *http://www.php.net/set-error-handler*; for more information about errors, see *http://www.php.net/manual/en/ref.errorfunc.php*.

20.8 Using a Custom Error Handler

Problem

You want to create a custom error handler that lets you control how PHP reports errors.

Solution

To set up your own error function, use `set_error_handler( )`:

```
set_error_handler('pc_error_handler');

function pc_error_handler($errno, $error, $file, $line) {
    $message = "[ERROR][$errno][$error][$file:$line]";
    error_log($message);
}
```

Discussion

A custom error handling function can parse errors based on their type and take the appropriate action. See Table 20-2 in Recipe 20.7 for a list of error types.

Pass `set_error_handler( )` the name of a function, and PHP forwards all errors to that function. The error handling function can take up to five parameters. The first parameter is the error type, such as 8 for E_NOTICE. The second is the message thrown by the error, such as "Undefined variable: html." The third and fourth arguments are the name of the file and the line number in which PHP detected the error. The final parameter is an array holding all the variables defined in the current scope and their values.

For example, in this code, $html is appended to without first being assigned an initial value:

```
error_reporting(E_ALL);
set_error_handler('pc_error_handler');

function pc_error_handler($errno, $error, $file, $line, $context) {
    $message = "[ERROR][$errno][$error][$file:$line]";
    print "$message";
    print_r($context);
}

$form = array('one','two');

foreach ($form as $line) {
    $html .= "<b>$line</b>";
}
```

When the "Undefined variable" error is generated, pc_error_handler( ) prints:

```
[ERROR][8][Undefined variable:  html][err-all.php:16]
```

After the initial error message, pc_error_handler( ) also prints a large array containing all the globals, environment, request, and session variables.

Errors labeled catchable in Table 20-2 can be processed by the function registered using set_error_handler( ). The others indicate such a serious problem that they're not safe to be handled by users and PHP must take care of them.

See Also

Recipe 20.7 lists the different error types; documentation on set_error_handler( ) at *http://www.php.net/set-error-handler*.

20.9 Logging Errors

Problem

You want to save program errors to a log. These errors can include everything from parser errors and files not being found to bad database queries and dropped connections.

Solution

Use error_log( ) to write to the error log:

```
// LDAP error
if (ldap_errno($ldap)) {
    error_log("LDAP Error #" . ldap_errno($ldap) . ": " . ldap_error($ldap));
}
```

Discussion

Logging errors facilitates debugging. Smart error logging makes it easier to fix bugs. Always log information about what caused the error:

```
$r = mysql_query($sql);
if (! $r) {
    $error = mysql_error();
    error_log('[DB: query @'.$_SERVER['REQUEST_URI']."][$sql]: $error");
} else {
    // process results
}
```

You're not getting all the debugging help you could be if you simply log that an error occurred without any supporting information:

```
$r = mysql_query($sql);
if (! $r) {
    error_log("bad query");
} else {
    // process result
}
```

Another useful technique is to include the __FILE__, __LINE__, __FUNCTION__, __CLASS__, and __METHOD__ "magic" constants in your error messages:

```
error_log('['.__FILE__.']['.__LINE__."]: $error");
```

The __FILE__ constant is the current filename, and __LINE__ is the current line number.

The __FUNCTION__ constant was added in PHP 4.3.0. From that PHP version through the rest of the PHP 4.x series, the __FUNCTION__ constant returns the current function name in lowercase; beginning in PHP 5, the constant returns the function name as it was declared. The __CLASS__ constant, which returns the current class name, was also introduced in PHP 4.3.0. __CLASS__ behaves exactly the same way as __FUNCTION__ in regard to case sensitivity in PHP 4.x and PHP 5.

PHP 5.0.0 introduced the __METHOD__ constant, which returns the current class method name. The method name returned is case sensitive to how it was declared.

See Also

Recipe 20.6 for hiding error messages from users; documentation on error_log() at *http://www.php.net/error-log*; documentation on "magic" constants at *http://www.php.net/manual/en/language.constants.predefined.php*.

20.10 Eliminating "headers already sent" Errors

Problem

You are trying to send an HTTP header or cookie using header() or setcookie(), but PHP reports a "headers already sent" error message.

Solution

This error happens when you send nonheader output before calling header() or setcookie().

Rewrite your code so any output happens after sending headers:

```
// good
setcookie("name", $name);
print "Hello $name!";

// bad
print "Hello $name!";
setcookie("name", $name);

// good
<?php setcookie("name",$name); ?>
<html><title>Hello</title>
```

Discussion

An HTTP message has a header and a body, which are sent to the client in that order. Once you begin sending the body, you can't send any more headers. So if you call setcookie( ) after printing some HTML, PHP can't send the appropriate Cookie header.

Also, remove trailing whitespace in any include files. When you include a file with blank lines outside <?php ?> tags, the blank lines are sent to the browser. Use trim( ) to remove leading and trailing blank lines from files:

```
$file = '/path/to/file.php';

// backup
copy($file, "$file.bak") or die("Can't copy $file: $php_errormsg);

// read and trim
$contents = trim(join('',file($file)));

// write
$fh = fopen($file, 'w')  or die("Can't open $file for writing: $php_errormsg);
if (-1 == fwrite($fh, $contents)) { die("Can't write to $file: $php_errormsg); }
fclose($fh)              or die("Can't close $file: $php_errormsg);
```

Instead of processing files on a one-by-one basis, it may be more convenient to do so on a directory-by-directory basis. Recipe 24.7 describes how to process all the files in a directory.

Another perfectly legitimate approach to ensuring included files don't have any trailing whitespace is to just leave off the closing ?> tag. If the included file is purely PHP, this method guarantees that you won't have to go back to that file to clean up inadvertent whitespace. See *http://www.php.net/manual/en/language.basic-syntax.instruction-separation.php* for a bit more discussion of this syntax.

If you don't want to worry about blank lines disrupting the sending of headers, turn on output buffering. Output buffering prevents PHP from immediately sending all output to the client. If you buffer your output, you can intermix headers and body text with abandon. However, it may seem to users that your server takes longer to fulfill their requests since they have to wait slightly longer before the browser displays any output.

See Also

Recipe 8.12 for a discussion of output buffering; Recipe 24.7 for processing all files in a directory; documentation on `header( )` at *http://www.php.net/header*.

20.11 Logging Debugging Information

Problem

You want to make debugging easier by adding statements to print out variables. But you want to be able to switch back and forth easily between production and debug modes.

Solution

Put a function that conditionally prints out messages based on a defined constant in a page included using the `auto_prepend_file` configuration setting. Save the following code to *debug.php*:

```
// turn debugging on
define('DEBUG',true);

// generic debugging function
function pc_debug($message) {
    if (defined('DEBUG') && DEBUG) {
        error_log($message);
    }
}
```

Set the `auto_prepend_file` directive in *php.ini* or your site *.htaccess* file:

```
auto_prepend_file=debug.php
```

Now call `pc_debug( )` from your code to print out debugging information:

```
$sql = 'SELECT color, shape, smell FROM vegetables';
pc_debug("[sql: $sql]"); // only printed if DEBUG is true
$r = mysql_query($sql);
```

Discussion

Debugging code is a necessary side effect of writing code. There are a variety of techniques to help you quickly locate and squash your bugs. Many of these involve including scaffolding that helps ensure the correctness of your code. The more complicated the program, the more scaffolding needed. Fred Brooks, in *The Mythical Man-Month* (Addison-Wesley), guesses that there's "half as much code in scaffolding as there is in product." Proper planning ahead of time allows you to integrate the scaffolding into your programming logic in a clean and efficient fashion. This requires you to think out beforehand what you want to measure and record and how you plan on sorting through the data gathered by your scaffolding.

One technique for sifting through the information is to assign different priority levels to different types of debugging comments. Then the debug function prints information only if it's higher than the current priority level:

```
define('DEBUG',2);

function pc_debug($message, $level = 0) {
    if (defined('DEBUG') && ($level > DEBUG) {
        error_log($message);
    }
}

$sql = 'SELECT color, shape, smell FROM vegetables';
pc_debug("[sql: $sql]", 1); // not printed, since 1 < 2
pc_debug("[sql: $sql]", 3); // printed, since 3 > 2
```

Another technique is to write wrapper functions to include additional information to help with performance tuning, such as the time it takes to execute a database query:

```
function db_query($sql) {
    if (defined('DEBUG') && DEBUG) {
        // start timing the query if DEBUG is on
        $DEBUG_STRING = "[sql: $sql]<br>\n";
        $starttime = microtime(true);
    }

    $r = mysql_query($sql);

    if (! $r) {
        $error = mysql_error();
        error_log('[DB: query @'.$_SERVER['REQUEST_URI']."][$sql]: $error");
    } elseif (defined(DEBUG) && DEBUG) {
        // the query didn't fail and DEBUG is turned on, so finish timing it
        $endtime = microtime(true);
        $elapsedtime = $endtime - $starttime;
        $DEBUG_STRING .= "[time: $elapsedtime]<br>\n";
        error_log($DEBUG_STRING);
    }

    return $r;
}
```

Here, instead of just printing out the SQL to the error log, you also record the number of seconds it takes MySQL to perform the request. This lets you see if certain queries are taking too long. See Recipe 21.1 for more discussion of timing code execution and for a PHP 4–compatible alternative to microtime(true).

Finally, you may also want to integrate PEAR's Log package, which provides an efficient framework for an abstracted logging system. PEAR Log predefines eight log levels: PEAR_LOG_EMERG, PEAR_LOG_ALERT, PEAR_LOG_CRIT, PEAR_LOG_ERR, PEAR_LOG_WARNING, PEAR_LOG_NOTICE, PEAR_LOG_INFO, and PEAR_LOG_DEBUG. The Log package provides a robust assortment of options for customizing error logging, including logging errors to SQLite and/or to a pop-up browser window.

See Also

Documentation on `define()` at *http://www.php.net/define*, `defined()` at *http://www.php.net/defined*, and `error_log()` at *http://www.php.net/error-log*; *The Mythical Man-Month* by Frederick P. Brooks (Addison-Wesley); main page for PEAR Log at *http://pear.php.net/package/Log*.

20.12 Using a Debugger Extension

Problem

You want to debug your scripts interactively during runtime.

Solution

Use the Xdebug extension. When used along with Xdebug's remote debugger client, you can examine data structure; set breakpoints; and step into, out of, or over sections of code interactively.

Discussion

The Xdebug extension provides a number of helpful features to aid in a development effort, such as code profiling that is compatible with Kcachegrind. In this recipe, focus on Xdebug's interactive debugging capability. In order to follow along with this recipe, you need to be able to compile and install a Zend extension, which means permissions to edit *php.ini* on your system. PHP's `dl()` extension-loading function does not work with Xdebug. Finally, examples in this recipe are intended to work with Xdebug 2.0.0.

Installing the Xdebug extension is a straightforward procedure. You can build from source, or you can install using the `pecl` command:

```
% pecl install xdebug-beta
```

Once you have the extension compiled and installed, you need to edit your *php.ini* file with the full path to the `xdebug.so` module, such as `zend_extension = /usr/lib/php/extensions/no-debug-non-zts-20050922/xdebug.so`.

For interactive debugging, you need to download a copy of the Xdebug source. The bundled Xdebug application *debugclient* is not installed by default with the *pecl* install procedure. This is because in many cases, the `xdebug.so` module is installed on a remote server, while the *debugclient* tool is typically installed on a separate machine. However, there is nothing that prevents the `xdebug.so` module from running alongside PHP and the web server in a local test environment.

Once you've downloaded the Xdebug source code that corresponds to the version of the module that was installed with the *pecl* command, unpack the source and `chdir` to the `debugclient` directory of the distribution. Issue the following commands:

```
% cd debugclient
% ./configure
```

```
% make
% sudo make install
```

The *debugclient* binary will install in /usr/local/bin. Test the installation by simply running the *debugclient* command. You should see something similar to:

```
% debugclient
Xdebug Simple DBGp client (0.9.1)
Copyright 2002-2005 by Derick Rethans.

Waiting for debug server to connect.
```

The *debugclient* tool listens for a connection from an Xdebug-enabled PHP script on port 9000 by default. You can ask *debugclient* to listen on another port by using the -p switch, like this:

```
% debugclient -p port
```

Just make sure that the setting in your script, or your *php.ini* file, matches the port that your *debugclient* is listening on.

Interactive debugging with Xdebug can be triggered through a command-line invocation of a PHP script, or it can be started by passing the proper values to a web server running Xdebug and a PHP script. To start an interactive session on the command line, you need to set a few environment variables before triggering the script:

```
% export XDEBUG_CONFIG="idekey=session_name remote_enable=1"
% php myscript.php
```

If you're debugging a web page running on a remote server, you just need to add XDEBUG_SESSION_START=*name* to the request URL. A browser cookie will be set with the name XDEBUG_SESSION. When the get or post variable of XDEBUG_SESSION_START is set or if the XDEBUG_SESSION cookie is present, the Xdebug extension will attempt to connect to the *debugclient* specified in *php.ini*'s xdebug.remote_host value.

Once a connection is made to the *debugclient*, the steps that follow are largely the same. The primary actions taken during interactive debugging are listed in Table 20-3.

Table 20-3. Common Xdebug commands

Command	Description
run	Starts or resumes the script until a breakpoint is reached, or until the end of the script.
step_into	Steps into the next statement. If there is a function call involved, Xdebug will break on the first statement in that function.
step_over	Steps to the next statement. If there is a function call on the line you were on when you issued the step_over command, the debugger will stop at the statement after the function call in the same scope as where the command was issued.
step_out	Steps out of the current scope and breaks on the statement after returning from the current function.
stop	Ends execution of the script immediately.
set_breakpoint	Sets a new breakpoint on the debugging session.

Command	Description
property_value	Gets a property value.
context_get	Returns an array of properties in a given context at a given stack depth. If the stack depth is omitted, the current stack depth is used.

With those options in mind, it's time to try debugging an application. Example 20-1 shows an overly complex application for saying hello to a visitor. The point of the over-complexity is not to demonstrate how you should greet visitors to your web site; it's just to give us some options for stepping over function calls while debugging interactively.

Example 20-1. Overly complex greeting application

```php
<?php
$user = 'Curly';

function sayHello($user, $greeting = 'Hello, %s!') {
  if (!validUser($user)) {
    $greeting = 'Hey! What are you doing here, %s?!';
  }
  printf($greeting, $user);
}

function validUser($user) {
  // do some validation here
  return true;
}

sayHello($user);
?>
```

We'll debug this program interactively after triggering it with a browser. See Recipe 20.16 if you need pointers on setting up a local test environment for this purpose. First, start up the *debugclient*:

```
% debugclient
Xdebug Simple DBGp client (0.9.1)
Copyright 2002-2005 by Derick Rethans.

Waiting for debug server to connect.
```

Now, load up Example 20-1 in a file named overhello.php and visit it with a browser, making sure to append the correct Xdebug values to the query string—for example, http://localhost/overhello.php?XDEBUG_SESSION_START=foo. Your waiting *debugclient* should register the connection and output the following:

```
Connect
<init fileuri="file:///Users/clay/Sites/overhello.php" language="PHP"
protocol_version="1.0" appid="4148" idekey="foo"><engine version="2.0.0beta5">
<![CDATA[Xdebug]]></engine><author><![CDATA[Derick Rethans]]></author><url>
<![CDATA[http://xdebug.org]]></url><copyright><![CDATA[Copyright (c)
```

```
2002-2005 by Derick Rethans]]></copyright></init>
(cmd)
```

You'll notice that your browser has not yet generated any output; it's waiting for you to continue with the debugging session. To do that, step into the program one line at a time. The DBGp protocol used by Xdebug requires that an identifier be sent with each request, so the following command will pass the identifier we've already started with back to the server:

```
(cmd) step_into -i foo
<response command="step_into" transaction_id="foo" status="break" reason="ok">
</response>
(cmd)
```

That response means that the Xdebug extension received your request to step forward a line, and has paused the execution waiting for the next debugging request. To confirm where you are in the execution, you may issue a stack_get request at any time:

```
(cmd) stack_get -i foo
<response command="stack_get" transaction_id="foo"><stack where="{main}"
level="0" type="file" filename="file:///Users/clay/Sites/overhello.php"
lineno="1"></stack></response>
(cmd)
```

The response from stack_get tells us that we're in the {main} portion of the script; in other words, we're not inside of a function or a class. We're running though the main file, and we're on line number 1. Looks good; let's move on to another line:

```
(cmd) step_into -i foo
<response command="step_into" transaction_id="foo" status="break"
reason="ok"></response>
(cmd)
```

debugclient again returns with an ok response, and sets the status to break again to wait for more instructions from us. So what's going on in this line?

```
(cmd) context_get -i foo
<response command="context_get" transaction_id="foo">
<property name="user" fullname="$user" type="uninitialized">
</property></response>
(cmd)
```

We can see from getting the context that the variable $user has come into the picture. The DBGp protocol is very careful about returning the values of variables and will not do so unless explicitly asked. Even then, you'll see that the values are *always* Base64-encoded to protect *debugclient* from any unexpected data:

```
(cmd) property_value -n user -i foo
<response command="property_value" transaction_id="foo"
type="null"></response>
(cmd)
```

We instruct Xdebug to give us the value of the variable $user, and it returns a null type. Why? Because the value of $user isn't actually set until *after* the second line; the *de-*

bugclient is currently reading line 2 from the beginning. So issue another `step_into` command, and ask for the `property_value` again:

```
(cmd) step_into -i foo
<response command="step_into" transaction_id="foo"
status="break" reason="ok"></response>
(cmd) property_value -n user -i foo
<response command="property_value" transaction_id=
"foo" type="string" encoding="base64">
<![CDATA[Q3VybHk=]]></response>
(cmd)
```

There's the base64-encoded value of `$user`, but how do we know what it contains? In a separate terminal window, just run a quick decoding of that value:

```
% php -r "echo base64_decode('Q3VybHk=');"
Curly
```

So far, so good. However, debugging a large program a line at a time like this could become a painful, time-consuming experience. So let's jump ahead to where the action is. To do that, we'll set a breakpoint and then run the program until it reaches that breakpoint:

```
(cmd) breakpoint_set -i foo -t call -m sayHello
<response command="breakpoint_set" transaction_id="foo" id="41480001"></response>
(cmd)
```

The `-t` switch lets Xdebug know that we're setting a breakpoint at a `call` type, and the `-m` switch sets the break at the point where the `sayHello` function is called. The response sets a unique ID for this breakpoint that we (or a full-blown IDE implementing the `DBGp` protocol) could use to refer back to this breakpoint. Now we can run the program until it pauses again, and then get our bearings again:

```
(cmd) run -i foo
<response command="run" transaction_id="foo" status="break" reason="ok"></response>
(cmd) stack_get -i foo
<response command="stack_get" transaction_id="foo"><stack where="sayHello" level="0"
type="file" filename="file:///Users/clay/Sites/overhello.php" lineno="5"></stack>
<stack where="{main}" level="1" type="file" filename=
"file:///Users/clay/Sites/overhello.php" lineno="16"></stack></response>
(cmd)
```

In our example program, we know that the `sayHello` function is defined on line 5 and called on line 16, so this response is in alignment with what we know about the example program. The debugger ran ahead to where the function was called, and then returned to where the function was declared so that we can step into that function and see what's going on in there. Let's do that now:

```
(cmd) step_into -i foo
<response command="step_into" transaction_id="foo" status="break" reason="ok">
</response>
(cmd) stack_get -i foo
<response command="stack_get" transaction_id="foo"><stack where="sayHello"
level="0" type="file" filename="file:///Users/clay/Sites/overhello.php"
```

```
lineno="5"></stack><stack where="{main}" level="1" type="file" filename=
"file:///Users/clay/Sites/overhello.php" lineno="16"></stack></response>
(cmd) context_get -i foo
<response command="context_get" transaction_id="foo"><property name="greeting"
 fullname="$greeting" address="60271800" type="string" encoding="base64">
<![CDATA[SGVsbG8sICVzIQ==]]></property><property name="user" fullname="$user"
address="60264872" type="string" encoding="base64"><![CDATA[Q3VybHk=]]>
</property></response>
(cmd)
```

This sequence of commands shows us that the program is now on line 16, and the sayHello function has been called. We're at the beginning of line 5 of the script, looking at the call to sayHello, noting what was passed into it, and preparing to go into the if( ) block that checks whether the $user is valid by running the validUser( ) function. Since we know that our simple program isn't finished yet, let's skip over that block and not waste time running through the incomplete function. After stepping over, check again to see where we are:

```
(cmd) step_over -i foo
<response command="step_over" transaction_id="foo" status="break"
reason="ok"></response>
(cmd) stack_get -i foo
<response command="stack_get" transaction_id="foo">
<stack where="sayHello" level="0" type="file" filename=
"file:///Users/clay/Sites/overhello.php" lineno="8">
</stack><stack where="{main}" level="1" type="file" filename=
"file:///Users/clay/Sites/overhello.php" lineno="16">
</stack></response>
(cmd)
```

As you can see, we're now on line 8, after the if( ) block. Let's go ahead and finish up by letting the program run its course:

```
(cmd) run -i foo
<response command="run" transaction_id="foo" status="stopped"
reason="ok"></response>
(cmd)
```

Finally, the run command returns a stopped status because the program ran the rest of the way through without encountering any additional breakpoints.

This is certainly a simple example, but you can see that it's possible to drill down into your application and see what's going on in real time with Xdebug. You may find that it is easier to use an Xdebug-enabled IDE, such as the free editor WeaverSlave, than it is to use *debugclient*. However, *debugclient* can provide a great deal of insight into your application in a hurry all by itself.

See Also

Documentation on Xdebug at *http://www.xdebug.org/*; on the DBGp protocol at *http://www.xdebug.org/docs-dbgp.php*; Xdebug-enabled editor WeaverSlave at *http://weaverslave.ws/*.

20.13 Writing a Unit Test

Problem

You're working on a project that extends a set of core functionality, and you want an easy way to make sure everything still works as the project grows.

Solution

Write a unit test that tests the core functionality of a function or class and alerts you if something breaks.

A sample test using PHP-QA's `.phpt` testing system is:

```
--TEST--
str_replace() function
--FILE--
<?php
$str = 'Hello, all!';
var_dump(str_replace('all', 'world', $str));
?>
--EXPECT--
string(13) "Hello, world!"
```

Discussion

There are a number of ways to write unit tests in PHP. A series of simple `.phpt` tests may be adequate for your needs, or you may benefit from more structured testing solutions such as PHPUnit or SimpleTest. We'll discuss each approach, but the first question is: why write a unit test in the first place?

Writing an application from scratch in any language is a lot like peeling an onion, only in reverse. You start with the center of the onion, and build layers on top of layers until you get to the finished product: an onion.

The more layers you build on top of your core, the more important it is for that core to continue functioning as you expect it to. The easiset way to ensure that the core of an application continues functioning as expected, especially after modifications, is through unit tests.

In the earlier example, we're testing that the `str_replace( )` function successfully replaces one string with another. The test doesn't care how the `str_replace( )` function is written; all that matters is that it works as expected on a recurring basis.

The easiest way to run the `.phpt` test is to save it in a file ending in `.phpt` (`str_replace.phpt`, for example), and then use PEAR's built-in `.phpt` execution tool, like this:

```
% pear run-tests str_replace.phpt
```

You'll see output like this:

```
Running 1 tests
PASS str_replace() function[str_replace.phpt]
TOTAL TIME: 00:00
1 PASSED TESTS
0 SKIPPED TESTS
```

You can test a number of features of your core functionality by creating multiple *.phpt* files, and executing:

```
% pear run-tests *.phpt
```

For full details on the structure of *.phpt* files, visit *http://qa.php.net/write-test.php*.

You can also write unit tests using the PHPUnit/PHPUnit2 unit testing framework. PHPUnit2 is for PHP 5 only, whereas PHPUnit will work under PHP 4 or PHP 5.

The example above could be written as a PHPUnit2 test like this:

```
require_once 'PHPUnit2/Framework/TestCase.php';

class StrreplaceTest extends PHPUnit2_Framework_TestCase
{
    public function testStrreplaceWorks()
    {
        $str = 'Hello, all!';
        $this->assertEquals('Hello, world!', str_replace('all', 'world', $str));
    }
}
```

Save this code in a file named StrreplaceTest.php. Once PHPUnit2 is installed, you can run the test like this:

```
% phpunit StrreplaceTest
```

That command will look for the file named *StrreplaceTest.php* and run the test defined within it.

PHPUnit is a very powerful unit testing framework that can do much more than run a simple test like in the example. For complete documentation, visit *http://www.phpunit.de*.

Another popular unit testing framework is called SimpleTest. By default, its tests are intended to be run in a web browser (though a command-line option exists as well). Our example test of the str_replace( ) function would be written like this using SimpleTest:

```
require_once 'simpletest/unit_tester.php';
require_once 'simpletest/reporter.php';

class TestStrreplace extends UnitTestCase
{
    function testStrreplace()
    {
        $str = 'Hello, all!';
        $this->assertEqual('Hello, world!', str_replace('all', 'world', $str));
    }
}
```

As you can see in this simple example, SimpleTest is quite similar to PHPUnit. However, the SimpleTest framework differs from PHPUnit in its full feature set, and it's best to conduct a thorough comparison of the two frameworks before deciding on which one is best for you. Learn more about SimpleTest at *http://www.lastcraft.com/ simple_test.php*.

See Also

Documentation on .phpt unit tests at *http://qa.php.net/write-test.php*; on PHPUnit and PHPUnit2 at *http://www.phpunit.de*; on SimpleTest at *http://www.lastcraft.com/ simple_test.php*.

20.14 Writing a Unit Test Suite

Problem

You want to be able to run more than one unit test conveniently on a regular basis.

Solution

Wrap your unit tests into a group known as a unit test suite.

Discussion

It's rare to have a program simple enough that a single unit test will fulfill all the testing needs that it will have during its lifespan. Over time, as applications grow there is a need to add more and more tests, either to test new functionality or verify that fixed bugs *stay* fixed.

Once your library of tests gets larger than a handful, you'll find it much more convenient to group your tests into a unit test suite. A test suite, despite its formal-sounding name, is just a wrapper around a bunch of tests that can all be run by referring to the name of the test suite.

Using the SimpleTest framework, let's create a test suite to test more than just the str_replace function in PHP. A number of tests related to string functions can be put in a single file. For example, in a file named **string_tests.php**, let's put:

```
class TestStringfunctions extends UnitTestCase
{
    function testStrreplace()
    {
        $str = 'Hello, all!';
        $this->assertEqual('Hello, world!', str_replace('all', 'world', $str));
    }

    function testSubstr()
    {
        $str = 'Hello, all!';
        $this->assertEqual('e', substr($str, 1, 1));
```

```
        }
    }
```

Now we've got two tests that will be run from the `TestStringfunctions` class. Let's create a similar file called **array_tests.php**, with the following tests defined in it:

```
class TestArrayfunctions extends UnitTestCase
{
    function testArrayflip()
    {
        $array = ('foo' => 'bar', 'cheese' => 'hotdog');
        $flipped = array_flip($array);
        $this->assertEqual('foo', reset($flipped));
    }

    function testArraypop()
    {
        $array = ('foo' => 'bar', 'cheese' => 'hotdog');
        $popped = array_pop($array);
        $this->assertEqual('hotdog', $popped);
        $this->assertEqual(1, sizeof($array));
    }
}
```

With four tests to run, it's time to put together a suite that will run all of these whenever we want to check to make sure things are working as they should be. Our test suite looks like this:

```
require_once 'simpletest/unit_tester.php';
require_once 'simpletest/reporter.php';

$test = new GroupTest('All tests');
$test->addTestFile('string_tests.php');
$test->addTestFile('array_tests.php');

if (TextReporter::inCli()) {
    exit ($test->run(new TextReporter()) ? 0 : 1);
} else {
    $test->run(new HtmlReporter());
}
```

Save this in a file named **test_suite.php**, and then run it with a browser that has PHP installed properly and paths set properly in the script to reflect the Simple Test installation location.

When run from a shell using the PHP CLI, the result should be similar to:

```
% php test_suite.php
All tests
OK
Test cases run: 4/4. Failures: 0, Exceptions: 0
```

Using this approach, you can grow your automated testing system to include a large number of tests and still be able to trigger them all through a single command.

Notice the use of the ternary operator when the tests are run in CLI mode; this method of running the unit test suite allows the script to return a success or failure condition when run as part of an external automated testing script.

See Also

Documentation on SimpleTest at *http://www.lastcraft.com/simple_test.php*; on PHPUnit and PHPUnit2 at *http://www.phpunit.de*, which covers test suite creation in PHPUnit.

20.15 Applying a Unit Test to a Web Page

Problem

Your application is not broken down into small testable chunks, or you just want to apply unit testing to the web site that your visitors see.

Solution

Write a series of unit tests around SimpleTest's `WebTestCase` class to test the finished output of your web site.

Create a file to test something about your web site, *example.com*. In a file called exampledotcom_tests.php, put:

```php
class TestOfExampledotcom extends WebTestCase
{
    // basic homepage loading
    function testHomepageLoading()
    {
        $this->assertTrue($this->get('http://www.example.com/'));
    }

    // test clicking on "FAQ", and the resulting generation of FAQ
    function testFaq()
    {
        $this->get('http://www.example.com/');
        $this->clickLink('FAQ');
        $this->assertTitle('Example FAQ');
        $this->assertWantedPattern('/have a question\?/i');
    }
}

require_once 'simpletest/web_tester.php';
require_once 'simpletest/reporter.php';

$test = new GroupTest('Web site tests');
$test->addTestFile('exampledotcom_tests.php');

if (TextReporter::inCli()) {
    exit ($test->run(new TextReporter()) ? 0 : 1);
} else {
```

```
        $test->run(new HtmlReporter());
}
```

Discussion

If you're dealing with a site that's driven in whole or in part by procedural PHP code, it is sometimes difficult to write a smaller unit test that tests encapsulated functionality. Instead, you just want to make sure that the web site is working; if it isn't, you'll debug from there.

Web-page unit testing is a handy technique that is useful whether or not your code base is easily broken into unit tests or not. After all, the real world environment doesn't always behave in the same way as your testing environment, so it can be beneficial to set up a cron job to run a Web Test suite.

The SimpleTest `WebTestCase` supports testing navigation, content, cookies, and form handling. It can even select frames within framesets to conduct tests within a particular frame.

If your site makes extensive use of JavaScript, take a look at Selenium, an open source testing framework designed to be run in a browser to test the complete user experience. Selenium offers a browser-based IDE that can record actions to automate test generation, and supports a wide range of browsers on Windows, Mac OS X, and Linux.

See Also

Documentation on SimpleTest at *http://www.lastcraft.com/simple_test.php*; the Selenium project page at *http://www.openqa.org/selenium/*.

20.16 Setting Up a Test Environment

Problem

You want to test out PHP scripts without worrying about bringing your web site down or contaminating your production environment.

Solution

Set up a test environment for your application on your desktop machine, using XAMPP.

Discussion

The complexity of setting up a localized running environment for your web application frequently deters developers from taking that step. The result is often a breakdown in development best practices, such as editing files on the production web site as a privileged user—never a good idea!

The XAMPP project provides single-installer solutions for four platforms: Windows 98/NT/2000/XP, Mac OS X, Linux (SuSE/RedHat/Mandrake/Debian), and Solaris.

The packages contain synchronized versions of Apache, MySQL, PHP and PEAR, phpMyAdmin, and eAccelerator.

With an easy, step-by-step installation procedure, the XAMPP project makes creating a web-application-running environment on your local machine a snap.

Dealing with a large dataset? Unfortunately, developers working with sites that deal extensively with content that changes frequently find that they let best practices development habits slip due to a lack of good test data to work with. Don't let this happen to you! Simply write a script that mirrors your data *structure* locally, and then periodically update your local copy of data with a subset snapshot of the complete data set. That way you're easily able to pull in a current copy of relevant data that's large enough to be used for real testing and development purposes.

See Also

The XAMPP project home page at *http://www.apachefriends.org/en/xampp.html*.

CHAPTER 21

Performance Tuning and Load Testing

21.0 Introduction

PHP is pretty speedy. Usually, the slow parts of your PHP programs have to do with external resources—waiting for a database query to finish or for the contents of a remote URL to be retrieved. That said, your PHP code itself may not be as efficient as it could be. This chapter is about techniques for finding and fixing performance problems in your code.

There's plenty of debate in the world of software engineeering about the best time in the development process to start optimizing. Optimize too early and you'll spend too much time nitpicking over details that may not be important in the big picture; optimize too late and you may find that you have to rewrite large chunks of your application.

A failsafe approach to this dilemma is to get into the habit of making good choices about approaching small problems; the benefits will add up in the end. Example 21-1 shows three ways to produce the exact same MD5 hash in PHP 5.1.2.

Example 21-1. Hashing three ways
```
// PHP's basic md5() function
$hashA = md5('optimize this!');

// MD5 by way of the mhash extension
$hashB = bin2hex(mhash(MHASH_MD5, 'optimize this!'));

// MD5 with the hash() function in PHP 5.1.2+
$hashC = hash('md5', 'optimize this!');
```

$hashA, $hashB, and $hashC are all 83f0bb25be8de9106700840d66f261cf. However, the third approach is over twice as fast as PHP's basic md5() function.

The dark side of optimization with head-to-head tests like these, though, is that you need to figure in how frequently the function is called in your code and how readable and maintainable the alternative is.

For example, in choosing hash functions, if you need your code to run on PHP versions earlier than 5.1.2, you either have to use md5() all the time or add a check that, based on PHP's version (and perhaps whether the mhash extension is installed), decides which function to use. The absolute time difference between md5( ) and hash( ) is on the order of a tenth of a millisecond. If you're computing thousands or millions of hashes at a time, it makes sense to insert the extra runtime calculations that choose the fastest functions. But the fraction of a fraction of a breath of time saved in a handful of hash computations isn't worth the extra complexity.

Optimization doesn't happen in a vacuum. As you tweak your code, you're not just adjusting raw execution time—you're also affecting code size, readability, and maintainability. There are always circumstances that demand screamingly fast execution time. More frequently, however, programmer time or ease of debugging is a more valuable commodity. Try to balance these concerns as you tackle optimization hurdles in your code.

Get started with integrating some easy analysis methods into your development routine. Recipe 21.1 shows you how to time the execution of a function, and Recipe 21.2 expands on that to illustrate timing overall program execution. Learn how to take these simple approaches even farther with Recipe 21.3, which covers the use of debugger extensions for application profiling.

An overview of how to stress test your web site in Recipe 21.4 reminds you that there's more to performance tuning than the code itself—network latency and hardware also play a big role.

One of the most common bottlenecks in many PHP scripts is misuse of regular expressions; Recipe 21.5 explains a few approaches to solving text-matching problems without incurring the overhead of regular expressions.

Recipe 21.6 covers the various PHP accelerators by explaining the common approaches used by the popular open source and commercial accelerators, and how you can expect to benefit from them.

21.1 Timing Function Execution

Problem

You have a function and you want to see how long it takes to execute.

Solution

Compare time in milliseconds before running the function against the time in milliseconds after running the function to see the elapsed time spent in the function itself:

```php
<?php

// create a long nonsense string
$long_str = uniqid(php_uname('a'), true);

// start timing from here
```

```php
$start = microtime(true);

// function to test
$md5 = md5($long_str);

$elapsed = microtime(true) - $start;

echo "That took $elapsed seconds.\n";
?>
```

Discussion

To determine how much time a single function takes to execute, you may not need a full benchmarking package like PEAR Benchmark (which is covered in Recipe 21.2). Instead, you can get the information you need from the `microtime()` function.

See Also

Using `microtime()`, including how it works in PHP 4, is discussed in Recipe 3.13; documentation on the `microtime()` function is at *http://www.php.net/microtime*; Recipe 21.2 looks at PEAR Benchmark.

21.2 Timing Program Execution

Problem

You have a block of code and you want to profile it to see how long each statement takes to execute.

Solution

Use the PEAR Benchmark module:

```php
<?php
require_once 'Benchmark/Timer.php';

$timer =& new Benchmark_Timer(true);

$timer->start();
// some setup code here
$timer->setMarker('setup');
// some more code executed here
$timer->setMarker('middle');
// even yet still more code here
$timer->setmarker('done');
// and a last bit of code here
$timer->stop();

$timer->display();
?>
```

Discussion

Calling `setMarker( )` records the time. The `display( )` method prints out a list of markers, the time they were set, and the elapsed time from the previous marker:

```
-------------------------------------------------------------------
marker    time index              ex time                   perct
-------------------------------------------------------------------
Start     1029433375.42507400     -                         0.00%
-------------------------------------------------------------------
setup     1029433375.42554800     0.00047397613525391      29.77%
-------------------------------------------------------------------
middle    1029433375.42568700     0.00013899803161621       8.73%
-------------------------------------------------------------------
done      1029433375.42582000     0.00013303756713867       8.36%
-------------------------------------------------------------------
Stop      1029433375.42666600     0.00084602832794189      53.14%
-------------------------------------------------------------------
total     -                       0.0015920400619507       100.00%
-------------------------------------------------------------------
```

The Benchmark module also includes the `Benchmark_Iterate` class, which can be used to time many executions of a single function:

```php
<?php
require 'Benchmark/Iterate.php';

$timer =& new Benchmark_Iterate;

// a sample function to time
function use_preg($ar) {
    for ($i = 0, $j = count($ar); $i < $j; $i++) {
        if (preg_match('/gouda/',$ar[$i])) {
            // it's gouda
        }
    }
}

// another sample function to time
function use_equals($ar) {
    for ($i = 0, $j = count($ar); $i < $j; $i++) {
        if ('gouda' == $ar[$i]) {
            // it's gouda
        }
    }
}

// run use_preg() 1000 times
$timer->run(1000,'use_preg',
                array('gouda','swiss','gruyere','muenster','whiz'));
$results = $timer->get();
print "Mean execution time for use_preg(): $results[mean]\n";

// run use_equals() 1000 times
$timer->run(1000,'use_equals',
                array('gouda','swiss','gruyere','muenster','whiz'));
```

```
$results = $timer->get();
print "Mean execution time for use_equals(): $results[mean]\n";
?>
```

The Benchmark_Iterate::get( ) method returns an associative array. The mean element of this array holds the mean execution time for each iteration of the function. The iterations element holds the number of iterations. The execution time of each iteration of the function is stored in an array element with an integer key. For example, the time of the first iteration is in $results[1], and the time of the 37th iteration is in $results[37].

To automatically record the elapsed execution time after every line of PHP code, use the declare construct and the ticks directive:

```
function profile($display = false) {
    static $times;

    switch ($display) {
    case false:
        // add the current time to the list of recorded times
        $times[] = microtime();
        break;
    case true:
        // return elapsed times in microseconds
        $start = array_shift($times);

        $start_mt = explode(' ', $start);
        $start_total = doubleval($start_mt[0]) + $start_mt[1];

        foreach ($times as $stop) {
            $stop_mt = explode(' ', $stop);
            $stop_total = doubleval($stop_mt[0]) + $stop_mt[1];
            $elapsed[] = $stop_total - $start_total;
        }

        unset($times);
        return $elapsed;
        break;
    }
}

// register tick handler
register_tick_function('profile');

// clock the start time
profile();

// execute code, recording time for every statement execution
declare (ticks = 1) {
    foreach ($_SERVER['argv'] as $arg) {
        print strlen($arg);
    }
}

// print out elapsed times
```

```
$i = 0;
foreach (profile(true) as $time) {
    $i++;
    print "Line $i: $time\n";
}
```

The `ticks` directive allows you to execute a function on a repeatable basis for a block of code. The number assigned to `ticks` is how many statements go by before the functions that are registered using `register_tick_function( )` are executed.

In the previous example, we register a single function and have the `profile( )` function execute for every statement inside the `declare` block. If there are two elements in `$_SERVER['argv']`, `profile( )` is executed four times: once for each time through the `foreach` loop, and once each time the `print strlen($arg)` line is executed.

You can also set things up to call two functions every three statements:

```
register_tick_function('profile');
register_tick_function('backup');

declare (ticks = 3) {
    // code...
}
```

You can also pass additional parameters into the registered functions, which can be object methods instead of regular functions:

```
// pass "parameter" into profile()
register_tick_function('profile', 'parameter');

// call $car->drive();
$car = new Vehicle;
register_tick_function(array($car, 'drive'));
```

If you want to execute an object method, pass the object and the name of the method encapsulated within an array. This lets the `register_tick_function( )` know you're referring to an object instead of a function.

Call `unregister_tick_function( )` to remove a function from the list of tick functions:

```
unregister_tick_function('profile');
```

See Also

http://pear.php.net/package/Benchmark for information on the PEAR Benchmark class; documentation on `register_tick_function( )` at *http://www.php.net/register-tick-function*, `unregister_tick_function( )` at *http://www.php.net/unregister-tick-function*, and declare at *http://www.php.net/declare*.

21.3 Profiling with a Debugger Extension

Problem

You want a robust solution for profiling your applications so that you can continually monitor where the program spends most of its time.

Solution

Use a profiling and debugging extension such as the Advanced PHP Debugger (APD) or Xdebug, both available from the PECL repository.

With APD installed, adding apd_set_pprof_trace( ) to the top of your script dumps a trace file in a configurable directory. Parsing that trace file gives you a breakdown of how time was spent during that run of the PHP script:

```php
<?php
$dumpdir = '/tmp';
$processid = posix_getpid();
ini_set('apd.dumpdir', $dumpdir);

// Prepare to output a basic report
$dumpfile = $dumpdir . '/pprof.' . $processid . '.0';

// Start the trace
apd_set_pprof_trace();

// Functions that we will profile
function pc_longString() {
    return uniqid(php_uname('a'), true);
}

function pc_md5($str) {
    return md5($str);
}

function pc_mhashmd5($str) {
    return bin2hex(mhash(MHASH_MD5, $str));
}

function pc_hashmd5($str) {
    return hash('md5', $str);
}

// Run the functions
$str = pc_longString();

$md5 = function_exists('md5') ? pc_md5($str) : false;
$md5 = function_exists('mhash') ? pc_mhashmd5($str) : false;
$md5 = function_exists('hash') ? pc_hashmd5($str) : false;

echo "now run:\n";
```

```
echo "  /usr/bin/pprofp -R $dumpfile\n";
echo "to view a report.\n";
```

Running the report generated by the pprofp tool, which is installed as part of the APD package, results in something like this:

```
% /usr/bin/pprofp -R /tmp/pprof.16704.0

Trace for /home/clay/phpckbk2/apd/md5.php
Total Elapsed Time = 0.00
Total System Time  = 0.00
Total User Time    = 0.00
```

%Time	Real (excl/cumm)		User (excl/cumm)		System (excl/cumm)		Calls	secs/ call	cumm s/call	Memory Usage	Name
100.0	0.00	0.00	0.00	0.00	0.00	0.00	1	0.0005	0.0042	0	main
77.8	0.00	0.00	0.00	0.00	0.00	0.00	1	0.0033	0.0033	33554432	apd_set_pprof_trace
4.6	0.00	0.00	0.00	0.00	0.00	0.00	1	0.0000	0.0002	0	pc_longString
2.6	0.00	0.00	0.00	0.00	0.00	0.00	1	0.0001	0.0001	0	php_uname
2.3	0.00	0.00	0.00	0.00	0.00	0.00	1	0.0000	0.0001	0	pc_mhashmd5
1.5	0.00	0.00	0.00	0.00	0.00	0.00	1	0.0001	0.0001	0	uniqid
1.5	0.00	0.00	0.00	0.00	0.00	0.00	1	0.0000	0.0001	0	pc_md5
1.5	0.00	0.00	0.00	0.00	0.00	0.00	1	0.0001	0.0001	0	mhash
1.3	0.00	0.00	0.00	0.00	0.00	0.00	1	0.0001	0.0001	0	md5
1.3	0.00	0.00	0.00	0.00	0.00	0.00	3	0.0000	0.0000	0	function_exists
1.2	0.00	0.00	0.00	0.00	0.00	0.00	1	0.0000	0.0001	0	pc_hashmd5
1.0	0.00	0.00	0.00	0.00	0.00	0.00	1	0.0000	0.0000	0	hash
0.6	0.00	0.00	0.00	0.00	0.00	0.00	1	0.0000	0.0000	0	bin2hex

Discussion

With APD installed, it's a simple matter to start a profiling session that will store reporting on application runtime. The output files generated by APD can be stored anywhere you want them—even in a dynamic location, if you want to integrate some conditional trace executions into your script. Just use ini_set('apd.dumpdir', '/path/to/writable/dump/directory') to pick a dump location prior to calling apd_set_pprof_trace( ).

The *pprof* output file is a machine-readable breakdown of how your script was processed. The output file is stored in the apd.dumpdir location with a naming convention of pprof.*process ID.file number*. The *file number* portion of the dump file is determined internally by APD, which will create sequential files as needed for each process being traced.

Process the output files with the bundled *pprofp* shell application to get some basic insight into what's taking the most time in your application. The longest-running functions are good places to start when looking for opportunities to optimize.

Beyond basic reporting on execution time, the *pprof* files can be converted to Kcachegrind-compatible files using the *pprof2calltree* conversion tool. Kcachegrind is a GUI application used to drill down deeply into applications to determine where bottlenecks are occurring.

A number of profiling extensions exist; for the most effective debugging and profiling experience, it's recommended to give each one a try to see which one suits your needs the best.

See Also

Documentation for APD at *http://www.php.net/manual/en/ref.apd.php*; the Xdebug profiling and debugging extension at *http://www.xdebug.org/*; the DBG extension at *http://dd.cron.ru/dbg/*; the Kcachegrind profiling visualization tool at *http://kcachegrind.sourceforge.net*.

21.4 Stress Testing Your Web Site

Problem

You want to find out how well your web site performs under a heavy load.

Solution

Use a stress-testing and benchmarking tool to simulate a variety of load levels.

Discussion

Stress testing is frequently confused with benchmarking, and it is important to recognize the difference between the two activities.

Benchmarking a web site is often a somewhat casual activity when performed by an individual developer. The most commonly used tool is the Apache HTTP server benchmarking tool, *ab*, which is designed to test how many requests per second an HTTP server is capable of serving. For example:

```
% /usr/bin/ab -n 1000 -c 100 -k
www.example.com/test.php
```

This test would return a report illustrating the average response time for requests to *http://www.example.com/test.php*, based on 1,000 requests, grouped in batches of 100 concurrent requests.

While that sort of test has value—it gives you a reasonable estimation of how many requests you can serve per second under normal load—it doesn't tell you much about how your entire web application will behave under heavy load. It only pounds on one URL at a time, after all.

Stress testing is a testing technique whose intent is to *break* your web application. By testing to a breaking point, you can identify and repair weaknesses in your application, or gain a better understanding of when you will need to add additional hardware. When combined with code profiling, you can also get an idea of what part of your application will need to scale first; i.e., will you need to add more servers to your database cluster before you need to add more frontend web server machines?

An excellent open source tool for stress testing is *Siege*. Siege can be configured to read a large number of URLs from a configuration file and run through them in order (regression testing), or it can read a list or URLs and hit them randomly, which better approximates real-world usage of a web site. Siege can also pound on a single URL in a similar fashion to *ab*.

If you are unable to install Siege on your system, Lincoln Stein's *torture.pl* script is a good alternative. Many of Siege's design concepts were inspired by *torture.pl*, and the two tools produce similar reports.

See Also

Source and documentation for Siege at *http://www.joedog.org/JoeDog/Siege*; *ab* at *http://httpd.apache.org/docs/2.0/programs/ab.html*; source and documentation for *torture.pl* at *http://stein.cshl.org/~lstein/torture/*.

21.5 Avoiding Regular Expressions

Problem

You want to improve script performance by optimizing string-matching operations.

Solution

Replace unnecessary regular expression calls with faster string and character type function alternatives.

Discussion

A common source of unnecessary computation is the use of regular expression functions when they are not needed—for example, if you're validating a form submission for a valid username and want to make sure that the username contains only alphanumeric characters.

A common approach to this problem is a regular expression:

```
<?php
if (!preg_match('/^[a-z0-9]*$/i', $username)) {
  echo 'please enter a valid username.';
}
?>
```

The same test can be performed much faster with the ctype_alnum( ) function.

Using code-timing techniques covered in Recipe 21.1, let's compare the above test with ctype_alnum( ):

```php
<?php
$username = 'foo411';

$start = microtime(true);

if (!preg_match('/^[a-z0-9]*/i', $username)) {
    echo 'please enter a valid username';
}

$regextime = microtime(true) - $start;

$start = microtime(true);

if (!ctype_alnum($username)) {
    echo 'please enter a valid username';
}

$ctypetime = microtime(true) - $start;

echo "preg_match took:  $regextime seconds\n";
echo "ctype_alnum took: $ctypetime seconds\n";
?>
```

This will output results similar to:

```
preg_match took:  0.000163078308105 seconds
ctype_alnum took: 9.05990600586E-06 seconds
```

ctype_alnum( ) is considerably faster; 9.05990600586E-06 is the same as 0.00000906 seconds, which is *18 times* faster than the preg_match( ) regular expression, with exactly the same result.

When applied to a complex application, replacing unnecessary regular expressions with equivalent alternatives can add up to a significant performance gain.

A good litmus test when you're coding and need to decide whether or not you need to use a regular expression is whether or not the match you're performing can be explained in a brief sentence. Granted, there are some matches, such as "string is a valid email address," which cannot be adequately verified without a complex regular expression. However, "check if string A contains string B" can be tested with several different approaches, but is ultimately a very simple test that does not require regular expressions:

```php
$haystack = 'The quick brown fox jumps over the lazy dog';
$needle = 'lazy dog';

// slowest
if (ereg($needle, $haystack)) echo 'match!';

// slow
if (preg_match("/$needle/", $haystack)) echo 'match!';

// fast
if (strstr($haystack, $needle)) echo 'match!';
```

```
// fastest
if (strpos($haystack, $needle) !== false) echo 'match!';
```

There is certainly a benefit to double-checking the `ctype` and `string` functions before making a commitment to a regular expression, particularly if you're working a section of code that will loop repeatedly.

See Also

Documentation on `ctype` functions at *http://www.php.net/manual/en/ref.ctype.php*; on `string` functions at *http://www.php.net/manual/en/ref.strings.php*; on regular expression functions at *http://www.php.net/manual/en/ref.pcre.php*.

21.6 Using an Accelerator

Problem

You want to increase performance of your PHP applications.

Solution

Install a code-caching PHP accelerator to allow PHP to avoid compiling scripts into opcodes on each request.

Discussion

PHP code accelerators do the bulk of their magic transparently by storing compiled versions of PHP scripts on disk or in shared memory in order to skip the compiling step with each request.

When the PHP interpreter is told to run a particular program, it reads the source code of the program and compiles it into a compact internal representation. Then, it executes the instructions in that compiled representation. When it's done executing the script, the interpreter throws away the compiled representation.

An accelerator, by contrast, keeps the compiled instructions around. The next time the PHP interpreter gets a request to run the same program, the accelerator steps in and checks whether it's saved a compiled version of that program. If so, it tells the PHP interpreter to skip recompilation and just execute the already compiled version. An accelerator can be configured to update its compiled representations based on different criteria, such as whenever the original program changes or only when you explicitly tell it to.

The three most popular freely available PHP accelerators are the Alternative PHP Cache (APC), eAccelerator, and the ionCube PHP Accelerator (PHPA). The freely available Zend Optimizer can also help with small performance increases by transparently correcting common but inefficient coding practices. However, the Zend Optimizer is not an accelerator.

There are a few important distinctions between the freely available accelerators that may influence your choice on which one to use. Issues such as Windows support, PHP 5 compatibility, Zend Optimizer compatibility, and functionality that goes beyond code caching may all be important in your decision on which accelerator to use. Benchmarks have shown that all the accelerators improve performance a roughly equivalent amount, so the deciding factor will most likely be one of these other issues.

APC and eAccelerator are open source projects with ongoing development. (eAccelerator is a fork of the Turck MMCache project, on which development has stopped.) The ionCube Accelerator is a commercial product. Developer responsiveness to bugs should also factor into your decision on which accelerator to use. Make sure to check the current status of open bugs with each accelerator and how those issues may affect you based on the version of PHP you're using, and the type of code (OOP versus procedural) your applications are based on.

Finally, it is important to recognize that accelerator compatibility often lags behind new PHP releases. If running the latest and greatest version of PHP is important to you, you may find that you are rarely able to take advantage of the benefits that an accelerator can provide.

See Also

The APC web site at *http://pecl.php.net/package/apc*; the eAccelerator web site at *http://www.eaccelerator.net/*; the PHPA web site at *http://www.php-accelerator.co.uk/*.

CHAPTER 22

Regular Expressions

22.0 Introduction

Regular expressions are an intricate and powerful tool for matching patterns and manipulating text. While not as fast as plain vanilla string matching, regular expressions
are extremely flexible. They allow you to construct patterns to match almost any con-
ceivable combination of characters with a simple—albeit terse and punctuation-
studded—grammar. If your web site relies on data feeds that come in text files—data
feeds like sports scores, news articles, or frequently updated headlines—regular expressions can help you make sense of those data feeds.

This chapter gives a brief overview of basic regular expression syntax and then focuses
on the functions that PHP provides for working with regular expressions. For a bit more
detailed information about the ins and outs of regular expressions, check out the PCRE
section of the PHP online manual (*http://www.php.net/pcre*) and Appendix B of *Learning PHP 5* by David Sklar (O'Reilly). To start on the path to regular expression wizardry,
read the comprehensive *Mastering Regular Expressions* by Jeffrey E.F. Friedl (O'Reilly).

Regular expressions are handy when transforming plain text into HTML and vice versa.
Luckily, since these are such helpful subjects, PHP has many built-in functions to handle these tasks. Recipe 9.10 tells how to escape HTML entities; Recipe 13.14 covers
stripping HTML tags; and Recipes 13.12 and 13.13 show how to convert plain text to
HTML and HTML to plain text, respectively. For information on matching and validating email addresses, see Recipe 9.4.

Over the years, the functionality of regular expressions has grown from its basic roots
to incorporate increasingly useful features. As a result, PHP offers two different sets of
regular expression functions. The first set includes the traditional (or POSIX) functions,
whose names each begin with `ereg` (for "extended" regular expressions; the `ereg` functions themselves are already an extension of the original feature set). The other set
includes the Perl-compatible family of functions, prefaced with `preg` (for Perl-compatible regular expressions).

The `preg` functions use a library that mimics the regular expression functionality of the
Perl programming language. This is a good thing because Perl allows you to do a variety

of handy things with regular expressions, including nongreedy matching, forward and backward assertions, and even recursive patterns.

In general, there's no longer any reason to use the ereg functions. They offer fewer features, and they're slower than preg functions. However, the ereg functions existed in PHP for many years prior to the introduction of the preg functions, so many programmers still use them because of legacy code or out of habit. Thankfully, the prototypes for the two sets of functions are identical, so it's easy to switch back and forth from one to another without too much confusion. (We list how to do this while avoiding the major gotchas in Recipe 22.1.)

Think of a regular expression as a program in a very restrictive programming language. The only task of a regular expression program is to match a pattern in text. In regular expression patterns, most characters just match themselves. That is, the regular expression rhino matches strings that contain the five-character sequence rhino. The fancy business in regular expressions is due to a handful of punctuation and symbols called *metacharacters*. These symbols don't literally match themselves, but instead give commands to the regular expression matcher.

The most frequently used metacharacters include the period (.), asterisk (*), plus sign (+), and question mark (?). (To match a literal metacharacter in a pattern, precede the character with a backslash.)

- The period means "match any character," so the pattern .at matches bat, cat, and even rat.
- The asterisk means "match 0 or more of the preceding object." (So far, the only objects we know about are characters.)
- The plus is similar to asterisk, but means "match *one* or more of the preceding object." So .+at matches brat, sprat, and even the cat inside of catastrophe, but not plain at. To match at, replace the + with a *.
- The question mark means "the preceding object is optional." That is, it matches 0 or 1 of the object that precedes it. colou?r matches both color and colour.

To apply * and + to objects greater than one character, place the sequence of characters that make up the object inside parentheses. Parentheses allow you to group characters for more complicated matching and also capture the part of the pattern that falls inside them. A captured sequence can be referenced by preg_replace( ) to alter a string, and all captured matches can be stored in an array that's passed as a third parameter to preg_match( ) and preg_match_all( ). The preg_match_all( ) function is similar to preg_match( ), but it finds all possible matches inside a string, instead of stopping at the first match. Example 22-1 shows a few examples of preg_match( ), preg_match_all( ), and preg_replace( ) at work.

Example 22-1. Using preg functions

```php
<?php
if (preg_match('{<title>.+</title>}', $html)) {
```

```
        // page has a title
    }

    if (preg_match_all('/<li>/', $html, $matches)) {
        print 'Page has ' . count($matches[0]) . " list items\n";
    }

    // turn bold into italic
    $italics = preg_replace('/(<\/?)b(>)/', '$1i$2', $bold);
    ?>
```

If you want to match strings with a specific set of characters, create a *character class* by putting the characters you want inside square brackets. The character class [aeiou] matches any one of the characters a, e, i, o, and u. You can also put ranges inside of square brackets to form a character class. The class [a-z] matches all lowercase English letters. The class [a-zA-Z0-9] matches digits and English letters. The class [a-zA-Z0-9_] matches digits, English letters, and the underscore.

So far, all the patterns we've seen match anything that contains text that corresponds to the pattern. That is, [a-z0-9]+ matches grapefruit and c3p0, but it also matches grr!!! and *******p. All four of those strings meet the condition that [a-z0-9]+ sets out: "one or more of a digit or lowercase English letter."

Anchoring your pattern enables matching against strings that *only* contain characters that the pattern describes. The caret (^) and the dollar sign ($) anchor the pattern at the beginning and the end of the string, respectively. Without them, a match can occur anywhere in the string. So while [a-z0-9]+ means "one or more of a digit or lowercase English letter," ^[a-z0-9]+ means "begins with one or more of a digit or lowercase English letter," [a-z0-9]+$ means "ends with one or more of a digit or lowercase English letter," and ^[a-z0-9]+$ means "contains only one or more of a digit or lowercase English letter." Example 22-2 shows a few character classes at work.

Example 22-2. Matching with character classes and anchors
```
    <?php
    $thisFileContents = file_get_contents(__FILE__);
    // http://php.net/language.variables gives a regular expression for
    // valid variable names in php. Beginning the pattern with \$ matches
    // a literal $
    $matchCount = preg_match_all('/\$[a-zA-Z_\x7f-\xff][a-zA-Z0-9_\x7f-\xff]*/',
                        $thisFileContents, $matches);
    print "Matches: $matchCount\n";
    foreach ($matches[0] as $variableName) {
        print "$variableName\n";
    }
    ?>
```

Example 22-2 prints each variable name it uses:
```
    Matches: 8
    $thisFileContents
    $matchCount
```

```
$thisFileContents
$matches
$matchCount
$matches
$variableName
$variableName
```

If it's easier to define what you're looking for by its complement, use that. To make a character class match the complement of what's inside it, begin the class with a caret. A caret outside a character class anchors a pattern at the beginning of a string; a caret inside a character class means "match everything except what's listed in the square brackets." For example, the character class [^aeiou] matches everything but lowercase English vowels.

Note that the opposite of [aeiou] isn't [bcdfghjklmnpqrstvwxyz]. The character class [^aeiou] also matches uppercase vowels such as AEIOU, numbers such as 123, URLs such as http://www.cnpq.br/, and even emoticons such as :).

The vertical bar (|), also known as the pipe, specifies alternatives. Example 22-3 uses the pipe to find various possibilities for image filenames in a block of text.

Example 22-3. Matching with |

```
<?php
$text = "The files are cuddly.gif, report.pdf, and cute.jpg.";
if (preg_match_all('/[a-zA-Z0-9]+\.(gif|jpe?g)/',$text,$matches)) {
    print "The image files are: " . implode(',',$matches[0]);
}
?>
```

Example 22-3 prints:

```
The image files are: cuddly.gif,cute.jpg
```

We've covered just a small subset of the world of regular expressions. We provide some additional details in later recipes, but the PHP web site also has some very useful information on Perl-compatible regular expressions at *http://www.php.net/pcre*. The links from this last page to "Pattern Modifiers" and "Pattern Syntax" are especially detailed and informative.

22.1 Switching from ereg to preg

Problem

You want to convert from using **ereg** functions to **preg** functions.

Solution

First, you have to add delimiters to your patterns:

```
preg_match('/pattern/', 'string')
```

For eregi() case-insensitive matching, use the /i modifier instead:

```
preg_match('/pattern/i', 'string');
```

When using integers instead of strings as patterns or replacement values, convert the number to hexadecimal and specify it using an escape sequence:

```
$hex = dechex($number);
preg_match("/\x$hex/", 'string');
```

Discussion

There are a few major differences between `ereg` and `preg`. First, when you use `preg` functions, the pattern isn't just the string `pattern`; it also needs delimiters, as in Perl, so it's /pattern/ instead.* So:

```
ereg('pattern', 'string');
```

becomes:

```
preg_match('/pattern/', 'string');
```

When choosing your pattern delimiters, don't put your delimiter character inside the regular expression pattern, or you'll close the pattern early. If you can't find a way to avoid this problem, you need to escape any instances of your delimiters using the backslash. Instead of doing this by hand, call `addcslashes()`.

For example, if you use / as your delimiter:

```
$ereg_pattern = '<b>.+</b>';
$preg_pattern = addcslashes($ereg_pattern, '/');
```

The value of `$preg_pattern` is now `<b>.+<\/b>`.

The `preg` functions don't have a parallel series of case-insensitive functions. They have a case-insensitive modifier instead. To convert, change:

```
eregi('pattern', 'string');
```

to:

```
preg_match('/pattern/i', 'string');
```

Adding the `i` after the closing delimiter makes the change.

Finally, there is one last obscure difference. If you use a number (not a string) as a pattern or replacement value in `ereg_replace()`, it's assumed you are referring to the ASCII value of a character. Therefore, since 9 is the ASCII representation of tab (i.e., \t), this code inserts tabs at the beginning of each line:

```
$tab = 9;
$replaced = ereg_replace('^', $tab, $string);
```

___

* Or {pattern}, <pattern>, |pattern|, #pattern#, or just about whatever your favorite delimiters are. If you use an opening pair character such as (, <, [, or { as the starting delimiter, PHP expects the corresponding closing pair character as the ending delimiter (), >,], or }). If you use another character as the starting delimiter, PHP expects the same character as the ending delimiter.

Here's how to convert linefeed endings:

```
$converted = ereg_replace(10, 12, $text);
```

To avoid this feature in **ereg** functions, use this instead:

```
$tab = '9';
```

On the other hand, `preg_replace( )` treats the number 9 as the number 9, not as a tab substitute. To convert these character codes for use in `preg_replace( )`, convert them to hexadecimal and prefix them with `\x`. For example, `9` becomes `\x9` or `\x09,` and `12` becomes `\x0c`. Alternatively, you can use `\t` , `\r`, and `\n` for tabs, carriage returns, and linefeeds, respectively.

See Also

Documentation on `ereg( )` at *http://www.php.net/ereg*, `preg_match( )` at *http://www.php.net/preg-match*, and `addcslashes( )` at *http://www.php.net/addcslashes*.

22.2 Matching Words

Problem

You want to pull out all words from a string.

Solution

The key to this is carefully defining what you mean by a word. Once you've created your definition, use the special character types to create your regular expression:

```
/\S+/          // everything that isn't whitespace
/[A-Z'-]+/i    // all upper and lowercase letters, apostrophes, and hyphens
```

Discussion

The simple question "What is a word?" is surprisingly complicated. While the Perl-compatible regular expressions have a built-in word character type, specified by `\w`, it's important to understand exactly how PHP defines a word. Otherwise, your results may not be what you expect.

Normally, because it comes directly from Perl's definition of a word, `\w` encompasses all letters, digits, and underscores; this means `a_z` is a word, but the email address `php@example.com` is not.

In this recipe, we only consider English words, but other languages use different alphabets. Because Perl-compatible regular expressions use the current locale to define its settings, altering the locale can switch the definition of a letter, which then redefines the meaning of a word.

To combat this, you may want to explicitly enumerate the characters belonging to your words inside a character class. To add a nonstandard character, use \xdd , where dd is a character's hex code.

See Also

Recipe 19.2 for information about setting locales and Recipe 19.13 for information about using UTF-8-encoded strings with the PCRE regex functions.

22.3 Finding the nth Occurrence of a Match

Problem

You want to find the *n*th word match instead of the first one.

Solution

Use `preg_match_all( )` to pull all the matches into an array; then pick out the specific matches in which you're interested, as shown in Example 22-4.

Example 22-4. Finding the nth match

```php
<?php
$todo = "1. Get Dressed 2. Eat Jelly 3. Squash every week into a day";

preg_match_all("/\d\. ([^\d]+)/", $todo, $matches);

print "The second item on the todo list is: ";
// $matches[1] is an array of each substring captured by ([^\d]+)
print $matches[1][1];

print "The entire todo list is: ";
foreach($matches[1] as $match) {
    print "$match\n";
}
?>
```

Discussion

Because the `preg_match( )` function stops after it finds one match, you need to use `preg_match_all( )` instead if you're looking for additional matches. The `preg_match_all( )` function returns the number of full pattern matches it finds. If it finds no matches, it returns 0. If it encounters an error, such as a syntax problem in the pattern, it returns `false`.

The third argument to `preg_match_all( )` is populated with an array holding information about the various substrings that the pattern has matched. The first element holds an array of matches of the complete pattern. For Example 22-4, this means that `$matches[0]` holds the parts of $todo that match /\d\. ([^\d]+)/: 1. Get Dressed, 2. Eat Jelly, and 3. Squash every week into a day.

Subsequent elements of the $matches array hold arrays of text matched by each parenthesized subpattern. The pattern in Example 22-4 has just one subpattern ([^\d]+). So $matches[1] is an array of strings that match that subpattern: Get Dressed, Eat Jelly, and Squash every week into a day.

If there were a second subpattern, the substrings that it matched would be in $matches[2], a third subpattern's matches would be in $matches[3], and so on.

Instead of returning an array divided into full matches and then submatches, preg_match_all( ) can return an array divided by matches, with each submatch inside. To trigger this, pass PREG_SET_ORDER in as the fourth argument. This is particularly useful when you've got multiple captured subpatterns and you want to iterate through the subpattern groups one group at a time, as shown in Example 22-5.

Example 22-5. Grouping captured subpatterns

```php
<?php
$todo = "
first=Get Dressed
next=Eat Jelly
last=Squash every week into a day
";

preg_match_all("/([a-zA-Z]+)=(.*)/", $todo, $matches, PREG_SET_ORDER);

foreach ($matches as $match) {
    print "The {$match[1]} action is {$match[2]} \n";
}
?>
```

Example 22-5 prints:

```
The first action is Get Dressed
The next action is Eat Jelly
The last action is Squash every week into a day
```

With PREG_SET_ORDER, each value of $match in the foreach loop contains all the subpatterns: $match[0] is the entire matched string, $match[1] the bit before the =, and $match[2] the bit after the =.

See Also

Documentation on preg_match_all( ) at *http://www.php.net/preg-match-all*.

22.4 Choosing Greedy or Nongreedy Matches

Problem

You want your pattern to match the smallest possible string instead of the largest.

Solution

Place a ? after a quantifier to alter that portion of the pattern, as in Example 22-6.

Example 22-6. Making a quantifier match as few characters as possible

```php
<?php
// find all <em>emphasized</em> sections
preg_match_all('@<em>.+?</em>@', $html, $matches);
?>
```

Or use the U pattern-modifier ending to invert all quantifiers from greedy ("match as many characters as possible") to nongreedy ("match as few characters as possible"). The code in Example 22-7 does the same thing as the code in Example 22-6.

Example 22-7. Making a quantifier match as few characters as possible

```php
<?php
// find all <em>emphasized</em> sections
preg_match_all('@<em>.+</em>@U', $html, $matches);
?>
```

Discussion

By default, all regular expression quantifiers in PHP are *greedy*. For example, consider the pattern <em>.+</em>, which matches "<em>, one or more characters, </em>", matching against the string I simply <em>love</em> your <em>work</em>. A greedy regular expression finds one match, because after it matches the opening <em>, its .+ slurps up as much as possible, finally grinding to a halt at the final </em>. The .+ matches love</em> your <em>work.

A nongreedy regular expression, on the other hand, finds a pair of matches. The first <em> is matched as before, but then .+ stops as soon as it can, only matching love. A second match then goes ahead: the next .+ matches work.

Example 22-8 shows the greedy and nongreedy patterns at work.

Example 22-8. Greedy versus nongreedy matching

```php
<?php
$html = 'I simply <em>love</em> your <em>work</em>';
// Greedy
$matchCount = preg_match_all('@<em>.+</em>@', $html, $matches);
print "Greedy count: " . $matchCount . "\n";
// Nongreedy
$matchCount = preg_match_all('@<em>.+?</em>@', $html, $matches);
print "First non-greedy count: " . $matchCount . "\n";
// Nongreedy
$matchCount = preg_match_all('@<em>.+</em>@U', $html, $matches);
print "Second non-greedy count: " . $matchCount . "\n";
?>
```

Example 22-8 prints:

```
Greedy count: 1
First non-greedy count: 2
Second non-greedy count: 2
```

Greedy matching is also known as *maximal* and nongreedy matching can be called *minimal matching*, because these methods match either the maximum or minimum number of characters possible.

The `ereg( )` and `ereg_replace( )` functions are always greedy. Being able to choose between greedy and nongreedy matching is another reason to use the PCRE functions instead.

While nongreedy matching is useful for simplistic HTML parsing, it can break down if your markup isn't 100 percent valid and there are, for example, stray `<em>` tags lying around.[†] If your goal is just to remove all (or some) HTML tags from a block of text, you're better off not using a regular expression. Instead, use the built-in function `strip_tags( )`; it's faster and it works correctly. See Recipe 13.14 for more details.

Finally, even though the idea of nongreedy matching comes from Perl, the `U` modifier is incompatible with Perl and is unique to PHP's Perl-compatible regular expressions. It inverts all quantifiers, turning them from greedy to nongreedy and also the reverse. So to get a greedy quantifier inside of a pattern operating under a trailing `/U`, just add a `?` to the end, the same way you would normally turn a greedy quantifier into a nongreedy one.

See Also

Recipe 22.6 for more on capturing text inside HTML tags; Recipe 13.14 for more on stripping HTML tags; documentation on `preg_match_all( )` at *http://www.php.net/preg-match-all*.

22.5 Finding All Lines in a File That Match a Pattern

Problem

You want to find all the lines in a file that match a pattern.

Solution

Read the file into an array and use `preg_grep( )`.

Discussion

There are two ways to do this. Example 22-9 is faster, but uses more memory. It uses the `file( )` function to put each line of the file into an array and `preg_grep( )` to filter out the non-matching lines.

[†] It's possible to have valid HTML and still get into trouble; for instance, if you have bold tags inside a comment. A true HTML parser would ignore them, but our pattern won't.

```
$pattern = "/\bo'reilly\b/i"; // only O'Reilly books
$ora_books = preg_grep($pattern, file('/path/to/your/file.txt'));
```

Example 22-10 is slower, but more memory efficient. It reads the file a line at a time and uses preg_match( ) to check each line after it's read.

Example 22-10. Efficiently finding lines that match a pattern

```
$fh = fopen('/path/to/your/file.txt', 'r') or die($php_errormsg);
while (!feof($fh)) {
    $line = fgets($fh);
    if (preg_match($pattern, $line)) { $ora_books[ ] = $line; }
}
fclose($fh);
```

Since the code in Example 22-9 reads in everything all at once, it's about three times faster than the code in Example 22-10, which parses the file line by line but uses less memory. Keep in mind that since both methods operate on individual lines of the file, they can't successfully use patterns that match text that spans multiple lines.

See Also

Recipe 23.5 on reading files into strings; documentation on preg_grep( ) at *http://www.php.net/preg-grep*.

22.6 Capturing Text Inside HTML Tags

Problem

You want to capture text inside HTML tags. For example, you want to find all the heading tags in an HTML document.

Solution

Read the HTML file into a string and use nongreedy matching in your pattern, as shown in Example 22-11.

Example 22-11. Capturing HTML headings

```
<?php
$html = file_get_contents('example.html');
preg_match_all('@<h([1-6])>(.+?)</h\1>@is', $html, $matches);
foreach ($matches[2] as $text) {
    print "Heading: $text \n";
}
?>
```

Discussion

Robust parsing of HTML is difficult using a simple regular expression. This is one advantage of using XHTML; it's significantly easier to validate and parse.

For instance, the pattern in Example 22-11 can't deal with attributes inside the heading tags and is only smart enough to find matching headings, so `<h1>Dr. Strangelove</h1>` is OK, because it's wrapped inside `<h1></h1>` tags, but not `<h2>How I Learned to Stop Worrying and Love the Bomb</h3>`, because the opening tag is `<h2>` while the closing tag is not.

This technique also works for finding all text inside reasonably well constructed `<strong>` and `<em>` tags, as in Example 22-12.

Example 22-12. Extracting text from HTML tags

```php
<?php
$html = file_get_contents('example.html');
preg_match_all('@<(strong|em)>(.+?)</\1>@is', $html, $matches);
foreach ($matches[2] as $text) {
    print "Text: $text \n";
}
?>
```

However, Example 22-12 breaks on nested headings. If *example.html* contains `<strong>Dr. Strangelove or: <em>How I Learned to Stop Worrying and Love the Bomb</em></strong>`, Example 22-12 doesn't capture the text inside the `<em></em>` tags as a separate item.

This isn't a problem in Example 22-11: because headings are block level elements, it's illegal to nest them. However, as inline elements, nested `<strong>` and `<em>` tags are valid.

Regular expressions can be moderately useful for parsing small amounts of HTML, especially if the structure of that HTML is reasonably constrained (or you're generating it yourself). For more generalized and robust HTML parsing, use the tidy extension. It provides an interface to the popular libtidy HTML cleanup library. Once tidy has cleaned up your HTML, you can use its methods for getting at parts of the document. Or if you've told tidy to convert your HTML to XHTML, you can use all of the XML manipulation power of SimpleXML or the DOM extension to slice and dice your HTML document.

See Also

Recipe 13.9 for information on marking up a web page and Recipe 13.11 for extracting links from an HTML file; documentation on `preg_match( )` at *http://www.php.net/preg-match* and on tidy at *http://www.php.net/tidy*.

22.7 Preventing Parentheses from Capturing Text

Problem

You've used parentheses for grouping in a pattern, but you don't want the text that matches what's in the parentheses to show up in your array of captured matches.

Solution

Put ?: just after the opening parenthesis, as in Example 22-13.

Example 22-13. Preventing text capture

```php
<?php
$html = '<link rel="icon" href="http://www.example.com/icon.gif"/>
<link rel="prev" href="http://www.example.com/prev.xml"/>
<link rel="next" href="http://www.example.com/next.xml"/>';

preg_match_all('/rel="(prev|next)" href="([^"]*?)"/', $html, $bothMatches);
preg_match_all('/rel="(?:prev|next)" href="([^"]*?)"/', $html, $linkMatches);

print '$bothMatches is: '; var_dump($bothMatches);
print '$linkMatches is: '; var_dump($linkMatches);

?>
```

In Example 22-13, $bothMatches contains the values of the rel and the href attributes. $linkMatches, however, just contains the values of the href attributes. The code prints:

```
$bothMatches is: array(3) {
  [0]=>
  array(2) {
    [0]=>
    string(49) "rel="prev" href="http://www.example.com/prev.xml""
    [1]=>
    string(49) "rel="next" href="http://www.example.com/next.xml""
  }
  [1]=>
  array(2) {
    [0]=>
    string(4) "prev"
    [1]=>
    string(4) "next"
  }
  [2]=>
  array(2) {
    [0]=>
    string(31) "http://www.example.com/prev.xml"
    [1]=>
    string(31) "http://www.example.com/next.xml"
  }
}
$linkMatches is: array(2) {
  [0]=>
```

```
  array(2) {
    [0]=>
    string(49) "rel="prev" href="http://www.example.com/prev.xml""
    [1]=>
    string(49) "rel="next" href="http://www.example.com/next.xml""
  }
  [1]=>
  array(2) {
    [0]=>
    string(31) "http://www.example.com/prev.xml"
    [1]=>
    string(31) "http://www.example.com/next.xml"
  }
}
```

Discussion

Preventing capturing is particularly useful when a subpattern is optional. Since it might not show up in the array of captured text, an optional subpattern can change the number of pieces of captured text. This makes it hard to reference a particular matched piece of text at a given index. Making optional subpatterns non-capturing prevents this problem. Example 22-14 illustrates this distinction.

Example 22-14. A non-capturing optional subpattern

```php
<?php
$html = '<link rel="icon" href="http://www.example.com/icon.gif"/>
<link rel="prev" title="Previous" href="http://www.example.com/prev.xml"/>
<link rel="next" href="http://www.example.com/next.xml"/>';

preg_match_all('/rel="(?:prev|next)"(?: title="[^"]+?")? href=
"([^"]*?)"/', $html, $linkMatches);

print '$bothMatches is: '; var_dump($linkMatches);
?>
```

See Also

The PCRE Pattern Syntax documentation at *http://php.net/reference.pcre.pattern.syn tax*.

22.8 Escaping Special Characters in a Regular Expression

Problem

You want to have characterssuch as * or + treated as literals, not as metacharacters, inside a regular expression. This is useful when allowing users to type in search strings you want to use inside a regular expression.

Solution

Use `preg_quote( )` to escape Perl-compatible regular-expression metacharacters:

```php
<?php
$pattern = preg_quote('The Education of H*Y*M*A*N K*A*P*L*A*N').':(\d+)';
if (preg_match("/$pattern/",$book_rank,$matches)) {
    print "Leo Rosten's book ranked: ".$matches[1];
}
?>
```

Use `quotemeta( )` to escape POSIX metacharacters:

```php
$pattern = quotemeta('M*A*S*H').':[0-9]+';
if (ereg($pattern,$tv_show_rank,$matches)) {
    print 'Radar, Hot Lips, and the gang ranked: '.$matches[1];
}
```

Discussion

Here are the characters that `preg_quote( )` escapes:

. \ + * ? ^ $ [ ] ( ) { } < > = ! | :

Here are the characters that `quotemeta( )` escapes:

. \ + * ? ^ $ [ ] ( )

These functions escape the metacharacters with backslash.

The `quotemeta( )` function doesn't match all POSIX metacharacters. The characters {, }, and | are also valid metacharacters but aren't converted. This is another good reason to use `preg_match( )` instead of `ereg( )`.

You can also pass `preg_quote( )` an additional character to escape as a second argument. It's useful to pass your pattern delimiter (usually /) as this argument so it also gets escaped. This is important if you incorporate user input into a regular expression pattern. The following code expects `$_GET['search_term']` from a web form and searches for words beginning with `$_GET['search_term']` in a string `$s`:

```php
$search_term = preg_quote($_GET['search_term'],'/');
if (preg_match("/\b$search_term/i",$s)) {
    print 'match!';
}
```

Using `preg_quote( )` ensures the regular expression is interpreted properly if, for example, a *Magnum, P.I.* fan enters `t.c` as a search term. Without `preg_quote( )`, this matches `tic`, `tucker`, and any other words whose first letter is `t` and third letter is `c`. Passing the pattern delimiter to `preg_quote( )` as well makes sure that user input with forward slashes in it, such as `CP/M`, is also handled correctly.

See Also

Documentation on `preg_quote( )` at *http://www.php.net/preg-quote* and `quotemeta( )` at *http://www.php.net/quotemeta*.

22.9 Reading Records with a Pattern Separator

Problem

You want to read in records from a file, in which each record is separated by a pattern you can match with a regular expression.

Solution

Read the entire file into a string and then split on the regular expression:

```
$filename = '/path/to/your/file.txt';
$fh = fopen($filename, 'r') or die($php_errormsg);
$contents = fread($fh, filesize($filename));
fclose($fh);

$records = preg_split('/[0-9]+\) /', $contents);
```

Discussion

This breaks apart a numbered list and places the individual list items into array elements. So if you have a list like this:

```
1) Gödel
2) Escher
3) Bach
```

You end up with a four-element array, with an empty opening element. That's because `preg_split( )` assumes the delimiters are between items, but in this case, the numbers are before items:

```
Array
(
    [0] =>
    [1] => Gödel
    [2] => Escher
    [3] => Bach
)
```

From one point of view, this can be a feature, not a bug, since the *n*th element holds the *n*th item. But, to compact the array, you can eliminate the first element:

```
$records = preg_split('/[0-9]+\) /', $contents);
array_shift($records);
```

Another modification you might want is to strip newlines from the elements and substitute the empty string instead:

```
$records = preg_split('/[0-9]+\) /', str_replace("\n",'',$contents));
array_shift($records);
```

PHP doesn't allow you to change the input record separator to anything other than a newline, so this technique is also useful for breaking apart records divided by strings. However, if you find yourself splitting on a string instead of a regular expression, substitute `explode( )` for `preg_split( )` for a more efficient operation.

See Also

Recipe 23.5 for reading from a file; Recipe 1.11 for parsing CSV files.

22.10 Using a PHP Function in a Regular Expression

Problem

You want to process matched text with a PHP function. For example, you want to decode all HTML entities in captured subpatterns.

Solution

Use `preg_replace_callback( )`. Instead of a replacement pattern, give it a callback function. This callback function is passed an array of matched subpatterns and should return an appropriate replacement string. Example 22-15 decodes entities between `<code></code>` tags.

Example 22-15. Generating replacement strings with a callback function

```
<?php
$html = 'The &lt;b&gt; tag makes text bold: <code>&lt;b&gt;bold&lt;/b&gt;</code>';
print preg_replace_callback('@<code>(.*?)</code>@','decode', $html);

// $matches[0] is the entire matched string
// $matches[1] is the first captured subpattern
function decode($matches) {
    return html_entity_decode($matches[1]);
}
?>
```

Example 22-15 prints:

```
The &lt;b&gt; tag makes text bold: <b>bold</b>
```

Discussion

The second argument to `preg_replace_callback( )` specifies the function that is to be called to calculate replacement strings. Like everywhere the PHP "callback" pseudotype is used, this argument can be a string or an array. Use a string to specify a function name. To use an object instance method as a callback, pass an array whose first element is the object and whose second element is a string containing the method name. To use a static class method as a callback, pass an array of two strings: the class name and the method name.

The callback function is passed one argument: an array of matches. Element 0 of this array is always the text that matched the entire pattern. If the pattern given to `preg_replace_callback( )` has any parenthesized subpatterns, these are present in subsequent elements of the matches array. The keys of the matches array are numeric, even if there are named subpatterns in the pattern.

The PHP manpage on `preg_replace_callback( )` suggests using `create_function( )` to create an anonymous function for use as a callback. Although this can be convenient, it is memory intensive if the call to `create_function( )` is inline with the call to `preg_replace_callback( )` and inside a loop. If you want to use an anonymous function with `preg_replace_callback( )`, call `create_function( )` once, storing the anonymous function callback in a variable. Then, provide the variable to `preg_replace_callback( )` as the callback function. Example 22-16 uses an anonymous function to apply the transformation in Example 22-15 to every line in a file.

Example 22-16. Generating replacement strings with an anonymous function

```php
<?php
$callbackFunction = create_function('$matches',
                        'return html_entity_decode($matches[1]);');
$fp = fopen('html-to-decode.html','r');
while (! feof($fp)) {
    $line = fgets($fp);
    print preg_replace_callback('@<code>(.*?)</code>@',$callbackFunction, $line);
}
fclose($fp);
?>
```

An alternative to `preg_replace_callback( )` is to use the e pattern modifier. This causes the replacement string to be evaluated as PHP code. We recommend you use `preg_replace_callback( )` instead, though, for the backreference-related reasons explained below.

Example 22-17 uses the e pattern modifier to do the same entity decoding in Example 22-15.

Example 22-17. Entity encoding matched text

```php
<?php
$html = 'The &lt;b&gt; tag makes text bold: <code>&lt;b&gt;bold&lt;/b&gt;</code>';
print preg_replace('@<code>(.*?)</code>@e',"html_entity_decode('$1')", $html);
?>
```

Things can get a bit tricky when you use the e modifier and include backreferences in the replacement string. There are multiple levels of escaping to be aware of (and, in some cases, to work around).

The first level of escaping is PHP's regular behavior that's at work whenever you construct a string. (Note that in Example 22-17, however, since $1 isn't a valid regular variable name, the $ doesn't need to be escaped even though the entire replacement string is delimited by double quotes.

The second level of escaping is how backreference replacements are delimited inside the replacement string. In Example 22-17, `html_entity_decode('$1')` becomes `html_entity_decode('<code>&lt;b&gt;bold&lt;/b&gt;</code>')`. This causes `html_entity_decode( )` to be called with one argument, a single-quoted string.

Both single and double quotes in the captured match are backslash escaped. The backreference replacements look a little different when they themselves contain single or double quotes. For instance, examine Example 22-18.

Example 22-18. Quote escaping in backreference replacements

```
<?php
$html = "<code>&lt;b&gt; It's bold &lt;/b&gt;</code>";
print preg_replace('@<code>(.*?)</code>@e',"html_entity_decode('$1')", $html);
print "\n";

$html = '<code>&lt;i&gt; "This" is italic. &lt;/i&gt;</code>';
print preg_replace('@<code>(.*?)</code>@e',"html_entity_decode('$1')", $html);
print "\n";
?>
```

Example 22-18 prints:

```
<b> It's bold </b>
<i> \"This\" is italic. </i>
```

Somehow, backslashes have crept into the second line. This is a consequence of how the e modifier works. As mentioned above, *both single and double quotes in the captured match are backslash escaped*. This means that, in the first call to `preg_replace( )` in Example 22-18, what's executed to calculate the replacement is:

```
html_entity_decode('<code>&lt;b&gt; It\'s bold &lt;/b&gt;</code>)
```

`html_entity_decode( )` is passed a single-quoted string with a backslash-escaped single quote in it. All is well—`'It\'s'` is really just `It's`. The second `preg_replace( )`, however, is problematic. What's executed to calculate the replacement is `html_entity_decode ('<code>&lt;i&gt; \"This\" is italic. &lt;/i&gt;</code>')`. In a single-quoted string, a backslash before a double quote represents not a literal backslash, but the two character sequence `\"`.

To work around this problem, use `str_replace( )` to replace `\"` with `"` in your code that's executed to calculate the replacement. (Don't use `stripslashes( )`—it also removes backslashes before other characters, which we don't want here.) Example 22-19 wraps `html_entity_decode( )` with a function that does just that.

Example 22-19. Fixing quote escaping in backreference replacements

```
<?php
$html = "<code>&lt;b&gt; It's bold &lt;/b&gt;</code>";
print preg_replace('@<code>(.*?)</code>@e',"preg_html_entity_decode('$1')", $html);
```

```
    print "\n";

    $html = '<code>&lt;i&gt; "This" is italic. &lt;/i&gt;</code>';
    print preg_replace('@<code>(.*?)</code>@e',"preg_html_entity_decode('$1')", $html);
    print "\n";

    function preg_html_entity_decode($s) {
        $s = str_replace('\\"','"', $s);
        return html_entity_decode($s);
    }
    ?>
```

The use of the `preg_html_entity_decode( )` function in Example 22-19 ensures that it prints correct results:

```
<b> It's bold </b>
<i> "This" is italic. </i>
```

One final note on escaping and the e pattern modifier: inside your replacement-calcu-lating expression, make sure to use single quotes (not double quotes) to delimit any strings that include backreference values. That is, use `preg_html_entity_decode('$1')`, not `preg_html_entity_decode("$1")`. Double quotes cause problems if the backreference value contains what looks like a valid variable name. Example 22-20 illustrates this problem.

Example 22-20. Variable names and double-quoted strings

```
    <?php
    $text = '<code>if ($temperature &lt; 12) { fever(); }</code>';
    print "Good: \n";
    print preg_replace('@<code>(.*?)</code>@e',"preg_html_entity_decode('$1')", $text);
    print "\n Bad: \n";
    print preg_replace('@<code>(.*?)</code>@e','preg_html_entity_decode("$1")' , $text);

    function preg_html_entity_decode($s) {
        $s = str_replace('\\"','"', $s);
        return html_entity_decode($s);
    }
    ?>
```

Example 22-20 prints:

```
Good:
if ($temperature < 12) { fever(); }
 Bad:

Notice: Undefined variable: temperature in example.php(6) : regexp code on line 1
if ( < 12) { fever(); }
```

With appropriate quoting, the first `preg_replace( )` works as expected: the only mod-ification to $text is that < is replaced by <. The second `preg_replace( )`, with double quotes around $1, is broken. The PHP interpreter thinks that the string to be passed to `preg_html_entity_decode( )` is "if ($temperature < 12) { fever( ); }". Since that's a double-quoted string, the PHP interpreter attempts to replace `$temperature` with the value of the corresponding variable, which, of course, doesn't exist.

So the moral of the "using the e modifier with `preg_replace( )`" story is twofold: correct for backslash-escaped double-quote characters and use single quotes to delimit strings inside your code expression to avoid accidental variable interpolation. This tricky quoting and interpolation behavior makes `preg_replace_callback( )` a friendlier option.

See Also

Documentation on `preg_replace_callback( )` at *http://www.php.net/preg_replace_callback*, on `preg_replace( )` at *http://www.php.net/preg_replace*, on `create_function( )` at *http://www.php.net/create_function*, and on the callback pseudo-type at *http://www.php.net/language.pseudo-types#language.types.callback*.

CHAPTER 23

Files

23.0 Introduction

The input and output in a web application usually flow between browser, server, and database, but there are many circumstances in which files are involved too. Files are useful for retrieving remote web pages for local processing, storing data without a database, and saving information that other programs need access to. Plus, as PHP becomes a tool for more than just pumping out web pages, the file I/O functions are even more useful.

PHP's interface for file I/O is similar to that of C, although less complicated. The fundamental unit of identifying a file to read from or write to is a filehandle. This handle identifies your connection to a specific file, and you use it for operations on the file. This chapter focuses on opening and closing files and manipulating filehandles in PHP, as well as what you can do with the file contents once you've opened a file. Chapter 24 deals with directories and file metadata such as permissions.

The code in Example 23-1 opens */tmp/cookie-data* and writes the contents of a specific cookie to the file.

Example 23-1. Writing data to a file

```php
<?php
$fh = fopen('/tmp/cookie-data','w')         or die("can't open file");
if (-1 == fwrite($fh,$_COOKIE['flavor'])) { die("can't write data"); }
fclose($fh)                                 or die("can't close file");
?>
```

The function fopen( ) returns a filehandle if its attempt to open the file is successful. If it can't open the file (because of incorrect permissions, for example), it returns false and generates an E_WARNING-type error. Recipes 23.1 through 23.3 cover ways to open files.

In Example 23-1, fwrite( ) writes the value of the flavor cookie to the filehandle. It returns the number of bytes written. If it can't write the string (not enough disk space, for example), it returns -1.

Last, `fclose( )` closes the filehandle. This is done automatically at the end of a request, but it's a good idea to explicitly close all files you open anyway. It prevents problems using the code in a command-line context and frees up system resources. It also allows you to check the return code from `fclose( )`. Buffered data might not actually be written to disk until `fclose( )` is called, so it's here that "disk full" errors are sometimes reported.

As with other processes, PHP must have the correct permissions to read from and write to a file. This is usually straightforward in a command-line context but can cause confusion when running scripts within a web server. Your web server (and consequently your PHP script) probably runs as a specific user dedicated to web serving (or perhaps as user nobody). For good security reasons, this user often has restricted permissions on what files it can access. If your script is having trouble with a file operation, make sure the web server's user or group—not yours—has permission to perform that file operation. Some web serving setups may run your script as you, though, in which case you need to make sure that your scripts can't accidentally read or write personal files that aren't part of your web site.

Because most file-handling functions just return `false` on error, you have to do some additional work to find more details about that error. When the `track_errors` configuration directive is `on`, each error message is put in the global variable `$php_errormsg`. Including this variable as part of your error output makes debugging easier, as shown in Example 23-2.

Example 23-2. Using file-related error information

```php
<?php
$fh = fopen('/tmp/cookie-data','w')        or die("can't open: $php_errormsg");
if (-1 == fwrite($fh,$_COOKIE['flavor'])) { die("can't write: $php_errormsg") };
fclose($fh)                                or die("can't close: $php_errormsg");
?>
```

If you don't have permission to write to the */tmp/cookie-data*, Example 23-2 dies with this error output:

```
can't open: fopen("/tmp/cookie-data", "w") - Permission denied
```

Windows and Unix treat files differently. To ensure your file access code works appropriately on Unix and Windows, take care to handle line-delimiter characters and pathnames correctly.

A line delimiter on Windows is two characters: ASCII 13 (carriage return) followed by ASCII 10 (line feed or newline). On Unix, it's just ASCII 10. The typewriter-era names for these characters explain why you can get "stair-stepped" text when printing out a Unix-delimited file. Imagine these character names as commands to the platen in a typewriter or character-at-a-time printer. A carriage return sends the platen back to the beginning of the line it's on, and a line feed advances the paper by one line. A misconfigured printer encountering a Unix-delimited file dutifully follows instructions and does a line feed at the end of each line. This advances to the next line but doesn't move the horizontal printing position back to the left margin. The next stair-stepped line of text begins (horizontally) where the previous line left off.

PHP functions that use a newline as a line-ending delimiter (for example, `fgets( )`) work on both Windows and Unix because a newline is the character at the end of the line on either platform.

To remove any line-delimiter characters, use the PHP function `rtrim( )`, as shown in Example 23-3.

Example 23-3. Trimming trailing whitespace

```php
<?php
$fh = fopen('/tmp/lines-of-data.txt','r') or die($php_errormsg);
while($s = fgets($fh)) {
    $s = rtrim($s);
    // do something with $s ...
}
fclose($fh)                              or die($php_errormsg);
?>
```

This function removes any trailing whitespace in the line, including ASCII 13 and ASCII 10 (as well as tab and space). If there's whitespace at the end of a line that you want to preserve, but you still want to remove carriage returns and line feeds, provide `rtrim( )` with a string containing the characters that it should remove. Other characters are left untouched. This is shown in Example 23-4.

Example 23-4. Trimming trailing line-ending characters

```php
<?php
$fh = fopen('/tmp/lines-of-data.txt','r') or die($php_errormsg);
while($s = fgets($fh)) {
    $s = rtrim($s, "\r\n");
    // do something with $s ...
}
fclose($fh)                              or die($php_errormsg);
?>
```

Unix and Windows also differ on the character used to separate directories in pathnames. Unix uses a slash (/), and Windows uses a backslash (\). PHP makes sorting this out easy, however, because the Windows version of PHP also understands / as a directory separator. For example, Example 23-5 successfully prints the contents of *C:\Alligator\Crocodile Menu.txt*.

Example 23-5. Using forward slashes on Windows

```php
<?php
$fh = fopen('c:/alligator/crocodile menu.txt','r') or die($php_errormsg);
while($s = fgets($fh)) {
    print $s;
}
fclose($fh)                              or die($php_errormsg);
?>
```

Example 23-5 also takes advantage of the fact that Windows filenames aren't case-sensitive. However, Unix filenames are.

Sorting out line-break confusion isn't only a problem in your code that reads and writes files but in your source code files as well. If you have multiple people working on a project, make sure all developers configure their editors to use the same kind of line breaks.

Once you've opened a file, PHP gives you many tools to process its data. In keeping with PHP's C-like I/O interface, the two basic functions to read data from a file are `fread( )`, which reads a specified number of bytes, and `fgets( )`, which reads a line at a time (up to an optional specified number of bytes). Example 23-6 handles lines up to 256 bytes long.

Example 23-6. Reading lines from a file

```php
<?php
$fh = fopen('orders.txt','r') or die($php_errormsg);
while (! feof($fh)) {
    $s = fgets($fh,256);
    process_order($s);
}
fclose($fh)                      or die($php_errormsg);
?>
```

If *orders.txt* has a 300-byte line, `fgets( )` returns only the first 256 bytes. The next `fgets( )` returns the next 44 bytes and stops when it finds the newline. The next `fgets( )` after that moves to the next line of the file. Without the second argument, `fgets( )` reads until it reaches the end of the line. (With PHP versions before 4.2.0, a line length is required. From PHP 4.2.0 up to 4.3.0, the length defaults to 1,024 if not specified.)

Many operations on file contents, such as picking a line at random (see Recipe 23.8) are conceptually simpler (and require less code) if the entire file is read into a string or array. The `file_get_contents( )` function reads an entire file into a string, and the `file( )` function puts each line of a file into an array. The trade-off for simplicity, however, is memory consumption. This can be especially harmful when you are using PHP as a server module. Generally, when a process (such as a web server process with PHP embedded in it) allocates memory (as PHP does to read an entire file into a string or array), it can't return that memory to the operating system until it dies. This means that calling `file_get_contents( )` on a 1 MB file from PHP running as an Apache module increases the size of that Apache process by 1 MB until the process dies. Repeated a few times, this decreases server efficiency. There are certainly good reasons for processing an entire file at once, but be conscious of the memory-use implications when you do.

Recipes 23.17 through 23.19 deal with running other programs from within a PHP program. Some program execution operators or functions offer ways to run a program and read its output all at once (backticks) or read its last line of output (`system( )`). PHP can use pipes to run a program, pass it input, or read its output. Because a pipe is read with standard I/O functions (`fgets( )` and `fread( )`), you decide how you want the input and you can do other tasks between reading chunks of input. Similarly, writing to a pipe is done with `fputs( )` and `fwrite( )`, so you can pass input to a program in arbitrary increments.

Pipes have the same permission issues as regular files. The PHP process must have execute permission on the program being opened as a pipe. If you have trouble opening a pipe, especially if PHP is running as a special web server user, make sure the user is allowed to execute the program to which you are opening a pipe.

23.1 Creating or Opening a Local File

Problem

You want to open a local file to read data from it or write data to it.

Solution

Use `fopen( )`, as in Example 23-7.

Example 23-7. Opening a file

```php
<?php
$fh = fopen('file.txt','r') or die("can't open file.txt: $php_errormsg");
?>
```

Discussion

The first argument to `fopen( )` is the file to open; the second argument is the mode in which to open the file. The mode specifies what operations can be performed on the file (reading and/or writing), where the file pointer is placed after the file is opened (at the beginning or end of the file), whether the file is truncated to zero length after opening, and whether the file is created if it doesn't exist, as shown in Table 23-1.

Table 23-1. fopen( ) file modes

Mode	Readable?	Writable?	File pointer	Truncate?	Create?
r	Yes	No	Beginning	No	No
r+	Yes	Yes	Beginning	No	No
w	No	Yes	Beginning	Yes	Yes
w+	Yes	Yes	Beginning	Yes	Yes
a	No	Yes	End	No	Yes
a+	Yes	Yes	End	No	Yes
x	No	Yes	Beginning	No	Yes
x+	Yes	Yes	Beginning	No	Yes

The x and x+ modes return `false` and generate a warning if the file already exists. They are available in PHP 4.3.2 and later.

On non-POSIX systems, such as Windows, you need to add a `b` to the mode when opening a binary file (as shown in Example 23-8), or reads and writes get tripped up on NUL (ASCII 0) characters.

Example 23-8. Safely reading a binary file

```php
<?php
$fh = fopen('c:/images/logo.gif','rb');
?>
```

Even though Unix systems handle binary files fine without the `b` in the mode, it's a good idea to use it always. That way, your code is maximally portable and runs well on both Unix and Windows.

To operate on a file, pass the filehandle returned from `fopen( )` to other I/O functions such as `fgets( )`, `fputs( )`, and `fclose( )`.

If the file given to `fopen( )` doesn't have a pathname, the file is opened in the directory of the running script (web context) or in the current directory (command-line context).

You can also tell `fopen( )` to search for the file to open in the `include_path` specified in your *php.ini* file by passing `true` as a third argument. Example 23-9 searches for *file.inc* in the `include_path`.

Example 23-9. Opening files in the include_path

```php
<?php
$fh = fopen('file.inc','r',true) or die("can't open file.inc: $php_errormsg");
?>
```

See Also

Documentation on `fopen( )` at *http://www.php.net/fopen*.

23.2 Creating a Temporary File

Problem

You need a file to temporarily hold some data.

Solution

Use `tmpfile( )`, as in Example 23-10, if the file needs to last only the duration of the running script.

Example 23-10. Creating a temporary file with tmpfile( )

```php
<?php
$temp_fh = tmpfile();
```

```
// write some data to the temp file
fputs($temp_fh,"The current time is ".strftime('%c'));
// the file goes away when the script ends
exit(1);
?>
```

If the file needs to last longer, generate a filename with tempnam( ), and then use fopen( ), as in Example 23-11.

Example 23-11. Creating a temporary file with tempnam()

```
<?php
$tempfilename = tempnam('/tmp','data-');
$temp_fh = fopen($tempfilename,'w') or die($php_errormsg);
fputs($temp_fh,"The current time is ".strftime('%c'));
fclose($temp_fh) or die($php_errormsg);
?>
```

Discussion

The tmpfile( ) function creates a file with a unique name and returns a filehandle. The file is removed when fclose( ) is called on that file handle, or the script ends.

Alternatively, tempnam( ) generates a filename. It takes two arguments: the first is a directory, and the second is a prefix for the filename. If the directory doesn't exist or isn't writable, tempnam( ) uses the system temporary directory—the TMPDIR environment variable in Unix or the TMP environment variable in Windows. Example 23-12 shows what tempnam( ) generates.

Example 23-12. Generating a filename with tempnam()

```
<?php
$tempfilename = tempnam('/tmp','data-');
print "Temporary data will be stored in $tempfilename";
?>
```

Example 23-12 prints:

```
Temporary data will be stored in /tmp/data-GawVoL
```

Because of the way PHP generates temporary filenames, a file with the filename that tempnam( ) returns is actually created but left empty, even if your script never explicitly opens the file. This ensures another program won't create a file with the same name between the time that you call tempnam( ) and the time you call fopen( ) with the filename.

See Also

Documentation on tmpfile( ) at *http://www.php.net/tmpfile* and on tempnam( ) at *http://www.php.net/tempnam*.

23.3 Opening a Remote File

Problem

You want to open a file that's accessible to you via HTTP or FTP.

Solution

Pass the file's URL to fopen( ), as in Example 23-13.

Example 23-13. Opening a remote file

```php
<?php
$fh = fopen('http://www.example.com/robots.txt','r') or die($php_errormsg);
?>
```

Discussion

When fopen( ) is passed a filename that begins with *http://*, it retrieves the given page with an HTTP/1.0 GET request (although a Host: header is also passed along to deal with virtual hosts). Only the body of the reply can be accessed using the filehandle, not the headers. Files can be read, not written, via HTTP.

When fopen( ) is passed a filename that begins with *ftp://*, it returns a pointer to the specified file, obtained via passive-mode FTP. You can open files via FTP for either reading or writing, but not both.

To open URLs that require a username and a password with fopen( ), embed the authentication information in the URL as shown in Example 23-14.

Example 23-14. Using a password with FTP or HTTP

```php
<?php
$fh = fopen('ftp://username:password@ftp.example.com/pub/Index','r');
$fh = fopen('http://username:password@www.example.com/robots.txt','r');
?>
```

Opening remote files with fopen( ) is implemented via a PHP feature called the *stream wrapper*. It's enabled by default but is disabled by setting allow_url_fopen to off in your *php.ini* or web server configuration file. If you can't open remote files with fopen( ), check your server configuration.

See Also

Recipes 13.1 through 13.7, which discuss retrieving URLs; documentation on fopen( ) at *http://www.php.net/fopen* and on stream wrappers at *http://www.php.net/ features.remote-files* and *http://www.php.net/wrappers*.

23.4 Reading from Standard Input

Problem

You want to read from standard input in a command-line context—for example, to get user input from the keyboard or data piped to your PHP program.

Solution

Use fopen( ) to open *php://stdin*, as in Example 23-15.

Example 23-15. Reading from standard input

```
<?php
$fh = fopen('php://stdin','r') or die($php_errormsg);
while($s = fgets($fh)) {
    print "You typed: $s";
}
?>
```

Discussion

Recipe 25.3 discusses reading data from the keyboard in a command-line context in more detail. Reading data from standard input isn't very useful in a web context, because information doesn't arrive via standard input. The bodies of HTTP post and file-upload requests are parsed by PHP and put into special variables. Non-file-upload post request bodies can also be read with the php://input stream, as discussed in Recipe 8.7.

See Also

Recipe 25.3 for reading from the keyboard in a command-line context; Recipe 8.7 for reading POST request bodies; documentation on fopen( ) at *http://www.php.net/fopen*.

23.5 Reading a File into a String

Problem

You want to load the entire contents of a file into a variable. For example, you want to determine if the text in a file matches a regular expression.

Solution

Use file_get_contents( ), as shown in Example 23-16.

Example 23-16. Reading a file into a string

```
<?php
$people = file_get_contents('people.txt');
```

```php
if (preg_match('/Names:.*(David|Susannah)/i',$people)) {
    print "people.txt matches.";
}
?>
```

Discussion

If you want the contents of a file in a string to manipulate, file_get_contents( ) is great, but if you just want to print the entire contents of a file, there are easier (and more efficient) ways than reading it into a string and then printing the string. PHP provides two functions for this. The first is fpassthru($fh), which prints everything left on the file handle $fh and then closes it. The second, readfile($filename), prints the entire contents of $filename.

You can use readfile( ) to implement a wrapper around images that shouldn't always be displayed. The program in Example 23-17 makes sure a requested image is less than a week old.

Example 23-17. Displaying recent images

```php
<?php
$image_directory = '/usr/local/images';

if (preg_match('/^[a-zA-Z0-9]+\.(gif|jpe?g)$/',$image,$matches) &&
    is_readable($image_directory."/$image") &&
    (filemtime($image_directory."/$image") >= (time() - 86400 * 7))) {

    header('Content-Type: image/'.$matches[1]);
    header('Content-Length: '.filesize($image_directory."/$image"));

    readfile($image_directory."/$image");

} else {
    error_log("Can't serve image: $image");
}
?>
```

The directory in which the images are stored, $image_directory, needs to be outside the web server's document root for the wrapper to be effective. Otherwise, users can just access the image files directly. The code tests the image file for three things. First, that the filename passed in $image is just alphanumeric with an ending of either *.gif*, *.jpg*, or *.jpeg*. We need to ensure that characters such as .. or / are not in the filename; this prevents malicious users from retrieving files outside the specified directory. Second, we use is_readable( ) to make sure the program can read the file. Finally, we get the file's modification time with filemtime( ) and make sure that time is after 86,400 × 7 seconds ago. There are 86,400 seconds in a day, so 86,400 × 7 is a week.[*] If all of these conditions are met, we're ready to send the image. First, we send two headers to tell

[*] When switching between standard time and daylight saving time, there are not 86,400 seconds in a day. See Recipe 3.12 for details.

the browser the image's MIME type and file size. Then we use `readfile( )` to send the entire contents of the file to the user.

See Also

Documentation on `filesize( )` at *http://www.php.net/filesize*, `fread( )` at *http://www.php.net/fread*, `fpassthru( )` at *http://www.php.net/fpassthru*, and `readfile( )` at *http://www.php.net/readfile*.

23.6 Counting Lines, Paragraphs, or Records in a File

Problem

You want to count the number of lines, paragraphs, or records in a file.

Solution

To count lines, use `fgets( )`, as in Example 23-18. Because it reads a line at a time, you can count the number of times it's called before reaching the end of a file.

Example 23-18. Counting lines in a file

```php
<?php
$lines = 0;

if ($fh = fopen('orders.txt','r')) {
  while (! feof($fh)) {
    if (fgets($fh)) {
      $lines++;
    }
  }
}
print $lines;
?>
```

To count paragraphs, increment the counter only when you read a blank line, as in Example 23-19.

Example 23-19. Counting paragraphs in a file

```php
<?php
$paragraphs = 0;

if ($fh = fopen('great-american-novel.txt','r')) {
  while (! feof($fh)) {
    $s = fgets($fh);
    if (("\n" == $s) || ("\r\n" == $s)) {
      $paragraphs++;
    }
  }
}
```

```php
print $paragraphs;
?>
```

To count records, increment the counter only when the line read contains just the record separator and whitespace. In Example 23-20, the record separator is stored in `$record_separator`.

Example 23-20. Counting records in a file

```php
<?php
$records = 0;
$record_separator = '--end--';

if ($fh = fopen('great-american-textfile-database.txt','r')) {
  while (! feof($fh)) {
    $s = rtrim(fgets($fh));
    if ($s == $record_separator) {
      $records++;
    }
  }
}
print $records;
?>
```

Discussion

In Example 23-18, `$lines` is incremented only if `fgets()` returns a true value. As `fgets()` moves through the file, it returns each line it retrieves. When it reaches the last line, it returns `false`, so `$lines` isn't incremented incorrectly. Because EOF has been reached on the file, `feof()` returns `true`, and the `while` loop ends.

Example 23-19 works fine on simple text but may produce unexpected results when presented with a long string of blank lines or a file without two consecutive line breaks. These problems can be remedied with functions based on `preg_split()`. If the file is small and can be read into memory, use the `pc_split_paragraphs()` function shown in Example 23-21. This function returns an array containing each paragraph in the file.

Example 23-21. pc_split_paragraphs()

```php
<?php
function pc_split_paragraphs($file,$rs="\r?\n") {
    $text = file_get_contents($file);
    $matches = preg_split("/(.*?$rs)(?:$rs)+/s",$text,-1,
                          PREG_SPLIT_DELIM_CAPTURE|PREG_SPLIT_NO_EMPTY);
    return $matches;
}
?>
```

In Example 23-21, the contents of the file are broken on two or more consecutive newlines and returned in the `$matches` array. The default record-separation regular expression, `\r?\n`, matches both Windows and Unix line breaks.

If the file is too big to read into memory at once, use the `pc_split_paragraphs_largefile( )` function shown in Example 23-22, which reads the file in 16 KB chunks.

Example 23-22. pc_split_paragraphs_largefile( )

```php
<?php
function pc_split_paragraphs_largefile($file,$rs="\r?\n") {
    global $php_errormsg;

    $unmatched_text = '';
    $paragraphs = array();

    $fh = fopen($file,'r') or die($php_errormsg);

    while(! feof($fh)) {
        $s = fread($fh,16384) or die($php_errormsg);
        $text_to_split = $unmatched_text . $s;

        $matches = preg_split("/(.*?$rs)(?:$rs)+/s",$text_to_split,-1,
                              PREG_SPLIT_DELIM_CAPTURE|PREG_SPLIT_NO_EMPTY);

        // if the last chunk doesn't end with two record separators, save it
        // to prepend to the next section that gets read
        $last_match = $matches[count($matches)-1];
        if (! preg_match("/$rs$rs\$/",$last_match)) {
            $unmatched_text = $last_match;
            array_pop($matches);
        } else {
            $unmatched_text = '';
        }

        $paragraphs = array_merge($paragraphs,$matches);
    }

    // after reading all sections, if there is a final chunk that doesn't
    // end with the record separator, count it as a paragraph
    if ($unmatched_text) {
        $paragraphs[] = $unmatched_text;
    }
    return $paragraphs;
}
?>
```

This function uses the same regular expression as `pc_split_paragraphs( )` to split the file into paragraphs. When it finds a paragraph end in a chunk read from the file, it saves the rest of the text in the chunk in `$unmatched_text` and prepends it to the next chunk read. This includes the unmatched text as the beginning of the next paragraph in the file.

The record-counting function in Example 23-20 lets `fgets( )` figure out how long each line is. If you can supply a reasonable upper bound on line length, `stream_get_line( )` provides a more concise way to count records. This function reads a line until it reaches a certain number of bytes or it sees a particular delimiter. Supply it with the record separator as the delimiter, as in Example 23-23.

Example 23-23. Counting records in a file with stream_get_line( )

```php
<?php
$records = 0;
$record_separator = '--end--';

if ($fh = fopen('great-american-textfile-database.txt','r')) {
    $done = false;
    while (! $done) {
        $s = stream_get_line($fh, 65536, $record_separator);
        if (feof($fh)) {
            $done = true;
        } else {
            $records++;
        }
    }
}
print $records;
?>
```

Example 23-23 assumes that each record is no more that 64 KB (65,536 bytes) long. Each call to `stream_get_line( )` returns one record, not including the record separator. When `stream_get_line( )` has advanced past the last record separator, it reaches the end of the file, so `$done` is set to `true` to stop counting records.

See Also

Documentation on `fgets( )` at *http://www.php.net/fgets*, on `feof( )` at *http://www.php.net/feof*, on `preg_split( )` at *http://www.php.net/preg-split*, and on `stream_get_line( )` at *http://www.php.net/stream_get_line*.

23.7 Processing Every Word in a File

Problem

You want to do something with every word in a file. For example, you want to build a concordance of how many times each word is used to compute similarities between documents.

Solution

Read in each line with `fgets( )`, separate the line into words, and process each word, as in Example 23-24.

Example 23-24. Processing each word in a file

```php
<?php
$fh = fopen('great-american-novel.txt','r') or die($php_errormsg);
```

```
    while (! feof($fh)) {
        if ($s = fgets($fh)) {
            $words = preg_split('/\s+/',$s,-1,PREG_SPLIT_NO_EMPTY);
            // process words
        }
    }
}
fclose($fh) or die($php_errormsg);
?>
```

Discussion

Example 23-25 calculates the average word length in a file.

Example 23-25. Calculating average word length

```
<?php
$word_count = $word_length = 0;

if ($fh = fopen('great-american-novel.txt','r')) {
  while (! feof($fh)) {
    if ($s = fgets($fh)) {
      $words = preg_split('/\s+/',$s,-1,PREG_SPLIT_NO_EMPTY);
      foreach ($words as $word) {
        $word_count++;
        $word_length += strlen($word);
      }
    }
  }
}

print sprintf("The average word length over %d words is %.02f characters.",
              $word_count,
              $word_length/$word_count);
?>
```

Processing every word proceeds differently depending on how "word" is defined. The code in this recipe uses the Perl-compatible regular expression engine's \s whitespace metacharacter, which includes space, tab, newline, carriage return, and formfeed. Recipe 1.5 breaks apart a line into words by splitting on a space, which is useful in that recipe because the words have to be rejoined with spaces. The Perl-compatible engine also has a word-boundary assertion (\b) that matches between a word character (alphanumeric) and a non-word character (anything else). Using \b instead of \s to delimit words most noticeably treats differently words with embedded punctuation. The term 6 o'clock is two words when split by whitespace (6 and o'clock); it's four words when split by word boundaries (6, o, ', and clock).

See Also

Recipe 22.2 discusses regular expressions to match words; Recipe 1.5 for breaking apart a line by words; documentation on fgets() at *http://www.php.net/fgets*, on preg_split( ) at *http://www.php.net/preg-split*, and on the Perl-compatible regular expression extension at *http://www.php.net/pcre*.

23.8 Picking a Random Line from a File

Problem

You want to pick a line at random from a file; for example, you want to display a selection from a file of sayings.

Solution

Use the pc_randomint( ) function shown in Example 23-26, which spreads the selection odds evenly over all lines in a file.

Example 23-26. Finding a random line of a file

```php
<?php
function pc_randomint($max = 1) {
  $m = 1000000;
  return ((mt_rand(1,$m * $max)-1)/$m);
}
?>

$line_number = 0;

$fh = fopen('sayings.txt','r') or die($php_errormsg);
while (! feof($fh)) {
    if ($s = fgets($fh)) {
        $line_number++;
        if (pc_randomint($line_number) < 1) {
            $line = $s;
        }
    }
}
fclose($fh) or die($php_errormsg);
?>
```

Discussion

The pc_randomint( ) function computes a random decimal number between 0 and $max, including 0 but excluding $max. As each line is read, a line counter is incremented, and pc_randomint( ) generates a random number between 0 and $line_number. If the number is less than 1, the current line is selected as the randomly chosen line. After all lines have been read, the last line that was selected as the randomly chosen line is left in $line.

This algorithm neatly ensures that each line in an *n* line file has a 1/*n* chance of being chosen without having to store all *n* lines into memory.

See Also

Documentation on `mt_rand( )` at *http://www.php.net/mt-rand.*

23.9 Randomizing All Lines in a File

Problem

You want to randomly reorder all lines in a file. You have a file of funny quotes, for example, and you want to pick out one at random.

Solution

Read all the lines in the file into an array with `file( )`, and then shuffle the elements of the array, as in Example 23-27.

Example 23-27. Randomizing all lines in a file

```php
<?php
$lines = file('quotes-of-the-day.txt');
$lines = shuffle($lines);
?>
```

Discussion

The `shuffle( )` function randomly reorders the array elements, so after shuffling, you can pick out `$lines[0]` as a quote to display.

See Also

Recipe 4.20 for `shuffle( )`; documentation on `shuffle( )` at *http://www.php.net/shuffle.*

23.10 Processing Variable-Length Text Fields

Problem

You want to read delimited text fields from a file. You might, for example, have a database program that prints records one per line, with tabs between each field in the record, and you want to parse this data into an array.

Solution

As shown in Example 23-28, read in each line and then split the fields based on their delimiter.

Example 23-28. Processing variable-length text fields

```php
<?php
$delim = '|';
```

```php
$fh = fopen('books.txt','r') or die("can't open: $php_errormsg");
while (! feof($fh)) {
    $s = rtrim(fgets($fh));
    $fields = explode($delim,$s);
    // ... do something with the data ...
}
fclose($fh) or die("can't close: $php_errormsg");
?>
```

Discussion

To parse the following data in *books.txt*:

```
Elmer Gantry|Sinclair Lewis|1927
The Scarlatti Inheritance|Robert Ludlum|1971
The Parsifal Mosaic|Robert Ludlum|1982
Sophie's Choice|William Styron|1979
```

Process each record as shown in Example 23-29.

Example 23-29. Processing a list of books

```php
<?php
$fh = fopen('books.txt','r') or die("can't open: $php_errormsg");
while (! feof($fh)) {
    $s = rtrim(fgets($fh));
    list($title,$author,$publication_year) = explode('|',$s);
    // ... do something with the data ...
}
fclose($fh) or die("can't close: $php_errormsg");
?>
```

If you supply a line-length argument to `fgets()`, it needs to be at least as long as the longest record, so that a record doesn't get truncated.

Calling `rtrim()` is necessary because `fgets()` includes the trailing whitespace in the line it reads. Without `rtrim()`, each `$publication_year` would have a newline at its end.

See Also

Recipe 1.14 discusses ways to break strings into pieces; Recipes 1.11 and 1.13 cover parsing comma-separated and fixed-width data; documentation on `explode()` at *http://www.php.net/explode* and `rtrim()` at *http://www.php.net/rtrim*.

23.11 Reading Configuration Files

Problem

You want to use configuration files to initialize settings in your programs.

Solution

Use `parse_ini_file( )`, as in Example 23-30.

Example 23-30. Parsing a configuration file

```php
<?php
$config = parse_ini_file('/etc/myapp.ini');
?>
```

Discussion

The function `parse_ini_file( )` reads configuration files structured like PHP's main *php.ini* file. Instead of applying the settings in the configuration file to PHP's configuration, however, `parse_ini_file( )` returns the values from the file in an array.

For example, when `parse_ini_file( )` is given a file with these contents:

```
; physical features
eyes=brown
hair=brown
glasses=yes

; other features
name=Susannah
likes=monkeys,ice cream,reading
```

The array it returns is:

```
Array
(
    [eyes] => brown
    [hair] => brown
    [glasses] => 1
    [name] => Susannah
    [likes] => monkeys,ice cream,reading
)
```

Blank lines and lines that begin with ; in the configuration file are ignored. Other lines with `name=value` pairs are put into an array with the name as the key and the value, appropriately, as the value. Words such as `on` and `yes` as values are returned as `1`, and words such as `off` and `no` are returned as the empty string.

To parse sections from the configuration file, pass `1` as a second argument to `parse_ini_file( )`. Sections are set off by words in square brackets in the file:

```
[physical]
eyes=brown
hair=brown
glasses=yes

[other]
name=Susannah
likes=monkeys,ice cream,reading
```

If this file is in */etc/myapp.ini*, then:

```
$conf = parse_ini_file('/etc/myapp.ini',1);
```

puts this array in $conf:

```
Array
(
    [physical] => Array
        (
            [eyes] => brown
            [hair] => brown
            [glasses] => 1
        )

    [other] => Array
        (
            [name] => Susannah
            [likes] => monkeys,ice cream,reading
        )

)
```

Another approach to configuration is to make your configuration file a valid PHP file that you load with require instead of parse_ini_file( ). If the file *config.php* contains:

```php
<?php

// physical features
$eyes = 'brown';
$hair = 'brown';
$glasses = 'yes';

// other features
$name = 'Susannah';
$likes = array('monkeys','ice cream','reading');
?>
```

You can set the variables $eyes, $hair, $glasses, $name, and $likes with a simple require 'config.php';.

The configuration file loaded by require needs to be valid PHP—including the <?php start tag and the ?> end tag. The variables named in *config.php* are set explicitly, not inside an array, as in parse_ini_file( ). For simple configuration files, this technique may not be worth the extra attention to syntax, but it is useful for embedding logic in the configuration file, such as the statement in Example 23-31.

Example 23-31. Logic in a configuration file

```php
<?php

$time_of_day = (date('a') == 'am') ? 'early' : 'late';

?>
```

See Also

Documentation on `parse_ini_file()` at *http://www.php.net/parse-ini-file*.

23.12 Modifying a File in Place Without a Temporary File

Problem

You want to change a file without using a temporary file to hold the changes.

Solution

Read the file with `file_get_contents()`, make the changes, and rewrite the file with `file_put_contents()`. This is shown in Example 23-32.

Example 23-32. Changing a file in place

```php
<?php
$contents = file_get_contents('pickles.txt');
$contents = strtoupper($contents);
file_put_contents('pickles.txt', $contents);
?>
```

Discussion

Example 23-33 turns text emphasized with asterisks or slashes into text with HTML `<b>` or `<i>` tags.

Example 23-33. HTML-ifying a file in place

```php
<?php
$contents = file_get_contents('message.txt');
// convert *word* to <b>word</b>
$contents = preg_replace('@\*(.*?)\*@i','<b>$1</b>',$contents);
// convert /word/ to <i>word</i>
$contents = preg_replace('@/(.*?)/@i','<i>$1</i>',$contents);
file_put_contents('message.txt', $contents);
```

Because adding HTML tags makes the file grow, the entire file has to be read into memory and then processed. If the changes to a file make each line shrink (or stay the same size), the file can be processed line by line, saving memory. Example 23-34 converts text marked with `<b>` and `<i>` to text marked with asterisks and slashes.

Example 23-34. Text-ifying a file in place

```php
<?php
$fh = fopen('message.txt','r+')          or die($php_errormsg);

// figure out how many bytes to read
$bytes_to_read = filesize('message.txt');

// initialize variables that hold file positions
```

```
$next_read = $last_write = 0;

// keep going while there are still bytes to read
while ($next_read < $bytes_to_read) {

    /* move to the position of the next read, read a line, and save
     * the position of the next read */
    fseek($fh,$next_read);
    $s = fgets($fh)                        or die($php_errormsg);
    $next_read = ftell($fh);

    // convert <b>word</b> to *word*
    $s = preg_replace('@<b[^>]*>(.*?)</b>@i','*$1*',$s);
    // convert <i>word</i> to /word/
    $s = preg_replace('@<i[^>]*>(.*?)</i>@i','/$1/',$s);

    /* move to the position where the last write ended, write the
     * converted line, and save the position for the next write */
    fseek($fh,$last_write);
    if (-1 == fwrite($fh,$s))              { die($php_errormsg); }
    $last_write = ftell($fh);
}

// truncate the file length to what we've already written
ftruncate($fh,$last_write)                 or die($php_errormsg);

// close the file
fclose($fh)                                or die($php_errormsg);
```

See Also

Recipes 13.12 and 13.13 for additional information on converting between plain text and HTML; documentation on fseek( ) at *http://www.php.net/fseek*, rewind( ) at *http://www.php.net/rewind*, ftruncate( ) at *http://www.php.net/ftruncate*, file_get_contents( ) at *http://www.php.net/file_get_contents*, and file_put_contents( ) at *http://www.php.net/file_put_contents*.

23.13 Flushing Output to a File

Problem

You want to force all buffered data to be written to a filehandle.

Solution

Use fflush( ), as in Example 23-35.

Example 23-35. Flushing output

```
<?php
fwrite($fh,'There are twelve pumpkins in my house.');
fflush($fh);
?>
```

Example 23-35 ensures that "There are twelve pumpkins in my house." is written to $fh.

Discussion

To be more efficient, system I/O libraries generally don't write something to a file when you tell them to. Instead, they batch the writes together in a buffer and save all of them to disk at the same time. Using fflush( ) forces anything pending in the write buffer to be actually written to disk.

Flushing output can be particularly helpful when generating an access or activity log. Calling fflush( ) after each message to logfile makes sure that any person or program monitoring the logfile sees the message as soon as possible.

See Also

Documentation on fflush( ) at *http://www.php.net/fflush*.

23.14 Writing to Standard Output

Problem

You want to write to standard output.

Solution

Use echo or print( ) print, as in Example 23-36.

Example 23-36. Writing to standard output

```
<?php
print "Where did my pastrami sandwich go?";
echo  "It went into my stomach.";
?>
```

Discussion

While print( ) is a function, echo is a language construct. This means that print( ) returns a value, while echo doesn't. You can include print( ) but not echo in larger expressions, as shown in Example 23-37.

Example 23-37. echo versus print

```
<?php
// this is OK
(12 == $status) ? print 'Status is good' : error_log('Problem with status!');

// this gives a parse error
(12 == $status) ? echo 'Status is good' : error_log('Problem with status!');
?>
```

Use *php://stdout* as the filename if you're using the file functions `$fh = fopen('php://stdout','w') or die($php_errormsg);`.

Writing to standard output via a filehandle instead of simply with `print( )` or `echo` is useful if you need to abstract where your output goes, or if you need to print to standard output at the same time as writing to a file. See Recipe 23.15 for details.

You can also write to standard error by opening *php://stderr*: `$fh = fopen('php://stderr','w');`.

See Also

Recipe 23.15 for writing to many filehandles simultaneously; documentation on `echo` at *http://www.php.net/echo* and on `print( )` at *http://www.php.net/print*.

23.15 Writing to Many Filehandles Simultaneously

Problem

You want to send output to more than one filehandle; for example, you want to log messages to the screen and to a file.

Solution

Wrap your output with a loop that iterates through your filehandles, as shown in Example 23-38.

Example 23-38. pc_multi_fwrite( )

```php
<?php
function pc_multi_fwrite($fhs,$s,$length=NULL) {
  if (is_array($fhs)) {
    if (is_null($length)) {
      foreach($fhs as $fh) {
        fwrite($fh,$s);
      }
    } else {
      foreach($fhs as $fh) {
        fwrite($fh,$s,$length);
      }
    }
  }
}

$fhs['file'] = fopen('log.txt','w') or die($php_errormsg);
$fhs['screen'] = fopen('php://stdout','w') or die($php_errormsg);

pc_multi_fwrite($fhs,'The space shuttle has landed.');
?>
```

Discussion

If you don't want to pass a length argument to `fwrite( )` (or you always want to), you can eliminate that check from your `pc_multi_fwrite( )`. The version in Example 23-39 doesn't bother with a `$length` argument.

Example 23-39. pc_multi_fwrite( ) without $length

```php
<?php
function pc_multi_fwrite($fhs,$s) {
  if (is_array($fhs)) {
    foreach($fhs as $fh) {
      fwrite($fh,$s);
    }
  }
}
?>
```

See Also

Documentation on `fwrite( )` at *http://www.php.net/fwrite*.

23.16 Escaping Shell Metacharacters

Problem

You need to incorporate external data in a command line, but you want to escape special characters so nothing unexpected happens; for example, you want to pass user input as an argument to a program.

Solution

Use `escapeshellarg( )` to handle arguments and `escapeshellcmd( )` to handle program names, as in Example 23-40.

Example 23-40. Escaping shell metacharacters

```php
<?php
system('ls -al '.escapeshellarg($directory));
system(escapeshellcmd($ls_program).' -al');
?>
```

Discussion

The command line is a dangerous place for unescaped characters. Never pass unmodified user input to one of PHP's shell-execution functions. Always escape the appropriate characters in the command and the arguments. This is crucial. It is unusual to execute command lines that are coming from web forms and not something we recommend lightly. However, sometimes you need to run an external program, so escaping commands and arguments is useful.

escapeshellarg( ) surrounds arguments with single quotes (and escapes any existing single quotes). Example 23-41 uses escapeshellarg( ) in printing the process status for a particular process.

Example 23-41. Using escapeshellarg( )

```
<?php
system('/bin/ps '.escapeshellarg($process_id));
?>
```

Using escapeshellarg( ) ensures that the right process is displayed even if its ID has an unexpected character (e.g., a space) in it. It also prevents unintended commands from being run. If $process_id contains 1; rm -rf /, then system("/bin/ps $process_id") not only displays the status of process 1, but also executes the command *rm -rf /*.

However, system('/bin/ps '.escapeshellarg($process_id)) runs the command */bin/ps 1; rm -rf*, which produces an error because "1-semicolon-space-rm-space-hyphen-rf" isn't a valid process ID.

Similarly, escapeshellcmd( ) prevents unintended command lines from execution. The command system("/usr/local/bin/formatter-$which_program"); runs a different program depending on the value of $which_program.

For example, if $which_program is pdf 12, the script runs */usr/local/bin/formatter-pdf* with an argument of 12. But if $which_program is pdf 12; 56, the script runs */usr/local/bin/formatter-pdf* with an argument of 12, but then also runs the program *56*, which is an error.

To successfully pass the arguments to *formatter-pdf*, you need escapeshellcmd( ): system (escapeshellcmd("/usr/local/bin/formatter-$which_program"));. This runs */usr/local/bin/formatter-pdf* and passes it two arguments: 12; and 56.

See Also

Documentation on system( ) at *http://www.php.net/system*, escapeshellarg( ) at *http://www.php.net/escapeshellarg*, and escapeshellcmd( ) at *http://www.php.net/escapeshellcmd*.

23.17 Passing Input to a Program

Problem

You want to pass input to an external program run from inside a PHP script. You might, for example, use a database that requires you to run an external program to index text and want to pass text to that program.

Solution

Open a pipe to the program with popen( ), write to the pipe with fputs( ) or
fwrite( ), and then close the pipe with pclose( ), as in Example 23-42.

Example 23-42. Passing input to a program

```
<?php
$ph = popen('/usr/bin/indexer --category=dinner','w') or die($php_errormsg);
if (-1 == fputs($ph,"red-cooked chicken\n"))    { die($php_errormsg); }
if (-1 == fputs($ph,"chicken and dumplings\n")) { die($php_errormsg); }
pclose($ph)                                     or die($php_errormsg);
?>
```

Discussion

Example 23-43 uses popen( ) to call the *nsupdate* command, which submits Dynamic
DNS Update requests to nameservers.

Example 23-43. Using popen( ) with nsupdate

```
<?php
$ph = popen('/usr/bin/nsupdate -k keyfile')               or die($php_errormsg);
if (-1 == fputs($ph,"update delete test.example.com A\n")) { die($php_errormsg); }
if (-1 == fputs($ph,"update add test.example.com 5 A 192.168.1.1\n"))
                                                          { die($php_errormsg); }
pclose($ph)                                               or die($php_errormsg);
?.
```

In Example 23-43, two commands are sent to *nsupdate* via popen( ). The first deletes
the *test.example.com* A record, and the second adds a new A record for
test.example.com with the address 192.168.1.1.

See Also

Documentation on popen( ) at *http://www.php.net/popen* and pclose( ) at *http://
www.php.net/pclose*; Dynamic DNS is described in RFC 2136 at *http://www.faqs.org/
rfcs/rfc2136.html*.

23.18 Reading Standard Output from a Program

Problem

You want to read the output from a program; for example, you want the output of a
system utility such as *route(8)* that provides network information.

Solution

To read the entire contents of a program's output, use the backtick (`) operator, as in
Example 23-44.

Example 23-44. Running a program with backticks

```php
<?php
$routing_table = `/sbin/route`;
?>
```

To read the output incrementally, open a pipe with popen( ), as in Example 23-45.

Example 23-45. Reading output from popen()

```php
<?php
$ph = popen('/sbin/route','r') or die($php_errormsg);
while (! feof($ph)) {
    $s = fgets($ph)                 or die($php_errormsg);
}
pclose($ph)                         or die($php_errormsg);
?>
```

Discussion

The backtick operator, which is not available in safe mode, executes a program and returns all its output as a single string. On a Linux system with 448 MB of RAM, the command $s = `/usr/bin/free`; puts the following multiline string in $s:

	total	used	free	shared	buffers	cached
Mem:	448620	446384	2236	0	68568	163040
-/+ buffers/cache:		214776	233844			
Swap:	136512	0	136512			

If a program generates a lot of output, it is more memory efficient to read from a pipe one line at a time. If you're printing formatted data to the browser based on the output of the pipe, you can print it as you get it. Example 23-46 prints information about recent Unix system logins formatted as an HTML table. It uses the */usr/bin/last* command.

Example 23-46. Printing recent logins with popen()

```php
<?php
// print table header
print<<<_HTML_
<table>
<tr>
 <td>user</td><td>login port</td><td>login from</td><td>login time</td>
 <td>time spent logged in</td>
</tr>
_HTML_;

// open the pipe to /usr/bin/last
$ph = popen('/usr/bin/last','r') or die($php_errormsg);
while (! feof($ph)) {
    $line = fgets($ph) or die($php_errormsg);

    // don't process blank lines or the info line at the end
    if (trim($line) && (! preg_match('/^wtmp begins/',$line))) {
        $user = trim(substr($line,0,8));
        $port = trim(substr($line,9,12));
        $host = trim(substr($line,22,16));
```

```
        $date = trim(substr($line,38,25));
        $elapsed = trim(substr($line,63,10),' ()');

        if ('logged in' == $elapsed) {
            $elapsed = 'still logged in';
            $date = substr_replace($date,'',-5);
        }

        print "<tr><td>$user</td><td>$port</td><td>$host</td>";
        print "<td>$date</td><td>$elapsed</td></tr>\n";
    }
}
pclose($ph) or die($php_errormsg);

print '</table>';
?>
```

See Also

Documentation on popen( ) at *http://www.php.net/popen*, pclose( ) at *http://www.php.net/pclose*, the backtick operator at *http://www.php.net/language.operators.execution*, and safe mode at *http://www.php.net/features.safe-mode*.

23.19 Reading Standard Error from a Program

Problem

You want to read the error output from a program; for example, you want to capture the system calls displayed by *strace(1)*.

Solution

Redirect standard error to standard output by adding 2>&1 to the command line passed to popen( ). Read standard output by opening the pipe in r mode. This is shown in Example 23-47.

Example 23-47. Reading standard error

```
<?php
$ph = popen('strace ls 2>&1','r') or die($php_errormsg);
while (!feof($ph)) {
    $s = fgets($ph)                  or die($php_errormsg);
}
pclose($ph)                          or die($php_errormsg);
?>
```

Discussion

In both the Unix *sh* and the Windows *cmd.exe* shells, standard error is file descriptor 2, and standard output is file descriptor 1. Appending 2>&1 to a command tells the shell to redirect what's normally sent to file descriptor 2 (standard error) over to file descriptor 1 (standard output). `fgets( )` then reads both standard error and standard output.

This technique reads in standard error but doesn't provide a way to distinguish it from standard output. To read just standard error, you need to prevent standard output from being returned through the pipe. This is done by redirecting it to */dev/null* on Unix and *NUL* on Windows, as in Example 23-48.

Example 23-48. Redirecting standard output

```php
<?php
// Unix: just read standard error
$ph = popen('strace ls 2>&1 1>/dev/null','r') or die($php_errormsg);

// Windows: just read standard error
$ph = popen('ipxroute.exe 2>&1 1>NUL','r') or die($php_errormsg);
?>
```

See Also

Documentation on `popen( )` at *http://www.php.net/popen*; see your *popen(3)* manpage for details about the shell your system uses with `popen( )`; for information about shell redirection, see the Redirection section of the *sh(1)* manpage on Unix systems; on Windows, see the entry on redirection in the Command Reference section of your system help.

23.20 Locking a File

Problem

You want to have exclusive access to a file to prevent it from being changed while you read or update it. If, for example, you are saving guestbook information in a file, two users should be able to add guestbook entries at the same time without clobbering each other's entries.

Solution

Use `flock( )` to provide advisory locking, as shown in Example 23-49.

Example 23-49. Using advisory file locking

```php
<?php
$fh = fopen('guestbook.txt','a')        or die($php_errormsg);
flock($fh,LOCK_EX)                      or die($php_errormsg);
fwrite($fh,$_POST['guestbook_entry']) or die($php_errormsg);
fflush($fh)                             or die($php_errormsg);
flock($fh,LOCK_UN)                      or die($php_errormsg);
fclose($fh)                             or die($php_errormsg);
?>
```

Discussion

The file locking flock( ) provides is called advisory file locking because flock( ) doesn't actually prevent other processes from opening a locked file, it just provides a way for processes to voluntarily cooperate on file access. All programs that need to access files being locked with flock( ) need to set and release locks to make the file locking effective.

There are two kinds of locks you can set with flock( ): exclusive locks and shared locks. An exclusive lock, specified by LOCK_EX as the second argument to flock( ), can be held only by one process at one time for a particular file. A shared lock, specified by LOCK_SH, can be held by more than one process at one time for a particular file. Before writing to a file, you should get an exclusive lock. Before reading from a file, you should get a shared lock.

If any of your code uses flock( ) to lock a file, then all of your code should. For example, if one part of your program uses LOCK_EX to get an exclusive lock when writing to a file, then in any place where you must read the file, be sure to use LOCK_SH to get a shared lock on the file. If you don't do that, then a process trying to read a file can see the contents of the file while another process is writing to it.

To unlock a file, call flock( ) with LOCK_UN as the second argument. It's important to flush any buffered data to be written to the file with fflush( ) before you unlock the file. Other processes shouldn't be able to get a lock until that data is written.

By default, flock( ) blocks until it can obtain a lock. To tell it not to block, add LOCK_NB to the second argument. Non-blocking locking is shown in Example 23-50.

Example 23-50. Non-blocking locking

```php
<?php
$fh = fopen('guestbook.txt','a')          or die($php_errormsg);
$tries = 3;
while ($tries > 0) {
    $locked = flock($fh,LOCK_EX | LOCK_NB);
    if (! $locked) {
        sleep(5);
        $tries--;
    } else {
        // don't go through the loop again
        $tries = 0;
    }
}
if ($locked) {
    fwrite($fh,$_POST['guestbook_entry']) or die($php_errormsg);
    fflush($fh)                           or die($php_errormsg);
    flock($fh,LOCK_UN)                    or die($php_errormsg);
    fclose($fh)                           or die($php_errormsg);
} else {
    print "Can't get lock.";
}
?>
```

When the lock is non-blocking, `flock( )` returns right away even if it couldn't get a lock. The previous example tries three times to get a lock on *guestbook.txt*, sleeping five seconds between each try.

Locking with `flock( )` doesn't work in all circumstances, such as on some NFS implementations and older versions of Windows. To simulate file locking in these cases, use a directory as an exclusive lock indicator. This is a separate, empty directory whose presence indicates that the datafile is locked. Before opening a datafile, create a lock directory and then delete the lock directory when you're finished working with the datafile. Otherwise, the file access code is the same, as shown in Example 23-51.

Example 23-51. Simulating locking with mkdir()

```php
<?php
// loop until we can successfully make the lock directory
$locked = 0;
while (! $locked) {
    if (@mkdir('guestbook.txt.lock',0777)) {
        $locked = 1;
    } else {
        sleep(1);
    }
}
$fh = fopen('guestbook.txt','a')           or die($php_errormsg);

if (-1 == fwrite($fh,$_POST['guestbook_entry'])) {
    rmdir('guestbook.txt.lock');
    die($php_errormsg);
}
if (! fclose($fh)) {
    rmdir('guestbook.txt.lock');
    die($php_errormsg);
}
rmdir('guestbook.txt.lock')               or die($php_errormsg);
```

A directory is used instead of a file to indicate a lock because the `mkdir( )` function fails to create a directory if it already exists. This gives you a way, in one operation, to check if the lock indicator exists and create it if it doesn't. Any error trapping after the directory is created, however, needs to clean up by removing the directory before exiting. If the directory is left in place, no future processes can get a lock by creating the directory.

If you use a file instead of directory as a lock indicator, the code to create it looks something like Example 23-52.

Example 23-52. Error-prone file locking

```php
$locked = 0;
while (! $locked) {
    if (! file_exists('guestbook.txt.lock')) {
        touch('guestbook.txt.lock');
        $locked = 1;
    } else {
        sleep(1);
```

```
        }
    }
```

Example 23-52 fails under heavy load because it checks for the lock's existence with `file_exists( )` and then creates the lock with `touch( )`. After one process calls `file_exists( )`, another might call `touch( )` before the first calls `touch( )`. Both processes would then think they've got exclusive access to the file when neither really does. With `mkdir( )` there's no gap between the checking for existence and creation, so the process that makes the directory is ensured exclusive access.

See Also

Documentation on `flock( )` at *http://www.php.net/flock*.

23.21 Reading and Writing Custom File Types

Problem

You want to use PHP's standard file access functions to provide access to data that might not be in a file. For example, you want to use file access functions to read from and write to shared memory. Or you want to process file contents when they are read before they reach PHP.

Solution

Write a stream wrapper that handles the details of moving data back and forth between PHP and your custom location or your custom format. A stream wrapper is a class that implements the methods that PHP needs to access your custom data stream: opening, closing, reading, writing, and so on. A particular wrapper is registered with a particular prefix. You use that prefix when passing a filename to `fopen( )`, `include( )`, or any other PHP file-handling function to ensure that your wrapper is invoked.

The PEAR Stream_SHM module implements a stream wrapper that reads from and writes to shared memory. Example 23-53 shows how to use it.

Example 23-53. Using a custom stream wrapper

```php
<?php
require_once 'Stream/SHM.php';
stream_register_wrapper('shm','Stream_SHM') or die("can't register shm");
$shm = fopen('shm://0xabcd','c');
fwrite($shm, "Current time is: " . time());
fclose($shm);
?>
```

Discussion

Stream wrappers are handy for non-file data sources, but they can also be used to preprocess file contents on their way into PHP. Mike Naberezny demonstrates a clever example of this as applied to templating. With short_open_tags turned off, printing an object instance variable in a template requires the comparatively verbose `<?php echo $this->property; ?>`. Mike's solution uses a stream wrapper that allows the @ character to stand in for echo `$this->`. Example 23-54 shows the stream wrapper code, Example 23-55 a sample template, and Example 23-56 a short demonstration of how the two work together.

Example 23-54. Stream wrapper for concise templates

```php
<?php
/**
 * Stream wrapper to convert markup of mostly PHP templates into PHP prior to include().
 *
 * Based in large part on the example at
 * http://www.php.net/manual/en/function.stream-wrapper-register.php
 *
 * @author Mike Naberezny (@link http://mikenaberezny.com)
 * @author Paul M. Jones  (@link http://paul-m-jones.com)
 */
class ViewStream {
    /**
     * Current stream position.
     *
     * @var int
     */
    private $pos = 0;

    /**
     * Data for streaming.
     *
     * @var string
     */
    private $data;

    /**
     * Stream stats.
     *
     * @var array
     */
    private $stat;


    /**
     * Opens the script file and converts markup.
     */
    public function stream_open($path, $mode, $options, &$opened_path) {

        // get the view script source
        $path = str_replace('view://', '', $path);
        $this->data = file_get_contents($path);

        /**
         * If reading the file failed, update our local stat store
         * to reflect the real stat of the file, then return on failure
         */
```

```php
    if ($this->data===false) {
        $this->stat = stat($path);
        return false;
    }

    /**
     * Convert <?= ?> to long-form <?php echo ?>
     *
     * We could also convert <%= like the real T_OPEN_TAG_WITH_ECHO
     * but that's not necessary.
     *
     * It might be nice to also convert PHP code blocks <? ?> but
     * let's quit while we're ahead.  It's probably better to keep
     * the <?php for larger code blocks but that's your choice.  If
     * you do go for it, explicitly check for <?xml as this will
     * probably be the biggest headache.
     */
    if (! ini_get('short_open_tag')) {
        $find = '/\<\?\= (.*)? \?>/';
        $replace = "<?php echo \$1 ?>";
        $this->data = preg_replace($find, $replace, $this->data);
    }

    /**
     * Convert @$ to $this->
     *
     * We could make a better effort at only finding @$ between <?php ?>
     * but that's probably not necessary as @$ doesn't occur much in the wild
     * and there's a significant performance gain by using str_replace().
     */
    $this->data = str_replace('@$', '$this->', $this->data);

    /**
     * file_get_contents() won't update PHP's stat cache, so performing
     * another stat() on it will hit the filesystem again.  Since the file
     * has been successfully read, avoid this and just fake the stat
     * so include() is happy.
     */
    $this->stat = array('mode' => 0100777,
                        'size' => strlen($this->data));

    return true;
}


/**
 * Reads from the stream.
 */
public function stream_read($count) {
    $ret = substr($this->data, $this->pos, $count);
    $this->pos += strlen($ret);
    return $ret;
}
```

```
/**
 * Tells the current position in the stream.
 */
public function stream_tell() {
    return $this->pos;
}


/**
 * Tells if we are at the end of the stream.
 */
public function stream_eof() {
    return $this->pos >= strlen($this->data);
}


/**
 * Stream statistics.
 */
public function stream_stat() {
    return $this->stat;
}


/**
 * Seek to a specific point in the stream.
 */
public function stream_seek($offset, $whence) {
    switch ($whence) {
        case SEEK_SET:
            if ($offset < strlen($this->data) && $offset >= 0) {
            $this->pos = $offset;
                return true;
            } else {
                return false;
            }
            break;

        case SEEK_CUR:
            if ($offset >= 0) {
                $this->pos += $offset;
                return true;
            } else {
                return false;
            }
            break;

        case SEEK_END:
            if (strlen($this->data) + $offset >= 0) {
                $this->pos = strlen($this->data) + $offset;
                return true;
            } else {
                return false;
            }
            break;
```

```php
            default:
                return false;
        }
    }
}
?>
```

Example 23-55. Sample template for the stream wrapper

```
<html> <?= @$hello ?> </html>
```

Example 23-56. Demonstration of the template stream wrapper

```php
<?php
/** Stream wrapper */
require_once dirname(__FILE__) . DIRECTORY_SEPARATOR . 'ViewStream.php';

/**
 * A very dumb template class just to demonstrate the concept.
 *
 * @author Mike Naberezny
 * @link    http://mikenaberezny.com/archives/40
 * @link    http://phpsavant.com
 */
class IdiotSavant {
    public function __construct() {
        if (!in_array('view', stream_get_wrappers())) {
            stream_wrapper_register('view', 'ViewStream');
        }
    }

    public function render($filename) {
        include 'view://' . dirname(__FILE__) . DIRECTORY_SEPARATOR . $filename . '.phtml';
    }
}

// Create a new view
$view = new IdiotSavant();

// Assign the variable "hello" to the scope of the view
$view->hello = 'Hello, World!';

// Render the view from a template.  Outputs "<html> Hello, World! </html>"
$view->render('ExampleTemplate');
```

See Also

Documentation on stream_register_wrapper( ) at *http://www.php.net/ stream_register_wrapper*; the PEAR Stream_SHM module at *http://pear.php.net/pack age/stream_shm*; Mike Naberezny's blog post "Symfony Templates and Ruby's ERb" at *http://www.mikenaberezny.com/archives/40*.

23.22 Reading and Writing Compressed Files

Problem

You want to read or write compressed files.

Solution

Use the `compress.zlib` or `compress.bzip2` stream wrapper with the standard file functions. Example 23-57 reads data from a gzip-compressed file.

Example 23-57. Reading a compressed file

```
<?php
$fh = fopen('compress.zlib://lots-of-data.gz','r') or die("can't open: $php_errormsg");
while ($line = fgets($fh)) {
    // $line is the next line of uncompressed data
}
fclose($fh) or die("can't close: $php_errormsg");
?>
```

Discussion

The `compress.zlib` stream wrapper provides access to files that have been compressed with the gzip algorithm. The `compress.bzip2` stream wrapper provides access to files that have been compressed with the bzip2 algorithm. Both stream wrappers allow reading, writing, and appending with compressed files. To enable the zlib and bzip2 compression streams, build PHP with `--withzlib` and `--with-bz2`, respectively.

In addition to the stream wrappers, which allow access to compressed local files, there are stream filters that compress (or uncompress) arbitrary streams on the fly. The `zlib.deflate` and `zlib.inflate` filters compress and uncompress data according to the zlib "deflate" algorithm. The `bzip2.compress` and `bzip2.uncompress` filters do the same for the bzip2 algorithm.

Each stream filter must be applied to a stream after it is created. Example 23-58 uses the `bzip2` stream filters to read compressed data from a URL.

Example 23-58. Reading compressed data from a URL

```
<?php
$fp = fopen('http://www.example.com/something-compressed.bz2','r');
stream_filter_append($fp, 'bzip2.uncompress');
while (! feof($fp)) {
    $data = fread($fp);
    // do something with $data;
}
fclose($fp);
?>
```

See Also

Documentation on compression stream wrappers at *http://www.php.net/wrappers.com pression*, on compression filters at *http://www.php.net/filters.compression*, and on `stream_filter_append( )` at *http://www.php.net/stream_filter_append*; the *zlib* algorithm is detailed in RFCs 1950 (*http://www.faqs.org/rfcs/rfc1950.html*) and 1951 (*http:// www.faqs.org/rfcs/rfc1951.html*).

CHAPTER 24

Directories

24.0 Introduction

A filesystem stores a lot of additional information about files aside from their actual contents. This information includes such particulars as the file size, directory, and access permissions. If you're working with files, you may also need to manipulate this metadata. PHP gives you a variety of functions to read and manipulate directories, directory entries, and file attributes. Like other file-related parts of PHP, the functions are similar to the C functions that accomplish the same tasks, with some simplifications.

Files are organized with *inodes*. Each file (and other parts of the filesystem, such as directories, devices, and links) has its own inode. That inode contains a pointer to where the file's data blocks are as well as all the metadata about the file. The data blocks for a directory hold the names of the files in that directory and the inode of each file.

PHP provides a few ways to look in a directory to see what files it holds. The `DirectoryIterator` class (available in PHP 5 and later) provides a comprehensive object-oriented interface for directory traversal. Example 24-1 uses `DirectoryIterator` to print out the name of each file in a directory.

Example 24-1. Using DirectoryIterator

```
<?php
foreach (new DirectoryIterator('/usr/local/images') as $file) {
    print $file->getPathname() . "\n";
}
?>
```

The `opendir( )`, `readdir( )`, and `closedir( )` functions offer a procedural approach to the same task, as demonstrated in Example 24-2. Use `opendir( )` to get to get a directory handle, `readdir( )` to iterate through the files, and `closedir( )` to close the directory handle. [*]

---

[*] PHP also has a `dir( )` class that mirrors the procedural approach (open, read, close) in its methods. Since `DirectoryIterator` is so much more capable, use that if you want an OO interface.

Example 24-2. Procedural directory iteration

```php
<?php
$d = opendir('/usr/local/images') or die($php_errormsg);
while (false !== ($f = readdir($d))) {
    print $f . "\n";
}
closedir($d);
?>
```

In this chapter, we generally use `DirectoryIterator` for examples.

The filesystem holds more than just files and directories. On Unix, it can also hold symbolic links. These are special files whose contents are a pointer to another file. You can delete the link without affecting the file it points to. To create a symbolic link, use `symlink( )`, as in Example 24-3.

Example 24-3. Making a symbolic link

```php
<?php
symlink('/usr/local/images','/www/docroot/images') or die($php_errormsg);
?>
```

The code in Example 24-3 creates a symbolic link called *images* in */www/docroot* that points to */usr/local/images*.

To find information about a file, directory, or link you must examine its inode. The function `stat( )` retrieves the metadata in an inode for you. Recipe 24.2 discusses `stat( )`. PHP also has many functions that use `stat( )` internally to give you a specific piece of information about a file. These are listed in Table 24-1.

Table 24-1. File information functions

Function name	What file information does the function provide?
file_exists( )	Does the file exist?
fileatime( )	Last access time
filectime( )	Last metadata change time
filegroup( )	Group (numeric)
fileinode( )	Inode number
filemtime( )	Last change time of contents
fileowner( )	Owner (numeric)
fileperms( )	Permissions (decimal, numeric)
filesize( )	Size
filetype( )	Type (fifo, char, dir, block, link, file, unknown)
is_dir( )	Is it a directory?
is_executable( )	Is it executable?
is_file( )	Is it a regular file?

Function name	What file information does the function provide?
is_link( )	Is it a symbolic link?
is_readable( )	Is it readable?
is_writable( )	Is it writable?

On Unix, the file permissions indicate what operations the file's owner, users in the file's group, and all users can perform on the file. The operations are reading, writing, and executing. For programs, executing means the ability to run the program; for directories, executing is the ability to search through the directory and see the files in it.

Unix permissions can also contain a setuid bit, a setgid bit, and a sticky bit. The setuid bit means that when a program is run, it runs with the user ID of its owner. The setgid bit means that a program runs with the group ID of its group. For a directory, the setgid bit means that new files in the directory are created by default in the same group as the directory. The sticky bit is useful for directories in which people share files because it prevents nonsuperusers with write permission in a directory from deleting files in that directory unless they own the file or the directory.

When setting permissions with chmod( ) (see Recipe 24.3), permissions must be expressed as an octal number. This number has four digits. The first digit is any special setting for the file (such as setuid or setgid). The second digit is the user permissions —what the file's owner can do. The third digit is the group permissions—what users in the file's group can do. The fourth digit is the world permissions—what all other users can do. To compute the appropriate value for each digit, add together the permissions you want for that digit using the values in Table 24-2. For example, a permission value of 0644 means that there are no special settings (the 0), the file's owner can read and write the file (the 6, which is 4 (read) + 2 (write)), users in the file's group can read the file (the first 4), and all other users can also read the file (the second 4). A permission value of 4644 is the same, except that the file is also setuid.

Table 24-2. File permission values

Value	Permission meaning	Special setting meaning
4	Read	setuid
2	Write	setgid
1	Execute	sticky

The permissions of newly created files and directories are affected by a setting called the *umask*, which is a permission value that is removed or masked out from the initial permissions of a file (0666) or directory (0777). For example, if the umask is 0022, the default permissions for a new file created with touch( ) or fopen( ) are 0644 and the default permissions for a new directory created with mkdir( ) are 0755. You can get and set the umask with the function umask( ). It returns the current umask and, if an argument is supplied to it, changes the umask to the value of that argument. Example 24-4 shows how to make the permissions on newly created files prevent anyone but the file's owner (and the superuser) from accessing the file.

Example 24-4. Changing the default file permissions

```
$old_umask = umask(0077);
touch('secret-file.txt');
umask($old_umask);
```

In Example 24-4, the first call to umask( ) masks out all permissions for group and world. After the file is created, the second call to umask( ) restores the umask to the previous setting. When PHP is run as a server module, it restores the umask to its default value at the end of each request. Windows has a different (and more powerful) system for organizing file permissions and ownership, so PHP's umask( ) function (like every other permissions-related function) isn't available on Windows.

24.1 Getting and Setting File Timestamps

Problem

You want to know when a file was last accessed or changed, or you want to update a file's access or change time; for example, you want each page on your web site to display when it was last modified.

Solution

The fileatime( ), filemtime( ), and filectime( ) functions return the time of last access, modification, and metadata change of a file, as shown in Example 24-5.

Example 24-5. Getting file timestamps

```
<?php
$last_access = fileatime('larry.php');
$last_modification = filemtime('moe.php');
$last_change = filectime('curly.php');
?>
```

A file's modification time can be updated with touch( ). Without a second argument, touch( ) sets the modification time to the current date and time. To set a file's modification time to a specific value, pass that value as an epoch timestamp to touch( ) as a second argument. Example 24-6 changes the modification time of two files without changing their contents.

Example 24-6. Changing file modification times

```
<?php
touch('shemp.php');           // set modification time to now
touch('joe.php',$timestamp); // set modification time to $timestamp
?>
```

Discussion

The `fileatime()` function returns the last time a file was opened for reading or writing. The `filemtime()` function returns the last time a file's contents were changed. The `filectime()` function returns the last time a file's contents or metadata (such as owner or permissions) were changed. Each function returns the time as an epoch timestamp.

The code in Example 24-7 prints the time a page on your web site was last updated.

Example 24-7. Printing web page modification times

```
<?php
print "Last Modified: ".strftime('%c',filemtime($_SERVER['SCRIPT_FILENAME']));
?>
```

See Also

Documentation on `fileatime()` at *http://www.php.net/fileatime*, `filemtime()` at *http://www.php.net/filemtime*, and `filectime()` at *http://www.php.net/filectime*.

24.2 Getting File Information

Problem

You want to read a file's metadata—for example, permissions and ownership.

Solution

Use `stat()`, as in Example 24-8, which returns an array of information about a file.

Example 24-8. Getting file information

```
<?php
$info = stat('harpo.php');
?>
```

Discussion

`stat()` returns an array with both numeric and string indexes with information about a file. The elements of this array are in Table 24-3.

Table 24-3. Information returned by stat()

Numeric index	String index	Value
0	dev	Device
1	ino	Inode
2	mode	Permissions
3	nlink	Link count
4	uid	Owner's user ID

Numeric index	String index	Value
5	gid	Group's group ID
6	rdev	Device type for inode devices (−1 on Windows)
7	size	Size (in bytes)
8	atime	Last access time (epoch timestamp)
9	mtime	Last change time of contents (epoch timestamp)
10	ctime	Last change time of contents or metadata (epoch timestamp)
11	blksize	Block size for I/O (−1 on Windows)
12	blocks	Number of blocks allocated to this file

The mode element of the returned array contains the permissions expressed as a base 10 integer. This is confusing since permissions are usually either expressed symbolically (e.g., *ls*'s -rw-r--r-- output) or as an octal integer (e.g., 0644). To convert the permissions to a more understandable format, use base_convert( ) to change the permissions to octal, as shown in Example 24-9.

Example 24-9. Converting file permission values

```php
<?php
$file_info = stat('/tmp/session.txt');
$permissions = base_convert($file_info['mode'],10,8);
?>
```

In Example 24-9, $permissions is a six-digit octal number. For example, if *ls* displays the following about */tmp/session.txt*:

```
-rw-rw-r--    1 sklar    sklar         12 Oct 23 17:55 /tmp/session.txt
```

Then $file_info['mode'] is 33204 and $permissions is 100664. The last three digits (664) are the user (read and write), group (read and write), and other (read) permissions for the file. The third digit, 0, means that the file is not setuid or setgid. The leftmost 10 means that the file is a regular file (and not a socket, symbolic link, or other special file).

Because stat( ) returns an array with both numeric and string indexes, using foreach to iterate through the returned array produces two copies of each value. Instead, use a for loop from element 0 to element 12 of the returned array.

Calling stat( ) on a symbolic link returns information about the file the symbolic link points to. To get information about the symbolic link itself, use lstat( ).

Similar to stat( ) is fstat( ), which takes a filehandle (returned from fopen( ) or popen( )) as an argument.

PHP's stat( ) function uses the underlying *stat(2)* system call, which is expensive. To minimize overhead, PHP caches the result of calling *stat(2)*. So if you call stat( ) on a file, change its permissions, and call stat( ) on the same file again, you get the same results. To force PHP to reload the file's metadata, call `clearstatcache( )`, which flushes PHP's cached information. PHP also uses this cache for the other functions that return file metadata: `file_exists( )`, `fileatime( )`, `filectime( )`, `filegroup( )`, `fileinode( )`, `filemtime( )`, `fileowner( )`, `fileperms( )`, `filesize( )`, `filetype( )`, `fstat( )`, `is_dir( )`, `is_executable( )`, `is_file( )`, `is_link( )`, `is_readable( )`, `is_writable( )`, and `lstat( )`.

See Also

Documentation on `stat( )` at *http://www.php.net/stat*, `lstat( )` at *http://www.php.net/lstat*, `fstat( )` at *http://www.php.net/fstat*, and `clearstatcache( )` at *http://www.php.net/clearstatcache*.

24.3 Changing File Permissions or Ownership

Problem

You want to change a file's permissions or ownership; for example, you want to prevent other users from being able to look at a file of sensitive data.

Solution

Use `chmod( )` to change the permissions of a file, as shown in Example 24-10.

Example 24-10. Changing file permissions

```
<?php
chmod('/home/user/secrets.txt',0400);
?>
```

Use `chown( )` to change a file's owner and `chgrp( )` to change a file's group. These are shown in Example 24-11.

Example 24-11. Changing file owner and group

```
<?php
chown('/tmp/myfile.txt','sklar');                // specify user by name
chgrp('/home/sklar/schedule.txt','soccer'); // specify group by name

chown('/tmp/myfile.txt',5001);                   // specify user by uid
chgrp('/home/sklar/schedule.txt',102);      // specify group by gid
?>
```

Discussion

The permissions passed to `chmod( )` must be specified as an octal number.

The superuser can change the permissions, owner, and group of any file. Other users are restricted. They can change only the permissions and group of files that they own, and can't change the owner at all. A non-superuser can also change only the group of a file to a group to which the user belongs.

The functions chmod( ), chgrp( ), and chown( ) don't work on Windows.

See Also

Documentation on chmod( ) at *http://www.php.net/chmod*, chown( ) at *http://www.php.net/chown*, and chgrp( ) at *http://www.php.net/chgrp*.

24.4 Splitting a Filename into Its Component Parts

Problem

You want to find a file's path and filename; for example, you want to create a file in the same directory as an existing file.

Solution

Use basename( ) to get the filename and dirname( ) to get the path, as shown in Example 24-12.

Example 24-12. Getting path components

```
<?php
$full_name = '/usr/local/php/php.ini';
$base = basename($full_name);  // $base is "php.ini"
$dir  = dirname($full_name);   // $dir is "/usr/local/php"
?>
```

Use pathinfo( ) to get the directory name, base name, and extension in an associative array, as in Example 24-13.

Example 24-13. Getting path components and file extensions

```
<?php
$info = pathinfo('/usr/local/php/php.ini');
// $info['dirname'] is "/usr/local/php"
// $info['basename'] is "php.ini"
// $info['extension'] is "ini"
?>
```

Discussion

To create a temporary file in the same directory as an existing file, use dirname( ) to find the directory, and pass that directory to tempnam( ). This is what Example 24-14 does.

Example 24-14. Creating a temporary file in a particular place

```
<?php
$dir = dirname($existing_file);
$temp = tempnam($dir,'temp');
$temp_fh = fopen($temp,'w');
?>
```

The `dirname()` function is particularly useful in combination with the special constant `__FILE__`, which contains the full pathname of the current file. This is not the same as the currently executing PHP script. If *usr/local/alice.php* includes *usr/local/bob.php*, then `__FILE__` in *bob.php* is `/usr/local/bob.php`. This makes `__FILE__` useful when you want to include or require scripts in the same directory as a particular file, but you don't know what that directory is and it isn't necessarily in the include path. Example 24-15 demonstrates.

Example 24-15. Including files relative to the current file

```
<?php
$currentDir = dirname(__FILE__);
include $currentDir . '/functions.php';
include $currentDir . '/classes.php';
?>
```

If the code in Example 24-15 is in the */usr/local* directory, then it includes */usr/local/functions.php* and */usr/local/classes.php*. This technique is particularly useful when you're distributing code for others to use. With it, you don't have to require any configuration or include path modification for your code to work properly.

Using functions such as `basename()`, `dirname()`, and `pathinfo()` is more portable than just splitting up full filenames on the / character because the functions use an operating-system-appropriate separator. On Windows, these functions treat both / and \ as file and directory separators. On other platforms, only / is used.

There's no built-in PHP function to combine the parts produced by `basename()`, `dirname()`, and `pathinfo()` back into a full filename. To do this you have to combine the parts with . and the built-in `DIRECTORY_SEPARATOR` constant, which is / on Unix and \ on Windows.

See Also

Documentation on `basename()` at *http://www.php.net/basename*, `dirname()` at *http://www.php.net/dirname*, `pathinfo()` at *http://www.php.net/pathinfo*, and `__FILE__` at *http://www.php.net/language.constants.predefined*.

24.5 Deleting a File

Problem

You want to delete a file.

Solution

Use `unlink()`, as shown in Example 24-16.

Example 24-16. Deleting a file

```php
<?php
$file = '/tmp/junk.txt';
unlink($file) or die ("can't delete $file: $php_errormsg");
?>
```

Discussion

The function unlink( ) is only able to delete files that the user of the PHP process is able to delete. If you're having trouble getting unlink( ) to work, check the permissions on the file and how you're running PHP.

See Also

Documentation on unlink( ) at *http://www.php.net/unlink*.

24.6 Copying or Moving a File

Problem

You want to copy or move a file.

Solution

Use copy( ) to copy a file, as shown in Example 24-17.

Example 24-17. Copying a file

```php
<?php
$old = '/tmp/yesterday.txt';
$new = '/tmp/today.txt';
copy($old,$new) or die("couldn't copy $old to $new: $php_errormsg");
?>
```

Use rename( ) to move a file, as shown in Example 24-18.

Example 24-18. Moving a file

```php
<?php
$old = '/tmp/today.txt';
$new = '/tmp/tomorrow.txt';
rename($old,$new) or die("couldn't move $old to $new: $php_errormsg");
?>
```

Discussion

On Unix, rename( ) can't move files across filesystems under PHP versions before 4.3.3. To do so, copy the file to the new location and then delete the old file. This is shown in Example 24-19.

Example 24-19. Moving a file across filesystems

```php
<?php
if (copy("/tmp/code.c","/usr/local/src/code.c")) {
  unlink("/tmp/code.c");
}
?>
```

If you have multiple files to copy or move, call copy( ) or rename( ) in a loop. You can operate only on one file each time you call these functions.

See Also

Documentation on copy( ) at *http://www.php.net/copy* and rename( ) at *http://www.php.net/rename*.

24.7 Processing All Files in a Directory

Problem

You want to iterate over all files in a directory. For example, you want to create a `<select/>` box in a form that lists all the files in a directory.

Solution

Use a DirectoryIterator to get each file in the directory, as in Example 24-20.

Example 24-20. Processing all files in a directory

```php
<?php
echo "<select name='file'>\n";
foreach (new DirectoryIterator('/usr/local/images') as $file) {
    echo '<option>' . htmlentities($file) . "</option>\n";
}
echo '</select>';
?>
```

Discussion

The DirectoryIterator yields one value for each element in the directory. That value is an object with some handy characteristics. The object's string representation is the filename (with no leading path) of the directory element. For example, if */usr/local/images* contains the files *cucumber.gif* and *eggplant.png*, Example 24-20 prints:

```
<select name='file'>
<option>.</option>
<option>..</option>
<option>cucumber.gif</option>
<option>eggplant.png</option>
</select>
```

A DirectoryIterator yields an object for *all* directory elements, including . (current directory) and .. (parent directory). Fortunately, that object has some methods that help us identify what it is. The `isDot()` method returns true if it's either `.` or `...` Example 24-21 uses `isDot()` to prevent those two entries from showing up in the output.

Example 24-21. Removing . and .. from output

```php
<?php
echo "<select name='file'>\n";
foreach (new DirectoryIterator('/usr/local/images') as $file) {
    if (! $file->isDot()) {
        echo '<option>' . htmlentities($file) . "</option>\n";
    }
}
echo '</select>';
?>
```

Table 24-4 lists the other methods available on the objects that a `DirectoryIterator` yields.

Table 24-4. DirectoryIterator object information methods

Method Name	Return value	Example
isDir( )	Is the element a directory?	false
isDot( )	Is the element either . or ..?	false
isFile( )	Is the element a regular file?	true
isLink( )	Is the element a link?	false
isReadable( )	Is the element readable?	true
isWritable( )	Is the element writable?	true
isExecutable( )	Is the element executable?	false
getATime( )	The last access time of the element.	1144509622
getCTime( )	The creation time of the element.	1144509600
getMTime( )	The last modification time of the element.	1144509620
getFilename( )	The filename (without leading path) of the element.	eggplant.png
getPathname( )	The full pathname of the element.	/usr/local/images/eggplant.php
getPath( )	The leading path of the element.	/usr/local/images
getGroup( )	The group ID of the element.	500
getOwner( )	The owner ID of the element.	1000
getPerms( )	The permissions of the element, as an octal value.	16895
getSize( )	The size of the element.	328742
getType( )	The type of the element (dir, file, link, etc.).	file
getInode( )	The inode number of the element.	28720

The data that the functions in Table 24-4 report come from the same underlying system calls as the data that the functions in Table 24-1 report, so the same cautions on differences between Unix and Windows apply.

See Also

Documentation on `DirectoryIterator` at *http://www.php.net/~helly/php/ext/spl/classDirectoryIterator.html*.

24.8 Getting a List of Filenames Matching a Pattern

Problem

You want to find all filenames that match a pattern.

Solution

Use a `FilterIterator` subclass with `DirectoryIterator`. The `FilterIterator` subclass needs its own `accept()` method that decides whether or not a particular value is acceptable. The code in Example 24-22 only accepts filenames that end with common extensions for images.

Example 24-22. Using a FilterIterator

```php
<?php
class ImageFilter extends FilterIterator {
    public function accept() {
        return preg_match('@\.(gif|jpe?g|png)$@i',$this->current());
    }
}
foreach (new ImageFilter(new DirectoryIterator('/usr/local/images')) as $img) {
    print "<img src='".htmlentities($img)."'/>\n";
}
?>
```

Discussion

The `FilterIterator` encloses a `DirectoryIterator` and only allows certain elements to emerge. It's up to the `accept()` method to return `true` or `false` to indicate whether a particular element (accessed with `$this->current()`) is OK. In Example 24-22, `accept()` uses a regular expression to make that determination, but your code can use any logic you like.

If your pattern can be expressed as a simple shell "glob" (e.g. *.*), use the `glob()` function to get the matching filenames. Example 24-23 finds all the text files in a particular directory.

Example 24-23. Using glob()

```php
<?php
foreach (glob('/usr/local/docs/*.txt') as $file) {
    $contents = file_get_contents($file);
    print "$file contains $contents\n";
}
?>
```

The glob( ) function returns an array of matching full pathnames. If no files match the pattern, glob( ) returns `false`.

See Also

Recipe 24.9 details iterating through each file in a directory recursively; documentation on `FilterIterator` at *http://www.php.net/~helly/php/ext/spl/classFilterIterator.html* and on glob( ) at *http://www.php.net/glob*; information about shell pattern matching is available at *http://www.gnu.org/software/bash/manual/bashref.html#SEC35*.

24.9 Processing All Files in a Directory Recursively

Problem

You want to do something to all the files in a directory and in any subdirectories. For example, you want to see how much disk space is consumed by all the files under a directory.

Solution

Use a `RecursiveDirectoryIterator` and a `RecursiveIteratorIterator`. The `RecursiveDirectoryIterator` extends the `DirectoryIterator` with a `getChildren( )` method that provides access to the elements in a subdirectory. The `RecursiveIteratorIterator` flattens the hierarchy that the `RecursiveDirectoryIterator` returns into one list. Example 24-24 counts the total size of files under a directory.

Example 24-24. Processing all files in a directory recursively

```php
<?php
$dir = new RecursiveDirectoryIterator('/usr/local');
$totalSize = 0;
foreach (new RecursiveIteratorIterator($dir) as $file) {
    $totalSize += $file->getSize();
}
print "The total size is $totalSize.\n";
?>
```

Discussion

The objects that the `RecursiveDirectoryIterator` spits out (and therefore that the `RecursiveIteratorIterator` passes along) are the same as what you get from `DirectoryIterator`, so all the methods mentioned in Table 24-4 are available.

See Also

Documentation on `RecursiveDirectoryIterator` at *http://www.php.net/~helly/php/ext/ spl/classRecursiveDirectoryIterator.html* and `RecursiveIteratorIterator` at *http:// www.php.net/~helly/php/ext/spl/classRecursiveIteratorIterator.html*.

24.10 Making New Directories

Problem

You want to create a directory.

Solution

Use `mkdir( )`, as in Example 24-25.

Example 24-25. Making a directory

```php
<?php
mkdir('/tmp/apples',0777) or die($php_errormsg);
?>
```

Discussion

The second argument to `mkdir( )` is the permission mode for the new directory, which must be an octal number. The current umask is taken away from this permission value to create the permissions for the new directory. So, if the current umask is `0002`, calling `mkdir('/tmp/apples',0777)` sets the permissions on the resulting directory to `0775` (user and group can read, write, and execute; others can only read and execute).

By default, `mkdir( )` only creates a directory if its parent exists. For example, if */usr/local/ images* doesn't exist, you can't create */usr/local/images/puppies*. To create a directory and its parents, pass `true` as a third argument to `mkdir( )`. This makes the function act recursively to create any missing parent directories.

See Also

Documentation on `mkdir( )` at *http://www.php.net/mkdir*.

24.11 Removing a Directory and Its Contents

Problem

You want to remove a directory and all of its contents, including subdirectories and their contents.

Solution

Use `RecursiveDirectoryIterator` and `RecursiveIteratorIterator`, specifying that children (files and subdirectories) should be listed before their parents, as in Example 24-26.

Example 24-26. Obliterating a directory

```php
<?php
function obliterate_directory($dir) {
    $iter = new RecursiveDirectoryIterator($dir);
    foreach (new RecursiveIteratorIterator($iter, RecursiveIteratorIterator::CHILD_FIRST) as $f) {
        if ($f->isDir()) {
            rmdir($f->getPathname());
        } else {
            unlink($f->getPathname());
        }
    }
    rmdir($dir);
}

obliterate_directory('/tmp/junk');
?>
```

Discussion

Removing files, obviously, can be dangerous. Because PHP's built-in directory removal function, `rmdir( )`, works only on empty directories, and `unlink( )` can't accept shell wildcards, the `RecursiveIteratorIterator` must be told to provide children before parents with its `CHILD_FIRST` constant.

However, that constant is not available before PHP 5.1. If you're using an earlier version of PHP, you can use the function in Example 24-27 for the same purpose.

Example 24-27. Obliterating a directory without RecursiveIteratorIterator

```php
<?php
function obliterate_directory($dir) {
    foreach (new DirectoryIterator($dir) as $file) {
        if ($file->isDir()) {
            if (! $file->isDot()) {
                obliterate_directory($file->getPathname());
            }
        } else {
            unlink($file->getPathname());
        }
    }
    rmdir($dir);
}
?>
```

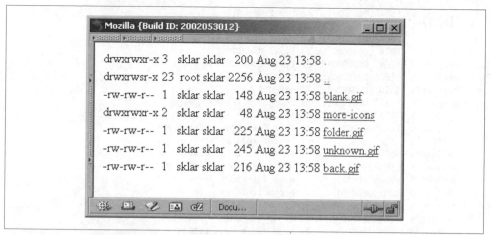

Figure 24-1. Web listing

See Also

Documentation on `rmdir()` at *http://www.php.net/rmdir* and on `RecursiveIteratorIt` `erator` at *http://www.php.net/~helly/php/ext/spl/classRecursiveIteratorIterator.html*.

24.12 Program: Web Server Directory Listing

The *web-ls.php* program shown in Example 24-28 (later in this recipe) provides a view of the files inside your web server's document root, formatted like the output of the Unix command *ls*. Filenames are linked so that you can download each file, and directory names are linked so that you can browse in each directory, as shown in Figure 24-1.

Most lines in Example 24-28 are devoted to building an easy-to-read representation of the file's permissions, but the guts of the program are in the `foreach` loop at the end. The `DirectoryIterator` yields an element for each entry in the directory. Then, various methods on the element's object provide information about that file, and `printf()` prints out the formatted information about that file.

The `mode_string()` functions and the constants it uses turn the octal representation of a file's mode (e.g., `35316`) into an easier-to-read string (e.g., `-rwsrw-r--`).

Example 24-28. web-ls.php

```php
<?php

/* Bit masks for determining file permissions and type. The names and values
 * listed below are POSIX-compliant; individual systems may have their own
 * extensions.
 */

define('S_IFMT',0170000);   // mask for all types
define('S_IFSOCK',0140000); // type: socket
```

```
define('S_IFLNK',0120000);    // type: symbolic link
define('S_IFREG',0100000);    // type: regular file
define('S_IFBLK',0060000);    // type: block device
define('S_IFDIR',0040000);    // type: directory
define('S_IFCHR',0020000);    // type: character device
define('S_IFIFO',0010000);    // type: fifo
define('S_ISUID',0004000);    // set-uid bit
define('S_ISGID',0002000);    // set-gid bit
define('S_ISVTX',0001000);    // sticky bit
define('S_IRWXU',00700);      // mask for owner permissions
define('S_IRUSR',00400);      // owner: read permission
define('S_IWUSR',00200);      // owner: write permission
define('S_IXUSR',00100);      // owner: execute permission
define('S_IRWXG',00070);      // mask for group permissions
define('S_IRGRP',00040);      // group: read permission
define('S_IWGRP',00020);      // group: write permission
define('S_IXGRP',00010);      // group: execute permission
define('S_IRWXO',00007);      // mask for others permissions
define('S_IROTH',00004);      // others: read permission
define('S_IWOTH',00002);      // others: write permission
define('S_IXOTH',00001);      // others: execute permission

/* mode_string() is a helper function that takes an octal mode and returns
 * a 10-character string representing the file type and permissions that
 * correspond to the octal mode. This is a PHP version of the mode_string()
 * function in the GNU fileutils package.
 */
$mode_type_map = array(S_IFBLK => 'b', S_IFCHR => 'c',
                       S_IFDIR => 'd', S_IFREG => '-',
                       S_IFIFO => 'p', S_IFLNK => 'l',
                       S_IFSOCK => 's');
function mode_string($mode) {
    global $mode_type_map;
    $s = '';
    $mode_type = $mode & S_IFMT;
    // Add the type character
    $s .= isset($mode_type_map[$mode_type]) ?
          $mode_type_map[$mode_type] : '?';

    // set user permissions
    $s .= $mode & S_IRUSR ? 'r' : '-';
    $s .= $mode & S_IWUSR ? 'w' : '-';
    $s .= $mode & S_IXUSR ? 'x' : '-';

    // set group permissions
    $s .= $mode & S_IRGRP ? 'r' : '-';
    $s .= $mode & S_IWGRP ? 'w' : '-';
    $s .= $mode & S_IXGRP ? 'x' : '-';

    // set other permissions
    $s .= $mode & S_IROTH ? 'r' : '-';
    $s .= $mode & S_IWOTH ? 'w' : '-';
    $s .= $mode & S_IXOTH ? 'x' : '-';

    // adjust execute letters for set-uid, set-gid, and sticky
```

```
    if ($mode & S_ISUID) {
        // 'S' for set-uid but not executable by owner
        $s[3] = ($s[3] == 'x') ? 's' : 'S';
    }

    if ($mode & S_ISGID) {
        // 'S' for set-gid but not executable by group
        $s[6] = ($s[6] == 'x') ? 's' : 'S';
    }

    if ($mode & S_ISVTX) {
        // 'T' for sticky but not executable by others
        $s[9] = ($s[9] == 'x') ? 't' : 'T';
    }

    return $s;
}

// start at the document root if not specified
$dir = isset($_GET['dir']) ? $_GET['dir'] : '';

// locate $dir in the filesystem
$real_dir = realpath($_SERVER['DOCUMENT_ROOT'].$dir);
// Passing document root through realpath resolves any
// forward-slash vs. backslash issues
$real_docroot = realpath($_SERVER['DOCUMENT_ROOT']);

// make sure $real_dir is inside document root
if (! (($real_dir == $real_docroot) ||
       ((strlen($real_dir) > strlen($real_docroot)) &&
        (strncasecmp($real_dir,$real_docroot.DIRECTORY_SEPARATOR,
         strlen($real_docroot.DIRECTORY_SEPARATOR)) == 0)))) {
    die("$dir is not inside the document root");
}

// canonicalize $dir by removing the document root from its beginning
$dir = substr($real_dir,strlen($real_docroot)+1);

// are we opening a directory?
if (! is_dir($real_dir)) {
    die("$real_dir is not a directory");
}

print '<pre><table>';

// read each entry in the directory
foreach (new DirectoryIterator($real_dir) as $file) {
    // translate uid into user name
    if (function_exists('posix_getpwuid')) {
        $user_info = posix_getpwuid($file->getOwner());
    } else {
        $user_info = $file->getOwner();
    }

    // translate gid into group name
```

```php
if (function_exists('posix_getgrid')) {
    $group_info = $file->getGroup();
} else {
    $group_info = $file->getGroup();
}

// format the date for readability
$date = date('M d H:i',$file->getMTime());

// translate the octal mode into a readable string
$mode = mode_string($file->getPerms());

$mode_type = substr($mode,0,1);
if (($mode_type == 'c') || ($mode_type == 'b')) {
    /* if it's a block or character device, print out the major and
     * minor device type instead of the file size */
    $statInfo = lstat($file->getPathname());
    $major = ($statInfo['rdev'] >> 8) & 0xff;
    $minor = $statInfo['rdev'] & 0xff;
    $size = sprintf('%3u, %3u',$major,$minor);
} else {
    $size = $file->getSize();
}

// format the <a href=""> around the filename
// no link for the current directory
if ('.' == $file->getFilename()) {
    $href = $file->getFilename();
} else {
    // don't include the ".." in the parent directory link
    if ('..' == $file->getFilename()) {
        $href = urlencode(dirname($dir));
    } else {
        $href = urlencode($dir) . '/' . urlencode($file);
    }

    /* everything but "/" should be urlencoded */
    $href = str_replace('%2F','/',$href);

    // browse other directories with web-ls
    if ($file->isDir()) {
        $href = sprintf('<a href="%s?dir=/%s">%s</a>',
                        $_SERVER['PHP_SELF'],$href,$file);
    } else {
        // link to files to download them
        $href= sprintf('<a href="%s">%s</a>',$href,$file);
    }

    // if it's a link, show the link target, too
    if ('l' == $mode_type) {
        $href .= ' -&gt; ' . readlink($file->getPathname());
    }
}

// print out the appropriate info for this file
```

```
printf('<tr><td>%s</td><td align="right">%s</td>
        <td align="right">%s</td><td align="right">%s</td>
        <td align="right">%s</td><td>%s</td></tr>',
        $mode,                  // formatted mode string
        $user_info['name'],     // owner's user name
        $group_info['name'],    // group name
        $size,                  // file size (or device numbers)
        $date,                  // last modified date and time
        $href);                 // link to browse or download
}

print '</table></pre>';
?>
```

24.13 Program: Site Search

You can use *site-search.php*, shown in Example 24-29, as a search engine for a small-to-medium-size, file-based site.

Example 24-29. site-search.php

```
<?php
class SiteSearch {
    public $bodyRegex = '';
    protected $seen = array();


    public function searchDir($dir) {
        // array to hold pages that match
        $pages = array();

        // array to hold directories to recurse into
        $dirs = array();

        // mark this directory as seen so we don't look in it again
        $this->seen[realpath($dir)] = true;

        try {
            foreach (new RecursiveIteratorIterator(
            new RecursiveDirectoryIterator($dir)) as $file) {
                if ($file->isFile() && $file->isReadable() &&
                (! isset($this->seen[$file->getPathname()]))) {
                    // mark this as seen so we skip it
                    // if we come to it again
                    $this->seen[$file->getPathname()] = true;

                    // load the contents of the file into $text
                    $text = file_get_contents($file->getPathname());

                    // if the search term is inside the body delimiters
                    if (preg_match($this->bodyRegex,$text)) {

                        // construct the relative URI of the file by removing
                        // the document root from the full path
                        $uri = substr_replace($file->getPathname(),'',0,strlen
```

```
                    ($_SERVER['DOCUMENT_ROOT']));

                    // if the page has a title, find it
                    if (preg_match('#<title>(.*?)</title>#Sis',$text,$match)) {
                        // and add the title and URI to $pages
                        array_push($pages,array($uri,$match[1]));
                    } else {
                        // otherwise use the URI as the title
                        array_push($pages,array($uri,$uri));
                    }
                }
            }
        }
    } catch (Exception $e) {
        // There was a problem opening the directory
    }
    return $pages;
    }
}

// helper function to sort matched pages alphabetically by title
function by_title($a,$b) {
    return ($a[1] == $b[1]) ?
            strcmp($a[0],$b[0]) :
            ($a[1] > $b[1]);
}

// SiteSearch object to do the searching
$search = new SiteSearch();

// array to hold the pages that match the search term
$matching_pages = array();
// directories underneath the document root to search
$search_dirs = array('sports','movies','food');
// regular expression to use in searching files. The "S" pattern
// modifier tells the PCRE engine to "study" the regex for greater
// efficiency.
$search->bodyRegex = '#<body>(.*' . preg_quote($_REQUEST['term'],'#').
                    '.*)</body>#Sis';

// add the files that match in each directory to $matching pages
foreach ($search_dirs as $dir) {
    $matching_pages = array_merge($matching_pages,
                        $search->searchDir($_SERVER['DOCUMENT_ROOT'].'/'.$dir));
}

if (count($matching_pages)) {
    // sort the matching pages by title
    usort($matching_pages,'by_title');
    print '<ul>';
    // print out each title with a link to the page
    foreach ($matching_pages as $k => $v) {
        print sprintf('<li> <a href="%s">%s</a>',$v[0],$v[1]);
    }
    print '</ul>';
```

```
    } else {
        print 'No pages found.';
    }
    ?>
```

The program looks for a search term (in $_REQUEST['term']) in all files within a specified set of directories under the document root. Those directories are set in $search_dirs. It also recurses into subdirectories and follows symbolic links but keeps track of which files and directories it has seen so that it doesn't get caught in an endless loop.

If any pages are found that contain the search term, it prints a list of links to those pages, alphabetically ordered by each page's title. If a page doesn't have a title (between the <title> and </title> tags), the page's relative URI from the document root is used.

The program looks for the search term between the <body> and </body> tags in each file. If you have a lot of text in your pages inside <body> tags that you want to exclude from the search, surround the text that should be searched with specific HTML comments and then modify $body_regex to look for those tags instead. Perhaps your page looks like what is shown in Example 24-30.

Example 24-30. Sample HTML page
```
    <body>

    // Some HTML for menus, headers, etc.

    <!-- search-start -->

    <h1>Aliens Invade Earth</h1>

    <h3>by H.G. Wells</h3>

    <p>Aliens invaded earth today. Uh Oh.</p>

    // More of the story

    <!-- search-end -->

    // Some HTML for footers, etc.

    </body>
```

To match the search term against just the title, author, and story inside the HTML comments, change $search->bodyRegex to what is shown in Example 24-31.

Example 24-31. Corresponding regular expression
```
    $search->bodyRegex = '#<!-- search-start -->(.*' . preg_quote($_REQUEST['term'],'#').
                '.*)<!-- search-end -->#Sis';
```

If you don't want the search term to match text that's inside HTML or PHP tags in your pages, add a call to strip_tags() to the code that loads the contents of the file for searching, as shown in Example 24-32.

Example 24-32. Stripping HTML and PHP tags

```
// load the contents of the file into $text
$text= strip_tags(file_get_contents($file->getPathname()));
```

CHAPTER 25

Command-Line PHP

25.0 Introduction

PHP was created for web programming and is still used mostly for that purpose. However, PHP is also capable as a general-purpose scripting language. Using PHP for scripts you run from the command line is especially helpful when they share code with your web applications. If you have a discussion board on your web site, you might want to run a program every few minutes or hours to scan new postings and alert you to any messages that contain certain keywords. Writing this scanning program in PHP lets you share relevant discussion-board code with the main discussion-board application. Not only does this save you time, but also helps avoid maintenance overhead down the road.

Beginning with version 4.3, PHP builds include a command-line interface (CLI) version. The CLI binary is similar to web server modules and the CGI binary but has some important differences that make it more shell friendly. Some configuration directives have hardcoded values with CLI; for example, the `html_errors` directive is set to `false`, and `implicit_flush` is set to `true`. The `max_execution_time` directive is set to 0, allowing unlimited program runtime. Finally, `register_argc_argv` is set to `true`. This means you can look for argument information in `$argv` and `$argc` instead of in `$_SERVER ['argv']` and `$_SERVER['argc']`. Argument processing is discussed in Recipes 25.1 and 25.2.

To run a script, pass the script filename as an argument:

```
% php scan-discussions.php
```

On Unix, you can also use the "hash-bang" syntax at the top of your scripts to run the PHP interpreter automatically. If the PHP binary is in */usr/local/bin*, make the first line of your script:

```
#!/usr/local/bin/php
```

You can then run the script just by typing its name on the command line, as long as the file has execute permission.

If it's likely that you'll use some of your classes and functions both for the Web and for the command line, abstract the code that needs to react differently in those different circumstances, such as HTML versus plain-text output or access to environment variables that a web server sets up. A useful tactic is to check if the return value of php_sapi_name( ) is cli. You can then branch your scripts' behavior as follows:

```
if ('cli' == php_sapi_name()) {
  print "Database error: ".mysql_error()."\n";
} else {
  print "Database error.<br/>";
  error_log(mysql_error());
}
```

This code not only adjusts the output formatting based on the context it's executing in (\n versus <br>), but also where the information goes. On the command line, it's helpful to the person running the program to see the error message from MySQL, but on the Web, you don't want your users to see potentially sensitive data. Instead, the code outputs a generic error message and stores the details in the server's error log for private review.

One helpful option on the command line is the -d flag, which lets you specify custom INI entries without modifying your *php.ini* file. For example, here's how to turn on output buffering:

```
% php -d output_buffering=1 scan-discussions.php
```

The CLI binary also takes a -r argument. When followed by some PHP code without <?php and ?> script tags, the CLI binary runs the code. For example, here's how to print the current time:

```
% php -r 'print strftime("%c");'
```

For a list of complete CLI binary options, pass the -h command:

```
% php -h
```

Finally, the CLI binary defines handles to the standard I/O streams as the constants STDIN, STDOUT, and STDERR. You can use these instead of creating your own filehandles with fopen( ):

```
// read from standard in
$input = fgets(STDIN,1024);

// write to standard out
fwrite(STDOUT,$jokebook);

// write to standard error
fwrite(STDERR,$error_code);
```

25.1 Parsing Program Arguments

Problem

You want to process arguments passed on the command line.

Solution

Look in $argc for the number of arguments and $argv for their values. The first argument, $argv[0], is the name of script that is being run:

```
if ($argc != 2) {
    die("Wrong number of arguments: I expect only 1.");
}

$size = filesize($argv[1]);

print "I am $argv[0] and report that the size of ";
print "$argv[1] is $size bytes.";
```

Discussion

In order to set options based on flags passed from the command line, loop through $argv from 1 to $argc, as shown in Example 25-1.

Example 25-1. Parsing commmand-line arguments

```php
<?php
for ($i = 1; $i < $argc; $i++) {
    switch ($argv[$i]) {
    case '-v':
        // set a flag
        $verbose = true;
        break;
    case '-c':
        // advance to the next argument
        $i++;
        // if it's set, save the value
        if (isset($argv[$i])) {
            $config_file = $argv[$i];
        } else {
            // quit if no filename specified
            die("Must specify a filename after -c");
        }
        break;
    case '-q':
        $quiet = true;
        break;
    default:
        die('Unknown argument: '.$argv[$i]);
        break;
    }
}
?>
```

In this example, the -v and -q arguments are flags that set $verbose and $quiet, but the -c argument is expected to be followed by a string. This string is assigned to $config_file.

See Also

Recipe 25.2 for more parsing arguments with *getopt*; documentation on $argc and $argv at *http://www.php.net/reserved.variables*.

25.2 Parsing Program Arguments with getopt

Problem

You want to parse program options that may be specified as short or long options, or they may be grouped.

Solution

Use PEAR's Console_Getopt class. Its getopt( ) method can parse both short-style options such as -a or -b and long-style options such as --alice or --bob:

```
$o = new Console_Getopt;

// accepts -a, -b, and -c
$opts = $o->getopt($argv,'abc');

// accepts --alice and --bob
$opts = $o->getopt($argv,'',array('alice','bob'));
```

Discussion

To parse short-style options, pass Console_Getopt::getopt( ) the array of command-line arguments and a string specifying valid options. This example allows -a, -b, or -c as arguments, alone or in groups:

```
$o = new Console_Getopt;
$opts = $o->getopt($argv,'abc');
```

For the previous option string abc, these are valid sets of options to pass:

```
% program.php -a -b -c
% program.php -abc
% program.php -ab -c
```

The getopt( ) method returns an array. The first element in the array is a list of all of the parsed options that were specified on the command line, along with their values. The second element is any specified command-line option that wasn't in the argument specification passed to getopt( ). For example, if the previous program is run as:

```
% program.php -a -b sneeze
```

then $opts is:

```
Array
(
    [0] => Array
        (
            [0] => Array
                (
                    [0] => a
                    [1] =>
                )
            [1] => Array
                (
                    [0] => b
                    [1] =>
                )
        )
    [1] => Array
        (
            [0] => program.php
            [1] => sneeze
        )
)
```

Put a colon after an option in the specification string to indicate that it requires a value.
Two colons means the value is optional. So ab:c:: means that a can't have a value, b
must, and c can take a value if specified. With this specification string, running the
program as:

```
% program.php -a -b sneeze
```

makes $opts:

```
Array
(
    [0] => Array
        (
            [0] => Array
                (
                    [0] => a
                    [1] =>
                )
            [1] => Array
                (
                    [0] => b
                    [1] => sneeze
                )
        )
    [1] => Array
        (
            [0] => program.php
        )
)
```

Because sneeze is now set as the value of b, it is no longer in the array of unparsed
options. Note that the array of unparsed options always contains the name of the program.

To parse long-style arguments, supply getopt( ) with an array that describes your desired arguments. Put each argument in an array element (leave off the leading --) and follow it with = to indicate a mandatory argument or == to indicate an optional argument. This array is the third argument to getopt( ). The second argument (the string for short-style arguments) can be left blank or not, depending on whether you also want to parse short-style arguments. This example allows debug as an argument with no value, name with a mandatory value, and size with an optional value:

```
require 'Console/Getopt.php';
$o = new Console_Getopt;
$opts = $o->getopt($argv,'',array('debug','name=','size=='));
```

These are valid ways to run this program:

```
% program.php --debug
% program.php --name=Susannah
% program.php --name Susannah
% program.php --debug --size
% program.php --size=56 --name=Susannah
% program.php --name --debug
```

The last example is valid (if counterproductive) because it treats --debug as the value of the name argument and doesn't consider the debug argument to be set. Values can be separated from their arguments on the command line by either a = or a space.

For long-style arguments, getopt( ) includes the leading -- in the array of parsed arguments; for example, when run as:

```
% program.php --debug --name=Susannah
```

$opts is set to:

```
Array
(
    [0] => Array
        (
            [0] => Array
                (
                    [0] => --debug
                    [1] =>
                )
            [1] => Array
                (
                    [0] => --name
                    [1] => Susannah
                )
        )
    [1] => Array
        (
            [0] => program.php
        )
)
```

This code uses $argv as the array of command-line arguments, which is fine by default. Console_Getopt provides a method, readPHPArgv( ), to look also in $argv and

$HTTP_SERVER_VARS['argv'] for command-line arguments. Use it by passing its results to getopt( ):

```
require 'Console/Getopt.php';
$o = new Console_Getopt;
$opts = $o->getopt($o->readPHPArgv(),'',array('debug','name=','size=='));
```

Both getopt( ) and readPHPArgv( ) return a Getopt_Error object when these encounter an error; for example, having no option specified for an option that requires one. Getopt_Error extends the PEAR_Error base class, so you can use familiar methods to handle errors:

```
require 'Console/Getopt.php';
$o = new Console_Getopt;
$opts = $o->getopt($o->readPHPArgv(),'',array('debug','name=','size=='));

if (PEAR::isError($opts)) {
    print $opts->getMessage();
} else {
    // process options
}
```

See Also

Recipe 25.1 for parsing of program options without *getopt*; documentation on Console_Getopt at *http://pear.php.net/manual/en/core.console.getopt.php*.

25.3 Reading from the Keyboard

Problem

You need to read in some typed user input.

Solution

Use *fopen( )* with the special filename *php://stdin*:

```
print "Type your message. Type '.' on a line by itself when you're done.\n";

$fh = fopen('php://stdin','r') or die($php_errormsg);
$last_line = false;  $message = '';
while (! $last_line) {
    $next_line = fgets($fp,1024);
    if (".\n" == $next_line) {
        $last_line = true;
    } else {
        $message .= $next_line;
    }
}

print "\nYour message is:\n$message\n";
```

If the Readline extension is installed, use readline( ):

```
$last_line = false; $message = '';
while (! $last_line) {
    $next_line = readline();
    if ('.' == $next_line) {
        $last_line = true;
    } else {
        $message .= $next_line."\n";
    }
}

print "\nYour message is:\n$message\n";
```

Discussion

Once you get a filehandle pointing to *stdin* with fopen( ), you can use all the standard file-reading functions to process input (fread( ), fgets( ), etc.). The solution uses fgets( ), which returns input a line at a time. If you use fread( ), the input still needs to be newline terminated to make fread( ) return. For example, if you run:

```
$fh = fopen('php://stdin','r') or die($php_errormsg);
$msg = fread($fh,4);
print "[$msg]";
```

And type in tomato and then a newline, the output is [toma]. The fread( ) grabs only four characters from *stdin*, as directed, but still needs the newline as a signal to return from waiting for keyboard input.

The Readline extension provides an interface to the GNU Readline library. The readline( ) function returns a line at a time, without the ending newline. Readline allows Emacs- and vi-style line editing by users. You can also use it to keep a history of previously entered commands:

```
$command_count = 1;
while (true) {
    $line = readline("[$command_count]--> ");
    readline_add_history($line);
    if (is_readable($line)) {
        print "$line is a readable file.\n";
    }
    $command_count++;
}
```

This example displays a prompt with an incrementing count before each line. Since each line is added to the Readline history with readline_add_history( ), pressing the up and down arrows at a prompt scrolls through the previously entered lines.

See Also

Documentation on fopen( ) at *http://www.php.net/fopen*, fgets( ) at *http://www.php.net/fgets*, fread( ) at *http://www.php.net/fread*, the Readline extension at *http://www.php.net/readline*, and the Readline library at *http://cnswww.cns.cwru.edu/php/chet/readline/rltop.html*.

25.4 Running PHP Code on Every Line of an Input File

Problem

You want to read an entire file and execute PHP code on every line. For example, you wish to create a command-line version of grep that uses PHP's Perl-compatible regular expression engine.

Solution

Use the -R command-line flag to process standard input:

```
% php -R 'if (preg_match("/$argv[1]/", $argn)) print "$argn\n";'
      php
      < /usr/share/dict/words

ephphatha
```

To execute a block of code before or after processing the lines, use the -B and -E options, respectively:

```
% php -B '$count = 0;'
      -R 'if (preg_match("/$argv[1]/", $argn)) $count++;'
      -E 'print "$count\n";'
      php
      < /usr/share/dict/words

1
```

Discussion

Sometimes you want to quickly process a file using PHP via the command line, either as a standalone project or within a sequence of piped commands. This lets you whip up a quick-and-dirty script to transform data.

PHP makes that easy using three command-line flags and two special variables: -R, -B, -E, $argn, and $argi.

The -R flag specifies the PHP code you want to execute for every line in the file. Within that block of code, you can access the line's text in the $argn variable.

As a basic example, here's a PHP script that takes HTML input, strips the tags, and prints out the result:

```
php -R 'print strip_tags($argn) . "\n"; ' < index.html
```

Since PHP automatically strips the newline from the end of the input, this code not only displays the results of strip_tags($argn), but also echos a newline.

It operates on the file *index.html*, which is passed in as standard input. There is no mechanism for specifying the file that you want processed.

This slightly more complicated example, which is a simple version of grep, shows how to accept input arguments via the $argv array:

```
% php -R 'if (preg_match("/$argv[1]/", $argn)) print "$argn\n";'
    php
    < /usr/share/dict/words

ephphatha
```

The first value passed preg_match( ) is /$argv[1]/, which is the first argument passed to the script. In this example, it's php, so this code is searching for all the words in the /usr/share/dict/words file containing php.

For what it's worth, ephphatha is an Aramaic word meaning "be opened."

Beyond the individual lines, you sometimes need to execute initialization or clean-up code. Specify this using the -B and -E flags.

Building on the grep example, this code counts the total number of matching lines:

```
% php -B '$count = 0;'
    -R 'if (preg_match("/$argv[1]/", $argn)) $count++;'
    -E 'print "$count\n";'
    php
    < /usr/share/dict/words

1
```

Inside the -B block, you initialize the $count to 0. It's then incremented in the -R block whenever there's a match. Finally, the total number is printed out in the -E block.

To find out the percentage of matching lines, in addition to the total, use $argi:

```
% php -B '$count = 0;'
    -R 'if (preg_match("/$argv[1]/", $argn)) $count++;'
    -E 'print "$count/$argi\n";'
    php
    < /usr/share/dict/words

1/234937
```

The $argi variable contains the current line number of the file, so inside the -E block, it's set to the total number of lines.

See Also

Documentation on Using PHP from the command line at *http://www.php.net/features.commandline.*

25.5 Reading Passwords

Problem

You need to read a string from the command line without it being echoed as it's typed —for example, when entering passwords.

Solution

On Unix systems, use */bin/stty* to toggle echoing of typed characters:

```
// turn off echo
`/bin/stty -echo`;

// read password
$password = readline();

// turn echo back on
`/bin/stty echo`;
```

On Windows, use the FFI extension to access _getch( ) from *msvcrt.dll*:

```
$ffi = new FFI("[lib='msvcrt.dll'] int _getch();");

while(true) {
    // get a character from the keyboard
    $c = chr($ffi->_getch());
    if ( "\r" == $c || "\n" == $c ) {
        // if it's a newline, break out of the loop, we've got our password
        break;
    } elseif ("\x08" == $c) {
        /* if it's a backspace, delete the previous char from $password */
        $password = substr_replace($password,'',-1,1);
    } elseif ("\x03" == $c) {
        // if it's Control-C, clear $password and break out of the loop
        $password = NULL;
        break;
    } else {
        // otherwise, add the character to the password
        $password .= $c;
    }
}
```

Discussion

On Unix, you use */bin/stty* to control the terminal characteristics so that typed characters aren't echoed to the screen while you read a password. Windows doesn't have */bin/stty*, so you use the Foreign Function Interface (FFI) extension to get access _getch( ) in the Microsoft C runtime library, *msvcrt.dll*. The _getch( ) function reads a character without echoing it to the screen. It returns the ASCII code of the character read, so you convert it to a character using chr( ). You then take action based on the character typed. If it's a newline or carriage return, you break out of the loop because the password has been entered. If it's a backspace, you delete a character from the end of the password. If it's a Ctrl-C interrupt, you set the password to NULL and break out of the loop. If none of these things are true, the character is concatenated to $password. When you exit the loop, $password holds the entered password.

The FFI extension is available as part of PECL. Windows users can download a pre-built DLL at *http://pecl4win.php.net/ext.php/php_ffi.dll*. Make sure you're using a version of FFI greater than 0.3, or this code won't work correctly.

The following code displays Login: and Password: prompts, and compares the entered password to the corresponding encrypted password stored in */etc/passwd*. This requires that the system not use shadow passwords:

```
print "Login: ";
$fh = fopen('php://stdin','r')   or die($php_errormsg);
$username = rtrim(fgets($fh,64)) or die($php_errormsg);

preg_match('/^[a-zA-Z0-9]+$/',$username)
    or die("Invalid username: only letters and numbers allowed");


print 'Password: ';
`/bin/stty -echo`;
$password = rtrim(fgets($fh,64)) or die($php_errormsg);
`/bin/stty echo`;
print "\n";

// nothing more to read from the keyboard
fclose($fh);

// find corresponding line in /etc/passwd
$fh = fopen('/etc/passwd','r')   or die($php_errormsg);
$found_user = 0;
while (! ($found_user || feof($fh))) {
    $passwd_line = fgets($fh,256);
    if (preg_match("/^$username:/",$passwd_line)) {
        $found_user = 1;
    }
}
fclose($fh);

$found_user or die ("Can't find user \"$username\"");

// parse the correct line from /etc/passwd
$passwd_parts = split(':',$passwd_line);

/* encrypt the entered password and compare it to the password in
   /etc/passwd */
$encrypted_password = crypt($password,
                            substr($passwd_parts[1],0,CRYPT_SALT_LENGTH));

if ($encrypted_password == $passwd_parts[1]) {
    print "login successful";
} else {
```

```
    print "login unsuccessful";
}
```

See Also

Documentation on `readline( )` at *http://www.php.net/readline*, `chr( )` at *http://www.php.net/chr*, on the FFI at *http://pecl.php.net/ffi*, and on `_getch( )` at *http://msdn.microsoft.com/library/en-us/vccore98/HTML/_crt__getch.2c_._getche.asp*;   on Unix, see your system's *stty(1)* manpage.

25.6 Program: Command Shell

The *command-shell.php* program shown in Example 25-2 (later in this recipe) provides a shell-like prompt to let you execute PHP code interactively. It reads in lines using `readline( )` and then runs them with `eval( )`. By default, it runs each line after it's typed in. In multiline mode (specified with -m or --multiline), however, it keeps reading lines until you enter . on a line by itself; it then runs the accumulated code.

Additionally, *command-shell.php* uses the Readline word-completion features to more easily enter PHP functions. Enter a few characters and hit Tab to see a list of functions that match the characters you've typed.

This program is helpful for running snippets of code interactively or testing different commands. The variables, functions, and classes defined in each line of code stay defined until you quit the program, so you can test different database queries, for example:

```
% php command-shell.php
[1]> require 'DB.php';

[2]> $dbh = DB::connect('mysql://user:pwd@localhost/phpc');

[3]> print_r($dbh->getAssoc('SELECT sign,planet,start_day FROM zodiac WHERE element
LIKE "water"'));
Array
(
    [Cancer] => Array
        (
            [0] => Moon
            [1] => 22
        )
    [Scorpio] => Array
        (
            [0] => Mars
            [1] => 24
        )
    [Pisces] => Array
        (
            [0] => Neptune
            [1] => 19
        )
)
```

The code for *command-shell.php* is in Example 25-2.

Example 25-2. command-shell.php

```php
// Load the readline library
if (! function_exists('readline')) {
    dl('readline.'. (((strtoupper(substr(PHP_OS,0,3))) == 'WIN')?'dll':'so'))
        or die("Readline library required\n");
}

// Load the Console_Getopt class
require 'Console/Getopt.php';

$o = new Console_Getopt;
$opts = $o->getopt($o->readPHPArgv(),'hm',array('help','multiline'));

// Quit with a usage message if the arguments are bad
if (PEAR::isError($opts)) {
    print $opts->getMessage();
    print "\n";
    usage();
}

// Default is to evaluate each command as it's entered
$multiline = false;

foreach ($opts[0] as $opt) {
    // Remove any leading -s
    $opt[0] = preg_replace('/^-+/','',$opt[0]);

    // Check the first character of the argument
    switch($opt[0][0]) {
    case 'h':
        // display help
        usage();
        break;
    case 'm':
        $multiline = true;
        break;
    }
}

// Set up error display
ini_set('display_errors',false);
ini_set('log_errors',true);

// Build readline completion table
$functions = get_defined_functions();
foreach ($functions['internal'] as $k => $v) {
    $functions['internal'][$k] = "$v(";
}
function function_list($line) {
    return $GLOBALS['functions']['internal'];
}
readline_completion_function('function_list');

$cmd = '';
$cmd_count = 1;
```

```
while (true) {
    // Get a line of input from the user
    $s = readline("[$cmd_count]> ");
    // Add it to the command history
    readline_add_history($s);
    // If we're in multiline mode:
    if ($multiline) {
        // if just a "." has been entered
        if ('.' == rtrim($s)) {
            // eval() the code
            eval($cmd);
            // Clear out the accumulated code
            $cmd = '';
            // Increment the command count
            $cmd_count++;
            // Start the next prompt on a new line
            print "\n";
        } else {
            /* Otherwise, add the new line to the accumulated code
               tacking on a newline prevents //-style comments from
               commenting out the rest of the lines entered
            */
            $cmd .= $s."\n";;
        }
    } else {
        // If we're not in multiline mode, eval() the line
        eval($s);
        // Increment the command count
        $cmd_count++;
        // Start the next prompt in a new line
        print "\n";
    }
}

// Display helpful usage information
function usage() {
    $my_name = $argv[0];

    print<<<_USAGE_
Usage: $my_name [-h|--help] [-m|--multiline]

  -h, --help: display this help
  -m, --multiline: execute accumulated code when "." is entered
                   by itself on a line. The default is to execute
                   each line after it is entered.

_USAGE_;
    exit(-1);
}
```

CHAPTER 26

PEAR and PECL

26.0 Introduction

PEAR is the PHP Extension and Application Repository, a collection of open source classes that work together. Developers can use PEAR classes to parse XML, implement authentication systems, make SOAP requests, send MIME mail with attachments, and a wide variety of other common (and not so common) tasks. A pear is also a tasty fruit.

PECL is the PHP Extension Community Library. PECL, pronounced "pickle," is a series of extensions to PHP written in C. These extensions are just like the ones distributed with the main PHP release, but they're of more specialized interest—such as an interface to the libssh2 library or the ImageMagick graphics library.

To find general information on PEAR, read the PEAR manual; to discover the latest PEAR packages, go to *http://pear.php.net*. The PEAR web site also provides links to mailing list archives, as well as RSS feeds that allow easy monitoring of new package releases.

Only a few core PEAR packages are bundled with the main PHP release. However, part of PEAR is a program called, appropriately enough, *pear*, that makes it easy for you to download and install additional PEAR packages. This program is also known simply as the PEAR installer. Recipe 26.1 shows how to use the PEAR installer.

Additionally, the PEAR installer allows you to use the PEAR class management infrastructure with your personal projects. By creating your own packages that follow the PEAR format, your users can use *pear* to download and install the files from your project's web site. If you distribute more than a handful of packages this way, you'll want to consider operating a formal PEAR channel server. The PEAR installer supports a wide variety of channel-specific features that are covered in recipes throughout this chapter.

PEAR requires PHP 4.2.0 or later, preferably with PHP built using the `--with-zlib` configuration flag. PEAR packages are available as gzipped `tar` archives, and are also available as uncompressed `tar` archives. The package installation process is more convenient in PHP environments with `zlib` capability.

This chapter explains how to find a PEAR package that you may want to use and how to install it on your machine. Because PEAR and PEAR channels offer many packages, you need an easy way to browse them. Recipe 26.2 covers different ways to find PEAR packages. Once you've found a package's name and determined which channel server it is on, Recipe 26.3 shows how to view package details and information.

Once you locate a package you want to use, you need to run *pear* to transfer the package to your machine and install it in the correct location on your server. Installing PEAR packages and PECL extensions are the subjects of Recipes 26.4 and 26.7, respectively. Recipe 26.5 shows how to discover if any upgrades are available to packages on your machine and how to install the latest versions. If you want to remove a package, see Recipe 26.6.

PHP has installed PEAR by default since PHP 4.3.0, so if you're running a version of PHP more recent than that, odds are that you can use PEAR without any additional setup.[*] PEAR has changed significantly since its initial inclusion with PHP 4.3.0, so it is strongly recommended that you upgrade to PEAR 1.4.9 or later. See Recipe 26.5 for details on upgrading PEAR. If you would prefer a clean PEAR install, refer to Recipe 26.1.

When installed during a PHP installation, PEAR installs *pear* in the same directory as *php* and places PEAR packages in *prefix/lib/php*.[†] To install PEAR in another directory, add `--with-pear=DIR` when configuring PHP. You may also install multiple instances of PEAR, which can come in handy in a shared server environment. Refer to Recipe 26.1 for details on installing multiple instances of PEAR.

Once a PEAR package is installed, use it in your PHP scripts by calling `require_once`. For example, here's how to include the `Net_Dig` package:

```
require_once 'Net/Dig.php';
```

Generally, if a package name contains an underscore, replace it with a slash, and add *.php* to the end.

Some packages may provide multiple class files, some of which should be used in certain scenarios, and not in others. The SOAP package is a good example of this; instead of requiring *SOAP.php*, you include *SOAP/Client.php* or *SOAP/Server.php*, depending on the needs of your script. Read the package documentation to determine if a particular package requires a specific inclusion approach depending on the usage scenario.

Because PEAR packages are included as regular PHP files, make sure the directory containing the PEAR packages is in your `include_path`. If it isn't, `include_once` and `require_once` can't find PEAR class files.

---

[*] If you disable building the command-line version of PHP with `--disable-cli`, PHP doesn't install PEAR.

[†] This is probably in one of */usr/local/lib/php*, */usr/lib/php*, or, in some Linux distributions, */usr/share/php*.

To view instructions and examples of how to use a particular PEAR package, check the PEAR web site at *http://pear.php.net/packages.php*. Many packages have end-user documentation complete with examples. The rest typically include at least a set of generated API documentation that provides examples of usage. If all else fails, read the top section of the package's PHP files; most contain an example of usage there as well.

Documentation for PECL extensions is not always as easy to find. Some PECL extensions are very well documented within the main PHP manual; the ClibPDF extension (available at *http://www.php.net/cpdf*) is an excellent example. Other PECL extensions are not documented at all, and usage must be gleaned by reading PHP test scripts included with the source bundles from the PECL web site. In extreme cases, you can only get the full idea of what an extension does by reading the extension source code.

The combination of PEAR and PHP provides a vast collection of high-quality reusable code that make both projects tremendous assets to the PHP community at large.

26.1 Using the PEAR Installer

Problem

You want to use the PEAR installer, *pear*. This allows you to install new packages, upgrade, and get information about your existing PEAR packages.

Solution

To execute a command with the PEAR installer, type the command name as the first argument on the command line:

```
% pear command
```

Discussion

Here's how to list all installed PEAR packages with the `list` command:[‡]

```
% pear list
Installed packages, channel pear.php.net:
=============================================
Package                       Version State
Archive_Tar                   1.3.1   stable
Console_Getopt                1.2     stable
DB                            1.7.6   stable
DB_DataObject                 1.8.4   stable
Date                          1.4.6   stable
File_Passwd                   1.1.6   stable
HTML_Common                   1.2.2   stable
HTML_QuickForm                3.2.5   stable
HTML_QuickForm_Controller     1.0.5   stable
HTML_Template_IT              1.1     stable
HTTP_Request                  1.3.0   stable
```

[‡] In early versions of *pear*, this command was `list-installed`.

```
HTTP_Session              0.5.1    beta
MDB2                      2.0.0    stable
Mail_Mime                 1.3.1    stable
Net_Socket                1.0.6    stable
Net_URL                   1.0.14   stable
Net_UserAgent_Detect      2.0.1    stable
PEAR                      1.4.9    stable
PHP_Compat                1.5.0    stable
Pager                     2.4.0    stable
XML_Parser                1.2.7    stable
XML_RPC                   1.4.0    stable
XML_RSS                   0.9.9    beta
XML_Serializer            0.18.0   beta
XML_Util                  1.1.1    stable
```

For a list of all valid PEAR commands, use `help`. Many commands also have abbreviated names; for example, `list` is also just `l`. These names are often just the first few letters of the command name. However, the PEAR installer now offers so many commands that it's safer to double-check the list of shortcuts until you get them memorized. You can review the list of *pear* shortcuts with:

```
% pear help shortcuts
```

pear has commands for both using and developing PEAR packages; as a result, there are many commands that you may not need. The `package` command, for example, creates a new PEAR package. If you only run other peoples' packages, you can safely ignore this command. See Table 26-1 for a list of frequently used commands.

Table 26-1. Common PEAR installer commands

Command name	Shortcut	Description
install	i	Download and install packages.
upgrade	up	Upgrade installed packages.
uninstall	un	Remove installed packages.
list	l	List installed packages.
list-upgrades	lu	List all available upgrades for installed packages.
channel-discover	di	Initialize an alternate PEAR Channel from its server.
list-channels	lc	List all locally configured PEAR Channels.
search	sp	Search for packages.

Like all shell programs, if you want to run *pear*, you must have permission to execute it. If you can run *pear* while running as root, but not as a regular user, make sure the group- or world-execute bit is set. Similarly, for some actions, *pear* creates a lock file in the directory containing the PEAR files. You must have write permission to the file named *.lock* located in that directory.

To find where your PEAR packages are located, run the `config-get php_dir` pear command. You can check the value of the `include_path` by calling `ini_get` ('include_path') from within PHP or by looking at your *php.ini* file. If you can't alter *php.ini* because you're in a shared hosting environment, add the directory to the include_path at the top of your script before including any PEAR files. See Recipe 20.5 for more on setting configuration variables from within PHP.

If you're behind an HTTP proxy server, configure PEAR to use it with this command:

```
% pear config-set http_proxy proxy.example.com:8080
```

You can configure PEAR installer settings using:

```
% pear set-config setting value
```

Here *setting* is the name of the parameter to modify and *value* is the new value. To see all your current settings, use the config-show command:

```
% pear config-show
Configuration (channel pear.php.net):
=====================================
Auto-discover new Channels      auto_discover       <not set>
Default Channel                 default_channel     pear.php.net
HTTP Proxy Server Address       http_proxy          <not set>
PEAR server [DEPRECATED]        master_server       pear.php.net
Default Channel Mirror          preferred_mirror    pear.php.net
Remote Configuration File       remote_config       <not set>
PEAR executables directory      bin_dir             /usr/local/bin
PEAR documentation directory    doc_dir             /usr/local/lib/php/doc
PHP extension directory         ext_dir             /usr/lib/php/extensions/↵
    no-debug-non-zts-20020429
PEAR directory                  php_dir             /usr/local/lib/php
PEAR Installer cache directory  cache_dir           /tmp/pear/cache
PEAR data directory             data_dir            /usr/local/lib/php/data
PHP CLI/CGI binary              php_bin             /usr/local/bin/php
PEAR test directory             test_dir            /usr/local/lib/php/test
Cache TimeToLive                cache_ttl           3600
Preferred Package State         preferred_state     beta
Unix file mask                  umask               22
Debug Log Level                 verbose             1
PEAR password (for              password            <not set>
maintainers)
Signature Handling Program      sig_bin             /usr/local/bin/gpg
Signature Key Directory         sig_keydir          /etc/pearkeys
Signature Key Id                sig_keyid           <not set>
Package Signature Type          sig_type            gpg
PEAR username (for              username            <not set>
maintainers)
User Configuration File         Filename            /home/foo/.pearrc
System Configuration File       Filename            /etc/pear.conf
```

For a brief description of each configuration option, use the config-help command.

If you don't have PEAR installed, or if you're in a shared-hosting environment and you're not able to upgrade or otherwise alter the system-wide PEAR installation, you need to bootstrap a fresh copy of PEAR. There's generally nothing wrong with doing a fresh PEAR installation on a shared host so long as you configure your copy to work within your shared environment. You may wind up with a PEAR package directory of */home/exampleuser/pear/php* instead of a more traditional installation location, but as long as your `include_path` values are set correctly to reflect that, there should be no problem with that approach.

To bootstrap a fresh copy of PEAR from the command line, run the following:

```
% lynx -source http://go-pear.org | php -q
Welcome to go-pear!

Go-pear will install the 'pear' command and all the files needed by
it.  This command is your tool for PEAR installation and maintenance.

Go-pear also lets you download and install the PEAR packages bundled
with PHP: DB, Net_Socket, Net_SMTP, Mail, XML_Parser.

If you wish to abort, press Control-C now, or press Enter to
continue:
```

This downloads a PHP script from the PEAR web site and hands it to PHP for execution. The program downloads all files needed to run *pear* and gets you up and running.

On some Unix systems, you may need to run *links* instead of *lynx*. If you have the command-line version of PHP installed, you may remove the `-q` flag to PHP; the CLI version automatically suppresses HTTP headers. If *go-pear* seems to hang, add `-d out put buffering=off` to the piped *php* command.

Installation on Windows is a two-step process:

```
C:\> php-cli -r 'readfile("http://go-pear.org");' > go-pear
C:\> php-cli go-pear
```

The *go-pear* script requires PHP 4.2 or greater. For the Windows installation, *php-cli* is the command-line version of PHP.

See Also

PEAR online documentation relating to installation procedures at *http://pear.php.net/ manual/en/installation.php*

26.2 Finding PEAR Packages

Problem

You want a listing of PEAR packages. From this list you want to learn more about each package and decide if you want to install it.

Solution

Browse packages at *http://pear.php.net/packages.php* or search for packages at *http:// pear.php.net/search.php*. Use *pear*'s `remote-list` command to get a listing of PEAR packages or the **search** command to search for packages. Explore listings of PEAR channel servers at PEAR Channel directory web sites *http://www.upear.com/* or *http://pear.php.net/channels/*.

Discussion

There are a few ways to review available PEAR and PEAR-compatible packages. First, to browse the listings of official PEAR packages in a directory-style fashion, go to *http://pear.php.net/packages.php*. From there you can burrow into each individual PEAR category.

Alternatively, you can search through the listings at the following address: *http://pear.php.net/search.php*. The search page allows you to search by package name, author, category and release date.

You can also ask the PEAR installer to provide you with a listing using the **remote-list** command:

```
% pear remote-list
Channel pear.php.net Available packages:
==========================================
Package                      Version
Auth_HTTP                    2.1.6
Auth                         1.3.0
Auth_SASL                    1.0.1
LiveUser                     0.16.11
Auth_PrefManager             1.1.4
Auth_RADIUS                  1.0.4


...

XML_Indexing                 0.3.6
XML_Feed_Parser              0.3.0beta
XML_RPC2                     0.0.7
XML_Query2XML                0.6.0
```

The short form of **remote-list** is **rl**.

You may also query compatible PEAR Channel servers for available packages using the **remote-list** command with the **-c** flag specifying the channel to query. In order to do so, you must first make the PEAR installer aware of the alternate channel server. For example:

```
% pear channel-discover pearified.com
Adding Channel "pearified.com" succeeded
Discovery of channel "pearified.com" succeeded
% pear remote-list -c pearified
Retrieving data...0%....50%....
Channel pearified Available packages:
======================================
Package                      Version
Editors_FCKeditor            2.2.0
Editors_TinyMCE              2.0.1
Icons_Silk                   1.3.0
```

```
...
Role_Web                    1.1.1
SimpleTest                  1.0.0
Smarty                      2.6.8
```

To search for package names from the command line, use the **search** command:

```
% pear search auth
Retrieving data...0%....50%....
Matched packages, channel pear.php.net:
=======================================
Package              Stable/(Latest)        Local
Auth                 1.3.0/(1.3.0 stable)   1.3.0 Creating an authentication
                                            system.
Auth_HTTP            2.1.6/(2.1.6 stable)   HTTP authentication
Auth_PrefManager     1.1.4/(1.1.4 stable)   1.1.4 Preferences management class
Auth_PrefManager2    -n/a-/(2.0.0dev1 alpha) Preferences management class
Auth_RADIUS          1.0.4/(1.0.4 stable)   Wrapper Classes for the RADIUS PECL.
Auth_SASL            1.0.1/(1.0.1 stable)   Abstraction of various SASL mechanism
                                            responses
```

This does a case-insensitive search of package names and returns the package name; the latest stable version; the latest version at any of dev, alpha, or beta states; the version you have installed locally (if any); and a short description about the package.

See Also

Recipe 26.3 to find more information about a package.

26.3 Finding Information About a Package

Problem

You want to gather information about a package, such as a description of what it does, who maintains it, what version you have installed, and which license it's released under.

Solution

If the package is installed on your machine, use the PEAR installer's **info** command:

```
% pear info Net_URL
```

Otherwise, use the **remote-info** command:

```
% pear remote-info SOAP
```

You can also view the package's home page on *http://pear.php.net*.

Discussion

The **info** command provides summary information about a package:

```
% pear info Net_URL
About Net_URL-1.0.14
====================
Provides              Classes:
Package               Net_URL
Summary               Easy parsing of Urls
Description           Provides easy parsing of URLs and their
                      constituent parts.
Maintainers           Richard heyes <richard@php.net> (lead)
Version               1.0.14
Release Date          2004-06-19
Release License       BSD
Release State         stable
Release Notes         Whitespace
Package.xml Version   1.0
Last Installed Version - None -
Last Modified         2006-05-08
```

If you don't have the package installed, ask the remote server for a description:

```
% pear remote-info Net_URL
Package details:
================
Latest      1.0.14
Installed   - no -
Package     Net_URL
License     BSD
Category    Networking
Summary     Easy parsing of Urls
Description Provides easy parsing of URLs and their
            constituent parts.
```

This request displays a slightly different set of information. It doesn't include the release data but does include the general PEAR category and the latest release number for the package.

The package home page provides a more complete view and also provides links to earlier releases, a change log, and browsable access to the package's CVS repository. You can also view package download statistics. Figure 26-1 shows a sample package information page.

See Also

Recipe 26.2 to search for packages.

26.4 Installing PEAR Packages

Problem

You want to install a PEAR package.

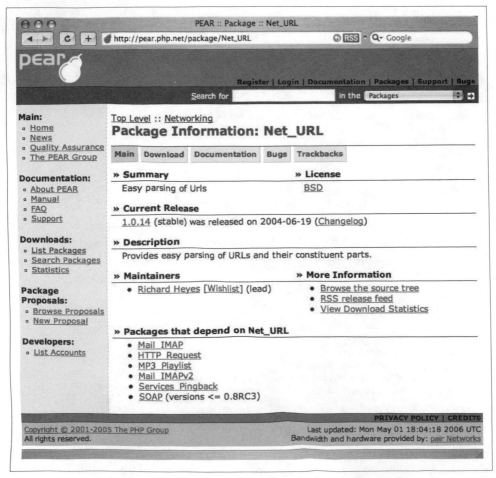

Figure 26-1. Net_URL Package Information page on the PEAR web site

Solution

Download and install the package from the appropriate PEAR Channel server using the PEAR installer:

```
% pear install Package_Name
```

You can also install from another PEAR Channel:

```
% pear install channel/Package_Name
```

You can also install from any location on the Internet:

```
% pear install http://pear.example.com/Package_Name-1.0.0.tgz
```

Here's how to install if you have a local copy of a package:

```
% pear install Package_Name-1.0.0.tgz
```

Discussion

To install PEAR packages, you need write permission where the packages are stored; this defaults to */usr/local/lib/php/*.

You can also request multiple packages at the same time:

```
% pear install XML_Parser XML_Tree
downloading XML_Parser-1.2.7.tgz ...
Starting to download XML_Parser-1.2.7.tgz (12,939 bytes)
.....done: 12,939 bytes
downloading XML_Tree-1.1.tgz ...
Starting to download XML_Tree-1.1.tgz (4,826 bytes)
...done: 4,826 bytes
install ok: channel://pear.php.net/XML_Tree-1.1
install ok: channel://pear.php.net/XML_Parser-1.2.7
```

When installing a package, PEAR checks that you have all the necessary PHP functions and PEAR packages that the new package depends on. If this check fails, PEAR reports on the dependencies:

```
% pear install MDB2_Driver_Mysql
 install MDB2_Driver_Mysql
Did not download dependencies: pear/MDB2, use --alldeps or --onlyreqdeps to
download automatically
pear/MDB2_Driver_mysql requires package "pear/MDB2" (version >= 2.0.1)
No valid packages found
install failed
```

As you can see from the error message, the PEAR installer made no attempt to download dependencies. This default behavior puts you in control by not assuming that you want to install or upgrade the related dependencies. The most convenient `install` command switch is `-o`, which is the shortcut for `--onlyreqdeps`, which installs all required dependencies.

Using the `-o` switch, the installation is now successful:

```
% pear install -o MDB2_Driver_Mysql
downloading MDB2_Driver_mysql-1.0.1.tgz ...
Starting to download MDB2_Driver_mysql-1.0.1.tgz (22,240 bytes)
........done: 22,240 bytes
downloading MDB2-2.0.1.tgz ...
Starting to download MDB2-2.0.1.tgz (91,219 bytes)
...done: 91,219 bytes
install ok: channel://pear.php.net/MDB2-2.0.1
install ok: channel://pear.php.net/MDB2_Driver_mysql-1.0.1
```

If you want to ignore the required dependencies, you can use the `-n` or `--nodeps` switches to tell the installer to ignore dependencies and install anyway.

See Also

Recipe 26.7 for information on installing PECL packages; Recipe 26.5 for more on upgrading an existing package; Recipe 26.6 to uninstall a package.

26.5 Upgrading PEAR Packages

Problem

You want to upgrade a package on your system to the latest version for additional functionality and bug fixes.

Solution

Find out if any upgrades are available and then tell *pear* to upgrade the packages you want:

```
% pear list-upgrades
% pear upgrade -o Package_Name
```

Discussion

Upgrading to a new version of a package is a simple task with the PEAR installer. If you know a specific package is out of date, you can upgrade it directly. However, you may also just want to check periodically to see if any new releases are available.

To do this, use the `list-upgrades` command, which prints out a table showing the channel server of the package, package name, local version number and state, version number and state of the remote upgrade, and size of the download of the upgrade:

```
% pear list-upgrades
pear.php.net Available Upgrades (stable):
==========================================
Channel       Package          Local           Remote          Size
pear.php.net  HTML_Table       1.6.1 (stable)  1.7.0 (stable)  13.7kB
pear.php.net  HTML_Template_IT 1.1.3 (stable)  1.1.4 (stable)  19.7kB
pear.php.net  Log              1.9.3 (stable)  1.9.5 (stable)  37kB
pear.php.net  Mail             1.1.9 (stable)  1.1.10 (stable) 16.5kB
pear.php.net  MDB2             2.0.0 (stable)  2.0.1 (stable)  90kB
pear.php.net  Pager            2.3.6 (stable)  2.4.1 (stable)  31kB
pear.php.net  PEAR             1.4.8 (stable)  1.4.9 (stable)  277kB
pear.php.net  Services_Weather 1.3.2 (stable)  1.4.0 (stable)  53kB
```

If you're up to date, *pear* prints:

```
Channel pear.php.net: No upgrades available
```

To upgrade a particular package, use the `upgrade` command. For example:

```
% pear upgrade MDB2
Did not download dependencies: pear/PEAR, use --alldeps or --onlyreqdeps to
download automatically
downloading MDB2-2.0.1.tgz ...
Starting to download MDB2-2.0.1.tgz (91,219 bytes)
...................done: 91,219 bytes
upgrade ok: channel://pear.php.net/MDB2-2.0.1
```

The short command for `list-upgrades` is lu; for `upgrade` it's up.

PEAR also has an RSS feed listing new and upgraded packages is available at *http://pear.php.net/rss.php*. An aggregated RSS feed listing new and upgraded packages available on the PEAR site and a variety of other PEAR Channels is available at *http://pearified.com/planet.xml*.

See Also

Recipes 26.4 and 26.7 for information on installing PEAR and PECL packages; Recipe 26.6 to uninstall a package; Recipe 12.12 for more on parsing RSS feeds.

26.6 Uninstalling PEAR Packages

Problem

You wish to remove a PEAR package from your system.

Solution

The uninstall command tells the PEAR installer to delete packages:

```
% pear uninstall Pager
uninstall ok: channel://pear.php.net/MDB2-2.4.1
```

Discussion

Uninstalling a package removes it completely from your system. If you want to reinstall it, you must begin as if the package was never installed.

If you try to remove a package another package depends on, PEAR will warn you and halt the uninstall process. For example, take a look at a sample PEAR installation:

```
% pear list
Installed packages, channel pear.php.net:
=========================================
Package            Version State
Archive_Tar        1.3.1   stable
DB                 1.7.6   stable
HTML_Common        1.2.2   stable
HTML_Table         1.7.0   stable
MDB2               2.0.1   stable
MDB2_Driver_mysql  1.0.1   stable
PEAR               1.4.9   stable
XML_Parser         1.2.7   stable
XML_Tree           1.1     stable
```

Now, try to uninstall the MDB2 package:

```
% pear uninstall MDB2
pear/MDB2 cannot be uninstalled, other installed packages depend on this
package
```

You can still force a package that has dependencies to uninstall by using the `n` flag or `--nodeps` flag to instruct the PEAR installer to ignore dependencies and uninstall anyway. Use this capability with caution.

There is no way to automatically roll back an upgrade to an earlier version of a package by using `uninstall`. Also, PEAR complains if you try install an earlier version of a package over a later one. To force the PEAR installer to overwrite a newer version of a package with an older one, use `install -f` or `install --force`:

```
% pear install DB-1.7.5
Skipping package "pear/DB , already installed as version 1.7.6
No valid packages found
install failed

% pear install -f DB-1.7.5
Downloading DB-1.7.5.tgz ...
Starting to download DB-1.7.5.tgz (124,767 bytes)
..........................done: 124,767 bytes
install ok: channel://pear.php.net/DB-1.7.5
```

The short command for `uninstall` is un.

See Also

Recipes 26.4 and 26.7 for information on installing PEAR and PECL packages.

26.7 Installing PECL Packages

Problem

You want to install a PECL package; this builds a PHP extension written in C to use inside PHP.

Solution

Make sure you have all the necessary extension libraries and then use the PEAR installer bundled command *pecl*:

```
% pecl install mailparse
```

To use the extension from PHP, add the appropriate line to your *php.ini* file:

```
extension=mailparse.so
```

Discussion

The frontend process for installing PECL packages is just like installing PEAR packages for code written in PHP. However, the behind-the-scenes tasks are very different. Because PECL extensions are written in C, the installer needs to compile the extension and configure it to work with the installed version of PHP. As a result, at present, you can build PECL packages on Unix machines if you have the necessary development tools installed and on Windows machines if you use MSDev.

Unlike PHP-based PEAR packages, PECL extensions don't automatically inform you when you lack a library necessary to compile the extension. Instead, you are responsible for correctly preinstalling these files. If you are having trouble getting a PECL extension to build, check the *README* file and the other documentation that comes with the package. The installer puts these files inside the *docs* directory under your PEAR hierarchy.

When you install a PECL extension, the *pecl* command downloads the distribution file, extracts it, runs *phpize* to configure the extension for the version of PHP installed on the machine, and then makes and installs the extension. It may also prompt you for the location of libraries:

```
% pecl install mailparse
downloading mailparse-2.1.1.tgz ...
Starting to download mailparse-2.1.1.tgz (35,883 bytes)
..........done: 35,883 bytes
9 source files, building
running: phpize
Configuring for:
PHP Api Version:        20031224
Zend Module Api No:     20041030
Zend Extension Api No:  220040412

...

Build complete.
(It is safe to ignore warnings about tempnam and tmpnam).

running: make INSTALL_ROOT="/var/tmp/pear-build-root/install-mailparse-2.1.1"
install
Installing shared extensions:
/var/tmp/pear-build-root/install-mailparse-2.1.1/usr/lib/php/20041030/
running: find "/var/tmp/pear-build-root/install-mailparse-2.1.1" -ls
8306920    4 drwxr-xr-x  3 root    root      4096 May  1 16:40 /var/tmp/pear-build-root/↵
    install-mailparse-2.1.1
4522201    4 drwxr-xr-x  3 root    root      4096 May  1 16:40 /var/tmp/pear-build-root/↵
    install-mailparse-2.1.1/usr
4522202    4 drwxr-xr-x  3 root    root      4096 May  1 16:40 /var/tmp/pear-build-root/↵
    install-mailparse-2.1.1/usr/lib
4522203    4 drwxr-xr-x  3 root    root      4096 May  1 16:40 /var/tmp/pear-build-root/↵
    install-mailparse-2.1.1/usr/lib/php
8306938    4 drwxr-xr-x  2 root    root      4096 May  1 16:40 /var/tmp/pear-build-root/↵
    install-mailparse-2.1.1/usr/lib/php/20041030
8306939  140 -rwxr-xr-x  1 root    root    136671 May  1 16:40 /var/tmp/pear-build-root/↵
    install-mailparse-2.1.1/usr/lib/php/20041030/mailparse.so

Build process completed successfully
Installing
'/var/tmp/pear-build-root/install-mailparse-2.1.1//usr/lib/php/20041030/mailparse.so'
install ok: channel://pecl.php.net/mailparse-2.1.1
You should add "extension=mailparse.so" to php.ini
```

PECL extensions are stored in different places than PEAR packages written in PHP. If you want to run *pecl*, you must be able to write inside the PHP *extensions* directory. Because of this, you may want to install these packages while running as the same user you used to install PHP. Also, check the execute permissions of these files; because most PEAR files aren't executable, your umask may not provide those executable files with the correct set of permissions.

If you're running PHP and PECL in a Windows environment, you may prefer to download precompiled DLLs for the PECL extensions you need from *http://pecl4win.php.net/*.

PHP's dl( ) can be used to load extensions at runtime, but it is deprecated. If possible, activate new extensions in the *php.ini* file.

See Also

Recipe 26.4 for information on installing PEAR packages; Recipe 26.5 for more on upgrading an existing package; Recipe 26.6 to uninstall a package; the PECL Windows Repository at *http://pecl4win.php.net*.

Index

Symbols

!== (nonidentity) operator, 120
" (double quotes), 1
   escaping, 2
   escaping in database queries, 309
$ (dollar sign), 145
   escaping, 2
$GLOBALS array, 479, 485
$HTTP_COOKIE_VARS arrays, 260
$HTTP_ENV_VARS arrays, 260
$HTTP_GET_VARS arrays, 260
$HTTP_POST_FILES arrays, 260, 282
$HTTP_POST_VARS arrays, 260
$HTTP_RAW_POST_DATA, 238
$HTTP_SERVER_VARS arrays, 260
$_COOKIE array, 232, 259
   global variable injection, 284
$_ENV array, 249
$_FILES array, 259, 281
$_GET array, 259
   global variable injection, preventing, 284
   required fields and, 262
   REST methods, serving, 465
   REST requests and, 462
$_POST array, 259
   global variable injection, preventing, 284
   required fields and, 262
   verifying data with hashes, 554
$_REQUEST array, 259
$_SERVER array, 239, 259, 466, 549
   detecting SSL, 566
   REST methods, serving, 467
   SOAP authentication, 482
$_SESSION array, 277

% (percent sign)
   format operators and, 68
   remainder operator, as a, 239
% (SQL wildcard), 309
%i specifier, 47
%n specifier, 47
& (ampersand), 606
   interpreting GET query stings, 237
' (single quotes), 1
   escaping in database queries, 309
( ) (parentheses), 653
* (asterisk), 642
+ (plus sign), 642
   GET query strings, 237
   merging arrays, 114
-> (arrow)
   accessing methods or variables, 180
   static properties and methods, defining,
      213
. (dot)
   concatenation operator, 3, 15
   regular expression metacharacter, 642
/ (forward slash), 665
   Perl m/ / pattern matching, 645
/i flag, 25, 645
:: (double colon), 211
   accessing methods or variables, 180
; (semicolon), using heredoc formats, 4
<<< (heredoc format), 2
   (see also heredoc format)
<img> source tag (see img source tag)
<option/> element, 278
<select/> element, 713
<textarea> form field, 24
= (equals), 142, 165

We'd like to hear your suggestions for improving our indexes. Send email to *index@oreilly.com*.

American Standard Code for Information (ASCII), 1
ampersand (&), 606
    interpreting GET query strings, 237
"An Overview on Globalizing Oracle PHP Applications" (Linsley, Peter), 594
anchoring patterns, 643
AND (logical), 606
anonymous FTP, 505
Apache, 251, 439
Apache HTTP server benchmarking tool (ab), 635
apache_note( ), 251
APC (Alternative PHP Cache), 638
APD (Advanced PHP Debugger), 633
apd_set_pprof_trace( ), 633
appendChild( ), 356
application MIME type, 497
Applied Cryptography (Schneier, Bruce), 560
arbitrary headers, 405
arbitrary methods, 406–408
arcs, drawing, 521–523
$argc, 729
arguments
    parsing, 729
    SOAP methods, accepting in, 470–472
$argv, 729
array( ), 103, 113
    temporary variables and, 144
ArrayAccess interface, 135
arrays, 101–139
    addFunction( ) method, bindind functions, 469
    appending, 113–114
    associative (see associative arrays)
    calculating differences of date parts, 71
    comma-separated data and, 17
    command-line arguments, parsing, 730
    commas, printing with, 116
    configuration files, parsing, 681
    controlling object serialization, 215
    deleting elements from, 109–111
    dumping variable contents, 153
    duplicate elements, removing, 129
    elements, checking if inside, 118
    environment variables and, 249
    error_reporting( ) and, 606
    exchanging values without temporary variables, 144

fixed-width field data records and, 20
functions, applying to each element in, 130–132
getdate( ), finding current data/time with, 59
iterating through, 107–109
Julian days and Gregorian calendars, converting between, 90
keys, 117
largest/smallest elements, finding, 121
localtime( ) return values and, 60
magic accessor methods and, 199
matching words with preg_match_all( ), 647
objects, 134–137
    checking if is an instance of a class, 220
paragraphs, counting, 674
printing correct plurals, 49
randomizing order, 129
    lines in files, 679
ranges of integers, initializing, 106
reading a file into, 293
reversing, 122
size, changing, 111–113
SOAP methods
    calling, 443
    passing to, 471
sorting, 123
    computable fields, 124–126
    multiple, 126–128
    using methods, 128
storing multiple elements in, 105
testing elements, 120
turning into a string, 115
unions/intersections/differences, finding, 132–134
values, finding the position of, 119
zero, not beginning with, 103
__call( ), using, 206
array_diff( ), 133
array_filter( ), 120
array_flip( ), 119
array_intersect( ), 271
array_intersection( ), 133
array_keys( ), 130
array_key_exists( ), 117, 143, 268, 270
array_map( ), 108, 134
array_merge( ), 113, 133
array_multisort( ), 126

call_user_func_array( ), 171, 204
CAL_FRENCH constant, 92
CAL_JEWISH constant, 93
CAL_JULIAN constant, 91
cal_to_jd( ), 90
capitalization (see case)
caret (^), 644
carriage return (\r), 2, 664
    trimming, 16
Cascading Style Sheets (CSS), 238
case
    controlling, 13
case-insensitivity
    regular expression pattern matching and,
        645
case-sensitivity, 645
    preg_split( ), 25
    XML, 351
CBC (Cipher Block Chaining), 558
CDB DBM backends, 294
ceil( ), 38
centered text, drawing, 527–532
CFB (Cipher Feedback), 558
<channel> element, 387
channel-discover PEAR command, 746
character classes, 643
character encoding, 588–590
characters
    escape sequences, 2
    escaping special with regular expressions,
        654
"Characters vs. Bytes" (Bray, Tim), 594
check boxes, 271–272
checkdate( ), 74, 273
chgrp( ), 709
chmod( ), 705, 709
chomp( ) (Perl), 17
chop( ), 17
chown( ), 709
chr( ), 737
Cipher Block Chaining (CBC), 558
Cipher Feedback (CFB), 558
circles, drawing, 521–523
class keyword, 178, 224
    abstract base classes and, 193
    interfaces, defining and, 192
classes, 177–227
    abstract base, 193–195
    access control, implementing, 184–187

accessing overridden methods, 207
aggregating objects, 203–207
autoloading class files, 222–224
cloning objects, 196–198
constants, defining, 210–212
constructors, 179, 182
destructors, 183
exceptions, creating, 598–601
instances, 220–222
instantiating an object dynamically, 224
interfaces, specifying, 191–193
introspecting object, 216–220
method polymorphism, using, 208–210
methods, returning, 203
preventing changes to, 187
property accesses, overriding, 198–202
references, 195
serialization, controlling, 214–216
static properties and methods, defining,
    212–214
XML schema datatypes, mapping to, 455
class_exists( ), 225
class_implements( ), 192
clean( ) (Cache_Lite), 324
CLI (command-line interface), 727
clone keyword, 196–198
cloning objects, 196–198
Coe, Katy, 472
comma-separated values (CSV), 17
    downloading, 31
    parsing, 19
command line, 727–739
    arguments, parsing, 729
    escaping shell metacharacters, 687
    getopt, passing arguments with, 730–733
    keyboards, reading from, 733
    passwords, reading from, 737–739
    running code on every line of an input file,
        735–736
command-line interface (CLI), 727
compact( ), 458
complex SOAP types, 446
compress.bzip2, 700
compress.zlib, 700
compressed files, 700
concatenation operator (see ., under Symbols)
config-show command, 747
configuration files, 680–683
configuration variables, 602–604

setting, 604
connect( ), 188
Console_Getopt class, 730
const keyword, 210
constants, 210
constructors, 179, 182
    accessing overridden methods and, 208
content encoding, 382
Content-Type header, 32, 355, 537
    character encoding, setting with, 588
    ImagePNG( ), sending images, 519
context_get Xdebug command, 616
"cookie jar" feature (cURL), 403
cookies, 339
    authenticating, 244–246
    debugging web pages, 615
    deleting, 233
    detecting SSL, 566
    reading values, 232
    setting, 230–232
    URL, fetching with, 403
Coordinated Universal Time (UTC), 57, 81
    offsets, 84
copy( ), 712
cos( ), 49
Costales, Bryan, 492
COUNT database function, 309
count( ), 108, 111
    functions that take a variable number of
        arguments, 163
CREATE SQL command, 466
createElement( ), 388
create_function( ), 174, 658
credit cards, validating from input and, 273
cross-site request forgeries (CSRF), 546
cross-site scripting (XSS), 275, 543
    avoiding cross-site scripting, 547
Cryptography: Theory and Practice (Stinson,
    Douglas R.), 560
CSRF (cross-site request forgeries), 546
CSS (Cascading Style Sheets), 238
CSV (comma-separated values)
    creating, 17
    downloading, 31
    parsing, 19
ctype_alnum( ), 636
ctype_digit( ), 264–266
cURL, 395, 400, 401, 441, 543
    CURLOPT_COOKIE option, 403

debugging SOAP requests, 446
finding stale links, 431
FTP, getting and putting files, 505
put, using with, 407
response headers, getting, 413
REST methods, executing, 441
sending headers, 405
timeouts, fetching URLs, 408
curly braces ({ })
    dynamic variable names and, 145
    interpolating strings and, 15
curl_close( ), 414, 506
curl_exec( ), 399, 413, 431
curl_init( ), 505
curl_setopt( ), 505
custom error handling, using, 608
custom file type, reading and writing, 695–
    699
CustomException class, 599

D

data persistence (see sessions)
data source name (DSN), 341
data sources (LDAP), 507
data stuctures, using complex SOAP types,
    446
databases, 291–334
    accessing connections, 324–326
    CSV (comma-separated values), 17–20
    DBM, 293
    encrypted data, 560–563
    identifiers, creating unique, 313–314
    logging information/errors, 311–312
    modifying data in SQL, 304
    paginated links, making, 319–322
    quotes, escaping, 309
    random rows, selecting, 41
    repeating queries efficiently, 305–308
    retrieving rows without a loop, 303
    rows, finding number of by a query, 308
    sessions, storing, 340
    SQL databases, 299–303
    SQLite, 297–299
    vs. LDAP, 508
date( ), 57–61, 63–69, 288, 474, 485
    finding day, week, month or year with, 72–
        74
    time zones and, 81
    Usenet, reading messages and, 503

mt_srand( ), 41
multidimensional arrays, sorting, 127
multipage forms, 276–277
multipart MIME type, 497
MySQL
    parsing dates and, 77
    test environments, setting up, 626
"The Mythical Man-Month" (Brooks, Fred),
        612
M_PI constant, 212

N

Naberezny, Mike, 695
name attribute (HTML checkboxes), 272
name element ($_FILES), 282
named placeholders, 306
namespaces, 447
    XML, debugging SOAP requests, 446
natcasersort( ), 124
natrsort( ), 124
natural log (base e), 43
NDBM DBM backends, 294
Network News Transport Protocol (see NNTP)
Net_Ping package (PEAR), 512
Net_Ping::checkhost( ), 512
Net_Ping::ping( ), 512
Net_Whois class, 514
Net_Whois::query( ), 514
new keyword, 178, 181
newlines, 664
    paragraphs, counting and, 674
    stripping, 656
    trimming, 16
    wrapping lines and, 27
    \n escape sequence, 2
newsgroups (Usenet), posting messages, 497
next( ) (XMLReader), 364
Niederst, Jennifer (Web Design in a Nutshell),
        55
nl2br( ), 503
NNTP (Network News Transport Protocol),
        495, 499
nodeType attribute, 365
non-Gregorian calendar, 90–94
nongreedy matching, 650
nonidentity (!==) operator, 120
note tables, 252
nsl namespace, 447
nsupdate command, 689

null, 16
null (variables), 141
null values
    SOAP methods, calling, 443
numbers, 35–56
    bases, 53–55
    checking variables for, 36
    exponents, calculating, 44
    floating-point, 37–39
    formatting, 45
    large or small, handling, 51
    logarithms, 43
    monetary values, formatting, 46
    operating on a series of, 39
    plurals, printing correct, 48
    random, generating, 40–43
    SOAP methods, passing to, 471
    trigonometry, calculating, 49–50
    validating form input, 264–266
number_format( ), 45, 580
numerical arrays, 101
NuSOAP, 442

O

object-oriented programming (OOP), 177
objects, 177–227
    abstract base classes, 193–195
    access control, implementing, 184–187
    accessing overridden methods, 207
    aggregating, 203–207
    arrays, 134–137
    autoloading class files, 222
    class constants, defining, 210
    cloning, 196–198
    constructors, 179, 182
    destructors, 183
    instances, 220–222
    instantiating, 181, 224
    interfaces, specifying, 191–193
    introspecting, 216
    method polymorphism, using, 208–210
    methods, returning, 203
    preventing changes to, 187
    property accesses, overriding, 198–202
    references, 195
    serialization, 214–216
    SOAP methods, passing to, 471
    sorting arrays and, 128

SOAPVar class, 477
SOAP_ENC_OBJECT, 448
SOAP_FUNCTIONS_ALL, 469
Solaris, 439
sort( ), 123
  multiple arrays, sorting with, 127
space-padding strings, 20
spaces, converting to tabs, 11
  (see also whitespace)
<span/> element, 417
special characters, escaping, 654
split( ), 24–27, 592
spliti( ), 25
spoofing (forms), 545
spreadsheets, generating/parsing CSV data,
    17–20
sprintf( ), 172, 541, 574–577
  money_format( ) and, 579
SQL databases, 291, 304
  commands, 466
  connecting to, 299–303
  querying, 300–303
SQL injection, 548
  vulnerablities, 543
SQLite, 292, 297–299
sqlite_master table, 298
square brackets ([ ]), 4
  character classes, matching with, 643
  configuration files, parsing, 681
  form elements with multiple options and,
      287
  HTML checkbox values and, 272
srand( ), 559
SSL, 565, 566
  detecting, 566
  encrypting mail with IMAP/POP3, 495
St. Laurent, Simon, 459, 488
stack traces, printing, 601
standard errors, reading, 691
standard output, 685, 689
stat( ), 707
statefulness, 335
stateless protocols, 259
static class method, creating a database
      connection, 324
static keyword, 213
static properties, 212–214
static variables, 146
stdin, 734

step_into Xdebug command, 615
step_out Xdebug command, 615
step_over Xdebug command, 615
Stinson, Douglas R., 560
stop Xdebug command, 615
strace(1), 691
stream context, 398
streams, 397
stream_filter_append( ), 425
stream_get_line( ), 675
stream_get_meta_data( ), 413
stream_set_timeout( ), 409
strfmon( ), 47, 580
strftime( ), 58, 63–69
  finding day, week, month or year with, 72–
      74
  localizing dates and times, 577
  money_format( ) and, 579
  time ranges, generating, 88
  time zones and, 81
strings, 1–33
  binary data, storing, 28–31
  breaking into pieces, 24–27
  bytes, processing, 8
  case, controlling, 13
  CSV data, 17–20, 31
  dates and times, parsing, 76–79, 76
  dumping variable contents as, 153–156
  encapsulating complex data types as, 152
  fixed-width field data, 20–24
  interpolating functions and expressions, 15,
      15
  reading a file into, 671–673
  reversing, 10
  SOAP methods, passing to, 471
  substrings
    accessing, 4
    extracting, 5
    replacing, 7
  tabs, expanding/compressing, 11
  time, formatting into, 58
  turning an array into, 115
  whitespace, removing, 16
  wrapping text and, 27
  XML, generating, 354
stripslashes( ), 153
strip_tags( ), 424, 650
strlen( ), 262, 592
strnatcmp( ), 125

U

V

W

web application security, 543–568
  cross-site scripting, avoiding, 547
  filtering input, 546
  form spoofing, protecting against, 545
  session fixation, preventing, 544
web automation, 395–434
Web Design in a Nutshell (Niederst, Jennifer),
    55
web pages, marking up, 416–419
web programming, 229–255
  automation, 395–434
  browsers, detecting different, 235
  buffering output to browsers, 247
  communicating within Apache, 251
  compressing web output, 248
  cookie authentication, using, 244–246
  cookies (see cookies)
  environment variables
    reading, 249
    setting, 250
  flushing output to browsers, 246
  GET query stings, 236
  HTML tables, generating with alternating
    row styles, 238
  HTTP authentication, using, 239–243
  POST requests, 237
  redirecting to a different location, 233–235
Web service helper, 472
web services, 439–460
  building, 461–488
Web Services Description Language (see
    WSDL)
WebTestCase class (SimpleTest), 624
WEEK( ) (MySQL), 74
WEEKDAY( ) (MySQL), 74
while loop, 107, 368
whitespace, 665
  removing, 16
whitespace (\s) metacharacter, 677
Windows (Microsoft), 439
  binary files, reading, 668
  directories in pathnames, 665
  Event Log, 605
  FFI extension, reading passowords, 737
  handling line delimiters, 664
  SMTP variables and, 491
  strftime( ) and date( ) format characters for,
    64

  XAMPP, using, 625
Windows XP, listing locales, 571
word boundries, 10
word-boundary (\b) metacharacter, 677
wordwrap( ), 27–28, 541
wrapping text, 27–28
wrap_html_tag( ), 159
WS-Security, 451
WSDL (Web Services Description Language)
  complex SOAP types, using, 447
  debugging SOAP requests, 446
  generating automatically, 472
  redefining endpoints, 451
  SOAP, calling methods, 441–445
wsdl-writer, 472
WSDL_Gen, 472
WWW-Authenticate header, 239

X

xajax, 430
XAMPP, 625
Xdebug, 602
Xdebug extension, 614–619
xdebug.remote_host value, 615
xdebug.so module, 614
XDEBUG_SESSION cookie, 615
XHTML, 353, 419, 420
XML (Extensible Markup Language), 351–393,
    426
  Atom feeds, writing, 389–393
  complex SOAP types, using, 447
  content encoding, handling, 382
  generating as a string, 354
  generating with DOM, 355
  large documents, parsing, 363–369
  namespaces (see XML namespaces)
  parsing documents
    basic, 358–360
    complex, 360–363
  reading RSS and Atom feeds, 383–385
  REST and, 441, 461
  schema datatypes, mapping, 455
  SOAPServer, instantiating, 468
  validating, 380–381
  writing RSS feeds, 386–389
  WSDL and, 442
  XML-RPC methods, calling, 456–459
  XPath, extracting information, 369–372
  XSLT, 372–379

Depending on their size, land iguanas reach maturity between 8 and 15 years of age. They congregate and mate during specific periods, which vary from island to island. The females then migrate to suitable areas to nest. After digging a burrow, the female lays 2 to 20 eggs in the nest. She then defends the covered nest site to prevent other females from nesting in the same spot.

Young iguanas hatch 85 to 110 days later and take about a week to dig their way out of the nest. Normally, if hatchlings survive the first year when food is often scarce and native predators such as hawks, egrets, herons, and snakes are a danger, they can live for more than 60 years. In reality, predation by feral cats is far worse because the young must survive and grow for at least three to four years before becoming large enough that cats can't kill them.

The cover image is a 19th-century engraving from the Dover Pictorial Archive. The cover font is Adobe ITC Garamond. The text font is Linotype Birka; the heading font is Adobe Myriad Condensed; and the code font is LucasFont's TheSans Mono Condensed.

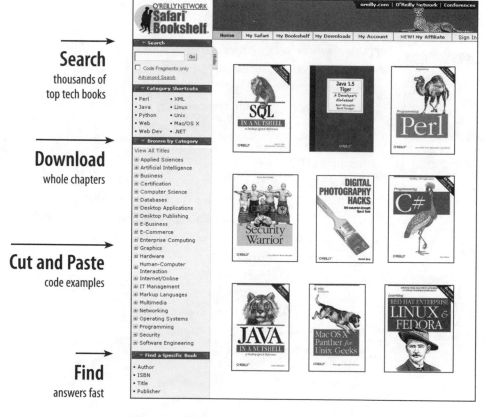

Related Titles from O'Reilly

Web Authoring and Design

ActionScript 3 Cookbook

Ajax Hacks

Ambient Findability

Cascading Style Sheets: The Definitive Guide, *2nd Edition*

Creating Web Sites: The Missing Manual

CSS Cookbook

CSS Pocket Reference, *2nd Edition*

CSS: The Missing Manual

Dreamweaver 8: Design and Construction

Dreamweaver 8: The Missing Manual

Essential ActionScript 2.0

Flash 8: Projects for Learning Animation and Interactivity

Flash 8: The Missing Manual

Flash Hacks

Head First HTML with CSS & XHTML

Head Rush Ajax

HTML & XHTML: The Definitive Guide, *5th Edition*

HTML & XHTML Pocket Reference, *3rd Edition*

Information Architecture for the World Wide Web, *2nd Edition*

Information Dashboard Design

Learning Web Design, *2nd Edition*

PHP Hacks

Programming Flash Communication Server

Web Design in a Nutshell, *3rd Edition*

Web Site Measurement Hacks

Our books are available at most retail and online bookstores.

To order direct: 1-800-998-9938 • *order@oreilly.com* • *www.oreilly.com*

Online editions of most O'Reilly titles are available by subscription at *safari.oreilly.com*

The O'Reilly Advantage

Stay Current and Save Money

Order books online:
www.oreilly.com/order_new

Questions about our products or your order:
order@oreilly.com

Join our email lists: Sign up to get topic specific email announcements or new books, conferences, special offers and technology news *elists@oreilly.com*

For book content technical questions:
booktech@oreilly.com

To submit new book proposals to our editors:
proposals@oreilly.com

Contact us:
O'Reilly Media, Inc.
1005 Gravenstein Highway N.
Sebastopol, CA U.S.A. 95472
707-827-7000 or
800-998-9938
www.oreilly.com

Did you know that if you register your O'Reilly books, you'll get automatic notification and upgrade discounts on new editions?

And that's not all! Once you've registered your books you can:

» Win free books, T-shirts and O'Reilly Gear

» Get special offers available only to registered O'Reilly customers

» Get free catalogs announcing all our new titles (US and UK Only)

Registering is easy! Just go to www.oreilly.com/go/register